The 2nd Royal Irish Rifles in the Great War

The 2nd Royal Irish Rifles in the Great War

JAMES W. TAYLOR

FOUR COURTS PRESS

Set in 10 on 12 point Ehrhardt for
FOUR COURTS PRESS LTD
7 Malpas Street, Dublin 8, Ireland
e-mail: info@four-courts-press.ie
http://www.four-courts-press.ie
and in North America by
FOUR COURTS PRESS
c/o ISBS, 920 N.E. 58th Avenue, Suite 300, Portland, OR 97213.

ISBN 1–85182–952–0

A catalogue record for this title
is available from the British Library.

Printed by Creative Print Design (Wales), Ebbw Vale.

Contents

LIST OF ILLUSTRATIONS   7
ACKNOWLEDGEMENTS   9
GLOSSARY   11

PART ONE

    Introduction   17
1   Mons   19
2   Le Cateau   31
3   The Aisne   39
4   La Bassée   51
5   First attack at Bellewaarde   59
6   Second attack at Bellewaarde   70
7   1916   78
8   Somme   85
9   Messines   92
10   Westhoek and Cambrai   100
11   St Quentin   111
12   The advance in Flanders   123

Appendices

   I   Officer casualties   134
  II   Casualties in the ranks   137
III   Medal roll   163
IV   Courts martial and discipline   169
  V   Operation Orders for the attack of 7 June 1917   181

PART TWO

Biographical details of the officers   189
Some other ranks   335

BIBLIOGRAPHY   347
INDEX   351

Illustrations

MAPS

1 The Western Front 21
2 Mons 23
3 Le Cateau 33
4 The Aisne 41
5 La Bassée 53
6 First attack at Bellewaarde 61
7 Second attack at Bellewaarde 71
8 Ovillers 87
9 Messines 93
10 Quarry Redoubt 113
11 The final advance 125

PLATES OCCUR BETWEEN PAGES 192 AND 193

1 2nd RIR Officers, Tidworth 1914
2 3rd RIR Officers, Dublin 1915
3 Kemmel, March 1915
4 Riflemen resting, summer 1915
5 Westoutre
6 Ramparts at Ypres
7 Walking wounded at a Field Ambulance
8 Lt.-Col. H.R. Charley
9 Lt. R.B. Marriott-Watson
10 Capt. J.C. Bowen-Colthurst
11 Lt.-Col. J. Evans
12 RQMS D.J. McAuley
13 Cpl D.J. McAuley
14 Rfn P. McAteer
15 Fr H.V. Gill
16 Capt. G. Lowry
17 2/Lt. J.F. Lucy

18 Lt.-Col. W.D. Bird
19 2/Lt. J.K. Watson
20 Capt. H.O. Davis
21 Rfn John Quinn and his brother Rfn Hugh Quinn

CREDITS

Campbell College, Belfast 20; Lt.-Col. W.R.H. Charley 8; Donal Hall 12, 13; Jesuit Archives Dublin 3, 4, 5, 6, 7, 15; Major D.P. Lucy 17; Dan Malloy 14; Bill Miles 21; Royal Inniskilling Fusiliers Museum 11; RUR Museum 1, 2, 9, 16, 18; Georgiana Sutherlin 10; Hugh Watson 19.

Acknowledgements

This book is dedicated to my wife, Maura Ryan, and our children, Adam and Emma. Without their continued support and understanding, I would not have initiated this project.

Special thanks must be conveyed to Lt.-Col. W.R.H. Charley OBE, JP, DL, Newtownards, and Alex Shooter, London, who were most helpful in providing information on the officers; to Fr Fergus O'Donoghue SJ, Irish Jesuit Archives, for permission to quote from Fr Gill's diary and to use some of his photographs; to Major D.P. Lucy for permission to quote from his father's book; to Georgiana Sutherlin, USA, for details provided about her father Capt. Bowen-Colthurst; to Donal Hall, Dundalk, and Paul McCandless, Newcastle, for many useful items supplied. My researcher, Tom Tulloch-Marshall, to whom I am as ever indebted, unearthed most of the information from the National Archives at Kew. Dr Timothy Bowman, King's College London, kindly gave the courts-martial list. Some good friends deserve special mention: Gerry Murphy, Naas, extracted most of the statistical data for the casualties, helped with photograph reproduction, and put the maps into a presentable format; Dan Malloy, Paisley, was most encouraging and acted as my unofficial proofreader over many versions of the book; Larry Gittens, Dublin, provided constant support; and particularly Keith Haines, Belfast, who went out of his way to help me as much as possible. Thanks also to Martin Fanning, Ronan Gallagher, Anthony Tierney, and Michael Adams of Four Courts Press.

Mention must also be made of the assistance given by: *In Éire*: Dr Michael Brennan, Frank Brophy, Bernard Browne, Dermot and Mary Byrne, Jean Callaghan, Adrian Carty, John Culleton, Liam Dodd, Oliver Fallon (Connaught Rangers Association), Jarlath Glynn, Jim Herlihy, Helen Kelly, Dr Máire Kennedy (Dublin City Public Libraries), Paschal Ledwith, Fr John Looby SJ (Clongowes Wood College), Alan Maguire, Senator Martin Mansergh, Séamus Moriarty, Dr Liz Mullins (Jesuit Archives), Michael O'Brien, Rita O'Brien, Jack O'Connell, Pat O'Daly, Major-General David N.C. O'Morchoe CB, MBE, Hazel Percival, Paul Rowley, Angela Ryan, John Sherwood, Sam Smyth, David Tucker, Cyril Wall, the staff of the Gilbert Library, the National Library of Ireland, and of the Wexford County Library; *in Northern Ireland*: Desmond Blackadder, Mrs Eveleigh Brownlow, James Davidson, Billy Ervine (Somme Association), Pat Geary (Friends School, Lisburn), Dr R.H. Jordan (Archivist of Methodist College), Capt. Jaki Knox MBE

(Royal Ulster Rifles Regimental Museum), Tommy McClimonds, Alan K. McMillan (Presbyterian Historical Society of Ireland), Amanda Moreno (Royal Irish Fusiliers Museum), Terence Nelson (RUR Museum), Mr R.J.I. Pollock (Headmaster, Campbell College), Bobby Rainey, Major George Stephens MBE, DL (Royal Inniskilling Fusiliers Regimental Museum), Catherine Switzer, Robert Thompson, David Truesdale, Carol Walker (Somme Association), Major Roy Walker MBE (RUR Association), and Robert N.C. Watts; *in Britain*: James Armstrong (Honourable Artillery Company), David Blake (The Cheshire Regiment Museum), Skeena Bowen-Colthurst, David Bownes (Royal Welch Fusiliers Regimental Museum), Ian Carter (Imperial War Museum), Peter Cluness, The Commonwealth War Graves Commission, A. Cox BEM (The Devonshire and Dorset Regiment), Jacyntha Crawley, Geoffrey J. Crump (The Cheshire Regiment Museum), Lt.-Col. C.D. Darroch DL (The Royal Hampshire Regiment Museum), Richard Davies (Liddle Collection), Peter Donnelly (King's Own Royal Regiment Museum), George Fraser (Durham Light Infantry Museum), Lt.-Col. R.J. Knox, Commander Victor M. Lake, Lt.-Col. C.P. Love (The Worcestershire Regiment Museum), Mr Nigel Lutt (Bedfordshire & Luton Archives & Records Service), Patricia McAtee, Col. Ian H. McCausland (The Royal Green Jackets Regimental Museum), Howard Martin, Alastair Massie (National Army Museum), Martin Middlebrook, William Miles, Capt. Michael Panter, Hugh Pitfield, Anthony Richards (Imperial War Museum), Tony Sprason (The Lancashire Fusiliers Museum), Rory Stephens, Hugh C. Watson, Tony Whitfeld, and Brian Woolerton; *in Belgium*: Aurel Sercu; *in Canada*: Michael Bowen-Colthurst and the National Archives of Canada; *in the USA*: Karen Copeland and Russell H. Schaller.

To all of these I express my sincere gratitude.

Glossary

ADS	Advanced Dressing Station
AWOL	absent without leave
Bar	additional award of the same medal
Bde	Brigade
BEF	British Expeditionary Force
BIFR	*Burke's Irish Family Records 1976*
BLGI	*Burke's Landed Gentry of Ireland 1958*
BM	Brigade Major
Bn	Battalion
bomb	hand grenade
Bomber	hand grenade specialist
CCS	Casualty Clearing-Station
CiC	Commander in Chief
CO	Commanding Officer
Coy	Company
CQMS	Company Quartermaster Sergeant
CR	Connaught Rangers
demonstrate	a feint attack
DCLI	Duke of Cornwall's Light Infantry
DCM	Distinguished Conduct Medal
draft	a group of men sent as reinforcements
DSO	Distinguished Service Order
duck-board	wooden planks used to make walkways in trenches or muddy ground
dug-out	a shelter made in the wall of a trench
enfilade	gunfire directed along a line from end to end
FA	field ambulance
fire trench	front-line trench
GHQ	General Headquarters
GOC	General Officer Commanding
GSO	General Staff Officer
GSW	gunshot wound
HAC	Honourable Artillery Company
H.E.	high explosive shells

keep	a heavily fortified position in a trench system
KIA	killed in action
KOYLI	King's Own Yorkshire Light Infantry
KOSB	King's Own Scottish Borderers
KRRC	King's Royal Rifle Corps
MB	Medical Board
MC	Military Cross
MGC	Machine Gun Corps
Minenwerfer	type of trench mortar
MM	Military Medal
MO	Medical Officer
MSM	Meritorious Service Medal
NCO	Non-Commissioned Officer
OC	Officer Commanding
OCA	Old Comrades Association
OiC	Officer in Charge
OR	Other Rank
OTC	Officers Training Corps
parados	the back of a trench
parapet	the front of the trench
pill-box	a reinforced concrete machine-gun post
POW	Prisoner of War
Pte	Private
QM	Quartermaster
RAF	Royal Air Force
RAMC	Royal Army Medical Corps
RASC	Royal Army Service Corps
RDF	Royal Dublin Fusiliers
RE	Royal Engineers
Regt	Regiment
RFA	Royal Field Artillery
RFC	Royal Flying Corps
RIF	Royal Irish Fusiliers
RIR	Royal Irish Rifles
R. Irish	Royal Irish Regiment
redoubt	a fortified strongpoint
RMC	Royal Military College
RMF	Royal Munster Fusiliers
RWF	Royal Welsh Fusiliers
RWK	Royal West Kent Regiment
RUR	Royal Ulster Rifles
S.A.A.	small arms ammunition
salient	a trench system projecting towards the enemy
sap	a narrow trench extending from a main trench

shrapnel	small metal balls ejected from a shell, usually while still in the air
SR	Special Reserve
TF	Territorial Forces
TMB	trench mortar battery
Town Major	an officer responsible for billeting arrangements in a town
UVF	Ulster Volunteer Force
WO	War Office or Warrant Officer
Zero-hour	the time for an attack to commence

PART ONE

The history of the 2nd Royal Irish Rifles, 1914–19

Introduction

This book has been compiled in two parts. The first covers the history of the 2nd Royal Irish Rifles, 1914–19. Part Two gives brief biographical details of the officers and some of the other ranks that served with the battalion during the war. Its purpose is to add some humanity to the story. Histories of this kind normally give the names of the officers who were involved but seldom, if ever, actually tell you who these men were.

To understand this narrative clearly it is first necessary to know the way the British Army was organized. In simple terms, the basic unit was a section – four of these made up a platoon of about fifty men and there were four numbered platoons in a company (which also included a Company HQ) giving a total strength of roughly 230. Naturally, as the war progressed, the battalion was seldom up to full strength. Four companies designated A, B, C, and D jointly formed a battalion (Platoons No. 1 to 16). The strength of a battalion was roughly 1,000 men when account is taken of headquarters, transport, supplies, signals, cooks, etc. There were initially four battalions in a brigade and three brigades in a division; which in this instance was the 7th Infantry Brigade of the 3rd Division, then 76th and 74th Brigade of the 25th Division, and later, in the autumn of 1917, the 108th and 107th Brigade of the 36th (Ulster) Division. About that time the strength of a brigade was reduced to three battalions.

Regimental Headquarters was little more than an administrative depot that served its battalions. The Royal Irish Rifles had twenty-one battalions during the Great War. The 1st and 2nd Battalions were the old regular units and had been formed by the amalgamation in 1881 of the 83rd (County of Dublin) and the 86th (County Down) Regiments of Foot. The 3rd, 4th, 5th, 17th, 18th, 19th, and 20th were Reserve Battalions; the 6th to the 16th were Service Battalions (for active service on a fighting front), and last was the 1st Garrison Battalion in India.

The usual rankings (and abbreviations) were:

Rifleman	Rfn
Lance Corporal	L/Cpl
Corporal	Cpl
Lance Sergeant	L/Sgt
Sergeant	Sgt

Company Sergeant Major	CSM Warrant Officer 2nd Class
Regimental Sergeant Major	RSM Warrant Officer 1st Class
Second Lieutenant	2/Lt.
Lieutenant	Lt.
Captain	Capt.
Major	
Lieutenant-Colonel	Lt.-Col., the CO of a battalion

Several members of the battalion played a prominent part in the 1916 Rising and their details in Part Two are necessarily brief. These include Major J. Rosborough, Capt. J.C. Bowen-Colthurst, Lt. S.V. Morgan, 2/Lt. W.L.P. Dobbin, and Rfn D.J. Bailey. A reading of the *1916 Rebellion Handbook* will provide much additional information. The differing accounts of the Battle of the Aisne between Capt. Bowen-Colthurst and Lt.-Col. Bird leave unanswered questions. The actions of Colthurst in Dublin during the Rising, his subsequent court martial, the commission of enquiry, and the debate as to his mental condition at the time remain highly controversial subjects that cannot be comprehensively covered here.

Some books and memoirs were written that could not, of course, be included in their entirety. The main ones that I can recommend are: *There's a Devil in the Drum* by J.F. Lucy, *The Burgoyne Diaries* by G.A. Burgoyne, and *War Reminiscences* by Fr H.V. Gill.

All the counties of Ireland are represented among the dead. The Irish character of the battalion varied as follows:

Year	Irish	Northern Ireland	Republic of Ireland
1914	83%	50%	33%
1915	75%	55%	20%
1916	80%	53%	27%
1917	62%	41%	21%
1918	48%	35%	13%

The records for some periods of the war are a little sketchy as, on occasions, there were few survivors left to tell the tale. Details for some actions had to be compiled from various sources that were not necessarily central to the overall picture. Where officers served with both 1st and 2nd RIR I have reduced their entries in this volume.

It was suggested to me that I should here give a brief overview of the war to place the story in a clearer context. The problem is that I had been trying to keep the size of the book within manageable proportions and was not prepared to excise new information in order merely to go over old ground. I was very fortunate on this occasion to find many more relations of participants and to make some wonderful friends along the way. The number of people who helped me, from all parts of these islands, has been simply amazing and this enabled me to complete the project at least a year ahead of schedule. What a contrast to when I set out alone on this journey so many years ago!

Mons

In the spring of 1914 the 2nd Battalion The Royal Irish Rifles was based at Bhurtpore Barracks, Tidworth, near Salisbury, under the command of a very capable Englishman, Lt.-Col. W.D. Bird DSO. He had been appointed Commanding Officer the previous September from the Royal West Surrey Regiment and it was not long before he was having difficulties with one of his senior officers, Capt. J.C. Bowen-Colthurst, over apparently trivial matters:

> He had little understanding of men and absolutely none of Irishmen. He was pitch-forked into the command of my Regiment, with a view to giving him accelerated promotion. The first command Lt.-Col. Bird issued when he arrived at Tidworth was to clear the billiard room as he desired to use it as a lecture room. He was informed by the Mess President that the billiard room was for the use of the officers to play billiards and not for his maps, diagrams and lectures.[1]

The country was in the depths of a political crisis brought about by Government attempts to introduce Home Rule to Ireland. Ulster unionists had vowed to oppose this, by force if necessary, and formed the Ulster Volunteer Force (UVF). In March 1914 many officers stationed at the Curragh in Co. Kildare had proffered their resignations rather than move against the UVF. It was feared that army and police barracks in the north of Ireland would be raided by the UVF in a bid to procure arms. Bird issued orders for the unit to get mobilized and was thought by Capt. Bowen-Colthurst to have offered the services of 2nd RIR for active operations in Ulster.

> I was commanding C Coy and was rude to the Colonel. The CO could have had me tried by court martial no doubt for insubordination, disobedience of orders, or any other charge he cared to have drawn up, for saying that I belonged to a Belfast regiment and was not going to order my men to fire on their own brothers and sisters and fathers and mothers, to please Messrs Asquith, Lloyd George, Sir John Simon, Winston Churchill or other politicians. I was an Irishman first and last and all the time, and I told Lt.-Col.

---

1 Bowen-Colthurst's quotes are from a letter he wrote to the Military Secretary, 31 January 1940, WO374/14934.

Bird that he did not understand the Irish and never would. Whoever appointed Bird to command an Irish battalion was capable of appointing a Brahmin to command a regiment of Pathans. Bird never forgot this ... As a Colonel of an Irish Regiment Lt.-Col. Bird proved himself by a thousand different follies an impossible individual and in April 1914 his crowning folly was volunteering the services of the Royal Irish Rifles he commanded for active service in Belfast and Ulster. Entirely on his own responsibility he ordered me and the other Company Commanders to prepare our Companies immediately to fight in Belfast. As far as I was concerned this was the final breach. I immediately informed Lt.-Col. Bird that his order was an impossibility, that the Regimental Depot was at Belfast, and that I as an Irishman declined to give my men orders to fire on the peaceful citizens at Belfast. It was forthwith reported to the WO by Lt.-Col. Bird but the order was withdrawn.

Colthurst apologized and the matter seemed to be settled. However, when war was declared he told Col. Bird that he preferred not to serve under his command on active service 'as I had discovered that no matter what I did it was wrong from Lt.-Col. Bird's point of view. He replied that it was too late to make a change.' This breakdown in their relationship was to have a serious effect on both the officers and the men under their command in the opening battles of the war.

The battalion was ordered to mobilize at 6 p.m., 4 August 1914. It formed part of 7th Infantry Brigade (Brigadier-General F.W.N. McCracken) in 3rd Division (Major-General Sir H.I.W. Hamilton), II Corps (General Sir H.L. Smith-Dorrien). The mobilization commenced the following day and was completed by the 9th. Lt. G. Lowry remembered:

> Our last days in England were spoilt by the inoculation for the prevention of enteric, which we all had to suffer. Minor as the prick of a little needle appeared at the time, it became a very major matter the next morning; and as the day advanced we felt so miserable that neither food nor drink appealed to us. Meanwhile, the mobilization had been carried forward with wonderful smoothness, and the British Expeditionary Force was completed for active service in record time to the last button. It was an amazing sight to see the Reserves of the Regiment, some of whom had returned to the Colours after years of civilian life, as thrilled with the prospect of active service as the youngest soldier.[2]

9896 Cpl J. Lucy, A Coy, observed:

> Our reservists came streaming in to make up our war strength; cheerful, careless fellows of all types, some in bowler hats and smart suitings, others in descending scale down to the garb of tramps. Soon, like us, they were

2 All Lowry's quotes are extracts of *From Mons to 1933*.

Map 1: The Western Front

uniformed and equipped with field kits, and the change was remarkable. Smart sergeants and corporals and beribboned veterans of the South African war hatched out of that crowd of nondescript civilians, and took their place and duties as if they had never left the army.[3]

At 2.30 p.m., on the 13th, the first half the battalion went by train to Southampton, where they embarked aboard the SS *Ennisfallen*, a Cork cattle steamer, and sailed at 8 p.m., reaching Le Havre at 5 a.m. the next day. They continued up the river Seine and reached Rouen at 7.30 p.m. where they disembarked and marched through the city and up a hill to the rest camp at Mont St Aignan. In the meantime the second half of the battalion left Tidworth an hour after the first had departed. Sailing from Southampton on the SS *Sarnia* at 4.15 a.m. the next morning, they reached Rouen at 6 p.m. without touching Le Havre, and marched the three miles to Mont St Aignan where they arrived shortly before the first half joined them. Here they remained throughout the 15th; a thunderstorm and heavy rain soon turned the ground at the camp into an impassable quagmire. 9872 Rfn J. Goss:

> The rain and subsequently the squelching mud in the camp made us all pretty miserable at the time, but such conditions were as nothing compared to those which the Unit had to endure in the succeeding years of the war.[4]

The other battalions of the brigade were 2nd South Lancashire Regt, 3rd Worcestershire Regt, and 1st Wiltshire Regt. Lt. Lowry was enjoying himself:

> That evening I visited Rouen in company with some brother officers, and had the good fortune to meet the officers of a French regiment, who joined us at dinner. It proved a hilarious evening, and we dined so well and drank so many toasts in our mutual admiration of each other that our Gallic comrades started to talk English with an Irish accent, and we in turn expressed ourselves in extraordinary French. The trouble came when our dinner party ended, for our comrades in arms insisted upon escorting us back to camp, creating such a turmoil in the process that we had great difficulty in preventing the guard from arresting the lot of us!

All boarded a train at Rouen on the 16th bound for Aulnoye (via Amiens) where they billeted in a large foundry at L'Usine Monbart, 1.5 miles from the station. The next day the brigade concentrated at the village of Marbaix. It was found that certain arrangements were necessary to ensure proper discipline, such as kit and iron rations being paraded at Reveille, followed by washing and water filling parades. On the 19th a route march was carried out in the morning; the weather was hot and security posts were put out on all roads. They moved to St Hilaire, 20 August,

---

3 Unless otherwise stated, all Lucy's quotes come from *There's a Devil in the Drum*.   4 All Goss's quotes come from his 'Narrative on the Battle of Le Cateau', *Quis Separabit*, Summer 1961.

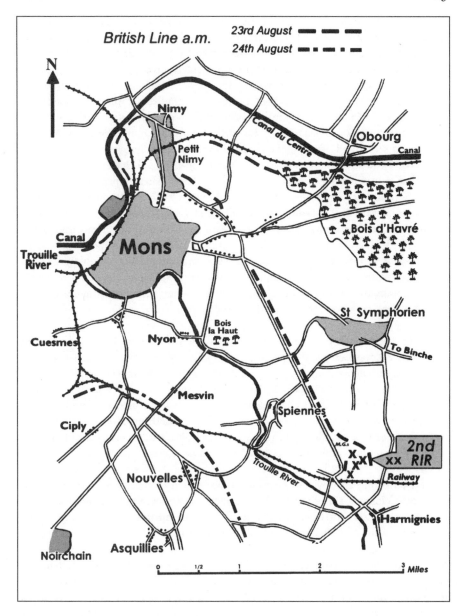

Map 2: The Battle of Mons

bivouacked in an orchard, and carried out a brigade route march, moving to Avesnes where the inhabitants gave them a great ovation. This march was a short one but, owing to the road being bordered by high trees, there was little air and the men felt the heat. At 1.30 a.m. on the 21st orders were received to join 7th Brigade at St Aubin, and from there march via the fortress of Maubeuge to fresh billets at Feignies. The total distance was about 17 miles and the troops were exhausted: this was due to an early start, 4.45 a.m., and that there was a long wait before occupying billets at 3.30 p.m. Their dinner was not ready until 8 p.m. The usual outposts were set up well in advance on the roads leading to the billeting area.

On the 22nd the brigade marched to Quévy-le-Petit and halted for about two hours then continued over heavy dusty tracks to Ciply where billets were taken up in the afternoon. The middle of the day had been very hot and sultry. Ciply was a small industrial village of about 1,000 inhabitants and lies about two miles south of Mons. Several aeroplanes were observed circling overhead but it was impossible to identify them. Reveille was at 2 a.m., Sunday, 23 August, because orders were to march at 4.30 a.m., but this was later delayed until 7 a.m. The men were advised that contact with the enemy was imminent: the battle of Mons was about to begin. Having marched a short distance beyond Nouvelles they halted and then proceeded about half way back to Ciply. According to Lowry:

> The information we received caused us often to deploy and re-form on the road. It was delightful to us all to feel that we were so soon to come to grips with an enemy who for years had been stressing its superiority and might, and the spirits of all ranks of the British Expeditionary Force were immensely high. Our first sight of war came at 11 a.m., when some riderless horses of our cavalry galloped through us, which we found out afterwards were the remains of a squadron of the 9th Lancers, who had heroically charged some German guns and suffered heavily in the process.

At 2 p.m. they marched to Harmignies where a report was received that some of the 15th Hussars (Cavalry Squadron of 3rd Division) had been driven back. Rfn Goss: 'Some of the horses were riderless. Practically all the returning cavalrymen and animals were wounded as a result of hand to hand action in some wooded country.' Sent forward to reinforce the Royal Scots on high ground north of Harmignies station, the Rifles commenced entrenching on the right flank of the British defences when the enemy's artillery opened at about 3.45 p.m. C and D Coys were in the firing line while A and B were in reserve on the Givry–Mons Road. These latter companies were afterwards brought up to prolong the line on the left occupying trenches near the road; D Coy was somewhat separated filling up a gap between two companies of the Royal Scots. The Rifles were now out on a limb as the Germans had crossed the Condé Canal, the 3rd Division had withdrawn to a new defensive line south of Mons, and they were separated from their own Brigade. The enemy attacked with the 75th Infantry Regt (1st Hanseatic) covered by artillery and with one machine gun crew on their left. Cpl Lucy:

The German infantry, which had approached during the shelling, was in sight, and about to attack us. Not a shot had been fired from our trenches up to now, and the only opposition to the Germans has been made by our field-gun battery, which was heavily engaged behind us, and making almost as much clamour as the enemy shelling. To my mind it seemed that the whole battalion must have been wiped out by that dreadful rain of shells, but apparently not. In answer to the German bugles or trumpets came the cheerful sounds of our officers' whistles, and the riflemen, casting aside the amazement of their strange trial, sprang to action. A great roar of musketry rent the air, varying in intensity from minute to minute as whole companies ceased fire and opened again ... The leading Germans fired standing, 'from the hip', as they came on. But their scattered fire was ineffective, and ignored. They crumpled up – mown down as quickly as I tell it, their rein-forcing waves and sections coming on bravely and steadily to fall over as they reached the front line of slain and wounded. Behind the death line thicker converging columns were being blown about by our field guns.

Our rapid fire was appalling even to us, and the worst marksman could not miss, as he had only to fire into the 'brown' of the masses of the unfor-tunate enemy, who on the fronts of two of our companies were continually and uselessly reinforced at the short range of three hundred yards. Such tac-tics amazed us and, after the first shock of seeing men slowly and helplessly falling down as they were hit, gave us a great sense of power and pleasure. It was all so easy. The German survivors began to go back here and there from the line. The attack had been an utter failure. Soon all that remained was the long line of the dead heaped before us, motionless except for the limb movements of some of the wounded.

Irish Times, 8 October 1914:

[17533 Rfn] William Hobson, of the 2nd Royal Irish Rifles, who is at pres-ent recuperating from a bullet wound in the shoulder at his home in Glasthule, Kingstown, tells an interesting story of the Battle of Mons. He received his wound in that engagement.

It was our first engagement, he said, we took possession of a hill and got orders to entrench. We had only dug a foot deep when the Germans started shelling us, but we continued digging under fire until we had got enough cover to lie behind. Under heavy fire we had to go back to our rifles and equipment and when we returned to the trench we lay flat from one o'clock on Sunday afternoon until twelve o'clock that night. When the Germans had covered the advance of their infantry they finished shelling. They must have thought we were all dead, they came on in such bunches. We gave them a burst of rapid firing and wiped out the majority. We escaped very luckily, five being killed and twelve wounded but our machine gun was smashed up. We forced them to retire, and stopped in the trenches until three o'clock in

the morning when we retired under orders. One of our men, said Private
Hobson, has been recommended for the Distinguished Conduct Medal.
When the man who was working the machine gun was killed he came up
and took his place under very heavy fire. At last the gun was smashed and
he had his hand blown off.

This account refers to 9558 Rfn John O'Connor whose citation reads: 'For gallantry at Harmignies under heavy shell and rifle fire. He fought his machine gun
for over three hours, doing important service.' Four men were killed – the battalion's first casualties – including 9471 L/Cpl G.T. McKinley from Shankill, Co.
Antrim:

> One of the Maxim operators was wounded. The German machine guns were
> much superior in numbers. Corporal McKinley went and dragged him out
> of danger and took his place. He had just knelt down when a venomous fire
> was directed on the guns. Poor McKinley was riddled with bullets; the very
> straps of his uniform were torn off him. He had over 100 wounds in him
> and his gun was smashed to atoms. We buried him there in the dark, and
> laid the broken fragments of the Maxim gun beside him.[5]

According to Lowry:

> At 12 noon we arrived at the village of St Waast, Mons, taking cover in a
> sunken road, where we waited in a blazing hot sun, listening to the steady
> boom of guns and waiting patiently for orders. My feelings at this time were
> mixed, for I had never been under fire before, and felt more afraid of being
> afraid than of being killed. It was an anxious time for all, and we were glad
> when orders arrived at last, by medium of a staff officer in a motor car, which
> caused us to fall in and double up a steepish road running at right angles to
> our left. Presently we gained the summit of the hill we had been ascending
> and, turning to the right, lined a ditch which ran along the side of the road.
> From here we were able to look down the valley below, and saw, to our great
> amazement, as far as the eye could see, a teeming mass of German soldiers,
> advancing with parade-ground efficiency. It was a thrilling introduction to
> an enemy we were destined to fight for four years; but we had little time for
> reflection, and opened fire at 800 yards range, with both rifle and machine-
> gun. The 'mad minute', by which name was known the British Army's stan-
> dard of musketry efficiency, which compelled every soldier to fire fifteen
> rounds a minute with great accuracy, at last showed its enormous value, for
> from each of our soldiers poured a stream of bullets into the advancing horde,
> who literally shivered with the shock and melted away line by line beneath
> our gaze. The enemy's artillery had not yet succeeded in finding our posi-
> tion; and we attempted in the brief intervals which were allowed us to

5 *Immortal Deeds.*

improve our only cover by the aid of the entrenching tool which, fortunately, every soldier carried, a tool which was to prove a veritable lifebuoy to the BEF during the earlier days of the Great War. Excellent as the accuracy of our riflemen was, and deadly as their fire became, it failed to stem the German weight of attack, and countless lines of their infantry moved steadily towards us over the bodies of those we had killed and wounded, displaying both superb discipline and bravery and also the utterly reckless manner with which the higher commands of the German Army regarded human life ... All the afternoon the German infantry came on, line after line as far as the eye could see, with a superb courage until, with our rifles almost red hot and our men tired with ceaseless firing, they succeeded in approaching to within 200 yards of our line. The German losses had been terrible, for our infantry-men had been accustomed to shoot with accuracy up to 1,000 yards, and our Army had never anticipated that an enemy could be found who would sac-rifice life in such profusion and be so well supplied with both artillery and gun ammunition. I can never think of those days now without remembering the ceaseless crackle of rifles along the British line, and the wonderful spirit of our soldiers notwithstanding that they must have appreciated that we were up against a mighty proposition. The enemy at one time came so close that we fixed bayonets in preparation for an assault, but before it could be deliv-ered our fire had taken such terrible toll that the surviving assailants retired before cold steel could be resorted to. All this while the German artillery had been gradually finding our position, and, just before darkness came, it became thoroughly unpleasant.

Col. Bird later recalled:

Here one company of R. Scots was found entrenched on ground where, owing to its convex shape, the effective field of fire was limited to about 300 yards. The remainder of the R. Scots were entrenched generally along the Givry–Mons road and some 300–400 yards further back than the company on the bluff. Two companies of 2nd RIR were ordered to occupy and entrench the bluff co-operating with the company of R. Scots and the remain-ing companies placed in a deep cutting where the road ascends to the bluff. The company flanking the position of the R. Scots and the machine guns had a good field of fire for about 2,000 yards, the other company a poor field of fire, the ground from about 1,000 to 3,000 yards being dead ... The German attack began at about 4 p.m., and just before or after this I received a message from Lt.-Col. McMicking, commanding R. Scots, that unless he received two companies he did not think he could hold his ground. The two reserve companies of the RIR were therefore sent to Lt.-Col. McMicking and report made to Brigadier-General McCracken as to the situation.

The German attack developed on the lines usually practised in 1914. Owing to the contour of the ground the enemy attacking the bluff were invisible from about 1,500 yards until they closed to 300 yards where they were checked. The company flanking the position of the main body of the R. Scots, and the machine guns, however, caused a good many casualties in the troops attacking the R. Scots. The enemy's artillery fire was fairly heavy, shrapnel only being used. The bursts, however, were high and accuracy poor, a good many shells bursting in the trees which lined the Mons road. Between 5 and 5.30 p.m. we were joined by a battalion of Grenadier Guards under Lt.-Col. Drummond and one of Irish Guards under Lt.-Col. G. Morris.

At nightfall the Germans brought up six machine guns, and made an attempt to advance but relinquished it as soon as our rapid fire was opened. I think they then fell back to cook leaving an outpost line opposite to us. At about 7.30 p.m. touch was obtained with a company of 2nd Division on the lower part of the bluff on our right. Between 8 p.m. and 8.30 p.m. an order was received from Brigadier-General McCracken that we were to fall back at 10 p.m. and I at once sent an officer to reconnoitre the route to the point from which we had advanced, where the bulk of our 1st line transport had been left. A report was also sent to Brigadier-General Doran who thereupon directed me not to withdraw until orders came from him to do so.

On receipt of these instructions I bicycled about 1½ miles down the road towards Mons and saw Brigadier-General Doran who informed me that I was to hold the bluff until his brigade had withdrawn and was then to retire ...

It was then arranged that we should be ready to retire at midnight, but should not move until orders were received from Doran. These arrived at about 2 a.m. We went to Nouvelles, because we *hoped* to find the 7th Brigade there. Actually we found our 1st line transport only.[6]

Bird's original intention was to fall back on Maubeuge but, when he learned the whereabouts of the 3rd Division, the Rifles marched across country in the direction of Bavai. In 1918 Bird made the following remarks on the tactics of August 1914:

One got so little sleep during the retreat and advance, when at best orders came in at midnight or a little earlier, and reveille was at 4 a.m., and physically one was so tired with marching, that the names of some of the smaller halting places reached at dusk and left at dawn have escaped me.

Our pre-war text books erred, I think, only in that the possibility of close fighting in long drawn out battles, such as occurred in the Russo-Japanese war, was not sufficiently considered. We were convinced that in well-developed Europe a war of movement would be fought, because, if for no other reason, the Germans seemed to contemplate this, and in addition most economists scouted the idea of a long drawn out struggle. Moreover there was the feeling that the dash of our men would be lowered were they taught in peace the slow methods of trench warfare.

6 Bird's quotes are from appendices attached to the war diary.

In principle, I think our system of holding a series of localities in a defensive position, and not a long continuous line was correct. But it was not sufficiently understood that covered communications between the localities and from there to the rear were also necessary. Within my brief experience the very extensive frontages taken up, which left no troops available as reserves prevented our principles from being put into practice as regards counterattack.

So little time, also, was available for entrenchment when we did stand to fight, that, as a rule, villages which seemed to afford some cover, were selected as our 'localities'. As a result the enemy's artillery was afforded a series of good targets on which fire could be and was concentrated, and our men, who perhaps were somewhat crowded in the villages, suffered accordingly. Speaking for myself it seemed to me that our means of intercommunication and arrangements for distribution of information were at fault.

During the retreat and advance I never knew the general position of our cavalry brigades or of the neighbouring infantry divisions; nor had I any idea as to our general intentions at Mons, the Marne or the Aisne; or before and after Le Cateau ... In two items of pre-war preparation our system was fully vindicated – viz. marching and rapid fire. The Germans never stood up to our rapid fire for more than a quarter of an hour, and we could not have done the retreat and advance had not march discipline been well taught in peace ... German tactics in attack appeared very like our own, in principle. They seemed to make deliberate preparation before launching an attack, bringing up guns and infantry onto the ground. The artillery preparation then began more or less simultaneously along the front of the attack, and where it was thought sufficient effect had been produced the infantry came on with all available machine guns. If the infantry attack did not succeed it was at once abandoned and more preparation commenced.

Orders were received on the 24th to withdraw and the Rifles were on their way by 2 a.m., reassembling at Nouvelles a few hours later. Col. Bird instructed that the men's packs, extra ammunition, picks and shovels, which had been carried down from the trenches, were to be abandoned. 'The weather was very hot causing considerable distress amongst the troops.'[7] That morning a German aeroplane flew over the battalion and was brought down by independent rapid fire. They retired 16 miles via Maladrie, Givry, Bavai, and St Waast to La Boiscrête and took up an outpost position. Bird noted:

Meanwhile the 1st line transport had unfortunately been swept down the Maubeuge road with the other masses of vehicles going in this direction, and was not recovered for several days ... We then moved to Bavai and took up a position on its outskirts until about 5 p.m., when the remainder of 7th Brigade appeared and we moved via St Waast to Le Plat de Bois with out-

7 3rd Division war diary.

posts towards La Flamengrie. Here some food was found dumped. Touch was established with the division on our left and the night passed without incident.

Rfn Goss:

> During the retreat the 2nd RIR was invariably acting as a rearguard and con-
> tinuously fighting during the day and marching at night. The fighting dur-
> ing the day was usually to assist in extricating guns and other horse-drawn
> vehicles, as well as covering up the retirement of the foot sloggers, from dif-
> ferent positions. We were continuously scouted upon by enemy cavalry –
> mostly Uhlans – of which there seemed to be endless numbers. In these rear-
> guard actions able assistance was received from units of the British Cavalry
> which was harassing the enemy at every opportunity. The Battalion reached
> Le Cateau where it subsequently marched to various points and eventually
> took up a defensive position between Caudry and Montigny.

The battalion formed the rearguard of 7th Brigade, 25 August, as they retired 30 miles with the Germans hot on their heels via Le Quesnoy, Romeries, Beaurain, Ovillers, Montay, through the central square of Le Cateau, Reumont, to billets at Maurois, arriving about 3.45 a.m. the next day. 'It had marched forty-five miles in forty-eight hours, after a previous day in action.'[8]

8 Falls. All of his quotes are from the regimental history.

2

Le Cateau

Col. Bird detailed subsequent events:

> At 7.30 a.m. I received a message from HQ 2nd Corps that we were to parade at once and march to Bertry. At Bertry Major Cory of HQ 2nd Corps was sent to guide us to a locality south of Caudry which was to be held in case the Germans broke through ... and proceeded to entrench from the stud farm one mile north of Montigny to the Caudry–Clary road. At about noon I was ordered to send half a company into Caudry and did so. At about 3 p.m. Major-General Hamilton came up and ... told me that he wished to clear Caudry and would place my battalion, such other troops of 7th Brigade ... as were not in the village, and also the Welsh Fusiliers and Middlesex (I think) at my disposal for this purpose, together with two batteries, that under Major Bruce, and another ... Before any definite action could be taken Lt.-Col. F. Maurice GSO 2 rode up with orders for the withdrawal of the division, and very soon afterwards Ligny was taken and the enemy opened fire on us from it. Major-General Hamilton then ordered me to withdraw the troops of 7th Brigade from Caudry and cover the retirement with my battalion and the two batteries.
>
> I accordingly sent orders for the evacuation of Caudry, placed my battalion in the enclosures near the stud farm and to the south of it, and posted Bruce's battery behind our right and the other behind our left. The latter battery did not wait long and the CO soon sent me word that he was withdrawing.
>
> At about 4.30 p.m., when Caudry had almost been cleared, the bulk of the artillery and infantry that had been defending Audencourt suddenly came streaming down the hill to the railway, then taking the road to Montigny. First came some guns and limbers at full gallop, the guns and limbers etc. covered with infantrymen, then the infantry in complete disorder. We watched them pass us, and as soon as they had cleared the slope down to the railway Major Bruce opened fire on the hillcrest between Audencourt and Caudry. The Germans made no attempt to pursue and after waiting about 20 minutes, since there was no sign either of more of our men or of any of the enemy coming from Audencourt or Caudry, I rode back and obtained Major-General Hamilton's permission to retire.

Earlier in the day B Coy and two platoons of A Coy were sent into Caudry under the command of Capt. C.L. Master. Lowry recalled:

> On Wednesday, August 26th, we advanced towards Caudry village at Le Cateau, delighted to be once again going the right way, as we had had enough of retreating, and wanted to stand and fight. Most of our brigade took up a position on the south side of Caudry, and my company of the Royal Irish Rifles and one of the Worcestershire Regiment entered the village, driving before us the Uhlans who occupied it with our fixed bayonets.

According to Rfn Goss:

> The Commander of the 2nd Army Corps had decided that it would be impossible to continue a safe and orderly retreat without making a stand and endeavouring to slow up the enemy advance. Although the troops were dog tired they responded splendidly and it was later competent military opinion that 'the results justified the means'.
>
> The position on the fateful 26th August was that the 3rd Division occupied the Troisville–Audencourt–Caudry line … The 7th Brigade (except the RIR) occupied the line north of Caudry. The Rifles, which had had practically continuous action since the retreat had commenced at Mons, had obtained a few hours rest and was then ordered to form part of a second line of defence on some high point on the Audencourt–Clary Road, about midway between Caudry and Montigny. Also in supporting defence with the Rifles at this point was a Battery (41st) of the Royal Field Artillery.
>
> In the meantime, a furious battle had developed and other units of the 7th Brigade were in the thick of it. These units were weakened by continuous frontal attacks 'en masse', and as a breakthrough was anticipated B and part of A Companies of the RIR were ordered forward into Caudry itself. I was one of those who went forward with this detachment to engage the enemy and, under heavy shell fire, we moved to a position on the right of the Worcesters. The position was serious and the 7th Brigade began to fall back, but with the help of the remainder of A Company and some companies of the R.I. Regiment the enemy was temporarily ejected from Caudry after some very savage fighting.
>
> Some time later (about 2 p.m.) severe fighting flared up again and under very heavy pressure the 7th Brigade fell back from the village of Caudry. The survivors of A and B Companies, RIR, had joined the Battalion and directions were then received apparently for the Rifles (assisted by units of the R.F. Artillery) to cover the withdrawal of the Brigade from the vicinity of the village. By this time the Rifles were the sole co-ordinated unit of a broken line of defence, and it was in a doubly difficult position because it later had to also cover the retirement of the R.F. Artillery units attached to it, and which had previously been shelling concentrations of the enemy

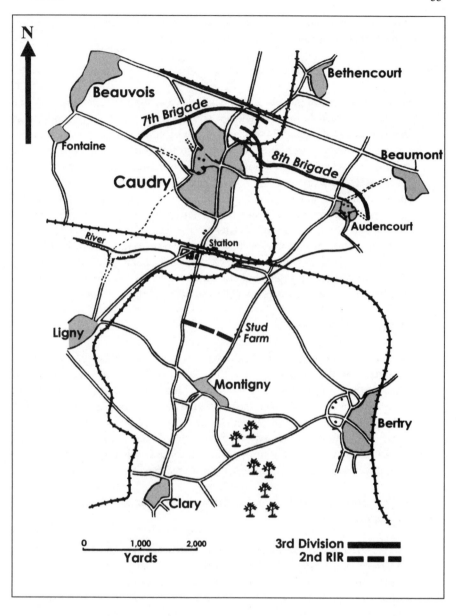

Map 3: The Battle of Le Cateau, 26 August 1914

north-east of Caudry itself. The Rifles eventually retired between 5 and 6
p.m. (via Serain) in the direction of Beaurevoir.

Capt. Master reported in the war diary:

> The orders were to proceed to the Market Square and await instructions but
> the area was heavily bombarded, several men being killed and wounded and
> many knocked down by the violence of the explosions. In order to minimize
> casualties the men were pushed forward to the northern edge of the town,
> where an advance position was taken up. Here they got in touch with the
> Worcestershire Regt on the left and mixed detachments on the right. In this
> position the detachment came under fire from German Infantry and machine
> guns, and also much shrapnel fire, the latter only doing damage. About 2
> p.m. Capt. Master received an order from a Major of 2nd Royal Irish Regt
> that, as the troops on the right had withdrawn from the village, he was also
> to retire ... The detachment covered the retirement of the 30th Brigade,
> RFA and certain stragglers and subsequently retired and joined the rest of
> the battalion and formed part of the vanguard to the 3rd Division.

Lt. Lowry gave this perspective:

> We received orders which required us to double until we reached a road
> commanding the approaches to the town. As we lay on our 'tummies' upon
> this, I saw to my dismay that we were within 100 yards of a gasometer so
> large in size that it seemed certain that it must be hit by any shells that
> missed us, with disastrous effect. However, as the day wore on it became
> clear that it bore a charmed life, for, although the enemy simply poured
> shells of all sizes into the town from three sides, this gasometer remained
> unhit, although the brave inhabitants suffered terribly.

The Transport got into difficulty at the stud farm north of Montigny. Lowry
told what happened next.

> A very gallant stand had been made by Major Charley and the Captain and
> Quartermaster Clark to save the transport, who, when surrounded, gave the
> thirteen men under their command all the ammunition they could find, 750
> rounds each, and for some hours held up the attack. They killed many of
> the enemy before they were eventually enfiladed and practically every man
> killed or wounded. Naturally, the loss of this transport very considerably
> increased the hardships of our retreat.

The following casualties had occurred: Major Charley and QM Clark were
wounded and captured, Lt. F.L. Finlay, 2/Lt. C.L.G. Mathews-Donaldson, and
29 men were wounded; 6 men had been killed. The retreat resumed for 18 miles

through Tronquoy, Clary, Elincourt, Serain, Ponchaux, to Beaurevoir, which the battalion reached in pouring rain at about midnight after forcing their way through masses of transport blocking the approaches. Many men tried to fall out and pick up biscuits and meat left in the bivouacs they passed, as they had had nothing to eat since some food reached them during the action at Le Cateau. Cpl Lucy observed a shell-shocked Capt. Colthurst:

> The officers at last began to feel the strain. One captain turns his whole company about and marches back towards the Germans. The commanding officer gallops after him, and the captain tells him he is tired of retreating. It is bad for the morale of the troops, so he prefers to fight and perish if necessary. The un-nerved captain is relieved of his command, and his gallantly docile company comes back to us under a junior, and joins the tail of the column.

Proceeding as brigade rearguard, the battalion headed off at 2 a.m., 27 August, through Belicourt, halting for four hours on the way at Hargicourt, then on via Jeancourt, Vendelles, Soyécourt, to Vermand, where they fed. They started out at 9 p.m. for Ham, arriving there at 4 a.m. on the 28th in very thick fog, crossed the Somme, then continued to Tarlefesse, a suburb of Noyon; this had been a march of 26 miles. Here they rested until noon on the 29th when they took up a line of outposts in the woods of Bois d'Autrecourt north of Salency. According to Col. Bird:

> The paths in the wood were narrow and overgrown, the wood very dense, and, as night began to come on, the wood became very dark. I therefore rode to the Brigadier, who was in Salency, and suggested that if a further retirement were in contemplation it would be as well to withdraw from the wood while we could see our way. He said, however, that we must remain in position and withdraw at 2 a.m. I pointed out the great difficulty of doing so and asked him to send a staff officer into the wood to report on the situation. This he refused to do.
>
> I then told one of my battalion interpreters, whom I had brought with me, to get two *gardes-forestiers* from the village and persuade them to come with us into the wood. I took one man to my second-in-command whom I put in charge of two companies and went to the remainder myself with the other man. Connecting files were placed at 25 yards interval between the groups and companies since it was so dark that one could not see one's hand even. Having drawn in the groups we began to retire at 2 a.m., the men moving in file and holding onto each other's clothing or rifles so as not to lose touch. At grey dawn we had cleared the wood and found ourselves, in a thick fog, in the valley of the Oise. Our guides, however, served us well and at about 6.30 a.m. we crossed the river at Varesnes, I think, just before the bridge was blown up, and here we found the rest of the brigade.

The Rifles acted as rearguard to the Division and marched via Blérancourt to Vic-sur-Aisne where they spent the night. Lowry remembered:

> So the retreat continued day after day, deploying at intervals, getting such good cover with the aid of our entrenching tools that the Germans suffered heavily from our rifle fire and never knew where it came from. Except for the exhaustion, it was really splendid fighting, combining as it did rapidity of movement with the maximum effect on the enemy, and the spirit of all ranks remained magnificently high throughout the time. In fact, the temptation throughout was not to retire in time, but to hang on to positions for too long a period ... In these last two days before reaching the forest of Crécy, the German advance had ceased to trouble us in any way, and we were saved the sad and familiar spectacle of families flying before the German hordes, carrying what they could save of their lares and penates with them, for it had proved a heart-breaking sight.

They set off again on the morning of the 31st via Montigny and Villers Cotterêts to a park near Coyelles. Two companies, C and D, were on outpost duty while the remainder of the battalion bivouacked. The march resumed on 1 September via Vauciennes, Lévignen to Villers-St Genest and, on the 2nd, via Bouillancy, Marcilly, Barcy, to Pringy. At 3 a.m. on the 3rd, the Rifles took up the rearguard position and moved to La Marche. The enemy's cavalry and infantry were reported one mile north of St Soupplets so they moved off at about 10 a.m. via Penchard, over the Marne at Meaux (the bridge being blown up as soon as they crossed), Boutigny, to Sancy. On 4 September the Rifles took up an outpost position covering Vaucourtois but withdrew during the night and resumed heading south to the east of Paris, via Crécy, Obélisque, Neufmoutiers-en-Brie to La Motte Farm about 1.5 miles north of Châtres. It was here that their first reinforcement of 150 men arrived from St Nazaire. The battalion had the unique honour of being received by the brigade at the close of their rear-guard action during the retreat from Mons by a special ovation. The road was spontaneously lined by troops from the other units who rushed out to shake hands with the officers and men. The long retreat was now over and it was time to go on the offensive: the Battle of the Marne had commenced and the German advance was being checked. Lt. Lowry's mood changed:

> To our great joy, the following morning we advanced towards the enemy. It had been very difficult to deal with the men, as for some time, like the officers – though we did not say so – they felt enraged at always being ordered to retire, as since Le Cateau we had not been permitted to have a really good biff at 'Jerry'.

The battalion set out on the morning of the 6th heading north-east via Neufmoutiers and Obélisque to Faremoutiers. On the 7th they continued via Coulommiers to Les Petites Aulnois, where a reinforcement of sixty men under

2/Lt. Magennis arrived, and the next day went through Rebais to Bussières. Some fighting by 8th Brigade was going on ahead of them but the 7th Brigade, in reserve, were not brought forward to engage the enemy. Some wounded Germans were picked up along the way. Col. Bird later recorded:

> 8th September. Apparently a body of Germans was east or south-east of La Ferte overnight and, taking advantage of the darkness, moved across our outpost front back over the Marne. As a result the S. Lancashire, and also General Gough's cavalry brigade which was east or south-east of 3rd Division, had some fighting, and on the morning of the 9th the 2nd R.I.R. were sent across the river at La Ferte to support the S. Lancashire. My orders were not to attack, but to come back over the Marne when relieved by 5th Division. At about noon Count Gleichen's brigade appeared and we repassed the river. After moving in an easterly direction we bivouacked near Bézu ... On the 9th September, 1914, the battalion ... was waiting on the road leading northward to Nanteuil-sur-Marne when a single airman landed in a stubble field close to us. He walked up to me, asked where the head-quarters of the 3rd Division was and whether he could borrow a horse in order to make a personal report to it. He told me that the Germans had a considerable force of infantry with guns on the hills north of the Marne, that the infantry were well hidden behind small woods, and that the Germans were preparing a surprise for us. We lent him the horse, and left a groom to wait for it who later brought the horse back to the battalion.
>
> 10th September. Another long day, uneventful except that one continu-ally passed German bivouacs covered with wine bottles, or houses whose gardens were also littered with bottles.

There now followed a series of moves over several days. On 10 September the Rifles marched via Chézy-en-Orxois to Montêmafroy and, the next day, to Grand Rozoy via Dammard, Neuilly-St Front, and Oulchy-la-Ville; the battalion being the advanced guard to the Brigade. The weather changed dramatically on the 11th when the temperatures dropped and heavy rain fell. The 12th saw them moving via Les Crouttes and Maast-et-Violane to Cerseuil where, due to the very wet weather, some of the men slept in a cave. On the 13th they marched three miles to Braisne where they bivouaced and continued the next day in heavy rain via Brenelle and Chassémy, east of Soissons, to Bois Morin. Then they turned off by a country road and moved towards the railway bridge over the Aisne near Ecluse. This bridge had been blown up so the river was crossed by an improvised footbridge made of a barge with planks alongside. The Germans opened fire as soon as the head of the column approached the bridge. The crossing was made in single file, which took a consid-erable amount of time. Cpl Lucy:

> We had hardly cleared the shelled area near the bridge when bullets began whistling about us. We must have been within a couple of hundred yards of

enemy riflemen but though we looked hard through the undergrowth we could not see them. We cursed them, and relying on the luck of soldiers, we bowed our heads a little, shut our jaws, and went stubbornly on. Quicker we went, on to our toes, and crouching lower ... Their rifles cracked sharply now, and the whistle and whine of bullets passing wide changed to the startling bangs of bullets just missing one ... Our own shells were now bursting a short distance ahead, just beyond a crest line clearly visible to us. This line marked the near edge of a large plateau, and as we made it in a last rush we found this plateau edge forming a small continuous cliff of chalk varying from two to four feet high, giving good protection from bullets, and fair cover from shell-fire. Automatically we halted here, and our officers ordered us to improve the position by digging.

According to Lowry:

It was not before we had got three companies across that the German gunners ended any further attempt on that bridge, impossible in the dark, and the river swollen with the carcasses of horses. We had a splendid fight that day, taking the hill and the wood on its summit before evening. The position was at the Maison Rouge farm, for we had crossed the river at the village of Hervilly. Our flank here swung round into a wood, and we lined a bank fronting a stubble field which led upward at a gentle slope to the village of Condé, which both commanded the hill we occupied and the river below.

Some men were wounded including Capt. Gifford and Lt. Cowley. D Coy was sent to occupy high ground at La Fosse Margnet on the left of the Wiltshires; A Coy followed and took up a position further to the left. Two platoons of D Coy moved forward and commenced entrenching but had to move back owing to being fired on by their own artillery. Capt. Soutry, A Coy, was slightly wounded along with a few others. There was an outburst of rifle fire during the night but nothing was seen.

3

The Aisne

Col. Bird described subsequent events:

> The German position on the Aisne was good. Their artillery commanded the flat marshy valley, all bridges were broken so that our guns could not cross and, as a result, when our infantry occupied the southern edges of the bluffs on the north of the valley, they found themselves without artillery support, close to entrenched infantry who could not be reached by our guns, and exposed to the full force of hostile artillery fire. The Germans, then, gained the time they required to bring up reinforcements, and when they arrived were able to attack in advantageous circumstances. The positions of the German infantry were selected to afford concealment and avoid fire, the field of fire from the trenches was restricted and they relied mainly on flanking machine gun and oblique field-gun fire to beat off our attacks. Placed at the front of a slope the Germans, however, suffered the usual drawback of difficulty of reinforcement and also of bringing up food and ammunition.
>
> At first the Germans burst their shrapnel high and did little harm, nor was their fire accurate. At the Aisne, however, the bursts were good but, even so, little damage was done in proportion to the ammunition expended. The H.E. was hardly more effective, that is the small shell fired at us. I thought the German pursuit slack and cautious. They ought to have taken my battalion on two if not three occasions. Apparently they did not march until late in the day – about noon – possibly owing to difficulties as to supplies, and as a result they only came up with us at nightfall, and we always made good our escape during darkness. I have only one other item to mention – the dreadful saltiness of the bully beef. After eating it an unquenchable thirst resulted which was very trying to men making long marches in hot weather and in a not-too-well watered country.

By nightfall the 3rd Division held high ground in a semi-circle about Vailly, the 7th Brigade being on the left, with its right on the Ostel road; 2nd RIR was due south of Rouge Maison. The Division's war diary reported that 'the weather from the 13th to the 21st September was wet and cold and the infantry in the trenches, being unable to take off their wet boots or to cook and being constantly under shell fire had a trying experience.' On the 15th a patrol from D Coy under Lt. Dawes was ordered forward to ascertain the whereabouts of the enemy and came under heavy fire; one man was killed while Dawes and another man were wounded. Cpl Lucy:

> We were ordered to fall in outside the caves, and out we went, shying a bit at the sight of blood-dripped stretchers propped against the wall of the cave mouth. Outside we saw some of our dead lying in grotesque positions ... A hollow in the ground about ten yards from the caves was filled with bandaged wounded, with whom we conversed ... I was looking keenly at this picture of our wounded, and thinking how good and brave they were, and also envying those with slight wounds who would go away back to England, or, with luck, to Ireland, when the scene suddenly changed. A rising tearing noise like that of an approaching train heralded the arrival of a heavy shell. Nearer and nearer it came and we all crouched down where we were. The wounded squirmed lower down in their hollow. We closed our teeth to the shattering burst, which seemed right on top of us, and then after a pause and a deep breath I slowly raised my head to see that the shell had exploded precisely over the hollow and killed every one of the wounded.

Lt. Lowry was with A Coy:

> The following morning the colonel, wishing to make sure whether we were up against the main body of the enemy and whether they were entrenched, ordered two companies to attack, including my own. There was practically no cover, and the ground was hard and bare, so we proceeded by short rushes ... The Germans were, however, waiting for us, and when we got to within a few hundred yards of their line they opened a perfect hail of machine-gun and rifle fire and shrapnel – a veritable tornado of flying, shrieking metal, well directed. Part of the company on our left got into the first line of German trenches, but were ultimately compelled to retire, as it was obvious that not only were the Germans dug in, but were in full force. Captain Bowen-Colthurst, who commanded this reconnaissance, was badly wounded in the assault, whilst two officers were killed and half the men killed or wounded; the machine-gun and shrapnel played havoc among us as we were getting back across the open valley ... In the days following there was no question as to what the Germans intended, as they attacked us continually, and their artillery was amazing in the way that they got on to our positions.

Col. Bird made this report in 1918:

> At daybreak on the 15th Brigadier-General McCracken came over the river, and I rejoined my battalion. On arrival at the hill crest I found the officers and men of A and D Companies standing about, and on asking what they were doing I was told that they thought the Germans had retired. I at once

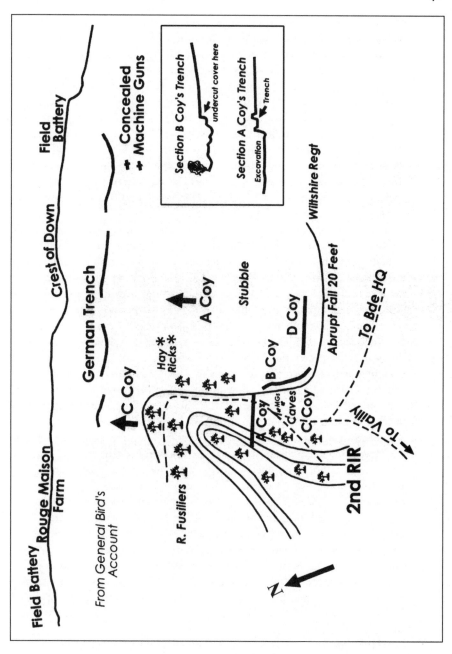

Map 4: The Aisne, 15 September 1914

ordered two officer's patrols to be sent out to clear up the situation. I then went a little north and found Major Spedding who pointed out the enemy's trenches in a hollow 700 yards from us and told me he had sent C Company to occupy the edge of a wood some 300 yards from the enemy.

I agreed that this was sound but demurred in regard to the officer selected [Capt. Colthurst] for this duty as I had no confidence in his judgement and feared he might make a rash attack. Major Spedding, however, assured me that strict orders had been given to him not to proceed beyond the wood. I then asked how long ago C Company had been sent off and he replied 20 minutes. As the distance to the edge of the wood was not more than a quarter of a mile and as no firing had been heard, I concluded that probably the Germans had retired, and ordered A Company to move forward east of the wood in support of C Company.

I now saw what I took to be a few Germans running away and, as this seemed to show that their trenches were still held, signalled to A Company to halt. No firing, however, took place, and I therefore sent my adjutant to the commander of A Company [Capt. Durant] to tell him to advance but to proceed with the greatest possible caution. Major Spedding now joined A Company, and with the M. Gun section the company moved forward. Almost immediately it began to attack by rushes and was met by heavy rifle, machine gun and artillery fire. The movements of the other company were hidden by the wood. About now the officer's patrols returned and reported one officer wounded and the enemy in force. As it was obvious that our partial attack could not succeed I sent my adjutant for B Company, which was in reserve at caves and hollows ... for I feared that the enemy could counter attack. He lost his way and could not find it, so I went and brought it forward myself and placed it in position to cover the retirement of the two other companies.

Meanwhile C Company had succeeded in rushing a trench and taking a few prisoners, but being met with heavy artillery fire and counterattacked was driven into the wood where A Company and the machine guns had been forced to take shelter. Those companies now streamed in disorder out of the wood and I rallied them 200 or 300 yards further back behind the crest. The Germans dropped several percussion shells among us as the men were rallying ... I understand that the OC C Company, who was wounded, subsequently stated that he was under the impression that he had been sent forward to attack the Germans. I asked the OC A Company, who was also wounded, when I met him at Home, why he had attacked, and he said that he had a faint recollection of having been told to advance with caution, but seeing the other company attacking he did so too.

Having made a report to Brigade HQ I rearranged my battalion ... and the men threw up cover with their entrenching implements. In the wood roots prevented much progress and outside it we were soon on solid rock. The reserve was in natural caves or hollows of which there were several near our line. Signal communication was established by our signallers with Brigade

HQ at the foot of the hill 800 yards away. My position was in a hollow near the machine guns.

The Germans shelled us a little with shrapnel and at about 10 p.m. there was an alarm of enemy attack and a good deal of firing. During the afternoon our patrols brought in some of the wounded who had been left between the German trenches and our own. The Company QMS reported during the day that they had rations ready at the foot of the hill and a party was sent for them. Subsequently a party was sent off each evening for rations at about 9 p.m. and returned with them at dawn when they were issued.

A damning complaint by Col. Bird was made in April 1915:

Captain J.C. Bowen-Colthurst showed, during the first few weeks of the campaign of 1914, that his military capacity and judgement were of so low a standard and his mind so lacking in balance that in my opinion he is not fit to be entrusted with the leadership of a company in the field. This officer so far broke down on the morning after the action at Mons, and his actions and demeanours exercised so dispiriting an effect on his men, that I was obliged to suspend him from the command of his company. Three or four days later, when the pressure of the enemy's pursuit had somewhat relaxed, and since Captain Bowen-Colthurst appeared to have recovered from his breakdown, I reinstated him in command of his company pending a decision by the Brigadier as to his future. I also verbally informed the Brigade-Major of the action that had been taken. Unfortunately an opportunity of threshing out the matter did not occur before Captain Bowen-Colthurst was disabled.

On this occasion Captain Bowen-Colthurst showed great want of judgement, although displaying, I believe, high personal courage. The circumstances were as follows: During the forcing of the passage of the Aisne, I was placed in command of the Wiltshire Regiment and my own Battalion, the two forming the advanced-guard of the 7th Infantry Brigade. On the afternoon of the 12th (?) September, the advanced-guard crossed the river and occupied the heights of the right bank near Vailly. Next morning soon after daybreak, the remainder of the 7th Infantry Brigade passed the Aisne, when I rejoined my Battalion. On reaching the heights I found that Major Spedding, the 2nd in command (now missing), had shortly before my arrival sent Captain Bowen-Colthurst's company forward to a distance of between 400–500 yards in front of the line held by the Battalion, for the purpose of occupying the northern edge of a copse which seemed to extend to a locality favourable for outflanking a German trench visible at about 750 yards from us.

When I demurred to the despatch of this Officer on such a mission – for throughout the campaign he had shown himself the least efficient and reliable of the company commanders – Major Spedding assured me that Captain Bowen-Colthurst had received definite orders not to proceed beyond the wood. It seems, however, that on reaching the edge of the wood Captain Bowen-

Colthurst saw a portion of the enemy's trenches, which were invisible from the line held by the R. Irish Rifles, lying about 250 yards to the front.

Without communicating with the Battalion headquarters Captain Bowen-Colthurst promptly led his company forward and captured this portion of trench. The enemy at once delivered a vigorous counter-attack supported by heavy Artillery fire, with the result that Captain Bowen-Colthurst's company was driven back with heavy loss, the whole of the officers (four) and about 75 NCOs and men being killed or wounded.

However, the war diary of 3rd Division states:

At 5.30 a.m. 2nd RIR reported about two platoons of enemy entrenching to their front. About 6 a.m. two companies 2nd RIR were pushed forward on the left to clear enemy out of wood south-east of Rouge Maison and between it and La Fosse Marguel. One company advancing through the wood was driven back by machine gun fire; the other company on its right advanced too far and was apparently enfiladed by shell fire and also suffered from the machine gun fire from La Rouge Maison. The 2nd RIR therefore took up their original position.

Capt. Colthurst made this statement in his defence:

I beg to point out that Colonel Bird does not know me well, out of 16 years service I have only served under him for a few months. I request therefore, that the opinions of the following officers – under whom I have served – be obtained in regard to my fitness for leadership in the Field ... I received verbal orders from Major Spedding (now missing) to advance through the wood with my Company – and to clear up the situation. In the absence of Colonel Bird, Major Spedding was commanding the Battalion at that time. Outposts had reported that the sound of wheels had been heard at night and it was believed that the enemy were retiring. Major Spedding and I both knew from the report of our Scouts on the previous evening that the nearest Germans were entrenched about 200 yards outside the wood. I had a piquet close to the front edge of the wood watching the Germans. I asked Major Spedding specially if he wished me to attack, and he replied 'Certainly!' On reaching the front edge of the wood I directed No. 9 Platoon to hold the edge of the wood and to open fire on the Germans in front. This was done with considerable effect and several Germans were seen to fall.

I was then reinforced by the Battalion Machine Guns, and I directed No. 9 Platoon and the Battalion Machine Guns to keep up the fire from the edge of the wood, No. 10 Platoon to work up the valley in the left and to attack the German right. Nos. 11 and 12 Platoons to remain in reserve in the wood under CSM Hart. The attack made by No. 10 Platoon was successful, and the whole of the occupants of the trench, some 20 Germans, were put out of action, six unwounded prisoners of the Prussian 64th Regiment were taken. A strong German 2nd line, some 300 yards away, was discovered behind the captured trench, and I directed No. 10 Platoon to fall back to the wood with their prisoners. Only two of my Platoons (about 80 men) were engaged in this attack, and of these only 1 Platoon advanced beyond the cover of the wood. The Platoon Commander of No. 10 (2nd Lt. Magenis) and the Battalion Scout Officer (2nd Lt. Swaine) who volunteered to go with him were both killed close to the captured trench. Lt. Peebles, Commanding No. 9 Platoon was subsequently wounded when the wood was shelled – but I have been unable to ascertain that there were more than 15 casualties, including officers, in the two Platoons during this attack and the firing and shelling which followed.

While this attack, which I was directing, was in progress, Major Spedding was himself directing another attack on the trenches to my right. This 2nd attack was being carried out by A Company – Major Spedding came up to Nos. 11 and 12 Platoons to advance through the wood and attack in conjunction with A Company the German trench on my right. This attack was unable to reach the German trench and suffered heavily. Although Major Spedding is now missing the fact that these two platoons of mine were led forward by Major Spedding himself, goes to prove that my attack on the left portion of the German trenches was in accordance with his orders.

The Germans then opened a very heavy shell fire on the wood and on our lines and the Company continued to suffer further casualties from shell fire throughout the day. The trench which had been captured by No. 10 Platoon was not re-occupied by the Germans until some 5 hours later ... I absolutely deny Colonel Bird's statement that I broke down after Mons or that I caused any of my men to become dispirited. Colonel Bird sent a note next day to the effect that I was to resume the command of my Company. I had not seen him again in the interval. With regard to the second incident referred to in Colonel Bird's report, namely the action at Vailly ... I attach six sworn statements by NCOs present, describing this incident, I would in conclusion point out that the incidents referred to occurred in August and September 1914; that the report was not written until April 1915, and that I did not receive it until July 1915.

The NCO statements were provided by Sgt A. Anderson, Sgt W. Flack, Sgt W. Rainey (all of No. 11 Platoon), Sgt J. Baines (No. 9 Platoon), Sgt W.J. Murphy (No. 10 Platoon), and CSM J. Harte (C Coy) at Portobello Barracks. This version was forwarded to the War Office by Major-General Sir Lovick Friend, Commanding the Troops in Ireland, with the following comments:

Forwarded and strongly recommended for favourable consideration. It is difficult to understand why Colonel Bird's report has been so long delayed – it is dated 8th April 1915 – although the incidents referred to occurred in August and September 1914, and there does not appear to be any strong reason for the report to be made after such a long delay. As to the incident on 15th September on the Aisne, I would point out that the Officer Commanding the Battalion (Major Spedding) evidently acquiesced in Captain Colthurst's action as he co-operated with him and supported his attack as much as he could. This action itself bears evidence of Captain Colthurst's great personal bravery and dash and resulted in the capture of a portion of the enemy's trenches, and if anything can be said against such action – it can only be to say that it was an excusable error of judgement.[1]

Cpl Lucy described Colthurst that day as he urged A Coy to support him:

... a tall gaunt captain with the light of battle in his eye. A very religious man he was too, always talking about duty, and a great Bible reader. Tall, sinewy, with pale face and pale-blue eyes, colourless hair, and a large, untidy, colourless moustache, he came at us looking for blood. He reminded me of a grisly Don Quixote. 'They have gone,' he cried jubilantly and with certainty, in a cracked voice, 'all the Germans have gone away, except about one platoon, which I have located in that wood to our left front. I intend to capture that enemy platoon with my company, but I want volunteers from A Company to move across the open to support me, while I work forward through the wood, which enters the left of my company line. Now, who will volunteer?' ... [After the attack] The warlike commander of the left company, bleeding from several wounds in various parts of his body, and looking more fanatical than ever, would not have any of his hurts dressed until he had interrogated his prisoners. He questioned them in German, and was removed from them with difficulty, and made to lie on a stretcher.

The truth appears to be that Colthurst made an attack with one platoon while Bird and Spedding thought the whole company was attacking. In consequence, Major Spedding committed further troops to an assault that was already being reversed. The delay in Bird making a report could well be attributed to the fact that he lost a leg in action shortly after the attack. Cpl Lucy commented:

... many stout riflemen died unknown and unsung who would have been decorated for bravery had their deeds been witnessed by officers. Up to the present very few of our regiment had been recommended. Our Colonel, admirable in other ways, believed in the policy that every man's best was his least in the way of duty.

The officer casualties in this action were: 2/Lts Swaine and Magennis killed; Capts Bowen-Colthurst, Durant, Lts Peebles and Varwell wounded. The Rifles remained in position on the hill, with D Coy replacing A Coy, and B moving to protect the left flank. The position was shelled throughout the day with some casu-

1 In these instances the quotes are from Capt. Bowen-Colthurst's file WO374/14934.

alties. The enemy attacked from 8 p.m. until 9.15 p.m. Falls described the situation at this time:

> The ugly day, with ceaseless wet adding to other miseries, ended in alarms, and a rattle of musketry along the front caused by the reports of German attacks which were probably no more than the movements of patrols. It had been disappointing. The 3rd Division had been ready for a new advance in co-operation with the 2nd on its right, but by now it had been decided that there could be no new attack that day. It was intended to continue the advance both on the 16th and 17th, but as a fact there was thereafter no serious attempt to go forward on the British front. The centre of interest was shifting northward, where the rival turning movements known as the 'race to the sea' were preparing. For the British all chance was gone with the arrival of strong German reinforcements on their front, while they were completely outgunned by the siege howitzers which the enemy was hastening forward.

Col. Bird outlined subsequent events:

> 16th September. This was a rainy and foggy day. The enemy's field artillery fired intermittently, ours not at all. Whenever the fog lifted we could see men in widely extended order, 30–40 paces apart being dribbled down the hill into the German trenches. We opened fire when the Germans were coming down in what we thought too large numbers and caused some casualties but at considerable expenditure of ammunition as the ranges were from 1,000–1,500 yards and visibility was poor. During the day I obtained the entrenching tools from our first line transport and the men improved their cover as far as they could. Touch was obtained with the R. Fusiliers on our left, and some more of our wounded were brought in by our patrols. In the evening we were informed that country people had reported that the Germans intended to attack during the night.
>
> 17th September. As nothing had happened by midnight I sent my adjutant with one private to ascertain whether there were signs of movement in the German lines. He went and actually fell into a German trench and found everyone asleep. I thereupon reported this to Brigade HQ. During the night the Germans shelled Vailly and the hillsides behind us with some heavy batteries probably near Jerlaux. The compass direction of the flash and estimated range, 4,500 yards, were reported to Brigade HQ. This shelling caused some casualties including Major Spedding, my senior major, who was in Vailly with the ration party and also to receive a draft of men said to be waiting there. This draft consisted of 1 officer and 6 men. During the morning my patrols reported no sign of movement in the German trenches and I therefore sent my adjutant to make a reconnaissance. He returned and said he could see no one and had stood in the open 300 yards from the trench without being fired at.

I accordingly ordered D Company to occupy the edge of the wood and patrol from it. The company commander took his company forward and sent word that he would like me to come and see the situation as the German trench appeared to be full of men. I went to the edge of the wood and, after consulting with him, ordered him to fall back as the company would have been much exposed and the roots of the trees made entrenching difficult. No sooner had the order been given than the enemy, who seems to have discovered our presence, began to shell the wood heavily and we had some casualties as we fell back. Our guns sent a few shrapnel onto the Germans and things then quieted down. A company of the Worcesters was sent to support me on this day and placed in the caves behind C Company. The night passed without incident, except for the usual shelling and was rainy.

18th September. Rain again fell, I think. The German artillery became more active and we were obliged to keep under cover most of the day. We lost a few men from artillery fire, and some of our patrols met German patrols in the wood ... An artillery subaltern came to our lines and I pointed out the direction of the enemy's guns as estimated and showed him a fuze we had picked up set at 1,500 metres. Another subaltern came up on 19th, I think, and these two were the only officers not belonging to my battalion, or attached to it, who visited our position. Nothing unusual occurred during the night of the 18th/19th.

19th September. Early on the 19th the Germans began to shell our position with shrapnel and continued, with pauses, to do so all morning. In the afternoon the shelling was more vigorous, the battery attacking us firing progressively at 1,500 metres, the usual procedure being two salvos short, one on our trenches, and one over. Probably the fact that the trees were 50–60 yards behind us made it difficult for them exactly to locate our position, but the fire was accurate, some shells bursting or grazing our parapets. The casualties were nevertheless comparatively few. Between 2 p.m. and 3 p.m. I was sent for to go to Brigade HQ and walked down the hill. The Germans were now occasionally sweeping the hill side with H.E. shells, probably 5.9″.

I returned at about 4 p.m. and got safely into the cave behind B Company's line and was waiting at the mouth of the cave for the shelling to moderate to go to my HQ. A H.E. shell now burst in a tree on B Coy's line which we had been unable to fell for want of tools and I and two other officers were wounded. At 6 p.m. the enemy attacked, bringing up machine guns, but was easily beaten off. Our artillery gave us no support at all and I believe was still on the south bank of the Aisne. [Officers wounded: Lt.-Col. Bird, Capt. Becher, Adjutant Lt. Dillon, and Lt. Cowley.]

There was a slight bombardment after daylight on the 20th and, at about 10 a.m., a severe attack took place supported by artillery that lasted a little over two hours. Both machine guns of 2nd RIR were put out of action and Capt. Becher was wounded. One company of the South Lancs came up in support. A report was received from the Wiltshires that the Germans had broken through on their right. Many casualties were caused by machine-gun fire from the wood, but a company of Worcesters was brought up by Capt. Goodman against the enemy's right and the Germans fell back immediately. Lt. Lowry gave more details:

> On the following Sunday morning, a lovely day, we heard music from the German lines and thought that 'Jerry' was going to church, but within a few minutes he started one of the most deadly attacks he had made on our line ... We were short of ammunition, with no artillery to speak of, and many rifles were difficult to handle as we had no oil for days and it was impossible to use them for rapid fire. However, we managed to get bayonets fixed, though in many cases this was difficult owing to the dirt, and kept our fire until the enemy were right upon us. We beat them off after four hours of the very best of hard fighting, but at a sad loss to our regiment of 200 officers and men – a company of the Worcesters which had been brought up in support also suffering heavily. It is interesting to state that we found from the officer in charge of the transport in the village of Hervilly that, no matter where the transport moved, the enemy artillery immediately ranged upon it with extreme accuracy. This we knew to be due to our lines being interwoven with spies – four German soldiers in uniform, indeed, being caught about this time on the Paris side of the Aisne; these were found secreted in a well-concealed dugout which was fully equipped with telephonic communications with both their own forces and also spies in this area.

The next day was quiet until a heavy attack took place about dusk supported by artillery and machine guns. This went on for two hours and there was intermittent firing all night. The Leicestershire Regt had relieved the battalion by 3 a.m., 22 September, and the Rifles marched down to Vailly. Casualties during the period 14–21 September were 3 officers and 44 other ranks killed; 12 officers and 226 other ranks wounded.[2] The Rifles crossed the Aisne and marched to Augy where they remained for the next few days, then relieved the South Lancs at Chassémy, 26 September, taking up the position at dusk. A, B, and D Coys were on outpost duty with C in reserve. At 4 a.m. on the 27th a report was received that the Germans were crossing the Condé bridge in large numbers; this worried all concerned but the report proved unfounded. Everything was quiet and, having been relieved by the Wiltshires on the afternoon of the 28th, they went to billets at Braisnes.

The battalion marched to Couvrelles on the 30th and, the next day, continued south to Grand Rozoy. There then followed a series of night marches: on 2 October via St-Rémy, Billy-sur-Ourcq, Chouy, to Noroy-sur-Ourcq; on the 3rd via Tröesnes, La Ferte Milon, Coyelles to Vaumoise; on the 4th via Crépy-en-Valois, Bethisy to

---

2 Killed: Major C.R. Spedding, 2/Lts Magenis and Swaine. Wounded: Lt.-Col. W.D. Bird, Capts C.M.L. Becher (twice), J.C. Bowen-Colthurst, H.N. Durant, H.L. Gifford, T.L.B. Soutry, Lt. and Adjutant S.S. Dillon, Lts V.L.S. Cowley (twice), C.R.B. Dawes, G.S. Norman, A.E. Peebles, and R.P. Varwell.

Verberie. The next day they crossed the Oise by the bridge of boats at Port Salut, entrained in cattle wagons at Longueil-Ste Marie by 2 a.m. on the 6th and headed west arriving at Noyelles-sur-Mer about 4.30 p.m. Orders were eventually received from Abbeville, over the station telephone, to detrain and find billets for the night at Noyelles. They marched east towards the enemy on the 7th via Sailly, Le Titre, Hautvillers to Le Plessiel; north to Regnauville on the 9th and on to Hesdin where the battalion was moved north-east by French lorries to Floringhem. There was a considerable lack of organization and a great deal of confusion; battalions and brigades got mixed up, but eventually the Rifles were sorted out at Floringhem and held an outpost line. Relieved by the Worcestershires on the afternoon of the 10th, they went into billets at Pernes where nine officers joined; then marched north on the 11th via Floringhem, Auchel, Lozinghem, Allouagne, Gonnehem to Hinges (north of Béthune). The next day, two companies of 2nd RIR marched with the South Lancs as advance guard, the other two at the head of the main body.

4

La Bassée

Falls writes:

> The Battle of La Bassée ... is overshadowed by the still more tremendous
> fighting which developed farther north. But it is a critical moment in the
> 'race to the sea'. Its results were disappointing, for with a shade of luck it
> would have succeeded at least in the consolidation of the Aubers ridge, which
> would have had an important influence upon the future campaign on the
> new British front. The three British corps were being directed, the II on La
> Bassée, the III upon Armentières, the I upon Ypres. The II Corps was to
> drive the enemy, not yet assembled in any considerable strength, from La
> Bassée and press on to Lille. The 3rd Division had deployed along the Aire
> Canal, its right on Hinges ... The orders issued by the Division ... were for
> the 8th Brigade, on the left, to advance in the direction of Herlies, on the
> Aubers Ridge, and the 7th to move into La Couture. The movement was to
> be a right wheel on the left flank to turn the flank of the enemy engaged
> with the 5th Division.

The Germans were encountered at La Couture, which was under shellfire. The
South Lancs crossed the Loisne and formed a bridgehead north of the stream; 2nd
RIR reinforcing them one company at a time. There were a few casualties including Capt. Master who was killed. This position was held during the night when
orders were received that the advance was to be continued next morning in conjunction with 8th Brigade, which had been held up and was still at Vielle Chapelle.
Owing to the streams and ditches it took some time to move the two battalions out
of the position at La Couture. The advance was contested but was carried to just
short of Croix Barbée, some of the Middlesex Regt and C Coy, 2nd RIR, occupying the houses near the crossroads. The Germans were holding Croix Barbée itself
and the woods to the south. Their artillery was behind and some of their trenches
ran in front of the village north of the La Couture Road. During the afternoon an
artillery officer brought information that the British were going to shell Croix Barbée
and requested that 2nd RIR be withdrawn from close proximity to the village. A
line was taken up from the group of houses midway between Croix Barbée and La
Couture. The Middlesex Regt was on the left, South Lancs on the right; three com-

panies were in the front line with one in reserve. Capt. Goodman, Capt. Smyth, and 2/Lt. Fitzgerald were wounded during the morning along with a few other ranks. The British artillery started before dark. A few Germans were seen advancing down La Couture Road but were soon driven back.

The Rifles went forward on the morning of 13 October under heavy machine gun fire and reoccupied the old position just short of Croix Barbée. Lt. Whitfeld was killed and Lt. Heron was wounded at this time. Soon after dark heavy firing broke out on the right and extended along the whole front, both sides firing heavily for two or three hours. This had originated with a French night attack on Vermelles. There was a pause on the 14th due to counter-attacks and the death of 3rd Division's commander who was replaced by Major-General C. MacKenzie. Orders were received, 15 October, that the advance was to be continued at 2 p.m. The Rifles moved to a short distance beyond Croix Barbée and came under some frontal and enfilade artillery fire, but there were few casualties. The line was held during the night from a point on the road a little south-west of the crossroads at Rouge Croix to the parallel road leading into the Neuve Chapelle–Estaires Road. They continued the next morning, halting for some time on the Neuve Chapelle–Fleurbaix Road, resuming in a slightly changed direction. They came under some shellfire near the Bois de Biez, but there were no casualties, and the line was held at night running north-east from the woods, with 1st Lincolnshire Regt on the left and South Lancs on the right.

The advance continued on the 17th to high ground at Haut Pommereau, on the slopes of Aubers Ridge, where they halted for some time and reconnoitred the village of L'Aventure. From here German reinforcements could be seen moving with a good deal of motor transport towards La Bassée along the road from Fournes. A message was received that the 8th Brigade was going to attack Herlies, and 2nd RIR advanced with the Brigade, three companies in front and one in reserve. The reserve company was left at L'Aventure, the other three being drawn off in the attack on Herlies but were eventually recalled and the line straightened out in conjunction with 7th Brigade; holding that night near Launoy. The battalion was relieved by 2nd King's Own Yorkshire Light Infantry at 5 a.m. on the 18th and marched back to Pont Logy, then moved forward about 7 p.m. and occupied the outpost line in front of Bois de Biez. This position was held until midday on the 19th when orders were received to go into billets about the Bois de Biez.

They marched at 2 a.m. on the 20th to L'Aventure, relieved 2nd KOYLI, and took up their former position. A considerable amount of shelling was endured during the day but there were no casualties. That night they fell back to a partially prepared line along the road running through Halpegarbe, leaving C Coy to hold the position, and proceeded to entrench. Three companies were in the firing line; C Coy, when it rejoined, was placed in reserve. Shells came from the right all day, enfilading the position, but no casualties were suffered. During the afternoon the enemy was seen moving across their front in a northerly direction. A certain amount of sniping came from the rear during the day, apparently from the woods north of the village. Orders were received to fall back at midnight on a prepared position at

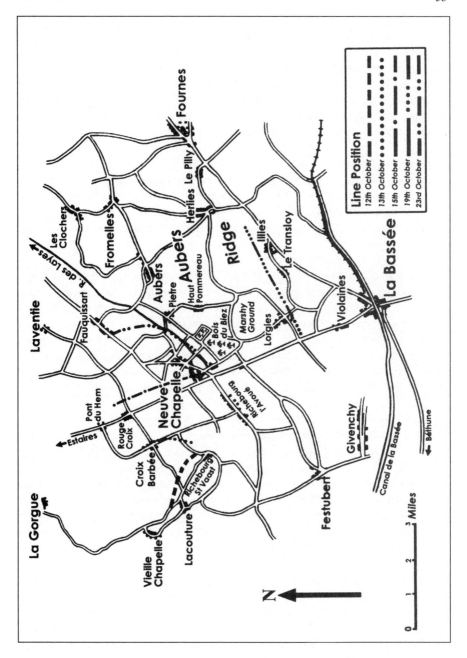

Map 5: The Battle of La Bassée

Neuve Chapelle, the movement to commence from the flanks of the Brigade. The RIR, being on the left, assembled at Halpegarbe and moved off soon after midnight.

They arrived at Neuve Chapelle on the 22nd, placing three companies in the trenches and one in reserve at the school. At 6 a.m., HQ and the reserve company moved to the chateau, near a fork in the road at the north end of the village, this being more central and made communication easier. Most of the day was spent in digging reserve and communication trenches, with a certain amount of rifle fire coming from an advanced German post. Cpl Lucy lamented:

> All we wanted now was a little time for final improvements to finish off the good work of the sappers, and we would smash anything that came at us ... But we got no time. It was the beginning of the end for us, for we had now arrived at the place of our destruction, and our fine battalion, still about seven hundred strong, perished here, almost completely, in the following five days.

The position had some disadvantages: the 8th Brigade on the left were echeloned back a considerable distance; a road on the left flank led towards the enemy and included several houses that had not been destroyed. This area was entangled and machine guns were entrenched so as to command as long a stretch of the road as possible. During the night the Rifles suffered friendly fire from the 8th Brigade: returning patrols were shot at by other units and some men were killed. Later that night there was heavy enemy firing along the line and the situation changed little over the next day. The Germans attacked that night but were repulsed. Lucy:

> We let them have it. We blasted and blew them to death. They fell in scores, in hundreds, the marching column wilting under our rapid fire. The groups melted away, and no man was able to stand in our sight within five minutes. The few survivors panicked, and tried to keep their feet in retreat. We shot them through the back. A red five minutes. No fire orders were given, as none was needed. Crowds of Germans at close range were plugged easily and rapidly by every one of us. The riflemen shouted as they fired: 'Come on boys. Let 'em have it', and the attack spluttered out, leaving lines and circles of corpses and wounded.

The German fire became heavier on the 24th and casualties increased. The recoil spring of the field gun in the centre of the front line of trenches broke and the gun went out of action, although the gun on the left remained. The enemy commenced a severe bombardment of Neuve Chapelle from their heavy guns at La Bassée and another to the left front. Soon after dark a determined German attack was made in considerable strength but was repulsed with heavy casualties 'judging by the noise made by German wounded lying in front of the trenches'.[1] Falls:

1 War Diary.

It was a wild evening of volleys fired at the flashes of the enemy's fire or at dim figures distinguished in the darkness, with ever and anon a momentary breakthrough, men meeting with shouts and oaths on the wet, slippery ground, thrusting at one another with bayonets. For an hour the affair was doubtful. Then gradually the enemy was shaken off, and by 6 p.m. the attack was definitely repulsed. It had been a fine example of obstinate courage and endurance.

The Corps Commander, General Smith-Dorrien, issued the following order on 25 October:

> During an attack by the enemy on the 7th Infantry Brigade last night the enemy came to close quarters with the Royal Irish Rifles, who repulsed them with great gallantry with the bayonet, and made several prisoners. The Corps Commander wishes to compliment the regiment on its splendid feat, and directs that all battalions of the corps shall be informed of the circumstances and of his high appreciation of the gallantry displayed.

The Germans succeeded in establishing themselves in the houses near the left flanks of the trenches and, on the morning of the 25th, rushed the end trench. They succeeded in capturing the remaining field gun there but only got to fire one round before it overturned, the recoil action having been purposely sabotaged by the British gunners. With the remains of B Coy in reserve, many having replaced casualties in the firing line, and a platoon of the Lincolns, the enemy was eventually driven out but the trench could not be reoccupied as the British artillery was shelling it and the rear ground. The War Diary noted:

> In fact this day our artillery shelled the trenches held by this battalion causing several casualties and it was some time before they could be stopped as the telephone line was cut by shell fire and orderlies took a long time getting back. The enemy's bombardment this day was more severe and our casualties heavy. The two machine guns were put out of action, the water jackets being damaged by rifle fire.

During these two days the following casualties occurred among the officers: Capts Reynolds, Kennedy and Lt. Rea were killed; Major Daunt suffered concussion, Lts Lowry and Laville were wounded. The battalion, which was previously very short handed, was now left practically without any officers. B Coy was in the trenches, D in support, while A and C were ordered back into billets at Richebourg St Vaast. At 3 a.m., 26 October, the enemy broke through the line in the vicinity of B and D Coys (commanded by Lts Finlay and Innes-Cross) and no further trace of these companies could be found. In the afternoon A and C were ordered up into the firing line. Four officers joined the battalion together with Major G.J. Ryan DSO, RMF, who took command. That night the enemy was driven back and the trenches were reoccupied. Cpl Lucy:

Once more the lines of German infantry, apparently inexhaustible, came over the field of dead, and again those of us still sound stood up to stave them off, but our strong ranks of riflemen were gone, and our weak fire caused alarmingly few casualties. The enemy swarmed everywhere in sight, and wearily, with bloodshot eyes and tired limbs, we destroyed them, shooting at one group, until we saw another threatening nearer. We shot and shot, and we stopped them once more on our company front, but they got in again on the left, and to some purpose ... One man, not waiting to be bayoneted by assaulting Germans got out of his trench to sell his life dearly. He was a noted fencer, and he was reported to have bayoneted six oncoming Germans, and held up the attack in his immediate vicinity, until a seventh German, refusing the challenge of cold steel, checked in his stride, stood back, and shot the Irishman through the forehead.

War Diary, 27 October:

The trenches to the left of A and C Coys being unoccupied by our own troops, the enemy, about 7 a.m., got round our left flank and rear, after these two Coys had suffered very severe losses from shrapnel, howitzer and rifle fire and Capt. Dixon had sent repeated messages for support; he was obliged to retire these 2 Coys into the village of Neuve Chapelle (250 yards in rear) to prevent the enemy getting round in rear of the Brigade. Only 2 officers and about 46 NCOs and men succeeded in getting back out of a total of 5 officers and about 250 NCOs and men. Capt. Davis being killed, Lt. Mulcahy-Morgan wounded and missing and Capt. Jonsson missing. The fighting strength of the battalion was now under 200. The battalion that evening went into billets at Richebourg St Vaast.

Owing to being heavily shelled on the 29th, the RIR moved three miles to La Couture where they were joined by the remainder of the Brigade. The next day Capt. Dixon took command from Major Ryan who returned to his regiment. At 1 p.m. the Rifles marched twelve miles north to Le Doulieu for the night. On 31 October they marched six miles to Merris and, the next day nine miles to Locre, for resting and reorganising. Four officers and 80 men joined at this time. Neuve Chapelle was lost and it would not be retaken until the following March when 1st RIR paid a terrible price.

At 9 a.m., 5 November, the battalion, with a fighting strength of about 250, marched through Ypres and east along the Menin Road to Hooge, to relieve the 7th Division in the firing line south of Heronthage Chateau. Lt. Eldred was mortally wounded, three men were killed and 14 wounded on the 7th; one man was killed and five wounded on the 9th. There was a large artillery and infantry attack by six German corps, 11 November. Cpl Lucy:

The magnificent Prussian Guards made a review of it. They executed their famous goose-step in the sight of their foe, and the field-grey waves came on ... The left of the Prussian Guard attack caught us ... We stopped the Germans on our front, and they were the finest troops of Germany, led by the flower of her noblest houses.

The RIR were only on the fringe of this battle but 15 men had been killed, 10 were wounded and 19 missing – over a quarter of its existing fighting strength. Over the next three days 9 men were wounded before the Rifles went into reserve at Hooge with a total strength of 130. Duties during this time included an officer and 30 men being sent to reinforce the West Kents on the 16th; one officer and 50 men to reinforce the KOSBs on the 18th. Falls:

> Both these battalions were involved in the heavy attack on the 17th, and both killed an extraordinary number of the enemy ... There is no record of the work of the riflemen who were sent to their aid, of whom, indeed, very few survived.

Cpl Lucy:

> My eyes weakened, wandered, and rested on the half-hidden corpses of men and youths. Near and far they looked calm, and even handsome, in death. Their strong young bodies thickly garlanded the edge of a wood in rear, a wood called Sanctuary ... Proudly and sorrowfully I looked at them, the Macs and the O's, and the hardy Ulster boys joined together in death on a foreign field.

By now the strength of the battalion was only forty strong. Relieved during the evening of 19 November by 5th R. Fusiliers, they spent the night in trenches near Divisional HQ, about two miles east of Ypres, where two men were wounded. The next morning they marched to Brigade HQ and then moved independently to Westoutre – a distance of fourteen miles. Over the next few days in billets, while resting and reorganising, reinforcements of 4 officers and 507 men joined. Cpl Lucy observed the problem with these new arrivals:

> Their misbehaviour caused through ignorance of the military code brought packs of trouble, and in one month our court-martial trials ran up to the incredible figure of thirty-two. Neglect of duty, absence, drunkenness, and insubordination were the common crimes. The serious ones were assaulting N.C.O.s, and desertion. We were dumbfounded.

Major J.W. Alston arrived on the 25th and took command. On the 27th they marched two miles to Locre, going into support billets, and went into the trenches near Kemmel on the 30th. The position held lay between the Kemmel–Wytschaete Road and the other road which branched from it at Maedelstede Farm, curved northward, then ran roughly parallel to it, past Rossignol Wood, to the main road from Neuve Eglise to Ypres. During this tour three men were killed and seven wounded before they were relieved by the Royal Scots and marched back about seven miles to reserve billets at Westoutre on 3 December. It was during their stay here that Fr H.V. Gill joined as chaplain, along with a reinforcement of 5 officers and 62 men, observing:

> There was plenty to do as there were nearly 1,200 Catholics in the Brigade. About 70 per cent of the men of 2nd RIR were Catholics. Chiefly from the North of Ireland, but with a large sprinkling from other parts of the Provinces ... [10 December] I find the officers very decent fellows – no Catholics except two promoted NCOs.

Three days were then spent in billets at Locre before they returned to the trenches on the 9th. This four-day tour resulted in the following casualties: Capt. Whelan and one man were killed, 11 were wounded and one missing. They returned to Locre for four days on the 12th where a draft of 190 men under Capt. G.A. Burgoyne joined. The next tour in the trenches, 15–18 December, resulted in the loss of six men killed in action, one died of other causes and 31 were wounded. 8666 Rfn J. Johnston was awarded the DCM, 'For conspicuous gallantry throughout the campaign. On 12th December 1914, near Kemmel, when acting as a stretcher bearer, he assisted to carry a wounded officer across fire swept ground, and again on the 16th idem performed a similar act of gallantry.' The German trenches were heavily bombarded on the 18th before 2nd RIR returned to Locre. Prior to moving to the trenches on the 24th, reinforcements of three officers and 90 men had joined. Christmas Day was quiet but there was no truce or fraternization with the enemy in this sector. Five men were wounded before the battalion moved to Westoutre on the 27th. Falls: 'So the year 1914 passed out in a period of comparative quiet, but in conditions of horrible discomfort and suffering, while each side was accumulating more munitions and assembling fresh forces.'

5

First attack at Bellewaarde

There followed a move to Locre on New Year's Eve before returning to the firing line on 4 January. Fr Gill counted his flock: 'The only other unit of the Brigade to have a large amount of RCs was the 2nd S. Lancs. Between both battalions there was over 1,000 RCs.' During the first two months of the year 10 officers and 273 men joined. 3056 L/Cpl Frank McKane wrote to his sister:

> I am now at the base for a rest after being six months on the continent. At Ypres I was slightly wounded, it was very fierce, and one day the Germans shelled our trenches for six hours without a halt, but did not move us, as we were hard to shift when well dug in, so Mr German came off second best.[1]

Fr Gill, 7 March:

> After dinner the Brigade Major, speaking of the Royal Irish Rifles, said they were 100 per cent a better battalion than a month before ... The Adjutant was at the Brigade HQ not long ago and he told me they said to him 'What's come over the Rifles recently; there is so much less crime?'

The cycle of moving between the trenches, Westoutre, and Locre continued until 12 March. By this time the Rifles' casualties since 1 January were Lt. J.C. Tyndall, 2/Lts H.S. Davy, C.A. Pigot-Moodie, and 15 men killed with 78 wounded. At 2.30 a.m., 12 March, the battalion marched to Lindenhoek and were held in reserve while an attack was made on Spanbroek Farm by 3rd Worcesters and 1st Wiltshires. The advanced German trenches were captured but could not be held and the RIR returned to billets after dark. On the afternoon of 13 March the battalion marched off to take over a new line near Dranoutre, but the order was cancelled just before the trenches were reached and the Rifles returned to Dranoutre late that night. The 7th Brigade was being held in Army reserve. The next day the battalion returned to Westoutre until the evening of the 16th when it moved to huts at Locre prior to going back into the trenches at Kemmel on the 17th. 4816 Rfn Robert Close wrote:

---

1 *Belfast News Letter*, 25 February 1915.

My regiment is doing fine work and cutting the enemy up like pork. I must say their snipers are good shots, but ours are every bit as good. On St Patrick's Day we had a football match, and afterwards proceeded to the trenches and arrived safe although the bullets were flying over our heads as thick as midges.[2]

3056 Sgt James Ewart:

On the 20th March my regiment was in the trenches, and at about 4.30, after having finished my tea, I heard the report of rifle grenades, of which the Germans fired about ten, but only one got the length of our trench. The enemy trenches were only about forty yards away and, owing to this, their artillery was ineffective. When I got wounded I thought my last hour had come, and had to wait until relief came up.[3]

Here they remained until 23 March when they moved to La Clytte. This tour had resulted in 5 men killed and 29 wounded. After six days, during which time four officers joined, the battalion marched on the evening of the 29th to Elzenwalle and went into the line between Voormezeele and St Eloi. By the time they returned to La Clytte on 4 April, 3 men had been killed and 10 wounded. They went into the firing line, 10 April, where, on the afternoon of the 15th, Major Alston was killed by a deflected bullet, while observing the enemy with a trench periscope, and Capt. Becher assumed command. Other casualties on this tour were 3 men killed, 2/Lt. C.R.E. Littledale and 26 men wounded. The battalion went to Canada Huts at Dickebusch on the 16th. On the evening of 20 April they marched back to the trenches where two men were killed, Capt. V.K. Gilliland and 19 men wounded.

The Rifles returned to Dickebusch, 25 April. The next day an enemy aeroplane passed over the huts and dropped five bombs, resulting in 14 injured men being admitted to hospital. Some troops were employed at digging work near the fire trenches by night; one man was killed and another wounded on the 27th. Major A.V. Weir joined on 28 April and took command. The battalion relieved 3rd Worcesters in the trenches on the night of the 30th. Reinforcements for April were 5 officers and 234 men.

At this time 2nd RIR established a new cemetery called Ridge Wood Military Cemetery. Ridge Wood was on the high ground between the Kemmel Road and Dickebusch Lake; the cemetery lies in a hollow on the western side of the ridge.

The trenches were shelled by the enemy, 2 May, resulting in 6 men killed and 29 wounded. The next day the shelling resumed again in reply to a few shells from the British side, casualties being 2 killed and 13 wounded. Relieved by 3rd Worcesters, 4 May, A, B and C Coys went to Dickebusch, while D was placed in

2 *Banbridge Chronicle*, 14 April 1915. He was killed on 7 May 1915.   3 *Banbridge Chronicle*, 14 April 1915.

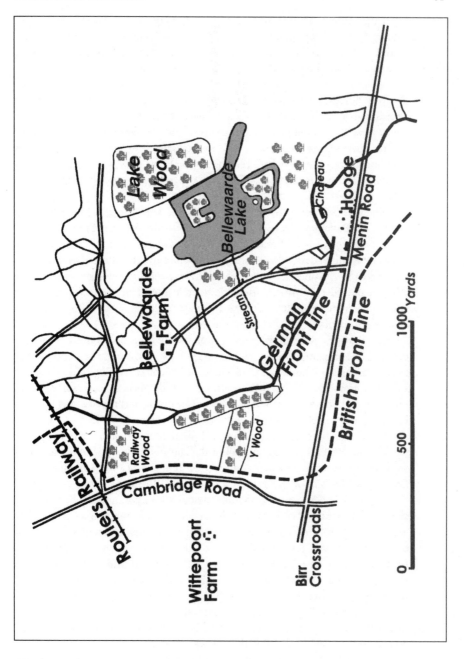

Map 6: First attack at Bellewaarde, 16 June 1915

reserve at Ridge Wood. Orders were received, 6 May, to temporarily join 13th Brigade. They marched to a point north of Hill 60 and relieved the Bedford Regt. As the guides were not well acquainted with the route the relief was not completed until 2.20 a.m., 7 May. Fr Gill gave the following account:

On May 6th the 2nd R.I. Rifles and the 2nd S. Lancs were lent to the 5th Division. It is always a disagreeable thing to be lent to another division, for the newcomers are looked on as outsiders and the authorities in command are not always broadminded enough to facilitate those who find themselves in strange surroundings where routing methods are often very different from what they are accustomed to. This trip proved no exception. Things were badly managed and we suffered in consequence.

When we left our camp at 3 o'clock no one knew exactly where we were going. The Battalion was to halt at a certain crossroads – itself a foolish order – and await the arrival of guides who would conduct us to the trenches. The company commanders, who had gone on before to reconnoitre the new position, were to return later and accompany the men to the trenches. As the evening passed it became evident that some hitch had occurred. The men got their tea and beguiled the time by singing dismal songs with references to dying warriors.

At about 9 o'clock a cycle orderly arrived with a note telling us where to go. The company officers could not get back in time as the horses could only go a certain distance. The orderly had spent several hours looking for us at our crossroad. At last we set off. At a neighbouring crossroads we were recommended by a road–control man not to delay as the place was shelled. He had hardly spoken when, 'whiz-bang', a shell passed a foot or two over my head. My horse gave a jump and all made a dive for the roadside. Luckily the shell was a dud and fell in the soft mud without exploding. Soon we had to dismount and proceed on foot. It was a beautiful night and the fireflies on the side of the path almost equalled the stars.

We reached Shrapnel Corner and made our way in single file along the side of Zillebeeke Lake. This part of the journey was most disagreeable. We were sheltered by a railway embankment but a constant stream of shells passed over our heads and fell around us. The sides of the path were covered with stretchers on which were wounded men and those who had been gassed. The latter presented a very painful sight. Men apparently unwounded coughing up white froth from lungs which had been eaten away by chlorine gas.

The Brigade HQ was 100 yards from the sheltered path and it was necessary to risk many shells to get there. There was utmost confusion; not only was there a battalion relief but the brigades were also changing over. No one seemed to know what was going on. At last we got on towards the trenches. The guide who had been assigned to us to show us the way did not appear to know where he was. He brought us along the top of the embankment although there was a sheltered path below, as we learned later. This place was fully exposed to shell and even rifle fire. A man lying dead with his face covered was not a reassuring welcome.

When our guide had brought us as far as he thought fit, he endeavoured to give verbal instructions for the remainder of the way, but he had to come along. We soon found ourselves under rifle fire from Hill 60 positions but at last reached Dormey House where the Battalion HQ was situated. The front trenches were a mile or so further on.

As appeared later on, HQ orderlies with our food supply continued straight on along the embankment almost to Hill 60 itself and into the hands of the Germans. The Bedfords, who were waiting for our relief, had sent away their supplies but shared with us half a bottle of whiskey and some Army biscuits ... It was now about 1 a.m. and an attempt to rush the German trench was timed for 2.30. The directions, which I saw, were apparently drawn up in a very casual manner on the back of an envelope. Some Germans were supposed to be in a portion of the front line trench which was held by the British on either side. The scheme was a simultaneous bombing on either flank, by the 2nd South Lancs and the 2nd Royal Irish Rifles, during which the occupied trench was to be rushed by the KOYLI. Owing to the delays already referred to, our company only reached the position five minutes before the time arranged for the attack. They found that the position was not as described. A long communication trench had to be passed through before the place occupied by the Germans was reached. As this trench was under German machine gun fire it had been allowed to get into a bad state of repair. The supply of bombs was deficient. The net result was several were killed and wounded. The party making the frontal attack disappeared. The whole thing had been badly planned and no proper preparation had been made.

We occupied this position for about a week. The main attack of the Germans took place on our left so that we did not come in for the heaviest part of the fighting.

D Coy on the right was ordered to join in the attack on Trench 46 at 2.50 a.m. by proceeding along a communication trench. They carried out their part well but the barricade did not blow up and they were met by heavy fire. Capt. Burgoyne, Lt. Leask and 16 men were wounded and 9 men were killed. The attack failed and there was a good deal of shelling from both sides for the rest of the day. The trenches were mortar-bombed by the Germans, 8 May; Capt. Gilliland and 4 men were killed, 2/Lt. G.W. Webb and 8 men were wounded. A battle was heard in the direction of Hooge, and there was a good deal of rifle and shell fire locally. The next day continued with more mortar bombs and a good deal of rifle fire from a section of Trench 46 held by the enemy: 3 men were killed and 21 wounded. Two bombs hit the parapet, 10 May, killing one man and wounding another. Lt. G.S. Norman went to hospital with concussion.

The trenches were again hit by trench mortars, 11 May, killing one man and wounding five. A group of Germans were spotted putting out wire and were fired

on leaving five dead on the ground. A further three men were wounded by the time
2nd RIR returned to La Clytte on the 12th. Fr Gill recorded:

> During the days of the 7th, 8th, 9th, 10th and 11th of May the Germans
> made repeated attempts to break through in front of Ypres. The 12th saw
> the climax of the attempt and its failure with the exception of forcing a slight
> readjustment of the British line. They had gained no advance. Both sides
> lost heavily. At times small bodies of Germans advanced along the Menin
> Road but never in any great numbers. Apart from the disadvantages of trench
> life, the time was not without interest. The regimental aid post was in a brick
> factory a few hundred yards from the Battalion HQ.

The battalion relieved 3rd Worcesters on the 16th. On this tour three men were
killed and seven wounded, including two killed and another wounded as a result of
British shells falling short on the 19th. The Rifles returned to Dickebusch at midnight on the 20th; A and C Coys were in Canada Huts, while B and D were billeted in farms. The farm occupied by D Coy was shelled, 24 May, killing 5 and
wounding 11. That evening the battalion relieved 3rd Worcesters. There was the
usual amount of sniping, 25 May, when four men were wounded. Fr Gill:

> Ypres. My next visit was on May 26th and I then found the town absolutely
> deserted and almost destroyed. It was being heavily shelled every day and,
> with the exception of some troops in the 'ramparts' and a few heavy batter-
> ies, there were not many soldiers there. But we heard about this time that
> we were 'for it' and that we were to take part in an attack on the trenches
> just North of Hooge, near Bellewaarde Lake. The object of the attack was
> to straighten out a small salient which the Germans had pushed out in our
> line. This was the first of three fierce attacks in which the Battalion took
> part in this truly terrible and desolate part of the front. Personally I think
> that the most vivid war picture left in my mind is the utter horror and des-
> olation of the Menin Road.

Casualties from sniping, 27 May, resulted in two killed and one wounded. Major
Weir left on the 29th to take over the post of Commandant of 7th Brigade Area,
handing over command to Capt. Becher. One man was wounded that day.
Reinforcements during May were 2 officers and 87 men.

Major E.M. Morris of the Devonshire Regt arrived, 1 June, and took command.
During the remainder of their time in the line one man was killed and another five
were wounded. The battalion was relieved on the 3rd by units of 85th Brigade and
marched to a bivouac south of the Vlamertinghe–Poperinghe Road. Over the next
few days large parties were furnished to carry barbed wire entanglements to the
Ypres Salient. On the 8th the battalion moved to a bivouac about 300 yards west
of the old camp. The CO, Adjutant, Machine Gun Officer, and two officers per
company, visited the new line of trenches to be taken over west of Hooge. Falls:

The British line at this period was in a curious position. From Hooge it followed the Menin Road to near Birr cross-roads, then turned at right-angles, running north, in front of Cambridge Road, to the Ypres–Roulers railway. The German position, though a salient within a salient, was strong, naturally as well as artificially, rising to a slight ridge, which in that flat country was dignified by the name of the Bellewaarde Spur, which took its name from the Bellewaarde Lake, a sheet of water some twelve acres in extent, with two large wooded islands upon it, lying south of the high ground. The British command decided that an attempt to nip off this minor salient, establishing a line which would run generally from Hooge, along the western side of the lake, across the Bellewaarde spur, to a point in the Ypres–Roulers railway a little in advance of the old position, would be worth while.

One officer of each company and the Machine Gun Officer remained overnight to guide 2nd RIR into the trenches on the evening of 9 June. During this tour one man was killed and 12 wounded. The battalion was relieved, 11 June, and returned to its bivouac, with the exception of B Coy, a party of C Coy attached and the machine gun team (about 250 all ranks) who had to remain, owing to the late arrival of the relieving unit, and the impossibility of getting clear before daylight. They did not rejoin until midnight the next day having lost one man killed and 7 wounded.

At 5.30 p.m., 15 June, 2nd RIR marched to the assembly trenches between Witteport Farm and the Ypres–Roulers railway to support 9th Brigade in an attack on Bellewaarde Spur. The artillery bombardment commenced at 3.20 a.m. on the 16th, lifting at 4.15 a.m. to the second objective, when the 9th Brigade assaulted and took the first three lines of German trenches. 2nd RIR supported the left of the attack: C Coy followed by D on the right, A followed by B on the left with orders to consolidate the first German line. C and D, under Capt. Farran and Lt. Eales, carried away by their keenness, pushed through to the third line, closing up with the assaulting troops. They were 'true Irishmen and unable to see a fight without joining in'.[4] These companies were then reorganized and withdrawn in perfect order to the first line, which they put in a state of defence. A Coy under 2/Lt. W.E. Andrews was similarly engaged on the left. Owing to the heavy artillery fire that soon developed, B Coy was unable to follow on quickly. They were formed up on Cambridge Road, 250 yards behind, preparatory to making another effort to get through, when they were shelled by enfilade fire causing about 35 casualties. The remainder of the company was then withdrawn and kept in support for the rest of the day. The War Diary boasted:

> During the day, from early morning to nightfall, the battalion was subjected to a terrific artillery bombardment. The men of all companies distinguished themselves by their discipline, coolness, and steadiness under the most trying circumstances. At no time during the day could it be said that they were

4 A.M. McGilchrist, *The Liverpool Scottish, 1900–1919* (Liverpool, 1930).

in any way shaken by their ordeal. For instance, at 3.30 p.m., after hours of bombardment, C and D Coys, with very short notice, were called upon to attack. It possessed just as much spirit and dash as their early morning attack. Both of these attacks were gallantly led by Capt. Farran, who was wounded and became missing, and 2/Lt. Eales.

A Coy consolidated and held the left flank of the German trenches, and handed them over to the Royal Scots at midnight. 2/Lt. Andrews was highly praised for the able way in which this difficult operation was carried out. Fr Gill recorded:

16 June 1915. At 3.00 on the morning a very intense bombardment commenced, and we knew that the attack had begun. The 7th Brigade was not taking part in the first line trenches, but were to follow up and occupy the trenches after the attacking parties had gone forward. But in the attack the eagerness of the 2nd RIRs brought them along with the attacking forces. They went past their objective and actually got to the fourth line of German trenches. This was the first opportunity the Battalion had since the earliest days of the war of showing that the old spirit was alive. They went forward with too great impetuosity and found themselves in front of some others whom they were supposed to support. They did not lose many in the first attack, but unfortunately an imprudent order was issued from a higher command to the effect that they were to fall back at once from the trenches they had reached. It was represented by those on the spot that this movement was not possible during the daytime without the risk of serious loss. The order was, however, insisted on and the men fell back. In doing so they had many casualties. The same result could have been obtained without these casualties by waiting a few hours until dusk ... At an early hour the wounded began to arrive at the dressing station. For two days and nights we were kept busy. I may not here enter on a description of the work at a dressing station during an attack. Terrible wounds are seen and at times it takes all one's strength of will to bear up under the strain of seeing hundreds of all sorts of cases who succeed each other in a constant stream to the rough operation table, where the essential dressings are carried out. All the available spaces were filled. The courtyards were crowded with 'walking cases' waiting to be brought back to the clearing stations and rest camps ... I met many officers and men, slightly wounded, walking back. Many of them carried souvenirs of German rifles, field glasses, etc., which they had got in the German dug outs.

Belfast News Letter, 9 July 1915:

An officer at the front with 2nd RIR wrote to a brother officer: 'We had a great attack on the 16th inst and distinguished ourselves. We were supposed to be in support but, when the attacking battalion advanced, our fellows jumped out of the trenches and raced forward, taking three German trenches in about 15 minutes. Eventually we had only one trench to our credit, where we remained until relieved that night. We had an awful shelling from the Germans. Your old Sergeant-Major Courtney was killed away well in advance of the third trench. This was the first time many of our fellows had seen Germans, and they did not think much of them. One fellow said to me: "Oh Sir, we should have gone to Berlin if only we had more men." This was the spirit throughout the battalion. The Corps Commander came to talk to the men, and was proud of us. Old Ballard came along too, and almost piped his eye over our good work.'

4/7413 Cpl Robert Platt outlined his experience in a letter to his father:

Since last I wrote to you we were in a charge and it was awful. We started out the night before and marched 13 miles. We arrived at the place about half past one in the morning so that we were put into an old trench and told to await orders, so you can have an idea that our nerves were strung to the highest pitch. So, the Germans started to rain shells into us but then our artillery opened fire on the German trenches. The row was awful. The whole sky was just in one great blaze with bursting shells. Sharp at three o'clock, the order came down our lines to fix bayonets and to load our rifles and, ten minutes later down came the order to charge, so we all rushed over the trench but a few of our boys fell on the parapet as the Germans had their machine guns trained on us but on we went and, as one fell, another took his place.

We arrived at the German trench and when it came to the steel they could not match it and I am proud to say that I put a few out with the bayonet myself. Although one does not think of it at the time, one does think of it after the excitement is over. We took over 200 prisoners and a couple of machine guns. I sent home a German sword. But we were not satisfied with one trench, we went on and took two more lines of them. They shelled us the whole day after we took them and they even sent loads of gas but we stuck on for what we had so dearly won.

I was to be recommended for the DCM for fetching in wounded under fire but the officer that took my name was killed shortly afterwards and I do not know how it will go now but I was promoted on the field by our own officer to Corporal. I was buried three times by shells and had to be dug out and I got a slight bullet wound in the thigh but I am out of hospital again and expect to go into action in a couple of days' time. The battle took place on 16th June. It was even worse than the charge we made at Hill 60. The Germans lost a good deal more than we did. The Brigade officer says the Rifles have made a name for themselves out here that will go down in history. All the English Regiments out here are very fond of the Rifles since we came out of the charge. [5]

5 *Ballymena Observer*, 30 July 1915.

Their performance was praised by the Corps Commander.[6] Rfn Mawhinney
wrote to a friend in Ardglass:

We were ordered to hold ourselves in readiness to go in support along with
the rest of our brigade ... and we got into our places in the reserve trenches
in the early hours of the morning of the 16th. Just as we took up our positions the enemy started throwing those so-called 'whizz-bangs', which are
meant to disorganize troops; then they sent over trench mortars, then came
grenades of all kinds, but these were nothing to the 'Jack Johnsons', 'Black
Marias' and high explosive shrapnel shells. At 2.30 our artillery started to
do their bit, and I tell you it was done, for in less than an hour from the
time it started our people had the first line rushed and taken at the point of
the bayonet. We had not much trouble in doing so, as our artillery had all
the German parapets blown in and most of the troops who held the trench
were buried in the soil and their dug-outs.

We had them properly taken by surprise, as when the first trench was
taken any of them who were left were in their stocking-feet. Then came the
sport when they came running in with their hands up shouting what was
meant for 'Mercy, mercy'. We let them come into the trench, and they were
in an awful state. We took the second line with a rush, and our people were
all bursting to go forward, though it was not our place to do so. There is
no doubt it was an awful ordeal, and I am sure there was not a bombardment like it in this campaign. It started at 2.30 and continued for 17 hours,
doing nothing but throwing over high explosives and lyddite shells and, what
was better, we saw the effect of our own artillery fire. It was something
awful. You could see nothing only bodies cut up and lying all over the place,
and they were retiring as fast as they could in a properly disorganized manner. The people we took prisoners were all properly worn-out and fed-up
looking; they were the clumsiest-looking things you ever looked at. There
was one fellow we captured who said: 'Allies very good; war no good. We
are fed up; are you?' Some say Germans have no food or smokes, but in one
of their dug-outs I found three bags full of loaves of bread and plenty of
tobacco, wine, rum, beer and German sausages.

Well, I suppose you are wondering what spirit our men took it in. They
were just bursting for the word to get over, and when we did get over there
was no such thing as running mad with excitement. We took it nice and cool,
and in fact the courage of our officers, NCOs and men was splendid. Our
officers were the first men on the bank and waited until we got in line, then
we all swept forward like a steel wall. After we were relieved from the trench
we were visited by some of our general officers, and they said they were proud

6 The following officers, and about 300 other ranks became casualties. Killed: Capt. E.C. Farran, 2/Lts
E.B. Kertland, F.C.P. Joy, and J.M. McIntosh. Wounded: Capt. C.M.L. Becher, Lts D.M. Anderson,
W.E.S. Howard, 2/Lts J.G. Bland, T.J. Considine, E.J. Hoare, A.A. Raymond, R.L. Vance, and C.H.
Wale.

of us and that our regiment was the talk of the army for the part it played in the taking of those lines of trenches. The GOC said that it was one of the roughest and most terrific bombardments which took place in this war.[7]

The net result of the battle was a gain of 250 yards on a front of 800 yards. The battalion marched to dug-outs on the 20th. Col. Morris departed, 23 June, and issued this farewell order:

> Lt.-Col. E.M. Morris ... wishes to sincerely thank all ranks for their support and assistance, during his short period of command, and begs them never to forget Neuve Chapelle, and Bellewaarde Farm on the 16th instant, when on both occasions their battalion covered themselves with glory.

Capt. Goodman took temporary command. That day 2nd RIR went into the trenches near Hooge, which were unrecognisable after the heavy bombardment. Major G.A. Weir DSO, 3rd Dragoon Guards, joined and assumed command on the 24th. Nine men were wounded on this tour. The battalion was relieved by 3rd Worcestershires on the night of 27 June. During the month 15 officers and 160 men had joined.

The Rifles entered the trenches, 1 July, and relieved 1st Wiltshires. The following afternoon the Germans fired gas shells on the trenches occupied by C Coy resulting in one death and eight men being admitted to hospital. Otherwise, four men were wounded on this tour. The battalion was relieved by 1st Wiltshires, 5 July, and marched to bivouac. A message addressed to the battalion was received, 6 July: 'The Corps Commander is pleased to hear of the success of your aggressive operations.' The next tour, 8–12 July, had casualties of two killed and six wounded. The battalion marched to the trenches near St Eloi (U23–26), 21 July, and relieved the KOSBs. The line held by 2nd RIR was changed and extended, 26 July. U23–24 were handed over to 3rd Worcestershires while U27–28 were taken over from 2nd Suffolk Regt. Reinforcements during July were 4 officers and 326 men.

7 *Northern Whig*, 8 July 1915.

6

Second attack at Bellewaarde

During the afternoon of 1 August, while the British artillery were registering, an enemy shell struck the parapet in U27, killing 2/Lts W.E. Andrews, A.A. Raymond, and two men, severely wounding Lt. D. Kirkpatrick, the Artillery Observing Officer and two other men. Fr Gill was nearby:

> There was to be a shoot in the afternoon. Sundays were often free from the horrors of war in the mornings but the evenings were devoted to 'hate'. On this morning the gunners came along to register on the object to be attended to in the evening. Several artillery officers came along and invited some of our officers to see the registering shots and to help them locate the position. I also set out to see the work. However I turned back to get some newspapers to bring to the men. I thus got separated from the party. However, I followed on after them until I got to a bifurcation in the trench where I forgot which way to turn. I sat down in the bottom of a trench and read a paper until someone should come along who could direct me. I was not encouraged by seeing a notice over my head 'Do not delay here, under machine gun fire', but I was safe in the bottom of the trench. When I did get to the front trench I met a group of officers passing along with periscopes. Taught by the death of Major Alston, I had a strong objection to being one of a party showing periscopes. I therefore gave out my papers and returned to our HQ. I had not been gone ten minutes when the group was shelled and I am sorry to say that four officers and men were killed. One other officer lost his leg and several others were badly wounded.

3/8697 L/Cpl Samuel V. Thompson:

> They started strafing early last week, and they have been mixing it ever since. For the past few days they have been using these liquid fire shells, and they must be about the limit. We have not been treated to any of them yet, but tonight we could get scores of them bursting along the line. A great sheet of flame about 30 yards square flies out of them ... We made some tea in the trenches and it was only by a lucky chance that we discovered we had been using the chemical stuff for the respirators instead of water. I didn't

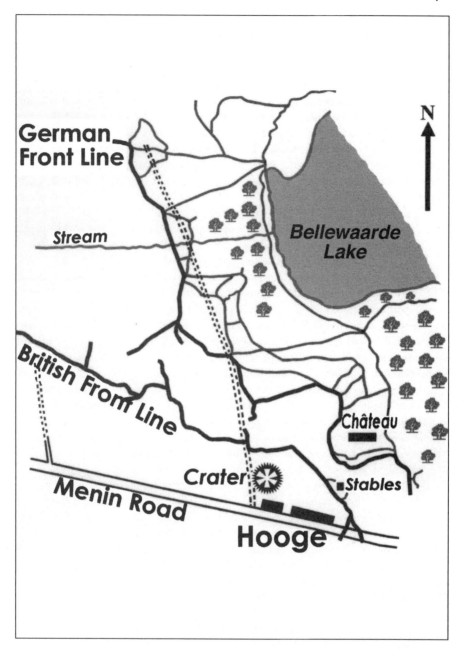

Map 7: Second attack at Bellewaarde, 25 September 1915

swear. I have passed that stage, and my hair is turning a beautiful shade of grey. I've got a table and a chair in the new dug-out. Unfortunately the billiard table is temporarily out of order.[1]

By the time of the relief, 2 August, additional casualties of 5 men killed and 26 wounded had been incurred. The battalion was in the support trenches near St Jean, 3–7 August, where two men were killed. Having been relieved by the HAC, they went to the Reserve Dugouts at the canal bank, Ypres. While there, 2/Lt. Seth-Smith and one man were wounded while with a working party. The battalion relieved 1st Wiltshires near St Jean, at that part of the line running through Wieltje, 11 August. On the night of the 15th, Lt. K. Ross's patrol met a German patrol about 300 yards out in no-man's-land: one German was killed and two captured of the 236th Regt, XXVI Reserve Army Corps. The Rifles were relieved on the night of the 19th by 2nd York and Lancs Regt. The RIR snipers had been busy this time and managed to kill six Germans. The tour casualties were one killed and 18 wounded.

During 20–22 August the battalion was kept ready to move off at one hour's notice, with a company as inlying picquet ready to move off at thirty minutes' notice. They marched to Ypres on the evening of the 24th relieving 2nd Leinster Regt in the support area. A, B and D Coys were placed in the Ramparts with C in dugouts on the south bank of Zillebeke Lake. The next day about six shells fell near the dugouts, killing one man and wounding five. On the 27th the Rifles moved forward to the trenches at Hooge. Throughout the relief there was some German bombing to prevent 1st Wiltshires and 2nd South Lancs from digging a trench in front of Chateau Stables. The Rifles' bombers retaliated successfully but one man was wounded. The next day some heavy shelling killed Capt. C.B. Williams and two men, wounding Lt. C.J. Wakefield and 17 others. On the night of the 29th a working party of RIR and 3rd Worcesters dug and connected up a new trench behind the south side of Chateau Stables. By the time of the relief on the 30th a further 11 men had been wounded. Reinforcements in August were 5 officers and 49 men.

The next tour at Hooge, 3–9 September, had the RIR suffering many casualties due to German retaliation for British shelling. Lt. Morton and 3 men were killed, 41 men were wounded; Col. Weir was slightly wounded but remained at duty. While at the Ramparts in Ypres one man was killed and two were wounded. On the 12th they moved back to their bivouac where three men were wounded on a working party. The battalion marched to bivouac under the cover of trees just west of Kruistraat, 23 September. The next day Operation Orders and plans for the impending attack were finally discussed.

The V Corps was attacking between the Menin Road and the Roulers railway. The 2nd Royal Irish Rifles was to be on the left flank of its division, and its objective was the southern half of the western shore of Bellewaarde Lake. Its advance, from the present British line covering Hooge, was to be,

---

1 *Drogheda Advertiser*, 14 August 1915.

therefore, in a north-easterly direction ... The attack was to be made by two companies – B on the right, and D on the left, with one, C, in support, to occupy our front line after it was launched, and A in reserve. The final objective was distant not more than 400 to 500 yards. The assault was to be preceded by an intense bombardment beginning at 3.50 a.m. Four mines were to be exploded along the whole front of the attack.[2]

The Rifles relieved the HAC in the trenches at 11.30 p.m., 24 September. The British artillery bombarded the front to be attacked from 3.50 a.m. until 4.20 a.m., lifting their fire gradually from the German front line to the support line commencing at 4.05 a.m. Four mines were exploded on the right – the first pair at 4.19 a.m. and the other pair thirty seconds later. The assault was delivered immediately. Fr Gill remembered:

> The attack, which was now beginning, was the biggest thing we had attempted since trench warfare began. The object was to improve the position at Hooge and at the same time 'demonstrate' in order to prevent troops being moved from this place to reinforce the enemy's forces at Loos where the main attack was to take place ... At 7 p.m. the CO gave the men a stirring address, and we all set out on foot to take up our position which was to be at the crater at Hooge. The weather was bad and the mud deep ... At the given time two companies had charged and had reached the German position. Some had got into the trenches. Others were held up by barbed wire, which was not cut. Some succeeded in regaining their own trench, some crept into shell holes to wait until dark. Some were taken prisoners. Apparently the attack had failed. But the main object had been attained, but at great cost.

At 4.14 a.m. the attacking companies crossed the parapet and deployed about 30 yards in front. Each company had two platoons in the front line, and two in the second line. The second line was just in front of the parapet. Six sections of bombers and two machine guns accompanied the attack.

> The reader who does not know his Ypres can have small conception of the conditions under foot, and many suppose that, since summer was not yet over, the 'going' was fairly sound. It cannot be too often insisted upon in the accounts of battles in the Salient that even in summer, even in dry weather, the hole made by a shell was brimful of water in a very short time. In this case there had been considerable rainfall recently, which meant that, even for those who avoided stepping into shell-holes, each footstep sank inches at least into the mud of the churned ground. The so-called 'rush' of the assault was in such cases often a very slow movement indeed. And here the opposing trenches were divided by 200 yards of this foul and adhesive clay.[3]

2 Falls.　3 Ibid.

The attack was met by heavy machine-gun fire. In the centre the Rifles reached the German second line, and occupied it with little opposition, but none of their bombers reached the objective as the German marksmen paid particular attention to men carrying the grenade-holding canvas buckets, and a bomb attack by the enemy forced those who had reached it to retire to the German first line, where one officer and some dozen men held on till dark. On the extreme flanks the attack was held up by wire and machine gun fire, and the men took what cover they could in shell holes close up to the German lines. Some of them rejoined after dark. At about 4.30 a.m., C Coy went forward, without orders or permission, to help the attacking companies, who were seen to have penetrated the enemy's line. They were met with heavy rifle and machine gun fire and few succeeded in reaching the others. Those that did found that there was only a handful left. A Coy then moved up, occupied the British front line trenches, and had to be restrained from trying to go forward to help their comrades. At about 6 a.m. some of RIR men could still be seen in the enemy's trenches, but after that hour nothing further could be seen of them, and although parties volunteered to go forward to find out what was going on in front, none succeeded in getting definite information, and headquarters remained in doubt as to the actual situation till evening. None of the signallers who accompanied the attack succeeded in getting back a message. The situation remained unchanged until dark, when those of the attacking companies, who were able, rejoined. One machine gun team had reached the German front line but they were either killed or captured, and the gun was found deserted by a man who came back from the German front line. He destroyed it with the butt of his rifle before retiring.

About midnight, the Wiltshires commenced the relief but the Rifles did not get back to camp until 6 a.m., 26 September. Capts W.P. O'Lone, H.G.C. Perry-Ayscough, Lts F.H.Bethell, R.F. Gavin, A.D. La Touche, 2/Lts J.G. Caruth, W.L. Orr, K. Ross, and M. Ross were killed; Capts W. Cupples, T.H. Ivey, H.N.Young, Lts G.W. Calverley, J.R. Tuckett, and 2/Lt. S.A. Bell were wounded. Other casualties were 46 men killed, 140 wounded, 150 missing, with 26 wounded and missing. During the month 6 officers and 64 men joined. General Sir E.H.H. Allenby KCB, V Corps Commander, addressed the troops on the morning of 27 September:

> Col. Weir, and the men of the Royal Irish Rifles, I have come to see how you look after your trying experience on Saturday last. I am glad to see you looking so fit and well. You are a fine soldierly looking lot of men. I want to thank you for your very gallant behaviour. Your attack was most brilliantly carried out and, though it did not succeed in the immediate object in view, it was quite successful in the main. You contained and occupied a large number of Germans, and especially guns, which otherwise would have been used in other parts of the line, where our troops and the French were attacking ... This attack against an almost impregnable position will, when history comes to be written, be looked on as one of the finest achievements of the whole war. Your gallantry has added to the already illustrious name, not only of the 2nd Battalion, but to the whole regiment of the Royal Irish Rifles.

The battalion marched, 1 October, via Kruisstraat to the trenches in front of Armagh Wood relieving 1/4th Lincoln Regt. The next afternoon German minen-werfers and light fieldguns shelled one part of the trenches for a quarter of an hour. Capt. F.M.S. Gibson, 2/Lt. A.E. Kemp, and Lt. D.T.C. Frew, RAMC, were wounded, although the latter remained at duty. This German activity continued over the next few days and, by the time of their relief on the 12th, three men had been killed and 27 wounded.

Col. Weir left to take command of 84th Brigade. On the 14th, Major-General A.L. Haldane CB, DSO, GOC 3rd Division, addressed the troops and congratulated them on their gallant conduct and magnificence. He bade farewell as they were leaving his command to join the 25th Division as it had been decided to mix the old units with the new.

> You are going to a more quiet part of the line, and you will be under an Irish General there, and perhaps he will understand you better than I do. You have a splendid fighting record throughout the campaign, being complimented by Sir John French and General Smith-Dorrien in Corps orders. The fighting in this part of the line during the last few months has been very severe, and the battalion has made history. When the history of the campaign has been written the name of the 2nd Battalion RIR will be written in large print ... Your Brigadier was ordered to hold the Germans in the Ypres salient, while the other corps made the attack further south. You attacked the strongest position in the enemy's line. We had not enough ammunition in our line to give you more support. The result was that the Germans' hidden machine guns and cleverly laid barbed wire traps were not demolished entirely ... Despite this you not only pierced the German lines, but actually held the first line trenches for 24 hours ... It was a splendid piece of work, and proves that Irishmen will always get to the Front, no matter what obstacles are in the way.

Major L.C. Sprague joined and took command. The Rifles marched via Poperinghe, Abeele, Godewaer, Velde, Fletre, Strazeele to Merris. They arrived on the night of the 16th and billeted in farm houses just north-east of Merris. On the 18th the Brigade was ordered to exchange with 76th Brigade in the 25th Division, II Corps. The GOC of II Corps, Sir Charles Fergusson, addressed the men, 21 October, and, on the 24th, the GOC of 25th Division, Major-General Sir B. Doran, inspected the battalion and welcomed it to his division. The battalion paraded at 9 a.m., 25 October, and marched via Oultersteen to Bailleul where they billeted. The next morning they marched to Le Bizet, near Armentières. The Belgian–French frontier passed through the village. On this day 2nd RIR transferred to 74th Brigade, now including 11th Lancashire Fusiliers, 13th Cheshire Regt and 9th Loyal North Lancashire Regt. Fr Gill described the new billets:

> A squalid industrial residential quarter. Many houses empty and hit by shells. The peculiar thing about this locality is that practically up to the firing line

there are people living in their cottages and working in the fields. Things are very quiet here in comparison to other places we have been in.

The Rifles went into the trenches at Le Touquet during the evening of the 27th and relieved 13th Cheshires. This was a very quiet tour; at night patrols went out but discovered nothing of importance.

> The new trenches marked an extraordinary change from those of Ypres. They were very quiet, and casualties were kept very low. The chief enemy was the wet, in a land lying for the most part only between 40 feet and 60 feet above sea level; whereas that of the Ypres Salient had been all over 100 feet, and in places considerably more. However, as this placid front was lightly held, it was generally possible to find comparatively sound ground for the posts. The discomfort, apart altogether from the shelling, was considerably less than in the Salient. Tours in the line were generally of six days' duration.[4]

During October 14 officers and 242 men joined. Fr Gill observed: 'Many Catholics and a good lot ... One RC Officer, now the only RC Officer with us.' Having been relieved on 2 November, they returned to Le Bizet. During their tour of 8–14 November the trenches were found to be very wet and the parapets subsided in parts. Capt. R. O'Lone was killed on the 11th while visiting a listening post. Otherwise there had been only one man wounded in this period. Over the next few days three men were wounded while on working parties that were furnished for drainage work. The battalion was inspected by the leader of the Home Rule Party, John Redmond MP, 19 November, and he congratulated them on their gallant conduct. Fr Gill was impressed:

> John Redmond arrived about 3 p.m. with Divisional General Doran and his son and private secretary. He made a speech to the men. He was glad to meet a regiment which contained men of every creed from different places in Ireland, especially the North. They were brothers-in-arms, and he was sure their harmony and unity in the great cause in which they were fighting was a happy omen of the relations which would exist between all in Ireland after the war. Seeing that the regiment is in great part from the North of Ireland and containing many Protestants the reception of Mr Redmond was very remarkable.

The battalion then marched to the firing line at Le Touquet and relieved 13th Cheshires that evening, but one man was killed and another wounded in the process. The trenches were found to be very wet and a considerable amount of work was required to repair them. The weather was reasonable although there was some frost.

4 Ibid.

A patrol went out on the night of the 22nd and gained some useful local information. Three men had been wounded and eight had joined before returning to Le Bizet on the 24th. During this time one man was accidentally wounded at a bomb throwing exercise, and a working party was shelled while repairing communication trenches on the 28th. The Medical Officer, Lt. Maurice MacKenzie, RAMC, rushed to them and while attending the wounded was killed by a shell. Two other men were killed and four wounded. Fr Gill:

> This morning we lost our M.O., Dr McKenzie, who was most popular and loved by all. He was sent for to attend a wounded RE Officer. He set out at once and met the party ten minutes walk up the road. He began dressing his wounds and, whilst doing so, a shell fell killing him and Sgt Doherty. Both were killed on the spot.

The next day 2nd RIR marched off by companies at half-hour intervals to relieve 13th Cheshires at Le Touquet. This was done to avoid being shelled unduly as the road to the firing line had been subjected to severe shell fire the day before. The trenches were in a fair condition, though still very wet. During the month 5 officers and 14 men joined. The tour ended, 4 December, and only one man had been wounded in the interim. Owing to the very wet state of trench 94, located at the bottom of the Lys Valley, it was decided to abandon most of it, and build redoubts just to the rear. D Coy provided continuous fatigues for this work. A lot of rain fell during the tour of 9–14 December; the trenches were wetter than ever and knee deep in mud. 2/Lt. C.H.W. Darling was killed, Lts J.A. Stewart, T.S. Jenkinson and three men were wounded. Le Bizet was slightly shelled during the 15th leaving one man killed and two wounded. Only one man was wounded on the tour of 19–24 December. Reinforcements during the month came to 5 officers and 86 men.

7

1916

The tour of 29 December to 3 January was quiet, with only one man being wounded, until the last day when, at about 11.30 a.m., the enemy shelled Battalion HQ at Surrey Farm. Not much damage was done to the buildings, though the house was struck. Shelling continued in the afternoon, chiefly in and around Le Bizet, resulting in the death of one man. The tour of 8–14 January was again quiet with casualties of five wounded, and a further two were wounded later at Le Bizet. An operation was carried out by a portion of the battalion in front of Le Touquet Salient on the 19th. The German front line trench ran just west of the main street of the village, some of the ruined cottages of which were within the British position. The objectives were to kill Germans, establish the identity of the enemy units, to capture or destroy any machine guns and to destroy any mine shafts found. In conjunction with this assault, a gas attack was launched against the enemy in front of the trenches held by 9th Loyal North Lancashires to the immediate north. This commenced at 4.30 p.m. and ceased about 5.15 p.m. At 4.35 p.m. a smoke attack commenced along the front until 5.05 p.m. This showed its disadvantages and advantages: it produced an intense enemy bombardment and machine gun fire, but certainly helped at least one party to get across to the German lines under cover of the smoke.

The artillery preparation commenced at 12.30 p.m. and ceased at 4.45 p.m. Its purpose was to cut lanes through the German wire, breach the enemy parapet at selected points of entry, destroy Crown Prince Farm and the counter-battery fire. The enemy retaliated almost immediately with artillery. Nine officers and 220 men took part in the assault, inclusive of two officers and eight men of the Royal Engineers who were to look for mine shafts, blow up machine gun emplacements and Machine Gun House. The points of entry were assaulted by two detachments: Northern Party (7 officers, 130 men) and Southern Party (2 officers, 90 men). Each had a 'Headquarters and Liaison Party': that of the Northern Party under Lt. E. Workman and that of the Southern Party under Capt. H.R.H. Ireland. Their role was to prepare the points of entry, pass back prisoners, and not to return until all the attacking parties had come back. A few casualties occurred from enemy shellfire before the assault commenced at 4.45 p.m. Both parties attacked and entered the enemy lines: no obstacles were met going in or coming back. Owing to the bombardment it proved extremely difficult to find the German trenches, which had been extensively destroyed. The first prisoner was brought back within five minutes. The Northern Party brought back three prisoners and the Southern Party eight. The assault was delivered with great dash and only a few casualties occurred when the men mounted the parapet to make the assault. Many Germans were killed but, at 5.05 p.m., the Northern Party reached Crown Prince Farm, a large building 100 yards east of the village in the German third line, and was met by a group of about 60 Germans and did not reach its objective. The counter attack lacked determination: the Germans had only approached to within fifty yards when they were fired at by an officer and four men of the Rifles, and some were seen to fall. The farm itself was too strongly held to be captured.

The Southern Party met with strong resistance from grenades and rifle fire, did not reach its objective of Machine Gun House and no mine shafts were discovered. The stronghold called Red Tile House in the second line was reached although there was some rifle fire and bombing from its ruins. Enemy dugouts were bombed killing many. The Southern Party brought back three more prisoners, and the Northern Party nine of the 181st Bavarian Regt. At 5.15 p.m. bugles were sounded as the signal to retire and all fell back at this time. The information gained, both from prisoners and captured documents, was exceptionally valuable. The officers that took part in this operation were Lt. Workman, 2/Lts O'Reilly, Phillips, Lennox, Broomfield, and the two RE Officers in the Northern Party, with Capt. Ireland, Lt. Erskine and 2/Lt. Cochrane in the Southern Party. Casualties were 2/Lts A.J. Lennox, C.H. Wale and 11 men killed, Lt. Workman and 2/Lt. H.W. O'Reilly died of wounds, and 2/Lts A.A. Broomfield, H. Phillips and 37 were wounded. Fr Gill:

> The following appeared in the Official Communiqué: 'A minor operation. A party of our troops at dusk raided the enemy trenches north of the River Lys and brought back several prisoners.' The above short notice was all the general public heard of an operation which cost the Battalion the lives of four officers and a dozen men. 200 RIRs were engaged in the raid, which was the first carried out by home troops. The Canadians were the first to raid the enemy trenches, and near this place, shortly before this time. The facts were as follows:
>
> For some time back there had been considerable doubt as to which German unit occupied the trenches opposite our lines. At this point the German and British trenches ran out abruptly into two salients opposite each other. At the heads of the salients the distance between the two was 60 yards. Both salients contained ruined cottages and the Germans had the river and a considerable village behind them, Frelinghien. Our right rested on the river. The object of the raid was to capture prisoners for identification, and to examine the nature of the enemy position. The programme of the attack was an elaborate one. For days beforehand detailed preparations had been made, and the scheme worked well. The trenches from which the Rifles were to make the raid were held by the 13th Cheshires. The capture of trenches was not part of the plan. Prisoners were to be taken. The raiding party were to spend half an hour in the German trenches.

At 8 a.m. the selected men began to go up in small parties to the place of assembly, so as not to attract attention, as aeroplane observers constantly flew over our position. The officers and men got into dugouts and fortified shelters, which had been prepared beforehand ... All were to be in their places in the front trench by 12 noon.

12.30 p.m. The preliminary bombardment began. This consisted of a not very heavy shelling by our field guns. There were, however, a great number of trench mortars throwing shells up to 50 pounds. The damage done by these bombs was enormous, and battered in their trenches, and smashed up the barbed wire sufficiently to enable the raid to take place. This was about 100 yards behind the front trenches in the cellar of a ruined house. Around this farm-house was assembled one of the two parties who were to go over the top. The place was specially marked by the enemy and was heavily shelled all day ... 3.30 p.m. The bombardment became more intense, and the 'heavies' began to play on the German salient. The German reply was vigorous, but evidently their artillery had to be brought up from some distance as their firing did not begin for some time. Only a few trench mortar bombs were sent back. On the whole the counter-bombardment did us little damage ... 4 p.m. The right attacking party left to take up their position in the front trenches. Three men were killed during the time of waiting in our farm; the other party also suffered.

4.30 p.m. A gas attack was launched by us about a mile to our right. No charge took place at this point, for the attack was intended to distract the German's attention and draw gunfire, which it succeeded in doing ... 4.35 p.m. A smoke cloud was launched on our immediate right to cover our men crossing the parapet.

4.42 p.m. Party over the top and just outside our wire.

4.45 p.m. The charge took place. At this time our Artillery, which had been playing on the enemy trenches, was raised, and began a *tir de barrage* behind the German lines to prevent reinforcements being rushed up.

4.55 p.m. Several men rushed down our trenches towards us with the first prisoners. There was a certain comic element in the midst of tragedy in the appearance of the Germans with their hands held up being urged on by our heroes with bayonets. Indeed there was no need to apply stimulants as the prisoners had not the slightest intention of attempting to escape ... At this time the German shelling all around our farm house became very intense. The communication trench to the rear was impossible.

7 p.m. Things became quieter and the walking cases, including a wounded German, began to get away ... I got back to our billets about 9 p.m. to find the Divisional General congratulating the CO on the success of the operation. Unfortunately three officers and a good many others were killed ... The result of it all was that some valuable information was obtained and heavy losses inflicted on the enemy. They were apparently taken completely by surprise. We got congratulations from all kinds of generals, and the Irish Rifles had established their reputation in the new division.

The next tour commenced, 21 January, and six men had been wounded by the 27th. On that day, probably because it was the Kaiser's birthday, the Germans shelled the front line and support trenches quite heavily from 7.30 a.m. until 2 p.m. Le Touquet railway station was hit as well as Battalion HQ. Capt. Borcherds and three men were wounded and another three killed before the battalion was relieved that night. On the 29th the Rifles went into the Divisional rest area at La Crèche, between Bailleul and Armentières. During the month one officer and 174 men had joined. There then followed a long rest period up to 5 March, during which time 6 officers and 80 men joined. The only notable event was on 9 February when the battalion was inspected by Sir Herbert Plumer, 2nd Army Commander. The battalion marched to Vieux Berquin, 6 March, en route south to join 3rd Army. On the 10th they continued south in falling snow to Ham-en-Artois and, on the 12th, to Bailleul-aux-Cornailles, just north of the Montreuil–Arras Road, which Fr Gill described as 'a very squalid place'. Two companies were placed at Monchy–Breton. On 14 March they arrived at XVII Corps area and billeted at Acq. The battalion was attached to 139th Brigade for fatigue duties, chiefly carrying stores and in work connected with mining in conjunction with the French. The next day they moved to Mont St Eloy and billeted for the day in huts. The details, such as Transport and Quartermaster, remained at Acq.

That evening the battalion marched to reserve trenches about 900 yards north of La Targette, east of the Béthune Road. The 16th was quiet although a deal of hostile aeroplane activity was noticeable during the day. On St Patrick's Day General Doran called round and brought shamrock, while usual fatigues for Mining Companies were carried out. A few shells fell on the 18th, wounding Lt. Moss, 2/Lt. Getty and three men. While reconnoitring the way from the reserve trenches to reinforce the front line in case of attack by the enemy, Lt. E.D. Price was hit and died of wounds. By the time the battalion was relieved on the 27th, further casualties of one man killed and two wounded had been incurred. Billets were at Chelers where the usual field training was carried out. During the month nine officers had joined. There followed a move to new billets at Ternas on 10 April where four officers joined. On the 22nd they went by bus to the Vimy Ridge area and relieved 4th Leicestershire Regt in very wet trenches that night. Falls described the position:

> This was a very disturbed area, and one of constant mining. Each side was trying to burrow under and blow up prominent points in its opponent's front line, but each was also continually blowing craters in the narrow 'no-man's-land', for which there generally followed sanguinary hand-to-hand battles.

A certain amount of shelling took place, 23 April, principally on the front line. The enemy were very active with trench mortars and caused some casualties. 2/Lt. P.E. Murray was wounded slightly but remained at duty, while four men were killed and 23 wounded. The situation was normal during the next day, but heavy shelling, minenwerfer and bombs were directed on their trenches unceasingly, but only one man was wounded. The Germans exploded a mine at 1.30 p.m., 25 April, on the immediate right of the RIR's sector. The enemy occupied it at once, put up loop-holes, and finally consolidated it. The trenches were very wet and somewhat dam-aged. Lt. A. Massey (RAMC), 2/Lt. H.E. White and four men were wounded. At 3.40 a.m. the next day, another enemy mine was exploded on the Rifles' left; the Germans occupied it and consolidated their position throughout the day. When the mine was exploded the enemy temporarily occupied about 100 yards of the British trenches but vacated them almost immediately. They reoccupied the trench a few moments later but were bombed out, and the line was retaken. The usual minen-werfer and shell fire was directed onto the British lines. 2/Lt. H.W.D. Stone and seven men were killed while Lt. T.S. Jenkinson, Lt. T.J.C.C. Thompson, 2/Lt. T.H. Grey, and another 32 men were wounded. This was the day the Easter Rising commenced in Dublin. Fr Gill:

> The news was naturally alarming, as it was not easy to find out exactly what had happened. On the whole, the event created very little comment. The full significance was not appreciated for some time.

Trench mortar and artillery activity continued unabated. Capt. G.S. Norman and Lt. W.P. Moss were both slightly wounded. The battalion was relieved that night and marched back to rest at Camblain L'Abbé, leaving two Lewis Gun teams in the line. On the evening of 28 April orders came to proceed to Cabaret Rouge. The battalion moved off within ten minutes and arrived about 12.15 a.m. on the 29th. The situation was by then normal, but previously during the night the enemy had sprung another mine on the front of 7th Brigade's sector. The Rifles remained in position until 3 a.m., 29 April, when three companies returned to Camblain L'Abbé; the fourth rejoined the next day. At this time the total strength was 31 Officers and 930 other ranks, one officer having joined during the month. The bat-talion relieved 13th Cheshires in the trenches, 3 May. Fr Gill was disturbed:

> We cannot think of anything else than the terrible things which have been going on in Dublin. Please God it is over now and that the Authorities will use – as I am sure they will – tact in dealing with it … Nothing has affected Irishmen out here more than this. I have no doubt things will soon be nor-mal again. But it has been a big lesson. Many who ought to have known bet-ter seem to have been asleep. But least said soonest mended. I pity the poor young lads who got entangled into so horrible an affair. I see the 16th Division have been in it. We too have had a bad week but, being an Irish regiment lost in an English Army corps, we never get any praise.[1]

This was a quiet tour, with only one man wounded, until 7.45 p.m., 5 May, when the Germans commenced a bomb attack. A red light was sent up and the enemy shelled very heavily, receiving an equal response from the British. This

1 Letter to the Fr Provincial, No. 47, 3 May 1916. See also Capt. Bowen-Colthurst's details.

resulted in the Rifles losing 5 men killed and 13 wounded, including Lt. P. Erskine. The men had to work continuously on the trenches which were very badly damaged. At 7.45 p.m. on the 9th, two large mines were sprung on their left in the lines of 9th Loyal North Lancs. A struggle ensued for the craters in which the North Lancs were generally successful; 2nd RIR's left company was able to lend assistance by supplying bombs, but two men were wounded in the process. At 2.30 a.m., 10 May, 13th Cheshires relieved the battalion which went into Brigade Reserve, placing ten platoons in Zouave Valley and six at Cabaret Rouge. That evening there was heavy shelling of the sector on their left. The Germans shelled the valley continuously during the 13th. At 7.14 p.m. they sprang a mine about 70 yards in front of 13th Cheshires who occupied the near lip of the crater. At their request two RIR platoons were sent up to reinforce the garrison. On the way in they came under intense heavy fire; a portion of them got through with great difficulty and, by 3.40 a.m., 14 May, had taken up their position. 2/Lt. A.G. Mitchell and 3 men had been killed, 2/Lts H.E. White, J.H.F. Sharkie, and 14 men were wounded.

The line was taken over from 13th Cheshires on the 15th. During the day the Germans shelled Zouave Valley at intervals. About 8.30 p.m. two mines were sprung in front of the North Lancs on the left, and detachments of 11th Lancashire Fusiliers occupied the crater. The Germans put up the usual barrage fire which was heaviest chiefly in the sector left of 2nd RIR. Three men were killed and 12 wounded. At 1.30 a.m., 16 May, the crater in front of the Rifles was taken over from 13th Cheshires. Throughout the day the enemy shelled the front and support lines with minenwerfers causing some damage. A great deal of work was done by 2nd RIR on the line including the communication trenches leading up to the new crater in front of them. The Germans knocked in the majority of the front line and communication trenches with shells and trench mortars on the 17th. About 11 a.m. they commenced a bombing attack on the mine crater; this was repulsed until 1.25 p.m. when, owing to casualties, the supply of bombs giving out, and reinforcements not arriving in time, the surviving officer and two men out of a garrison of twenty-four retired and established themselves in a sap head leading from the main fire trench. A Lewis gun and one man had previously been sent away from the crater. A counter attack was ordered to take place at 9 p.m. but, owing to the necessarily hurried arrangements, the condition of the trenches, and the lack of jumping off accommodation, the attack became disorganized and failed. The artillery preparation had lasted at intervals from 6 p.m. till 9 p.m. The crater was very strongly held by the enemy with bombs and machine guns. A second attack was organized but instructions were received that, should the objective be too difficult and the chances of success slight, it was not to take place. This being the case the second assault was cancelled. Casualties incurred were 18 killed, 73 wounded, and 5 missing.

Throughout the 18th and 19th the enemy bombarded the trenches occupied by 2nd RIR; many areas were badly damaged and casualties of 7 men killed and 14 wounded occurred. The Rifles were then relieved by 1/7th London Regt and proceeded to billets at Acq. It was thought that the enemy activity during the previous three days had been done to test the British strength. The battalion moved via

Aubigny and Penin to Averdoingt, 20 May, and arrived at about 3.10 a.m. the next morning. About 7 a.m., 22 May, an urgent message arrived ordering 2nd RIR to Bailleul-aux-Cornailles where the Brigade was concentrating, as it was understood that the enemy had made an attack on the sector which the battalion had vacated on the 19th; at noon they were sent back to Averdoingt. On 31 May the Rifles moved back to Bailleul-aux-Cornailles. During the month 4 officers and 19 men had joined. There then followed a series of moves that was to bring the Rifles to the Somme area: 14 June to Ecoivres, on the 15th to Maizicourt (near Auxi-le-Chateau), 17th to Fransu, 18th to St Léger (near Domart), 24th to Canaples, 25th to Bonneville, 28th to Mirvaux, and on the 30th to Harponville. During June 8 officers and 119 men joined.

8

Somme

At the beginning of July the Rifles were in billets at Senlis with a total strength of 38 officers (including the Medical Officer and Chaplain) and 1028 other ranks. They did not take part in the first day of the Somme battle where many of the regiment's units had suffered terribly. On the 3rd they moved to Bouzincourt and, on the afternoon of the 6th, marched through Albert and bivouacked about half a mile east of it, until 11 p.m. when 20 officers and 603 other ranks proceeded to the assembly trenches at La Boisselle preparatory to making an attack the next morning. Falls described the strategic situation:

> As a result of the first day's fighting, though neither Ovillers nor the neighbouring fortress of La Boisselle had been taken, a dint in the enemy's line had been made between them. On July 2nd the 19th Division captured half of La Boisselle, and the 12th some of the trenches in front of Ovillers. South of the former village the advance had been more considerable, and our line was facing more nearly north than east, as at the start. On the 5th the whole of La Boisselle was in our hands. To open wider the breach, the 74th Brigade, at the disposal of the 12th Division, was to be employed. It was to attack almost due northwards, from La Boisselle toward the eastern side of Ovillers.

Fr Gill recorded:

> It would be impossible to describe the various attacks which took place during the following days. We pushed forward by the aid of bombs, bayonets, and artillery several kilometres, captured many Germans and killed many more. There was little sleep for anyone during these days. The opening day of the attack it began to rain. Soon the ordinary horrors of this kind of fighting were augmented by the indescribable mud and squalor which torrents of rain produced in the trenches. The subsoil was chalk and soon the hollows of the trenches began to fill up with a white liquid mud like thick whitewash. There was no question of keeping dry. The stretcher-bearers arrived with their loads of wounded. They could not be got down into the dug out and had to be dressed in the trenches and wait there until the squads

from the dressing station could take them further back. It was necessary to harden one's heart.

At 8 a.m., 7 July, the battalion occupied the assembly trenches vacated by 9th Loyal North Lancs and 13th Cheshires which had gone into the attack. A and B Coys were behind the Cheshires on the left and C and D behind the North Lancs on the right. At 9.50 a.m. the Rifles went forward and occupied the line that had been captured. Casualties were 2 officers and 28 men killed, 4 officers and 116 men wounded, 17 men missing.[1] The line was held throughout the following day until 6 p.m. A Coy was brought from the left to the right flank and, with the remainder of the battalion and two companies of 11th Lancashire Fusiliers, were ordered to advance to a particular trench but, through difficulty in identifying it, the force really assembled in a line 600 yards too far that had been given as the objective to be gained by a future night attack. At 8.40 p.m. the assault was launched, one company of the Lancashire Fusiliers followed by 2nd RIR; the position that was taken took all night to consolidate. As the battalion was too far forward, in error, there was no connection with troops on the right and left. During the night and the day of the 9th they were subjected to a continuous barrage from their own artillery who, owing to difficulty of communication, were unaware of their presence in that position. Casualties were one officer and 7 men killed, 2 officers and 22 men wounded, 11 men were missing.[2]

> Rifleman G. Bell ... says he would have written sooner only he had got a lot of shifting about. He was wounded in the leg, but not too badly and was progressing favourably. He was in the big push for two days. The fighting was very fierce; in fact it was like 'hell let loose'. He never saw anything like it before, and during the fighting there was a continual downpour of rain, and the men were up to their knees in mud. It was fine to see the Germans running and the British troops after them. They were 'beating the brains' out of the Germans now, and no doubt many of them would be delighted to be out of it.[3]

At about 4 p.m., 9 July, the Germans attacked in two parties from Contalmaison Wood and outflanked 2nd RIR, which forced them to retire to their original objective that was being held by a company of Lancashire Fusiliers with the 8th North Staffords on the right. The enemy bombed vigorously but the retirement was carried out in good order. The casualties on this day were one officer and 12 men killed, 3 officers and 62 men wounded, 45 men were missing.[4] The Rifles were relieved in the early hours of 10 July and marched to billets at Senlis. On the 14th, they moved through Bouzincourt and Albert to the Usna Hill trenches, taking over

---

1 Officers killed: 2/Lts W.W. Vernon, J. Watson. Wounded: Capt. H.R.H. Ireland, Lt. W.P. Moss, 2/Lts J.L. MacLaughlin and C.E. Wilson.   2 Lt. W.C. McConnell killed; 2/Lts P. McMahon and D.O. Turpin wounded.   3 *Banbridge Chronicle*, 29 July 1916.   4 Capt. W.A. Smiles killed; 2/Lts J.M. Clarke, P.E. Murray, and P. Windle wounded

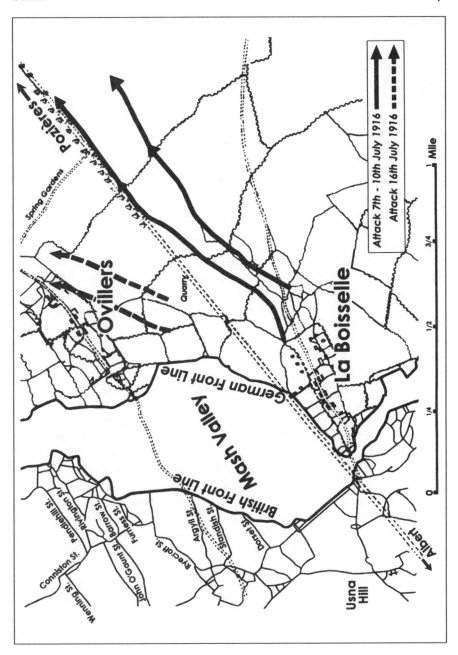

Map 8: The Battle of the Somme

the frontline at Ovillers the next day. Casualties were two men killed and three wounded. Fr Gill:

> This time we went to the trenches in full daylight down the road from Albert, now no longer shelled. We now felt that we had got into the German lines, which had seemed so impregnable, but not very far! ... The Germans in the south-east corner of Ovillers still held out. In spite of the heavy bombardment they had been able to hold on in their deep dugouts, or rather they were unable to get away ... During this night several attempts were made to take the German trench, but some of their machine guns were still in action and, in spite of heavy losses, we made no progress.

At 1 a.m., 16 July, 2nd RIR, in conjunction with two companies of 13th Cheshires, took part in an attack. The battalion formed up in six lines on a half-company front in the following order: D, A, C. B Coy remained as trench garrison. The foremost line reached the enemy's wire but, owing to very heavy machine gun fire from the front and from the right of their own trench that was held by the enemy, were forced to return. From 9 a.m. to 4 p.m., RIR bombers endeavoured to dislodge an enemy bombing post, but only made an advance of ten yards in that time, a new barricade being constructed. The bombers, weakened by considerable casualties, were then reinforced by two squads from 11th Lancashire Fusiliers. Another attack was made, considerable use being made of rifle grenades, which succeeded in dislodging the enemy at about 7 p.m. Here they captured two officers and 126 other ranks of the 15th Regiment (Prussians). During this operation 9641 Cpl G.A. Reading distinguished himself and was awarded the Military Medal.[5] This successful operation enabled 2nd RIR to secure the south-eastern perimeter of Ovillers, the right flank of the battalion linking up with 5th Royal Warwickshire Regt. Two officers and 4 men were killed, 3 officers and 42 men wounded, and another 6 were missing.[6] Fr Gill explained the events of 16 July:

> The position was somewhat as follows. Some of the Warwicks were separated from us by some 100 yards of trench occupied by the Germans. Only a parapet separated the British and Germans at either end. A heavy gunfire from our batteries made it impossible for the Germans to retire. It was resolved to try stronger measures. A little earlier we had sent down a fatigue party to bring up a supply of rifle grenades, and a new attack was made. A brisk fire was opened on the German trench. At the same time a heavy shower tended to damp the spirits of the garrison, who were evidently hard pressed. The effect was dramatic. Suddenly a burly German appeared holding a long pole on which was a white flag. Our men raised a cheer and were about to rush the trench. Our CO ordered all to 'stand to' with fixed bay-

---

5 Killed in action, 4 April 1917.   6 Officer killed: 2/Lts T.E. Barton and J. Lecky; wounded: Capt. D.H. Kelly, 2/Lts R.U. Bennett and T.H.E. Gallwey.

onets in case there might be some trick. But the Germans had had enough
… They were German Guards, who had made a good fight, but did not look
up to much after all they had gone through.

The battalion was relieved at midnight and arrived at Bouzincourt by 6.30 a.m.,
17 July. That evening they marched to Forceville, bivouacked for the night, then
went to billets at Beauval. The Divisional Commander inspected the Brigade on
the 19th and congratulated them on their good work. The Brigade marched to Bus-
en-Artois, 21 July, and to Mailly-Maillet Wood on the 24th. In the evening the
Rifles took over trenches opposite Beaumont Hamel, their right flank at Mary
Redan. By the time they moved back to Mailly-Maillet Wood on the 30th, 19 men
had been wounded. During July reinforcements of 12 officers and 268 men joined.

On 5 August the Rifles marched to a camp at Bertrancourt. Two days later they
went into trenches in front of Auchonvillers until the 10th when they moved to a
camp at Bus-en-Artois. On the 15th they went to Acheux and, on the 18th, to
Hedauville. The next day they marched to dugouts at Northern Bluff (east bank of
the Ancre) relieving 7th West Riding Regt. The battalion had to provide numerous
carrying and working parties in the river valley that was under intermittent shell fire.
D Coy occupied strong points on the west bank of the Ancre. On the 26th the battalion marched to billets at Bouzincourt, paraded at 4 a.m., 28 August, and marched
via Aveluy to the trenches in front of Ovillers. The day was quiet except for almost
incessant German shelling, particularly on the right. To their right flank were the
Anzacs of 4th Brigade and on the left 11th Lancashire Fusiliers. Connection was
made with the Anzacs by means of patrols; the front line on the right was only held
lightly with Lewis guns and small posts due to the shelling. The trenches were wet
and badly knocked about. Casualties during the month were 2 officers and 41 men
wounded, 7 men killed; reinforcements were 3 officers and 24 men.

Having been relieved on 1 September, A and C Coys occupied dugouts in
Ovillers and C and D dugouts at Donnet Post in Brigade Reserve. Working parties were provided around the clock working on the front line and communication
trenches. Six men had been wounded by the time 2nd RIR moved back to camp
on the 6th. In the period 7–12 August, the battalion moved to Acheux Wood,
Puchevillers, Beauval, Berneuil, to Domqueur where they commenced a period of
training. On 25 September they went via Beauval to Forceville, to Hedauville the
following day, then to Bouzincourt on the 27th. That evening they relieved 8th
West Yorkshire Regt in the line above Thiepval Wood. During this tour there was
heavy shelling and, by the time of the relief on the 30th, 2/Lt. J.F. Stein and 6
men had been killed, 2/Lt. K. Elphick and 14 men were wounded. Three officers
and 36 men joined during the month.

Only two companies got away to Englebelmer; the others were retained and did
not rejoin until 2 October. The following few days were spent at work details and
training. The Rifles left Ovillers Post on the 6th and went into reserve; two companies were located in Ovillers, one in Mouquet Farm and one in a nearby trench.
The next day some shells fell in the vicinity of the two forward companies so B

Coy moved up and occupied a trench near Pozières Cemetery. The remaining company was moved up from Ovillers on the 8th and occupied a trench near Mouquet Farm. Working parties were provided throughout the day and night. The Rifles entered the front line at Hessian Trench on the 13th placing one company in reserve in Zollern Trench. The line was improved and a new trench was commenced joining up the right of the battalion to the left of 55th Brigade. The front line was slightly reorganized on the 18th as an assault from Hessian Trench on the enemy's Regina Trench was planned. In consequence 2nd RIR extended to the west, taking over about 200 yards more of the line. The trenches were in a bad state owing to the wet; all efforts were concentrated in deepening and improving the front line in preparation for the intended attack. 2nd RIR was relieved during the early morning of 21 October by 11th Lancashire Fusiliers, 13th Cheshires, and 9th Loyal North Lancs preparatory to these battalions taking part in the attack together with a portion of 53rd Brigade on the right, and 75th Brigade on the left. The Rifles did not actually form part of the attacking wave, its task being to re-occupy and hold Hessian Trench and supply carrying parties to the remainder of the Brigade after the objective had been gained. When the attack commenced, two platoons each from A and B Coys moved from Zollern Trench into Hessian Trench and took up the original front, the remainder of the battalion moved up and proceeded with the work of carrying over bombs, ammunition, water, and consolidating material to Regina Trench, which had been successfully assaulted. The work was carried out satisfactorily under very heavy shell-fire, in some parts over a distance of from four to five hundred yards. The battalion also furnished escorts for conducting prisoners to Brigade HQ. Having been relieved on the 22nd, they moved to a camp near Albert. Casualties for this period: 2/Lts C.R. Cooney, F.R. Fowler and 6 men had been killed; Lt. J.R. Tuckett, 2/Lt. S.A. Bell, a/RSM Murphy and 87 men were wounded, 5 were missing. The next day the battalion moved by bus to Harponville, then marched on the 24th to Beauval. General Sir Douglas Haig inspected the Brigade and thanked individual commanding officers for the good work their units had done during the recent operations. On the 30th the Rifles went to Camdas Station, took a train to Caestre, then marched to Thieushouk. During October 4 officers and 12 men joined.

November commenced with a move to Shaexhen on the north side of Meteren. On the 2nd they marched to a camp three miles from Nieppe on the Bailleul–Nieppe Road. The next day they marched to Ploegsteert Wood and occupied positions in support of the North Lancs who were holding the front line. HQ was placed at Creslow Farm, A Coy in Everest, Dead House, and Boyd forts (Hunter's Avenue), B in dugouts about Plugstreet Hall, C in Regent, Eel Pie, Eccles and Reading forts (Hunter's Avenue), D in Toronto Dugouts and Rotten Row. HQ moved closer towards the front line to Lewisham Lodge, 6 November, and C Coy moved to dugouts around Gloucester House. On the 7th the Rifles entered the front line placing their HQ at Hope House. Gas was discharged along the Divisional front, commencing at 4.25 a.m., 10 November, and lasting about 25 minutes, accompanied by three minutes combined artillery, trench mortars and Stokes guns bombardment commencing at 4.30 a.m. Apparently very little impact was made on the enemy. Later that morning 2nd RIR was relieved in the line and took up the support positions. Orders were issued, 13 November, for a new method of holding the line: two companies of the RIR were to hold the front line on the left of the brigade front with the other two in support in St Andrew's Drive and Rotten Row Dugouts. The North Lancs were to hold the right line in a similar way. Col. Sprague handed over command to Major J. Evans, 21 November, and Major Goodman took command on the 25th. During November the casualties were 6 men killed and 13 wounded, while 4 officers and 67 men joined.

On 7 December 5009 Rfn S. McBride was executed for desertion. Having been relieved on the 14th, the Rifles marched to huts at Regina Camp where the majority were employed in and about the front line on working parties. Billets at Nieppe were occupied on the 22nd and working parties continued. Brigadier-General Bethel visited on Christmas Day. During December one man was killed while an officer and six men were wounded. Reinforcements of 4 officers and 318 men arrived, including 65 from 1/9th London Regt.

9

Messines

The fighting strength of 2nd RIR at the start of the year was 8 officers and 490 men. They marched from Nieppe, 2 January, and manned the trenches in the Ploegsteert left subsector. During this tour Lt. Leach and 2/Lt. Jackson were killed. Having been relieved by 11th Lancashire Fusiliers on the 6th the battalion went into support at Creslow Farm, Ploegsteert, where Major-General Bainbridge presented Military Cross ribbons to Lts Wilkins and Marriott-Watson.

The Rifles relieved 11th Lancs in the trenches during 10–14 January, then marched to reserve billets at Regina Camp where training of companies and specialists was carried out. During the next tour, 18–22 January, the Germans became very active with artillery and particularly trench mortars during the latter days. After returning to the support area in Ploegsteert Wood, HQ was placed at Creslow Farm, with A Coy at Gloster House, B was holding forts along Hunter's Avenue, C was at Plugstreet Hall, D at Touquet Berthe with one platoon at Keeper's Hut Barricade. At 1.15 p.m. the enemy commenced to bombard the line with artillery and trench mortars. About 4.30 p.m. this became intense and at 5 p.m. an SOS rocket was sent up from the right subsector. Reinforcements had been called for by 13th Cheshires at 3.15 p.m. but the Brigade did not think the situation critical enough for reinforcements to be sent up at that time. The bombardment became intense about 4.30 p.m. and D Coy was ordered to reinforce Keeper's Hut Barricade. At 5.15 p.m. C Coy was ordered to reinforce the forts in Hunter's Avenue. Around 5.30 p.m., OC 11th Lancs informed Col. Goodman that the enemy had entered his trenches south of St Ives Avenue and asked for reinforcements, so A Coy was sent up to St Andrew's Drive at 7.30 p.m. Information was received thirty minutes later that the enemy had been expelled so the three companies that were sent up to reinforce were requisitioned for working parties to repair damage done to the trenches. As much work as possible was done during the night and the companies returned to their respective positions in the support area at daylight. 2/Lts M.J. McDonnell and W.J.S. Tydd had both been mortally wounded. The Rifles relieved 11th Lancs in the line, 26–30 January, then moved to Regina Camp. Other rank casualties during January were 2 killed and 18 wounded (including 4 self-inflicted wounds). Reinforcements of 7 officers and 98 men joined.

On 2 February they moved back to reserve at Romarin Camp where training commenced in practice attacks near Bailleul. There was an accident on the train-

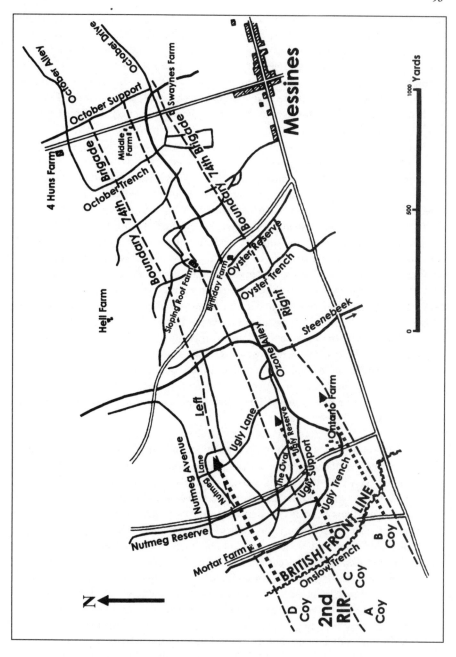

Map 9: The Battle of Messines, 7 July 1917

ing field, 15 February, when 9641 Sgt G.A. Reading and 40960 Rfn R. Cruickshank
were injured by the premature explosion of a Mills bomb; 2/Lt. E.J. Williams was
also slightly hurt but remained at duty. The battalion moved to Courte Croix, just
south-south-east of Fletre, 20 February, to Ebblinghem the next day, and then to
Tatinghem on the 22nd for more training. Further moves took place to Staple, 20
March, the Strazeele area on the 21st, Nieppe on the 23rd, and Oosthove Farm on
the 28th. Working parties were furnished throughout this period. During February
and March reinforcements totalling 12 officers and 97 men had joined.

A further move took place to the Noote Boom area south-west of Bailleul, 6 April.
The battalion went into the line on the 13th, taking over the sector held by 8th
Border Regt, placing HQ at a ruined house called St Quentin Cabaret. By the time
of their relief on the 19th, 4 men had been killed, 6 wounded and 3 were missing.
The Rifles moved from reserve at Aldershot Camp back to Noote Boom for train-
ing on the 30th. Reinforcements of 69 men joined during April.

The battalion moved into support at Neuve Eglise, 10 May, relieving 2nd
Auckland Infantry Regt. From 16–19 May they were in the front line before going
into reserve at Bulford Camp. During the night of the 17th, 6876 Cpl William
Beckett had earned the DCM: 'When returning with a reconnoitring patrol he went
back, under heavy fire, and rescued a Co. Sergeant Major and another man, and
brought them to safety.' Having gone to a camp in the Ravelsberg area, 24 May,
the battalion moved the next day to Bailleul, then by rail to Watten before marching to billets at Tournehem where practice attacks were carried out. On the 29th
they took a train from Watten to Bailleul and then marched to La Crèche for more
training. During the month 7 officers and 6 men joined; casualties were 2 men
killed, 18 wounded and 3 missing. On 5 June the battalion marched to bivouacs at
Bremerschen. Fr Gill observed:

> We soon moved up to take up a position in front of Neuve Eglise. These
> trenches were near the base of Messines Ridge where we took part in the big
> attack six weeks later. This village was on a ridge parallel to the Messines
> Ridge and was pleasantly situated. The village and church had been destroyed
> and the troops lived in wooden huts. My own billet was somewhat behind,
> near a little shop just off the Bailleul–Nieppe Road. The camps were called
> after Aldershot and Bulford. We did our turns in the trenches in the ordinary
> way and things were very quiet. The chief feature of the trench work was the
> frequent patrols to the German trenches, which were sometimes entered.
> Active preparations were in progress for the coming attack. Broad and nar-
> row gauge railways had been constructed and vast supplies of all sorts of
> ammunition were being accumulated. Miles of wooden corduroy roads were
> made over soft ground and, in general, the intense activity, pointing to a big
> attack, was everywhere visible. There was hardly a ditch which did not hide
> an ammunition dump, and many of them were sent up by German shells.
>
> Endless streams of lorries and frequent trains passed along. No attempt
> was made to hide the preparations. New railway lines were ballasted with white

sand which must have shown up clearly on aerial photographs. Indeed a captured document showed that the Germans were well prepared for the attack.

One morning the Brigadier sent for the CO and myself and asked if we thought it likely that any of the Irish would think of deserting and if it would be advisable to talk to the men. It was, I suppose, an aftermath of the trouble in Ireland the year before. I said that nothing could do greater harm than to suggest that any of the men were thought capable of treachery. As a matter of fact no further step was taken. Later on, when the attack was over, it was discovered that a sergeant of an English regiment had given information to the enemy. We were free from anything of this kind ... 6 June. Owing to the proximity of all the units of the Brigade, I had excellent opportunities of giving the sacraments to all who were there. That day we were addressed by the Brigadier and got orders to march to the assembly trenches at the foot of Messines Ridge. About dusk we marched down to the Wulverghem Road and took up our positions slightly north-east of Messines. I went to the advanced dressing station where I would have the best chance of finding the wounded. There was little or no sleep for anyone that night.

The Rifles lined up by the Westhoek–Neuve Eglise–Wulverghem Road, with a strength of 21 Officers and 616 men. At 9.30 p.m. they moved into the assembly area where B (Capt. Thompson), C (Lt. Anderson) and D (Lt. Fry) companies were placed in Onslow Trench with A (Capt. McKeown) in support at Fusilier Trench. By 11 p.m. everyone was in position.

At Zero, 3.10 a.m., 7 June, the battalion pushed forward to the attack in accordance with Operation Orders No. 38 (see Appendix V) and quickly closed up to the barrage. When it lifted from the front line the waves followed and passed over the German first line meeting little opposition. A mine had been exploded under Ontario Farm at Zero which effectively shattered the enemy support trench there. The waves followed the barrage which was 'as perfect as could be'. Each objective was taken in a similar manoeuvre to the first with little opposition. A few small pockets of resistance made the advance 'a little interesting'. The final objective was reached and taken by the scheduled hour, and consolidation of the captured trenches began. The task was a difficult one as the enemy lines were almost obliterated. The 9th Loyal North Lancs leap-frogged the battalion at this stage. Enemy shelling up to the time of taking the final objective was negligible; the only difficulty experienced during the first hour of the attack was the maintenance of direction due to darkness and dust and smoke from the barrage. At Zero plus 90 minutes 2nd RIR moved forward to occupy and consolidate Occur Support and Avenue. It was then observed that the North Lancs were meeting with fierce resistance from four machine guns at Middle Farm. Capt. Thompson took B Coy and immediately pushed forward, working around the farm on the right flank and attacking from the rear. This operation was entirely successful and resistance at the farm was completely broken.

The move to Occur Support and Avenue was accomplished without difficulty and work on consolidation was continued throughout the remaining part of the day and night. The Rifles took 200 prisoners (3rd Bavarian Division), five machine guns, and two trench mortars.[1] Casualties were 2 officers and 23 men killed or died of wounds, 5 officers and 216 men wounded. Fr Gill:

> Perhaps no action in the British zone has been more written about than the attack we are about to describe. It was in one way the most successful of all the attacks. The casualties were slight in comparison with other attacks and the limited objective was speedily secured. The method employed necessitated a prodigality of guns and material which could not often be obtained. The success was chiefly an artillery one and the amount of guns and ammunition brought into action was probably unequalled in any other action. The weather, which was fine and not too hot, was also an important element in the success. Both sides attached great importance to the Messines–Wytschaete Ridge and the British offensive to be made later on in the year depended on the capture of the position. Documents found in the German trenches showed that the attack was expected, but its overwhelming strength was evidently unsuspected. The length of the front to be attacked was about ten miles and included many positions which had been very strongly fortified during the previous years of the war. In addition to the unparalleled artillery preparation, nineteen great mines had been made under the German positions. It has been calculated that there was a gun of greater or lesser calibre to about every yard and a half of the whole front. There was a machine gun to every fifty yards, so that the whole front was sprayed with machine gun fire during the attack. About seven million rounds of machine gun fire passed over the heads of the attacking party ... One of the features of this attack was the creeping barrage. Each gun had its objective and, according to an accurately worked out timetable, the range of the guns was gradually extended so as to allow the shells to fall just in front of the advancing infantry. The machine guns were in positions further back so as to catch reinforcements or cut off the retreat of the Germans. It may be stated that the timetable was accurately adhered to. Each of the battalions had its definite objective at which it was to halt and consolidate while fresh troops pushed on and went through them to further objectives ... All were in their places well before the Zero hour which was fixed for 3.10 a.m., summer time, June 7th. At this hour dawn was just beginning. I had taken up my position in the advance dressing station which was in two large elephant shelters not far from the trenches. We had the misfortune to have the greater part of a Lewis gun team knocked out by a shell on their way up to the trenches, but apart from this there were few casualties. The night had been relatively quiet and there was the ordinary bombardments such as took place every night. As the hour drew near the tension naturally became greater, and then it began! Suddenly the ground

---

1 2/Lts S.J.V. O'Brien and W.J. Dobbie were killed; Capt. T.J.C.C. Thompson, 2/Lts R.S.H. Noble, H.C. Mallett, H. Marshall, and E.J. Williams were wounded.

rocked from side to side and the peculiar swaying movement told that the mines had been exploded. The attack had begun. I do not think that anyone who was present will ever forget that time. From all sides the guns began to blaze. I went to the door of the dressing station. It was still almost night. From every direction tons of flame leaped out. Every wood and tree was outlined by the fire from the guns which seemed to be everywhere. Standing as I was between the guns and the trenches the sight was one never to be forgotten. The roar of the guns and the sudden breaking of the storm after the quiet of night was indescribable. I, of course, could only see one corner of the great inferno. Others who saw the spectacle from places like the top of Kemmel Hill have described the wonderful sight. It was easy to imagine the effect of such a fire on the enemy trenches. They were for the most part obliterated but, as they were held comparatively lightly, the number of killed was not as great as might have been expected. I remained at the dressing station for some hours attending on such wounded as had been brought in. A good deal of gas from gas shells hung about the place. I then set out to follow in the wake of the attack to see what could be done for wounded on the field. A sharp counter-barrage had been set up by the Germans so that the going was none too good. I got over our first line trench and made my way across what had just ceased to be no-man's-land. One of the first casualties I came across was one of our officers lying on his face dead. I stopped to take out of his pack any personal belongings which might be valued by his relatives. I also took a small bottle of rum which might turn in handy and then came a serial comic incident. At the bottom of a sap or shell hole lay a sergeant belonging to an English regiment. I thought he was badly wounded and endeavoured to arouse him. I bethought me of my little flask of rum and proceeded to administer a dose, but the hero only grunted and turned away his head. I then thought that perhaps water was what he needed and opened his water bottle. But alas for the weakness of human nature, it was nearly half full of rum. The gallant sergeant was merely speechless. I hope no one responsible for his conduct found him. I emptied out the precious liquid and left him where he was. It is not to be concluded from this incident that these attacks took place under the influence of Dutch courage. It was usual to give a small tot of rum during the night duty under strict supervision and no doubt this sergeant helped himself to the supply entrusted to him for others. I continued on my way to the Steenbeeke which seemed to have disappeared. There was merely a series of shell holes containing water with a slight trickle from one to another. The ground was, however, sufficiently soft to bog a tank which lay helpless in the mud. I had no clear idea where I could find the battalion. Soon, however, I saw some of them in front of me. Amongst them was an officer who had led the difficult part of the attack who was awarded the DSO.[2] He had been wounded in the head and was being

2 Capt. T.J.C.C. Thompson.

helped back to the dressing station. He was unfortunately killed in the retreat of the Fifth Army the following year. Presently I joined the attacking party who were already consolidating their objective and resting after the attack. The position was simply a ditch which the Germans had converted into a trench and was not very suitable as the ground was swampy. I found that the casualties had been few. We had had, in fact, a walkover but there was a good deal of shell fire falling around us. Our position, nearly due north of Messines, was near the right flank of the front along which the advance had been made and was under gun fire from the German batteries which had been able to retain their positions near Warneton in front of Ploegsteert Wood. There was no cover of any sort where we were, yet it needed considerable encouragement to get the men to dig in. The period following an attack is one of reaction and the fatigue of the effort begins to make itself felt. The CO and his staff were in the trench affording little or no shelter. Others were in shell holes. There was one good shell hole which we proceeded – some shells falling near – to deepen and enlarge. This became the Battalion HQ for a few days. The German shelling was systematic and seemed to follow a fixed cycle which was repeated over and over during the day. Many shells fell near us and there was no knowing where the next might land. Some officers and men were unfortunately killed, in fact nearly all our casualties took place during the days following the attack. We had led the advance and were now in reserve, as the others had passed through and taken up more forward positions. My own location was very suitable, as I found, as I was in touch with the Brigade and the main path from the more forward positions passed through our line so that I met the wounded being carried back from other units ... Some large tanks were scattered near us. I do not think the tanks did very much that day except draw fire. One of them caught fire near us and had to be deserted by its crew. The officer ran over and told our CO that it would be well to move as the flames and smoke would certainly draw enemy fire. Our Colonel replied magnificently that the Infantry could not move off on account of shell fire – whatever others might do! Looking down from our newly-won high ground, we could appreciate the advantage it had been to the Germans. We could see the country for miles back to the next ridge. There were several disabled tanks in the soft ground below us.

Nothing of note happened during the 8th and work on consolidation was continued. The German artillery activity increased, especially during the latter part of the day, but no concentrated effort was made in 2nd RIR's sector. By the time they withdrew to bivouacs on 11 June there had been additional casualties of 2/Lt. P. McMahon killed, Lt. E. Brown and 23 men wounded. Fr Gill:

> Mass in transport lines. I remember insisting on the need of being always ready and that even in their position of relative safety. One of the Quarter Masters, whose duty it was to accompany the ration party to the trenches,

which meant a short stay there, who was at Mass that morning, was killed that evening.

The Rifles moved into the support trenches of 75th Brigade, south-east of Messines, on the 12th. Five men had been wounded by 14 June when the battalion was relieved at midnight by 8th Loyal North Lancs. The next tour in the front line west of Warneton, 17–20 June, was a more unpleasant experience and resulted in seven men being killed, 2/Lts S. Mercer, W.H. Calwell and 15 men being wounded. While in support a further three men were killed and three wounded. On the 22nd the battalion moved to the transport lines on the Wulverghem–Neuve Eglise Road. Over the next few days they moved via Caudescoure, Molinghem and Estree-Blanche before arriving for a period of training at Fruges on the 26th. Reinforcements for June were 2 officers and 69 men.

On 8 July billets at Radinghem were taken over. They marched to the vicinity of Delette and Reclinghem on the 12th and carried out Brigade exercises in the afternoon, camping during that night at Passion Village. The exercises were repeated again the next day before returning to billets in the evening. The battalion moved by lorry, 14 July, to Pioneer Camp west of Ypres. For the next ten days large working parties were furnished for making roads in the forward area. Casualties during this time were two men killed, Capt. Knox and 30 men wounded. On the 25th they moved to bivouacs for further training before moving to Dominion Camp on the 29th and Swan Chateau on the 30th. The Rifles were left out of the great attack of 31 July and were employed in the construction of corduroy tracks near Hooge and laying water pipes along the Menin Road from Birr Crossroads eastwards. Enemy shelling was heavy in the vicinity of Hooge where three men were wounded. During the month 4 officers and 235 men joined bringing the fighting strength up to 15 Officers and 459 men. On 4 August they moved into the Ramparts at Ypres.

10

Westhoek and Cambrai

Fr Gill:

I got back to Swan Chateau and accompanied the Battalion to dug-outs in the Ypres ramparts just north of the Menin Gate. These ramparts were very strong and afforded excellent protection, but the area outside was under more or less continuous shell fire. Our transport experienced this. When waiting to be loaded up just before the Battalion set out to the trenches from their dug-outs, a shell fell among the horses causing great damage to both men and horses. One of our best transport men was killed.[1] The horses of another driver, who had himself been wounded, stampeded through the ruins but, in spite of his wounds, the driver held on to them. When he was discovered by the transport officer he was completely indifferent to his own wounds and was binding up those of the horses with his own field dressings! Six horses were killed or had to be shot. There is a picture published by one of the great Illustrateds representing an artillery man saying goodbye under shell fire to one of his horses which had been mortally wounded. It hardly exaggerates the attachment which existed between the men and their horses. Consequently the condition of the horses of the British Army was the envy of the French who are less sentimental in this respect. The man I refer to was removed to the F.A. to have his wounds dressed, and was marked down for the base, and probably for home. However, he escaped from the F.A. and hid in the transport lines for some days, until he deemed it safe to declare himself. He wanted to look after his horses! It is the only case I know of a man refusing a chance to be sent down. I am glad to say he was awarded a Military Medal.

As the Rifles were going into the line at Westhoek Ridge on the night of 5 August the Germans put down a heavy barrage catching A Coy at Chateau Wood resulting in two men being killed and four wounded. Fr Gill: 'During the night we had the misfortune to lose our M.O. [Lt. A.B. Ross, RAMC], a Scotsman loved and respected by all. He was the second doctor killed with the Battalion. A sad

1 7303 Rfn P. McAteer.

thing was that he had been suddenly recalled from leave and only arrived a day or two before.' Heavy intermittent shelling continued throughout 6–8 August resulting in additional casualties: Lt. E. Brown and 7 men were killed, 77 were wounded. An active operation was ordered for the 9th with the objective of capturing and holding about 500 yards of the German line. Rain fell during the evening and the attack was postponed for twenty-four hours. A lot of preparatory work was needed, although the time was limited, but the assembly trenches were dug and much other necessary work was finished in good time. Zero hour was fixed for 4.35 a.m., 10 August. Falls explained:

> The Brigade was to attack upon a front of 2,000 yards, south of the Ypres–Roulers railway line. The distance of its objective varied considerably along its front, being about 450 yards on the right, 650 in the centre, and 250 on the left. With a frontage so wide, the Brigade used all its four battalions … The 2nd Royal Irish Rifles had to go the extreme distance, and had, moreover, to take the village of Westhoek itself; and, if Westhoek were hard to find on the ground, at least the 'pill boxes' might be expected to be thicker on its site than elsewhere. The Battalion's advance was to be made in four waves, A Company in rear forming the fourth.

The battalion, led by Major Rose, was formed up in its assembly position by 3.05 a.m. At Zero the Rifles advanced to the attack. Two strong concrete dugouts at Westhoek were quickly rushed by special parties detailed by C Coy and the enemy holding them, taken completely unawares, offered little resistance. The waves pushed forward to Jabber Support; most of the enemy who were holding this line fled, making no attempt to fight. Rushing blindly back, they were caught in the British barrage and annihilated. A German machine gun, that had just come into action on the left, was dealt with by B Coy; 2/Lt. T. McAlindon having led a determined rush put the gun team to flight. The advance continued with the waves keeping close to the barrage and the fighting chiefly consisted of mopping up concrete dugouts, of which there were many, but at no time did the Germans put up any real resistance. Their morale had been badly shaken by the effect of the heavy barrage and, before they had time to organize themselves, the attacking waves were upon them. The main objective, the Black Line, was taken by about 5.20 a.m. and rapid consolidation began. Contact was immediately established with 13th Cheshires and 9th Loyal North Lancs on the right and left respectively. At 10 a.m. the enemy was seen coming over Anzac Ridge and down the forward slope towards Hannebeeke Valley presumably with the intention of massing for a counter-attack. This concentration continued throughout the day and at 3.30 p.m. a feeble effort was made by the Germans to move forward, but broke down under machine gun and rifle fire with the help of artillery support which came later. At 7.30 p.m. a more determined effort was made under cover of a smoke barrage and a heavy bombardment of the front line and Westhoek Ridge. The SOS signal was sent up but the British artillery did not respond. Shortly thereafter a British aeroplane appeared and

dropped an SOS signal, whereupon the artillery immediately opened a heavy barrage that completely broke up the attack and almost wiped out the enemy whose
remnants could be seen running in all directions. Many casualties were also inflicted
by small arms fire.

At 4.15 a.m. on the 11th, the enemy pushed forward strong patrols but only
two of them reached the firing line. One, consisting of about twelve men, got within
bombing distance but was quickly wiped out by grenades and the bayonet. The
other patrol of twenty men retreated to a dugout as soon as firing commenced. The
Rifles sent out their own patrol and the Germans surrendered without a fight. The
battalion was relieved that night by 8th Border Regt, moving first to Ypres and
later to Halifax Camp. Total casualties, 5–11 August, were 4 officers and 30 men
killed, 5 officers and 295 men wounded, and 17 missing.[2] The battalion strength
coming out of the line was reduced to 10 Officers and 148 men. Four officers and
150 men of the German 90th Reserve Infantry Regt had been captured together
with a 77mm gun and five machine guns. 2/Lt. J. Lucy, B Coy, gave the following account from his perspective:[3]

> At the first streak of dawn on 10th August 1917, my platoon of Irishmen,
> thirty strong, went forward in the first wave of the attack on Westhoek
> Ridge. In twenty minutes we reached the German second line, which had
> been churned to ground-level by the British artillery bombardment. Parts of
> men's bodies, rags of uniforms and smashed war gear marked the line of the
> vanished trench. The remnants of the shocked garrison staggered by us to
> the British rear with uplifted, shaking hands.
>
> Our own trench, which we had left intact, had by now also been flat-
> tened out by the enemy counter-barrage. At the second German line I
> counted my men, and found we were only eight in all; the enemy machine-
> gunners of the concrete pill-boxes had raked us as we passed through their
> network of strong points in the mud. My Company Commander [Capt.
> Jeffares] – a Wexford man, whose left hand was shattered by a bullet, and
> who carried a green flag emblazoned with a gold harp in his right – joined
> us forward on the fighting front, and ordered us back in line with his other
> platoons, echeloned right and left to our rear. In the excitement of battle,
> my fellows had overrun the final objective. We went back and took post
> behind a shell-pocked German pill-box, where we mounted our Lewis gun
> and posted a sentry. The shelling had died down, and the rest of the morn-
> ing was quiet. Two weak counter-attacks were attempted during the after-
> noon, but our field guns broke them far to our front. Hostile scouts and
> snipers then became busy and crawled close to our posts.
>
> I checked a runner behind the cover of our pill-box and warned him to
> live up to his name while crossing the danger space between our post and

2 Lt. A.B. Ross, RAMC, Lts E. Brown, S.V. Morgan, and 2/Lt. P.J. McKee were killed; Capt. R.T.
Jeffares, 2/Lts P.D. Alexander, R. Carruthers, B.J. Murphy, and R.S. Walsh were wounded.   3 *Quis
Separabit*, November 1938.

the next on the left, which we had just then discovered as having been marked down by a newly-arrived sniper. He smiled his thanks and had taken only a few steps when I saw his steel helmet flicked into the air like a piece of cardboard, and he checked, lurched, fell over to his left, and rolled away down a little slope into a pool of water – shot through the head.

We all felt grateful when night found us still in possession of the captured ground. I mounted double sentries and the remainder of us slept deeply. At half-past four in the morning I was awakened by a loud crash, blasphemy and shouting. The enemy were attacking my little post and had already killed one of my sentries with a stick-bomb. There were Germans front and rear of us. In the half-light we could see some who had passed through our line standing and kneeling and firing into our backs from a distance of a few yards. The stick-bomb had come from that group. We dealt with them first and shot down several, including an officer and a sergeant. The rest suddenly bolted back through us towards their own side, some even leaping over our entrenched heads.

A platoon of ours on the right joined in the fight, and quite a large body of Germans, caught in the open, were seen rushing into the nearest deserted pill-box in what was now 'No-man's-land'. My orderly had put in a lot of firing in this surprise raid. He had killed both the officer and the sergeant, and now I sent him behind to search the body of the officer. He brought back pistol, field-glasses and papers, and then went out on his own to look at the other dead. I was horrified a few minutes later to see him sawing at a finger to remove a ring. Enraged, I covered him with my revolver, threatening to take his life for such an act. His irresponsible replies showed that he had no idea of the ghoulishness of his behaviour, but he took serious notice when I reminded him that we could possibly be captured in the vicinity of mutilated corpses.

The Germans in the pill-box remained quiet, and came out to surrender about mid-day. There was a second officer who came to me with his hands up, so quickly in his startling field-gray uniform that my right hand closed over my pistol grip. I released my grip and waved his hands down, and we talked in broken French. He was a very handsome young fellow, with mild grey eyes and straight face lines, as in the statues of the youths of ancient Greece, and his first act after surrender was to remove his becoming, but rather cumbersome, steel helmet, which he replaced with a flat 'Broderick'. I took his parabellum, a nice new one dated 1916, his ammunition, and any papers he had. He then offered me a very neat and elaborate little first-aid hold-all, fitted with shining forceps and scissors, which I refused with thanks. Then a shrapnel sprayed around us, and he quietly changed headgear again, making me laugh at the solemn way he did it.

He looked very relieved at my laughter, and laughed too, and, the ice effectively broken, he asked me very earnestly if the English were always gentlemen. This was rather hard on one of my race, but I said 'Yes'. I wondered if the propaganda merchants on both sides knew how unfair and cruel their lies were to newly-captured prisoners – most helpless of men. I assured the German that he would be perfectly all right if he could escape his own shells in rear of us, for there seemed to be a perpetual box-barrage behind us on Bellewaarde Ridge. He saluted me perfunctorily in the German sailor-like way, and went off happily. Several times he turned round to face and salute me as he made his way up the dangerous slope in rear ... His Corps, as far as I remember, was the 25th Regiment, of which a fighting patrol of two officers and twenty-five men had raided my little party of eight. They lost one officer, one sergeant, and five men killed. I did not note their wounded.

We were relieved that night, and each of my tired men, given the option, refused to take back a German machine-gun in good condition, which we found abandoned close to our post. I ordered a few rifle bullets to be shot into its mechanism, and we left it there for any future occupants of that part of the line, who might be keen on war trophies. We hurried back independently by platoons, and night was gone before we had our soldiers settled into the rampart dugouts at Ypres; for it took hours to get clear of the mud and shell holes of the forward area.

The next morning another subaltern and myself were shelled while breakfasting above ground in a sandbagged hut. I finished my meal rapidly, muttered: 'To hell with war. I'm going downstairs', and entering a deep dugout, I threw myself on a chicken-wire mattress, and slept the round of the clock. I woke up in a fog caused by the evaporation of mud and water from my soiled clothing.

After lunch a battalion conference was called to discuss the battle, and at its conclusion the part we had played was brought home to us for the first time. On the battle front one never knew what was happening. We had captured the redoubtable 'Black Line' at Westhoek, one of the nastiest positions in the Salient. Westhoek was noted as a strong point of pill-boxes, and had repulsed a British attack ten days before. We lost over fifty per cent of our fifteen officers and over seventy per cent of our five hundred men. We captured four enemy officers and 150 men. Some platoons had brought back German machine-guns, and five of these were stacked near battalion headquarters. Other platoons, like mine, had not bothered to collect trophies ... I went off to tell my fellows that they had smashed the Westhoek strong point, which other regiments had failed to take. They were far more interested in the quality of the Irish stew they were eating than in my proud commentary of the fact that our regiment was being cited in higher formation orders for gallantry in the late assault.

Fr Gill:

The following detailed account of the attack is from an official document and gives a good idea of the strenuous nature of these operations.

4.25 a.m. 2nd Royal Irish Rifles rushed Westhoek together with two strong points and took the garrison before the enemy realized that they were being attacked. At Point J.7.87.61 an unsuspected machine gun in an emplacement was encountered which opened fire on advancing waves. An officer rushed at it firing his revolver and the team fled. Those of the enemy, who were not killed by our barrage on Jabber Support, fled as our waves closed on them and were caught in our barrage, our men firing at them from the hip as they ran and very few escaped. All enemy beyond this had taken cover in good emplacements and dug outs about the Black Line, which was immediately cleared with very little opposition and the occupants taken prisoner. The Red Line could not be identified as Jabber Reserve did not exist or could not be recognized. In consequence of which the outpost line pushed on and took up a line behind our protective barrage.

Counter-attacks on August 10th and night of 10th/11th. 2nd Royal Irish Rifles reported that about 10 a.m. the enemy were seen coming over Anzac Ridge and down the slope, at first in sections, and afterwards in larger bodies and that it was obvious that they were massing for a counter-attack. These concentrations continued throughout the day. At about 5.30 p.m. a feeble effort to come forward was made but failed under machine gun fire and artillery support. The enemy, however, continued to send troops forward into the Hannebeeke Valley and opened a very heavy bombardment on and behind Westhoek Ridge.

At 5.40 p.m. SOS signals were sent up by 2nd Royal Irish Rifles. At 5.50 p.m. the OC this Battalion sent by runner the following message: W.12 10th. Enemy massing in Hannebeeke Valley A.A.A. SOS has gone up A.A.A. Enemy has been accumulating in enormous bodies since 10 a.m. A.A.A.

This message reached Advanced Brigade HQ at 6 p.m. and was immediately telegraphed to Brigade HQ. At 5.55 p.m. Artillery Liaison Officer attached to 2nd Royal Irish Rifles sent a pigeon message reporting enemy massing in Hannebeeke Valley and calling for artillery action on J.2.d., J.2.c., and J.8.b. 3rd Worcestershire Regt reported by pigeon at 6.16 p.m. Enemy in strength apparently gathering for counter-attack between J.8.d.9.9. and J.8.b.9.8. and Polygon Veld.

Our artillery opened on these areas shortly after 6 p.m. and an intense fire was concentrated on them at 6.45 p.m. Enemy artillery began to close down and our artillery were ordered to cease fire at 7.15 p.m. At 7.30 p.m. 2nd Royal Irish Rifles saw that another determined effort was being made to counter-attack under cover of a smoke barrage and renewed bombardment of the front line and Westhoek Ridge. The SOS signal was sent up but, on this occasion, elicited no response from our artillery, probably through its not having been seen through the smoke barrage put up by the enemy in the valley west of Westhoek Ridge.

OC 2nd Royal Irish Rifles sent SOS through visual and pigeon shortly before 8 o'clock and 3rd Worcesters also got SOS through to Advanced

Brigade HQ at 8.03 p.m. At about the same time one of our aeroplanes appeared and dropped the SOS signal, whereupon our artillery immediately opened a heavy barrage which completely broke up the attack and almost wiped out the enemy, whose remains could be seen running in all directions.

About 4.15 a.m. on the 11th, the enemy pushed forward strong outposts only two of which made any effort to get to our lines. One, consisting of about 12 ORs got to within bombing distance and commenced to bomb our line but were quickly answered with bombs and afterwards finished off with the bayonet. The other consisted of one officer and 19 ORs were fired at, returned to a dug out and a patrol was sent out and took this party who surrendered without showing much fight.

For the remainder of the month the battalion carried out training in the Steenvoorde area. Reinforcements of 4 officers and 52 men arrived during August, bringing the total strength up to 25 officers and 554 men, and the trench strength to 10 officers and 289 men. At the beginning of September they moved back towards Ypres, passed the night at Cornwall Camp near Ouderdom, and entered the line on the night of the 2nd relieving 23rd London Regt on Westhoek Ridge. At 7.30 p.m., 6 September, the Germans opened a heavy barrage on the sector held by 2nd RIR and, under cover of this barrage, attempted an attack. Artillery support was requested and brisk small arms fire was opened on the advancing infantry. Fortunately the front-line troops had suffered few casualties and the attack quickly melted away, no German having reached the front line. Artillery activity continued until 8.45 p.m. when everything went quiet. Six patrols were sent out during the night to capture a prisoner but were unsuccessful and no identifications were secured. Total casualties for this period were 3 men killed, 19 wounded and one missing, before being relieved on the night of the 8th and moving to Micmac Camp. Fr Gill:

Finally left Westhoek trenches and came to camp near the old Canada Huts of two years earlier which had by this time disappeared. A rather unpleasant incident took place about this time. We happened to be near another battalion, the name of which need not be mentioned. One afternoon, two officers strolled over and proposed a few athletic contests for the next day. The officer detailed to look after our sports was rather tired and out of sorts after a strenuous time in the trenches and certainly not in form to deal with sporting characters. They suggested a tug-of-war and a few boxing items. This was agreed to although we had no tug-of-war team and very few boxers. We had been very badly knocked about in the trenches and, indeed, had very few men left. We had one good boxer and our Regimental Sergeant Major was a good sprinter so, in our turn, we suggested a 100 yard race but they had no one, etc. The next day they turned up with a powerfully trained tug-of-war team and a number of good boxers. We were badly beaten in every event in the presence of many 'gold hats' of their division whom they had brought to witness their triumph. We discovered later that this battalion was noted for this trick. They kept a well-trained tug-of-war team and boxers in transport jobs, which kept them out of the trenches and enabled them to keep in training. They would, as in our case, propose to the simple minded a few 'friendly' events. In this case they went off with 600 francs in bets and stakes. It was a thoroughly unsporting act and, I am glad to say, uncharacteristic of the Army as a whole. This regiment had done well in the field. Their men were not to blame but their 'sporting' officers.

On the 11th the battalion moved by bus to the Caestre area, then marched the next day to Steenbecque. They arrived for training at Raimbert, a mining village connected with the mines of Marles, on the 13th. Word came through that 2nd RIR was to be transferred to the 36th (Ulster) Division. Fr Gill described the reaction:

> Our repose was disturbed by some bad news which reached us. We were to be transferred into the 36th (Ulster) Division. This news came as a surprise and disagreeable shock to almost everyone in the Battalion ... The prospect of a change into a political division was not pleasant, nor did the outlook appear very bright. Everything possible was done to have the decision changed, but without success ... there were not many Catholics in the other battalions except the 1st RIR.

The battalion moved to Béthune, 4 October, and moved into the line relieving 22nd Royal Fusiliers in the Cambrin sector the next day. During this tour Capt. R.T. Jeffares was killed. In addition, five men were wounded including two by self-inflicted wounds. On relief by 13th Cheshires, 12 October, the Rifles moved into the support lines, where one man was wounded, and returned to the firing line on the 18th. A company from the Portuguese Expeditionary Force was attached for instruction. Fr Gill:

> October 1917. One day, when I went into the dugout of one of the officers of one of the front line companies, I found a discussion going on concerning the absence of two men who had been out on patrol the night before. In the midst of this discussion a commotion was heard on the stairs and finally one of the men in question got, or was got, into the place. He was apparently very much exhausted and could only be got to give an account of himself after libations of hot tea. His story was that he and his companion lost their way and, as morning was approaching, they got into a shell hole to wait until the next night. However, one of them got tired and probably hungry and crawled back across no-man's-land in daylight. He reported that the other man had been wounded in the head, but not seriously, and that he had left him in a shell hole smoking a cigarette. The Captain of the company thought it was up to him to make an effort to get in the missing man and got the returned wanderer to point out from the parapet the direction he had come from. No very clear indication was forthcoming. I was

consulted as to the advisability of the attempt. I heard that such an excursion would be risky and imprudent since, if the Germans saw any movement, it would probably end in lives being lost without any advantage to the man in the shell hole, where he was apparently alright and could wait where he was for four or five hours until dusk.

However, this advice was not taken and the officer brought me aside and 'made his soul', and then, with his orderly, crawled cautiously through the barbed wire. However, his search was in vain and, after some time, returned safely, being unable to locate the shell hole. About 4 p.m. the absentee returned little the worse of his adventure. Evidently the Germans were not keeping a sharp look out in this section. The CO was extremely annoyed at this uncalled for bravery, and the Divisional General sent in a note saying that, while he was much impressed by the gallantry of the officer in question, he wished once more to insist on the regulation that company officers were not to go out on patrol without expressed permission. All's well that ends well.

Patrols continued to be sent out and, on the night of 22 October, it was the turn of 2/Lts A. Davison and C.R.W. McCammond with instructions to try and capture a prisoner. The next morning there was still no sign of Davison or his eight men. About 7.15 p.m. three men of the patrol succeeded in returning. Patrols under 2/Lts J.A. Moreland and T.C. Wallis went out to try and find traces, but were unsuccessful. It was not until after the war that the mystery was fully resolved when Davison made his report. He had left from the fire-bay as instructed but had difficulty getting through the wire. They headed towards the German trenches and, after some time, were fired on from what appeared to be the direction of the British line. They went further towards the enemy and were fired on heavily, though this quietened down to sniping. After a short while they started back towards their own line but, when they got to the wire, they found it to be very thin and discovered they were actually at the German trench. After retreating back through the wire they were fired on, one man being killed and two wounded. Moving in the opposite direction they came on the enemy line again, as he had lost his bearings. It was decided to shelter in two shell holes with the wounded and three of his men got away at dawn. A German aeroplane spotted them about 8 a.m. and 'gave us away'. The Germans signalled for them to come in and, as he was only seventeen yards from their wire and covered by two parties of Germans, he gave himself up.

Enemy artillery and trench mortars were unusually active, 24 October, before the Rifles went into reserve that afternoon. A and B Coys moved to Beuvry, and C and D to Annequin. A patrol under 2/Lt. J.J. Stanley went out that night from 13th Cheshires line, after preparatory fire by Stokes trench mortars, to try and find traces of the missing patrol. Rifles identified as belonging to two of the missing men were recovered. On 25th, 2/Lt. Wallis and six men went out but no further trace of the missing patrol was found. The next day C and D Coys moved to Beuvry and working parties were provided to bury cables between Cambrin and Annequin. Reinforcements of 6 officers and 147 men joined during the month. The battalion moved back into the line, 31 October, with a trench strength of 21 officers and 491 men.

Over the next few days the British artillery was active cutting the enemy wire and listening posts were sent out at night. Gas was discharged from cylinders by the Royal Engineers at 10.15 p.m., 6 November, during which time the front line held by the Rifles was cleared except for six posts. Casualties totalled seven men wounded including one self-inflicted. The battalion went into support on the afternoon of the 8th placing A, B, and C Coys at Annequin with D at Factory Dugouts. On the 10th they moved to Béthune and were billeted in the tobacco factory at Rue de Lille. The battalion proceeded by bus to 3rd Army area, 13 November, on transfer to 108th Brigade in 36th (Ulster) Division, and billeted in Arras with HQ at 20 Rue de Coclipas. 2/Lt. Lucy returned from leave:

> I had all kinds of commissions to perform for my fellows in France, one special request being to bring out a supply of Irish flags with harps only inscribed on them ... Our battalion was due to be transferred to the Ulster Division, which was considered to be poisonously loyal by many of our southern officers, hence the flags ... The battalion was in bivouac east of Arras, in reserve for the battle of Cambrai when I got back ... We gave a great dinner the night before the battle, and invited a good many officers of the Ulster division to join us. They came, and affected no surprise at our very Irish table, decorated with green flags and other national emblems, and we had a very merry evening.

The next day they moved via Bapaume, Le Transloy, Rocquigny, and Bus to 36th Divisional Area at Ypres. 2nd RIR encamped at Little Wood where 17 officers and 515 men joined on its amalgamation with 7th RIR, which was being disbanded. A further 22 men joined while training and reorganization took place over the next few days. On the 16th they all moved to huts in the Barastre area; on the 19th to a camp near Lebucquière; on the 20th to some fields in the vicinity of Hermies where they remained in reserve during the first day of the Cambrai battle. The night was spent at Yorkshire Bank of the old British front line before a move to Spoil Heap and the Hindenburg Line. At 7 a.m., 22 November, the battalion moved 1,000 yards north up the Hindenburg Line where it remained until evening then crossed the Bapaume–Cambrai Road to support 12th RIR.

On the morning of the 23rd, 12th RIR attacked the village of Mœvres with 2nd RIR in support. When the attack was held up, three companies of 2nd RIR went forward and fought their way about three quarters of the way through the village, but had to come back because their flanks were in the air. Thirty minutes later D Coy moved forward up the trench to the west of the village with the high ground as their objective, but the German resistance was too great. 2/Lt. W. Rainey and 16 men were killed; Capts J.B. McArevey, G.B.J. Smyth, 2/Lts T. McAlindon, T.M. Stuart and 99 men were wounded and 7 were missing. Having been relieved in the early morning of the 24th the Rifles marched to a position near Hermies.

There then followed a series of moves, firstly towards Amiens as it was considered
the battle had ended, then back to the lines to defend against the German counter-
attack: 26th to Beaumetz-les-Loges in falling snow, 27th to Rocquigny, 29th to
Simencourt, 30th to Gomiecourt, 1 December to Rocquigny, 2nd to Metz-en-
Coutre, 3rd to a reserve line west of Couillet Wood. Early on the morning of 4
December 2nd RIR moved north to the reserve line in the vicinity of Beauchamp
and marched to the trenches at Couillet Valley that night.

The Rifles arrived in the firing line at 3 a.m., 5 December, and relieved the
King's Own Scottish Borderers in the old German line. Work was done on the outpost line, which was a new trench begun by the KOSBs, enemy patrols being very
active during the night. Late on the 7th, the Rifles took over an extra piece of line
from 10th RIF and readjusted the line. Col. Goodman fell ill, 9 December, and
Major E.H. Carson took command. Fr Gill:

> During this time we lost our CO who had been in command for over a year.
> He had done excellent work and had the interest of every man at heart. All
> were genuinely sorry at his departure. His disappearance was typical of the
> sudden changes which took place during the war. He had been greatly over-
> worked and had to 'go down'. When the time came he said to the next in
> command 'Is that you?' as he entered the dug out 'Well, I'm off', and thus
> ended his connection with the Battalion during the war. Nothing makes one
> feel far from being indispensable better than a war.

On the night of the 12th the battalion went into reserve where nine men joined.
2/Lts J. Lucy and P. Phillips had been wounded, and four Germans were captured.
The next afternoon the Rifles moved up into the support line, relieving 10th RIR,
and were themselves relieved on the night of the 14th by troops of the Naval
Division, moving to Metz for the night. The following day they marched to camp
at Etricourt and, on the 17th, moved to Mondicourt by rail, and marched to billets at Warlincourt. Here time was spent at training and clearing roads of snow.
Snow fell again on Christmas night and, the next morning, work recommenced on
the Warlincourt–Grincourt–La Belle Vue Road. While in this area, an officer and
thirty men joined.

The Ulster Division was now transferred to XVIII Corps, 5th Army. The battalion transport proceeded in advance, 27 December, halting for the night at
Puchevillers. Early next morning the remainder marched to Mondicourt, where
they entrained, and travelled via Doullens, Camdas, and Amiens to Boves, then
marched through snow to billets at Gentelles. In the meantime the Transport travelled by train from Mondicourt at 1 p.m., 28 December, got snowed in between
Camdas and Amiens, and didn't rejoin until the 30th. The year ended with the battalion in billets where training was being carried out. Working parties were deployed
on the Gentelles–Boves and Gentelles–Cachy roads. The total strength was 36 officers and 801 men and the trench strength was 11 officers and 549 men.

11

St Quentin

Fr Gill noticed a change: 'I have not so many Catholics in the Battalion, but they are even better than family, I think.'[1] On Sunday, 6 January, Capt. Ogier and sixty men of the Jersey contingent were reposted to 2nd Hampshire Regt. The Rifles left Gentelles the next day marching via Cachy, Villers Bretonneux, Marcelcave, and Wiencourt to Guillaucourt where training was to resume. The 8th saw renewed snowfall and frost as Lt.-Col. P.G.A. Cox DSO, RDF, arrived and took command. A thaw commenced on the evening of the 9th and continued throughout the following day. Another move took place, 11 January, via Harbonnieres, Lihons, Chaulnes and Curchy to the Nesle area. B and C Coys billeted in Herly while A and D were in Billancourt. Two days later they marched via Bacquencourt, Ham and Estouilly to the little hamlet of Pithon where C and D Coys billeted; A and B were at Estouilly. The whole battalion was placed in huts at Fluquieres on the 15th. The Divisional Commander, Major-General O.S.W. Nugent, inspected the troops on the 22nd. Fr Gill was not impressed:

> The most important domestic event at this time was an inspection by the Divisional General. Since our arrival no notice had been taken of the Battalion. Having been 'old soldiers' and used to a considerable amount of notice and congratulations, this action was resented. When the GOC did come, his speech was such as to still further annoy the men. Some of them had decorated their billets with the sign of the 36th Division: a red hand. It was noticed that this was replaced by the sign of our old division – after his departure. The CO spoke to the brigadier on the impression the address had made.[2] The only consolation he got was to be told by that officer that he had never heard the general so complimentary before! As we learned later, his praise was always well salted with abuse. This general soon after got an appointment, no doubt a higher one, in India.

Training was completed by the 25th and the men were then set to work on the Battle Zone defences at a line of trenches east of Roupy. Col. Cox assumed command of 108th Brigade during the Brigadier-General's absence on leave, and Major

1 Letter to the Fr Provincial, No. 66, 4 January 1918. 2 Brigadier-General C.R.J. Griffith CMG, DSO.

Rose became temporary CO. On the afternoon of January 28th the battalion marched via Happencourt and Grand Séracourt to Railway Cutting, relieving 10th Inniskilling Fusiliers in Brigade reserve at dugouts in the area. The following day they moved via Essigny to the firing line and relieved 11th Inniskilling Fusiliers. This was a quiet tour – only two men were wounded – with wiring work being carried out and a couple of night patrols. Relieved by 11/13th RIR, 4 February, they moved into reserve in dugouts at Essigny Station. This was a time of major reorganization in the British Army. Due to the shortage of reinforcements being released to the BEF, brigade strength was reduced to three battalions. Many units were being disbanded or amalgamated. Lt. T.H. Witherow, 8/9th RIR, was not a happy man:

> That day, the 6th February, I will always remember as one of the most depressing that I have ever come through. We received orders to join the 2nd Battalion Royal Irish Rifles which had some time previous come into our Division ... We were such a happy crowd that it is difficult to realize the feeling of depression that settled down on everybody at the prospect of parting ... I was by no means favourably impressed by my first visit to my new unit ... We were looked upon as strangers by most of the officers who were not originally Ulster Division officers at all and who were not inclined to look at things from the Ulster point of view. They were most careful to distribute us all over the battalion so that we could not collect together in a clan. Although I was senior to several company commanders and therefore ought to have got a company things were so arranged that I should only be a platoon commander. Only officers from Sandhurst were fit to command companies in a regular battalion.

In total, 2 officers and 123 men joined on disbandment of 8/9th RIR. 2nd RIR was transferred to 107th Brigade, 8 February, and moved into their reserve area at Roupy, behind the line on the left of the canal. Lt. Witherow, D Coy, described the position:

> This line was rather peculiar in some ways. The front line was a long distance away from the reserve line where headquarters was situated; the means of communication being a long winding trench, very muddy, with the result that it took ages to reach the front line ... Like the sector on the other side of the Canal, the whole country was dominated by the ruins of the Cathedral of St Quentin so that the enemy were able to see every movement. In the neighbourhood of company headquarters, which was on the top of a rise and therefore in full view of the enemy, there were many trenches which were only half dug and when we proceeded to use them to get about, the enemy snipers immediately became active and shots came unpleasantly near. This was the worst sector that I had been in for sniping.

Fr Gill observed that the character of the 36th Division had changed utterly from its original composition:

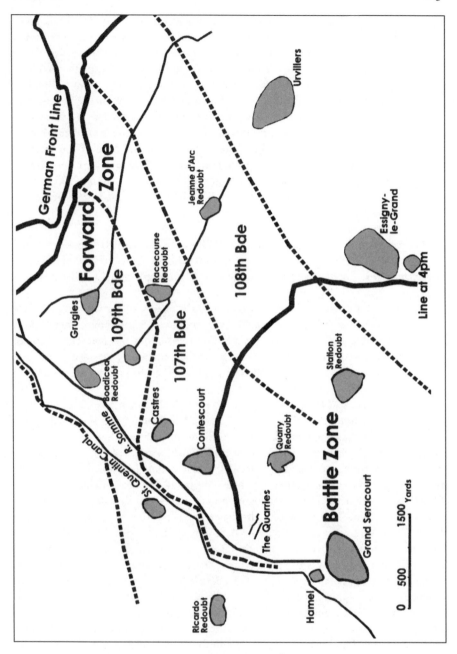

Map 10: Quarry Redoubt, 21 March 1918

A marked change had come over the constitution of the 36th Division to which we belonged. Battalions like the 2nd Royal Irish Rifles were moved out of other divisions and put into the Ulster Division – which had failed to obtain recruits – in order to keep it up to strength. Out of the nine battalions for sometime before March 21st no less than five were old regular battalions which had no sort of sympathy whatever with the religious or political aims of the original Ulster division. Those set free by the arrival of the new battalions became Pioneer Battalions ... A census of religions at this time showed that in the Ulster Division, at the time of the German advance, there were between 3,000 and 4,000 Catholics. When this division came from Ireland their boast was that there was not a single RC in their ranks. The four RC Chaplains were SJ's [Jesuits] and the three interpreters were French priests.

On the evening of February 9th the battalion relieved 10th RIR, placing C and D Coys in the front line, with A as the Counter-Attack Coy and B as the Passive Resistance Coy. For the next four nights patrols were sent out. Lt. Witherow:

> From this dugout we had a good view of the enemy sniper who was so active in this sector. About half a mile away there was a prominent enemy post, well wired, and which being on a hill overlooked our position. We could see the Bosche sentry looking over the parapet, but every attempt to hit him was in vain and only induced reprisals so we had to give up the attempt.

Only one man had been wounded by the time the battalion moved on the night of the 15th to Fluquieres village. Fr Gill noticed that 'there was not much fighting, the country was open and dry and, on the whole, the weather was good'. The area had recently been taken over from the French Army and the defences were not up to British standards. There were no reserve trenches and these had to be made. A new system of defence was being prepared for the anticipated German offensive, now that the enemy was being heavily reinforced by troops coming from the Russian front. This involved a three-tier line consisting of a Forward Zone, a Battle Zone, and a Reserve Line, one battalion of the brigade being allocated to each area. The Forward Zone would, in effect, be the old front line and be manned in the normal way. It was designed so that the enemy would have to assault it to make progress and was expendable. The Battle Zone was now the main area of defence and was quite a distance to the rear of the Forward Zone. It was lightly manned but could be quickly reinforced in the case of an attack – this allowed most of the troops to shelter in billets. It had strong redoubts and defensive positions within its area. The Reserve Line held reinforcements that could be directed to assist the areas most under threat in the Battle Zone. It was hoped that this system would hold the enemy until French troops arrived in force. That was the theory but Fr Gill observed the true situation:

Another cause of disquiet was the system of defence. There were very few troops in reserve. As far as my personal observations went during visits to Divisional and Corps HQ there were practically no reserves to be seen. It was indeed announced that the main shock would have to be withstood by the divisions actually holding the trenches. The line was held as follows. Of each of the three brigades, one battalion was in the forward trenches, one in reserve, and the third in support between the two. Each battalion of the brigades took their turn in each of these positions. Conditions were not satisfactory in the trench system.

The front line was not held as a continuous line manned all along as was the usual case, but was held by a series of detached posts. These posts were supposed to command the gaps between them, and chiefly by machine guns. Each of these posts was an independent unit. Two companies of the battalion were in positions a little behind these forward positions and were to come up if necessary in support. There was no cover but rather ill-constructed trenches. These positions were more or less surrounded by barbed wire. The support positions were arranged on somewhat the same plan. The battle zone consisted of strong points some three thousand yards behind the forward positions. These were surrounded by barbed wire, so that there were only a few places in which one could leave or enter.

There was no system of communication trenches between the forward area and this position. In fact there was no question or possibility of the battalion holding the front line being supported or relieved – or of getting away – except at night. I understood that the forward battalion was expected to hold out at least forty-eight hours before there would be any question of relief! It is not surprising that the people in the front trenches had anxious views on the whole position, and as the time of the attack was, of course, unknown, everyone in the division had an interest in the matter.

Shortly before the attack I felt it my duty to make arrangements with the other chaplains as to the best positions to take up. Three of the chaplains lived with battalions and the fourth with an Artillery unit. Now it was quite clear to me that anyone who might happen to be in the front line when the attack took place would never get back alive. But the chaplain's duty was with the brigade as a whole and he therefore had to make arrangements so as to avoid being killed without necessity! I mention this fact as typical of the mental attitude of those who were obliged to face realities. It was a toss up as to which battalion of each brigade would be sacrificed. Whatever be the rights or wrongs of the method it is true that one third of the Fifth Army was killed or captured by the Germans in their initial onslaught.

The 107th Brigade held the centre of 36th Division's sector. On February 21st the battalion moved to billets in the ruined village of Grand Séracourt which was on the canal. D Coy was just across the canal on the opposite side in a little hamlet called Hamel. Working parties were furnished daily until the 28th when the battalion moved into support at the Quarries. Additional reinforcements during the month were six officers and 104 men. The total strength was now 41 officers and 967 men, with a fighting strength of 20 officers and 684 men, the trench strength being 18 officers and 551 men.

2nd RIR relieved 1st RIR in the Battle Zone on March 1st and worked on strengthening the defences. On the 6th they took over the firing line with HQ being placed in the railway embankment at Grugies and advanced HQ in the Quarry. Patrols were sent out most nights. The battalion was relieved on the evening of 14 March by 15th RIR and moved to Grand Séracourt; D Coy was placed at Somme Dugouts on the canal bank, C at Hamel, with A and B in Grand Séracourt. Casualties for this tour were one man killed and 14 wounded. Training commenced and 104 men joined. The Roman Catholics of 1st and 2nd RIR were united at Mass on St Patrick's Day for the first time since 1854 and shamrock was distributed throughout the division. A football match was played in the morning that 1st RIR won 2–1. Fr Gill was apprehensive:

> I buried a Sergeant and we had sports on high ground from which we could clearly see St Quentin, and no doubt the Germans were watching us at play. The *tag* was approaching. Adopting the tactics of a prize fighter we hurled defiance at the foe! Typewritten notices were distributed and ordered to be placed by patrols in front of the German trenches! I never heard which department of the Higher Command was responsible for this childish device.

At 4 p.m., 20 March, a warning was received that the long-awaited German offensive was expected to open the following morning, after information had been received from prisoners and deserters. Fr Gill explained:

> Information had been received by the authorities which they looked on as reliable. It appeared that two soldiers had come in from the German trenches – Alsatians, it was said – bringing the news that the attack was to begin about midnight that night.

At 5 a.m., 21 March, the German bombardment, which had been continuing intermittently throughout the night, intensified. At 6.30 a.m. orders were received to man the battle stations and companies moved independently to previously arranged points of assembly; HQ was in the Quarry east of Grand Séracourt. Lt. C.R.W. McCammond was wounded and gassed, while 2/Lt. M.A. McFerran was killed in the neighbourhood of Grugies as he endeavoured to clarify the situation. It was unlucky for the defenders that a dense fog made it impossible for them to see any of the enemy troop movements until they were upon the Forward Zone; the British Artillery was firing blind in most places. Fr Gill moved forward:

> There was a most unusual and dense fog, which made it almost impossible to make our way. With shells falling all round, the journey was not a pleas-

ant one. Soon we had to put on our gas masks, which made things much worse. We had great difficulty in locating ourselves, and after many false moves reached the headquarters of the 1st RIR. We got directions here and soon reached 2nd RIR at the other side of the road. The 15th RIR were in the front trenches and were consequently either killed or taken prisoners -- quite according to plan. This part of the programme worked well. We found our people in dug-outs made in the side of a chalk quarry. An indication of the way the Germans had mapped out the ground it is interesting to note that, at the very beginning of the attack, this quarry was heavily shelled. Although, up to this time, it had escaped attention. The shells fell with an accuracy which proved that the range had been carefully taken beforehand. Then began an anxious time of waiting. Gas shells were falling all around.

The 5th Army, in the southern area of the attack, was seriously undermanned and the forward areas were quickly overrun. The Germans reached the Battle Zones with alarming rapidity. Orders were received at 2 p.m. to take up position along the Grand Séracourt–Essigny Road. The battalion was not yet in contact with the enemy, but was being heavily shelled with both gas and high-explosive shells. A thick mist rendered all observation exceedingly difficult. At 4 p.m. they were ordered to assume their former position in the Quarry. D Coy advanced at 7 p.m. on Contescourt to attempt to recapture the village. The enemy put up a stubborn resistance, and at the same time advanced to the attack, under cover of a very heavy gas bombardment. In spite of a gallant effort no ground was gained; heavy losses were inflicted on the enemy, but both officers of D Coy, Lt. G.E. Lynch and 2/Lt. W.L.P. Dobbin, were killed, and all the remainder of the company, with the exception of about forty men were missing. Within a few minutes of their advancing to the attack, orders were received from 1st RIR to cancel the assault, but these were not received in time to be acted on. Under orders from 107th Brigade, 2nd RIR fell back at 11 p.m. on the Le Hamel–Happencourt Road. Defensive positions were taken up, and the night passed quietly. Fr Gill:

> The telephone wires had, of course, been cut as usual during the first few minutes of the bombardment, so that communications were completely cut off. A young 'Intelligence Officer' was sent up the road to find out what was happening. He never came back. He was an excellent young fellow, most popular with everyone. Then came the news that the Germans had got through on our right and that we were to take up a position about half a mile to the right of our present one, near to Grand Séracourt. The Advanced Dressing Station in the village was quite near and the MO in charge there handed it over to our regimental MO and departed.
>
> But we only remained in this position a short time. The order came through to return to our former position. One company was ordered to counter-attack just in front of our post. This cost us many men and two excellent officers.

In the meantime the dressing station was without an MO as ours had to accompany the Battalion. Wounded were still arriving and it was necessary to have someone in charge. It was now getting on to 8 p.m. The day had been long, eventful and fatiguing. Just as I was settling down for some rest, I got a message from the Adjutant of the Battalion telling me that they were moving to a new position and that the best way for me to get into touch with them was to join the transport at Bray St Christophe. I am sorry to say the Adjutant was killed shortly after.

We set off and we were just in time as, very soon afterwards, the whole Field Ambulance had to get on the move. We crossed the canal at Pont Tugny, a very awkward place intersected by a number of streams. Here we were told that there was no use in going to Bray – there were no transports there ... It was now evident that a general retirement was in progress but there was no sign of any panic, neither was there any sign of reinforcements.

The battalion, under orders, withdrew at 11 a.m., 22 March, to an old French trench system, south-east of Happencourt. The mist had by this time cleared and the Germans, spotting this movement, shelled them on the move, but without inflicting many casualties. Here they remained until dusk; the position was exceedingly difficult to hold, as the enemy had it under direct observation from the front. No troops were on the right and there were no obstacles in front. At 6 p.m. Major Rose, who commanded the battalion, was wounded. At dusk the enemy, who had made some minor attacks during the afternoon, advanced in force, and orders were received to withdraw to Sommette-Eaucourt, via Cugny and Pithon. On nearing Sommette-Eaucourt, information was received that the battalion was to go to Cugny, where the battalion billeted and Capt. T.J.C.C. Thompson assumed command. Falls described the general situation:

> The great breakthrough had begun, and was to be completed the moment the Germans forced the line of the Somme and the Crozet Canal, as they did early on the 23rd ... Owing to an error on the part of a brigade on the left of the 36th Division and of some engineers, not only was the main bridge at Ham not properly demolished, but the crossing of the river at this point was not guarded. The enemy speedily crossed here, and was also across the Crozet Canal at several points at 11.30 a.m.

The battalion re-organized and a defensive position north-east of the village was taken up at 10 a.m. The remnants of D Coy, together with 67 reinforcements under the command of Lt. J.K. Boyle, were in reserve to the north-west. At noon reports were received that enemy cavalry patrols had entered Flavy-le-Martel and Brigade orders directed that Cugny was to be held at all costs. With the exception of one or two minor attacks, the afternoon passed quietly, although hostile aeroplanes were very much in evidence. At 6 p.m. the Germans attacked in force and, after a stiff fight, were repulsed on 2nd RIR's front, but later they succeeded in driving back the troops on the right and occupied positions between 2nd RIR and Cugny. A party of C Coy under Lt. R.B. Marriott-Watson, which was returning to the village at 8.30 p.m., came in contact with a strong party of the enemy. He spoke to them in German, which enabled his group to get to close quarters to rush and disperse them. At 10 p.m. the battalion withdrew to a line 300 yards west of Cugny. No contact could be established with troops on either flank but the night passed quietly, although the enemy could be heard, evidently in force, in the immediate front.

At 6 a.m., 24 March, touch was established with troops who had moved forward during the night. Enemy machine-gun fire was very heavy during the morning, but no infantry advanced on 2nd RIR's front, although on the right and left they succeeded in making progress. Flanks were slightly withdrawn to form a defensive position but, at 2 p.m., the Germans advanced in overwhelming strength, preceded by a very heavy artillery bombardment, to the front and both flanks. Although 2nd RIR put up a stubborn resistance, all with the exception of about twenty men were killed or taken prisoner. The Divisional history recorded what happened:

> Having withdrawn from the eastern to the western skirts of Cugny overnight, the battalion had steadfastly maintained its position, almost entirely unsupported. After beating off an enemy attack at ten in the morning, it was discovered that ammunition was woefully short, and orders were issued to fire at especially good targets only. Captain Thompson, deliberately exposing himself to encourage the men on the menaced right flank, which was being again attacked, was killed, as also was Lieutenant Marriott-Watson. Captain Bryans now assumed command. Messages sent up from the 1st Rifles in rear, ordering the battalion to withdraw, did not reach it. The men who bore them were killed or wounded. In any case, it was the opinion of Captain Bryans that a retirement across the bare, open country between Cugny and the village of Villeselve, with the Germans on three sides of him, was impossible.
>
> From noon onwards was a lull, which was occupied in reorganization of the line. Then, about 2 p.m., preceded by a violent barrage of artillery and machine-gun fire, supported by an attack from low-flying aeroplanes, an assault was launched, the Germans sweeping in from the left in overwhelming numbers, despite the gaps cut in their ranks by fire. 'Many,' writes Captain Bryans, 'had only their bayonets left. Rather than wait for the end, they jumped from the entrenchments and met it gallantly. It was an unforgettable sight. We were overwhelmed, but not disgraced.'
>
> After a desperate hand-to-hand fight, the little band was simply engulfed … Of about a hundred and fifty men on their feet when the attack began, it is estimated that over a hundred were killed or wounded.[3]

3 Capt. T.J.C.C. Thompson, Lts J.K. Boyle, R.B. Marriott-Watson and M.E.J. Moore were killed; Capt. J.C. Bryans and 2/Lt. E.C. Strohm were taken prisoner.

The 107th Brigade Major reported back at 4.35 p.m.:

> All troops are retiring in disorder except 1st and 2nd R. Irish Rifles. 2nd R.
> Irish Rifles appear to be cut off, and it is doubtful if the 1st Battalion can
> get away as the troops on both flanks have retired.

Fr Gill:

> I heard that the 2nd RIRs were at Cugny, south-east of Ham, and set out to
> get into touch with them. I had a considerable distance to go but, with the
> help of various motor cars, I got as far as Guiscard, which was still about 7
> kilometres from them. I found the Brigade HQ here and did not get encour-
> aging news. I was asked to bring some maps to them if I did reach them.
> Several despatches had failed to be delivered. I hoped to find the MO on my
> way up. It soon became evident that I was not destined to get in touch with
> them and I was, besides, rather played out. There was a slow but general
> movement towards the rear taking place ... When I got back I met a ration
> party about to set out to find the Battalion. I told them that I feared they had
> gone. I was unfortunately right. The order had been given that Cugny was to
> be held at all costs and they had done so. Of the whole 750 or so, only a very
> few came back. They had been killed or taken prisoner. One felt a lump in
> one's throat. The Battalion had, of course, been gradually renewed many times
> but no such sudden extinction as this had taken place. It was said that German
> agents had got in amongst the British disguised as English officers and were
> spreading rumours calculated to help their advance ... [25 March] We marched
> from Margny after a restless day. The MO and a few of his staff were almost
> all that returned from the Battalion. The rest had been cut off, surrounded
> by Germans and fighting to the last.

Officers and men who had returned from leave, courses, and various assign-
ments, and had been fighting with other units, were collected and reorganized as a
battalion. Col. Cox assumed command of this force consisting of eight officers and
forty men. They went to Avricourt, where the Transport joined, and bivouacked
in a field. Lt. Witherow:

> Amid the roar of the guns, which during these days never ended, we con-
> tinued our march in the evening. In the neighbourhood of Roye we were in
> the sector where the old French line had been previous to the enemy retire-
> ment on the Somme. The country was therefore interlaced with old trenches
> and communication trenches which ought to have now proved useful in stop-
> ping the enemy advance when he eventually reached that sector. The men
> were very fatigued with the continual marching and it was with a feeling of
> relief that the village of Guerbigny, where we were to spend the night, came
> into sight ... Here at last we were assured of rest as the line was being held

by the French soldiers who were fresh and held a good line. But our hopes were soon to be dashed to the ground as early in the morning the alarm sounded and the battalion was ordered to fall in in the town square. The Germans had again broken through the lines of the French on a wide front and were advancing in the direction of the village, so the tired Division had again to buckle to and prepare once again to stop the onflowing tide.

On the morning of March 26th, the situation being somewhat obscure, a section of four officers and fifty men under the command of Capt. P. Murphy took up a defensive position between Guerbigny and Erches. 1st RIR was on the left but no troops were on the immediate right; two infantry brigades and one French cavalry regiment were believed to be in front. The afternoon and evening passed quietly, but immediately after dark large columns of men and transport could be seen passing down the road from Erches to Guerbigny, about 100 yards to the right of the position occupied by Capt. Murphy's section. For some time these were believed to be French but a patrol discovered they were German having encountered an Uhlan patrol. About 9 p.m. rifle and machine gun fire east of Erches died away, and at the same time the patrol sent to Guerbigny reported that the enemy held that area. With the Germans on three sides, the section moved left and took up a position to the rear of 1st RIR. The remainder of the night passed quietly although many enemy patrols were encountered.

At 5.30 a.m., 27 March, a ration party under CQMS R.G. Somers missed its way and got into Erches Village, where it was twice charged by enemy cavalry patrols. He beat them both off, killing two Uhlans himself, and delivered the rations, only one of his men being wounded. The enemy attacked in force on three sides at 9 a.m. and, after a short but severe fight, the section withdrew, first to a position 2,000 yards north-east of Saulchoy-sur-Davenscourt, and finally to a position east of Hangest-en-Santerre. Capt. Murphy was wounded early in the operations, and Lt. C.O. Crawford assumed command. They were relieved by 102nd Chasseurs Alpins, 11.30 a.m., and withdrew to Sourdon, where the Transport rejoined.

In the meantime the remainder of the battalion, under Lt.-Col. Cox, moved out at 1 p.m. on the 28th and occupied a defensive position near Coullemelle; the enemy was not encountered. After a very wet and miserable night they withdrew about 6 p.m. on the 29th to Chaussoy-Epargny. Fr Gill:

March 29th Good Friday. We remained a greater part of the day at Sauvillers. In the afternoon a small remnant of the Battalion, with one or two officers, joined us. As we were finishing dinner at 8 p.m. word came that we were to move off. It was an all-night march but we were helped by motor lorries.

All marched to Oresmaux and then by lorry to Vallennes, arriving about 6 a.m. on the 30th. At 4.45 p.m. they moved by route march to Saleux where a miserable night was passed in the open. The next day they went by train to Gamaches, then marched to billets at Maisnieres on the north-west coast not far from Abbeville. Lt. Witherow:

> How lovely to be away from war once again and to feel the joy of life this Easter morning. Here was a rich rural country without any outward signs of war whatsoever and we might have been route marching in Ireland … Drafts now began to pour in, men being also received from the Y.C.V.s [14th RIR] and the 10th Battalion. The men from home were mere boys of 18 years of age and under who had been rushed out during the crisis from the home-training battalions.

Fr Gill:

> A short march brought us to the little village of Maisnieres where we remained a day or two. Next morning I had Mass for those who had survived. Instead of the hundreds who filled the church before, there were less than thirty.

Total recorded casualties during these operations were 6 officers missing, 3 killed and 4 wounded; among other ranks 10 were killed, 64 wounded, and 628 missing (many of whom had been killed). A draft of 9 officers and 256 men joined from the Entrenching Battalion. Reorganization was carried out during the morning of April 3rd and, at 6 p.m., the battalion marched to Fluquieres where it entrained at 9 p.m. for Flanders; arriving about 10 a.m. the next morning at Proven Station. An hour later they moved by lorry to Siege Camp in II Corps area. Fr Gill:

> April 1918. Our troubles were far from being over. In a few days we were once more made up to strength, chiefly by aid of the men who had been transferred into the working corps before the attack, when the Brigades were reduced from four to three battalions. There were very few Catholics among this large reinforcement and before many months were passed my flock was once more numerous.[4]

---

4 Letter to the Fr Provincial, No. 68, 8 April 1918, noted that there were 2,000 to 3,000 Catholics in the Ulster Division before the attack. There had been 300 RCs of the RIR at Mass beforehand, and only 25 turned up at his first Mass after the offensive.

The advance in Flanders

The battalion proceeded to the line in the Poelcapelle Sector, 5 April, relieving 1st Gloucester Regt in the left sub-sector. Lt. Witherow, now commanding D Coy, described the area:

> We crossed the canal and soon crossed what had been the old front line and no-man's-land for two years of terrible fighting. Now there was hardly a trace of the line and the whole ground was occupied with camps, dumps and building and stores of all varieties. When we topped the low ridge which was in front what a sight met our eyes. What a scene of desolation and ruin. The country rose gradually to the Passchendaele Ridge but what was in August ... a green and pleasant land was now one huge desolate waste as far as the eye could reach. Nothing but shellholes and more shellholes. In this vast expanse of country shellhole touched shellhole, each being filled with water, and the only means of transport was over a few roads which looked like white strips of ribbon spread over the landscape ... Then all over the country at intervals were narrower stripes, these being duckboard tracks, about two feet broad, and were the only means of communication for the infantry between the front line and the rear ... Off these wooden tracks it was impossible to advance without being drowned ... We proceeded for miles along the wooded track towards the front line ... Of course it was impossible to have anything approaching a continuous line. Little posts were held here and there where there happened to be a dry spot. Battalion, Company and Platoon headquarters were usually in a concrete dugout rising like an island from the midst of the surrounding mud and water. Between these dugouts and the posts occupied by the men paths were made winding zig-zag round the lips of the shellholes.

Patrols and work on improving the trenches were carried out every day until they came back to man the Battle Zone on the night of the 12th. Battalion HQ was established at Bochcastel and a draft of 306 men joined. During the night of the 15th the 109th Brigade, who were holding the line, withdrew through 2nd RIR leaving the battalion to hold the line, which then became the Outpost Line. On the night of the 17th they were relieved by 2nd Battalion, 18th Regiment of Belgians, and proceeded to Siege Camp. Total casualties for this tour were Lt. J. Cordner killed in action, one man killed accidentally, and 11 men wounded.

Two hundred of the men that had joined at Maisnières were sent back to II Corps Reinforcement Camp. During the afternoon of the 20th the battalion proceeded to the Support Line and relieved 1st RIR. An enemy attack was expected on the 22nd and all ranks were prepared for any emergency. At 1 a.m. the next day they moved forward and relieved 15th RIR in the Outpost Line west of Steenbeek. During this tour work was carried out in strengthening positions and daily patrols were sent out. On the 26th a patrol captured a German officer and two men. The next day the support company was relieved and 2nd RIR withdrew through 1st RIR, leaving that unit to hold the Outpost Line. Casualties for this tour: Capt. L.A.H. Hackett and 2/Lt. V.E. Gransden were killed, 18 men had been wounded. The battalion proceeded to Brigade Reserve at Wagner Camp where a draft of ten men joined.

2nd RIR relieved 15th RIR at Canal Bank on the night of 30 April; one company relieving a company of 1st RIR. Working parties were furnished for 107th Brigade HQ. This remained the situation until the night of the 6th May when the battalion was relieved by 1st RIR, and proceeded to the Outpost Line. This line was held until the night of the 11th when they proceeded to the support area at Canal Bank East. Work was carried out at demolitions east of the canal where carrying parties were furnished. On the night of the 17th they withdrew to Steenje Camp via Brielen and Elverdinghe, going into Divisional Reserve. During May an Instructional Class was established under the supervision of Major C.W. Garner at the battalion transport lines where, under selected NCO Instructors, untrained men of recent reinforcements, partially trained signallers and Lewis gunners, received instruction for a fortnight, when they were replaced by others from the battalion. Total casualties for this tour: 2/Lt. E.A. Cochrane and seven men were wounded, four men were killed.

Working parties were furnished for work on the Green Line, while training was carried out by the remainder. Steenje Camp, which the battalion occupied, was renamed Seaborn Camp. The battalion moved to the Outpost Line in the Right Sub-Sector on the night of 29 May. At this time the total strength of the battalion was 35 officers and 1,140 men, although the number actually present was 22 officers and 784 men. Precautionary patrols were sent out in the early hours of June 1st. A soldier was accidentally killed while the investigation of a stoppage in a Lewis gun was being carried out. On the night of the 2nd, a reconnaissance patrol was sent out under 2/Lt. N.B. Munn and five other ranks accompanied by Major H. Musgrave DSO, Royal Engineers, a Staff Officer of II Corps HQ. The objective was to reconnoitre a road and try to locate a suspected enemy post at Jasper Farm. The party proceeded via the light railwayline then up track No. 5 and along the road, where the patrol was heavily bombed and Major Musgrave was killed. At this juncture the patrol scattered and took cover in shell holes; no enemy was seen. 2/Lt. Munn personally carried the body of Major Musgrave towards his line but fell exhausted about half way, having himself been wounded in about twelve places.

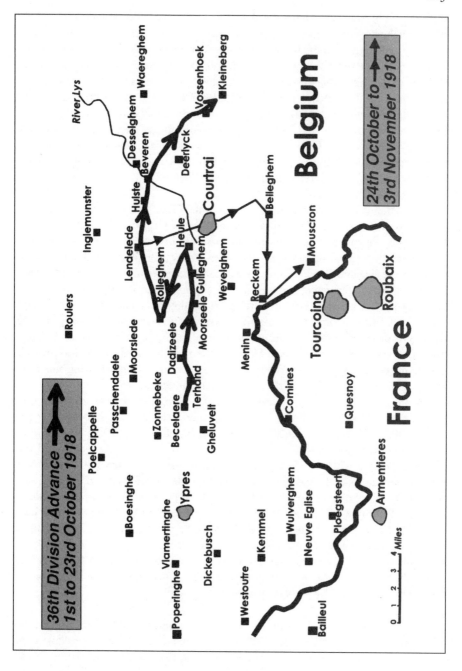

Map 11: The final advance

With the aid of 2/Lts H. Marshall and L.J. Ricks the body was brought back. Three other members of the patrol were also wounded. On the night of June 5th the battalion was relieved by units of 4th Carabiniers and proceeded to Reading Station, where troops entrained for Coutek then marched to Corps Reserve billets at Road Camp for training. Other casualties during this tour were four men wounded.

On the 13th the battalion moved to Peterborough Camp in the Proven area and was engaged in work on the Blue Line. At this time it was expected that II Corps' front would be attacked, and all preliminary arrangements were made to meet any surprise of this nature. They marched to Tunneller's Camp on the 21st. The battalion, less the administrative portion, moved to the Cassel and Rubrouck areas for musketry training during the period 24–8 June. Two officers and three men joined during the month.

The battalion marched, 3 July, to a camp in the Cassel Area. On the 5th advance parties, consisting of the CO, Signals and Intelligence Officers, one officer and four NCOs per company, proceeded to reconnoitre the positions in the Schaexken–Fontaine Houck Line to be taken over on the night of the 6th. They stayed in the line and acted as guides when the remainder followed, relieving 128th Infantry Regt of the French Army in the support line, Right Brigade Sector. Working parties were engaged at cutting crops, digging trenches, revetting, and wiring in the support line. On the 15th dispositions in support were changed. The frontage widened with 2nd RIR taking over more line from 1st RIR; the Battle positions then extended from Fontaine Houk on the right to Ermitage on the left. Col. Cox returned to England and Major Clendining took command. During this time Lts A. Collings and C.R.W. McCammond were wounded.

On the 23rd the battalion relieved 1st RIR holding the Brigade front line system placing HQ at Kopje Farm. Two companies were in front: one on the right with its HQ at Haute Poste Farm, the other on the left with its HQ at Salvo Farm. A third company was in the counter attack position, HQ at Risky Farm, and the fourth in reserve with its HQ at Runaway Farm. On the evening of July 29th, a patrol of four other ranks was sent out under Lt. D.B. Walkington and 2/Lt. J.N.G. Stewart to identify the opposing units. A German post was found in a farmhouse that appeared to be held by about ten men. The patrol rushed them and took four prisoners; two being killed in no-man's-land on the way back as they showed fight when an enemy machine gun opened fire. The remaining Germans were either killed or wounded. The next day the Germans heavily shelled the Rifles' front, especially the HQ of B Coy at Haute Poste Farm where there were some casualties including Lt. E. Morrow being wounded. Fr Gill:

> Shortly before I went away, a tragic event happened. By one of the peculiarities of war methods, it often happened that less care was taken to strengthen the dug outs near the front line than in positions further back. One of the companies holding the trenches had their HQ in a miserable ruined cottage with little or no protection. A considerable number of men were located there. The previous day the Battalion had made a successful

raid on an enemy position and had been complimented on the result. It would seem that their movements had been observed by the Germans. The next day a sudden and intense bombardment fell on the cottage and many men were buried in the mass of falling walls, roof, etc. This attack lasted the best part of an hour. I had come up and was in the Battalion HQ when two officers rushed in, looking more dead than alive, to report what had taken place. I went along with the MO to see what could be done. After a considerable amount of trouble some of the men were got out alive but, unfortunately, others could not be got at. They had probably been killed at once as it was during daylight and in sight of the enemy. It was extremely difficult to do much without attracting attention and further casualties.

The battalion was relieved on the night of July 31st and went into Brigade reserve at Wigwam Copse, commencing work on the Blue Line. Seven officers had joined during the month. Companies were placed at Tibets Farm, Roberts Farm, Senlac Farm, and a farm at Noote Boom. On August 4th a party consisting of three officers, fifteen men and a bugler attended Terdeghem Church for an Anniversary Service commemorating the outbreak of the war. 2nd RIR relieved 1st RIR in the Support Line, 8 August, from Fontaine Houck on the right to Ermitage on the left in the 107th Brigade sector. On the 10th 2/Lt. Gough and ten men attended a Special Divine Service at Divisional HQ at Terdeghem and were afterwards on parade when the King was inspecting troops in 2nd Army area. On the 14th the battalion's area was heavily gas shelled, particularly in the vicinity of A Coy's HQ. Capt. C.E. Barton, 2/Lts R.A. Gough, C.H. Lane, F.T. Poole, and 60 men were gassed. Capt. Barton and 2/Lt. Lane later died from the effects. The battalion was temporarily attached to 108th Brigade for tactical purposes, 16 August, in their left front line sector. 1/41145 Rfn William C. Gillman was awarded the DCM at this time: 'On the 20th August, 1918, W. of Bailleul, though wounded himself, he dressed a comrade's wounds under heavy shell fire. During this time he was twice buried, but continued to work with great coolness, and finally took the man to the dressing station. He showed a very good example to the other men of the company.'

Relieved by 1st RIR, 21 August, 2nd RIR moved to the support line of 107th Brigade placing HQ at La Manche Copse, A Coy at Vanilla Farm, C at Roberts Farm, D at Blighty Farm, and B as the nucleus garrison. Lt. W.H. Calwell and 2/Lt. R.I. Johnston were mortally wounded on the 24th. Lt.-Col. J.H. Bridcutt DSO joined and took over command on the 25th. On the night of the 27th the battalion went to billets in the training area. News was received at the end of the month that the Germans had fallen back on the Bailleul front and 2nd RIR moved to the Mont Noir and Mont Kokereele area, billetting at Wolfhoek and taking up a position in reserve to the 109th Brigade. During August 15 officers and 147 men had joined.

The battalion proceeded to Cyprian Farm, 1 September, moved forward to Brigade support the next day, and entered the front line relieving 9th RIF early on the 6th. The battalion, assisted by one company of 1st RIR, carried out an operation as described in the War Diary:

By 3.30 p.m. 6th September, 1918 half an hour before Zero the troops were in position. Three Companies in the Firing Line: A, B, C 2nd R. I. Rifles. Two Companies in Support: D Company 1st R. I. Rifles; D Company 2nd R. I. Rifles. These two Companies were concealed behind bushes on or near the jumping off line. At scheduled time the guns opened and troops that were not exactly in their places moved from their concealment to get there ready to advance when the barrage lifted. According to time table the barrage lifted and the troops advanced in small wormlike columns picking their way through the undergrowth and uncut wire moving steadily forward until their objectives were reached when Battle Outposts were pushed forward as near as possible to the standing barrage line, the troops consolidating Hanbury Support Trench. When darkness came on Patrols were pushed forward to gain touch with the Bosche. He was found to be holding a piece of trench in the trench system U.d.central at the same time a considerable amount of M.G. fire was coming from the direction of (a) The Crater in U.1.a. (b) Mortar Farm in N.36.d. (c) Trench system T.6.b. A good deal of the latter was taking the men in rear and naturally they began to think the Bosche was surrounding them. To counteract this I ordered my left supporting Company (D Company 1st RIR) to form a defensive flank between the support and front line – this was done in a very efficient manner by Capt. P.J. Cullen.

The objectives were all taken except Gabion Farm. Some little delay was experienced in establishing a post here as it was difficult to tell or recognize the exact spot but inside 1 hour this had been done and the post put out and handed over on relief. On the left flank Boyle's Farm and Crater was given as an objective – this was taken but on examination of the ground the Company Commander on the spot decided it would be very much better to hold the trench system which runs some 30 to 40 yards West of these two places. I personally examined this by daylight and could not help but support his opinion and agreed to his action on the grounds that his men were being very badly shot at from the left rear chiefly from the trenches in T.6.b. also that Boyle's Farm was denied the Bosche.

Casualties were 2/Lts W. Eaton, H.D. Mitchell and 18 men killed, Lts W.F. Hunter, V.C. Young, and 148 men wounded. 7/1226 Sgt Herbert Higgins gained the DCM:

During the operations in the Messines sector on 6th September, 1918, he was employed as Scout Sergeant, and rendered invaluable service. He maintained communication with the firing line from the commencement until the finish of the battle, and made a very valuable reconnaissance, which enabled it to be decided how to deal with the left flank, that had become exposed to the enemy, who were advancing to get between the advance and the support lines. He led his scouts forward after the battle to ascertain that the enemy had been mopped up between the front and support lines, the ground being a nest of old trenches. He was gassed but remained at duty.

As the enemy showed no sign of counter-attacking, the company of 1st RIR withdrew. Companies of 2nd RIR were then arranged with A Coy holding the right front line, B holding the left front, C in left support, and D in King Edward Trench (right support). The battalion went into reserve at Neuve Eglise on the 8th, moving into support on the 12th, to billets in the Piebrouck–Rossignol area early on the 16th, to the St Sylvestre area on the 19th, to Esquelbecq on the 20th, and to Tunneller's Camp on the 26th. They located to the vicinity of Hell Fire Corner east of Ypres, 28 September, and remained in an open field for the remainder of the night being subjected to fire from hostile aircraft, Lt. H. Cumming being wounded. The next morning they marched to Westhoek Ridge and to the Becelaere area on the 30th. Other casualties in September were 10 men killed, 132 wounded, and 10 missing. Reinforcements of 139 men joined during the month.

The battalion attacked at dawn, 1 October, A and C Coys passing through D and B, but was unable to make any advance on account of machine gun fire from Clarbrough House and Wheatley Corner. Col. Bridcutt and Lt. Buttle were killed, Capt. A.E. Kemp and Lt. F.K. McKeeman were wounded. Having been relieved that day by 1st RIR, the battalion marched to Brigade reserve at Terhand where Major J.D. McCallum DSO took temporary command. The battalion had suffered about 183 casualties. On the 3rd October, 2nd RIR moved into Brigade support south-east of Terhand, and into reserve in the Reutel area, west of Becelaere, on the 5th. Lt-Col Becher took command on the 7th. The battalion moved forward on the 13th and, at 5.35 a.m. the next morning, took part in the general attack. They advanced through a thick mist in artillery formation, passed through 15th RIR at Moorseele, coming into Brigade support, and advanced to a line running north and south to the west of Gulleghem.

At 9 a.m., 15 October, the attack was resumed. The battalion advanced in Brigade support, passed through 1st RIR at 3.30 p.m., and resumed the attack capturing Heule and the Corps first objective. A patrol under 2/Lt. C. Rule was sent out, entered Courtrai and found that all the bridges crossing the river Lys had been destroyed. That day 5/8207 Rfn Walter Gudgeon earned the DCM:

> For conspicuous gallantry and cool courage. In the attack on Gulleghem on 15th October, 1918, when his platoon was held up by two enemy machine guns, he immediately rushed out with his gun, and, lying down in the roadway, opened fire. Before finishing one magazine a stoppage occurred in his gun. He calmly proceeded to take off the butt, rectified the stoppage, and continued firing, being exposed to the fire of two guns all the time. Eventually he beat off the enemy guns out of their position, and enabled his platoon to advance.

Early the next morning 108th Brigade passed through 2nd RIR and resumed the advance. The battalion, less C Coy which remained at Heule to collect salvage, withdrew and spent the following day in cleaning and resting. C Coy rejoined on the 18th and the Rifles marched to the Lendelede area where they remained until the morning of the 20th when they advanced in Brigade reserve. At 9 a.m., 22 October, the battalion advanced with three companies in line and one in support attacking and taking Klijtberg Hill. Having been relieved at dusk on the 23rd, they withdrew to Bavichove. Over the next few days they moved via Lendelede and Marcke, arriving at Reckem on November 1st. Fourteen officers joined during the month.

The battalion finally came to a halt at Mouscron on November 3rd. This was to be their base until they returned to England. Over the intervening period the troops were kept occupied with military, educational and recreational training. The war ended on the 11th but the only entry in the War Diary was: 'During the morning the Battalion carried out a Rehearsal parade prior to the Divisional Commander's Inspection.' A Thanksgiving Service was held in the Casino Palace, Roubaix, 17 November, to which 2nd RIR sent representatives and afterwards marched past the Acting Army Commander, Lt.-General C. Jacob KCB. Fr Gill rejoined for a short while:

> I found the Post Corporal of the Battalion at the Brigade Post Office and was glad to come across an old friend once more and went with him to the Rifles. This was in the little town of Mouscron where the Brigade was billeted. I met many old friends including Colonel Becher who had left us in 1915 and who was now, after having served in the East, in command. It was like coming home again, for I had felt out of it all the time I had been away. The Battalion had taken its part in the final advance and lost their commanding officer, whom I had not met, in the advance. They had fought at Neuve Eglise and in front of Ypres, over the old ground and right up to Roulers and had followed the retiring Germans up to the Armistice. I did not regret to have missed it as I should have done a year or so before. For I was tired out and would not have been equal to the work. No one seemed to be very clear as to what would happen next but it gradually became clear that we were not to be one of the divisions going into Germany, which was a disappointment. We were to settle down where we were and to keep in training. Plans for educating these soldiers were being worked out. A beginning was being made to form classes but as everything from books to benches were missing it was not surprising that little progress was made. From the chaplain's point of view there was not much to do, now that the danger of death had become normal. The special privileges for Holy Communion without fasting and a need of General Absolution naturally ceased. We had evening devotions and opportunities for the Sacraments according to the ordinary usage. As the whole Brigade was assembled together there was no need for long journeys ... The life was rather monotonous. In the morning there was some drill and practice. After their early dinner the men played football. Now that the war was virtually over a great deal of reality of the life had worn off ... I got away in the early morning of December 5th and spent a few days in London on my way home. I obeyed the telegram to

return home with very different feelings to those which I had four years earlier when I got the wire ordering me to the front. Many changes had taken place in the Battalion during that time. Only too many old friends had been killed. There were some who had been through good and bad times with me and it was not without regret that I said goodbye to them and to the Battalion. I was glad that circumstances had conspired to make it possible for me to end my military life with the same unit which I had joined so many years before, and with which, through exceptional circumstances, I had remained in when the division was changed. I said goodbye to the 2nd Royal Irish Rifles on December 5th 1918, four years to the day since I first joined them at Westoutre. I had always been treated with the greatest kindness. I wished them goodbye and good luck.

The replacement chaplain was Revd F.J. Irwin SJ. An officer and 135 men marched to Roubaix, 7 December, and formed a guard of honour as the King was passing through the town. The 16th was taken up by a Divisional parade and inspection by the Corps Commander at Halluin Aerodrome. Eighteen men were demobilized during December, 92 in January, 158 in February and 28 in March. Regular lectures were given on the 'Dangers of Venereal Disease'. On February 1st HRH The Prince of Wales visited the battalion. A popular bus service to Lille was commenced for anyone wishing to visit the city. A dancing class was formed for all interested ranks and lessons were held in the large hall at Rue St Germaine; civilian musicians being engaged for this purpose. Another popular attraction was the performances given by Miss Lena Ashwell's Concert Party. Orders were received to reduce the strength to a cadre.

A total of 10 officers and 189 men were selected to join 12th RIR in the Army of the Rhine in Germany. The majority of these departed on February 22nd. As there were now only a few details left representing 2nd RIR, they were formed into one company under the command of Capt. Teele. By the 24th the numbers actually remaining were 13 officers, 6 warrant officers, 13 sergeants, 4 corporals and 64 men. Orders were received, 16 March, for the cadre to go to Dunkirk for embarkation. The remaining thirty Riflemen were attached to 15th RIR. The cadre entrained at Mouscron Station at 12.30 p.m., St Patrick's Day. The bands of 1st RIR and 2nd Inniskilling Fusiliers were in attendance at the station to see them off. They arrived at Dunkirk at 2 a.m., detrained at 8 a.m., and proceeded to a camp for a hot meal and a bath, later proceeding to No. 2 Camp. Here they remained until the afternoon of March 26th when they embarked for Southampton on the troopship *Koursk*.

Among the cadres which have just arrived in England from the western front is that of the 2nd Royal Irish Rifles (old 86th Royal County Down Regiment), and it is now stationed at the Hutments Camp, Thetford, Norfolk. Seven officers and 38 other ranks from the 3rd Special Reserve have joined the battalion. It will gradually be brought up to strength, and it is expected that during the autumn it will begin its tour of foreign service, possibly at Malta.

The commanding officer is Lt.-Col. C.M.L. Becher DSO, who was a captain at the beginning of the war, and the other officers who accompanied him home were: Major C.W. Garner, Capt. and Adjutant R. Watts MC, Capt. W.B. Teele MC, Lt. J.J. Reilly MM, and 2/Lt. J.N.G. Stewart MC. Warrant-officers and NCOs: RSM D. Miller DCM, CSM M.M. Doherty, CSM W. Baillie, ARQMS J. Turner MM, CQMS T. Stapleton, Cr-Sgt (O.R. Sgt) P.J. Cleary, Sgt A.J. Highman MM, Sgt T. McClelland, Sgt H. Duffy, Sgt F. O'Callaghan, Sgt T. Long.[1]

The battalion was reformed at Thetford on July 1st. In September they sailed for Mesopotamia (now Iraq) under Lt.-Col. A.D.N. Merriman and were soon engaged in the Arab Rebellion of 1920–1. It would be fourteen years before they returned to the UK as 2nd Royal Ulster Rifles.

1 *Down Recorder*, April 1919.

Appendices

I   Officer casualties   134

II   Casualties in the ranks   137

III   Medal roll   163

IV   Courts martial and discipline   169

V   Operation Orders for the attack of 7 June 1917   181

APPENDIX I: OFFICER CASUALTIES

This list contains only those officers who died while attached to the battalion and were members of the regiment unless otherwise stated. There were several others who were killed after they had transferred to other units. The battalion's war ended on 23 October 1918 and, up to that time, 326 officers had served on various occasions. Of these 87 were killed (excluding two medical officers) – a rate of over 26 per cent.

Major James William Alston	15.4.1915
Capt. William Ernest Andrews	16.6.1915
Capt. Charles Erskine Barton	23.8.1918
2/Lt. Thomas Eyre Barton	16.7.1916
Lt. Frank Harry Bethell, Connaught Rangers	25.9.1915
2/Lt. John George Bland	9.7.1915
Capt. John Kemmy Boyle (as a POW)	21.10.1918
Lt.-Col. John Henry Bridcutt, Bedfordshire Regiment	1.10.1918
Lt. Edward Brown	7.8.1917
Lt. Albert Edwin Buttle	2.10.1918
Lt. Walter Henry Calwell	27.8.1918
2/Lt. James Gordon Caruth	25.9.1915
2/Lt. Charles Richard Cooney, R. Dublin Fusiliers	9.10.1916
Lt. James Cordner	16.4.1918
Capt. William Cupples, R. Inniskilling Fusiliers	25.9.1915
2/Lt. Claude Henry Whish Darling	12.12.1915
Capt. Henry Ouseley Davis	27.10.1914
2/Lt. Howard Samuel Davy	15.2.1915
2/Lt. Averell Digges La Touche	25.9.1915
2/Lt. William Dobbie	7.6.1917
Lt. William Leonard Price Dobbin	21.3.1918
2/Lt. William Eaton	6.9.1918
2/Lt. John Sturgess Eldred, Leinster Regiment	27.11.1914
2/Lt. Kevin Elphick	28.9.1916
Capt. Edmond Chomley Lambert Farran	16.6.1915
2/Lt. Francis Reginald Fowler, Leinster Regiment	18.10.1916
Lt. Robert Fitz-Austin Gavin	25.9.1915
Capt. Valentine Knox Gilliland	8.5.1915
Lt. Victor Eric Gransden	26.4.1918
Capt. Leäro Aylmer Henry Hackett	24.4.1918
2/Lt. Sydney Maxwell Innes-Cross	27.10.1914
Lt. Patrick Arthur Dudley Jackson	4.1.1917
Capt. Richard Thorpe Jeffares	6.10.1917
2/Lt. Rowland Ivan Johnston	28.8.1918
2/Lt. Frederick Charles Patrick Joy	16.6.1915
Capt. Herbert Alexander Kennedy	28.10.1914

2/Lt. Edwin Blow Kertland	16.6.1915
2/Lt. Charles Henry Lane	21.8.1918
Capt. Ernest Walter Vindin Leach	2.1.1917
2/Lt. John Lecky	16.7.1916
2/Lt. Alfred James Lennox	19.1.1916
Lt. Gilbert Edwin Lynch, Durham Light Infantry	21.3.1918
Lt. William Clark McConnell	9.7.1916
2/Lt. Martin Joseph McDonnell	24.1.1917
2/Lt. Maurice Anderdon McFerran	21.3.1918
2/Lt. James Marshall McIntosh	16.6.1915
Lt. Patrick Joseph McKee	10.8.1917
Lt. Maurice MacKenzie, RAMC	28.11.1915
2/Lt. Patrick McMahon	11.6.1917
2/Lt. Richard Henry Cole Magenis	15.9.1914
2/Lt. Richard Brereton Marriott-Watson	24.3.1918
Capt. Charles Lionel Master	12.10.1914
2/Lt. Arthur Gorman Mitchell	13.5.1916
2/Lt. Homer Dean Mitchell	6.9.1918
Capt. Samuel Valentine Morgan	10.8.1917
Lt. William John Edward Morton	5.9.1915
Lt. Edward Spread Mulcahy-Morgan	27.10.1914
2/Lt. Bernard Joseph Murphy, R. Munster Fusiliers	18.8.1917
2/Lt. Sidney Joseph Vincent O'Brien	7.6.1917
Lt. Robert James O'Lone	11.11.1915
2/Lt. Walter Percy O'Lone	25.9.1915
2/Lt. Herbert Wilson O'Reilly	20.1.1916
2/Lt. Walter Leslie Orr	25.9.1915
Capt. Henry George Charles Perry-Ayscough, R. Inniskilling Fusiliers	25.9.1915
2/Lt. Charles Alfred Pigot-Moodie, Rifle Brigade	13.1.1915
Lt. Ernest Dickinson Price, R. Irish Regiment	19.3.1916
2/Lt. William Rainey	23.11.1917
Lt. Arthur Augustus Raymond	1.8.1915
Lt. Vivian Trevor Tighe Rea	25.10.1914
Lt. Andrew Beaconsfield Ross, RAMC	5.8.1917
2/Lt. Kenneth Ross	25.9.1915
2/Lt. Melbourne Ross	25.9.1915
Capt. William Alan Smiles	9.7.1916
Capt. George Bostall Jenkinson Smyth	22.10.1918
Major Charles Rodney Wolfe Spedding	19.9.1914
2/Lt. John Joseph Stanley	9.12.1917
2/Lt. John Francis Stein	28.9.1916
2/Lt. Herbert William Detagau Stone, Connaught Rangers	26.4.1916
2/Lt. Henry Poyntz Swaine	15.9.1914
Capt. Thomas John Chichester Conyngham Thompson, R. Irish Fusiliers	24.3.1918

2/Lt. William John Sterne Tydd, Connaught Rangers   22.1.1917
Lt. Joseph Charles Tyndall, R. Dublin Fusiliers   2.3.1915
2/Lt. William Wood Vernon, Connaught Rangers   8.7.1916
2/Lt. Clifford Hardwicke Wale   19.1.1916
2/Lt. James Watson   7.7.1916
Capt. John Percy Whelan   11.12.1914
Lt. Arthur Noel Whitfeld   14.10.1914
Capt. Charles Beasley Williams   28.8.1915
Lt. Edward Workman   26.1.1916

APPENDIX II: CASUALTIES IN THE RANKS

This list is as comprehensive as I could reasonably make it. It has been compiled from the database of the Commonwealth War Graves Commission, *Ireland's Memorial Records*, and *Soldiers Died in the Great War*. These records are incomplete and not entirely accurate, especially in terms of the battalion with which men served, the date of death, and whether they were killed in action or died of wounds received on an earlier day. I know that all are not included as I could not always match the listings to the numbers of casualties given in the War Diary. Many records were lost during the time when the details were transferred from the War Office to the Imperial War Graves Commission. Men were often moved between battalions, especially when they returned from sick leave. Thus you can find men listed in the records as being from 2nd RIR yet must have died while serving with 1st RIR. From mid 1916 the War Office no longer listed the battalions of a regiment when supplying the casualty lists.

Later in the war, particularly from 1917 onwards, men were transferred in from other regiments or corps but they are recorded as only having served with their original unit. In some instances they are shown as attached to the RIR but the number of the battalion is not stated. A rough analysis of the 221 men who are noted as having previously served in other units shows that the largest groups came from the Lancers (47), KRRC (29), RASC and London Regt (28 each). The four-digit numbers of the other men are problematic: some would originally have had a prefix such as 3/ (for 3rd RIR) to denote the battalion with which they originally served. It is not, therefore, safe to make assumptions based on the numerical sequences.

I have identified 1,411 deaths of other ranks up to the end of the war on 11 November 1918. Total deaths, therefore, including officers are at least 1,500 and, of those, roughly 1,056 (70 per cent) were Irishmen: this coincides well with the fact that 71% enlisted in Ireland. Although the battalion was at war for only a little over four months of 1914, it will be noted that they suffered more casualties in this period than the total for any other year of the war. The format I have used is the date on which men died – the alphabetical and cemetery orders are already available elsewhere.

August 1914

23rd   7115 Rfn John Henry McCrea, 9471 L/Cpl George Thomas McKinley (see main text), 8771 L/Cpl Patrick Sharkey (shrapnel, the first RIR man killed). (The war diary recorded 4 killed.)

26th   9995 Rfn Thomas Chittick, 7451 Cpl Arthur Patrick Doran, 7300 Rfn David McClintock, 7585 Rfn John McCoskrie, 6165 Rfn Thomas Rainey. (The war diary recorded 6 killed.)

September 1914

14th   8120 Rfn Michael Leavy.

15th   8877 Rfn David Brown, 8980 Rfn James Cassidy, 6731 Rfn James Chittenden, 10050 Rfn Archibald Crawford, 7031 Rfn George Green, 7198 Rfn Arthur Hammill, 6601 Rfn James Higgins, 9895 L/Cpl Denis Lucy, 4588 CSM David

Andrew Lyness LSM, GCM (A Coy), 7598 Rfn Bernard McAlea, 10099 L/Cpl Francis McClurg, 8739 Rfn Francis McCullough, 8250 Rfn Hugh McGreevy, 7924 Rfn Thomas Malone, 9849 Rfn John Murphy, 9749 Rfn Constantine Murray, 7533 Rfn John Pender, 10146 Rfn Edward Ryan, 6370 Rfn Walter Wilkinson.

16th 9819 Rfn John Joseph Murphy, 8266 Rfn Llewelyn Roberts.

17th 7210 Rfn John Gallagher (died of wounds).

18th 8490 Rfn John Martin.

19th 8828 Rfn Henry Douglas, 7231 Rfn George Neill.

20th 5936 Rfn Edward Anderson, 9977 Rfn William Bennett, 7350 Rfn Henry Bishop, 9441 Rfn Edward Brady, 7011 Rfn John Clarke, 8294 Rfn Philip Clarke, 5692 L/Cpl John Connolly, 10101 Rfn James George Coulter, 7129 Rfn William Cutts, 10103 L/Cpl Jeremiah Foley, 8347 L/Cpl Samuel Greenaway, 8521 Rfn Joseph Hanna, 7142 Rfn James Harris, 8672 Rfn John Lynch, 15065 Rfn James McCormack (died of wounds), 6420 Rfn William McCready, 7529 Rfn Alfred McCullough, 7476 Rfn Robert McKay, 6847 Rfn Thomas Martin, 5319 Rfn Daniel Nelis, 9003 Rfn John Regan, 4353 Rfn James Scott, 8857 Rfn John Scott, 8206 Rfn Robert Smeaton, 7232 Rfn John Vaughan, 6358 Rfn Thomas White.

21st 7519 Rfn Patrick Duffy, 10051 L/Cpl John Dunphy, 7818 Cpl Joseph Hanley (died of wounds), 10175 Rfn Patrick Lynch (died of wounds, age 17), 8994 Rfn William McAllister, 7194 Rfn Peter McAteer, 9966 L/Cpl Henry Moore, 6493 Rfn William Phillips, 10190 Rfn Patrick Rafferty, 10070 Rfn George Alfred Swain.

22nd 8367 Rfn George McGrane (died of wounds).

25th 7205 Rfn Michael Bowes (died).

27th 6897 Bandsman George Goulter Gunning (died of wounds and tetanus).

28th 6931 Rfn Joseph Kane (died of wounds received at Mons).

29th 8560 Rfn John Reid Stitt (dysentery).

October 1914

12th 6561 Sgt James Ruddock.

14th 7990 Rfn Charles Adams, 7944 Rfn Edward Adams (died of wounds), 6220 Rfn John Gallagher, 9276 Rfn Robert Gowdy, 8151 L/Cpl John Johns (died of wounds, formerly 8815 R. Irish), 7759 Rfn William Murray, 9290 Sgt Frederick White.

15th 6081 Rfn Patrick Quinn, 5002 Rfn John Smith (died of wounds).

16th 7634 Rfn Joseph Gardner.

17th 6836 Rfn Thomas Evans, 6920 Rfn Albert Edward Gloster, 7678 Rfn David McClelland (died of wounds), 6587 Rfn George Raynham.

21st 8297 Rfn Patrick Smyth.

23rd 7170 Rfn James Stevinson Poag.

24th 9756 Cpl Jack Altman (Jewish), 8073 Rfn Edward Galway, 9329 Rfn Patrick Joseph Gibbons, 5844 Rfn Robert Green, 8068 Rfn Joseph Richardson, 8336 Rfn Joseph Patrick Robinson.

25th 9204 Sgt Robert Adair, 7880 Rfn Joseph Robert Albon, 8988 Rfn Patrick Bannon, 9004 Rfn Samuel Elliott, 10068 Rfn Thomas Fox, 6884 Rfn Hugh Gorman, 6299 Rfn Richard Greer, 6660 Rfn William Hetherington, 7554 L/Cpl Robert Jamieson, 8290 Rfn Thomas Kearney, 7061 Rfn John Baptist Stanislaus Keogh, 9801 Rfn Peter Kirwan, 8845 L/Cpl William McCann, 8400 Sgt Robert Cunningham McFarlane, 8989 Rfn David Mahon, 6121 Rfn Andrew Masterson, 9087 Rfn Thomas O'Keefe, 9955 Rfn Thomas O'Reilly, 7942 Rfn John Perry, 8262 Rfn Daniel Robinson, 8976 Rfn Patrick Scanlon, 8417 Rfn James Templeton, 8619 Rfn William Tumblety, 7787 Rfn Thomas Woods.

26th 10102 Rfn William Barry, 7241 L/Cpl Joseph Beeley, 7842 Rfn Robert Bell, 9107 Sgt Anthony Boylan, 8311 Rfn William Bratchford, 9945 L/Sgt William Burns, 8432 Rfn William Clarke, 8484 Rfn Hugh Connor, 6656 Rfn John William Coulson, 10011 Rfn Henry Greer Cree, 7308 Rfn Patrick Deighton, 8267 Rfn Richard Delaney, 9258 Rfn Samuel Easton, 10042 Rfn William Ellison, 7037 Rfn James Fiddis, 9572 Sgt Patrick Joseph Flynn, 7180 Rfn Robert James Foley, 8747 Rfn John Greer, 2/6954 Cpl James Henry, 6826 Rfn John McAlindon, 7768 Rfn Michael McDonnell, 7290 Rfn James McKenna, 7254 Rfn Patrick Malone, 9056 Sgt Richard Henry Martin, 7164 Rfn Allister Mearnes, 6925 Rfn Edward Meehan, 9887 L/Cpl Thomas Gray Mellefont, 10100 Rfn John Joseph Moynihan, 7803 Rfn Michael Murphy, 7371 Rfn Patrick O'Neill, 6932 Rfn John O'Rawe (Leeds Policeman), 8972 Rfn Patrick Partridge (served in the South African War), 7125 Rfn Timothy Patton, 8164 Rfn Joseph Rice, 7296 Cpl David Robinson, 7253 Rfn John Rourke, 6599 Rfn Frank Sawkins, 8400 Rfn Matthew Scott, 7775 Rfn John Shanks, 6772 Rfn James Lewis Sloan, 8185 L/Cpl Samuel Spratt, 8958 Rfn Thomas Spratt, 9950 L/Cpl Edward Paul Stack, 7797 Rfn Bernard Sullivan, 7244 Rfn Alfred Swann, 6486 Rfn Ernest Burrowes Tytherleigh, 8639 Rfn Percy John Walsh, 10090 Rfn James Ward, 8301 Rfn John Joseph Wheeler.

27th 8449 Rfn William Armstrong, 6168 Rfn Joseph Bell, 7784 L/Cpl Alexander Boyd, 18136 L/Cpl Patrick Leslie Brennan, 9064 Rfn John Butler, 8781 L/Cpl Joseph Byrne, 7077 Rfn William Byrne, 6983 Rfn Alexander Campbell, 7073 Rfn John Campbell, 8199 Rfn Robert Carlisle, 9975 Rfn Lawrence Carolan, 9020 Rfn Patrick Clarke, 6598 L/Cpl Caleb Collins, 8952 Rfn William Thomas Condit, 8069 Rfn Thomas Cooke, 8015 Rfn John Crossett, 8000 Rfn Patrick Curran, 9113 Rfn John Daly, 10189 Rfn Martin Delaney, 7805 Rfn James Dillon, 10121 Rfn Jeremiah Donovan, 8102 L/Cpl Andrew Doyle, 7100 Rfn Thomas Dunne, 5634 Rfn Thomas Easton, 10111 Rfn Hugh Epplestone (*Belfast News Letter*, 9.7.1915: 'A brother is at the Front, and another is a POW in Germany.'), 6839 Rfn Bernard Fearan, 6444 Rfn Robert Getty, 6845 Rfn John Golden, 7415 Rfn Thomas Gourley, 8867 Rfn Patrick Govers, 6503 CSM Henry Green, 9109 Rfn John Hall, 7267 Rfn Joseph Henry Halligan, 7234 Rfn James Harrison, 6899 Rfn Edward Harvey, 6633 Rfn William Hempenstal, 8004 Rfn Frank Hogg, 10118 Rfn Daniel Horgan, 6324 Rfn William Hunt, 5138 Rfn William Hurley, 6780 Rfn James Kelly, 10104 Rfn Bartholomew

Kenneally, 8728 Rfn Joseph Lavery (served in the South African War), 9111 Sgt Robert Lee, 7876 Rfn John Linehan, 6652 Rfn Frank Lowe, 8989 Rfn Alexander Lundy (died), 7583 Rfn James McAllister, 8120 Rfn William McCabe, 7243 Rfn Frederick McCracken, 10147 Rfn James McGlade, 5893 Rfn William James McIlwrath, 8945 L/Cpl Daniel McIvers, 7934 Rfn Thomas Joseph MacInerney, 5994 Rfn Daniel McKenzie, 5736 Rfn Patrick McLaughlin, 8335 Rfn James McNally, 8256 Rfn William McNally, 7902 Rfn John Madden, 7814 Rfn John Magner, 8486 L/Cpl Hector Claude Marsh, 9304 Rfn Patrick Millard (formerly 8290 R. Irish), 8016 Rfn John Mooney, 8705 Rfn George Morrison, 9054 Rfn John Mulgrew, 7073 Rfn John Murphy, 9017 L/Cpl John Murphy, 6882 L/Cpl William Thomas Nowlan, 5803 Rfn Edward O'Neill, 9183 Rfn James O'Neill, 10218 Rfn Richard O'Neill, 6507 Rfn Thomas Robert Palmer, 10116 Rfn Joseph Paul, 7556 Rfn Charles Frederick Payne, 9016 Rfn Thomas Quail (served in the South African War), 8393 Rfn Alfred Reilly, 7689 Rfn John Reilly, 7334 Cpl Patrick Reilly, 7442 Sgt George Reynolds, 7064 Rfn William Reynolds, 9733 Rfn Michael Ryan, 6101 Rfn Robert James Scott, 3995 Rfn William Shirlow, 6696 Rfn Herbert Edgar Skipper, 6176 Rfn Edward Smyth, 6126 Rfn John Stokes (served in the South African War), 8868 Rfn Patrick Swift, 7275 Rfn Andrew Taggart, 7075 Rfn William George Taylor, 8441 Rfn Samuel Turner, 8079 Rfn Hugh Walker, 8191 Rfn Thomas Charles James Walker, 7993 Rfn John Warren, 8270 Rfn John Watters, 10074 Rfn George Westlake (died of wounds), 8333 CSM Percival Williams, 7154 Rfn Christopher Wilson, 9036 Rfn William Wilton, 6479 Rfn Andrew Wright.

28th   10237 Rfn Joseph Tyrrell, 8117 Rfn Willliam Watt.

30th   5664 Rfn William Joseph Delaney.

31st   8679 Rfn Joseph Haggan, 6499 Rfn Michael O'Meara (died of wounds).

November 1914

1st   8782 Rfn John McDonnell (died), 6615 Rfn Ernest Walker (died of wounds).

4th   7491 Rfn Arthur Phipps (died of wounds, formerly 8299 Worcester Regt).

5th   7477 Rfn Bernard Quilton (died of wounds).

6th   8080 Rfn James Galway (died in the UK).

7th   9719 Cpl Robert Elphick (died in the UK of wounds received at Neuve Chapelle), 8675 Rfn John Lyons.

8th   8122 Rfn Luke Delaney, 7905 Rfn Andrew Hutchinson, 7597 L/Cpl Samuel Parkinson (died of wounds).

9th   7587 Rfn John Irvine (died of wounds; member of LOL 1055).

10th   9209 Rfn William Wigston (died of wounds).

11th   8955 Rfn Robert James Adair, 10106 Rfn Daniel Cahill, 8213 Rfn George Cole, 9087 Rfn William John Crainey, 8995 Cpl James Dickey, 9406 Rfn Thomas Dunne, 9153 Rfn Samuel Ferris, 10330 Rfn Michael Forde, 7223 Rfn William Wolfe Kennedy, 7252 Rfn James Macartney, 8769 Rfn William John McIlroy, 8264 Rfn James Alexander Stewart, 8983 Rfn James White, 9088 Rfn Francis Williamson.

13th 7383 Rfn Joseph McCunnin, 9963 Rfn Robert Martin.

14th 8840 Rfn Robert McIntyre (died of wounds).

16th 8810 Rfn Bernard McKillops (died of wounds), 6226 L/Cpl Robert Stannage.

18th 8204 Rfn William J. Agnew (died).

23rd 10969 Rfn Samuel Jamison.

25th 7108 Rfn John Beggs.

27th 9110 Rfn Patrick Cummins.

28th 8121 Rfn Patrick McGuigan (died of wounds in the UK).

December 1914

1st 6612 Rfn James Patton.

3rd 3416 Sgt John Graham, 8252 Rfn George Harkness (died), 4905 Rfn Shaw Martin.

6th 8180 Rfn Samuel Nelson (*Irish Times*, 22.12.1914: 'wounded at the battle of Mons, and was invalided home, rejoining his regiment in November').

7th 10261 Rfn Anderson McIlwaine (*Irish Times*, 30.12.1914: 'died from wounds received on the 6th December. Private McIlwaine, who was only 17 years of age, joined the Army in November 1913, and was sent to the front with a draft of Rifles last month. Mr McIlwaine has two other sons with the Colours, Gunner Alexander McIlwaine, HMS *Bellerophon*, and Private James McIlwaine, Royal Irish Rifles').

9th 7139 Rfn Patrick McCoy.

12th 9136 Rfn Thomas Macauley, 9458 Rfn John Blair McFarlane (died of wounds).

13th 4528 Rfn Robert Shanks (died of wounds).

16th 6338 Sgt William Black (*Burgoyne*: 'shot because he was too drunk to be careful'), 7233 Rfn Terence Hynes, 10060 Rfn William Weldon.

17th 4253 Rfn Francis Duffy (*Burgoyne*: 'a pig of a man took a jar of rum to bed with him, and was found dead next morning'), 6569 Rfn Thomas Harvey, 6808 Cpl Michael McGivern, 6183 Rfn Francis Murphy, 5697 Rfn Hill Quinn.

18th 7228 Rfn Bernard Doran, 5623 Rfn John Foster (age 56), 3213 Rfn James McCullough, 7165 Rfn William John McJury (died of wounds).

20th 10335 Rfn Thomas Lambert (died of wounds).

27th 10372 Rfn Alfred Moore (died of wounds).

30th 9844 Rfn Harry Kinsella.

January 1915

5th 8252 Rfn Henry Cohen (Jewish), 4767 Rfn Thomas McCafferey.

6th 12383 Rfn Charles Kavanagh, 3773 Rfn John Young (enteric fever).

8th 6844 Rfn James Burns (*Burgoyne*: 'hit just above the heart by a bullet which enfiladed the trench').

12th 6743 Rfn James McGrath (age 17. *Frontier Sentinel*, 23.1.1915: 'a member of the Newry National Volunteers, joined the Army at the outbreak of war, and volunteered for active service. He proceeded to the front ... about three months ago, and there he sustained frostbite, which was so severe that he had to be removed to Fazakerley Hospital, Liverpool. His condition, however, was hopeless, and in the course of a few weeks he passed away').

13th 6188 Rfn John Wright (died in the UK).

14th 7518 Rfn George McFarland, 4865 Sgt Frank Neill (a Reservist, buried when a shell hit his dugout), 6594 Rfn Jeremiah Porter.

16th 7021 Rfn Edward Cotter (*Burgoyne*: 'shot slap through the top of his head from side to side').

17th 6078 Rfn William Vance (died of wounds).

22nd 6296 Rfn Francis Farrell (died of wounds).

24th 8588 Rfn Thomas Hugh Heaney (enteric fever).

30th 14466 Rfn George Edwin Berry, 5569 L/Cpl Ernest Hurrell, 8892 Cpl Philip Wyman.

31st 6446 Rfn James MacKenzie Irwin (died of wounds).

February 1915

4th 3959 Rfn Edward Gaynor (died).

9th 5303 Rfn John Hanlon DCM (Previously Rfn 2618. *Belfast News Letter*, 1.3.1915: 'died at No. 8 Clearing Station ... from chronic nephritis.' Awarded the DCM in the South African War: 'for having, in a reconnaissance near Stormberg, in January, 1900, when Rifleman McLoughlin's horse had been shot, gone back, under heavy fire, and assisted McLoughlin back to his section').

10th 7305 Rfn Francis Hunter (died of wounds).

11th 8390 Rfn Luke Clarke (died of wounds)

16th (1 killed per war diary).

17th 8238 Rfn David Ennis.

21st 4768 Rfn Samuel James Gillespie (enteric fever), 5204 Rfn Samuel McKee (died of wounds), 7753 Sgt John Seiles (*Burgoyne*: 'A Company lost a Sergeant killed and one man wounded the day before yesterday. In the mist they went out to bury two Gordons just in front of their wire. The mist lifted and the Germans shot them').

23rd 16805 L/Cpl William McAtamey (died of wounds, served in the South African War).

March 1915

1st 10399 Rfn Joseph Kelly (died of wounds).

2nd 9373 Rfn Francis King, 8670 Rfn Francis McLarnon.

3rd 9445 Rfn Thomas Mangan (died of wounds in the UK).

4th 7227 Rfn Richard Nailor (died).

8th 10234 Rfn John Hughes (executed by the Germans).

10th 10408 Rfn George Aucutt, 10358 Rfn William Fitzpatrick, 10137 L/Cpl James Gahan, 13306 Rfn John McCarthy, 8596 Rfn David McEwan, 7299

Rfn Alan Waddie, 1406 Rfn Victor Leonard Watts. (These were probably killed with 1st RIR, as 2nd RIR was in billets.)

11th 10328 Rfn Charles Donohoe, 10332 Rfn Hugh Doran, 7931 Rfn Bartholomew Forde, 7409 Rfn William Phipps. (These were probably killed with 1st RIR.)

12th 6043 Rfn David Carlisle, 10401 Cpl Frederick William Nalty. (These were probably killed with 1st RIR.)

18th 8997 Rfn Robert Smyth.

20th 9351 Rfn James Maguire.

21st 5783 Rfn Laurence Burns (died of wounds), 4723 Rfn Peter McCrory, 5350 Rfn John McQuade.

23rd 8239 Rfn Edward Higgins (died of wounds), 9135 Rfn William Quinn.

31st 10354 Rfn William Aherne (*Burgoyne*: 'Shot him through the back of the head and made a horrible mess. He lived for six hours in spite of it but he never spoke a word and was unconscious all the time').

April 1915

2nd 8981 Rfn Hugh McCrory (*Burgoyne*: 'was shot in the knee and bled to death').

3rd 4945 Rfn Joseph Bingham (*Burgoyne*: 'Stupid fellow was sniping at a sniper, and after firing a shot, instead of ducking down behind the parapet, he kept his head up to see the success of his shot, kept it up for an appreciable time, and his target shot the top of his head off'), 6586 L/Cpl Thomas McClartney.

10th 5205 L/Cpl David Walsh (died of disease).

13th 4730 Rfn Ezekel Nesbitt (*Burgoyne*: 'A bullet had hit him in the mouth as he was digging behind a parapet').

15th 4969 Rfn James Gracey (died of wounds).

17th 6587 Rfn Michael Doran (died of wounds).

20th 5694 Rfn Robert Andrews (age 17. *Burgoyne*: 'shot through the lung'.).

21st 10429 Rfn Charles Haskins (*Burgoyne*: 'Contrary to orders, one of my men … hops out of a small trench … to this spring with his water bottle. A bullet immediately hits him in the arm and enters his body below the waist … he died three hours later').

24th 5329 Rfn Richard Simpson Smyth.

27th 8634 Rfn James McIlroy (*Burgoyne*: 'one man working at the furthest range got a bullet through the centre of the chest; he died in half an hour').

30th 16793 Rfn James Cooke, 9613 Cpl Joseph Courtney (died of wounds).

May 1915

1st 6781 Rfn Peter Carroll (died in the UK).

2nd 7782 Rfn John Boulger, 5565 Rfn James Carmichael, 13050 Rfn Robert Henry Kennedy, 8699 Rfn James McIldoon, 5244 Rfn Joseph Mackell, 6365 Rfn John Rainbird. (All by shell fire.)

3rd 2/8744 Rfn Thomas Baker, 9007 Rfn Robert Kavanagh, 9942 Rfn George Williams. (All by shell fire.)

4th   6631 Rfn Thomas Nutley (died of wounds).
7th   4816 Rfn Robert Close (brother of 3973 Rfn W. Close, 1st RIR, KIA
       29.5.1915), 5508 Rfn Thomas Cochrane, 5313 Rfn James Hughes, 2373 Rfn
       Andrew William Kennedy, 4864 Rfn James McCollum (died of wounds),
       7137 Rfn Daniel McDonald, 7948 Cpl James Mason, 5818 Rfn Michael
       O'Hara, 7094 Rfn William Sloan, 9385 Rfn Thomas Spence.
8th   5465 Rfn Robert Bradford, 6607 Rfn William Duff, 10049 Rfn Thomas Gale,
       10277 Rfn James McFall.
9th   1524 Rfn Albert Ashworth, 5459 Rfn William Farrell, 8366 Rfn Patrick
       Johnston, 1375 Rfn James Kennerley, 1447 Rfn John McAuley, 6272 Rfn
       John McCreedy, 4908 Rfn Robert McGeown, 9836 Rfn Joseph Madden, 7417
       Rfn Robert Millar (age 17), 8705 L/Cpl George Nelson, 13311 Cpl Thomas
       O'Flynn, 5383 Rfn John Pyper, 6502 L/Cpl James Riddell, 1357 Rfn William
       Walford, 5088 Rfn William Henry Wallace. (Some of these were probably
       killed with 1st RIR as the war diary recorded 3 killed and 21 wounded.)
10th   5586 Rfn Hugh John Brown, 9974 Rfn Alfred Clegg (died of wounds), 3799
       Rfn Stanley Heaney, 10459 Rfn Patrick Reilly. (Some of these may have been
       wounded with 1st RIR the previous day as the war diary recorded 1 killed
       and 1 wounded.)
11th   9146 Rfn James Kennedy, 4735 Rfn William James Orr (Reservist. *Banbridge
       Chronicle*: 'the deceased leaves a wife and six children.' Brother-in-law of
       18/301 Rfn Samuel McBride, 13th RIR, died of wounds, 20.5.1917.), 6339
       Cpl William J. Roy (died of wounds in the UK).
13th   8513 Rfn James Mills.
17th   8552 Cpl William Porter.
19th   1/8404 Rfn Michael O'Toole, 4770 Rfn Patrick Weir (died of wounds in the
       UK). (The war diary noted 2 killed by British artillery.)
24th   1787 Rfn Michael Gilmore, 7070 Rfn William Jameson, 6857 Rfn David
       Jones, 10340 Rfn Thomas McCormack, 6766 L/Cpl Robert McKee (served
       in the South African War with the RAMC). (All by shell fire.)
27th   5845 Rfn James Morton. (The war diary recorded 2 killed by sniping.)
28th   1381 Rfn George Frith, 9526 Sgt John Mullen (died of wounds).
31st   6305 L/Cpl James Jardine (Reservist. Wounded in the leg by a splinter from
       a shell and died of illness.).

June 1915
2nd   5165 Rfn William Babes, 8879 Rfn James Davison Close (died of wounds in
       the UK, age 17), 7201 Rfn John Tilney.
8th   1686 Rfn Reginald Percy Elcombe (died of wounds).
10th   10352 Rfn Henry Bracken.
12th   10319 Rfn James Patrick Smith.
16th   7128 Rfn Joseph Booth (died of wounds), 6980 L/Cpl Thomas Brady, 10250
       Rfn John Cole, 6545 L/Cpl Patrick Condon, 5849 Rfn William Cotter, 9687
       L/Cpl Daniel Coughlan, 8074 CSM James Thomas Courtney (D Coy), 10287

Rfn Patrick Cregan, 15289 Rfn Francis Daly, 7335 Rfn Francis Dunne, 10432 Rfn Peter Fields, 5510 Rfn James Fitzsimmons, 6322 Rfn Patrick Fitzsimmons, 5521 Rfn William John Gilchrist (member of LOL 916), 6970 Rfn John Harvey, 6528 Cpl William Harold Henderson, 7153 Rfn James Heron, 9369 Rfn Arthur Hollingsworth, 10221 Rfn Daniel Hoystead, 10373 Rfn Edward Hudson (age 17), 17211 Rfn Leo Irwin, 8622 Cpl Samuel Irwin, 6467 Rfn Hugh Johnston, 1788 Rfn Joseph Jones, 5559 Rfn Samuel King, 8835 Cpl George Laird, 5047 Rfn Daniel Lappin (Friends School, Lisburn, War List: 'Orangeman and member of the 1st Lisburn battalion, UVF. He was a reservist in 5th RIR and was called up at the start of the war, serving in 2nd RIR along with his brother William [died of wounds 24.6.1915].'), 5921 Rfn Robert Loughlin, 2318 Rfn Matthew McCartney, 7044 Rfn Archibald McCormick, 8423 Rfn Robert McDowell, 7873 CSM James Joseph McGibney, 5078 Cpl Patrick McGreevy, 7599 Cpl John McIlroy, 9223 L/Cpl William McIlroy, 10217 Rfn Thomas McKenzie, 5722 Rfn John McKeown, 6768 Rfn John McKeown, 4894 Rfn Joseph Malcomson, 4/6319 Rfn William Martin, 7017 Cpl George Morgan, 8731 Rfn James Morrow, 5542 Rfn Thomas Mullan, 6095 Cpl Hugh Murray, 5233 Rfn William Henry Nicholson, 5189 Rfn Joseph Owens (died of wounds), 2572 Rfn Peter Rodgers, 5221 Rfn John Joseph Smyth, 4601 Rfn John Thompson, 6253 Rfn James Vint, 8097 Rfn Archibald Walker, 2503 Rfn Frederick Watling, 10369 Rfn Peter West, 1265 Rfn William Winstanley, 15706 Rfn Philip Camillus Wynne.

17th 9781 Rfn Daniel O'Brien (died of wounds).

18th 6376 Rfn John Reilly (died of wounds).

19th 9033 Rfn Thomas James Dalton (died of wounds).

21st 8895 Rfn Samuel Maynard (died of wounds, age 17).

22nd 3377 Rfn Alfred Britton (died of wounds, age 16).

24th 8786 Rfn Andrew Kirkland (died of wounds), 5377 Rfn William Lappin (Friends School, Lisburn, War List: 'Orangeman and member of the 1st Lisburn battalion, UVF. He enlisted at the start of the war in 5th RIR and was sent to the front on the 26.12.1914 … from gunshot wounds to the leg.').

28th 7312 Rfn Archibald Young (died of wounds).

July 1915

2nd (The war diary recorded 1 man died from the effects of gas poisoning.)

5th 9047 Rfn Robert Johnstone (served in the South African War. Shot in the eye and operated on in France for an internal ailment. Died at Derbyshire County Infirmary.), 7287 Rfn David Trimble.

7th 5818 Rfn Robert Hugh Adair.

10th 4966 Rfn Frank Bunton (formerly 10321 Lancers), 10276 Rfn Daniel McFall.

11th 9097 Rfn John Catherwood (died of wounds).

17th 10191 L/Cpl William Thompson (died of meningitis while a POW).

20th 5545 Rfn William Hall.

24th 8683 Sgt Martin Butler.

25th   4925 Rfn Henry Gallery (died of wounds).
26th   5013 Rfn Frederick James Fido (formerly 12242 Lancers).
27th   9631 L/Cpl William Lynas.
28th   5164 L/Cpl Kenneth Ward (formerly 5763 Lancers).
31st   4766 Rfn Thomas Smith (died in the UK)

August 1915
1st   5645 Rfn John Kearney, 5147 L/Cpl Joseph William Tatam (formerly 4059 Lancers). (Both by shell fire.)
3rd   8975 Rfn James Joseph Doherty.
5th   (The war diary noted 1 killed.)
8th   2437 Rfn George Arthur Green (died of wounds in the UK, age 17).
9th   10451 Rfn William Hassan, 7027 Rfn Joseph McDermott (died of sickness).
19th   8809 Rfn Patrick Mulholland.
25th   10302 Rfn Charles Thompson.
28th   10418 Rfn Thomas Dines, 8851 Sgt Thomas O'Rourke. (Both by shell fire.)
29th   5393 Rfn John Magee (died of wounds received at Hooge).
30th   5143 Rfn Leonard Joseph Stapleford (died of wounds in the UK, formerly 4050 Lancers).

September 1915
4th   6200 Rfn William Gibbons (shell fire).
5th   4979 Rfn Leslie Clark (died of wounds, formerly 4001 Lancers), 5138 Rfn Frank Smith (formerly 10589 Lancers). (Both by shell fire.)
8th   3962 Rfn Herbert Collins.
10th   5006 Rfn William Megaw (died of wounds at No. 28 CCS. Enlisted August 1914 and had served for some time in the Navy.).
11th   5790 Rfn John Kirgan.
13th   5115 Rfn Charles Archibald Walter Quiney (died of wounds, formerly 18082 Lancers).
25th   4943 Rfn Harold William Athey (formerly 4044 Lancers), 5863 L/Cpl Thomas Atkinson, 4949 Rfn Jubal Bartlett (formerly 3533 Hussars), 4974 Rfn Samuel Baxter, 4950 Rfn George Frederick Beard (formerly 4993 Lancers), 9784 Rfn James Behan, 4956 Rfn James Bland (formerly 7065 16th Lancers), 4960 Rfn Charles Henry Bramall (formerly 4843 Lancers), 17216 L/Cpl Samuel Brolly, 6581 Rfn John Burns, 2521 Rfn Thomas Carroll, 4977 Rfn Albert Victor Clark (died of wounds), 5185 Rfn John Samuel Clarke (formerly 4071 Lancers), 4983 Rfn Sidney Thomas Clarke (formerly 12632 Reserve Cavalry Regt), 4987 Rfn Arthur Collie (formerly 4085 Lancers), 1665 L/Cpl James Alfred Connolly (age 17), 2/10295 Sgt William H. Cowden (he was the fourth of five sons of Mr S. Cowden, then aged 81, all serving in the war, alongside two grandsons), 9199 CSM Joseph John Cullen (*Lucy*: 'He led his men right up to the second line, and a German stickbomb broke open his chest.'), 5748 Rfn William James Darragh, 1359 Rfn James Dorber, 1388

Rfn Patrick Doyle, 7006 Rfn Patrick Earls, 5012 Rfn Sidney Charles Farren (formerly 6879 Lancers), 4835 Rfn Robert Flanigan (previously invalided home with frostbite. His twin brother, 789 Rfn John Flanigan, 13th RIR, was killed in action 1.7.1916.), 9943 Rfn James Gibson, 5031 Rfn Arthur James Hammond (formerly 6720 Lancers), 5034 Rfn William Charles Harding (formerly 7106 Lancers), 3190 Rfn James Huey, 5049 Rfn John Hunter (formerly 3993 Lancers), 14451 Cpl Frederick Hurford, 2767 Rfn Robert Jenkins, 4938 Rfn William Jones, 8718 Cpl Joseph Kitson, 8184 Cpl Charles Hemy Lettington, 6923 L/Cpl Patrick McCarron, 5511 L/Cpl William M'Clurg (served five years with 2nd RIR prior to the war and was invalided home from India.), 7501 Sgt William McCrory, 5705 Rfn Thomas Mackey, 9444 Sgt Edwin Mess, 5088 Rfn Robert Mitchell (formerly 4550 Lancers), 8807 Rfn James Leo Moan (died of wounds), 1440 Rfn Michael Murphy, 4587 Rfn Peter Murray, 5093 Rfn James Henry Nugent (formerly 7189 17th Lancers), 10174 Rfn John O'Connor, 5096 Rfn James Thomas O'Gara (formerly 4034 Lancers), 5197 L/Cpl James Alexander Parker, 5073 Sgt James Powell, 7012 Rfn Benjamin Rodgers, 5132 Rfn Trevor Shaw (formerly 8489 Lancers), 6055 Sgt William Shearer DCM (*London Gazette*, 30.3.1915: 'For conspicuous gallantry on all occasions, especially near Hooge, on 11th November, 1914, when he took a message into the trenches whilst exposed to most destructive fire. His absolute fearlessness has been most noticeable in dangerous situations'), 7087 Rfn George Summerville, 4167 Rfn Joseph Stewart (died of wounds), 5451 Rfn Thomas Stewart (age 17), 1517 Rfn Charles Storey, 8956 Rfn Daniel Stuart, 5150 Rfn Charles Thomas (formerly 4334 Lancers), 4872 Rfn Ezekiel Thompson, 8916 Cpl William Toole, 5154 Rfn Cyril Francis Tribble, 1583 Rfn James Turner, 5161 Rfn Arnold Walker (formerly 6500 16th Lancers), 4/311 Sgt Stanley Watson, 5176 Rfn Herbert Wright (formerly 4018 Lancers).

26th   6890 Rfn William McCrory (died of wounds).
27th   5087 Rfn James Mullaly (died of wounds, formerly 10300 Lancers).
28th   7233 L/Cpl Thomas Thompson (died of wounds).
29th   5131 Cpl George Stevens (formerly 10354 Lancers).

October 1915

1st   6389 Rfn James Brown (died of wounds received 25.9.1915).
2nd   4958 Rfn Thomas William Box (formerly 8346 Lancers), 9349 Rfn Robert Martin (died of wounds), 5191 Rfn William Weir (died of wounds).
4th   5225 Rfn William Sanders (died of wounds in the UK).
5th   5115 L/Cpl Joseph Wilson McNeice (died of wounds in the UK).
6th   7141 Rfn John Boyd (died of wounds in the UK), 3/5105 Rfn Ernest Frank Pinnington (died of wounds, formerly 7672 Lancers).
11th   5055 Rfn George William Jessop (formerly 8274 16th Lancers), 6815 Rfn Robert Warnock.
13th   1519 Rfn Daniel Hannen (died of wounds in the UK).

November 1915

7th   4990 Rfn Charles Christopher Corbin (died of wounds in the UK, age 17, formerly 8578 Lancers).

19th   9468 L/Cpl James Bohill (member of Irish National Volunteers, Drogheda).

20th   18996 Rfn James Brewster.

26th   6609 Rfn John Ledwidge (died of wounds).

27th   5779 Rfn Samuel Saulters (died of wounds in the UK).

28th   9002 L/Sgt Francis Doherty (*Fr Gill*: 'This morning we lost our MO, Dr McKenzie, who was most popular and loved by all. He was sent for to attend a wounded RE Officer. He set out at once and met the party ten minutes walk up the road. He began dressing his wounds and, whilst doing so, a shell fell killing him and Sgt Doherty. Both were killed on the spot. The latter was a splendid Catholic and was the greatest help to me ... The Sgt was absolutely devoted to the sick and wounded.'), 8644 Cpl George Erskine, 6637 L/Sgt James Mullan (died of wounds).

December 1915

15th   10357 Rfn Thomas O'Connor (shell fire).

23rd   5396 Rfn James Hutton.

25th   7161 Rfn John James Willy (died in the UK).

January 1916

3rd   10077 Rfn William Eustace (shell fire).

16th   5156 Rfn Sidney Tucker (died of wounds).

19th   4843 Sgt William Allely, 3904 Rfn Robert Coburn, 8478 Rfn Lawrence Cullen, 4843 Sgt Robert Flanagan, 7761 Cpl Thomas Geraghty, 1335 Rfn George McAdam, 5147 Rfn William Nesbitt, 13318 Rfn Walter John Nicholas, 9504 Rfn William Reavey, 8631 L/Cpl James Walsh, 10123 Rfn Matthew James Watson.

21st   5242 Rfn Moses Thompson (died of wounds).

22nd   6466 Rfn Patrick McDonnell.

23rd   4/6565 Rfn Thomas McTaggart (died in the UK).

27th   6644 L/Cpl Daniel Doyne, 2290 Rfn Moses Murphy.

28th   5884 Rfn Thomas Donnelly (died of wounds), 5090 Rfn James Hall (died of wounds).

February 1916

1st   5323 Rfn George Young (died of wounds).

March 1916

19th   7584 Rfn William Murphy.

22nd   7585 Rfn David Keating (died of wounds).

April 1916

23rd   8651 Cpl John Joseph Behan, 7412 Rfn Patrick James Lennon, 5172 Rfn Victor Willsher.

24th 7449 Rfn David Gillespie (died of wounds).

26th 7723 Rfn Thomas Joseph Byrne (formerly 100115 RFA), 9445 Rfn Joseph Church, 7829 Rfn Lawrence Cotton, 8833 CQMS Robert Gamble (killed during the Rebellion in Dublin; served in France from August 1914 and had been twice wounded), 14444 L/Cpl Patrick Gougerty, 9574 L/Cpl James Reid, 7372 Rfn Herbert Smith (age 17), 9157 Rfn Patrick White.

27th 6751 Rfn William Cardy, 8489 Rfn Owen Corrigan, 3912 Rfn Samuel Gribben, 5531 Rfn Samuel Irvine (Reservist. Friends School, Lisburn, War List: 'A widower, he was survived by three young children who appear to have been looked after by his parents'), 9387 Rfn Ebenezer Jones, 1642 Rfn William Lochrie, 3216 Rfn William Moore (brother of Rfn Robert Moore, 1st RIR, KIA 9.5.1915. Other brothers, George and Tommy, also served.), 10618 Cpl Henry Smith.

28th 6774 Rfn John Hanna, 8680 L/Cpl Henry Kilgariff (died of wounds), 7342 Rfn James Mackey.

29th 2287 Rfn Michael McMenamon (died of wounds).

May 1916

1st 8509 Rfn Christopher Gleeson (age 17).

3rd 7890 Rfn Thomas O'Bryne.

4th 5429 Rfn David John Whiteside.

5th 8741 Rfn Joseph Docherty (formerly 18077 R. Inniskilling Fus.), 6994 Rfn Patrick Joseph Dougherty, 5736 Rfn John McColl, 6400 Rfn John Morrison.

7th 8977 Rfn Martin Turley (died of wounds).

12th 5549 Rfn William Millar.

13th 9437 Cpl John Brown, 5353 Sgt Samuel O'Hara.

14th 7005 Rfn James Alexander Mooney.

15th 8818 Rfn Joseph Dillon, 8741 Rfn Joseph Docherty (formerly 18077 R. Inniskilling Fus.), 5007 Rfn Charles William Radford English (age 17, formerly 7598 Lancers), 7209 Rfn George McEnaney (died of wounds).

16th 7300 Rfn Randolph Albert Matthews (died of wounds), 7430 Rfn Christopher O'Connor (died in the UK).

17th 4982 Rfn William Thomas Carver (formerly 16187 Hussars), 5855 Rfn Francis Clarke, 11143 Rfn William Robert Crumlin, 4999 Rfn Arthur Dorrington (formerly 7467 Lancers), 6667 Rfn John Doyle, 1864 Rfn Patrick Johnson, 7194 Rfn James Kelly, 10839 Rfn Richard Little, 11327 Rfn Francis Neagle, 5095 Rfn Ernest Odell (formerly 7482 Lancers), 7581 Rfn Charles Pollock, 5381 Cpl Robert Poots (died of wounds. Brother of 798 Rfn William J. Poots, 15th RIR, KIA 21.3.1918.), 5361 Rfn Samuel Price, 11016 Rfn Patrick Smyth, 3929 L/Cpl William Somerville, 5121 Rfn James Wilson.

19th 16799 Rfn William Stephen Chapman (died of wounds), 8174 Rfn Edward McManus (died of wounds), 10461 Rfn Charles McNally, 5/5592 Rfn Aubrey Manson (*Banbridge Chronicle*, 23.6.1916, reported that his brothers Sidney and Clarence were also serving.), 6823 Rfn William Smyth, 5715 Rfn Patrick

Starkey, 5151 L/Cpl Arthur Edwin Thomas (formerly 16873 Hussars), 19998 Rfn John Tully.

20th   9010 Rfn James Dolan.

21st   11036 Rfn Archibald Moore (died of wounds).

29th   3381 Rfn Joseph Gilmore (died of wounds), 7546 Cpl Francis McGovern (died in the UK).

June 1916

2nd   7551 Rfn William Laverty (died of wounds).

11th   6989 Rfn Michael Low (died).

23rd   2946 Rfn Thomas Glenny (died in the UK).

30th   8454 Rfn John McLoughlin.

July 1916

1st   2318 Rfn James McGuinness, 2328 Rfn George Alfred Tanner.

7th   7778 Rfn Edward Anderson, 8560 Rfn Thomas Arnold, 7859 Rfn John Barr, 4633 Rfn Bernard Blaney, 8333 Rfn James Brennan, 6858 CSM John Alfred Byers MC, 8968 L/Cpl Edward Commack, 11014 Rfn David Walter Crothers (wounded in August 1915 while with 6th RIR), 7214 Sgt George Davis MM, 7147 Cpl Patrick Delaney, 8687 Sgt George Doherty, 5600 Rfn John Duffy, 8507 Rfn John Dunlea, 8994 Rfn Patrick Eagers (age 17), 10838 Rfn James Furphy, 2587 Rfn Robert Henderson, 7851 Rfn Michael Kenny, 18364 Rfn William Lamond, 10730 Rfn Andrew Larrissey, 6776 Rfn William Lowry, 1650 Rfn Matthew McCarrick, 5480 Rfn Leonard McComb, 7605 L/Cpl Robert James McGreechan, 8480 L/Cpl William McIlwaine, 5874 Rfn James McKinley, 6916 Rfn Alexander McRoberts, 1329 Rfn John James Matthews, 8647 Rfn John Moran, 6523 Rfn Robert Rainey, 7126 Rfn Robert Scott, 7764 Rfn John Slattery (formerly 100328 RFA), 7707 Rfn Michael Sullivan (formerly 100094 RFA), 5758 Rfn John Waterfield, 5173 Rfn William Winder.

8th   3/4412 Rfn William John Benson (*de Ruvigny*: 'Fifth son of James Benson of Bellevue, Shinrone, King's County, schoolmaster, by his wife, Catherine, daughter of James Wilson. Born Shinrone 15.11.1894. Educated at the Scriptural School there; was a grocer's assistant'), 4967 Rfn Reginald Lancelot Bush (formerly 6799 Lancers), 7421 Rfn Patrick Joseph Carroll, 7301 Rfn Charles Crymble, 7845 Rfn Thomas Cullen, 7876 Rfn George Doherty, 14435 Rfn Michael Ganley, 8137 Rfn Michael Keating, 5059 Rfn John Arthur King (formerly 16726 Hussars), 11245 Rfn William Lindsay, 9115 Rfn Harry McDowell, 7561 Rfn John McLoughlin, 8623 Rfn Thomas Mann, 7180 Rfn James Stevenson.

9th   6769 Rfn George Baxter, 1394 L/Cpl Edward Richard Beddoes, 6841 Rfn David Boyd, 9476 L/Cpl William Burns, 5233 Rfn Thomas Croke (died of wounds), 5086 Rfn Robert Dennison, 8981 Rfn Joseph Flynn, 5020 L/Cpl Ernest Stewart Garrett (formerly 6747 Lancers), 10469 Rfn John Garville, 5026 Rfn Percy Cecil Grant (formerly 8590 Reserve Cavalry Regt), 2935

Rfn William James Hawthorne (died of wounds), 8213 Sgt Thomas Howell, 8637 Rfn Robert Kernaghan (age 17), 3104 Rfn William King, 9126 Rfn Samuel Kirkpatrick, 5387 Rfn Patrick McAleavey, 11331 Rfn James Henry McCann, 8033 Rfn Oliver Milligan, 6832 Rfn Joseph Miskimmins, 8542 Cpl George Moore, 8016 Rfn John Moore, 5331 Rfn William Murphy, 5220 Rfn James O'Rourke, 6827 L/Cpl Patrick Quinn, 6810 Rfn Charles Reid, 10003 L/Cpl James Reilly, 10394 Rfn Joseph Ruxton, 2673 Rfn John Shannon, 10531 Cpl John Skinner (wounded at Gallipoli), 8866 Rfn Simon Thompson, 5795 Rfn Hugh Weir, 6505 Rfn Richard Williams, 8504 Rfn Christopher Wisely, 5178 L/Cpl John Godwin Wrigley (formerly 7425 Lancers), 7571 Rfn William Young.

15th 8465 Rfn Arthur Coupland (died of wounds), 4998 Rfn Herbert Glen Dormer (formerly 6327 Lancers), 11366 Rfn William James Gray (died of wounds), 8503 Rfn Michael Hughes, 5938 L/Cpl Robert Nixon Leckey, 10580 Rfn Charles McIlwrath, 8873 L/Cpl Thomas Nugent, 2465 Rfn James O'Hare.

16th 3852 Rfn James Crawford, 6740 Rfn Joseph Grant (died of wounds), 7199 Rfn William Hanna, 7716 Rfn Michael O'Sullivan (formerly 100094 RFA), 6779 Rfn John Rodgers (died of wounds), 5125 Cpl George Rule, 10110 Rfn John Sloan (died of wounds), 4923 Rfn John Walker.

18th 5555 Rfn Robert Millar Templeton (died of wounds).

19th 7285 Rfn Thomas Crumpton (died of wounds).

22nd 10031 Rfn Henry John Wallace (died as a POW).

23rd 5159 Rfn Ernest Henry Vicker (died of wounds, formerly 17th Lancers).

30th 8777 Rfn John Hughes (died of wounds).

August 1916

1st 7830 Rfn James Mearns, 9078 Rfn Patrick Morrison. (Both died of wounds in the UK.)

2nd 4/7298 Rfn Thomas W.A. Best.

8th 6363 Rfn Alexander Luke.

22nd 5766 Rfn Francis Adair.

28th 14424 Rfn Albert Holbrook, 5452 Rfn James McGagharty.

30th 10225 Cpl Edward Byrne, 5737 Rfn George Cleary (died of wounds), 9293 L/Cpl James McAuley, 4885 Cpl William McKee (died of wounds), 4849 Rfn Joseph Murray, 7897 Rfn Joseph Peters, 4876 L/Cpl John Prentice.

September 1916

4th 8273 Rfn Louis James (died of wounds, formerly 100154 RFA).

7th 8522 L/Cpl William Knox.

25th 5089 Rfn Percy Mullin (formerly 11468 Lancers).

27th 737 Rfn Andrew Brady (died of wounds), 5399 Rfn James George Jennings (Reservist, died of wounds).

28th 7854 Rfn William James Burns, 7909 Rfn Thomas Holohan. (The war diary recorded 3 killed.)

29th 19927 Rfn John Patrick O'Reilly, 4710 Rfn James Wright. (The war diary recorded 3 killed.)

30th 2/7245 Sgt George Love (died of wounds), 9645 Rfn James Lynn.

October 1916

2nd 5113 Rfn Frederick Pidden (died of wounds, formerly 6724 Lancers).

6th 8753 Rfn Peter Casey (died of wounds in the UK).

7th 3755 Rfn James Horner.

12th 9220 Rfn John Heron, 5235 Rfn Daniel Shannon.

16th 2697 Rfn James Fay (died of wounds).

17th 6581 L/Cpl Robert Fitzsimmons, 7460 Rfn James Grinen (died of wounds, formerly 11603 RIF).

19th 5418 L/Cpl Thomas William Hunte (died of wounds, formerly No. 124 British West Indian Regt. Born in British Guiana, where he was a customs officer.).

20th 1433 Rfn James Bolton (died of wounds), 2599 Rfn Michael Reilly, 6964 Cpl George Walsh (died of wounds).

21st 13550 Rfn Arthur Barker (died of wounds).

26th 10355 Rfn Patrick Cotter.

November 1916

19th 14543 Rfn George Graham, 8012 Rfn Michael McGrath.

24th 11548 Sgt Samuel Baird, 6699 Rfn Patrick Byrne, 8767 Rfn Thomas Gray (died of wounds), 7610 Rfn Francis Smith.

December 1916

1st 5075 Rfn Maurice Edwin Mann (died of wounds, formerly 6729 Lancers).

3rd 9077 L/Cpl Thomas Caldwell.

7th 5009 Rfn Samuel McBride (executed).

12th 5367 Rfn James Fitzsimmons.

14th 10255 Rfn John Doherty (died of wounds in the UK).

23rd 8227 Rfn Joseph Murphy (died).

January 1917

14th 5980 Rfn Robert Storey (died in the UK).

20th 10955 Rfn Joseph Breen (died of wounds).

22nd 5082 Rfn Walter Richard John Meakin (formerly 4025 Lancers).

23rd 44143 Rfn Frederick Sewell (died of wounds, formerly 6510 London Regt).

27th 3/16691 Rfn William McKeown.

28th 5962 Rfn Patrick Kennedy (died of wounds), 9500 Rfn Patrick O'Hara.

29th 3/8313 Rfn David Stone (died of wounds).

February 1917

–

March 1917
11th   4618 Rfn Thomas Delaney (died in the UK).

April 1917
4th   2/9641 Sgt George Alfred Reading MM.
15th   7922 Rfn William McGrady.
16th   5373 Rfn Samuel Craig.
18th   40941 Rfn Hugh Nicholl (formerly 31750 Hussars).
19th   4941 Rfn James Casey.
20th   2576 Cpl Frank Fox.
26th   9144 Rfn Stanislaus Edgerton (attached 74th TMB), 6833 Rfn John Miskelly.

May 1917
17th   (The war diary recorded 1 killed and 1 missing believed killed.)
18th   44102 Rfn Herbert James Brown (formerly 6148 London Regt), 5029 Cpl Daniel Hadwin (formerly 7064 16th Lancers), 9550 Rfn John Hart.
20th   4/7731 Cpl James O'Dwyer (died of wounds, formerly 100136 RFA).
21st   4/9711 Rfn James Kinney (died of wounds).

June 1917
6th   3/10181 Cpl James Breen (died of wounds).
7th   7453 Rfn David Ayre, 7849 Rfn James Bannon, 5554 Sgt William Joseph Campbell, 7106 Rfn Herbert Cathcart, 8205 Rfn Robert Coates, 5933 L/Cpl Richard Augustus Despard, 9997 Rfn William John Finn, 9926 Rfn David Fowler, 11593 Rfn Samuel Gibson, 2579 Rfn James Hughes (died of wounds), 9631 Rfn Samuel Jones, 9706 Rfn Daniel Lyons, 10654 Rfn Samuel McCaugherty (died of wounds), 9386 Rfn Francis William Mulligan, 7505 Rfn Patrick Joseph O'Donohoe, 44133 Rfn William Poole (formerly 5763 London Regt), 5393 Rfn Frederick Rawl (died of wounds), 10972 Rfn Samuel Sloan.
8th   18/1647 Rfn Samuel Wallace Anderson, 3965 Rfn John Elliott (died of wounds), 9465 Rfn George English (died of wounds, formerly 10419 Irish Guards), 9436 Rfn John Fitzpatrick (died of wounds), 3/5540 Rfn John Flaherty, 9400 Rfn John Foster (died of wounds, formerly 6002 ACC), 5160 L/Cpl Bertie Vokes (formerly 8398 Lancers), 8884 Rfn William Wilson (died of wounds).
9th   10269 L/Cpl Michael Murphy (died of wounds).
10th   4944 L/Cpl Frederick Thomas Athersuch, 44103 Rfn Frederick Barton (formerly 5949 London Regt), 3/7550 CQMS James Kelly, 40635 Rfn James Kelly (formerly 17729 Yorks. Regt), 7924 L/Cpl Paul Monnier, 9936 Rfn Christopher Mulligan, 5565 Rfn Thomas James Murphy, 5939 Cpl William Lawrence Pitkethley, 44159 Rfn George Daniel Willis (died of wounds, formerly 5783 London Regt).
16th   4184 Rfn Thomas James Mitchell (died of wounds, A Coy).
18th   9402 Rfn Richard Bready (formerly 6803 ACC), 4/2977 Sgt John Cullen (died of wounds), 389 Rfn Alexander Doggart, 9470 Rfn Thomas John Gault, 9489 Rfn William Henry Hart.

20th 5823 Rfn Robert Boyd. (The war diary recorded 2 killed.)

22nd 9704 Rfn Bernard McAllister (age 17), 8471 Rfn Francis Macken, 5358 Rfn Alfred Noble (died of wounds).

July 1917

2nd 7102 Rfn John Millar (died of wounds).

17th 42634 Rfn William Charles Canton (formerly S/23759 Rifle Bde), 42635 Rfn William Henry Collen (died of wounds, formerly S/23757 Rifle Bde), 6846 Rfn James McCullough, 42477 Rfn George Wood (formerly R/34801 KRRC).

18th 10349 Rfn John McLoughlin (died of wounds).

23rd 42627 Rfn John Tumber (died of wounds, formerly S/24321 Rifle Bde).

August 1917

5th 9595 L/Cpl James Leech, 2/7303 Rfn Patrick McAteer, 3977 Rfn Robert John Patterson.

6th 42494 Rfn George Albert Brookes, 2/42500 Rfn Audrey Hamilton Harcourt Burrage (died of wounds), 7810 Rfn Samuel Colhoun, 9495 Rfn George Cross (died of wounds, formerly 13032 RIF), 42602 Rfn Thomas Ford (formerly SS/6393 RASC), 4434 Rfn Patrick Johnston (died of wounds), 10528 Rfn James McClelland (age 17), 9021 L/Cpl Joseph O'Reilly (died of wounds), 7703 Rfn George William Turner (died of wounds, formerly 100065 RFA).

7th 2772 Rfn John Collins, 6667 Rfn Felix Doran (died of wounds), 3/8725 Sgt Frank Elliott (died of wounds. His two brothers were KIA: Rfn Joseph Elliott, 13th RIR, 4.8.1917, and Pte William Elliott, 2nd Inniskilling Fus., 26.8.1914.), 8152 Sgt James Henry Taylor.

8th 10556 Rfn Andrew Campbell (formerly S/19111 Argyll & Sutherland Highlanders), 5423 Rfn Stanley Curran (*Banbridge Chronicle*, 1.9.1917: 'Deceased's father is serving with the Transport attached to the [9th] Royal Irish Rifles. A brother, Rifleman James Curran [767, 13th RIR], was killed on July 1st of last year at the battle of the Somme, and another brother, David, is an A.B. in the Navy and has seen active service in the North Sea and Mediterranean.'), 2594 L/Cpl Richard Whitworth.

9th 44109 Rfn George Basil Edser (formerly 6411 London Regt), 10907 Rfn Daniel McKie, 42509 Rfn Charles Laurence Wells (formerly R/22767 KRRC).

10th 7464 Rfn Leo Boyle, 7906 Rfn Samuel Brown (*Northern Constitution*, 18.8.1917: 'He had been almost two years in khaki and was lately home on recuperation from frost-bite.'), 42633 Rfn Arthur Ernest Buckoke (formerly S/25100 Rifle Bde), 4972 Rfn Michael Callahan (formerly 10325 Lancers), 10455 Rfn John Francis Cooney, 8923 Rfn Daniel Cull, 6718 L/Cpl Joseph Dixon, 6920 L/Cpl James Donaldson (died of wounds), 9412 Rfn John Thomas Douglas, 10423 Rfn Joseph Dunne, 5553 Rfn William Gault, 10663 Rfn John Greer, 10827 Rfn John Hamilton (formerly 6919 Argyll & Sutherland Highlanders), 5681 Rfn Thomas Hannigan, 42614 Rfn George

Richard Hearn (formerly R/28626 KRRC), 42501 L/Cpl Frederick Henry James (formerly 29513 Gloucester Regt), 9789 Rfn Charles Lavery, 40953 Rfn Edward Lennox (formerly 24918 Hussars), 4971 Rfn William McCormack, 9716 Cpl Edward McLoughlin, 9697 Rfn Patrick Maguire (age 17), 8996 Rfn Harry Marsden, 44125 Rfn Sydney James Mitchenall (formerly 6442 London Regt), 40964 Rfn John Moncur (formerly A/632 RASC), 43022 Cpl Isaac Moore (formerly 18859 Inniskilling Fus.), 9636 Rfn George O'Brien, 7513 L/Cpl Andrew O'Conner, 42643 Rfn Albert Pipe (formerly 30560 KRRC), 5829 Rfn Michael Sheridan (died of wounds), 44147 Rfn George Smith (formerly 6414 London Regt), 7896 Rfn Robert White, 9389 Rfn Kennedy Wilkinson (formerly 7341 Army Cyclist Corps), 9526 Rfn Frederick Williams (Jewish).

11th 42641 Rfn James Cutler (formerly R/26803 KRRC), 5027 Rfn William Edmund Gronow (formerly 11073 Lancers), 7667 Rfn John Jones (formerly 99931 RFA), 9579 L/Cpl James McDonagh, 9273 Rfn John McPhillips (died of wounds), 8441 Cpl Francis Moore (died of wounds), 8962 Cpl Lawrence Leo Murphy, 42622 Rfn Claude Oliver (formerly S/21949 Rifle Bde).

12th 9976 Rfn Thomas Calpin, 10384 Rfn Michael Loughran (died of wounds), 10684 Rfn Samuel Lynas, 5845 Rfn Daniel McBride (died of wounds).

15th 47048 Rfn Archie Elliott (formerly S/23309 Rifle Bde).

16th 42651 Rfn Edward Sidney Gask (formerly S/20735 Rifle Bde), 42619 Rfn Percy Henry Arthur Kent (formerly S/21661 Rifle Bde), 41880 L/Cpl Gustave Wilson (formerly 19269 Essex Regt).

17th 8288 Rfn John Fagan, 45271 Rfn John James Woods (formerly 269860, 7th The King's Liverpool Regt).

18th 5619 CSM Robert H. Wallace (died of wounds, C Coy, served in the South African War).

24th 42476 Rfn Richard Brandon Read (died of wounds, formerly S/29012 Rifle Bde).

29th 5264 Rfn Thomas Henry Turkington (died of wounds).

September 1917

4th 7626 Rfn Horace Webb (died of wounds, formerly 77037 RFA).

6th 42615 Rfn William Hirst (formerly R/12275 KRRC), 49945 Sgt James Henry Anderson Watson (formerly 2318 RASC).

8th 6874 Rfn Benjamin Fox (died in the UK).

9th 5778 Rfn James Barkley (died in the UK).

29th 17/79 Rfn Alex Crawford.

October 1917

7th 18306 Rfn James O'Donoghue (died of wounds).

17th 11408 Sgt George McClenaghan (died of wounds).

25th 7943 Rfn Henry Corlett.

November 1917

21st   47124 Rfn Arthur James Allan (died of wounds, formerly 6924 Wilts Regt).

23rd   40029 L/Cpl Joseph Carton MM, 9406 Cpl James Clancy, 7660 Sgt Thomas
Costley (formerly 99917 RFA), 43023 Rfn Thomas Courtney (formerly 2971
R. Inniskilling Fus.), 7006 Rfn Walter Erskine, 7356 L/Cpl David Fitzgerald,
10436 Rfn Walter Holmes, 8235 Rfn George Hutchinson, 4155 L/Cpl Albert
LeFeuvre (from Jersey), 11052 Rfn James McCullouch, 44120 Rfn Edmund
Mahoney (formerly 5624 London Regt), 6740 L/Cpl Patrick Massey, 9493
Rfn Reginald Arthur Mauger (from Jersey), 4359 Rfn Joseph Moy (from
Jersey), 7898 Rfn John O'Toole, 4834 Rfn William Robinson (died), 7911
L/Cpl Albert Smith, 10296 Rfn James White.

24th   8359 Rfn William Wales (died of wounds).

December 1917

2nd   5259 Rfn James Neill.

24th   8367 Rfn Thomas Rochfort (died in the UK).

January 1918

14th   5717 Rfn Robert Costello MM (died of wounds).

16th   40669 Rfn Albert Edwin Osborne (formerly 10201 Yorks Regt).

February 1918

27th   7566 Rfn Edward Rooney.

March 1918

3rd   40949 Rfn James Petrie Caithness (formerly 2496 RASC).

11th   10299 Rfn William Casey.

20th   4849 CSM David Ferris (died of wounds).

21st   3968 Rfn Joshua Brush (served in the South African War), 5568 L/Cpl James
Buchanan, 43780 L/Cpl William Charles Cook (died, formerly 7006 London
Regt), 10551 Rfn Andrew Gibson, 40010 L/Cpl Alfred House MM (formerly
22815 RIF), 5631 L/Cpl Hugh O'Neill, 9244 Rfn Thomas Phillips (died,
formerly 5944 ACC), 43980 Rfn Harold Victor Thomas Reynolds (formerly
6183 London Regt), 9584 Rfn William Taplin, 5554 Rfn William Topping.

22nd   40958 Rfn Maurice Llewellyn Joseph (formerly 2246 RASC), 8902 Cpl Robert
Patterson, 1441 Rfn John Ryan (died of wounds).

23rd   3598 Rfn Thomas Breen, 49949 Rfn James Petrie Caitness (formerly 2496
RASC), 7657 Rfn Albert Cartwright (formerly 99914 RFA), 188 Rfn John
Graham (formerly 8th/9th RIR), 6469 Sgt George Esaud Jennings, 19987
Rfn John McLean, 9583 L/Cpl Henry Quigley MM and bar, 8582 Sgt John
Smyth.

24th   47612 Cpl James Oliver Armiger (formerly 3758 Hussars), 47613 Rfn Ralph
Baker (formerly S/34219 RASC), 1690 Rfn Harry Barham, 10516 Rfn Victor
Barnes, 11248 Rfn Henry Bell, 1379 Rfn John Best, 47667 Rfn Frederick

Bonner (formerly S/30598 RASC), 5865 Rfn Michael Butler, 7706 Rfn Philip Campbell (died), 47633 Rfn William James Carter (formerly S/4/994879 RASC), 5/42596 Rfn Francis Chadwick (formerly SS/20298 RASC), 4981 Cpl Lawrence Clarke MM (formerly 13229 Hussars), 10350 Rfn Henry Clifford, 9859 Rfn Timothy Coleman, 10762 Rfn Joseph Collins, 43530 Rfn Albert William Cotton (formerly 7082 London Regt), 45277 Rfn Charles Crawley (formerly 8733 King's Liverpool Regt), 1274 Sgt Thomas Crowe, 5610 Rfn James Patrick Curran, 47672 Rfn Arthur Eric Curtis (formerly SS/1213 RASC), 47637 Rfn John Harry Daniels (formerly S/4/094580 RASC), 10401 Rfn Frank Donaghy, 5881 Rfn William Donnelly, 10532 Rfn William Duggan, 42475 Rfn Frank Fewtrell (formerly TR/13/71548 110th I.R), 41894 Rfn Harry William Freeman MM (formerly 26798 Northamptonshire Regt), 11006 Rfn James Furphey, 47641 Rfn Thomas Edward Garton (formerly S4/070849 RASC), 10030 Rfn John James Girvan, 8517 Rfn Thomas Green, 5930 Rfn Albert Griffen (died of wounds), 43858 Rfn Charles Hamilton (formerly 6533 London Regt), 47606 Rfn Amos Harrop (formerly 131951 RGA), 47646 Rfn Horace Heath (formerly S4/044631 RASC), 6127 Rfn Stephen Heneghan, 10360 L/Cpl Mark Hinksman, 6469 Rfn Robert Hopps, 9843 Rfn Edward Humphreys, 47604 Rfn William Hurst (formerly 32080 Leicestershire Regt), 4881 Rfn Thomas Johnston (formerly 2186 NIH), 5920 Rfn James Kennedy, 6987 Rfn Michael James Kirby, 14910 Rfn John Lawlor, 45291 Rfn William Lee (formerly 8737 The King's Liverpool Regt), 5848 Cpl James McAleese, 6910 Rfn Frederick McCallum, 20640 Rfn Hugh McConnell, 9384 Sgt Andrew McCormick (formerly 11th/13th RIR), 10857 Rfn John McGill, 9776 Rfn Hugh McGinn, 3875 Rfn John McGivern (died), 9307 Rfn Thomas McGivern, 40970 Rfn Patrick McGlynn (formerly 31774 Reserve Cavalry Regt), 8485 L/Cpl Peter McLoughlin, 528 Rfn Francis McTier, 249 Rfn Robert McVea, 6157 Rfn Edward Magee, 7916 Rfn John Magill, 9438 Rfn John Maloney, 47620 Rfn Andrew Marshall (formerly S4/128500 RASC), 47618 Rfn Archie Matthews (died of wounds, formerly S4/125238 RASC), 6174 Rfn William Matthews, 13274 Rfn Richard Mellon MM, 4606 Rfn Samuel Monks, 1392 Rfn Thomas Morrison, 41906 Rfn John William Munton (formerly 30886 Northamptonshire Regt), 11369 Rfn David Murray, 40644 Rfn John Thomas Onions (formerly 12483 Yorks Regt), 43951 Rfn William James Osborne (formerly 6411 London Regt), 10306 Rfn Daniel O'Callaghan (died), 41776 Rfn Frederick Albert Pomroy (formerly 5197 London Regt), 465 Rfn Edward Redmond, 20677 Rfn David Robinson, 10508 Rfn Christopher Scally, 10151 Rfn William Seeley, 4940 Rfn Thomas Silcock, 8228 Rfn Arthur Small, 4787 Rfn John Smith, 41872 Rfn Martin Elijah Spooner (formerly 32930 Essex Regt), 40019 Rfn Albert Staunton (formerly 3496 RIF), 47622 Rfn Charles Henry Vaughan (formerly S4/039827 RASC), 5898 Rfn Samuel Voga (died), 6048 Rfn Henry Wakefield, 4846 Rfn Edmund White, 47069 Rfn Arthur William Widdicombe (formerly T4/092835 RASC), 47608 Rfn William John

Willett (formerly T4/035788 RASC), 9101 L/Cpl John Wilson, 2949 Rfn John Winsley, 17089 L/Cpl Christopher Wood, 8297 Rfn Joseph Woods, 869 Rfn Samuel Young MM.

26th   5507 Rfn Alfred Savage (died of wounds).

27th   7440 Rfn William Belton (died of wounds), 1674 Rfn George Chambers (died of wounds), 9790 Rfn Francis Gourley (died of wounds), 8838 Rfn John Jiles (died of wounds), 47649 Rfn Alfred Reginald Larner (died of wounds, formerly S/4/070387 RASC), 6039 Rfn Walter McAuley (died of wounds), 26 Rfn Samuel McSheffrey (died of wounds as a POW. A member of LOL 930, he had five children), 9993 Rfn Robert Patton (died).

28th   8967 Cpl John Brady (died of wounds), 9065 Rfn Daniel Butler, 41876 Rfn William Ratcliff (died of wounds, formerly 24050 Essex Regt), 47658 Rfn Charles Sargeant (died of wounds, formerly S4/058474 RASC).

30th   11616 Rfn Robert McCoy.

31st   43758 Rfn Frederick Walter Carter (died of wounds, formerly 7037 London Regt), 47128 Rfn William Cragg (died, formerly R/4/066858 RASC).

April 1918

2nd   47629 Rfn John Cuthill (died of wounds, formerly S/4/094827 RASC), 45275 L/Cpl William Halton (died of wounds, formerly 8696 KLR).

4th   9461 Rfn John Bond (died of wounds).

10th   8480 Rfn Samuel Cronin.

11th   7567 Rfn William Fryers (died of wounds).

13th   20/85 Rfn Wason Ross.

16th   5709 L/Cpl William McGarrell MM (died of wounds).

17th   54232 Rfn Stephen Frederick Brooks (accidentally killed).

20th   9147 Rfn John McKinley (died).

22nd   576 L/Cpl Robert Foreman (died of wounds), 9/43519 Rfn Hubert Frank Horwood (died of wounds, formerly 4029 London Regt).

May 1918

4th   5480 Rfn Timothy Dougherty (died in the UK).

7th   54270 Rfn Edward Eke (formerly S/36111 Rifle Bde).

9th   5652 Rfn Walter Graydon, 54121 L/Cpl Harold Musgrave Stone.

10th   10170 Rfn Nicholas Chapman (POW, died in Switzerland), 42248 Rfn Walter Lion, 1206 Rfn Hugh McCullough.

11th   54024 Rfn William Whiston (died of wounds, formerly R/21020 KRRC).

29th   4432 Rfn Michael Price (died).

30th   8636 Rfn Daniel McLernon (died in the UK).

June 1918

1st   54239 Rfn William Charles Brown (*War Diary*: 'Accidentally killed whilst investigation of a stoppage in a Lewis Gun was being carried out.'), 44936 Rfn Alfred Henry Egan (died of dysentery, formerly 3934 London Regt).

3rd 47673 Rfn Sydney Cowley (died, formerly S/4/109945 RASC).

5th 7026 Rfn Daniel Rodgers (died as a POW).

10th 7663 L/Cpl Arthur Spencer (died of wounds, formerly 99926 RFA).

14th 41654 Rfn Harry Hughes (died, formerly 28197 East Lancs. Regt).

22nd 41832 Rfn Charles Frank Older (died as a POW, formerly 6135 London Regt), 4931 Rfn William George Reilly (died of wounds as a POW).

24th 7353 Rfn Thomas Ellis (died of wounds as a POW).

26th 993 Rfn William Crothers (died as a POW).

27th 54172 Rfn Charles William Houghton (died of wounds, attached XI Corps Works Bn, formerly R/42361 KRRC).

July 1918

1st 1914 Cpl William Bickerstaff (died as POW in Germany).

2nd 40934 Rfn Christopher McAvoy (died, formerly 24912 Hussars).

14th 7362 Rfn Patrick McEvoy (died of wounds as a POW).

15th 19467 Rfn Isaac Doole (died of wounds), 10013 Rfn Henry Nolan (died as a POW).

19th 6917 Rfn Samuel Nelson (died of wounds), 45855 Cpl Barnard Henry George Treasure (died of wounds, formerly S/4/070287 RASC).

23rd 54233 Rfn Victor Wallace Broom (died of wounds), 20182 Rfn Thomas Smith.

24th 41564 Rfn Cyril Stephen Harmer (died of wounds, formerly 5978 Norfolk Regt).

25th 8991 Rfn John Johnston (died of wounds as a POW).

30th 14207 Rfn Samuel James Clarke, 54204 Rfn Stanley Collins (formerly TR/9/25465 45th T.R. Bn), 4902 Sgt Robert James Gibson, 1506 Rfn David McIlroy, 54020 Rfn William Smith (formerly R/1231 KRRC).

August 1918

8th 54206 Cpl Arthur John Edwards (formerly 7th RIR).

9th 7/41857 Rfn George E. Westrop (died, formerly 24616 Suffolk Regt).

10th 12622 Rfn John Campbell (died).

16th 54126 Rfn Arthur Burton (died of wounds, formerly 12847 KRRC).

17th 1645 Rfn Francis Sydney Barker (died of wounds), 54195 Rfn Charles Monk (died of wounds, formerly R/42396 KRRC).

18th 4555 Rfn William Browne MM, 6283 Rfn Samuel Cordner, 14252 Rfn Samuel Courtney, 47640 Rfn Ernest Richard Faircloth (died, formerly S/255262 RASC)

19th 3105 Rfn Thomas Boulton (died of wounds), 42245 Rfn Alfred Percy Kent.

20th 54032 Rfn Herbert Thomas Allen (died of wounds, formerly 37402 KRRC), 54181 Rfn John Robert Jacques (died of wounds, formerly R/42365 KRRC).

22nd 10186 L/Cpl Hugh Cecil Scott (POW, died of pneumonia in Switzerland).

24th 2316 Rfn John Walker (died).

30th 4209 L/Sgt Robert Simms (died in the UK).

September 1918

6th   10025 Rfn Joseph Adams, 9162 Rfn Matthew Andrews, 52479 Rfn George
Baldwin (formerly 41114 R. Warwickshire Regt), 43154 Rfn George Edward
Barlow, 54002 Rfn Arthur Harold Blake, 17285 Rfn Ernest Bloxsom, 42655
Rfn Frederick George Burgess (formerly S/31645 Rifle Bde), 5261 Cpl Percy
Burke (served with 2nd RIR from September 1914. His brother, 14137 Sgt
Frederick G. Burke, 11th RIR, was KIA 1.7.1916.), 54087 Rfn Leslie John
Burnett, 54143 Rfn George Sidney Coburn, 20889 Rfn David Crothers, 54264
Rfn Walter Dowie (formerly S/36030 Rifle Bde), 7902 L/Cpl Thomas
Ferguson, 47126 Rfn George Forsythe (formerly 168 RIR), 520 Rfn Albert
Gilmore, 5799 Rfn Thomas Gore, 54098 Rfn Frederick Gregory (formerly
R/42206 Rifle Bde), 20835 Rfn John Charles Hewitt, 10038 L/Cpl James
Hillen, 41848 Rfn George Percy Howard (formerly 5561 London Regt), 17937
Sgt Lester Jackson, 5915 Rfn James Kavanagh MM (age 17), 11364 Rfn James
McCandless, 767 Rfn Thomas McMahon, 15572 Rfn Thomas Maxwell,
44131 Rfn Jesse Parsons (formerly 6324 London Regt), 10523 Rfn Aubrey
Patterson, 5971 Cpl Josiah Rush, 7840 Rfn Alexander Scott, 43331 Rfn Walter
Henry Short (formerly 4834 London Regt and was a postman in West
Kensington.), 1720 Rfn Robert Smyth, 43337 Rfn Samuel Spicer (formerly
4836 London Regt), 13542 Rfn Robert Stewart, 75 Rfn Joseph Uprichard,
3753 L/Cpl Edward McKindry Walker MM, 6390 Rfn Richard Williams (died
of wounds), 44164 L/Cpl. Arthur Thomas Wright.

7th   44954 Rfn William Henry Cramer (formerly 8194 London Regt), 9181 Rfn
Edward Friel (died of wounds), 9786 Rfn Patrick Hughes (died of wounds),
44383 Rfn Joseph Massicks (formerly 20315 KORLR).

8th   9636 Sgt Ernest George Keen.

9th   14379 Rfn George Donnelly, 20271 Rfn Charles Major (died of wounds).

12th   54067 Rfn Charles Gerald O'Connell (formerly 1918 KRRC).

18th   959 Rfn John Stevenson Hartley.

23rd   9/15244 Sgt Robert McCullough DCM (died of wounds)

27th   8862 L/Cpl Hugh Magee (died of pneumonia).

28th   12575 Cpl Edward Barnes MM.

30th   11079 Rfn Frederick Herbert Allison, 2799 Rfn Michael Byrne, 1421 Rfn
Thomas Docherty, 10593 Rfn James Hayes, 7506 Rfn George Jones (died of
wounds, B Coy), 20346 Rfn John Kane (died of wounds), 44116 Rfn John
Latter (formerly 6449 London Regt), 2399 Rfn Wesley McConnell, 22875
Rfn George McGhee, 22682 Rfn James McGovern, 54211 Rfn Frederick
Stanley Richardson (formerly S/36079 Rifle Bde), 6065 Sgt John Albert
Saunders, 54129 Rfn Charles Smith (formerly 12876 KRRC), 41834 Rfn John
Stillman (formerly 6678 London Regt).

October 1918

1st   42662 Rfn John Clive Alford, 1120 Rfn Michael Donovan (died of wounds),
54173 Rfn William Frederick Husk (formerly R/42304 KRRC), 22871 Rfn

John Kirkpatrick, 19706 Rfn James Gabriel Murdock, 20876 Rfn John Scullion (age 17).

2nd   9404 Rfn Edward Dixon (formerly 11461 ACC), 54030 Rfn Samuel Hainsworth Pickup (formerly G/6212 KRRC).

3rd   5843 L/Cpl William Russell (died of wounds).

4th   9999 L/Cpl Alfred Wallace Harry Edwards, L/54014 Rfn Joseph Martin (died of wounds, formerly A/201771 KRRC).

5th   47664 Rfn Isaac Bowers (formerly S/4/040972 RASC), 8922 Rfn John Gittens (died of wounds as a POW), 3036 Rfn Robert Nelson (died of wounds), 54026 L/Cpl Walter Bruce Short (formerly SR/218467 RASC), 52635 Rfn Edward Tooze (formerly 41275 R. Warwickshire Regt), 6220 CSM Thomas Bell Willis.

6th   54178 Rfn Edwin Clarence Hawkridge (died of wounds, formerly R/42394 KRRC).

7th   10352 Rfn Michael McGibbon (died of wounds).

11th   54010 Rfn Harry Gaskell (died of wounds, formerly R16499 KRRC),

54066 Rfn Norman Strafford Moorhouse (died of wounds, formerly R/42246 KRRC).

12th   8785 Rfn Thomas Murphy (died of wounds as a POW).

14th   20661 Rfn Ernest Ellison, 40940 Rfn James Edward McCauley (died of wounds, formerly 31704 Hussars), 54080 Rfn Edwin Vaughan Williams (formerly TR/9/26141 45th T.R.).

15th   13959 Rfn William John Arneill, 54145 Rfn Albert Callcut, 54205 Rfn Albert William Darby (formerly 316433 RASC), 9388 Sgt Hugh Fraser Henderson, 15406 Rfn Thomas David McFarland, 54069 Rfn Alfred Noel Pearson (died of wounds, formerly R/42247 KRRC), 6668 Cpl Patrick Tyer (died of wounds).

16th   54038 Rfn Harry Maynard Chandler (served as Bellham, died of wounds), 5051 Rfn Frank Taylor Hill (died of wounds, formerly 5527 Lancers), 11336 Rfn Richard Scullion.

19th   18795 Cpl Robert Smyth (died of wounds).

21st   54128 Rfn Frederick James Jennings (formerly 13079 KRRC), 22161 Rfn Hugh Lowry, 54196 Rfn William Hatherly Meier (formerly R/42315 KRRC).

22nd   40201 Rfn Robert Ackinson (formerly R/21548 KRRC), 54221 Rfn William Bartlett, 23994 Rfn James Morris Bauld, 47557 Rfn William John Brown (formerly 33105 Suffolk Regt), 11049 Rfn Matthew Carrol MM, 54268 Rfn Charles John Edwards (formerly S/35956 Rifle Bde), 8796 Cpl James Graham, 14880 Cpl David John Hewitt, 54177 Rfn William George Mark Hill (formerly R/42363 KRRC), 10365 Rfn Samuel Hutchinson MM, 54109 Rfn John Denis Lonergan (formerly R/42215 KRRC), 22331 Rfn William McClean, 2450 Rfn Thompson Mathers, 44150 Rfn Edgar Thomas (formerly 6199 London Regt), 52642 Rfn Clarence Hubert Westley (formerly 41282 R. Warwickshire Regt).

23rd   11050 Rfn Allan Edward Baker, 43448 Sgt Hugh Christie MM (died of wounds, formerly 1586 R. Scots), 11121 Rfn Thomas Little (died of wounds).

24th 43589 L/Cpl George Gillings (died of wounds, formerly 6283 London Regt).
25th 42621 Rfn Robert George Lee (died of wounds, formerly R/28776 KRRC).
30th 50183 Rfn James Frederick Braund, 47645 Rfn Albert Hooley (died in the UK), 5/5210 Rfn Patrick Sterling (died in the UK).

November 1918
3rd   8462 Sgt James Lynch (died in the UK).
11th 583 Rfn William Irwin (died of wounds).
18th 4/6971 Rfn James Donnelly (died in Germany).
28th 54163 Rfn Arthur Edward Fry (died of wounds).

December 1918
16th 7688 Rfn Hugh Traynor (died).
23rd 54065 Rfn Albert Francis McEwen (died of wounds, formerly R/42181 KRRC).

January 1919
22nd 40057 Rfn Joseph Taylor (died in the UK).

March 1919
1st   47638 Rfn Bertram John Dean (died in the UK, repatriated POW).

APPENDIX III: MEDAL ROLL

The following list of awards and decorations was compiled from the War Diary and the regimental histories. It includes those made after the diary ended or awarded after the person had left the battalion. I have excluded awards that were obviously for service with another unit.

OFFICERS

2/Lt. F. Adams	MC 15.2.19.
Major J.W. Alston	Mentioned in Despatches 22.6.15.
Lt. A.M. Anderson	MC 3.6.19. French Croix de Guerre avec etoile en Bronze 19.6.19.
Major C.M.L. Becher	Mentioned in Despatches 9.12.14.
Lt.-Col. W.D. Bird	Mentioned in Despatches 9.12.14. French Legion d'Honneur, Croix d'Officier 3.11.14.
2/Lt. A.A. Broomfield	MC 15.3.16.
Lt. L. Browne	MC 18.2.15. Mentioned in Despatches 17.2.15.
Lt. G.W. Calverley	DSO 25.8.16. Mentioned in Despatches 4.1.17.
Capt. V.L.S. Cowley	Mentioned in Despatches 9.12.14.
Lt. G.V. Fitzgerald	Mentioned in Despatches 14.1.1915.
QM & Capt. H.W. Foster	MC 1.1.18. Mentioned in Despatches 4.1.17, 25.5.17.
Major H.R. Goodman	Mentioned in Despatches 9.12.14, 25.5.17, 12.12.17. DSO 17.9.17.
Lt. W.C. Hill	MC 12.3.17.
Major S.S. Hill-Dillon	DSO 18.2.15. Mentioned in Despatches 9.12.14.
Capt. E.J. Hoare	MC 10.8.21.
Lt. W.F. Hunter	MC 1.2.19.
Capt. H.R.H. Ireland	MC 15.3.16.
Capt. R.T. Jeffares	Mentioned in Despatches 21.12.17.
2/Lt. M.C. Kearns	Mentioned in Despatches 17.2.15.
Lt. A.E. Kemp	MC 15.2.19.
Lt. E.W.V. Leach	Mentioned in Despatches 4.1.17.
Capt. S.E. Lewis, RAMC	Mentioned in Despatches 9.12.14.
2/Lt. E.B.K. Loyd	Mentioned in Despatches 27.5.17.
2/Lt. T. McAlindon	MC 26.9.17.
Lt. J.B. McArevey	MC 26.9.17.
2/Lt. M.A. McFerran	MC 4.2.18.
Capt. W.A. Malone	MC 26.7.18.
2/Lt. R.B. Marriott-Watson	MC 1.1.17.
Lt. H. Marshall	Mentioned in Despatches 9.7.19.
2/Lt. J. Martin	Mentioned in Despatches 14.1.15.
Capt. C.L. Master	Mentioned in Despatches 9.12.14.

Lt. M.E.J. Moore	MC 27.3.18
2/Lt. J.A. Moreland	MC 4.2.18.
Lt. W.P. Moss	MC 1.1.17.
2/Lt. N.B. Munn	MC 16.9.18.
Lt. P. Murphy	Mentioned in Despatches 21.12.17.
Capt. G.S. Norman	MC 1.1.17. Mentioned in Despatches 22.6.15.
Lt. R.J. O'Lone	Mentioned in Despatches 1.1.16.
Lt. G.W. Panter	Mentioned in Despatches 1.6.16.
Capt. R. deR. Rose	MC 26.9.17. BAR 16.9.18. Mentioned in Despatches 16.9.18.
2/Lt. C. Rule	French Croix de Guerre 19.6.19.
Lt. R.C. Scott	MC 1.2.19.
Lt. G.B.J. Smyth	Mentioned in Despatches 28.12.18.
Major C.R.W. Spedding	Mentioned in Despatches 9.12.14.
2/Lt. J.N.G. Stewart	MC 15.10.18.
Capt. W.B. Teele	MC 1.2.19.
Capt. T.J.C.C. Thompson	DSO 16.8.17.
Capt. C.J. Wakefield	Mentioned in Despatches 1.1.16.
Lt. D.B. Walkington	MC 15.10.18.
2/Lt. T.C. Wallis	MC 26.9.17.
2/Lt. R.S. Walsh	MC 26.9.17.
Capt. R. Watts	MC BAR 1.2.19. French Croix de Guerre a l'Ordre Division 9.12.18.
Lt. A.N. Whitfeld	Mentioned in Despatches 9.12.14.
Capt. C.F. Wilkins	MC 1.1.17. DSO 1.1.18. French Croix de Guerre 19.6.19. Mentioned in Despatches 21.12.17, 20.12.18.
Lt. E. Workman	MC 15.3.16.
2/Lt. J. McH. Wright	MC 1.2.19.
Lt. R.A. Young	MC 16.8.17.

OTHER RANKS

13956 Cpl H. Anderson	MSM 6.9.19.
7795 Rfn A. Atkinson	MM 18.10.17.
40202 Rfn A. Atcheson	Mentioned in Despatches 9.7.19.
43492 Rfn J. Bain	MM 11.2.19.
8222 Sgt J. Barrett	Belgian Croix de Guerre 4.9.19.
4948 Rfn E. Bartaby	MM 18.10.17.
6985 Rfn W.R. Baxter	Mentioned in Despatches 9.7.19.
13990 L/Cpl B. Beattie	MM 29.8.18.
6876 Cpl W. Beckett	DCM 26.7.17.
8651 L/Cpl J.J. Behan	Mentioned in Despatches 9.12.14.
4951 Sgt G.H. Bellis	DCM 19.10.17.

4953 Sgt R. Bevan	MM 18.10.17.
7473 QMS B. Booth	MSM 1.1.17. Mentioned in Despatches 21.12.17.
9/14140 Sgt R.B. Bowers	MSM 3.6.19.
902 Rfn P. Boyd	MM 11.2.19.
4647 Sgt T. Burney	MSM 18.1.19.
6858 CSM J.A. Byers	MC 27.7.16.
40949 Rfn J.P. Caithness	MM 21.8.17.
5111 Rfn J. Caldwell	MM 21.8.17.
7436 Rfn W.J.A. Campbell	BAR to DCM 30.1.16.
9975 Rfn L. Carolan	Mentioned in Despatches 17.2.15.
7991 Rfn J. Carroll	Mentioned in Despatches 22.6.15.
7991 CSM J. Carroll	MSM 17.2.17.
11049 Rfn M. Carroll	MM 11.2.19.
7752 Cpl H. Carthy	DCM 15.3.16. MSM 1.3.19.
43448 Sgt H. Christie	MM 11.2.19.
4981 L/Cpl L. Clarke	MM 18.10.17.
5164 Sgt J. Clarke	MM 14.5.19.
8078 Sgt J. Coleman	Mentioned in Despatches 1.1.16.
9397 Cpl P. Conlon	DCM 16.8.17.
8229 Sgt M. Corr	MSM 17.6.18.
5717 Rfn R. Costello	MM 18.10.17.
43023 Rfn T. Courtney	MM 18.10.17.
7165 Sgt J.J. Crozier	MM 21.8.17.
3383 Sgt A. Cullen	MM 11.2.19.
7759 Rfn J. Curtin	DCM 16.8.17.
7214 Sgt G. Davis	MM 1.9.16.
16445 L/Cpl G. Douglas	Belgian Croix de Guerre 4.9.19.
6222 Sgt H.J. Duffy	Mentioned in Despatches 9.7.19.
8725 Cpl F. Elliott	French Croix de Guerre 1.5.17.
8536 L/Cpl A. Farrell	MM 28.7.17.
5937 Rfn T. Fay	MM 18.10.17.
4849 CSM D. Ferris	Mentioned in Despatches 24.5.18.
8721 L/Cpl T. Galloway	MM 28.7.17.
6770 Rfn T. Gamble	MM 28.7.17.
9213 Sgt T. Gardiner	Mentioned in Despatches 28.12.18, 9.11.19.
6959 Rfn A. Gare	Mentioned in Despatches 17.2.15.
41145 Rfn W.C. Gillman	MM 19.3.18. BAR 17.6.19. DCM 1.1.19.
17744 Sgt J. Gowdy	MSM 17.6.18. MM 29.8.18.
7127 Rfn W. Gray	French Medaille Militaire 1.12.14.
9461 Rfn D. Griffiths	MM 30.1.20.
8207 Rfn W. Gudgeon	DCM 12.3.19.
4536 Rfn T. Hall	MM 18.10.17.
5740 L/Cpl S. Harbinson	Mentioned in Despatches 1.1.16.
7081 CSM W.J. Harris	Belgian Croix de Guerre 12.7.18.

7648 Sgt E. Henry	Mentioned in Despatches 9.12.14. Russian Medal of St George, 2nd Class 26.8.15.
1226 Sgt H. Higgins	MM and BAR 13.8.18. DCM 16.1.19.
5043 Sgt A.J. Highman	MM 29.8.18. MSM 13.6.19.
47489 Rfn J. Hogden	MM 11.2.19.
42617 Rfn S. Hoffman	MM 18.10.17.
9114 Cpl P. Humpson	Mentioned in Despatches 1.1.16.
10365 Rfn S. Hutchinson	MM 14.5.19.
24053 Rfn J. Irvine	Belgian Croix de Guerre 26.11.19.
8666 Rfn J. Johnston	DCM 1.4.15.
8027 Rfn E.J. Johnstone	MM 28.7.17.
5980 Rfn T. Kane	Mentioned in Despatches 9.7.19.
5915 Rfn J. Kavanagh	MM 16.8.17.
5357 Rfn H. Kernaghan	MM 21.8.19.
9867 Rfn T.K. Kierans	MM 11.2.19.
6782 Rfn P. Killeen	MM 19.11.17.
5041 Rfn J. Leggett	MM 11.2.19.
5067 Rfn T. Lewis	MM 30.1.20.
2662 Rfn A. Lockett	MM 16.7.18.
41157 L/Cpl J. Longhurst	MM 11.2.19.
8066 L/Cpl D. Lorimer	Mentioned in Despatches 1.1.16.
7428 Rfn J. Lynskey	Mentioned in Despatches 1.1.16.
47356 Rfn P. McCabe	French Croix de Guerre a l'Ordre Division 9.12.18. DCM 12.3.19.
10791 Rfn W. McCabe	MM 21.8.17.
9362 Sgt J. McCambey	MM 21.12.16.
9367 CQMS J. McCamley	MSM 17.6.18.
8985 CSM S. McCrea	DCM 25.8.17.
15244 Sgt R. McCullough	DCM 16.1.19.
10411 Rfn J. McDermott	MM 18.10.17.
3/8841 Rfn M. McDermott	MM 29.7.16.
7674 Sgt A. McFarland	MM 18.10.17.
7359 L/Cpl W. McFarlane	Mentioned in Despatches 14.1.15.
7873 CSM J.J. McGibney	Mentioned in Despatches 22.6.15.
9732 Rfn A. McGrath	Mentioned in Despatches 15.2.15, 18.1.19.
936 Rfn R. McHarg	MM 20.10.19.
25697 Rfn W.J. McIlwaine	MM 11.2.19.
8848 Rfn W. McIlwraith	MM 21.8.17.
2/16801 Cpl R. McKee	MM 21.9.16.
9362 L/Cpl M. McNulty	MM 28.7.17.
8722 L/Cpl T.P. McTeague	DCM 22.10.17.
5997 Sgt T. Magill	DCM 3.6.19.
8708 Rfn H. Meneilly	MSM 17.6.18.
43100 Rfn A. Millar	MM 14.5.19.

10064 RSM D. Miller	DCM 3.6.18. BAR 16.1.19. MSM 24.9.21.
5/5822 Rfn A. Mills	Russian Medal of St George, 3rd Class 15.2.17.
4184 Rfn T.J. Mitchell	Mentioned in Despatches 1.1.16.
54110 Rfn J. Mitchen	MM 13.3.19.
7339 L/Cpl C. Morley	Mentioned in Despatches 17.2.15, 1.1.16.
7450 L/Cpl H. Murray	Mentioned in Despatches 9.12.14.
43318 Rfn A. Nichols	MM 11.2.19.
9558 Cpl J. O'Connor	DCM 17.12.14. Mentioned in Despatches 9.12.14. Russian Cross of the Order of St George, 3rd Class 26.8.15.
6781 Rfn M. O'Gara	MM 18.10.17.
10298 L/Cpl P.J. O'Hare	Mentioned in Despatches 25.5.17.
7511 Sgt W. O'Lone	DCM 1.4.15.
7954 Rfn J. O'Rawe	MSM 18.1.19.
8003 Sgt J. O'Shea	MM 28.7.17.
43592 Rfn W. Oatway	MM 18.10.17.
5644 Cpl J. Owens	MM 13.3.18. BAR 13.11.18.
9132 Bdsmn H. Palmer	Mentioned in Despatches 22.6.15.
4071 Rfn S. Parks	MM 20.8.19.
7048 Rfn T. Paterson	MM 13.3.18.
9027 Sgt S.J. Pedlow	MSM 17.6.18.
9401 L/Cpl W. Pitman	MM 11.2.19. Italian Bronze Medal 12.9.18.
11129 Rfn T. Preston	MM 18.10.17.
44135 Rfn H. Quarterman	MM 18.10.17.
8556 Sgt H.F. Quee	DCM 16.1.19.
9583 Rfn H. Quigley	MM 18.10.17. BAR 13.3.18.
12405 Sgt D. Quinn	MM 15.2.19.
9285 Sgt J. Quinn	Mentioned in Despatches 1.1.16.
2/9641 a/Cpl G.A. Reading	MM 1.9.16.
7036 Sgt J. Reilly	MM 29.8.17.
5121 L/Cpl J. Roberts	MM 18.10.17.
5219 Rfn J. Roberts	MM 18.10.17.
8690 Rfn W.H. Rodgers	Russian Medal of St George, 4th Class 26.8.15.
6955 Rfn D. Russell	Mentioned in Despatches 22.6.15.
7982 L/Cpl F. Salinger	MM 13.3.18.
3/1525 Rfn W.H. Salt	MM 18.10.17.
10803 Cpl J. Scott	Mentioned in Despatches 14.6.18.
9763 Rfn W. Scott	MM 13.3.18.
6055 Rfn W. Shearer	DCM 1.4.15.
9996 Rfn F. Sheridan	MM 18.10.17.
8593 L/Cpl G. Sinclair	MM 18.10.17.
3/8582 Sgt J. Smith	MM 18.10.17.
6928 Rfn J. Smyth	MM 18.10.17.
7104 L/Cpl J. Smyth	MM 18.10.17.

8551 CQMS R.G. Somers	DCM 3.9.18.
10/13508 RQMS T.H. Stafford	MSM 17.6.18.
44037 L/Cpl A.R. Tait	DCM 12.3.19.
9746 Cpl W. Taplin	MM 14.5.19.
8380 Sgt W.H. Taylor	DCM 14.1.16.
9759 L/Cpl J. Thompson	Mentioned in Despatches 1.1.16.
7174 Rfn T. Trueman	DCM 15.3.16.
9647 a/RQMS J. Turner	MM 18.10.17. MSM 18.1.19.
3753 Rfn E.M. Walker	MM 17.9.17.
9927 Sgt J. Walsh	MM 18.10.17.
4883 Cpl J. Weldon	Belgian Croix de Guerre 26.11.19.
9970 L/Cpl J. Welsh	Serbian Gold Medal 15.2.17.
6720 Sgt J. Whelan	MM 18.10.17.
40032 Cpl H. Williams	MM 11.2.19.
10485 Rfn R. Wilson	DCM 15.3.16.
6436 L/Cpl J.A. Wright	DCM 22.10.17.
9098 Cpl W.S. Wood	MM 28.7.17. BAR 23.7.19.
10564 Rfn S. Woodside	MM 11.2.19.

APPENDIX IV: COURTS MARTIAL AND DISCIPLINE

Abbreviations

FP1 Field Punishment No. 1
FP2 Field Punishment No. 2
HL Hard labour
PS Penal servitude
SO Superior officer
S Sections of the Army Act, Part 1.
S6 Offence in respect of military service.
S11 Neglect to obey an order.
S13 Fraudulent enlistment.
S18 (1) Malingering. (2) Wilfully injures himself or another soldier. (3) Delaying recovery. (4) Stealing, embezzling, or receiving stolen money, goods or property. (5) Any other offence of a fraudulent nature or any other disgraceful conduct.
S40 Conduct, disorder, or neglect to the prejudice of good order and military discipline.
S41 Stealing and embezzlement.

Field general courts martial

Date	Name	Charge	Sentence
4.9.14 Sancy	L/Cpl J. McIrvine	Absent from parade.	10 days FP2.
	Bugler P. Byrne	Drunkenness.	21 days FP1.
	Bugler J. Behan	Drunkenness.	2 days FP1.
	CQMS J.A. Byers	Neglect of duty.	Acquitted.
24.9.14 Augy	Rfn P. Donnelly	Drunkenness.	42 days FP1.
	Rfn W. Burns	Drunkenness.	42 days FP1.
	Rfn A. McIlroy	Drunkenness.	42 days FP1.
	Rfn E. Burns	Drunkenness and absent from parade	1 year HL, commuted to 3 months FP1.
23.10.14 Richebourg St Vaast	Rfn H. Donnelly	Drunkenness.	9 months HL, commuted to 3 months FP1.
	Rfn P. Maguire	Drunkenness.	9 months HL, commuted to 3 months FP1.
	Rfn J. Magill	Drunkenness.	9 months HL, commuted to 3 months FP1.
	Rfn J. Keenan	Drunkenness.	9 months HL, commuted to 3 months FP1.
	Rfn H. Colquhoun	Drunkenness.	9 months HL, commuted to 3 months FP1.
	Rfn F. Waugh	Drunkenness.	9 months HL, commuted to 3 months FP1.
	Rfn A. McIlroy	Drunkenness.	9 months HL, commuted to 3 months FP1.
	Rfn H. Hoare	Stealing.	28 days FP1.
	Rfn C.J. Condit	Insubordination and striking a SO.	2 years PS.

Date	Name	Charge	Sentence
	Rfn W. Hanna	Drunkenness and threatening to shoot.	1 year HL.
1.11.14 GHQ in the field	Sgt R. Kelly	Leaving post.	Reduced.
2.11.14 Le Mans	Rfn J. Melville	Drunkenness.	3 months FP1.
19.11.14 in the field	Sgt D. Smeeth	Drunkenness.	18 months HL and reduced; commuted to 12 months FP1.
23.11.14 Le Mans	Rfn J. Boyd	Drunkenness.	3 months FP1, 1 month remitted.
30.11.14 Locre	Rfn J. Hamilton	Losing equipment by neglect.	7 days FP2 and stoppage of pay.
	Rfn P. Smith	Drunkenness.	21 days FP1.
	Sgt J. Boyd	Drunkenness.	Reduced to Cpl.
	Rfn W. Armour	Insubordinate.	14 days FP1.
	Rfn M. Byan	Absent on parade and losing property by neglect.	7 days FP2 and stoppage of pay.
	Rfn J. Lemon	Drunkenness.	14 days FP1.
	Rfn P. McCoy	Drunkenness and threatening to shoot.	42 days FP1.
	Rfn J. Robinson	Drunkenness.	21 days FP1.
6.12.14 Westoutre	Rfn J. MacDermott	Breaking out of camp.	12 months HL.
	Rfn W. Murphy	Breaking out of camp.	12 months HL.
	Rfn F. Waugh	Breaking out of camp.	12 months HL.
	Rfn M. Doran	Breaking out of camp.	3 months FP1.
	Rfn J. O'Regan	Breaking out of camp and losing property.	3 months FP1.
21.12.14 Locre	Rfn G. Jameson	Drunkenness and theft.	48 days FP1.
30.12.14 Boulogne	Cpl S. Doherty	Drunkenness.	Reduced.
30.12.14 Westoutre	Cpl H. Murray	Miscellaneous.	Severely reprimanded. Quashed.
	Cpl W. Baxter	Miscellaneous.	Severely reprimanded. Quashed.
	Rfn T. Martin	Miscellaneous.	90 days FP1.
2.1.15 Locre	Rfn J. Ireland	Absent and breaking out of barracks.	90 days HL. Commuted to FP0.
	Sgt J. Johnston	Absent and breaking out of barracks.	90 days Hl and reduced. HL commuted to FP1.
	Rfn H. Dempsey	Absent and breaking . out of barracks	90 days HL, commuted to FP1.
	Rfn J. Bradley	Absent and breaking. out of barracks.	90 days HL, commuted to FP1.
	Rfn A. Brennan	Absent and breaking out of barracks.	90 days HL, commuted to FP1.
	Rfn S. McAllister	Absent and breaking out of barracks.	90 days HL, commuted to FP1.
	Rfn M. Fennessy	Absent and breaking o out of barracks.	90 days HL, commuted to FP1.
	Rfn G. Cinnamond	Absent and breaking out of barracks.	90 days HL, commuted to FP1.
	Rfn E. Bloomer	Absent and breaking out of barracks.	6 months HL, commuted to 90 days FP1
	Rfn D. McDonnell	Absent and breaking out of barracks.	6 months HL, commuted to 90 days FP1.
	Rfn D. Milligan	Absent and breaking out of barracks.	6 months HL, commuted to 90 days FP1.
	Rfn W. Wilkins	Absent and breaking out of barracks.	6 months HL, commuted to 90 days FP1.
	Rfn A. McKeown	Absent and breaking out of barracks.	6 months HL, commuted to 90 days FP1.

Date	Name	Charge	Sentence
4.1.15 Locre	Sgt R. McCall	Drunkenness and S40.	Not guilty.
	Rfn T. Waugh	Drunkenness.	2 years HL.
	Rfn G. Golden	S40.	2 years HL, 1 year remitted.
	Rfn L. Craig	S40.	2 years HL, 1 year remitted.
	Rfn F. Browne	Striking a SO.	2 months FP1.
	Cpl P. Mathews	Drunkenness.	Reduced.
	Rfn W. Miller	Absent and breaking out of camp.	12 months HL.
	Rfn J. McCleland	Drunkenness, insubordinate and threatening.	2 years HL.
11.1.15 Locre	L/Cpl T.J. Uprichard	Drunkenness.	28 days FP1.
20.1.15 Locre	Rfn R. Boyd	Absent and breaking out of barracks.	2 years HL.
	Rfn S. McBride	Absent and breaking out of barracks.	2 years HL.
	Rfn R. McFadden	Absent and breaking out of barracks.	2 years HL.
	Rfn G. Graham	Drunkenness.	90 days FP1.
26.1.15 Locre	Sgt D. Mills	Drunkenness.	Reduced to Cpl.
	Cpl P. Lappin	S40.	42 days FP1 and reduced. FP remitted.
	Rfn G. Cinnamond	Disobedience.	2 years HL, commuted to 3 months FP1.
	Rfn J. Young	Absent and breaking out of barracks.	2 years HL.
	Rfn H. Beattie	Disobedience.	2 years HL, commuted to 3 months FP1.
	Rfn A. McLoughlin	Disobedience.	18 months HL, commuted to 3 months FP1.
	Rfn S. McAlister	Disobedience.	18 months HL, commuted to 3 months FP1.
28.1.15 Boulogne	Rfn J. Stevenson	Quitting post.	6 months HL.
28.1.15 Locre	Rfn T.J. Uprichard	Absent and breaking out of barracks.	2 years HL, commuted to 3 months FP1.
	Rfn J. Scott	Drunkenness, absent and breaking out of barracks.	90 days FP1.
	Rfn S. Price	Drunkenness, absent and breaking out of barracks.	60 days FP1.
	Rfn R. Hurley	Sleeping at post.	90 days FP1.
	Rfn T. Daly	S40.	2 years HL.
	Rfn T. McCormack	S40.2.	90 days FP1.
4.2.15 Locre	Rfn S. McKie	Cowardice.	Death. Quashed.
	Rfn A. McClean	Drunkenness and striking a SO.	2 years HL.
	Rfn J. McGiven	Drunkenness.	90 days FP1.
	Rfn D. Milligan	Drunkenness.	90 days FP1.
	Rfn W. Murphy	Drunkenness.	48 days FP1.
	Rfn P. McKenna	Drunkenness and striking a SO.	2 years HL.
	Rfn W. O'Hanlon	Absent and breaking out of camp.	2 years HL.
	Rfn P. Sterling	Cowardice.	Death. Quashed.
24.2.15 Locre	Rfn J. Hagan	Insubordination and striking a SO.	18 months HL.
8.3.15 Locre	Sgt R. McCann	S40.	Reduced.
	Rfn A. Drennan	Desertion.	Death. Commuted to 10 years PS.
	Rfn J. McKeown	Drunkenness.	90 days FP1.

Date	Name	Charge	Sentence
9.3.15 Locre	L/Cpl W. Tweedie	Drunkenness and striking a SO.	4 years PS.
	Rfn M. McCarrick	S40.	90 days FP1.
	Rfn R. Thom	S40.	90 days FP1.
	Rfn J. Woods	Sleeping at post.	3 years PS.
12.3.15 Rouen	Cpl J. McComb	Absent and breaking out of barracks.	Reduced.
14.3.15 Locre	Rfn P. McCarron	S40.	90 days FP1.
	Rfn A. Morrow	S40 and drunkenness.	42 days FP1.
	Rfn W. Close	S40 and drunkenness.	42 days FP1.
	Rfn M. Buckley	Desertion.	Death. Quashed.
19.3.15 Rouen	Rfn R. Hart	S6.10.	56 days HL, commuted to FP.
	Rfn G. Reading	S6.10.	56 days HL, commuted to FP.
	Rfn F. McGovern	S6.10 and insubordination.	56 days HL, commuted to FP.
27.3.15 Dickebusch	Rfn G. Young	Desertion.	Death. Commuted to 15 years PS.
	Cpl W. Windrum	S40.	Reduced. Quashed.
23.4.15 Boulogne	Rfn R. Farley	Drunkenness.	56 days FP1, sentence remitted.
9.5.15 Dickebusch	L/Cpl W. Spence	S40.	42 days FP1.
	Rfn J. Lamb	Disobedience.	90 days FP1.
28.5.15 Rouen	Rfn J. Fitzpatrick	Theft.	90 days FP1.
1.7.15 Etaples	L/Cpl T. Thompson	Drunkenness.	28 days FP1.
12.7.15 Proven	Sgt J. Fife	Drunkenness.	6 months HL and reduced. HL remitted.
	Sgt W. Attley	Drunkenness.	90 days FP1 and reduced. FP remitted.
	L/Cpl T. Russell	Drunkenness.	90 days FP1 and reduced. 60 days FP remitted.
17.7.15 In the field	A/Cpl G. Gilliland	Striking a SO.	3 months FP1.
29.7.15 Etaples	Rfn J. Diver	Drunkenness.	28 days FP1.
26.8.15 In the field	Rfn E. Bennett	Miscellaneous.	Not guilty.
2.9.15 Etaples	Rfn A. McGrath	Drunkenness.	35 days FP1.
17.9.15 Brandhoek	Sgt J. Morgan	S40.	Reduced. Mitigated to reduction to Cpl only.
20.10.15 Bailleul	A/Sgt P. Humpson	Desertion.	2 years HL and reduced.
21.10.15 Cassel	Rfn J. Byrne	S40.	42 days FP1.
24.10.15 Cassel	Rfn M. Kane	S40.	28 days FP1.
27.10.15 Cassel	Rfn McDonagh	S40.	Not guilty.
1.11.15 Etaples	Rfn J. Driver	Drunkenness.	56 days FP2.
1.11.15 Armentieres	A/Cpl A. Armstrong	Desertion.	3 years PS. Commuted to 1 year HL, guilty of absence only.
27.11.15 Armentieres	Sgt W. Mills	Absent and breaking out of barracks.	18 months detention and reduced. Detention remitted.
	L/Cpl M. Hinksman	Absent and breaking out of barracks.	3 months HL, commuted to 1 month FP1.
7.12.15 Havre	A/CSM A.J. Wilson	Theft.	1 year HL.
8.12.15 Armentieres	Rfn W. Tweedie	Drunkenness, absent and breaking out of barracks.	3 years PS and £1 fine. Reduced to 1 year HL.
13.12.15 Armentieres	Rfn W. Darragh	Drunkenness, striking a SO and resisting escort.	12 months HL.
14.12.15 Rouen	Rfn R.J. Harte	Absent and breaking out of barracks.	3 months FP2.
19.12.15 Pont de Nieppe	Rfn J. Best	Absent and breaking out of camp.	6 months HL, commuted to 3 months FP1.
23.12.15 Pont de Nieppe	Sgt J.J. Behan	S40.	Reduced to Cpl.
	A/Sgt J. Coleman	Drunkenness.	Reduced.
24.12.15 Rouen	A/L/Cpl A. McQuade	S40.	Not guilty.

Date	Name	Charge	Sentence
28.12.15 Etaples	Rfn P. Rowan	Drunkenness.	28 days FP1.
29.12.15 Pont de Nieppe	Rfn J. Moore	Desertion.	7 years PS. 4 years remitted.
8.1.16 Pont de Nieppe	Sgt R. Irvine	Drunkenness.	Reduced.
17.1.16 Pont de Nieppe	A/Cpl M.J. Murphy	Desertion.	4 years PS. Commuted to 1 year HL, absent only.
23.1.16 Pont de Nieppe	Cpl J. Morgan	Absent and breaking out of barracks and disobedient.	6 months HL and reduced. Quashed.
24.1.16 Calais	Rfn P. Brougham	Absent and breaking out of barracks.	42 days FP1.
13.2.16 In the field	Rfn W. Buchanan	S40.	30 days FP1.
16.2.16 Bailleul	Rfn M. Lyons	Desertion.	6 months HL, absent only. Commuted to 3 months FP1.
	L/Cpl P. O'Kane	Drunkenness.	60 days FP1. 30 days remitted.
	Rfn T. Hennessey	S13.	3 months HL, suspended sentence.
17.2.16 Bailleul	Rfn P.Elley	Desertion, drunkenness and escaping confinement.	Death. Commuted to 10 years PS.
18.2.16 Calais	Rfn H. Rice	Desertion and losing property.	2 years HL.
18.2.16 Bailleul	Rfn T.J. Higgins	Desertion.	90 days HL, absent only. Commuted to FP1.
1.3.16 Bailleul	L/Cpl S.J. Bradley	Absent and breaking out of camp.	90 days FP1. 60 days remitted.
9.3.16 Etaples	Rfn P. Rowan	Drunkenness.	2 months FP1.
13.3.16 Bailleul aux Cornailes	Rfn H.J. Smith	Desertion.	Death. Commuted to 10 years PS, suspended sentence.
29.3.16 Chelers	L/Cpl A.J. Highman	S40.	7 days FP2. Sentence quashed.
5.4.16 Chelers	Sgt J.J. Wade	Drunkenness.	Not guilty.
	L/Cpl T. Hinds	Disobedience.	6 months HL.
5.5.16 In the field	Rfn J.W. Kirby	Striking a SO.	42 days FP1.
27.5.16 Bailleul aux Cornailes	Rfn H. Lewis	Desertion.	2 years HL, commuted to 3 months FP1, absent only.
	Rfn H. McCrystal	Quitting post.	Not guilty.
3.6.16 In the field	Rfn R.H. McAuley	Desertion.	56 days FP1, absent only.
	Rfn P. McLoughlin	Desertion and S13.	1 year HL. 6 months remitted.
4.6.16 In the field	Rfn J. Cummins	Drunkenness and losing property.	Not guilty.
8.6.16 In the field	Rfn A. Matthews	Desertion.	6 months HL, suspended sentence, guilty of absence only.
9.6.16 In the field	Rfn P. O'Kane	Absent and breaking out of camp.	6 months HL, commuted to 84 days FP1.
12.6.16 In the field	Sgt T.B. Graham	S18.5(3).	1 year HL and reduced.
22.6.16 In the field	Rfn R.H. McAuley	Escaping confinement.	56 days FP1.
23.6.16 Rouen	Rfn T.P. Hinds	Absent and breaking out of camp.	28 days FP1.
	Rfn J. Walker	Absent and breaking out of camp.	28 days FP1. 14 days remitted.
24.6.16 In the field	Sgt H. Bennett	Drunkenness.	Reduced.
27.6.16 In the field	Cpl J. Dunlea	Drunkenness.	Reduced and 10s fine. 10s fine remitted.
	Sgt W. Hawthorne	Drunkenness.	Reduced and £1 fine. £1 fine remitted.
	L/Cpl J. Cummins	Drunkenness.	3 months HL, commuted to 84 days FP1.
6.8.16 In the field	Rfn T. Kane	Desertion.	Death. Commuted to 1 year HL, suspended sentence.
	Cpl R. Graham	S40.	Reduced.

Date	Name	Charge	Sentence
10.8.16 In the field	Rfn T. Murland	S40.	90 days FP1.
17.8.16 In the field	Rfn N. Hunter	Insubordination.	2 years HL, suspended sentence.
15.8.16 In the field	Rfn A. McKirley	Absent and breaking out of camp.	Not guilty.
18.8.16 In the field	L/Cpl J. Fegan	Drunkenness.	35 days FP1.
29.8.16 In the field	Rfn T. Burke	S40.	28 days FP1.
30.8.16 Boulogne	Rfn P. Rowan	Drunkenness.	90 days FP1. 30 days remitted.
4.9.16 In the field	Sgt W.J. Nash	Drunkenness.	1 year HL, commuted to reduction to Cpl.
	Rfn T. Jackson	Drunkenness.	Not guilty.
14.9.16 In the field	Rfn T. Lavery	S40.	7 days FP1.
	L/Cpl J. Tipping	Drunkenness.	14 days FP1.
	Rfn W. Armour	Drunkenness.	10 days FP1.
18.9.16 Havre	Rfn J. Apritchard	Drunkenness and S11.	28 days FP1.
18.9.16 In the field	L/Cpl J. Smith	Drunkenness and S11.	28 days FP1.
26.9.16 In the field	Rfn J. Dologhan	Drunkenness.	14 days FP1.
2.10.16 Havre	Rfn J. McKernan	Absent and breaking out of barracks.	84 days FP1.
9.10.16 Havre	Rfn G. Caddell	Drunkenness.	42 days FP1.
20.10.16 In the field	Rfn J. Diver	Absent and breaking out of camp, drunkenness.	6 months HL, commuted to 3 months FP1.
25.11.16 In the field	Rfn J. McCann	Desertion.	60 days FP1. Mitigated to 28 days FP2, absent only.
	Rfn S. McBride	Desertion.	Death.
7.12.16 Languervillette	Rfn A. Marshall	S40.	Not guilty.
1.12.16 In the field	Rfn D. Murdoch	S13.	1 year HL, commuted to 56 days FP1.
8.12.16 In the field	Rfn M. Murray	Drunkenness.	28 days FP2.
	Rfn J. Smith	Drunkenness.	28 days FP1 and £1 fine.
30.12.16 In the field	Rfn W. Wilson	Absent and breaking out of camp.	3 months FP1.
29.1.17 Havre	Rfn G. Cinnamond	Drunkenness and resisting escort.	28 days FP1 and £1 fine.
31.1.17 In the field	Rfn A. Moore	Drunkenness.	Reduced.
5.2.17 Cassel	Rfn F. Durant	S40.	42 days FP1.
	Rfn F. Devlin	S40.	28 days FP1.
	Rfn O. Grant	S40.	28 days FP1.
11.2.17 In the field	Rfn J. Norton	Disobedience.	18 months imprisonment, suspended sentence.
12.2.17 In the field	Rfn T. Kane	Threatening and theft.	6 months HL. Theft charge quashed.
9.3.17 In the field	Rfn J. Snoddy	Absent and breaking out of camp.	28 days FP1.
15.3.17 In the field	Rfn J. Diver	Quitting post.	3 months FP1.
25.3.17 In the field	Cpl J. Morgan	Drunkenness.	Reduced.
10.4.17 In the field	Rfn M. Egan	Absent, breaking out of camp, losing property.	3 months FP1 and stoppage of pay for 35 days.
28.4.17 In the field	Rfn E. Cleary	Drunkenness, theft and S40.	30 days FP1.
	Rfn J. Worsfield	Drunkenness and theft.	30 days FP2.
	Rfn J. Finnegan	S11 and S40.	40 days FP1.
16.5.17 In the field	Cpl E. Bartaby	Drunkenness.	28 days FP1 and reduced.
21.5.17 Dieppe	Rfn W. Halleran	Drunkenness.	90 days FP1.
24.5.17 Havre	Sgt J. Smith	Drunkenness.	Reduced to Cpl.
16.6.17 In the field	Rfn J. Moore	Violence to SO, resisting escort.	2 years HL, suspended sentence.
2.7.17 Busseboom	Rfn J. Peoples	Absent and breaking out of camp.	90 days FP1.
12.7.17 In the field	Rfn W. McGeown	Theft.	1 year HL, suspended sentence.

Date	Name	Charge	Sentence
19.7.17 Ouderdom	Rfn T. Morrissey	Absent and breaking out of camp.	3 months FP1.
29.8.17 In the field	Rfn E. Quinn	S40.	90 days FP1.
23.9.17 In the field	Rfn T. Morisey	Desertion and losing property.	10 years PS and stoppage of pay.
25.9.17 Havre	Rfn E. McElkinney	Absent, breaking out of camp, losing property.	42 days FP1 and stoppage of pay.
2.10.17 In the field	Rfn A. Allen	Absent, breaking out of camp, losing property.	2 years HL and stoppage of pay, commuted to 90 days FP1.
	Rfn J. Snoddy	Desertion and losing property.	7 years PS and stoppage of pay, suspended sentence.
23.10.17 In the field	Rfn D. Murphy	S40.	32 days FP1.
	Rfn J. Smyth	S40.	35 days FP1. 14 days remitted.
28.10.17 In the field	Rfn J. Barbour	Theft.	Not guilty.
15.11.17 In the field	L/Cpl J. Quigg	S40.	21 days FP1.
22.11.17 In the field	Rfn J. Barbour	Resisting escort and S40.	56 days FP1, commuted to FP2.
27.11.17 In the field	Rfn R. Ferguson	S40.	28 days FP1.
	Rfn J. Lyons	Striking a SO and drunkenness.	6 months HL.
4.1.18 In the field	Cpl F. Pomroy	S40.	Reduced.
5.1.18 In the field	Rfn J. McGuinness	Absent and breaking out of camp.	56 days FP1.
20.1.18 In the field	Rfn J. Smith	Absent and breaking out of camp.	10 days stoppage of pay.
24.1.18 In the field	Rfn J. Donnelly	Absent and breaking out of camp.	1 year HL, commuted to 90 days FP1.
1.2.18 In the field	Rfn W. Topping	Absent and breaking out of camp.	Not guilty.
	Rfn T. Leggett	Absent and breaking out of camp.	28 days FP1.
	Rfn J. McCandless	Absent and breaking out of camp.	2 months FP1.
	Cpl T. McTeague	Absent and breaking out of camp.	Reduced.
	L/Cpl D. Atkinson	Absent and breaking out of camp.	21 days FP1.
11.2.18 In the field	Rfn G. Ryan	Drunkenness.	28 days FP1.
25.2.18 In the field	Rfn A.P. McGrath	Drunkenness and resisting escort.	28 days HL.
3.3.18 In the field	Rfn J. Marron	Desertion.	2 years HL, suspended sentence, guilty of absence only.
14.3.18 In the field	Rfn R. Clarke	Absent and breaking out of camp.	35 days FP2.
18.3.18 In the field	Rfn P. Cassidy	Absent and breaking out of camp and S40.	28 days FP1 and 42 days stoppage of pay.
15.4.18 In the field	Cpl D. Robson	Drunkenness.	Reduced.
6.5.18 In the field	Rfn W. Birrell	Manslaughter and S40.	56 days FP1.
27.5.18 In the field	L/Cpl A.J. Moore	Absent and breaking out of camp.	1 year HL. 6 months remitted, suspended sentence.
	Rfn J. McCoy	Drunkenness, S40 and S41.	10 years PS.
14.6.18 In the field	L/Cpl E.J. O'Connor	Absent and breaking out of camp, escaping confinement.	56 days FP1.
	Rfn J. Kelly	Absent and breaking out of camp,	56 days FP1.
	Rfn D. Murdoch	Striking a SO, insubordinate and threatening, disobedient.	6 months HL, commuted to 90 days FP1.
25.6.18 In the field	Rfn M. Shelley	Striking a SO and S40.	56 days FP1.
8.7.18 In the field	Cpl D. Finlay	Drunkenness.	Reduced.
	L/Cpl R. Lavery	Drunkenness.	40 days FP2.
	Rfn J. Morrissey	Absent and breaking out of camp.	Not guilty.
9.7.18 In the field	Rfn R.W. Hughes	Desertion.	90 days FP1, guilty of absence only.
	Rfn M. Ward	Desertion (2).	Not guilty.
12.7.18 In the field	Rfn J. Martin	Striking a SO, theft.	2 years HL.
25.7.18 In the field	Rfn A. Cherry	Absent and breaking out of camp.	35 days FP1.
28.7.18 In the field	Rfn R. Bean	Desertion.	5 years PS, commuted to 2 years HL, suspended sentence.
2.8.18 In the field	Rfn H. Davis	Manslaughter and S40.	Not guilty.
22.8.18 In the field	Rfn R. Davison	Disobedience.	35 days FP1.

Date	Name	Charge	Sentence
23.8.18 In the field	Rfn F. Hall	Sleeping at post.	1 year HL, suspended sentence.
	Rfn S.J. Turner	Absent and breaking out of camp.	9 months HL, suspended to 90 days FP1.
11.9.18 In the field	Rfn M. Ward	Theft and S40.	6 months HL.
26.9.18 In the field	Rfn A. McCullough	Absent and breaking out of camp.	28 days FP1.
	Rfn B. Kelly	Desertion.	42 days FP1, guilty of absence only.
1.11.18 In the field	Sgt W. Coombs	Drunkenness.	Reduced.

General courts martial

Date	Name	Charge	Sentence
22.5.18 In the field	Lt. V.C. Young	Disobedience, leaving post and S40.	Cashiered. Commuted to severe reprimand.
21.6.18 Proven	Lt. K.D. Leslie	Drunkenness.	Dismissed from the Army.

A rough analysis of the 270 Field General Courts-Martial produced the following:

OFFENCE	AMOUNT	PERCENTAGE
Cowardice	3	1
Desertion	35	13
Absence	57	21
Striking or violent	16	6
Disobedience	7	2
Quitting post	4	2
Drunkenness	70	26
Theft	4	2
Misc. and multiple offences	71	26
Sleeping at post	3	1

These cases show the offences that were considered of serious concern and warranted deterrent action by the CO. This list excludes cases that were settled by agreement between the CO and the person concerned without recourse to a formal trial. The final sentences, or results, of these courts-martial are summarized below:

Death	1
Penal Servitude	9
Hard labour	33
FP1	145
FP2	11
Reduced/reprimanded	29
Fines	2
Quashed/not confirmed	8
Suspended sentence	14
Not guilty/acquitted	16

Trial of 5009 Rfn Samuel McBride

Rfn McBride had been sentenced to two years imprisonment with hard labour, 25.1.1915, on a charge of desertion, but was released on suspension 3.1.1916. His situation was to be reviewed regularly. Staff Capt., 74th Infantry Bde, to OC 2nd RIR, 20.10.1916: 'Please report on the conduct of this man during the past six months ... and state whether during the recent operations he has performed such acts as would merit the remission of the sentence.' Lt.-Col. Sprague replied that day: 'The rifleman's conduct during the period in question has been unsatisfactory, and he will probably be brought before a FGCM as soon as I am able to collect all available evidence.'

The trial was delayed, as explained by a Brigade Staff Officer: 'In the first instance two witnesses were called for from Base and the Base wrote back to say that only one was available, would he be sufficient. Base was then written to again and asked to send up both witnesses as soon as available. Eventually only one witness was obtained.' A FGCM was convened, 25.11.1916, under Major D.G. Robinson DSO, 13th Cheshire Regt. The other members were Capt. J.A. Ferguson, 2nd RIR, 2/Lt. M.C. Perks, 9th LNL, and 2/Lt. O.F. Dawson, ASC. The charge was 'When on active service "Deserting His Majesty's Service" in that he, in the field, between 15th and 17th May 1916 absented himself from the front line trenches until apprehended by the Canadian Stationary Hospital Police, at Outreau, near Boulogne, on 17th September 1916 in uniform.' A plea of not guilty was entered.

Lt. R.A. Young, 2nd RIR, appeared as prosecutor. His first witness was 7550 Sgt J. Kelly, 2nd RIR:

> During May 1916 I was acting Sergeant of A Company. The accused was there in No. 1 platoon of this company. We were on the Vimy Ridge Sector.
>
> On a date about 15th–17th May, I cannot remember exactly which day, the accused's platoon had been withdrawn, in accordance with the routine we had been following for some time, from the trenches and were resting in a reserve position some 800 yards behind the front line. The routine we had been following was for two platoons to be in the front line and two out on each day. Two were drawn back each morning until 'Stand To' in the evening.
>
> On the day in question the accused's platoon was back and the ordinary custom was followed, viz., they fell in at 'Stand To' to carry material up to the front line at 4.30 p.m. Immediately after 4.30 p.m. I received a report from the accused's platoon Sergeant, who is now away wounded, about the accused. In consequence I made a report to the Company Officer and on the following morning I searched for the accused and found that he was absent. I went round all the Brigade dressing stations to look for him but could not find him, nor could I find any trace of his having passed through any dressing station.
>
> I did not see the accused again until about September 21st 1916. He was then under arrest in the Guard Room at Domqueur. I remained with the

Company all the time from May to September and I should have known if he had been present at any time.

During the time we were on the Vimy Ridge in May we were under heavy fire. The accused's platoon had suffered severely, especially from trench mortars. On the day the accused went absent there was heavy shelling in the valley where his platoon were resting. We remained in the Vimy Ridge sector for only about three days after the accused disappeared and then we went right back.

34298 L/Cpl E.R. Knight, No. 2 Canadian Stationary Hospital:

On September 17th 1916 I was doing police duty at Cutreau near Boulogne. About 12.30 a.m. I passed near the men's mess (of the hospital staff) when I heard a noise inside the tent which should have been empty. I waited a moment and then saw the accused come out of the tent. I took him to the guard room. He made several statements to me but I did not pay any attention to them. I could not say how he was dressed then. I saw the accused in the Guard Room on the following morning. He was dressed in a khaki coat and riding breeches. He had no rifle or equipment. He had a cap on but no badges or shoulder lettering. The accused was detained in the guardroom until handed over to the APM Boulogne on the same day.

8561 Cpl F. Todd, 2nd RIR:

On 19th September 1916 I left Domqueur with an escort and on arriving on September 20th at the Punishment Barracks Boulogne the accused was handed over to me. I took him in charge and went back with him to Domqueur where his battalion was.

None of the witnesses were cross examined. Rfn McBride then made the following statement in his defence:

While we were on the Vimy Ridge I was very tired and very sore in my feet. I had a headache and I felt bad all over. I went into a dug out and lay down and went to sleep. When I woke up I saw some KRR men and asked them if they had seen the Irish Rifles. They told me they were gone out so I tried to find out where the Regiment was but there was no one who could tell me where they were. I had been in the dug out about a day and a half. I then made my way with great difficulty and after struggling all over the place I reached Boulogne. I found my way into a tent by a hospital and then I was arrested.

(Cross examined.) I did not report to an officer of another unit because I did not know what to do at the time. I had been with my platoon on the Vimy Ridge up to the time I went into the dug out. I knew I should have to go up to the front line that evening. I was very tired and I went into the dug out about 3.30 p.m. I left my rifle and equipment at St Eloi where I slept the night after I left. I left them because they were taken away from me during the night. My health was pretty good while I was wandering about. I managed to get something to eat here and there from soldiers whom I saw. I was trying all the time to find the Irish Rifles. I told a lot of NCOs and men I had lost my rifle. I did not know I ought to report to an officer or to anyone who could tell me what I ought to do. I had no intention whatever of leaving the regiment. I walked along the roads and by day I made no attempt to conceal my movements. I have been out here since December 1914.

He was found guilty and sentenced to death. Evidence of character was then provided. Lt. Young: 'The accused tells me that his age is 26, and that he enlisted on October 12, 1911 in the Special Reserve.' Sgt Kelly was recalled: 'I have known the accused since February 1916. He has been in my platoon since then. So far as I have known him he has always been a good, steady and willing soldier.' He also wrote the following statement, 27 November:

I have known this Rifleman previous to and since his desertion. I have always found him a willing worker and all-round good soldier, and willing at all times to volunteer for any dangerous work to be carried out. I was a Cpl in his platoon before his desertion and I have been his Platoon Sgt since he rejoined.

Sgt D. Miller, 28 November:

Rfn McBride first joined this battalion on the 1st of January 1915, he was then posted to my Coy. I always found him a good and willing worker, both in and out of the trenches. I lost sight of Rfn McBride about the end of January 1915.

I saw Rfn McBride in action on Vimy Ridge, about the 8th of May 1916. He was then carrying bombs to the front line. On this occasion he was working very hard. The enemy's activity with minenwerfers and trench mortars had a most demoralising effect on the majority of men in my Coy.

Major Goodman, OC 2nd RIR, to 74th Bde, 28 November:

I attach statements of Sgts Kelly and Miller, the only NCOs in the battalion who can give any information concerning Rfn McBride. Rfn McBride has served with the Expeditionary Force from 6.12.14 to 20.1.15 when he absented himself and was awarded 2 years imprisonment – to prison 2.2.15, escaped from prison 1.5.15, readmitted to prison 2.5.15 and released under suspension … rejoined battalion 4.1.16 and served until he deserted 17.5.16. On the evidence and the man's previous record, the presumption is that he did absent himself to avoid returning to the firing line. I can give no reason why the extreme penalty should not be inflicted in this case beyond that in the interest of the battalion discipline I do not consider an example necessary.

As far as I have been able to judge in so short a time the discipline of the battalion is good. And I believe during this campaign their discipline in action has always been good, it has most emphatically been so during the short periods I have served with it. There have been five previously convicted cases of desertion in the battalion.

Brigadier-General H.K. Bethell, commanding 74th Infantry Bde: 'I am of the opinion that the crime was deliberately committed … and that there is no reason why the extreme penalty should not be inflicted.' Major-General Bainbridge, Commanding 25th Division, 29 November: 'I recommend that the sentence be carried out.' Lt.-General Gordon, Commanding IX Corps, 1 December: 'I consider that this is a case of deliberate desertion and I recommend that the sentence be carried out.' The sentence was confirmed by General D. Haig, 4 December. The execution took place at 7.10 a.m., 7 December. Capt. F. Robinson, APM, 25th Division: 'I hereby certify that the sentence was carried out in my presence.' 2/Lt. Marriott-Watson, 2nd RIR, certified that the sentence had been promulgated that day. Hyde Park Corner (Royal Berks) Cemetery, Comines-Warneton, Hainaut, A.17. File ref: WO71/529.

APPENDIX V: OPERATION ORDERS FOR THE ATTACK OF 7 JUNE 1917

SECRET OPERATION ORDER NO. 38
by Lt. Col. H.R. Goodman, Commanding, 2nd Battn The Royal Irish Rifles
Reference Sheet 28 S.W. 2 & 4, Edition 4A, Wytchaete and Messines, 1/10,000 and Map
A, 1/5,000 attached.
June 3rd, 1917.

1. INTENTION

The 25th Division will on Zero Day capture the enemy system opposite its sector up to a line north and south through Despagne Fme. The New Zealand Division will attack on the right of the 25th Division and the 36th (Ulster) Division on its left. The 4th Australian Division will then capture the enemy's system on the 25th Divisions and New Zealand's front up to a Green line inclusive (Odious, Odd and Owl Trenches).

The 74th Brigade on the right will capture the enemy first and second lines of defence. The 7th Brigade on the left will capture enemy first and second lines of defence. The 75th Brigade will then pass through and capture enemy third system. The 2nd Royal Irish Rifles on the right and 13th Cheshire Regiment on the left will lead the attack of the Brigade. The dividing line between the 2nd Royal Irish Rifles and the 13th Cheshire Regiment is shown by the centre green dotted line on Map A.

2. OBJECTIVES

The Battalion's objectives are as follows:

(a) Ugly Trench.
(b) Ugly Switch.
(c) Ugly Support.
(d) Ugly Reserve.
(e) Ugly Lane.
(f) River Steenebeeke.

Companies Objectives and Consolidation Tasks are shown on attached Table Appendix 1).

On the battalion gaining its furthermost objectives, (i.e. S.P. in Ozone Alley and River Steenebeeke) the 9th Loyal North Lancs will pass through the battalion and take their objectives:

(a) Steenebeeke Trench.
(b) Occur Trench.
(c) Intermediate Trench.
(d) October Trench.
(e) October Support.
(f) Ozone Alley.

3. INFANTRY ACTIONS

The battalion will move up to Bremerschen between 9 a.m. and 11 a.m. and bivouac there 1 night. On the following day the battalion will parade at 6 p.m. and move down and assemble in jumping off trench in the following order: HQ Unit, D Company, C Company, B Company, A Company. Assembly to be complete by 11 p.m.

Route to Wulverghem in red on Map 1A (copy issued to OC Companies). From Wulverghem to entrance of Snipe Avenue, route runs north of Souvenir Fme and is indicated by a line of white flags, thence down Snipe Avenue and Stone Street. The battalion will move in a continuous stream in single file with no interval. Absolute silence to be maintained. No smoking after arrival at Snipe Avenue.

Assembly Trenches are allotted and will be occupied as follows:

A Company – Lancashire Trench, covering the left half of B Company and the Right half of C Company.

Flanks of Companies in assembly trenches will be indicated:

A Company – 2 white flags; B Company – 2 yellow flags; C Company – 2 blue Flags; D Company – 2 red flags.

Boundary between the Battalion and 13th Cheshires Regiment is indicated by Green board.

4. COMPASS BEARINGS

i From left of battalion's assembly trench to left of objective Ugly Trench, 67 degrees (true).

ii From centre of assembly trench to centre of objective Ugly Trench, 60 degrees (true).

iii From right of assembly trench to right of objective (Ontario Fme), 47 degrees (true).

iv From left of assembly trench to Sloping Roof Fme, 63 degrees.

v From right of assembly trench to Sloping Roof Farm, 46 degrees. Officers concerned will set their compasses on these bearings in accordance with the variation of their respective compasses.

5. ATTACK

(a) At Zero all companies will fix swords.

(b) B Company will advance in lines of Platoon – Sections in file – 20 yards interval between Sections – 30 yards distance between Platoons. No's 1 and 3 Sections of each Platoon will advance to the Southern flank of Ozone Alley. No's 2 and 4 Sections of each Platoon to the Northern Flank. The 2 leading Platoons will envelope and mop up vicinity of Ontario Fme: The 3rd Platoon will advance above ground along either flank of Ozone Alley as far as S.P., C.31.d.25.30. closely following creeping barrage. On completion of mopping up at Ontario Fme: 1 Bombing Section and 1 Rifle Section will work along Ozone Alley and mop up. 1 Rifle Section and 1 Bombing Section will mop up all ground 100 yards South of Ozone Alley. Remaining 2 Rifle Sections and 2 Lewis Gun Sections will advance above ground along both flanks of Ozone Alley, pass through Platoon at S.P. C.31.d.25.30 to junction of Ozone Alley and Oyster Trench.

(c) B Company's Consolidation Task – siting and digging, a C.T., from C.31.d.80.50 (junction of Ozone Alley and Oyster Trench), to C.32.a.15.00. (just north of Sloping Roof Fme)

(d) C and D Companies will advance simultaneously in 3 waves – leading waves objective, Ugly Support. 1 Platoon will temporarily remain in Ugly Trench to mop up any dugouts that may possibly still exist in Ugly Trench and Ugly Switch. 2nd Waves Objective, that portion of The Oval in battalion's frontage, and Ugly Reserve. 3rd Waves Objective, Ugly Lane. Each wave will consist of one complete Platoon per company. Care must be taken to maintain direction, and Platoons of D Coy must do a rapid right incline and move quickly at first to close on creeping barrage.

(e) A Company will leap-frog over C and D Companies in two waves. Objectives S.P. and dugouts about Ozone S.P., C.31.d.25.30. Leading wave 1 Platoon 30 yards in rear of C and D Companies 3rd Wave, followed by remaining 2 Platoons at 30 yards distance. On gaining objectives, 1 Platoon will advance to the Steenebeeke, will clear battalion's sector of all wire, and will render it passable for Infantry. Remaining 2 Platoons will construct a S.P. about Ozone S.P., C.31.d.25.30.

At Zero plus 50, C and D Companies, Lewis Gun Sections of A and B Companies, will form up in Artillery Formation on the eastern side of the Steenebeeke, will advance and take over Intermediate Trench from the 9th Loyal North Lancs. A and B Companies, less their Lewis Gun Sections, will continue their consolidation tasks.

6. CARRYING PARTIES

Each Company will have two Carrier Gangs. Each gang will consist of 1 NCO and 11 men. Badges 4" wide will be worn by these Parties on the right arm:

A Coy ... White.
B Coy ... Yellow.
C Coy ... Blue.
D Coy ... Red.

Loads as follows:

		Total per Company
NCOs	A light load of rockets and flares	2 loads.
3 men	8 drums L.G. SAA each	24 drums.
	3 boxes rifle grenades	6 boxes.
3 men	2 boxes SAA and 4 drums L.G.	5 boxes & 4 drums.
5 men	10 tins water	20 tins.
Each man will carry 10 sandbags in addition		110 sandbags.

These gangs will follow in rear of their companies, and as soon as they have dumped their loads will be available for fighting. There is to be no movement in the rear other than of runners and stretcher bearers before Zero plus 5 hours.

7. LEWIS GUNS

2 Lewis Guns and 24 full drums of ammunition will remain at battalion Headquarters.
2 Guns will be sent to Brigade Headquarters. No L.G. Personnel is required for these Guns.

8. ARTILLERY

For Artillery barrage time table see Appendix C. The normal rate of advance of the creeping barrage will be 100 yards in 5 minutes, but the pace of the barrage will vary in order to conform with the advance of the Ulster Division on the left of the 25th Division. Between the enemy's front and support lines it will be 100 yards in 1½ minutes.
2 New Zealand batteries will bombard Ozone S.P. from Zero to Zero plus 14 minutes (this is in addition to our own bombardment).

9. MACHINE GUNS

6 Guns of the 74th MGC will be sited about 500 yards in rear of the British Front Line, and will form a portion of the Divisional M.G. Barrage assisting the artillery. At Zero 2 M.G.s will advance with the rear wave of A Coy. Orders have been issued by the Brigade to the OC regarding the tactical handling of these guns.

10. TRENCH MORTARS

2 Stokes will advance with the rear wave of A Coy. Orders have been issued by the Brigade to the Officer Commanding as to the tactical handling of these Mortars.

11. BATTN HQ

At Zero hour, Company Headquarters in Surrey Lane, Zero plus 30, Ugly Reserve. 2 Headquarters signallers and 2 runners will go forward with the last wave of A Company, and will establish themselves in Ugly Reserve, and will then establish communication with Battalion Headquarters in Surrey Lane.

12. MEDICAL

During assembly march to Zero plus 15, Battalion Aid Post at Battalion Headquarters. Zero plus 39 minutes – Junction of Ugly Reserve and Ozone Alley where it will remain. A.D.M.S. is arranging to have 36 RAMC Bearers at Brigade Advance dressing Station (Pont St Quentin). These will move up to the old British Front Line at Zero plus 30 minutes. From Zero to Zero plus 3 hours, battalion stretcher bearers will be responsible for carrying wounded down to the old British Front Line. RAMC will arrange to evacuate from here. From Zero plus 3 hours onwards, Battalion Stretcher Bearers will be responsible for carrying wounded back to Oval. RAMC will arrange to evacuate from here.

13. DRESS AND EQUIPMENT

Fighting Order as per attached Table (Appendix B).

14. DUMPS

Brigade Dump – T.6.c.3.6.

15. PRISONERS & STRAGGLERS

All prisoners will be sent down under escort to Brigade Headquarters. The escort will not exceed 10 per cent of the personnel of each batch. Batches should not consist of less than 10. A receipt will be obtained for each batch sent in. Full use will be made of carrying parties and slightly wounded.

The Regimental Police will establish Stragglers Posts of 1 NCO and 2 men – (1) About Junction of Teale Avenue with Day Street. (2) Junction of Surrey Lane with Medicine Hat Trail.

At Zero plus 1½ hours these posts will move forward to junction of Surrey Lane with British Front Line. These posts will collect stragglers into squads and forward them to their companies under a reliable Soldier. (Copies of Orders for Stragglers for Battle Stragglers Posts, issued to NCOs i/c of Posts).

16. COMMUNICATIONS

The Signalling Officer will arrange for the system of communications and co-operation with contact aeroplanes as laid down in Appendix B of Brigade Operation Order.

17. SYNCHRONIZATION OF WATCHES

Four signallers will report to Brigade Signalling Officer at Brigade Battle Headquarters at Zero minus 2 hours. (Brigade Battle Headquarters Midland Trench), and will then communicate correct time to OC Companies.

18. GENERAL

All ranks are reminded they are fighting for:

(i) The Allied cause of humanity against highly organized, disciplined, and educated savages.
(ii) For their women and children.
(iii) For the honour of Ireland.

Victory depends on:

(i) Surprise. To effect this there must be absolute silence during assembly and afterwards until Zero.
(ii) Hugging the creeping barrage closely and coolly whilst strictly preserving formation.
(iii) Closest co-operation between all ranks of all arms.
(iv) Frequent, brief, clear reports being received by Company and Battalion Commanders and Brigade Headquarters to enable opportunities and critical situations to be immediately dealt with.
(v) The display of initiative and drive on the part of all ranks, and non-existence of the 'Wait and see policy'.
(vi) Hard, fast, determined scientific fighting.

19. PASSWORD

Password: 'Vimy'.

20. ZERO HOUR

Zero Day and hour will be notified later.
Acknowledge.

G.D. Jones, Lt.,
Adjutant, 2nd Battn, The Royal Irish Rifles.

APPENDIX C: ORDERS FOR BATTLE STRAGGLERS POSTS

1. Collect all stragglers (armed and unarmed) seen moving to the rear through the line of posts. Stragglers will be re-armed with rifles and ammunition taken from the wounded, or from the nearest Advanced dressing Station. Stragglers will be re-formed under cover, or at the Divisional Collecting Station and sent forward as circumstances permit.
2. Every man on battle straggler post duty should know the position of the Posts on his right and left, the nearest dressing station, field ambulance, and the nearest way to them. He should know where the A.P.M. is to be found.
3. All wounded men, and those who appear to be suffering from gas poisoning, will be taken to the nearest advance dressing station, or to the Divisional Collecting Station, unless they can produce a printed medical tally, showing the nature of the wound, or disability, in which case they are to be allowed to proceed.
4. Examine all individual NCOs and men passing to and from the trenches both by day and by night, and ascertain their business. Sacks and bundles carried by men coming from the trenches are to be examined, and if found to contain plunder the men are to be arrested, and either handcuffed or placed in close confinement. Men in possession of revolvers or field glasses which look like the property of officers are to be detained pending investigation.
5. Ascertain the names and units of all Officers passing the post at night.

6. Prevent all civilians from passing the line of posts towards the front. Arrest all civilians seen coming from the direction of the front, and hand them over to the French Gendarmes. If their behaviour excites suspicion they are to be searched. All papers, etc., found on them are to be tied into a packet and handed over to the Gendarmes or Military Police. No passes are to be accepted from civilians under any circumstances.

7. Arrest all civilian found wandering about in the vicinity of the line of posts between 8 p.m. and 5 a.m.

8. Officers and men in French uniform are not to be allowed to pass the line unless in possession of a pass.

9. Control the traffic at the post, seeing that cross roads are kept clear for reinforcing troops, and that loaded ammunition carts or lorries, supply vehicles or ambulances are given a clear passage. The intervals between the posts are to be patrolled at uncertain times both by day and by night. The first stragglers to come in should be retained to assist battle posts, if it appears that large numbers of stragglers will have to be dealt with.

APPENDIX I

COY A

Objective: S.P. and dugouts about Ozone S.P. (O.31.d.25.30) and Steenbeeke.

Special points to be dealt with: Strong Point at O.31.d.25.30.

Consolidation tasks: 1 Platoon clearing battalion's sector of Steenbeeke of all wire and making it passable for Infantry. 2 Platoons constructing S.P. at C.31.d.25.30.

COY B

Objective: Ontario Farm, Ozone Alley, junction of Ozone Alley, and Oyster Trench.

Special points to be dealt with: Ozone Alley.

Consolidation tasks: Mopping up Dugouts at Ontario Farm: mopping up ground to 100 yards south of Ozone Alley. On completion of mopping up, siting and digging a C.T. from C.31.d.80.50 (junction of Ozone Alley and Oyster Trench) to C.32.a.15.50 (just north of Sloping Roof Farm).

COY C

Objective: Ugly Trench, Ugly Support, Ugly Reserve, Ugly Lane.

Special points to be dealt with:

Consolidation tasks: 1 Platoon to mop up Ugly Trench and Ugly Switch. 1 Platoon to mop up Ugly Support. 1 Platoon to mop up its sector of Ugly Reserve.

COY D

Objective: Ugly Trench, Ugly Support, Ugly Reserve, Ugly Lane.

Special points to be dealt with: S.P. and dugouts in Oval.

Consolidation tasks: 1 Platoon to mop up its sector of Ugly Reserve. I Platoon to mop up dugouts in Oval. 1 Platoon to mop up in Ugly Lane.

LIST OF OFFICERS OF 'POINTER' GOING INTO ACTION

HEADQUARTERS	1. Lt.-Col. H.R. Goodman.	Commanding.
	2. Lt. R.A. Young.	Signalling Officer.
	3. 2nd Lt. G.D. Jones	Asst. Adjutant.
	4. Lt. A.B. Ross.	Medical Officer.
A COMPANY	1. Captain W.W. MacKeown.	Commanding Coy.
	2. 2nd Lt. P. McMahon	2nd in Command.
	3. 2nd Lt. S.J.V. O'Brien.	
	4. 2nd Lt. S. Mercer.	

B COMPANY	1. Captain T.J.C.C. Thompson.	Commanding Coy.
	2. Lt. E. Brown.	2nd in Command.
	3. 2nd Lt. W. Dobbie.	
	4. 2nd Lt. R.S.H. Noble.	
	5. 2nd Lt. W.H. Calwell.	
C COMPANY	1. 2nd Lt. A.M. Anderson.	Commanding Coy.
	2. 2nd Lt. H. Marshall.	
	3. 2nd Lt. W. Rainey.	2nd in Command.
	4. 2nd Lt. E.J. Williams.	
D COMPANY	1. 2nd Lt. G.F. Fry.	Commanding Coy.
	2. 2nd Lt. L.J. Ricks.	2nd in Command.
	3. 2nd Lt. H.C. Mallett.	
	4. 2nd Lt. T.C. Wallis.	

APPENDIX A: STORES IN BRIGADE DUMP

T.6.C.3.6.

S.A.A.	100 Boxes.
Mills No.5	400 Boxes.
Mills No. 23	200 Boxes.
Sandbags	10,000.
Wire, barbed	100 Coils.
Stakes, corkscrew, Short and Long	500.
Stokes ammunition	500 rounds.
Very Light Ammn.	20 Boxes 1″. 10 Boxes 1½″.
Knife Rests, Collapsible	300.

APPENDIX B: FIGHTING ORDER

1. Packs will contain the following:
   (1) Unexpired portion of the day's rations.
   (2) Iron Rations.
   (3) Soap and Towel.
   (4) Pair of laces.
   (5) Shaving Kit.
   (6) Pair of Socks.
   (7) Canteen.
2. Waterproof sheets will be carried inside packs.
3. Supporting straps of packs to be worn.
4. Each man will carry:
   (1) 170 Rounds of S.A.A.
   (2) 2 Sandbags.
   (3) 2 Bombs. (Men of bombing squad 8 Bombs each, except carriers, 12 each. Rifle grenade men each to carry 8 rifle grenades and 12 rounds of special blank cartridges. S.A.A. to be reduced in these cases by 50 rounds).
   (4) Steel Helmets will be painted.
   (5) Box Respirator.
   (6) Field Dressing.
   (7) All Water Bottles must be filled.

(8) Men must be cautioned to use their rations and water sparingly, as it is probable they will go 48 hours at least on the rations carried in their packs.

(9) In addition to the above, Companies must be in possession of:
    (a) Wire Cutters – 12 per Platoon, which must be attached to the person or rifle.
    (b) 12 pairs of Hedging Gloves per Company, which must be tied to the left wrist.
    (c) 2 Black and Yellow Distinguishing Flags per Platoon.
    (d) Grenadiers, Mills Grenade Retracting Hook [?]. Arrangements must be made for carrying these.

(10) Officers will carry all available Very Light Pistols, and 5 rounds S.O.S. Very Light Ammunition (RED) and 10 white. Officers Servants will carry 5 rounds RED and 15 white. Each N.C.O. will carry a flare.

(11) Tools – Regimental. Each Lewis Gun Team 1 shovel. Bombers and Rifle Grenadiers – nil. Riflemen 1 pick to 4 shovels strapped on packs.

(12) 24 Bill Hooks per battalion.

NOTE   (a) Blank ammunition for rifle grenades must be kept separate from ball ammunition.
    (b) Each grenadier should carry a piece of oily rag for oiling rods just before use.
    (c) Each Platoon to carry 3 'P' Bombs, to be used under supervision of OC Platoon, only if other means to clear dugouts fail.
    All men of Rifle Section to carry a pick or a shovel. 1 pick to 4 shovels.

APPENDIX C: ARTILLERY BARRAGE TIME TABLE

1.   At Zero an intense barrage will be put down on enemy front line (Nutmeg to Ugly Trenches).

2.   The barrage will lift off the various enemy lines and S.P.s and infantry will capture same at the following times:

All objectives on the same line must be taken simultaneously:

(a) Nutmeg and Ugly Trenches. (Yellow line).	Zero plus 3½ minutes.
(b) Nutmeg and Ugly Support.	Zero plus 5 minutes.
(c) Nutmeg and Ugly Reserves. (Grey line).	Zero plus 7 minutes.
(d) Nutmeg and Ugly Lane.	Zero plus 12 minutes.
(e) Ozone Strong Point.	Zero plus 16 minutes.
(f) Along Steenebeeke where it crosses Ozone Alley to the Road O.51.a.80.13. (Pink line).	Zero plus 30 minutes.
(g) Sloping Roof Trench. (Purple line).	Zero plus 57 minutes.
(h) Intermediate Trench.	Zero plus 1 hour 17 minutes.
(i) October Trench. (Orange line).	Zero plus 1 hour 40 minutes.
(j) October Support. (Blue dotted line).	Zero plus 1 hour 55 minutes.
(k) October Alley. (Blue line).	Zero plus 2 hours 10 minutes.
(l) October Avenue. (Black line).	Zero plus 4 hours 10 minutes.
(m) Line Of Strong Points. (Black dotted line).	Zero plus 5 hours 30 minutes.
(n) Odious, Odd & Owl Trenches. (Green Line).	Zero plus 10 hours 20 minutes.

SECRET

TO ALL RECIPIENTS OF OPERATION ORDER NO. 58

With reference Operation Order No. 38. Following amendments: Para 5(f) at Zero plus 50 read at Zero plus 70. Before 'Intermediate' insert 'Occur' and Para 6 total number of sand-bags should read 220.

From OC 2nd Royal Irish Rifles. 6/6.

PART TWO

Officers who served with the Battalion during the war

Adams Lt. Frank MC. Born 22.9.1889 at Courtrai, Belgium. Educated at the Belgian State School and Westcliff College, Ramsgate. Enlisted at Newcastle, Co. Down, as Rfn 19/577 into 19th RIR, 3.8.1916. Single, height 5 foot 7½ inches, weight 153 pounds, chest 37–40 inches, linen salesman. Address 48 Elmwood Avenue, Belfast. His father was a retired merchant. To No. 7 Officer Cadet Bn at Fermoy, 5.5.1917, and commissioned to 19th RIR 29.8.1917. Posted to 10th RIR. Joined D Coy, 2nd RIR, 2.4.1918. MC, *London Gazette*, 15.2.1919: 'For gallantry and good leadership on October 1st, 1918, south of Dadizeele. He was in command of one of two platoons that were instrumental in the capture of the enemy position at Carton Farm. He led his platoon splendidly in face of heavy fire, and on the position being secured, he superintended the mounting of his Lewis guns in the roof of a building and silenced enemy machine-gun fire from Sowerby Farm, thereby allowing the company on his left to arrive at their position without undue loss.'

Promoted Lt. 1.3.1919. Demobilized 23.5.1919. He was admitted to St Bernard's Mental Hospital in Southall, 31.3.1938, as a voluntary patient suffering from depression. His address was c/o Mr F. Gregory, 53 Lanark Villas, Maida Vale, London. His brother George was residing at 90 Salisbury Avenue, Belfast. Died 1971. File ref: 339/88208.

Adams Lt. George Henry. Served as No. 10802 in 2nd KRRC and later as 19811 in the MGC. Promoted to 2/Lt. in 1st RIR 26.6.1918. Joined 2nd RIR during October 1918. After the war he was Commandant of a POW camp. Promoted Lt. 26.12.1919. Retired January 1925. Reserve of Officers 24.8.1939 to October 1940. Closed file.

Agnew Capt. Andrew Eric Hamilton. The only child of Andrew G.H. Agnew, 66 Upper Leeson Street, Dublin. Commissioned into 2nd RDF. Joined 2nd RIR 10.2.1915. Later served with 3rd RDF and as a recruiting officer. Attached GHQ Forces in the UK. Mentioned in Despatches. Resided at his father's house at 4 Warrenpoint, Clontarf, Dublin. Married Marion Rose Anna Nielson Hamilton Hedderwick, The Manor House, Weston Turville, Tring, Bucks, 5.6.1918, at St Mary's, Weston Turville. Died at The Manor House, 3.11.1918, from septic pneumonia. Gross value of the estate £488. File ref: 339/19085.

Alexander Capt. Percy Douglas. Disembarked France 8.11.1914 and served at Pte L/2659 in 17th Lancers and later as a Cpl in 2nd RIR. Rejoined 2nd RIR on promotion to 2/Lt., 31.5.1917. Wounded 10.8.1917. Appointed Lt., on probation, Indian Army 31.5.1918. Promoted Lt., Indian Army, 30.11.1918. Awarded the GSM with S. Persia clasp. Closed file.

Alston Major James William. Born February 1874, the son of Robert Douglas and Margaret Elizabeth Alston. Commissioned to the RIR from Sandhurst, 10.10.1894. Promoted Lt. 3.2.1897, Capt. 17.10.1902, and Major 28.10.1912. Served in the South African War, chiefly in the Orange River Colony, and had the Queen's Medal with two clasps and the King's Medal with two clasps. Served in India and France with 1st RIR. Married Daisy Adela 15.4.1912. Transferred to 2nd RIR, 22.11.1914, and took command three days later. *War Diary*, 15.4.1915: 'Major J.W. Alston proceeded to the trenches for the day, to observe the enemy's position. At 5 p.m., while observing with a trench periscope, a bullet obviously aimed for the top glass of the periscope, struck a sandbag on the parapet and, being deflected, struck the Major in the head above the left ear. He never recovered consciousness or spoke, and died at 5.15 p.m.' Dickebusch New Military Cemetery, Ieper, D.11. File missing.

Anderson Capt. Andrew Millar MC. Born 3.2.1880 at Belfast. Married Mabel Sophia Proctor at Stoke Newington 20.1.1904. Their daughter Eileen Mabel May was born 30.11.1906. Enlisted as Pte 2180 in 18th London Irish Rifles, 31.8.1914. Address 9 York Buildings, Adelphi, London; height 5 foot 8½ inches, chest 34½–37 inches, theatrical manager. Appointed L/Cpl 17.2.1915. To France, 9.3.1915, promoted Cpl that day, and Sgt 13.7.1915. To Cadet School 18.8.1915. Commissioned 18.9.1915 and posted to 2nd RIR. Embarked Boulogne–Folkestone on leave 5.6.1916. He wrote a letter to the WO, 7 June, from 12 Ingram Road, Thornton Heath: the previous February he had applied for a 'rest' and was told to apply via his CO. When he saw the unit MO he was told to apply for a MB, which he did, but was informed that these were no longer held in France and that he should go 'sick' in the normal way. As he wasn't sick, he didn't do this but still needed a rest. He thought he was going to have a nervous breakdown. MB at Croydon War Hospital, 19.6.1916, granted two months leave due to neurasthenia. He wrote, 22.6.1916, stating that he wanted to proceed to Ireland but his rail warrant was out of date because he was delayed due to visiting his daughter at school on the south coast, and attending the MB. Reported for duty with 3rd RIR 20.8.1916. Promoted Lt. 1.1.1917, certified fit for general service 6.1.1917, and presumably rejoined his unit.

Rejoined 2nd RIR from hospital and assumed command of C Coy, 13.1.1918. Admitted to No. 112 FA, 31.7.1918, with shell shock . 'Could not control himself when under shellfire bringing his Coy out of the line ... His dugout received a direct hit two days ago and he was buried.' MB at Etaples, 14.8.1918, recommended three weeks leave. Relinquished his commission 1.1.1920. At that time he was living at Stranorlar, Co. Donegal. Awarded the MC in the King's Birthday List 3.6.1919. French Croix de Guerre avec Etoile en Bronze 17.6.1919.

By 1934 he was living at Bonnie Rock, Western Australia. Applied, and was accepted, for enrolment in the Emergency Reserve, 18.9.1939. Letter to the WO from 21 Canonbury Square, London, 16.2.1944, advised that he was serving as an Aircraftman in the RAF as the Army would not accept him due to age. File ref: 339/43057.

Anderson Major David Mitchell DL, LL D. Educated at Wellington. Commissioned to 5th RIR. Address, The Park, Dunmurry, Co. Antrim. Member of Dunmurry Presbyterian Church. Promoted Lt. 10.1.1915. Joined 2nd RIR 28.3.1915 on his first overseas posting. Wounded 16.6.1915. Promoted Capt. 24.3.1916. On leave from 2nd RIR 5.6.1916. Joined 1st RIR, 4.9.1917, and was transferred to England, sick, 1.11.1917. Later attached to the Indian Army. Two brothers also served: Lt. Robert N. (2nd Cavalry Reserve), and Capt. William A. (RAMC). Died 1.5.1977, aged 85, at his home, Creevy Rocks, Saintfield, Co. Down. *Belfast News Letter*, 4.5.1977: 'husband of Marian and father and grandfather of Elizabeth and Diana Armytage.' *Blackthorn* 1977: 'For many years he was Chairman of Anderson & McAuley Ltd., the well-known Belfast department store.' File missing.

Andrews Capt. William Ernest. Born 25.2.1891, the son of Archibald and Mary Andrews, Moyallon, Gilford, Co. Down. Educated at the Royal School, Armagh, being prefect in his last year. Passed exam into the Indian Police, 1910, and was stationed at Canton in defence of the British Consulate during the Chinese Rebellion. Became Assistant Commissioner of Police, Free Malay States. Commissioned to 3rd RIR, 16.12.1914, and posted to 2nd RIR 1.4.1915. T/Lt. and T/Capt. 16.6.1915. *War Diary*, 16.6.1915: 'A Coy Commander, 2/Lt. W.E. Andrews, who commanded this portion of the line, deserves the highest praise for the able way in which this difficult operation was carried out.' Lt. and T/Capt. 31.7.1915. *War*

1. Officers of the 2nd RIR at Tidworth, St Patrick's Day, 1914
(*back row*) 2/Lt. Innes-Cross, Lt. Norman, Lt. Whitfeld, Lt. Cowley, Capt. Hill-Dillon,
2/Lt. Swaine, 2/Lt. Teele, Lt. Thomas, 2/Lt. Mathews-Donaldson
(*front row*) Capt. Soutry, Capt. Bowen-Colthurst, Capt. Goodman, Col. Bell,
Capt. Reynolds, Lt. Peebles, Capt. Whelan, Capt. Masters

2. Officers of the 3rd Royal Irish Rifles, Dublin, 1915 (*back*) 2/Lt. L.M. Bayly,
2/Lt. J.B. McArevey, 2/Lt. N.F. Hone, 2/Lt. J.F. Stein, 2/Lt. W.L.P. Dobbin,
2/Lt. W.H. Chawner, 2/Lt. H.E. Keown, 2/Lt. W.P.B. Darley, 2/Lt. W.F. Hogg
(*centre*) 2/Lt. C.S.W. Watson, 2/Lt. F.M. Moore, 2/Lt. P. Erskine, 2/Lt. G.H.P.
Whitfeld, 2/Lt. O. O'N. Cassidy, 2/Lt. E.W.V. Leach, 2/Lt. J.F. Healy,
2/Lt. T.H.E. Gallwey, 2/Lt. A.C. Worthingon, 2/Lt. D. Motherwell, 2/Lt. V.T. Forsythe,
2/Lt. T.F. Boyhan; (*front*) Capt. W.B. Teele, Lt. R.B. Hayward, 2/Lt. J.R.A. McFerran,
Lt. (Adjt.) S.V. Morgan, Major J. Rosborough, Lt.-Col. W.E.C. McCammond,
Major J.G.S.W. Samman, Capt. R.P. Varwell, Capt. (QM) H.W. Foster, Lt. G.W. Webb,
2/Lt. H.G.W. Greer.

3. Lt.-Col. Alston, Capt. Hutcheson, Lt. MacKenzie (RAMC), Capt. Becher and QM
Templeton at battalion HQ, Kemmel, March 1915

4. Men of 2nd RIR resting, summer 1915

5. Westoutre

6. The ramparts at Ypres

7. Walking wounded at a field ambulance near Ypres, 1915

8. *(left)* Lt.-Col. H.R. Charley   9. *(right)* Lt. R.B. Marriott-Watson

10. *(left)* Capt. J.C. Bowen-Colthurst   11. *(right)* Lt.-Col. J. Evans

12. *(left)* RQMS D.J. McAuley   13. *(right)* Cpl D.J. McAuley

14. Rfn P. McAteer and his wife

15. Fr H.V. Gill with his batman, Rfn D. Doyle

16. *(left)* Capt. G. Lowry   17. *(right)* 2/Lt. J.F. Lucy

18. Lt.-Col. W.D. Bird

19. *(left)* 2/Lt. J.K. Watson   20. *(right)* Capt. H.O. Davis

21. Rfn John Quinn (standing), and his brother Rfn Hugh Quinn

Diary 1.8.1915: 'During the afternoon, while our Artillery were registering, an enemy shell struck the parapet ... killing 2/Lt. W.E. Andrews.' See main text. *Irish Times*, 9.8.1915: 'He was sent to China to learn the language, preparatory to entering the Federated Malay Police in the Malay States. He played his part in the suppression of the Canton Rebellion, and before leaving the East on sick leave, was in charge of the police of the whole of the Penang State. As soon as he recovered his health in England, he joined the Royal Irish Rifles ... He spent his last leave at the Royal School, Armagh, as his people had gone to the north of England and to Canada. Mr Andrews was a fine rugby player. He represented Ulster in the School's Inter-provincial before joining Knock Club, Belfast, which he assisted for two seasons.'

A letter from Miss Anne W. Richardson, Moyallon House, 7.8.1915: 'I am the nearest friend he had in Great Britain and helped to educate him and I am not sure that he left the address of his father and mother who have gone to Canada.' The WO replied that his father had been notified. The parents were at 662 Hochelaga Street West, Moosejaw, and later moved to 647 Athabasca Street, Saskatchewan, Canada. Mr Andrews, who administered the estate, gross value £119.97, was notified that his son was buried behind the Stable Building of Lankhof Chateau near Ypres. White House Cemetery, St Jean-Les-Ypres, Ieper, Lankhof Chateau Memorial. File ref: 339/28803.

Arnott Capt. Sir Lauriston John, Bt. Born 27.11.1890 at Stoke Bishop, Westbury, Bristol, the second son of John Alexander Arnott (1853–1940), a ship owner (Bristol Steam Navigation Co.), and Caroline Sydney, eldest daughter of Sir Frederick Martin Williams MP, Tregullow, Cornwall. His grandfather, Sir John Arnott, was a Scot from Aughermuchty near Glasgow, who gave his name to the famous department store in Dublin. The family lived at 12 Merrion Square, Dublin, and Woodlands, Cork. His father was proprietor of the *Irish Times* and the Phoenix Park Racecourse, Dublin. Educated at Wellington College. Applied for the Royal Military Academy, 25.4.1909, and received his commission in 1910. He was dealt with by the GOC Lowlands Division, 24.6.1913, on a charge of misconduct through heavy drinking at Stobbs Camp. All leave was stopped for one year and no clemency was to be shown for any repetition. He was a Lt. in 1st Cameronians (Scottish Rifles) when he was placed under arrest by the OC, 19.3.1914, having been witnessed by fellow officers as being 'Drunk and was misbehaving himself' in the Alhambra Theatre. A report by OC Lowland Division, to HQ Scottish Command, stated that he had been visited in Dublin by Sir John Arnott. He had made a 'most urgent appeal' that his son should be allowed to resign his commission in order to avoid a trial and the disgrace to the family. The OC also stated that he was concerned for the good name of the Cameronians. Arnott's resignation was approved 1.5.1914.

Enlisted as Rfn 1312 in 3rd RIR, 3.11.1914. Height 5 foot 11 inches, chest 35–37½ inches, weight 147 pounds. Appointed L/Cpl, 6.11.1914, and a/Sgt, 9.11.1914. Went overseas and joined D Coy 2nd RIR two days later. Wounded in the leg at Kemmel 27.12.1914. Returned to the UK on leave, 3.1.1915, until he was promoted to a commission 24.3.1915. Wounded while serving with 1st RIR, 24.6.1915, and embarked Dieppe–Dover 29.7.1915. GSW, compound fracture of the right arm. Promoted Capt. 18.9.1915. His brother, Capt. John Arnott MC, was killed in action, 30.3.1918. He returned to 2nd RIR, 7.4.1918, and assumed command of D Coy. *Witherow*: 'He turned out to be an exceedingly nice man but unfortunately strongly addicted to one evil. He was very popular with all but in my case I had still to command the company in everything but name. I had all the work to do but the Captain was so nice and appreciated the position that we got on well together. He had previously been badly wounded in the arm and it had not properly healed and caused him much pain. Indeed he was not at all fit for active service.' MB at Le Havre Base, 25.5.1918, rated him B3. Appointed Assistant Commandant and Adjutant, Divisional Reception Camp. MB, 12.3.1919: his service was no longer required due to his wound disability. He succeeded as 3rd Baronet on the death of his father, 26.7.1940.

Died of a heart attack at his home Shearwater, Baily, Co. Dublin, 2.7.1958. He never married. *Irish Times*, 3.7.1958: 'On his return to Ireland from the First World War, Sir Lauriston became a director of the *Irish Times Ltd.*, and was its managing director from 1940 until 1954. After that date he remained on the board as a director and took an active interest in the newspaper. A keen sportsman, he maintained the Arnott family connection with the Phoenix Park Race Club, of which he was chairman for many years. He was also interested in golf and was a former chairman and president of the Leinster Golfer's Alliance. He devoted a lot of his time to charitable institutions, and particularly, service charities ... During the second World War he was an officer in the North Co. Dublin Battalion of the Local Defence Force.' File ref: 339/15777.

Baker Lt. Arthur Lancelot. Born 22.6.1893. Educated at Aravon School, Bray, Co. Wicklow. Entered Trinity College, Dublin, 1912. Applied for a commission 5.8.1914. Height 5 foot 3 inches, weight 127 pounds, chest 34–37 inches, student. Address, Rockfort, Sandycove, Co. Dublin. Commissioned to 3rd RDF, 15.8.1914, and promoted Lt. 22.2.1915. Left 5th RDF, 16.3.1915, joined 2nd RIR 28.3.1915, and went to hospital 1.4.1915: bronchitis, measles, and dental trouble. Embarked for Southampton 13 May. MBs at King George V Hospital, Dublin, found him suffering from acute dermatitis and ulceration of the mouth. Joined 5th RDF at the Curragh, 21.9.1915, and certified fit for general service 16.10.1915. Left 5th RDF, 5.3.1916, and embarked Calais–Dover 8.3.1916 with bronchitis, influenza, and laryngitis.

Arrived at Salonika 3.2.1917. Posted to No. 10 Infantry Bde Depot 20.2.1917. Ordered to join No. 1 Entrenching Bn 5.5.1917. Posted to 9th King's Own Royal Lancs 3.7.1917. To No. 68 FA with bronchitis, 27.7.1917, and to No. 48 General Hospital the next day. To Base Depot at Salonika 6.9.1917. Posted to Karasonli as Railhead Commandant 10.9.1917; to Labour Corps Base Depot 14.12.1917, and to a POW camp at Agrasit 20.12.1917. To No. 31 CCS with malaria 15.1.1918. Posted to duty at No. 2 POW camp at Pazarkia, 23.1.1918, to GHQ 8.2.1918, and No. 1 Turkish POW Camp 16.6.1918. Appointed Adjutant and QM of POW camp 23.7.1918. Promoted Capt. 28.8.1918. Embarked on leave to the UK 6.10.1918. His father wrote to the WO, 6.11.1918, saying that Baker was due to return to Salonika but was unfit to travel and had a doctor's certificate saying he would be unfit for three months. Granted sick leave to 27.11.1918. MB at Dublin 7.12.1918: debilitated following influenza and ordered to return home and await orders. MB at Weelsby Camp near Grimsby, where he was stationed with 3rd RDF, 10.3.1919: fit for home service.

Court martialled at Newcastle-on-Tyne, 4.7.1919: 'Conduct to the prejudice of good order and military discipline, in that he, at Ponteland Camp, on the 26th day of May 1919, improperly permitted a woman to enter his quarters at about 23.30 hours and remain there until about 10.00 hours on the 27th day of May 1919.' Found guilty and sentenced 'To be severely reprimanded'. Discharged 21.9.1919, rated A1, single. Relinquished his commission 1.4.1920, retaining the rank of Capt. Court martialled at Peshawar 2–5.12.1921. Capt., Indian Army Reserve of Officers, commanding No. 125 Bde Supply Section. Charged that between 30.12.1920 and 4.4.1921 he had so negligently performed his duties in respect to the supply and issue of charcoal as to cause the loss to the public of 1,998 maunds of charcoal worth 5,493 Rupees and 2 Annas. Found guilty, sentenced to be severely reprimanded and to have stoppages of pay until the amount had been made good in respect of the loss of 639 maunds.

A letter from the Commandant, Special Constabulary (C.1.), Belfast, 19.3.1923, requested details of his service record as Baker had applied to be Adjutant to one of his battalions. His father wrote to the WO, 2.4.1925, saying that a DSO was received at the house during 1920 or 1921, for his son, and as he was in India it was returned 'in error'. Baker was then at home and had 'asked about it'. The return of the medal was requested. Baker wrote, 21.4.1925, referring to his father's letter and asked for the medal to be forwarded to 18 Ormiston Crescent, Knock, Belfast, where they were both living. WO informed him that there was no record of this DSO ever having been awarded. Mrs B.E. Kettle, Brooklands, Waldegrave Road, Teddington, Middlesex, visited the WO, 26.8.1925, and wrote to them the following day: she was trying to get in touch with Baker, whom she titled Major, DSO, MC. WO replied that she must have been referring to Capt. A.L. Baker, RDF, who was demobilized in 1919, and told her to write to him c/o War Office.

An undated note from Mr H. Dobinson MC, Far Eastern Dept., Foreign Office, London, enquired about the record of Major A.L. Baker DSO, who stated he was on the Prince of Wales' staff in India. He was known to have been in Venice recently and to have served under Colonel Slattery of the Albanian Police. They wanted to test the accuracy of certain statements he had been making with a view to getting trade credits, including saying that he was an intimate friend of Mr Dobinson. 'He keeps changing lodgings without leaving any address.' WO advised that it was not practice to disclose details but they were unable to trace any officer 'as described'. They thought it may be Capt. A. Lancelot Baker, RDF, who had not been appointed to the DSO.

Baker wrote from 27 Radcliffe Square, Earls Court, London, 22.2.1927, applying unsuccessfully for his name to be placed on the Reserve of Officers. He titled himself Capt., ex RDF and Indian Army. The Film Covering Company Ltd., Ealing, wrote, 14.1.1929, asking for credentials and military decorations for Baker, who had applied for a position. Baker told them he had served with the RDF and held a WO appointment with the Gendarmerie of Albania, and served with distinction. The WO replied that they would not furnish any information, but if Baker applied they would consider it. Metropolitan Police to WO, 30.12.1930: Baker had been charged with obtaining £90.23 from Modern Cars Ltd., Great Portland Street, under false pretences. He had been remanded on bail until 6.1.1931 and they wanted his military history confirmed for the magistrates. The WO gave very basic details and said that he also served in the Indian Army, his court martials were not mentioned. A police note implied that Baker had claimed a DSO and MC. WO replied that there was no record of Baker having these awards. The Met advised, 5.5.1931, that Baker had been remanded pending possible restitution. He was in court, 21.7.1931, was fined £10 and ordered to pay 50 Guineas costs or, in default, three months hard labour. Seven days were allowed to pay the fine. The WO made a submission to the King, 13.8.1931, to remove Baker's rank upon civil conviction. As of 20.8.1931 the fine had not been paid and the police were unable to trace him. The India Office was advised of the situation. Baker was arrested 14.10.1931 and placed in prison at Wormwood Scrubs. The earliest date of release was set at 30.12.1931; expiration of sentence 13.1.1932. Next of kin, father, at Galwally, Belvoir Park, Belfast. The WO wrote to the Prison Commission, Home Office, 22.10.1931, asking them to advise Baker that he had been stripped of his rank. He applied for the Army Officers Emergency Reserve 19.6.1939, but was not accepted. File ref: 339/23857.

Barclay Capt. Leslie George De Rand. Commissioned to 4th RIR, 8.9.1897, and promoted Lt. 22.3.1899. Served in the South African War 1900–2. Operations at Cape Colony and Orange River Colony, May–November 1900; Orange River Colony, November 1900 to

31.5.1902. Queen's Medal with two clasps and King's Medal with two clasps. Commissioned to 2nd RIR, 19.9.1900, and promoted Lt. 16.7.1904. Reserve of Officers, 6.9.1905. Member of Freemason Lodge 40, Belfast. Promoted Lt., 2nd RIR, 7.8.1914. Reported sick, 15.11.1914, and invalided home. In 1915 he compiled and published *History of the Scottish Barclays*. Promoted Capt. 28.9.1915 and employed at the Depot. With 4th RIR in 1917. Attached HQ Northern District. *Belfast News Letter*, 6.3.1917, reported that he was best man, the previous day, at the wedding of Major L.G.B. Rodney, 1st RIR, and Gwendolen Agnes Leslie at Belmont Presbyterian Church. Rejoined 2nd RIR and took command of C Coy, 28.8.1918. Reserve of Officers 1919. Closed file.

Barrett Lt. & QM William. Born 19.7.1874, the son of William Joseph and Mary Barrett, 9 Colestown Street, Bridge Road, Battersea, London. Enlisted 29.7.1893 as Gunner 98387 in the RFA and posted to 2nd Battery. Height 5 foot 6½ inches, chest 34–36 inches, weight 136 pounds. To 12th Battery 17.10.1893. Various postings followed. Promoted Bombardier 5.8.1895 and Sgt 20.10.1900. Married Beatrice Maud Macklin at Agra, India, 20.11.1901. Served in India 24.2.1899 to 22.4.1905. All other pre-war service was at home. His son Alexander Reginald was born at Bradford 22.11.1906. A WO memo, 10.4.1913, referred to a proposed design of 'Observation Ladder' put forward by BQMS Barrett, 124th Battery, 28th Bde, RFA, Kildare: not to be adopted for consideration because a new type of observation vehicle was being introduced, but Barrett should be thanked for the trouble he had taken over the matter.

Memo from OC 124th Battery to WO, 4.12.1913: recommended that Barrett be allowed to extend his service beyond 21 years. Among 'exceptional abilities' listed: in September 1910 he mobilized 31st Bde RFA Ammunition Column, and demobilized, with clear account; in January 1911 he compiled a book for submission to the WO regarding the organization of a Field Artillery Ammunition Column; in May 1911 he compiled mobilization tables designed to simplify the mobilization of an 18-pounder QF Battery; in December 1911, the ladder as above. The application was not accepted because of the lack of vacancies. Discharged 28.7.1914. Held the Long Service and Good Conduct Medal. Awarded a pension of 12.5 pence per day for life.

Re-enlisted as QMS 52123, 9.9.1914. Occupation shown as Messenger. Memo from GOC Training Centre at Aldershot, 20.11.1914, recommended Barrett for service as a 2/Lt. Posted to 14th Divisional Ammunition Column HQ, 10.4.1915, as RSM. To BEF France 21.5.1915.

Mentioned in Despatches *London Gazette*, 29.12.1916. An undated WO telegram to OC RFA Officer Cadet School, St John's Wood, London, stated that Barrett would be joining for a Quartermaster's course at Aldershot 30.3.1917. Applied for a commission 8.2.1917. Address 18 Burntwood Lane, Wandsworth Common, London. Returned to the UK 22.2.1917. Passed '7th QM Class held at Aldershot 15 May to 11 June 1917'. Commissioned 25.6.1917 and served with 7th RIR as QM from 8 July. Joined 2nd RIR 14.11.1917. Left 8/9th RIR, 11.4.1918, also noted as 36th Bn MGC. Rank shown as Lt. and QM. Embarked Calais–Dover, 23.4.1918, sick. MB 4.7.1918: granted leave until 25.7.1918 when he was to rejoin HQ MGC at Grantham. Ordered to report to POW Camp, Dorchester, 16.8.1918. He was serving at Port Talbot as of 7.11.1918. A note, 15.11.1918, stated that he was to remain with the POW Camp at Frith Hill. Joined 52nd Graduated Training Bn (Gordon Highlanders) at Portsmouth 19.2.1919. Discharged 5.12.1919, rated A1, last served with 17th Royal Fusiliers. Reserve of Officers 18.1.1922. File ref: 339/104235.

Barton Capt. Charles Erskine. Second son of Charles William Barton JP, DL, Glendalough House, Annamoe, Co. Wicklow. BLGI. Husband of Norah Grace Deane Barton. Brother of

T.E. Barton below. Educated at St Columba's College, Dublin. His elder brother, Robert Childers Barton (1881–1975), resigned his commission at the time of the 1916 Rising, was Sinn Féin MP for West Wicklow 1918–22, Minister for Agriculture in the First Dáil (1919–21), and was a delegate and signatory of the Anglo-Irish Treaty in 1921. Their cousin, Robert Erskine Childers (1870–1922), author of *The Riddle of the Sands*, brought a shipment of arms from Germany for the Irish Volunteers in July 1914; served in the Royal Navy during the war; elected to Dáil Éireann in 1921 and appointed secretary to the Irish delegation that negotiated the Treaty; during the Civil War he was arrested at Glendalough House estate, court-martialled for possession of a revolver and executed by the Free State Forces. His son, Erskine Hamilton Childers (1905–1974), was later elected President of Ireland.

Promoted Lt. 17.9.1914. *Free Press*, 11.12.1915: 'Capt. Barton first served as a Second Lieutenant in the 3rd Royal Scots Fusiliers (Militia) from 1902 to 1904. He volunteered on the outbreak of the present war in August 1914 and was gazetted First Lieutenant in the 4th Bn Royal Irish Rifles. He went to the front in April where he served with the 1st Royal Irish Fusiliers till June 26th when he was invalided home suffering from gas poisoning. He was promoted Captain on 1st October 1915 and is now at Carrickfergus pending his recall to the front.'

Served during the Easter Rising. Returned to France during 1916. The war diary does not say when he joined 2nd RIR but it mentions that he was in hospital 17–26.1.1917. Gassed 14.8.1918 and died at No. 5 British Red Cross Hospital 23.8.1918. Age 35. *Irish Life*, 27.9.1918: 'Capt. C. Erskine Barton … resided at Ruane, New Ross, and was a magistrate for the County of Wexford.' Effects to his widow at 7 Prince of Wales Terrace, Bray, Co. Wicklow. Terlincthun British Cemetery, Wimille, Pas de Calais, II.D.41. File ref: 339/2985.

Barton 2/Lt. Thomas Eyre. Brother of C.E. Barton. Joined the Royal Naval Armoured Car Division in October 1914. Served as a Petty Officer. Discharged 11.11.1915 upon disbandment of the Corps. Applied for a commission 23.11.1915. Joined 2nd RIR 21.5.1916. Killed in action 16.7.1916. *de Ruvigny*: ' … third and youngest son of the late Charles William Barton … by his wife, Agnes Alexandra Frances, daughter of the Revd Charles Childers, of Nice, France; Canon of Gibraltar; born Glendalough House aforesaid, 15 August 1884; educated Fettes College, Edinburgh, and Trinity Hall, Cambridge; joined the Royal Naval Air Service October 1914, and served with the Armoured Car Section in Gallipoli; was invalided home in November 1915, with fever; gazetted 2/Lt. Royal Irish Rifles 14 December; went to France 15 May 1916.'

A WO telegram to his home, 16.7.1916, advised that he was slightly wounded at duty, 10 July, and requested details of his next of kin. Another telegram, 19.7.1916, notified that he was missing from 16 July. His identity disc was recovered but nothing else. Died intestate. Next of kin was his mother. Siblings were Frances (39), Dulcibella (37), Robert (36), Charles (34), all at the same address. Witness statements: 5266 Rfn J. Graham, a/Cpl No. 1 Platoon, at Horton County of London War Hospital, Epsom. On 16 July they went over and were held up by barbed wire. He saw Barton dead about 50 yards from their trenches. 1369 Rfn J. O'Brien, A Coy, at Havre Hospital. He saw Barton killed instantly by machine gun fire about midnight 16 July. 7747 Rfn J. O'Sullivan, B Coy Machine Gun Section, saw Barton hit by shrapnel 9.7.1916 in the trenches (see above); Barton shouted 'Go ahead boys'. He didn't see Barton again. Someone else told him Barton was killed the same day. 7446 Sgt W. Hall said they advanced 'about three minutes past one on Sunday morning, July 16th. We opened fire with machine guns and so lay down until orders came to charge. Then we all got up and cheered and were away. Lt. Barton fell dead almost at once.' 4420 CSM W. Toal saw Barton killed by a shell that knocked him into a shell hole. The senior next of kin was later shown as his brother Robert.

WO advised, 8.4.1920, that Barton had been exhumed from a point just north-west of Ovillers and reburied in Ovillers Military Cemetery, Somme, IX.K.8. File ref: 339/50402.

Battershill Lt. Fred Luntley MC, DCM. Born 25.4.1868 at Dartmouth, Devon. Another document gave his date of birth as 1860. Educated at Dartmouth Grammar School. His father was a farmer. Prior to 1899 he was a Trooper in the Royal 1st Devon Yeomanry and Cavalry. Served as a Lt. in the South African Light Horse, November 1899 to July 1902, later joining the Reserve of Officers. Served as Capt. and Adjutant with 2nd Imperial Light Horse throughout the German SW Africa Campaign. Applied for a commission 11.5.1916. Permanent address Kruges, Transvaal, South Africa, where he was a farmer and horse breeder. Correspondence address, 65 Richmond Road, Bayswater. Appointed T/Lt., 23.5.1916, as Regimental Transport Officer and told to hold himself in readiness pending orders to proceed overseas. Posted to 8th RIR. Left unit, 3.7.1917, and embarked Boulogne–Folkestone the next day. A doctor's note stated that he was suffering from nervous debility. Certified fit to return to the BEF 28.7.1917. MC *London Gazette*, 28.12.1917.

Joined 2nd RIR 12.7.1918 and went to FA 'sick' four days later. Posted to No. 162 POW Coy, Labour Corps, 21.8.1918. To Abbeville, 13.10.1918, and posted to No. 315 POW Coy. Rated 'B2 Permanent' 29.11.1918. To the UK for demobilization, 6.11.1919, and relinquished his commission 6.5.1920. At that time he was married and his address was Grand National Hotel, Johannesburg, Transvaal. His son, Lt. L.W. Battershill, Devonshire Regt, wrote to the WO, 17.7.1931, saying that his father was retired and requested his full service record. WO refused because his father was still alive. File ref: 339/58669.

Beale Lt. Donald Olaf Christopher. Born 29.4.1888 at Frant, Sussex, the son of Louis Stephen Beale, a builder, and Mary Ann *née* Davison. Educated at Skinner's School, Tunbridge Wells, and University School, Hastings. Joined Inns of Court OTC, Berkhamstead, 4.1.1915, as Pte 2556. Height 5 foot 7¾ inches, chest 34¼–36½ inches, surveyor. Applied for a commission 24.3.1915. Permanent address, Linden, Tunbridge Wells, Kent (his father's home). Although he was married, he gave his father as the next of kin. Discharged to a commission in 5th RIR 10.4.1915. Served with 12th RIR. Promoted Lt. 24.12.1916. Left unit, 29.7.1917, and embarked for the UK aboard the *St Andrew* 1.8.1917. He was suffering from synovitis and inflammation of a knee joint. Home address, Jarvis Brook, Sussex. MB at 3rd Western General Hospital, Cardiff, 5.10.1917: granted three weeks leave and to then join 5th RIR. Instructed to return to his unit 30.1.1918. Joined 2nd RIR early October 1918. Wounded 14.10.1918: GSW to scalp and concussion. Embarked Calais–Dover 20.10.1918. Last served with 5th RIR. Discharged 11.2.1919; rated B, home address, Haslemere Grange, Hackfield. File ref: 339/48376.

Becher Lt.-Col. Cecil Morgan Ley DSO. Born 9.7.1870, the only son of Mr J.P. Becher. *Becher's Brook* at Aintree is named after his family. Educated at Christ's Hospital. Commissioned 21.4.1900. Served in the South African War receiving the Queen's Medal with four clasps. *Laurie*: 'Whilst the South African War was progressing, the Royal Irish Rifles was called upon to furnish a representative detachment to proceed to Australia, to form part of the Imperial Representatives Corps, which was composed of troops of all arms from the United Kingdom and India. This corps attended all the celebrations connected with the inauguration of the Australian Commonwealth ... This party consisted of twenty-three non–commissioned officers and men, and was commanded by 2/Lt. Ley Becher.' Left England in November 1900 and returned in April 1901.

Promoted Lt., 22.3.1904, and Capt. 22.1.1909. Adjutant Liverpool Regt 23.5.1910. Wounded 19th and 20.9.1914 while commanding A Coy, 2nd RIR. In Lucy's book he was called Oakes: 'Captain Oakes was well liked by us all. He was never without an eyeglass, and he spoke in a very deep rich voice, like a tragic actor. He was genuinely very fond of us, and would, I think, have given his life for the most humble private soldier. He was the grandest type of Englishman ... Captain Oakes was wounded in the left leg, but he refused to leave us ... He called the remains of our once strong company from the caves, and stood on a slight prominence near the outlet. He looked more dramatic than ever. I think he felt dramatic, and enjoyed that feeling. At any rate, there he stood, his monocle still in his now red-rimmed eye, his face drawn and dirty with many days' growth of beard, a revolver in each hand, and a second wound in his left leg. He waved his left revolver grandly in a magnificent sweep towards the front line, and said in a deep voice: "A Company, man the earthworks." His strange appearance and weirdly expressed order amused us even then, and seeing us smiling as we went past him his whole manner changed, in a habitual endearing way he had, and he said simply, as if to each man singly: "The Germans are very fond of my left leg." This time, however, he received no quarter from his NCOs and men, and he was scolded and bullied into retiring from the firing line, protesting to the last.' To hospital at the Astoria, Paris. Rejoined 24.12.1914.

Burgoyne 22.4.1915: 'He is a real old fashioned type of "Foot-slogging" muddle-headed officer.' Slightly wounded 16.6.1915. Promoted Major 1.9.1915. Appointed T/Lt.-Col., 28.11.1915, when he arrived at Salonika, and took command of 6th RIR until the battalion was disbanded 15.5.1918. Mentioned in Despatches 9.12.1914 and 6.12.1916. Awarded the DSO, *London Gazette*, 1.1.1917, for distinguished service in the field. Commanded 2nd RIR 6.10.1918 to 31.3.1919. Married Winifred, only daughter of Ernest Page KC, Recorder of Carlisle. Employed with the Leicester Regt in the Armies of Occupation. Belgian Officier de l'Ordre de Leopold avec Croix de Guerre 24.10.1919. Retired 1920. Died at Surrey 3.7.1952.

Quis Separabit, winter 1952: 'Many of the 2nd Battalion will remember his distinctive figure awaiting their arrival in Southampton from Khartoum in a snowstorm in 1933 and all who corresponded with him will not forget the style which he used and the Latin quotations which seemed to flow so easily from his pen. I learnt quite a lot of the ancient tongue in that way. It was not until I became Colonel of the Regiment that I realized how much interest he took in Regimental affairs and what efforts he made to get the Kennedy Trust ironed out. [See H.A. Kennedy.] For many years he had been sole surviving Trustee and spared no trouble to get the scheme put on a satisfactory basis. As time dragged on he sometimes despaired of the matter being settled before his death, but he had the satisfaction of seeing a suitable scheme in operation – with two years to spare ... To his wife and family we give our deep sympathy in their great loss.' – General J.S. Steele. His medals are in the regimental museum. File missing.

Bell Capt. Samuel Allen. The sixth son of James Bell, Grovehill, Ballymena. Promoted from 8119 Colour-Sgt, 2nd RIR, to 2/Lt. 18.11.1914. Posted to D Coy. Slightly wounded 25.9.1915. *Irish Times*, 13.10.1915: 'He was wounded in the head by shrapnel ... and he is now in a hospital in Lincoln.' Rejoined 23.5.1916. Promoted Lt. 4.10.1916. Wounded in action 21.10.1916. *Irish Times*, 26.10.1916: ' ... is one of two brothers who are serving. The other is Captain (the Revd) John Bell MA, King's Own Lancaster Regiment, parish minister of Carlton Church, Uddingston, Scotland. Second Lieutenant Bell ... served for seven years in the Army, and studied for the Presbyterian Church from 1911 to the outbreak of the war [at Glasgow University], when he rejoined the Army and was given a commission.' T/Capt. 5.8.1918. Employed 4th Monmouthshire Regt. File missing.

Bennett Major George Guy Marsland MC. Home address, Carrigart, Pinner, Middlesex. Commissioned to 4th RIR 29.9.1914. Joined 2nd RIR 2.6.1915. Promoted Lt. 22.1.1916. Joined 7th Bde MG Coy 6.1.1916. *Belfast News Letter*, 10.5.1918, reported that he had been wounded while serving with the MGC. Mentioned in Despatches, *London Gazette*, 21.5.1918. Ended the war as a/Major in the MGC. MC awarded for service with 4th Bn MGC, *London Gazette*, 3.6.1919. By 1938 he was residing at Sunnyside, Sunningdale, Berks. File missing.

Bennett Capt. Reginald Urban. Born 1892, the son of Urban William Bennett. Enlisted as Pte 6338 in 5th Scottish Rifles TF, 19.2.1912. Age 19 years 11 months, height 5 foot 8⅝ inches, chest 31½–35 inches, civil servant serving with the Commissioners of Customs and Excise, member of the Civil Service Cadet Corps, London. Mobilized 5.8.1914. L/Cpl 3.10.1914. Embarked for France 4.11.1914. A/Cpl 4.3.1915, and a/Sgt 4.11.1915. To Cadet School, GHQ France, 10.11.1915, and appointed 2/Lt. in 13th Cheshire Regt, 12.12.1915. Attached 2nd RIR. Wounded 16.7.1916, embarked Le Havre–Southampton aboard SS *Salta*, and admitted London General Hospital suffering from wounds and shock. Went on sick leave and resided with his father at 16 Windsor Road, Wanstead, London. Joined 3rd Cheshires at Birkenhead 18.9.1916. Fit for general service 19.1.1917. MB at Etaples, 18.5.1918, granted three week's leave. He was an a/Capt. with 1st Cheshires when he was wounded at Gouzeaucourt, 28.9.1918, GSW left forearm. Admitted to No. 3 General Hospital at Le Treport, being evacuated to the UK 6.10.1918. Discharged 12.6.1919, rated A1, single. File ref: 339/51211.

Bethell Lt. Frank Harry. Born 18.5.1896, the eldest son of 1st Baron of Romford (Sir John Henry Bethell 1861–1945, Knight 1906, Baronet 1911), Park House, Wanstead, Essex. His father was JP Essex, first mayor of East Ham, Liberal MP, Romford Division, Essex, 1906–18, and East Ham (N) 1918–22. A director of Barclays Bank Ltd., Royal Exchange Assurance, and chairman of Frederick Hotels Ltd.

He was in the OTC at Harrow. Commissioned to 3rd CR, 15.8.1914, and promoted Lt. 6.4.1915. Admitted to No.14 General Hospital, Wimereux, 11.5.1915, with German measles. To Cambridge Hospital, 17.5.1915, suffering from debility. He had recovered from the measles, but was 'suffering from wounds in the face caused by an extraction of teeth and requires consecutive treatment for three weeks'. Joined 8th CR 2.7.1915. Posted to 2nd RIR 23.9.1915 and reported as missing two days later. The British Red Cross received a report from the German Red Cross in Berlin (who received the information from a comrade in his section) that Bethell 'was killed at Hooge on 25 September 1915 by a splinter from a grenade'.

His father later resided at Bushey House, Bushey, Herts, and enquired to the WO, 29.6.1921, about a service gratuity for 112 days' service in his first year (1914) and 62 days in the second year (1915). His younger brother, John Raymond Bethell (1902–65), became 2nd Baron. Menin Gate Memorial. File ref: 339/26280.

Bird Major-General Sir Wilkinson Dent KBE, CB, CMG, DSO. Born 4.5.1869, the son of Capt. J.D. Bird, 20th Hussars, and Kathleen Shortt. Educated at Wellington and Sandhurst. Commissioned in The Queen's (Royal West Surrey Regt) 22.8.1888. Promoted Lt. 1.12.1890, Capt. and Brevet Major 1897. *The Distinguished Service Order*: 'He served under the Niger Company in the Niger Expedition, 1897, taking part in the expeditions to Egbon, Bida and

Ilorin. He was Mentioned in Despatches (*London Gazette*, 11 June 1897); was given the Brevet of Major 16 June 1897, and received the Medal and clasp. He took part with the 1st Bn of the Queen's in the operations on the North-West Frontier of India, 1897–8, serving with the Mohmand Field and Tirah Expeditionary Forces (Medal and two clasps). He was on Special Service in South Africa, 15 July 1899 to 16 August 1900, with the Rhodesian Regt. He was severely wounded; Mentioned in Despatches (*London Gazette*, 19 April 1901); received the Queen's Medal with three clasps, and was created a Companion of the Distinguished Service Order (*London Gazette*, 19 April 1901): "Wilkinson Dent Bird, Capt. and Brevet Major, Royal West Surrey Regt. In recognition of services during the recent operations in South Africa." The insignia were presented by the King 29 October 1901. Capt. and Brevet Major Bird passed the Staff College in 1901. He was specially employed at the War Office from 1 January 1902 to 26 April 1903; was Chief Instructor and Staff Officer, School of Musketry, Hythe, 27 April 1903 to 8 June 1905; was Professor, Staff College, India, 24 June 1905 to 13 January 1909; was given the Brevet of Lt.-Col. 18 December 1909; was G.S.O., Second Grade, War Office, 23 January 1910 to 23 September 1913; was promoted to Major 29 September 1910; Lt.-Col., Royal Irish Rifles, 24 September 1913 to 7 June 1915; Colonel 2 June 1913 (by antedate). He served in the European War, with the 2nd Bn Royal Irish Rifles, in 1914 and was severely wounded; was Mentioned in Despatches; was appointed ADC to the King, with the Brevet rank of Colonel, 18 February 1915. He was specially employed at the War Office, 16 April 1915 to 7 June 1915; was G.S.O., First Grade (temporary), War Office, 8 June 1915 to 3 February 1916; Director of Staff Duties, War Office (temporary), and Temporary Brigadier-General, 4 February 1916 to 31 December 1917. Lt.-Governor and Secretary, Royal Hospital, Chelsea, 19 May 1918, and Temporary Major-General. He was created a CB in 1916, and a CMG in 1918. Is an officer of the Legion of Honour and has the French Croix de Guerre. He has the Royal Geographical Society's Diploma, and has published *Lectures on the Strategy of the Franco-German and Russo-Japanese Wars*; also *A Précis of Strategy*. He married, in 1902, Winifred Editha, daughter of Major J.B. Barker, and they have two daughters.' Other publications were *Direction of War*, and *A Chapter of Misfortunes in Mesopotamia 1915*.

Irish Life, 22.1.1915: 'He also served in the North-West Frontier of India, for which he was awarded the medal with two clasps. During the South African War he was present at the Relief of Mafeking, where he was severely wounded.' This wound caused him to lose the use of an arm. Transferred to 2nd RIR, 23.9.1913, when he took over command of the battalion. Wounded, losing a leg, 19.9.1914. Retired from the Army and made a KBE in 1923. He was Colonel of The Queen's Royal Regt 1929–39. Resided at *Glenturf*, Middleton Road, Camberley.

Belfast Telegraph, 1939: 'Captain Falls ... stated that the loss of Colonel Bird was a very serious one. "Sagacious, determined, and swift of decision, he had brought the battalion through some very tight places. Its debt to him was high."' Died 6.1.1943. Closed file.

Bland 2/Lt. John George. Born 14.5.1889 at Hornsey, London, the son of George and Eliza Ann Bland. Educated at City of London School and was a clerk in the City Corporation Office at the Guildhall in 1904. His sport was hockey and, up to the outbreak of the war, he was organist at Colebrook Row Chapel, Islington. Enlisted as Pte 5906 in the HAC, 14.11.1912, height 5 foot 10 inches, chest 37–39½. Address given was his father's residence at 27 Granville Road, Stroud Green, London. Mobilized 5.8.1914. Went overseas with 1st HAC to St Nazaire 18.9.1914. Commissioned in the RIR, 11.2.1915, and joined 2nd RIR 12.4.1915. Appointed Coy Bombing Officer. Wounded 16.6.1915, bullet wound to the chest and left shoulder, and admitted to No.2 Canadian Stationary Hospital, Le Touret. Died 9.7.1916. His last letter indicated that he hoped to be sent home in the very near future, but a blood clot passed to his lung and caused his death. His father administered a gross estate of £765. Etaples Military Cemetery, Pas de Calais, I.B.1. File ref: 339/28230.

Bond 2/Lt. Thomas Robinson. Commissioned to 3rd RIR 26.6.1918. Joined 2nd RIR in October 1918. To 12th RIR in the Army of the Rhine 22.2.1919. Closed file.

Borcherds Capt. Douglas Bower De Alverez. Born 2.11.1881. *Irish Times*, 30.1.1916: 'He is the second son of Mr Peter Borcherds JP, of Wynberg, South Africa, and the brother-in-law of Captain the Hon. A.S. Fitzgerald of the Royal Irish Regiment.'

Educated at a college in Cape Town and an agricultural school in the Cape Colony. Served as a Trooper in the Western Province Mounted Rifles, Cape Colony, 15.1.1901 to 29.4.1901. Worked for the Cape Colony and Transvaal Civil Service. Applied for a commission 26.12.1914. Single, permanent address Westons, Clacton-on-Sea, Essex, 'Agricultural Expert'. First appointment as a Lt., 4th CR, 26.1.1915.

Joined 2nd RIR 1.10.1915. Promoted Capt. 30.11.1915. Wounded by shellfire 27.1.1916. Home address Cambrian House, Clonmel, Co. Tipperary. MB at No. 1 London General Hospital, 25.2.1916: superficial flesh wound to neck and right shoulder; shell fragment removed from right forearm, and shell fragment still lodged in thigh. All wounds were healed and movement was perfect; general condition good but suffering from neurasthenia. Joined 4th CR at Fermoy, 8.4.1916.

Judge Advocate's form, 13.11.1917, noted he was severely reprimanded at a court martial for drunkenness. Confidential report by OC 6th R. Irish, December 1917: '[Borcherds] has rejoined the battalion under my command. I wish to report that this officer is not fit to be placed in charge of men in the line, as he has been some considerable time in the tropics he suffers very much from cold and is by no means himself in cold weather; he is naturally of a highly strung nervous temperament and has been blown up and wounded with the result that he is quite unfit to carry out the duties required of him. I am unable to place any confidence in him either in the offensive or to repel an attack. I believe him to be capable of instructing in musketry and think he might be employed on home service.' Forwarded to HQ 16th Division by OC 47th Bde 19.12.1917, 'it is most undesirable that an officer of this type should be retained with the Expeditionary Force'.

Joined 4th CR at Nigg 28.1.1918. Disembarked from SS *Himalaya* at Alexandria, 13.10.1919, and was Officer Instructor in agriculture, Imperial School of Instruction, Cairo. Admitted to hospital 23.11.1919 with neurasthenia. Embarked Alexandria–Dover 4.1.1920 aboard HS *Assage*. MB 25.2.1920 at the Military Hospital, Fermoy: neurasthenia, 'wounded and concussed in January 1916. Never quite fit since. Now feeling much improved.' Discharged 31.5.1920. Last served with CR attached Depot Royal Fusiliers.

Claimed repatriation to South Africa. Letter from WO, 31.12.1920, to Borcherds, c/o K.H. Borcherds, Mines Office, Salisbury, S. Rhodesia: everything possible would be done regarding repatriation of his wife and family to Cape Town. A deferment was granted to them until 1.2.1921 on medical grounds, and if his son was still not fit to travel by that date then another deferment would be granted. No details are on file about this problem. K.H. Borcherds may be Kenneth Havelock Borcherds, 4th CR, who served in the war with 8th R. Inniskilling Fusiliers, RIF, and 5th CR.

Applied to the WO for a record of service 1.9.1932. Gave his address as c/o Hon. Mrs Fitzgerald (his sister), 46 Boundary Road, London. He wrote to WO, 4.10.1936, asking for a position having heard there were vacancies due to the 'reconstruction of the fighting force'. Address, 44 Gloucester Gardens, London. WO advised that there were no openings for him. File ref: 339/55174.

Bowen-Colthurst Capt. John Colthurst. Born 12.8.1880 at 13 Morrisson's Quay, Cork, the eldest son of Robert Walter Travers Bowen JP, and Georgina de Bellasis *née* Greer (1855–1920), Oakgrove House, Killinardrish, Co. Cork. The family name was changed to Bowen-Colthurst in 1882 under the will of Joseph Colthurst of Dripsey Castle, Coachford, Co. Cork. Educated in Germany and at Haileybury (1894–8). He was a Cadet at Sandhurst and passed out second with honours in 1899. Height 6 foot 3½ inches, religion Church of Ireland. Commissioned to 1st RIR, 12.8.1899, and promoted Lt. 20.8.1900. Served in the South African War 1900–1 and was captured at Reddersburg. Released at Pretoria by Lord Robert's advance. Received the Queen's Medal with four clasps (Transvaal, Orange Free State, Cape Colony, and South Africa 1902). Served in India with 1st RIR 1901–8. On 20.5.1904 he, and a machine gun detachment of one sergeant and six men, proceeded to Tibet with the mission under Brigadier-General R. Macdonald CB. He received a medal and clasp for this service at and around Gyantse. Promoted Capt. 21.12.1907. Married The Hon. Rosalinda Laetitia Butler, youngest daughter of Lord Dunboyne, at Quin, Co. Clare, 2.4.1910. Their children were Robert St John (18.4.1911), Theobald George (29.8.1914), Dorinda Katherine (15.11.1912), and David Lesley (31.10.1919).

Wounded 15.9.1914. See main text. Embarked Rouen-Southampton aboard the *St David*, 19 September. MB at the Herbert Hospital, Woolwich, 5.10.1914: GSW left side of chest, front of right upper arm and right forearm; forearm broken. MB at Cork Military Hospital, 18.11.1914: the wounds were healed but movement in his right arm was limited. MBs at King George V Hospital, Dublin, 1.12.1914, 5.2.1915 and 25.3.1915: he was suffering from 'nervous exhaustion the result of active service'; unfit for home service. His only brother, Capt. Robert MacGregor Bowen-Colthurst, 4th Leinster Regt, was killed in action 15.3.1915. Left 3rd RIR for Salisbury, 9.4.1915, to take up duties as Brigade Major.

Certified fit for general service at Tidworth, 5.5.1915, 'slight impairment of movement of right forearm but otherwise recovered'. Served as a Brigade Major with 111th Infantry Bde to 9.7.1915. A confidential WO memo, 17.9.1915, stated that he was not to be promoted or to join the BEF, and should be so informed. This was due to an adverse report made by Col. Bird regarding his behaviour at Mons and the Aisne. Served with 3rd RIR at Portobello Barracks, Dublin, and was engaged on recruiting duties. He murdered six civilians during the Easter Rebellion after having a complete mental breakdown (see Lt. W.L.P. Dobbin). Efforts were made by the authorities to play down the episode but Major Sir Francis F. Vane, RMF, having been ignored in Dublin, brought the matter to the attention of Lord Kitchener who ordered that Colthurst be arrested on a charge of murder. His trial started on 6 June at Richmond Barracks, Dublin. Timothy M. Healy KC: 'Lord Cheylesmore presided, and as regards the defence of insanity raised on behalf of the prisoner two things impressed me; First: that Colthurst was proved to have become a "Bible convert" in India after a wild life. Second: that in 1914, in the retreat from Mons, he refused to go back, and led his men towards the Germans. He sat throughout the trial with clouded brow, gazing downwards. I do not think he was shamming madness, although I at first suspected it. The tribunal convicted, but declared him insane, and he was sent to Broadmoor Asylum, from which few emerge.'

1916 Rebellion Handbook: 'Major-General Bird was questioned as to the general character of the accused, and his demeanour in 1914. Witness said that he found him eccentric.

Accused seemed to be unable to concentrate his mind on a subject, and was certainly at times eccentric. Apart from that, he was a man of high character, and set a very good example to everybody ... Dr Parsons ... found him labouring under considerable excitement and restless. He did not seem to realize his position in regard to the present charge ... he told me that on Wednesday morning he went to bed at three and read his Bible, and that he came across a passage in it which seemed to have exercised a very powerful influence on his mind. The passage was to the effect: "And these my enemies which will not have me to rule over them, bring them forth and slay them." So far as I could gather from him the way that affected his mind was that it was his duty to slay men who would not have His Majesty to rule over them ... Witness said that the accused made it quite clear to him that he (accused) had done right and carried out his duty. His words were to the effect that in any other country except Ireland it would be recognized as right to kill rebels.'

Found guilty but insane and committed at His Majesty's pleasure to Broadmoor Asylum for the Criminally Insane. His service was terminated, 10 June, and he was admitted to King George V Hospital until he left for Broadmoor, 5 July. His address at that time was Dripsey Castle. A Royal Commission of Inquiry was held in Dublin, 23–31 August, under the Chairman, Sir John A. Simon. Released from Broadmoor 26.1.1918; an internal WO note stated that he was in a private asylum at Chobham. He was placed there involuntarily as a condition of his release. A Home Office note, 1.5.1918, stated that he was then quite sane. He requested a MB, 4.3.1919, as it was his intention to move to Canada at an early date. His address at that time was Crugmeer, Stanpit, Christchurch, Hants. By 24.4.1921 he was at Carnarvon House, Swanage, Dorset, when he acknowledged receipt of permission to travel to British Columbia. He intended to sail from Southampton on 26th. His home at Oakgrove had been destroyed by the IRA, 4.7.1920, and, in view of the current state of affairs in Co. Cork, he didn't want to stay there.

He lived for a few years at Terrace, BC, before moving to Sooke on Vancouver Island. His income derived from pensions and investments. He travelled to South America and Asia and, in April 1940, met Priscilla Marie Bekman of Iowa (1906–90), who was teaching at Ferris Girls School, Yokohama, Japan. His wife died 1.8.1940. Priscilla returned to the USA and they married in January 1941. They moved to Sooke and had two children: Georgiana (1942) and Alfred Greer (1945). Greer died in a boating accident in 1958. He had a small fruit ranch that he ran as a hobby. He made many complaints against General Bird for holding a personal grudge and making a damning report against him. Died of a coronary thrombosis 11.12.1965. His address was R.R.1., Three Mile Road, Penticton. *Vernon News*, 17.12.1965: 'Penticton paid its respects to the memory of its last South African War veteran at funeral service Wednesday for John Bowen-Colthurst, 85. The service in the Lutheran Church of our Redeemer, Penticton, was filled to capacity ... The Royal Canadian Legion, Branch 40, conducted its ceremonial at the graveside.' File ref: WO374/14934, PIN26/21245 and HO144/21349.

Boyle Capt. John Kemmy MC. Born in 1897, the son of Michael and Nora Mary Boyle, 12 Upper Gardiner Street, Dublin. His father was employed in the Veterinary Branch of the Department of Agriculture and Technical Instruction for Ireland. Attended the Officer's Instruction School, Trinity College, Dublin, and joined the RDF in September 1915, being afterwards transferred to the RIR. Served in Dublin during the 1916 Rebellion. Commissioned to 7th RIR, which he joined 24.8.1916. Wounded 9.9.1916. Joined 1st RIR 22.6.1917. Wounded 16.8.1917 and awarded the MC, *London Gazette*, 8.1.1918: 'For conspicuous gallantry and devotion to duty. He showed the greatest coolness under fire, and led his company with ability and courage. When the enemy counter-attacked he organized counter-attacks upon them, thereby regaining all the ground which had been temporarily lost.' Mentioned in Despatches twice.

Irish Life, 23.11.1917: 'He is the elder son of Mr M.F. Boyle, DATI, 80 Pembroke Road, Dublin, and was educated at the Christian Brothers School, North Richmond Street, and Blackrock College.' Joined 2nd RIR 6.2.1918. Wounded 24.3.1918 and taken prisoner. Died of pneumonia following influenza 21.10.1918. Cologne Southern Cemetery, Germany, VII.C.21.

Boyle Lt. Thomas Mulholland. Born 10.8.1883, the son of Thomas Muir Boyle, 4 Summerville Terrace, Dalkey, Co. Dublin. Educated at the Boy's College, Southampton, and High School, Dublin. By 1916 his father was a retired civil servant, Ordnance Survey Department. Enlisted as Pte 9277 in the Inns of Court OTC, 3.2.1916. Land agent's clerk, weight 160 pounds, height 6 foot ½ inch, chest 35–37 inches. Applied for a commission 22.7.1916. To No. 7 Officer Cadet Bn 11.8.1916. Commissioned to 5th RIR 19.12.1916. First overseas date 19.2.1917. A note, 23.3.1917, shows valvular disease of the heart, slightly irregular heartbeat and 'feels dizzy if he hurries'. Joined 2nd RIR 29.5.1917. Admitted to No. 39 General Hospital 6.7.1917: synovitis of the knee: fell and twisted it during physical drill. Embarked Calais–Dover 13.7.1917 aboard *Peter de Connick*. MBs at 2nd Southern General Hospital, Bristol: 15.8.1917, swelling disappeared but joint still stiff; unfit for service; transferred to Ashton Convalescent Hospital, Bristol; 10.9.1917, three weeks leave then report to 3rd RIR at Belfast. Promoted Lt. 19.6.1918. MBs at Fargo: 5.7.1918, condition unchanged, 20 per cent permanent disability; 20.2.1919, knee greatly improved, fit for general service, to rejoin his unit at Durrington. Discharged 26.3.1919, rated A1, married, address 58 Hardcastle Street, Belfast. Resigned his commission 30.1.1920. File ref: 339/67523.

Braddel Lt. Claude. Born 28.9.1886. Educated at Methodist College, Belfast. Applied for a commission 10.3.1915. Single, permanent address c/o Northern Banking Company, Seafield Avenue, Monkstown, Co. Dublin. 'I have for sometime past been drilling with the Irish Rugby Football Union Volunteer Corps'. Commissioned to 5th RIR 13.5.1915. Joined 2nd RIR 19.4.1916. To FA 30.5.1916. Embarked Rouen–Southampton aboard HS *St Patrick* 7.6.1916. Address, c/o Mrs C. Tracy Dunn, 23 Clifton Gardens, Maida Vale, London. MB at 4th London General Hospital, 9.6.1916, gave a date of wounding, shell shock, as 18.5.1916 at Vimy Ridge. 'This officer is of very nervous temperament and is not fit temperamentally for active service at the front.' MB at Millbank, 4.7.1916, recorded that he had a nervous breakdown in France. Since returning to the UK his feet had turned septic but were healed. He was very weak.

He wrote to the WO, 27.7.1916, advising his address as Clonkirk, Knockbreda Park, Belfast. Reported to 5th RIR 10.8.1916. Promoted Lt. 1.7.1917. A note by Capt. N.A. Stewart, RAMC, 29.10.1917: Braddel was fit for general service since 18.7.1917 but was of a nervous temperament and not physically strong. MB 30.10.1917: he had an operation for tonsillitis but his throat was still inflamed. Certified fit for general service, 22.2.1918, and ordered to rejoin his unit. A note the same day stated Braddel had complained about his nerves and that sudden noise or excitement would upset him. Last served in France with 16th RIR. Discharged 1.2.1919, rated A1, married, permanent address Northern Bank House, Donegall Square, Belfast. Relinquished his commission 11.6.1920. File ref: 339/48377.

Bratby 2/Lt. William David. Served as a Sgt (L/12827) in 4th Middlesex Regt. Promoted 2/Lt., 19.9.1917, and posted to 7th RIR. Interviewed at Albert by an RFC officer, 10

November, with a view to joining that corps. Joined 2nd RIR, 14.11.1917. To England and struck off the strength 8.1.1918. Closed file.

Bridcutt Lt.-Col. John Henry DSO. Born 7.5.1874, the son of John Bridcutt, Berick, near Benson, Oxfordshire. Enlisted as Guardsman 9509 in the Coldstream Guards 3.7.1893. Height 5 foot 10¼ inches, weight 136 pounds, chest 35–37 inches, clerk. Severely reprimanded for using bad language towards the RSM on parade 15.2.1895, neglect of duty on Barrack Guard 22.6.1895, and neglect of duty when on escort duty 12.2.1896. Promoted Cpl 4.10.1896, L/Sgt 15.4.1897, Sgt 30.4.1898, and Colour-Sgt 12.12.1899. All service up to 2.1.1900 was in the UK, apparently with the 4th Bn. Posted to 1st Bn in South Africa until 4.10.1902. Mentioned in Despatches, *London Gazette*, 10.9.1901 and 29.7.1902. Received the Queen's Medal with five clasps and the King's Medal with two clasps. Married Florence Martha Scott 18.10.1902. Children: Eva born 2.7.1903 (died the following day), Henry Owen Scott 5.5.1904, Norah 20.3.1911, and Beatrix Phyllis 4.12.1912. Posted to 2nd Bn, 11.10.1905, and appointed Sgt Major. Awarded the Long Service and Good Conduct Medal and the 1911 Coronation Medal. A testimonial by the Adjutant 2nd Coldstream Guards, 21.8.1913, noted that he was very hardworking, entirely trustworthy, tactful, intelligent, a good disciplinarian, had plenty of initiative, and was an efficient organizer. Appointed Garrison Sgt Major, London District, 15.8.1914. Home service 5.10.1902 to 5.3.1915.

Appointed 2/Lt. in Somerset Light Infantry, 6.3.1915, and transferred to the Bedfordshire Regt that day. Went overseas with 7th Bedfordshires 27.7.1915. Promoted Lt. 29.10.1915. A/Adjutant 1.5.1916. Mentioned in Despatches, *London Gazette*, 15.6.1916. Took part in the attack at Pommiers Redoubt 1–3.7.1916. His CO, Lt.-Col. G.D. Price, made the following entry in their war diary: 'This officer was my right-hand man previous to and during the assault. He took five German prisoners single-handed – organized and led two bombing parties against Montauban Avenue. He was tireless in seeing to the organization of the strong points and arranging for the comforts of the men.' Promoted Capt. 10.9.1916. Took part in the attack 27–8.9.1916 that led to the capture of Thiepval and the Schwaben Redoubt. Appointed T/Major and to command 7th Bedfordshires from 19.10.1916. Mentioned in Despatches, *London Gazette*, 4.1.1917 and 23.7.1917. Appointed OC of all specialist officers, 4.1.1917. DSO *London Gazette*, 4.6.1917 'for distinguished service in the field'. Commanded the battalion during the attack at Hooge 9.8.1917. Appointed a/Lt.-Col. and to command 12th Middlesex Regt from 8.9.1917. Seconded for duty with XVIII Corps Reinforcement Camp, 23.11.1917, and was Commandant from 8.12.1917. To Base Camp at Dieppe, 5.7.1918, to command 2nd Reinforcement Training Camp. Joined 2nd RIR and assumed command 25.8.1918. Killed in action 1.10.1918, 150 yards north of Carlton House, and was buried in Molenhoek Military Cemetery, north of Becelaere. His widow was at 11 Delmeny Avenue, Norbury, London.

Mr G.T. Thorn, 55 Hill Street, Coventry, contacted the WO, 26.1.1927, asking for his uncle's record of service on behalf of his mother, Bridcutt's sister, as she was dangerously ill. Dadizeele New British Cemetery, Moorslede, West-Vlaanderen, III.E.17. File ref: 339/24093.

Broomfield Col. Arthur Allen OBE, MC. Born 8.12.1894 at Hartley, Wintney, Hants. He was studying forestry in Exeter when war broke out. Joined the Public Schools Bn and completed a short course at Sandhurst before being commissioned to 5th RIR, 14.5.1915. Joined 2nd RIR 26.11.1915. Awarded the MC for his part in the attack of 19.1.1916, *London Gazette*, 14.3.1916: 'For conspicuous gallantry when leading a raid. He entered the enemy's trenches with a party of 15 men, killed many of them and took some prisoners. He himself with his orderly captured one Officer and one man. He displayed great coolness, courage and power of leadership. During the raid he was wounded.' Slightly wounded and went to hospital, sick, the next day. Promoted Lt. 1.7.1917. Served with 5th Tank Bn in the Tank Corps and promoted Capt. After the war he went to India with No. 1 Armoured Car Coy and later transferred to the Indian Army in which he served until his retirement in 1946. Married his wife Ruth in 1934. Awarded the OBE in 1945. Resided at Richmond in Yorkshire where he died *c.*1970. Closed file.

Brown Lt. Edward. Born 6.8.1892, the eldest son of Robert and Mary Brown, Pond Park, Lisburn, Co. Antrim. *Irish Life*, 31.8.1917: 'Before the war he was employed by Messrs William Heney & Co., Brunswick Street, Belfast [linen and cambric manufacturers] ... He was a member of the South Antrim Regiment UVF, and was a signalling instructor at the Old Town Hall, Belfast.' Commissioned to 11th RIR 16.11.1914. Height 5 foot 6¾ inches, chest 33–35 inches, weight 136 pounds, single. *Belfast News Letter*, 4.7.1917, reported that he was a nephew of Edward Leathem, Belfast City Council. Posted to B Coy, 11th RIR. Promoted Lt. 1.4.1916. Joined B Coy, 2nd RIR, 7.5.1917. Wounded twice, 8.6.1917, but remained at duty. Killed in action by a grenade 7.8.1917. The estate, gross value £326, was administered by his father, who was manager of Messrs. R. McBride & Co., Alfred Street, Belfast (finishing and stitching works). The Huts Cemetery, Ieper, II.B.13. File ref: 339/21120.

Browne Major John Plunkett. 4th R. Inniskilling Fusiliers. Embarked for France 17.10.1914. Capt. Browne joined 2nd RIR 2.11.1914. Reported sick 14.11.1914. Also served with 1st Garrison Bn R. Irish Regt that sailed for Gallipoli 6.9.1915. Closed file.

Browne Capt. Lindsay MC. Born 18.4.1890. Commissioned to 4th RIR 25.5.1912. Promoted Lt. 20.2.1913. Joined 2nd RIR 10.10.1914. Mentioned in Despatches, 14.1.1915, 'for gallant and distinguished service in the field'. Awarded the first MC to the Regiment, 18.2.1915, for his actions at Neuve Chapelle. *Belfast News Letter* 19.2.1915: '2nd RIR attached to the 4th Bn is at Holywood, Co. Down.' Promoted Capt. 16.5.1915. Relinquished his commission on account of ill health, 26.4.1916. Address The Hall, Rushbrook, Bury St Edmunds. File missing.

Bryans Capt. Joseph Charles. Served as Pte 1551 in the Liverpool Regt and joined the BEF 24.2.1915. Commissioned to 3rd RIR 1.8.1917. Served with 7th RIR from 7.10.1917 and joined 2nd RIR 14.11.1917. Appointed a/Capt. 27.12.1917. Missing in action, POW, 24.3.1918. He was in command of the remnants of the battalion that day. By July 1918 he was at Berne (see M.E.J. Moore). Promoted Lt. 1.2.1919. Closed file.

Bryans Lt. Thomas Edmond. Born 4.7.1895 at Smithborough, Co. Monaghan. Educated at McCrea, and Magee College, Londonderry. Listed as 12th RIR. Short Service Cadet with 17th RIR, posted 19.1.1916. Single, height 5 foot 7¾ inches, weight 133 pounds, chest 30–32 inches. His father was deceased. Rfn No. 1925 with 7th RIR 5.10.1916. Rejoined 17th RIR, 20.3.1917. With the BEF in 9th RIR, 27.4.1917. Appointed L/Cpl 19.7.1917. Posted to 8/9th RIR 21.1.1918. Admitted to No. 7 Officer Cadet Bn, 8.2.1918. Commissioned to 3rd RIR 26.6.1918. Joined 2nd RIR in October 1918. Promoted Lt. 1.2.1919. Arrived at Depot Coy CLC from the Rhine Army, 5.8.1919. Reported to No. 331 POW Coy, 6.8.1919. Attached from No. 708 Labour Coy, 31.1.1920. File ref: 339/73094.

Burgoyne Major Gerald Achilles. Born 3.2.1874, the eldest son of Peter Bond Burgoyne, Broadlands, Ascot. Had a brother named Cuthbert. Educated at Rugby. He was a descendant of 'Gentleman Johnny' Burgoyne, the soldier, dramatist, and politician who lost the battle of Saratoga during the American War of Independence. He was originally called to the Bar (barrister of the Middle Temple) but never practised. In 1892 he was commissioned in the Militia with the Duke of Cambridge's Own (Middlesex) Regt. Four years later he joined 3rd Dragoon Guards with which he went to South Africa, returning with an ivory inlaid Cape Dutch chair given to him by a Boer farmer's wife for not carrying out his orders to burn her farm. Joined 4th RIR (1910–20). He had a son by his first marriage.

Joined 2nd RIR 13.12.1914. Slightly wounded by a grenade 7.5.1915. Sick leave for two months with shell-shock. Rejoined 4th RIR 2.7.1915. Appointed T/Major, 2.2.1916. After the war he joined the Royal College of Heralds and became Cork Pursuivant of Arms. In 1922 he married Clarice, widow of Capt. Charles T. Waters, Admiralty Register for Ireland, and had one daughter. Died in March 1936, aged 62, bombed by the Italian Air Force while he and his mules were convoying a Red Cross unit in Ethiopia. *Who Was Who* gives his address as Corfe Cottage near Taunton, Somerset. After his wife died, his daughter, Claudia Davison, found his war letters and had them published as *The Burgoyne Diaries*. File missing.

Burke Lt.-Col. Charles James DSO. Born at Armagh, 9.3.1882, third and youngest son of Michael Charles Christopher and Amy Jervaise Burke, Ballinahone House, Armagh, and Co. Galway. Educated King's School, Bruton. *The Distinguished Service Order*: 'He served in the South African War of 1899–1902; was present at operations in the Transvaal (Queen's Medal with two clasps). He joined the Royal Irish Regt., as Second Lieutenant from the Militia, 26.9.1903; became Lieutenant 15.6.1904; was employed with the West African Frontier Force 22.7.1905 to 6.12.1909; became Captain 22.12.1909. He took up flying in 1910, and was employed with the Aeroplanes and Balloon School 22.11.1910 to 31.3.1911, and flew the first aeroplane purchased by the British Government. He served with the Air Bn Royal Engineers, Digits Formation, 1.4.1911 to 12.5.1912; joined the Royal Flying Corps 12.5.1912. During these periods he was twice injured in aeroplane accidents 7.1.1911 and 1.8.1912. He was given the Brevet of Major 3.6.1913. He served in the European War ... became Temporary Lieutenant-Colonel 9.11.1914 ... created a Companion of the Distinguished Service Order (*London Gazette*, 18.2.1915) ... He was appointed Commandant of the Central Flying School 1.2.1916 ... He was a member of the Royal United Service Institution and Meteorological Society, and an Associate Fellow of the Aeronautical Society.' He married Beatrice Osborn, third daughter of William Shakespeare, 42 Princess Gardens, London, and Yately, Hants, 28.4.1909, at London. They had four children: Amy Beatrice (born 18.1.1910), Vivienne Doreen (27.9.1911), Michael Robert James (16.9.1912), and Charles Graham (3.1.1914). He went to France in August 1914 in command of No. 2 Squadron (Wing Commander, 2nd Wing HQ), RFC. His DSO was awarded 'for services (RFC) in connection with operations in the field'. Unfit for service 7.7.1915 until 17.10.1915.

de Ruvigny: ' ... being attached to the RFC until May 1916; took a pilot's certificate of the French Aero Club the following November.' Joined 2nd RIR 26.6.1916. To CCS 30.6.1916. Promoted Major 24.10.1916. Killed in action while commanding 1st East Lancashire Regt 9.4.1917. His home address was Battlefield, Newbury, Berks. *Irish Times*, 23.4.1917: ' ... his sister being Mrs Charles Maunsell, Finniterstown, Adare, Co. Limerick. Colonel Burke was the officer in command of the Royal Flying Corps squadron which went to Limerick for manoeuvres in the September of 1913, and had an extended stay there before returning to Scotland.' Mentioned in Despatches 20.10.1914, 9.12.1914, 24.3.1915, and 22.5.1917. Point-du-Jour Military Cemetery, Athies, III.C.2. File ref: AIR76/66.

Buttle Lt. Albert Edward. Born 6.1.1895, the youngest son of John and Annie Buttle, Templeshannon, Enniscorthy, Co. Wexford. His father was director of Buttle Bros & Co. Ltd., Bacon Curers and Merchants. Educated at the Model School, Enniscorthy, and Newtown School, Waterford. Enlisted in 12th Royal Inniskilling Fusiliers 1.4.1915. Height 5 foot 9 inches, chest 34½–37 inches, weight 134 pounds, blue eyes, dark hair, shop assistant. Left Newtownards, 22.8.1915, to join the Officers School of Instruction, Queen's University Cadet Corps, Belfast. *Free Press*, 18.11.1915: 'In social circles Mr "Bertie" Buttle, as he was best known, was a prime favourite, while, latterly, his favourite outdoor pastime was motor cycling, at which he was regarded as extremely clever. He had been only a week at the depot when his intelligence and superior education attracted the attention of his officers and he was right away made a Lance Corporal. Four weeks later he was made a full Corporal and, quite recently, he was promoted to the Cadet Corps.'

Commissioned to 17th RIR, 23.8.1915, and promoted Lt. 1.7.1917. Joined C Coy, 2nd RIR, 7.8.1918. *Free Press*, 28.9.1918: 'Lt. Bertie Buttle ... was slightly wounded in the recent successful advance ... his indisposition was only of some hours duration and was able to join his company almost immediately.' *de Ruvigny*: 'Served with the Expeditionary Force in France and Flanders from 16 June 1916, taking part in the Battles of the Somme in July; was invalided home 9 January 1917; was subsequently offered his discharge as being medically unfit, but again volunteered for foreign service, and rejoined his regiment in France, 29 May 1918, and died at No. 3 Australian Casualty Clearing Station, 2 October following, of wounds received in action the previous day.'

Free Press, 12.10.1918: 'He left early in 1916 with his regiment for France where he took part in several severe engagements. His constitution, never very robust, failed to withstand the hardships of the battlefield, and he was obliged to leave for England where he remained on service for some months. His next removal was to Tipperary, where he was promoted to the rank of Lieutenant and remained for almost 12 months. Feeling that the object for which he had joined the army was not being achieved while he remained on home service, he made application to be allowed to proceed to the front. His application was refused on medical grounds but so keenly anxious was he to be with those engaged in the gigantic struggle on the western front, now happily moving to a desired point of success, he renewed his application and, after repeated refusals, it was acceded to. He again took his place in the firing line and, early in September, was slightly wounded but quickly recovered ... Prior to joining the army he had been actively associated with his father and uncle in the management of their extensive business. In social circles he was extremely popular. He was an accomplished musician and assisted frequently at public and other classes of entertainment.'

His widowed mother administered the gross estate of £829. Haringhe (Bandaghem) Military Cemetery, Poperinghe, West-Vlaanderen, III.B.3. File ref: 339/46660.

Calverley Lt. Geoffrey Walter DSO. Born 22.2.1896 at 72 Lower Mount Street, Dublin, the son of Walter Calverley Bladys Calverley (died 1906) and Edythe Agnes Calverley. Educated at St Michaels, Westgate, 1906–10; Charterhouse to 1912 (where he was in the OTC), and Loudwater, Westgate, to 1913. Entered the RMC as a gentleman cadet, 8.7.1913, applying for a regular commission 14.9.1914. Gazetted to 3rd RIR. Joined 2nd RIR 19.12.1914. Promoted Lt., 15.3.1915, and went to hospital with diarrhoea, 1.4.1915. Evacuated to the UK 22 April. Rejoined 2nd RIR 29.8.1915. Wounded 25.9.1915. Admitted to No. 1 Red

Cross Hospital at Le Touquet with severe shrapnel wounds to his back and buttocks. Arrived in the UK, 2 October, and admitted to the Hon. Mrs Guests Hospital, 26 Park Lane, London. Reported to 4th RIR, 25.1.1916, and rejoined 2nd RIR 10.6.1916.

DSO, *London Gazette*, 25.8.1916, for actions at La Boisselle, 7–16.7.1916: 'For conspicuous gallantry during several days of fighting. He led his company with great dash, and successfully beat off enemy counter-attacks. He helped to organize bombing attacks, which broke down the enemy's resistance, and led to the capture of a large number of prisoners.' Admitted to No. 1 Red Cross Hospital, 7.8.1916, with a dislocated right shoulder due to a fall from his horse. Returned to the UK 11.8.1916. Joined 1st RIR, 1.12.1916. Mentioned in Despatches 4.1.1917. Slightly wounded by gas poisoning, 8.3.1917, admitted to No. 8 General Hospital, Rouen, and later evacuated to the UK. Applied for flight training at the School of Military Aeronautics, Reading, 18.4.1917. Joined No. 1 Squadron, 1 May, and was gazetted a Flying Officer, 30 June. Died in a flying accident, 7.1.1918, in a Sopwith Scout from the Royal Flying School near Upavon, Wiltshire: 'got into a spin at too low altitude to recover'. The only next of kin was his sister Sybil Mona Calverley, Clontarf, Brockhill Road, Hythe, Kent. Gross estate £14,708.96. Buried at Upavon Church, grave No. 15.

Calwell Lt. Walter Henry. Born at Belfast 24.4.1885, the son of Walter and Rebecca Busby Calwell, Spafield, Holywood, Co. Down. His father was a linen warehouse manager. Educated at Sullivan Schools, Holywood. Enlisted at Pte 75159 in 29th Bn, 2nd Canadian Expeditionary Force, 4.11.1914. Rancher (also listed as Superintendent of Sewer Works), height 5 foot 6 inches, chest 38–42 inches, weight 146 pounds. Discharged from the CEF on appointment to a commission in 5th RIR, 18.12.1916. Trained at No. 7 Officer Cadet Bn. His father was next of kin. Joined B Coy, 2nd RIR, 13.3.1917. Wounded 18 June. *Belfast News Letter*, 28.6.1917, reported that he was not dangerously wounded and was in hospital in London. His brother, Lt. Theophilus L. Calwell MC, 9th Royal Fusiliers, was killed in action 7.10.1916. Another brother, W.K. Calwell, served with the RAMC.

Promoted Lt. 3rd RIR 1.8.1917. Rejoined 2nd RIR 18.8.1917. Wounded 24.8.1918 and died at No. 62 CCS three days later. His widowed mother administered the estate, gross value £793. Effects included a pipe, cigarette case, black cat mascot, and false teeth. *Irish Life*, 13.9.1918: 'He was in Vancouver at the outbreak of war and at once joined the Canadian Contingent and was through much severe fighting ... and was twice badly wounded.' Arneke British Cemetery, Nord, III.D.7. File ref: 339/59694.

Carruthers Lt. Robert. Born 18.1.1885 at Corporation Road, Carlisle, Cumberland. Educated at the Higher Grade School, Carlisle, and by private tuition. Married Ella Sahra Garland, 8.6.1908, at Donegall Road Presbyterian Church, Belfast. Enlisted as Rfn (Cadet) 17/1744 in 17th RIR, 1.11.1915. Height 5 foot 6¾ inches, chest 33½–36 inches, weight 135 pounds, defective teeth, Government Surveyor, Board of Agriculture and Fisheries. Address, 1 Holywood Terrace, Shore Road, Belfast. His father was deceased and had been a butcher. Next of kin was his mother, Agnes, 16 Castle Street, Carlisle. She was later replaced as next of kin by his second wife, Ella Carruthers. Applied for a commission 31.7.1916. To No. 7 Officer Cadet Bn 5.10.1916. Gazetted a 2/Lt. 28.2.1917. Joined 2nd RIR 7.8.1917. Wounded 11 August and embarked Calais–Dover two days later. MB at Caxton Hall 20.8.1917: superficial shell splinter wound right scapula, superficial bayonet wound outside of right knee; both wounds healed. Also contusion of the left knee from debris 'knocked up by whiz bang', and had diarrhoea from drinking shell-hole water. Sent for treatment at Randalstown. MB 24.9.1917: the wounds were healed but he had stiffness in his shoulder. MB at Southampton

War Hospital 26.11.1917: he complained of lassitude and general malaise with looseness of bowels. Required indoor hospital treatment. MB at British Red Cross Hospital, Netley, 14.12.1917: greatly improved and fit for home service; currently serving at the Ordnance Survey Office, Southampton. Transferred to the RE 4.1.1918. Last served with No. 2 Field Survey Bn RE. Discharged 4.4.1919, rated A1. File ref: 339/73095.

Carson Lt.-Col. Ernest Hope DSO, MC. Born at Aldershot 19.8.1871. Height 5 foot 7 inches. Served during the rebellions in Mashonaland (medal) 1896, and Matabeleland (clasp) 1897, Boer War 1899–1901 (medal and six clasps), 1914 rebellion in South Africa, German South West Africa 1914–15, Egypt and Salonika 1916. Married 11.5.1908. At the outbreak of the Great War he was a Staff Officer for the Rhodesian Reserves. Served as Adjutant in 1st Rhodesian Regt during the South Africa Rebellion and the German South West Africa campaign. Promoted Capt. in 4th RIR, 7.10.1915. Posted to Alexandria, 1.1.1916, and took charge of details of 29th Bde. Joined 6th RIR in the field at Salonika, 18.2.1916, and took command of B Coy. Admitted 31st FA 12.4.1916, 'VDH' (heart). Admitted No. 1 Canadian Stationary Hospital, 13.5.1916, with rheumatism. Embarked Salonika–Malta–Southampton aboard HMHS *Oxfordshire*, 26.5.1916, and disembarked 26.6.1916. Address, 7 Vale Road, Ramsgate. By 21.7.1916 he was at The Beechwood, Harrogate. He wrote to the WO from the Regent Palace Hotel, 15.8.1916. He was going to call to see them the following day to discuss his future employment. He was recovered but had a doctor's advice not to return to Salonika. He believed he could carry out more responsible work than he had so far been doing.

To France 1.2.1917 and served with 7th RIR. CO from 18 October. Joined 2nd RIR, 14.11.1917, and took command 9.12.1917. Accepted for service with the Tank Corps 19.1.1918. Embarked Southampton–Le Havre 18.6.1918. Served as T/Major with 15th Bn Tank Corps. To Tank Depot, 26.8.1918, and to England, 5.9.1918. Applied for a position at the Tank Corps Training Centre, Woolwich, in March 1919. At that time the next of kin was his wife at 16 West Kensington Mansions, West Kensington. The second was his sister, Miss Carson, 31 Earls Court Square, Earls Court. Posted to the North Russian Detachment 27.7.1919. Awarded the DSO, 11.11.1919 (*London Gazette*, 3.2.1920), 'For distinguished service in connection with military operations in Finland and the Baltic States.' Demobilized 5.6.1920. Address, Salisbury, Rhodesia. By 1947 his address was Haslemere, Hasfield Street, The Gardens, Cape Town, South Africa. File ref: 339/64817.

Caruth 2/Lt. James Gordon. Born at Ballymena 3.9.1896, the eldest son of James Davis and Mrs C.H. Caruth, Hugomont, Ballymena, Co. Antrim. Served as a Sgt in the Cheltenham College OTC, junior division, and left after three years, 28.7.1914. Applied for a commission, 9.8.1914, and was gazetted 15.8.1914. Height 5 foot 9½ inches, weight 150 pounds. Joined 2nd RIR in July 1915. Killed in action 25.9.1915. *Irish Life*, 26.11.1915: 'He was educated at Oakfield Preparatory School, Rugby, and Cheltenham College, where he played in the School Cricket 2nd XI, and football in the 1st XV. He was champion gymnast of the school in March, 1914, and represented his school at Aldershot for the Public Schools Shield in April, 1914.' His father claimed the effects as being the only relative. Menin Gate Memorial. File ref: 339/27463.

Charley Col. Harold Richard CBE, DL. Son of William Charley JP, DL, Seymour Hill, Dunmurry, and Ellen Anna Matilda (1839–90), daughter of Edward Johnson JP, Ballymacash, Lisburn. BIFR. The family had been engaged in the linen industry since 1822. Commissioned 28.9.1895, promoted Lt. 13.11.1897 and Capt. 10.12.1902. Adjutant 1st RIR 1904–6. Adjutant

5th RIR 13.5.1910. Promoted Major 17.9.1913. Member of Freemason Lodge 86, Downpatrick, and later Lodge 10, Belfast. His leg was struck by a shell and broken 26.8.1914. See main text. Captured and taken to Boy's College, Cambrai, until 10 September; Notre Dame Ambulance, then Mme Brunot's Ambulance to 23 November; St Vincenz Hospital, Limburg, to 10.2.1915; Mainz Hospital to 19 February; Citadel to 26 February; Mainz Hospital to 16 March; Citadel to 11 May; Neisse Camp to 3 August; Gnadenfrei to 10.3.1916; Neisse Hospital to 15 June; Gnadenfrei to 22 July. Passed the Swiss Board, went to Constance, Heidelberg, and then interned at Mürren, Switzerland, 11.8.1916. Repatriated to Dunmurry in September 1917, and was sent back to Mürren as the officer in charge of technical instruction for British internees. Appointed acting Commissioner and then Commissioner of the British Red Cross in Switzerland 1918. After the war, March–August 1919, he was appointed manager of the British Red Cross in Berlin to supervise the repatriation of Britons interned in Germany. It was at his instigation that Cyril Falls was persuaded to write volume 2 of the regimental history. Died at his home, The Trees, Helen's Bay, Co. Down, 13.4.1956.

Quis Separabit, 1956: 'He was born on April 4th, 1875, the second youngest of a family of eleven. The Charley family, originally Chorleys, from Chorley in Lancashire, came over to Northern Ireland in the seventeenth century and settled in Finaghy and Dunmurry. His father William Charley was a well-known linen manufacturer. In 1887 Harold Charley joined his elder brothers at Cheltenham College, where he gained his first XV colours, was head of his house, and became a College Prefect. He went to the RMC Sandhurst in 1893 and had Winston Churchill as one of his brother cadets. In 1895 he joined the 1st Battalion The Royal Irish Rifles at Brighton.

'From 1901 till 1903 he was on the staff at the Regimental Depot in Belfast commanded by the late Lt.-Col. Stokes. While here he followed the County Down Staghounds, and was a prominent point-to-point rider and polo player. He then rejoined the 1st Battalion in India, and, as Adjutant took part in an outstanding march 300 miles across the top of India from Meerut to Fyzabad. A road map which he drew on this occasion is now in the Regimental Museum.

'In 1910 he was appointed Adjutant of the South Down Militia in Downpatrick, and there assisted Colonel Bob Wallace, the Commanding Officer, to compose the words of the famous song *The Terrors of the Land*. On promotion to Major he joined the 2nd Battalion at Tidworth in 1914, and a few days after the outbreak of war he left with them for Flanders as OC B Company. On August 26th, leading his company in a rearguard action at Le Cateau in the retirement of the BEF from Mons, he was wounded and captured by the Germans. He remained a prisoner of war until 1916, when he was interned in Switzerland. Shortly after his arrival in Switzerland he organized workshops for British internees and for this valuable work received the CBE.

'In August 1919 he assumed command of the 1st Battalion at Rugely. He completed his term in 1923 and retired within the next year. Lt.-Col. Charley was a most enlightened commanding officer and during his term in command introduced many innovations long before they became customary in the Army. Among them were the issue of permanent passes to riflemen, permission to wear plain clothes, voluntary church parades and company welfare meetings. All these things developed a tremendous esprit de corps in the Battalion.

'Almost immediately after his retirement he was appointed to command the North West Brigade of the Special Constabulary (C.1.s). In 1925 the "C.1.s" were disbanded and then he became County Commandant of Country Antrim [until 1939] and City Commandant of Belfast "B" Specials – now known as the Ulster Special Constabulary, and remained as City Commandant until 1951, a total of 56 years in uniform.

'He did a great deal for the Regiment in all sorts of ways – not least after he had retired – and that will always be remembered. From 1924 till 1949 he was Chairman of the Regimental Association and, in recognition of his service, he was presented with his portrait in uniform and made a vice-president. Practically every day during those 26 years he visited the Association office and was mainly responsible for building it up to the thriving condition in which it is today. He attended almost every Stormberg Day, Depot Old Soldiers' Day and other parades that the Association arranged. He took a prominent part in building up the Benevolent Fund and in the special week he organized in 1945, he reached his target of £10,000; a magnificent achievement.

'The Regiment meant everything to him and he showed it in many ways. For instance, green was his favourite colour and he disliked the red of heavy infantry. He even arranged to have the car number plates IA 83 and IA 86, and used these to the end. In addition, outbuildings and gates at his home were painted dark green with black fittings. It would not be fitting to speak of Harold Charley's work for the Regiment without also referring to the very great services rendered by his wife who shared in full his devotion to it. She organized the Royal Ulster Rifles Comforts Fund and the Prisoners of War Fund in the late war and during the 1st Battalion's year in Korea. In recognition of her work she was appointed an Honorary Life Member of the Regimental Association after the war, and in 1952 was awarded the MBE. Harold Charley was the beau ideal of a Regimental Officer and it was a great satisfaction to him to see his son Robin firmly established in the Regiment [from 1943] and showing signs of weaving his life around its interests in the same way as he himself had done. – J.Y.C.'

His son, Lt.-Col. W.R.H. Charley OBE, JP, DL, provided the following additional information: 'He was on a German train and remembered being taken out onto the platform when over the border in Germany and old German women coming up and spitting on him as he lay on a stretcher. He was badly treated as a prisoner of war. Luckily he could speak German and, after recovering from tetanus and still on crutches, he became interned in Switzerland ... [1919–23] This was also the time of partition in Ireland and, after the assassination of Sir Henry Wilson, the Commanding Officer's life was on several occasions threatened by the IRA. He gave up command of the battalion on 23 May 1923 and on 9 June married Phyllis, the daughter of Robert S. Hunter of *Ma Vie*, Cooden, Sussex, and Dunmurry. He was then promoted Colonel and placed on half pay until 1 October 1924 when he retired ... He settled down at Warren House, Dunmurry ... He was a member of the Northern Ireland TA Association for many years and, shortly before the war was appointed Hon. Colonel of the Antrim Coast Regt RA TA.

'At the beginning of the 1939–45 war he was Chairman of the Northern Ireland Officers' Selection Board ... In 1940 he raised and commanded the Belfast LDVs later known as Home Guards, and organized the local HG defence of Belfast in the event of invasion. He formed battalions and raised sub units ... He was appointed a Deputy Lieutenant for County Antrim in 1946 and was also a member of the County Antrim Grand Jury. As a Freemason he was a member of Royal Arch Chapter and ... was also a member of Eldon Loyal Orange Lodge VII ... For the last two years he had been in failing health ... His daughter, June Charley, died in 1954 aged 26.' Closed file.

Chatterton Capt. Edward Victor Horace P. Served in the South African War. Promoted Capt., 3rd RIR, 5.8.1905. Army List 1912 shows him as Extra ADC to Sir Walter Egerton KCMG, Governor of Southern Nigeria. Joined 2nd RIR 21.11.1914. Returned to 3rd RIR early 1915 having been injured by a horse. Army Lists 1919 show Assistant Instructor, Military Convalescent Hospital. Closed file.

Chatterton Capt. George Alleyn. Served in the South African War 1901–2, receiving the Queen's Medal with five clasps. Promoted 2/Lt., 30.4.1902, and Lt., 12.4.1906. Retired on appointment to the SR, 5th RIR, 2.4.1910. Promoted Capt. 12.9.1914. Joined 2nd RIR 1.11.1914. Reported sick 16.11.1914 and posted to 5th RIR. According to 2/Lt. W.V.C. Lake, who was with 5th RIR at Holywood Barracks in May 1915: 'My own Company Commander was a Captain Chatterton, who in peace time had been a Gentleman Jockey and had ridden in the Grand National. He owned a very high-spirited pedigree mare, which took some handling at the head of our company and behind the band. One night, when Captain Chatterton became rather boastful as a result of imbibing much liquor, he was challenged to ride one of the Transport mules from the stables into the Mess, along the corridor (which had gas lamps all the way along) and into the Billiard Room. He did it, and also took the animal back to the stables. Anyone who knows how stubborn these animals can be will appreciate the equestrian skill required.' Rejoined 2nd RIR 10.6.1916. Joined 1st RIR, 18.12.1917, and was posted to C Coy. On sick leave with trench foot, 17.1.1918, and rejoined 6.7.1918. Later served with 5th RIR. File missing.

Clark Major & QM Walter MBE. Awarded the King George V Coronation Medal 1911. *Quis Separabit*, April 1928: 'Born in August 1872; enlisted in The Royal Irish Rifles in 1892; served in the ranks 11 years 3 months, in the rank of Warrant Officer 10 years 9 months, including Regimental Sergeant-Major; gazetted Lieutenant and Quartermaster, 2nd Battalion Royal Irish Rifles in April 1914; promoted Captain in July 1917; served in the Great War 1914–21, with the BEF, France; captured at Le Cateau [wounded 26.8.1914, see main text] … retired 30.6.1927. On retirement Capt. Clark was appointed Quartermaster, 18th London Regiment (London Irish Rifles).' Awarded the MBE in the 1939–46 Birthday Honours List. *Corbally*: 'Known, universally and affectionately, as "Pa".' Closed file.

Clarke Lt. Jack Moore. Born 2.10.1889, the son of Canon Clarke, Killead Vicarage, Crumlin, Co. Antrim. Educated at Stratford-upon-Avon. Permanent address Killead; correspondence address, 147 My Lady's Road, Belfast. Served two years in the UVF. Applied for a commission 23.4.1915. Gazetted to 17th RIR 14.5.1915. Joined 2nd RIR 16.2.1916. Suffered a bullet wound to the right side of his neck 9.7.1916. Admitted 1st London General Hospital, 13 July, and discharged to sick leave a week later. At this time part of a shrapnel ball was known to be lodged deep in the back of his neck. Reported for duty with 10th Somerset Light Infantry, Salisbury, 22.11.1916. Certified fit for general service 16.2.1917. His brother, 2/Lt. Edward Rupert Clarke, 4th Royal Fusiliers, was killed in action 9.4.1917.

Wounded at Messines, 7.6.1917, while serving with 8th RIR; GSW right thigh. Embarked Calais–Dover, 9 June, aboard the *Newhaven*. Promoted Lt. 1.7.1917. Reported for duty at Military Convalescent Hospital, Holywood, 9.10.1917. Certified fit for general service 20.11.1917. Left unit 19.8.1918, 'Royal Irish Rifles 36th Division' suffering from diarrhoea. Embarked Calais–Dover, 4 September. MB 23.9.1918: diarrhoea gone but 'looks anaemic'; recommended three weeks leave, then to report to OC 3rd RIR at Larkhill. Discharged 17.6.1919, rated A1, single, electrical engineer. File ref: 339/1300.

Clendining Lt.-Col. Hamilton DSO. Member of Freemason Lodge 418, Belfast. Commissioned to 17th RIR 23.8.1915. Served with 10th RIR. Promoted Major 3.12.1916. Assumed the duties of Second-in-Command of 2nd RIR, 11.6.1918. Took command, T/Lt.-Col., 10 July to 25 August. Left 2nd RIR on leave, 27.9.1918, prior to joining Senior Officers' School at Aldershot. Mentioned in Despatches 28.12.1918, and awarded the DSO, *London*

Gazette, 1.1.1919. He attended the 36th (Ulster) Division Officers OCA annual dinner and signed the guest book as a past member of 10th RIR. File missing.

Cochrane Lt. Ernest Alexander. Born 29.7.1893 at Belfast. His father was a loom moulder. Educated at Mount Pottinger and the Technical Institute, Belfast. Enlisted in the Inns of Court OTC as Pte 8080, 1.12.1915. Next of kin was his grandmother, Mrs Eliza Johnston, Ravenna, Cregagh Road, Belfast. Height 5 foot 7½ inches, chest 36–38½ inches, weight 148½ pounds. Applied for a commission 4.9.1916. Book-keeper, permanent address, Ravenna; correspondence address, Inns of Court OTC, Berkhamstead, Herts. To No. 7 Officer Cadet Bn 4.11.1916. Gazetted a 2/Lt. in 5th RIR 25.4.1917. No overseas service prior to this date. Served with 7th RIR until posted to 49th TMB, 28.9.1917. Joined 2nd RIR 14.11.1917. Left 11.5.1918, GSW left forearm. Rejoined 5th RIR at Larkhill in August. Admitted to 2nd Western General Hospital, Manchester, 10.4.1919. MB 26.6.1919: syphilis, originating in Belfast during March 1919; to continue mercury treatment. MB 21.8.1919: 'Now quite cured'. Ordered to report for duty at the Depot. Discharged 11.4.1919, rated A1, single. Relinquished his commission 1.4.1920. File ref: 339/71065.

Cochrane Lt. John Stewart. Son of the Revd John Cochrane, Guildford, Co. Down. Entered Trinity College, Dublin, 1914. 2/Lt. in 16th RIR 4.2.1915, and 18th RIR 22.3.1915. To the BEF 25.12.1915. Joined 2nd RIR 2.1.1916. To hospital, sick, 20.2.1916. Probably served with 7th RIR. Promoted T/Lt., a/Capt, 1.7.1917, and Lt., 5th RIR, 26.10.1918. Address Tullylish, Templepatrick, Co. Antrim. Closed file.

Collings Capt Alfred MC. Born at Scarborough, Yorkshire, 11.5.1897. He served with the 5th York Territorials and had been voluntarily discharged. Enlisted at Belfast as Rfn 10/14237 in 10th RIR, 11.9.1914. Salesman, single, Church of England, height 5 foot 5 inches, chest 32–34½ inches, weight 117 pounds, hazel eyes, red hair. Next of kin was his mother, Isabel, 93 Victoria Road, Scarborough. Promoted Sgt 23.9.1914. Gazetted a 2/Lt. in 10th RIR, 11.11.1914. Promoted Lt. 25.5.1916. Wounded in the jaw and chest at Thiepval 1.7.1916. *Irish Times*, 8.7.1916: ' … is a son of Mrs J.H. Collings, Tudor House, Victoria Road, Scarborough, and before the war was in business in Belfast with Messrs. Hanna and Browne.' Embarked Le Havre–Southampton aboard HMS *Asturias*, 4 July, and admitted to Cambridge Hospital at Aldershot. A shrapnel wound broke the rim of his jaw and knocked out eight teeth; a bullet also entered through his cheek and damaged his tongue and lip, exiting through his open mouth. The injuries were rated severe but not permanent. Granted leave and went to Tudor House. MB at York, 13 September: still required dental treatment. By October he was serving with 3rd RIR. MC, *London Gazette*, 14.11.1916: 'For conspicuous gallantry in action. He handled his men with great determination under heavy fire. When his Company Commander was wounded, he led the company on till he himself was wounded.' Certified fit for general service 6.2.1917. Promoted Capt. 5.5.1918. Joined 2nd RIR 12.7.1918. Wounded in action 16.7.1918: buried by a shell explosion, contusions to left shoulder, face, and back; severe bruising left thigh. Relinquished his commission on account of ill health in January 1919. File ref: 339/14174.

Connon Major & QM Alexander Ruddiman. Enlisted 1893. Promoted from 2/4622 RQMS to H/Lt. 20.5.1918. *London Gazette*, 3.6.1935: Major (QM) A. Connon, having attained the age for retirement, is placed on ret. pay.' In 1936 he was residing at 141 Cornwall Avenue, Blackpool, N.S. Awarded the Jubilee Medal 1938. Closed file.

Considine 2/Lt. Talbot John. Born 30.11.1884 at Denny Street, Tralee, Co. Kerry, the son of Sir Heffernan James Fritz Considine CB, MVO, DL (1846–1912) and Emily Mary (died 1903), daughter of John Hyacinth Talbot JP, DL, MP, of Castle Talbot, and Ballytrent, Co. Wexford. His father was Deputy Inspector-General of the Royal Irish Constabulary. His step-mother was Eliza, daughter of Sir John Power, Edermine, Enniscorthy, Co. Wexford. Educated at Beaumont College, Old Windsor, Berkshire. Applied for a commission 10.8.1914. Height 5 foot 6½ inches, chest 34½–37 inches, weight 138 pounds, Roman Catholic. Permanent address Derk, Pallas Green, Co. Limerick; correspondence address: Grosvenor House, Monkstown, Co. Dublin. Occupation, 'Distillery', John Power & Son Ltd., Dublin. Appointed a 2/Lt. in 5th RDF.

Joined 2nd RIR 25.3.1915. Wounded 16.6.1915 by shrapnel balls to the head, shoulder, and thigh. Granted leave of absence until 22.10.1915 and went to Derk. Received gratuities of £187.50 and £62.50. Declared fit for general service, 28.9.1916, and posted to 1st RDF. *Belfast News Letter*, 5.2.1917, reported that he had been wounded. Discharged 9.4.1919, rated A1, single, farming at Derk. Two of his brothers were killed in action: Lt. Christopher Daniel Considine, 2nd RDF, 25.5.1915, and Capt. Heffernan James Considine MC, 2nd R. Irish, 27.10.1916. Another brother was an ambulance driver in France. His brother-in-law was Lt.-Col. E.C. Lloyd DSO, R. Irish, and a cousin was Lt.-Col. H.W.D. MacCarthy-O'Leary DSO, MC, RIF, both of whom commanded 1st RIR during the war. File ref: 339/23863.

Coomber 2/Lt. George Scott. Born 20.11.1877 in Bermuda. Enlisted as Pte 5677 in the RIF 20.7.1896. Church of England. Served in the South African War, 23.10.1899 to 31.3.1902. Awarded the Queen's Medal with four clasps and the King's Medal with two clasps. Returned to the UK 1902. Married Annie Jane 27.1.1904. Posted to India 25.4.1904. Children were William Scott (born 23.4.1905) and George Alexander (21.6.1911). Returned to the UK 11.10.1914. Promoted from Colour-Sgt to 2/Lt., 3rd RIF, 21.5.1915. Joined C Coy, 2nd RIR, 12.6.1915. To hospital, 23.6.1915, suffering from concussion and deafness as a result of shelling on 16 June. Embarked Le Havre–Southampton aboard HS *Salta*, 28 June. Home address, 2 Charlton Terrace, Inchicore Road, Dublin. Granted leave until he reported to 4th RIF at Belfast, 10 September. Promoted Lt. 12.5.1916. Placed on the Home Service List 13.3.1917. Serving at Portobello Barracks, Dublin, 24 March. Reported for duty with the Ministry of Labour, Dublin, 25.11.1918. He wrote to Lt.-Col. F.R.M. Crozier, Controller, Appointments and Training Branch (Ireland), 6.9.1919, asking to be registered for employment as an Officer in the Infantry Records Dept. He was presently seconded to the Ministry of Labour, ATB, in Dublin. As he was married with children he preferred to be employed in Dublin, but any appointment would suit. This application was forwarded to the WO but there were no vacancies. Discharged 2.12.1919, 2nd RIF attached 'A.T.B. Ireland', rated E, address, 11 Charlton Terrace, Inchicore. He reported for duty at Dublin Records Office, 2 February, was placed on the half-pay list and retained his position in the Dublin office. Appointed Staff Lt., Class HH, 5 September. Applied to be put on the retired list, 1.4.1921, while he was being employed on the civil list of the office. Granted retired pay of £200 per annum plus a bonus. In 1952 his son submitted an application on his behalf for a pension in respect of an ulcerated leg which was claimed to be an aggravated wound from the Boer War. This was refused as there was no medical evidence to back it up. File ref: 339/30003.

Cooney 2/Lt. Charles Robert. Born 13.3.1894, the only son of James L. Cooney, 3 High Street, Moneymore, Co. Derry. Educated at Cookstown Academy. Senior grade certificate of education, Irish Board, 1911. Served with the Dublin Metropolitan Police at Dublin Castle.

Resided at 1 Annadale Park, Fairview, Dublin, the home of Revd Charles Robert Cooney. *Irish Times*, 16.10.1916: 'Prior to receiving his commission he held a Civil Service appointment in Dublin in the Finance Department of the Dublin Metropolitan Police Office.' Applied for a commission, 17.9.1915, and reported to the school of instruction at Ipswich, 2.11.1915, before being posted to 6th RDF. Commissioned to 7th RDF. Joined 2nd RIR 25.7.1916. Killed by a shell 9.10.1916. Thiepval Memorial. File ref: 339/45585.

Cordner Lt. James MC. Son of the Revd Joseph Cordner, Drumbo Manse, Lisburn, Co. Down. Commissioned to 17th RIR 7.6.1915. Joined 2nd RIR 16.2.1916. To FA with shell shock 23.5.1916, admitted No. 1 Red Cross Hospital at Le Touquet the following day, and evacuated to the UK 29 May. *Friends School Roll of Honour*: 'He lived at Drumbo Manse and had spent some time in Canada before returning to Ireland to study for the ministry. Although he became a minister in the United Free Church, Lisburn, he volunteered for combat service and was presented with a sword of honour by the congregation in June 1915. He did recruiting work while attached to 17th RIR. '

Served with 10th RIR. *Witherow*, April 1917: 'He was such a cheery fellow and, as his cheeriness was infectious, he was a valuable companion.' Awarded the MC early 1918 and was a Company Commander. Date of return not known but he was killed by shell fire while serving with 2nd RIR, 16.4.1918. His will, dated 13.4.1918, left everything to his fiancée, Miss Bertha A.M. Templeton, 71 Belmont Church Road, Strandtown, Belfast. She wrote to the WO: 'As the above left everything to me … I shall be obliged if you will kindly inform me if I am entitled to the "Blood Money" or if same will go to Lt. Cordner's father.' The WO replied that the amount due from Army Funds was £146.49. As this exceeded £100 they had no power under the Regimental Debts Act 1873 and there must be a grant of probate or letters of administration. 'No such grant as "Blood Money" has been authorized for issue by this Department.' *Friends School Roll of Honour*: 'He was the son of Joseph Cordner of Bannside, Portadown. There is an address to him in Drumbo Presbyterian Church where he was the minister … from 1911–26 and thereafter in Canada and Clifton Street, Belfast. He died on the 27.5.39 and his wife on the 31.1.77 aged 100.' Minty Farm Cemetery, Langemark–Poelkapelle, 11.C.2. File ref: 339/32227.

Cowley Lt.-Col. Victor Leopold Spencer DSO, MC. Born 7.6.1889 at Ealing, Middlesex, the only son of Major A.V. Cowley, King's Own (Royal Lancaster Regt). Educated at the Dragon School, Oxford (1901–3), and Repton (1903–8). Spent a year at the Royal Military Academy, Woolwich (Sandhurst Coy), where he was awarded the Sword of Honour on commissioning to the RIR, 6.11.1909. Played hockey for Kent 1908–9 and Surrey 1923–6. Promoted Lt. 24.1.1914. Member of the Army Officer's Soccer Team v Holland 1914. Wounded 14.9.1914 and 19.9.1914. Married Dorothy Sibyl Gertrude, youngest daughter of Lt.-Col. R.H. Thurlow, Kilgour, Acton Lodge, Andover, and grand-daughter of Henry Smyth, Cairnburn, Co. Down, in February 1915. Promoted Capt. 1.10.1915. Seconded to the MGC during 1916 and appointed chief instructor in November 1916. *Belfast News Letter*, 19.5.1917, reported that he had been wounded. Awarded the MC 1.1.1918. At this time his father was serving with the Labour Corps. DSO *London Gazette*, 3.6.1919. Mentioned in Despatches 9.12.1914, 28.12.1918, and 10.7.1919. Took part in the Fencing (Epee, Sabre, Bayonet) Olympia three times between 1930 and 1935. In 1938 he was residing at Green's Old Farm, Bucklebury Common, Berks. Later moved to Norden House, Kingsbridge, South Devon.

Blackthorn, 1975: 'After five years in the Regiment during which he showed himself to excel in athletics and sporting activities, he reached the final of the Army Officers' heavyweight boxing competition in 1914 ... Twice wounded at the Battle of the Aisne, where he was listed as officially killed, he was posted home until February 1917. After a period as instructor at the Small Arms School Western Command and then with the Machine Gun School on its formation, he returned to France in February 1917 with the 31st Division where he formed and commanded 31st Division Machine Gun Battalion ... After the war his services included two periods at GHQ India; the first as Commandant of the Machine Gun School, Ahmednagar, and the second as Commandant of the Small Arms School, Pachmari. He was later Adjutant of The London Irish Rifles. Retiring in 1935 after commanding the Depot at Armagh, Colonel Cowley was recalled to the service in 1939. From September 1941 to December 1942 he commanded Swansea Garrison and December 1942 to February 1943 he commanded the Barrow Garrison. In 1943 he served on the Home Guard Staff, being GSO1 (HG) NW District during the whole of 1944. He finally retired in March 1945. His death on 15th January, 1975 in his eighty-sixth year means that the Regiment has lost a very outstanding former officer who was throughout his life devoted to his family and to The Regiment.

'M.J.P.M.C. [Lt.-Col. Pat Corbally] writes: "To a very young officer Victor Cowley was indeed a formidable figure. Of venerable seniority (he joined the Regiment comfortably before the first World War): of massive stature and gigantic proportions: very much decorated and be-medalled: and of apparently invincible skill at all athletic and sporting activities ... behind this imposing façade there lay a gentle and kindly nature motivated by a great love of animals and children. Victor was very devoted to his family as indeed he was to his Regiment. It was a great sorrow to Victor when his wife died and in writing to me on that occasion he expressed a will to follow her as soon as possible. That wish has now been granted."' Closed file.

Cox Lt.-Col. Patrick Godfrey Ashley DSO. Born 10.10.1872 and entered the Army 21.2.1894. Served in the South African War 1899–1902 as a SR Officer (employed with the Mounted Infantry). Operations in Orange Free State including actions at Vet River (5–6.5.1900) and Zand River; Transvaal in May and June 1900 including actions near Johannesburg, Pretoria and Diamond Hill (11–12.6.1900); Transvaal, east of Pretoria (July–November 1900); Orange River Colony 27–9.11.1900; Cape Colony and Orange River Colony 30.11.1900 to 31.5.1902. Mentioned in Despatches 10.9.1901 and 29.7.1902. Awarded the Brevet of Major, 22.8.1902, Queen's Medal with four clasps and the King's Medal with two clasps. Retired from the Rifle Bde 15.2.1911. At the beginning of the Great War he commanded 6th RDF. Temporarily acting Commander of 30th Bde in 10th (Irish) Division, Serbia, late 1915. Mentioned in Despatches, *London Gazette*, 28.1.1916, 13.7.1916, and 6.12.1916. DSO, *London Gazette*, 1.1.1917, for distinguished service in the field. Joined 2nd RIR 8.1.1918 and assumed command. Took temporary command of 108th Infantry Bde 26.1.1918. Proceeded to the Senior Officers' School, Aldershot, 10.7.1918. Awarded French Croix d'Officier, Legion of Honour 4th Class. Placed on the Reserve of Officers list 19.10.1919. File missing.

Crawford Capt. Charles Oliver MC. Attended Foyle College. Gazetted a 2/Lt. in 17th RIR 4.10.1915. Served with 9th, 8/9th, and 2nd RIR. MC, *London Gazette*, 26.9.1915: 'For conspicuous gallantry during operations. He organized a party in the dark, and succeeded in getting ammunition up to the front line. Later, he led a charge in order to rescue some bombs which had fallen into the enemy's hands and were badly needed. He has also done fine work against enemy bomb attacks.' Served as a Lt. in the Supply and Transport Corps. Assumed temporary command of 2nd RIR 27.3.1918. Appointed a/Capt. and Adjutant 17.6.1918. Awarded a Bar to his MC. Later served as a Capt. in 2nd Punjabis, Indian Army. Closed file.

Crawford 2/Lt. Joseph. Enlisted as Rfn 12/17495 in 12th RIR. Promoted Cpl. Gazetted a 2/Lt. 25.6.1918. Joined 2nd RIR during October 1918. Closed file.

Crowley 2/Lt. Thomas P. 3rd Leinster Regt. Joined 2nd RIR 24.7.1916. To FA 2.9.1916. Most likely returned to serve with the Leinster Regt. Closed file.

Cumming Lt. Howard. Born at Belfast 13.12.1897, the son of Samuel and Eliza Cumming. His father was a building contractor. Educated at Mercantile College and Municipal Technical Institute. Attested as Rfn 19/549 in 19th RIR, 18.4.1916. Height 5 foot 8½ inches, chest 33½–35½ inches, weight 132 pounds, vision 6/6 both eyes with glasses, 6/18 without, builder's apprentice. Applied for a commission 20.5.1916. He was living at his parents' house at 77 Antrim Road, Belfast, and had served twenty months with Belfast OTC. First class shot: he had completed a two-month intensive training course. Mobilized 1.7.1916. To No. 7 Officer Cadet Bn at the Curragh 3.7.1916. Transferred to MGC Officer Cadet Bn 30.9.1916. 'Not suitable for MGC, returned to former Cadet Bn.' Commissioned to 17th RIR, 18.12.1916. MB at Belfast 1.3.1917: septic problem, unfit for any service for six weeks. He was in hospital as of 10.4.1917 with septic poisoning to his arm, following a vaccination, and had not yet served overseas. Posted to 10th RIR, 17.4.1917. Left unit 23.3.1918, GSW left arm at Ham. MB at The Prince of Wales Hospital, Marylebone, 3.4.1918: the wound was 'flesh, slight', clean and healed. Rejoined 17th RIR at Larkhill 25.5.1918. Promoted Lt. 19.6.1918. Joined 2nd RIR 24.8.1918. Wounded 30.9.1918, GSW left foot and left shoulder. Embarked Boulogne–Dover, 6.10.1918, and admitted to 1st Eastern General Hospital, Cambridge. MBs: 10.10.1918, foot septic, shoulder wound, slight flesh; 28.10.1918, 'The wounds have healed and he has recovered', but to remain in hospital and await instructions. Transferred to the UVF Hospital, Belfast, 11.11.1918. MB 4.12.1918: currently at the Officers Convalescent Hospital, Gilford, Co. Down. Ordered to take three weeks leave and then report to 3rd RIR. Discharged 4.4.1919, rated A1, single. Address, Montrose, Downview Avenue, Belfast. File ref: 339/64700.

Cupples Capt. William. Born 23.9.1895 at 145 Terment Street, Belfast, the son of William and Mary Cupples *née* Balmer. His father was a pawnbroker's assistant (later a pawnbroker). Educated at Methodist College and matriculated at Queen's University, Belfast, 1912. Applied for a commission 6.8.1914. Single, serving in Belfast University OTC, height 5 foot 8 inches, chest 33–36 inches, weight 158 pounds, medical student. Address 10 North Parade, Belfast. First appointed to 3rd R. Inniskilling Fusiliers, 15.8.1914. Later resided at his parents' home, 98 Clifton Park Avenue, Belfast. Promoted Lt. 10.4.1915, and Capt. 24.7.1915.
  Joined 2nd RIR 22.9.1915. Wounded and missing 25.9.1915. Lt. W.N. Harrison, R. Inniskilling Fusiliers, was at 1st London General Hospital, 25.2.1916. He said that Cupples was seen to go over the top with his hat off. It was thought that he was taken prisoner. Harrison had heard this from another officer 'who spoke of this youth and how brilliant he was'. The WO wrote to his father, 11.8.1916, stating that, as no further news had been received, consideration must be given to accepting death for official purposes. He replied 'I am still making enquiries and hope that he will yet turn up, as I have never had any news of his death, and some of the men in the 2nd Rifles have told me that he was taken prisoner.' He was waiting for a reply to a letter which he had sent to 7083 Rfn W. Miller who was in his son's company, was taken prisoner the same day, and had recently been transferred to Switzerland. WO advised that they had noted his views and the matter would be deferred. They regretted that they could hold out no hope of Cupples being a POW but would be pleased to hear any further news.

John Cupples, manufacturer's agent, 3 College Street, Belfast, wrote, 27.2.1919, that his brother was reported wounded and missing and the family had no information for years. He had interviewed his brother's orderly but he could tell him no more than that William had been taken prisoner by the Prussian Guards. WO to father, 29.3.1919: they could hold out no hope and asked him to reconsider accepting death had occurred. Father agreed but wanted the official notification sent to his son John. The parents later lived at 124 Malone Road, Belfast. Menin Gate Memorial. File ref: 339/23123.

Daly 2/Lt. James Joseph. 3rd Leinster Regt. Joined 2nd RIR 25.7.1916. Wounded 30.8.1916. Rejoined 12.9.1916. Struck off the strength 7.11.1916. Closed file.

Darling 2/Lt. Claud Henry Whish. Born 13.4.1895 at Winkle, Chester, the second son of the Revd Oliver W. and Edith Darling. Nephew of Col. H.N. Dunn, RAMC, and Revd J. Lindsey Darling, Rector of the Mariner's Church, Kingstown; also related to Col. Carr-Ellison of the Irish HQ Staff. Educated at Braidlea, Stoke Bishop, Bristol; Monckton Coombe School, near Bath, where he was a member of the OTC, and on the *Worcester* training ship for the Mercantile Marine. While in training his eyesight was found to be deficient and he was obliged to resign. Joined the 8th Hussars as a trooper, 8.5.1913, being sent to the 4th Hussars at the Curragh. Permanent address Chelsea Lodge, Duncannon, Co. Wexford. Correspondence address D Squadron, 10th Reserve Cavalry Regt, The Curragh, Co. Kildare. Applied for a commission at the outbreak of war and was gazetted to 3rd RIR, 10.3.1915. His brother Lt. W.O.F. Darling was killed with 1st RIR, 16.10.1915. Went to France at the end of September and joined 2nd RIR 29.10.1915. Shot through the head 12.12.1915. *Irish Times*, 17.12.1915: 'His Colonel writes: "He was sniped when trying to find some drier piece of trench for his men."'

Irish Life, 28.1.1916: ' ... son of the late Revd Oliver W. Darling, Killesk Rectory, Duncannon, Co. Wexford, and a grandson of Dr George Newman Dunn, of Duncarrig, Kinsale, Co. Cork.' Died intestate, leaving Peregrine George Ellison Darling and Katherine Ellison Darling (half-brother and half-sister, both minors) as his only next of kin. Letters of Administration were granted to his step-mother, Violet Caroline Darling, as guardian of the next of kin, her children. Tancrez Farm Cemetery, Ploegsteert, I.G.10. File ref: 339/42944.

Daunt Lt.-Col. Richard Algernon Craigie DSO. Born 1.10.1872 at Dawlish, Devon, the son of Lt.-Col. Richard Daunt, Knockerhowlea, Co. Cork, and Charlotte Isabella Craigie. Educated at Haileybury College. Gazetted to the RIR 7.3.1894, and was employed in Malta, India, and Ireland. Served in the South African War, 1899–1902, and was on the Staff, as Divisional Signalling Officer, 3rd Division, South African Field Force, 1900. Operations in Cape Colony, south of Orange River, 1899 to 1900; Orange Free State, February to May 1900; Orange River Colony to November 1900; Transvaal to 31.5.1902. Mentioned in Despatches, *London Gazette*, 16.4.1901; received the Queen's Medal with three clasps and the King's Medal with two clasps and was created a Companion of the Distinguished Service Order, *London Gazette*, 19.4.1901, 'For services during operations in South Africa'. Married Ellen Georgina Ferozepore, daughter of Capt. H.J. Cooper, Suffolk Regt, at Tarporley, Cheshire, 4.2.1903. They lived at Lauston, Pentire, Newquay, Cornwall, and had two children: Richard Hubert, born 31.12.1903, and Moira Bridget.

He was Adjutant of Militia and SR at Newtownards, 2.1.1904 to 1.1.1909, being promoted Lt. 1.2.1897, Capt. 11.10.1902, Major 5.9.1912, and T/Lt.-Col. 19.10.1914. Joined the BEF, 14.8.1914, and commanded 2nd RIR from 21.9.1914. Suffered concussion,

24.10.1914, and invalided with shell shock to the UK. Joined 3rd RIR at Wellington Barracks, Dublin, 12.4.1915. Promoted Lt.-Col. 27.5.1915. Returned to the front and took command of 1st RIR, 13.6.1915, being placed on the sick list, 26.2.1916, suffering from shell shock. Mentioned in Despatches 15.6.1916 and again assumed command of 1st RIR 28.4.1917 to 27.6.1917. *Whitfeld*: '29 September 1917. Daunt has gone home. He didn't hit it off with Heneker [8th Division Commander].' Returned to England on account of ill health, 30.8.1917, and was appointed to 4th Army HQ. At the end of 1918 he was commanding the Depot at Belfast. Retired August 1919. Fellow of the Royal Astronomical Society. Died at Newquay following an operation 4.7.1928.

Davies Lt. Percy John Llewellyn. 4th R. Inniskilling Fusiliers attached to 1st RIR. Posted to 2nd RIR 25.11.1914. To hospital, sick, 3.2.1915, and transferred to Berthen Convalescent Depot two days later. Rejoined 16.2.1915. To hospital, sick, 2.4.1915. Later served in the Labour Corps with the rank of Camp Superintendent. Closed file.

Davis Capt. Henry Ouseley. Born 15.9.1884 at Church Road, Holywood, Co. Down, the eldest son of Henry Davis, merchant and manufacturer, and Mary *née* Ouseley. Educated at Portora Royal School, Enniskillen, September 1896 to July 1900; Belfast Mercantile College, September–December 1900; Campbell College, January 1901 to November 1903. Applied for admission to Sandhurst 31.8.1903. Address Abingdon, Holywood. He was a member of the HQ Staff of the UVF at Craigavon and approached Campbell College in that capacity, 26.3.1914, to ask if it might be used as a hospital if civil war broke out. By July 1914 medical supplies were moved in and UVF nurses practised in the school's sanatorium. Davis was asked to guard the school over the summer against attacks – not from military incursions, but from suffragettes. Joined 2nd RIR from 3rd RIR 10.10.1914.

Bond of Sacrifice: ' ... a great-grandson of the late Major-General Sir Ralph Ouseley ... He was gazetted to the Royal Dublin Fusiliers in August, 1905, and posted to the 2nd Battalion, becoming Lieutenant in June, 1908. His recreations were cricket and golf. He resigned his commission in 1910, and on the outbreak of the war was gazetted Captain in the 5th Battalion Royal Irish Rifles at the end of August, 1914, being attached to the 2nd Battalion for service in September. He was killed in action by shrapnel on the 27th October, 1914.'

Next of kin: widowed mother (residing at Abingdon), sister Mary Louise, brothers Harold Newel and Frederick José. Letter from José, 11.4.1921, advised that he had received a letter from the Imperial War Graves Commission asking for details of Henry's height, build, colour of hair and any physical peculiarities that may assist in establishing his identity. He enquired as to where he could get this information. He issued a reminder, 30.4.1921, then wrote to the Secretary of State for War, 9.5.1921, enclosing copies of the two letters to the WO and asked him to resolve the matter. A letter from IWGC, 25.5.1921, said that papers only show Henry's height; if José had any further particulars regarding physical description he should forward them. An IWGC letter to Sir Edward Carson explained that their intention had been to open a grave to try to get an identification, which was why they had asked for the information. Memorial plaque in Holywood Parish Church. Le Touret Memorial. File ref: 339/6278.

Davison 2/Lt. Alexander. Born 10.1.1895 at Belfast, the son of Hugh Joseph Davison, a salesman, and Maggie Erwin *née* McMurtry, 10 Castleton Terrace, Belfast. Educated at Belfast Academical Institution. Enlisted as Rfn 14/14351 in 14th RIR, 12.9.1914. 'Apprentice Manager Linen Trade', height 5 foot 9 inches, chest 35–37½ inches, weight 130 pounds, single. (At his application for a commission his height was recorded as 5 foot 10 inches, weight 144 pounds, and expanded chest 36 inches.) Appointed L/Cpl 30.8.1915. To BEF France 3.10.1915. Applied for a commission, 25.5.1916. Reprimanded, 21.7.1916, for 'Leaving arms and equipment unprotected on line of march.' Posted to 19th RIR, 5.9.1916, and to No. 5 Officer Cadet Bn at Cambridge, 5.10.1916. Gazetted a 2/Lt. in 3rd RIR 28.3.1917 and later attached to 2nd RIR. Sent out on patrol, 22.10.1917, and was taken prisoner. See main text. POW at Karlsruhe. Repatriated 4.12.1918 and rated A. Address 10 Castleton Terrace, Antrim Road, Belfast. Reported that he had been captured unwounded at Annequin, La Bassée Canal. No blame attached for his capture. Reported to 3rd RIR 3.2.1919. Discharged 27.3.1919. Relinquished commission 13.8.1920. File ref: 339/67525.

Davy 2/Lt. Howard Samuel. Born at St Peter's, Tunbridge Wells, 15.8.1893, the son of Henry John and Elizabeth Rosa Davy, 22 Church Road, Tunbridge Wells, Kent. *Bond of Sacrifice*: 'He was educated at Skinner's School, Tunbridge Wells, where he was a member of the OTC.' Employed as a clerk with Barclays Bank, 54 Lombard Street, London. Resided at Holmcroft, Chelmsford Road, Woodford. Admitted to the HAC 29.1.1912; his number was initially 691 and later 5827. The family address was 52 Grove Hill Road, Tunbridge Wells. Single, height 6 foot 1 inch, chest 32–36½ inches. Mobilized 5.8.1914 and embarked at Southampton 18.9.1914. Appointed a L/Cpl in No. 4 Coy, 1st HAC 1.1.1915. Joined 2nd RIR as an officer on probation, 11.2.1915, and was discharged to a commission in 2nd RIR the following day. *Burgoyne* 15.2.1915: 'Poor Davey was shot through the head this morning and died in his trench at midday. I had warned him about bullets coming along the trench from the left … He was shot bang through the head from front to rear.' Kemmel Chateau Military Cemetery, Heuvelland, West-Vlaanderen, D.38. File ref: 339/23555.

Dawes Capt. Charles Reginald Bethel. Born 12.5.1888 at Osnaburg House, York Town, Frimley, Surrey, the son of Bethel Martin and Elizabeth Isabella Maud Dawes *née* King. His father was later a Colonel on half pay at Sandhurst. Joined 3rd RIR from the militia and gazetted a 2/Lt., 11.12.1909. Promoted Lt. 27.5.1914. Went overseas with 2nd RIR and suffered bad gunshot wounds in the left arm and right thigh, 15.9.1914. Joined 3rd RIR at Dublin, 7.4.1915. Returned to 2nd RIR but sent to hospital, sick, 29 June to 7 July. To hospital, sick, 9.8.1915. Contracted pneumonia in Paris, 25.8.1915, and returned to the UK, 9 September, being unfit for service. Arrested in Paris for being drunk, 2.11.1915. He was carrying papers which said that he had been granted one month's leave by a MB and had been ordered to wear plain clothes for this period. It was inferred that he was in uniform when arrested. Court martialled at Rouen for drunkenness, 19 November, pleaded guilty and received a severe reprimand. Ordered to return to the UK where he took up residence in Jermyn Court Hotel, Piccadilly Circus, London. Posted to 5th RIR in Belfast 7.4.1916. Joined 1st RIR, 20.7.1916, and was appointed Town Major of Fouqereuil, 4.8.1916. There is a brief note on his file dated 2.12.1916 from Lt.-Col. E.C. Lloyd, OC 1st RIR, which refers to an earlier confidential report from Lloyd to the GOC, France, reporting unsatisfactory performance by Dawes. A letter was sent from the Office of the CiC, France, to the WO reporting Dawes as unfit for service with the BEF: 'I request that he may not be sent to rejoin the forces under my command'. Another report noted that his work as a Town Major had been unsatisfactory, and that 'he has previously received an adverse report when in the front line trenches'.

Went AWOL, 3.2.1917, and was arrested in uniform in London, 18.2.1917. Court martial held in Belfast, 27 March to 4 April. His plea of not guilty was accepted but there is no explanation of the case on his file. He was severely reprimanded. Went AWOL 28.12.1917 to 6.1.1918 and again 23.1.1918 to 10.2.1918. A note from the GOC Southern Command stated that proceedings had been delayed due to the need to investigate reports that cheques issued by Dawes were being returned unpaid. Court martialled at Perham Down, 11.4.1918, found guilty and severely reprimanded. Reported as owing a mess bill of £21, his CO gave him one day's leave to arrange finances. Instead he went AWOL 16.8.1918. Arrested at the Craven Hotel, London, 9 September. His father called at the WO and said that his son's health had deteriorated and that he was not responsible for his actions. Court martialled at Durrington Camp 5.10.1918. Dawes claimed that he was shell-shocked but the MB examined him and declared him A1, with no sign of any mental problems. Found guilty and dismissed from the Army.

Deacon Lt. Charles Henry. Born 21.11.1891, the son of Revd John Joseph and Gertrude Deacon, Rathmullan Rectory, Clough, Co. Down. Educated Campbell College (1904–10) and was School Prefect. Served as L/Cpl in the Junior Division OTC at Campbell, September 1909 to October 1910. Joined 36th Division RE Divisional Signal Company, 20.11.1914, as a Motorcyclist Dispatch Rider and Signaller. Later promoted Cpl. Applied for a commission, 17.5.1915, and made 2/Lt. in 17th RIR the next day. Single. To BEF June 1916 attached to 8th RIR. Left unit, 2.7.1916, GSW to the head at Thiepval. Embarked Le Havre–Southampton aboard HS *Salta*, 6 July, and admitted to Worsley Hall Hospital, near Manchester. MB at 2nd Western General Hospital, Manchester, 30 July: he was struck on the head by a piece of shrapnel. Not operated on and thought that fragments of metal were still in his head. Suffered from slight dizziness and headaches. He was at home by 20 August. MB at Belfast, 11.11.1916: a fragment of shrapnel had been removed from his head but he still suffered from headaches. Certified fit for general service, 25.1.1917, and appears to have served with 15th RIR.

Appointed T/Lt., 1.7.1917, and promoted Lt. 28.5.1918. Joined 2nd RIR 24.7.1918. Left to join the Army of the Rhine with 12th RIR 22.2.1919. The next day his son, Gerald Charles Murray Deacon, was born. Discharged 15.9.1919, rated A1, married, address Rathmullan. Obtained his BA from Trinity College, Dublin, 1920. He was a master at Campbell College, 1920–39, and at the prep school (Cabin Hill) 1939–57. Vice-master 1950–7. In 1938 he was residing at 25 Stormont Park, Belfast. Retired 25.7.1957. His nickname was 'Marley' (from his bald head), and he donated a handbell – for calling in pupils – which became known as the 'Marley Bell'. He had a brother John, born 1893. Another brother, Lt. Samuel Murray Deacon, born 1896, served with the RIF and the King's Own (Royal Lancaster) Regt.

The Junior Campbellian, July 1957: 'For the last eight years of his service in Campbell he was Housemaster of Dobbin's. At the outbreak of the second World War, he elected to stay in Belfast instead of going with Campbell to exile in Portrush. These years at Cabin Hill were, we hope and believe, the happiest and most successful of his life as a schoolmaster. During the war years, when Cabin Hill trebled in size and raised its age limit to 18 plus from 13 plus, his experience proved invaluable. As second master, he was always cheerful and willing to take on any job that suddenly called for help and – during the war years in particular – these jobs were many and unexpected ... When we reverted to prep school status, much to our pleasure he decided to stay with us for the remainder of his service ... We hope, too, that Mrs Deacon and Maeve and Gerald, who have all helped us so much in the past, will keep on coming to see us.'

Junior Campbellian, July 1981: 'We heard with deep regret of the deaths of Mr Deacon on Monday, 13th April, and his beloved wife Connie, to whom he had been married for sixty-four years, on Saturday, 11th April ... His quiet and selfless devotion to his wife, who was a semi-invalid for many years, was a source of inspiration to all who had the good fortune to know him.' File ref: 339/30953.

Digges La Touche 2/Lt. Averell. Born 24.12.1884 at Carnacavill, Maghera, Newcastle, Co. Down, the youngest son of Major Everard Neal (Bengal Infantry and Assam Commission) and Clementine Digges La Touche *née* Eager, 56 Highfield Road, Rathgar, Dublin. BIFR. Nephew of Lt.-Col. Henry Averell Eager, Burrendale, Newcastle, who died during the Boer War of wounds received at Stormberg while commanding 2nd RIR. Educated at Bedford Grammar School, Mountjoy School, and the Royal College of Science, Dublin, where he received certificates in mineralogy, mathematics, machine construction, heat and advanced chemistry (June 1903). Member of LOL 357 and Royal Black Preceptory 460. Employed as a manager at Joshua Watson's, maltsters, Leighlinbridge, Co. Carlow. Applied for a commission in 5th RIR 28.8.1914. Single, height 5 foot 9½ inches, chest 31½–34½ inches, weight 126 pounds. *Irish Times*, 1.10.1915: 'He was a well-known golfer, was a semi-finalist for the Irish Close Championship in 1906 and 1911, and tied for scratch prize in the Irish Open Amateur Championship in 1908.' Joined 2nd RIR 28.6.1915. Killed in action 25.9.1915. Effects included a pipe.

   Named on the Newcastle war memorial. His widowed mother had a plaque erected to the memory of her sons and husband in St Patrick's Catherdal, Dublin. Another plaque is located in the Church of Ireland at Monasterevan, Co. Kildare, where she was living (The Gable House) at the time of their deaths. In acknowledging receipt of the Plaque and Scroll, 13.1.1919, she mentioned that his elder brother 'gave his precious life for God and the Empire at the Battle of Lone Pine, Gallipoli, and I have none left in this world': 2/Lt. the Revd Dr Everard Digges La Touche, 6th Reinforcements, 2nd Battalion, Australian Imperial Force, was killed in action 7.8.1915. Menin Gate Memorial. File ref: 339/27468.

Dixon Major Charles Stewart. Commissioned to 1st RIR 4.5.1898. Promoted Lt., 2nd RIR, 24.2.1900, and Capt. 18.7.1904. Joined 2nd RIR from 3rd RIR 10.10.1914. Commanded 2nd RIR 30.10.1914 to 24.11.1914 when he was placed on the sick list due to concussion. Promoted Major 27.5.1915. On half-pay list 4.6.1916 to 29.1.1917. Employed at the Record Office according to the 1918–19 Army Lists. File missing.

Dobbie 2/Lt. William James. Born 1882 at Partic, Glasgow, the son of William Dobbie. Enlisted as Rfn 6160 in the RIR 28.5.1900. Age 18 years 1 month, apprentice plumber, single, Church of England, height 5 foot 5½ inches, chest 34–35 inches, weight 118 pounds. Siblings were Albert, aged 4, and Jennie, aged 6. Appointed L/Cpl 27.10.1900. Certified in mounted infantry duties 3rd Class 11.4.1901, and 2nd Class 18.12.1902. Promoted Cpl 2.6.1902, L/Sgt 15.11.1902, and Sgt 4.10.1904. Married Francis Matilda Smith at Rathmines, Dublin, 11.3.1905. A daughter, Esther Winifred, was born at Dublin, 20.10.1906, but died young. Promoted Colour-Sgt 6.7.1909. Married Maud Elizabeth Ebbage at East Dulwich, 10.12.1910. There is no further information on file about his previous wife. Appointed CSM 29.8.1914. Children, Violet Florence 27.9.1911, Elsie Maud 18.9.1912, William Jame 1914 (died young), and Maud Emma 19.3.1916. All service since enlistment had been in the UK.

   To 2nd RIR 1.2.1916. Recommended for a permanent commission by Col. Goodman, 8.2.1917: 'This WO is very steady and reliable. A good disciplinarian. Is very good in front line, has good powers of organization, is a good leader and gets good work out of the men. I would like this WO as a commissioned platoon commander in this battalion.' Appointed 2/Lt., 24.2.1917, and took up duties with B Coy that day. Killed in action 7.6.1917. Effects included a set of upper and lower dentures. His will, witnessed by 9211 Sgt J.J. Wade 2nd RIR, 23.3.1916, left everything to his widow. At that time she was residing at 16 Goodrich Road, East Dulwich, London. St Quentin Cabaret Military Cemetery, Heuvelland, West-Vlaanderen. File ref: 339/86185.

Dobbin Lt. William Leonard Price MC. Born Victoria, Australia, the son of William Wood Dobbin and Emily Josephine Cuzens Dobbin. Gazetted a 2/Lt. in 3rd RIR 26.6.1915 and was in Dublin during the 1916 Rising. *Inglorious Soldier*: 'tall, slight, fresh complexioned ... friendly, gentle, gracious.' Left to join 2nd RIR 25.6.1916. He was recalled from France, 28.8.1916, to give evidence before the Simon Commission, the sittings of which were postponed for his return on 31st. *1916 Rebellion Handbook*: 'Dobbin ... stated that he was at Portobello Barracks on the 26th April, in command of the main guard. There were, he thought, eight civilian prisoners in the guardroom. He did not know either Skeffington, Dickson, or MacIntyre. He saw the accused [Capt. Bowen-Colthurst] going into the guard-room that morning. He came out again, and then said to witness, to the best of his belief, "I am taking these men out of the guardroom, and I am going to shoot them, as I think it is the right thing to do," or words to that effect. Witness, continuing, said that at the back of the guardroom was a yard enclosed by a wall ten or twelve feet high. The three men were taken out into the yard, and he heard shots fired as from the yard. He went into the yard and saw three men lying dead there ... Cross-examined by Mr Chambers, the witness said he and other men were constantly on duty for three days ... witness said that when Capt. Colthurst came out of the guardroom he appeared in an excited state, which was not his usual manner ... Did you notice anything about one of these bodies? I did. What was it? I noticed a movement of one of the legs of Sheehy-Skeffington. What did you do then? I sent for an officer to the orderly room ... What was the answer received by you? The order was that I was to shoot again. Who sent the order? Capt. Colthurst ... What did you do then? I stood by four men of my guard, and I complied with the order.'

Returned to 2nd RIR 4.9.1916. To 74th Infantry Bde HQ 5.2.1917. MC, 1.1.1918, for gallantry and devotion to duty. Rejoined 2nd RIR, 27.1.1918, and posted to D Coy. Promoted to Lt. 7.2.1918. *Witherow*: 'Then there was a young Sandhurst Lieutenant called Dobbin who was rather famous as being in charge of the firing party that shot Sheehy-Skeffington during the Dublin Rebellion. He was a very nice fellow indeed and we got on well together.' Killed by shellfire 21.3.1918, age 20. *Belfast News Letter*, 5.4.1918, reported that his sister was Mrs William McLaughlin, Jordanstown. *Irish Times*, 10.4.1918: 'Major W.W. Dobbin, Governor HM Borstal Institution, Clonmel, Co. Tipperary, has been informed by the War Office that his only son ... was killed.' Major Dobbin MBE later resided at Osborne, Dunmurry, Co. Antrim. Pozières Memorial. File missing.

Downing Capt. William Martyn. Born 4.11.1879, the son of William M. Downing, Rollo House, Holywood, Co. Down. Member of Freemason Lodge 34, Belfast, and Lodge 337, Groomsport. Enlisted as Rfn 17587 in 13th RIR, 14.9.1914. Manufacturer's agent, height 5 foot 8¼ inches, chest 33–36 inches, weight 152 pounds. Applied for a commission 23.9.1914. Under previous military experience he put '5 years Scoutmaster in B.P. Boy Scouts. Organized Holywood & District local association (Sir Robert Kennedy KCMG, President). Joined UVF when organized. Acted in all ranks. Half Coy Commander from June 1913. Company Commander from April 1914.' Gazetted a 2/Lt. in 9th RIR, 1.10.1914, and promoted Lt. 1.2.1915. Employed on Base Duty from 14.4.1916. Embarked Le Havre–Southampton aboard the *Formosa*, 6.11.1916, to have an operation on a hernia. Reported for duty with 17th RIR at

Ballykinler Camp, 5.2.1917. Appointed a/Capt., 8th RIR, 22.6.1917. B Coy commander, 8/9th RIR. Went on leave, 10.10.1917, during which time he got married. On his return he was attached to Divisional HQ as Burial Officer. Rejoined and assumed command of B Coy 26.12.1917. Left for six months leave in England, 5.1.1918. Joined 2nd RIR 17.8.1918. To Harfleur Base with bronchitis 4.11.1918. MB at Le Havre 7.11.1918: 'unlikely to become fit.' Transferred to the Labour Corps 25.11.1918. Embarked Calais–Dover, 3.1.1919, suffering from rheumatism, and admitted to Reading War Hospital. Last served with the Labour Corps, attached Staff, Dorchester. Discharged 26.6.1919. Commercial traveller, rated B1. He attended the 36th (Ulster) Division Officers' Old Comrades' Association annual dinner in 1928, signing himself as a past member of 9th RIR. File ref: 339/19178.

Drought Capt. John Bertie Armstrong. Born 8.2.1885 at 15 Kensington Garden Terrace, London, the son of John Armstrong Head Drought and Annie Gertrude *née* Turner. Educated at Winchester College and Sandhurst. Applied for the RMC 4.3.1903. Address, The Deane House, Sparsholt, Winchester; religion Anglican. Commissioned into 3rd RIR, 27.1.1905, and stationed at Dublin until 16.11.1906. Promoted Lt. 27.4.1907. At Aldershot to 24.1.1909. Married Olive Gore. Stationed at Belfast 23.6.1909 to 9.4.1914. A letter from OC 4th RIR to HQ No. 11 District, 8.4.1914, advised that Drought had applied to retire on temporary retired pay. He asked for him to be promoted Capt. in 4th RIR as he was keen to retain him and was short two captains. Rank shown as Lt. and Adjutant 3rd RIR Depot. Address, Delaford Manor, Iver, Bucks. Member of the Conservative Club. The WO approved his retirement 23.4.1914, and granted a pension of £100 per annum for a maximum of ten years. Promoted Capt. 2.5.1914.

Joined 2nd RIR 27.10.1914. To sick list suffering from concussion, 4.11.1914, and disembarked at Southampton two days later. Joined 4th RIR at Holywood 23.11.1914. Entered hospital there, 28 November, due to fainting and an irregular heartbeat. He wrote to the WO, 1.2.1915, from the Marine Hotel, Bray, Co. Wicklow, advising that he would be there until his leave expired. A MB at Dublin, 12.3.1915, ordered him to rejoin 4th RIR. Subsequent monthly MBs did not find him fit for general service until 11.4.1916 and being only occasionally fit for light duty. A letter from the MO at Carrickfergus to OC 4th RIR, 22.7.1916, reported that Drought 'is suffering from disordered action of the head ... In my opinion the greater part of his trouble is due to the injudicious use of alcohol and I recommend that he be granted three months leave in order that he may undergo treatment, preferably in an institution'. He also had sciatica. Drought stated that he was willing to undergo the recommended treatment and that he drank because of insomnia.

MB at Belfast, 31.7.1916, noted that he had 'Nervous Debility', marked muscular tremors and that he suffered from severe insomnia. The Board recommended three months leave for '(special) treatment'. OC 4th RIR agreed with the recommendation on condition that Drought was treated 'under restraint'. The OC himself was not hopeful and recommended that the leave should be unpaid. Brigadier-General Northern Command to HQ Irish Command: he was not optimistic; 'I consider his retention in the Army inadvisable in every way'. WO to CiC Forces in Ireland: Drought to be relegated to retired pay. Admitted for treatment to the Military Hospital, Victoria Barracks, Belfast, 2.8.1916, and passed fit for home service 30.10.1916. The next day he requested the restitution of his pay and wrote to the WO stating that he was discharged from hospital, 18.10.1916, but was not being paid. MBs at the Curragh Military Hospital found him only fit for home service. Admitted to hospital 18.4.1917: 'he was extremely tremulous (hands and tongue), and it was feared he would give way to violence'. A letter from OC, Military Hospital, to Irish Command, 12.6.1917, advised that he was very much better; they didn't want to detain him and requested instructions. Drought had expressed a wish to be invalided out of the Army. At that time he was Musketry Officer at the Curragh.

MB 22.6.1917: disability shown as shell shock 'following as nervous debility'. It was noted that he suffered nervous debility prior to 1914, following an accident. WO to Irish Command: to relinquish his commission on account of ill health. A letter from Lt.-Col. W.G. Murray DSO, District Musketry Officer, to PMO Curragh Camp, 24.7.1917, informed that he had not seen Drought the worse for drink during the last 4½ months that he had been under his command; generally supported him and said that he was good at his duty. Drought wrote to the WO the same day noting that he was gazetted out (*London Gazette*, 19.7.1917) and asked how he should go about applying for a pension and gratuity. WO replied that, in view of the circumstances under which he relinquished his commission, he was not entitled to a gratuity but a pension application could be forwarded.

Died at his home, Millcrest, Stone Cross, Sussex, 21.12.1949. *Quis Separabit*, Summer 1950: 'Following his retirement, he entered the ranks of Sporting Journalism, and for the last ten years held the position of shooting Editor to *Country Life*. Among the foremost writers on his subject, his recent publication *A Sportsman looks at Ireland* (published by *Country Life*, 1949), embraces both shooting and fishing experiences, and can be confidently recommended as delightful reading to all who are interested.' Another of his books was *Rough Shooting*. File ref: 339/6124.

Durant Lt.-Col. Hugh Norcott. Gazetted a 2/Lt. 29.1.1902, promoted Lt., 7.4.1906, and Capt. 11.3.1910. Adjutant 2nd RIR 25.1.1911. A Coy Commander. Wounded in the arm 15.9.1914. *Lowry*: ' ... it was not till towards dusk that we found Durant lying badly wounded near a haystack some hundred yards to our front. He had been visited by some German officers, who had treated him courteously.' Taken prisoner. Promoted to Major 8.9.1916. By 1920 he was on retired pay. *Quis Separabit*, May 1948: ' ... died very suddenly at his home at Storrington, Sussex, on 24th March 1948.' Left a widow. File missing.

Eales Major Charles Herbert Harberton. Born 16.1.1895 at Exmouth, the son of W.H.L. and Mary B. Eales, 10 Camden Grove, Kensington. His father worked for the Indian Court Service in Burma. Commissioned 2/Lt., Unattached List Indian Army, and attached 4th RIR until he left for the BEF 16.3.1915. Joined 2nd RIR 23.3.1915. Commended for gallantry for his part in the attack of 16.6.1915. To hospital, sick, 24.6.1915. Promoted Lt. 1.9.1915. Qualified as a first class machine-gun instructor at Dublin, 25.9.1915. Served in Mesopotamia 1918. Joined 10th Queen Victoria's Own Guides, India, 1918. Mentioned in Despatches, *London Gazette*, 1.1.1916 and 12.1.1920. Passed fit for promotion to Capt., March 1929. His sister, Mrs S.M. Jacobs, lived at Jullunder. Married Vere Edith Ogilvy at St Francis Church, Maine Tal, 15.5.1932. Substantive Major 15.8.1932. Children: John David Harburt, born 22.2.1934 at Saugor, India, and Mary Anne Vere, born 13.8.1935 at Aberdeenshire. File ref: L/MIL/14130 and 9/301.

Eames Major Thomas Bunbury Gough Fairfax. Born 20.6.1871. Served in Sierra Leone, West Africa, in the Mendiland Expedition of 1898–9 and received the medal with clasp. Appointed 2/Lt. in the Connaught Rangers from the Militia 21.4.1900. Seconded that day for service with the Sierra Leone Frontier Police. Promoted Lt. 5.4.1902. Joined 2nd CR 1.3.1905. Promoted Capt. 18.2.1909 and Major 1.9.1915. Served in France, August 1915 to August 1916. He also served as a Capt. in the Royal Engineers. Joined 2nd RIR 3.11.1915.

Egyptian Expeditionary Force May–September 1918. Retired 9.6.1920. Died at Castlebar, Co. Mayo, 7.4.1933. Closed file.

Eaton 2/Lt. William. Born 24.3.1894, the son of Charles and Elizabeth Eaton, 25 Bruton Street, Moss Side, Manchester. Enlisted as Pte B.2427 in the Rifle Bde 31.8.1914. Designers apprentice, cotton trade; height 5 foot 9 inches, chest 33–36¾ inches, weight 138 pounds. Posted to 7th Rifle Bde 3.9.1914. Sentenced to seven days confined to barracks and four days loss of pay for being absent off pass from midnight till 1.15 a.m., 13.4.1915, at Aldershot. Seven days confined to barracks for 'Omitting to shave himself', Alton, 21.4.1915. Forfeited five days pay for having a dirty rifle in camp, 13.6.1915. Forfeited three days pay for losing his smoke helmet at Vlamertinghe, 22.6.1915. Returned to England and posted to the Depot, 1.8.1915, to 5th Rifle Bde, 7 September, and to their 2nd Bn, 6 October. Admitted to No. 25 FA with bronchitis 21.2.1916. Posted to No. 8 Infantry Base Depot at Le Havre, 21 March, and rejoined his unit 27 April. Appointed L/Cpl 24.8.1916.

GSW left knee 24.10.1916, admitted to No. 14 CCS and to No. 18 General Hospital at Camiers that day; to No. 6 Convalescent Depot at Etaples 31 October. Posted to No. 47 Infantry Base Depot, 16 November, and rejoined 2nd Bn, 30 November. Applied for a commission, 24.12.1916. Returned to the UK 10.1.1917, and joined No. 13 Officer Cadet Bn at Newmarket, 9 March. Discharged to a commission in 18th RIR, 31.7.1917. GCM at Reading, 29.11.1917, while attached to the Pioneer School of Instruction: 'Drunkenness, in that he, at Reading on the 23rd October, 1917, was drunk.' Found guilty and sentenced to be dismissed from His Majesty's Service. File notes indicate that mitigation was pleaded, in that Eaton had taken suddenly ill. There are no detailed notes on file. Commuted to forfeiture of seniority and to date from 29.11.1917.

Joined 2nd RIR 24.8.1918. Killed in action 6.9.1918. Single, intestate, gross value of estate £115. Kandahar Farm Cemetery, Neuve Eglise, Heuvelland, West-Vlaanderen, I.A.7. File ref: 339/100593.

Edwards Lt. Cyril Kendrick. Born 7.12.1897 at Ackville, The Mount, Castlereagh, Belfast, the son of Joseph Kendrick and Gertrude Emily Edwards *née* Charnley. His father was a chief draughtsman. Educated at Belfast Academical Institution. Applied for a commission 9.2.1915. Civil engineer's apprentice, Church of England, height 6 foot ¾ inch, chest 35–37½ inches, weight 145 pounds. Currently a Cadet in Belfast University OTC. Address, The Leete, Hampton Park, Belfast. Gazetted a 2/Lt. in 4th RIR, 6.3.1915. Joined 2nd RIR 21.9.1915. Promoted Lt. 29.7.1916. Town Major at Bertrancourt, 24.7.1916 to 19.8.1916. Left 2nd RIR, 25.8.1916, with catarrh and bronchial problems. Granted sick leave and returned to Belfast. Reported to 4th RIR, 4.11.1916. Later certified fit for duty in a warm climate.

Embarked Marseilles–Salonika, 15 January. Joined 2nd Garrison Bn RIF 28.1.1917. Admitted to No. 143 FA, 26.6.1917, and No. 35 CCS the next day. To No. 43 General Hospital 28 June, and Officer's Convalescence Home 2.7.1917. To No. 3 Infantry Base Depot, 14 July, and rejoined unit 18 July. Appointed a/Capt. 20.7.1917. Reported to 2nd Garrison Bn King's Liverpool Regt, 21.9.1917. Relinquished acting rank, 24.9.1917, when he was seconded to the MGC. To No. 3 Base Depot for course of instruction, 31 October, and returned 17 November. Attached 277th MG Coy 25.2.1918. To Lewis Gun School, Salonika, 21 July. Rejoined MG Coy 21.8.1918. Ordered to attend a training course at the MG School, Grantham, and embarked for the UK 5.9.1918. Admitted No. 79 General Hospital at Taranto, 10–19.9.1918. Struck off strength of British Salonika Force 18.10.1918. Demobilized from MGC 6.1.1919. Rated GS at discharge, single.

He wrote to WO, 2.3.1937, from The Forge, Newforge, Malone Road, Belfast, asking if he was eligible for a commission in one of the new Northern Ireland TF units. He was then managing director of a mechanical and electrical engineering business, Edwards & Edwards, which he had set up. Told to apply direct to GOC NI. He was called up sometime after 1.9.1939 and sent to France. Applied for an appointment late 1939. A memo from the Deputy Assistant Director of Ordnance Services to WO, 16.11.1939, asked that he should be interviewed and assessed, with a view to him joining Ordnance Services. Attached were letters from the Assistant General Manager, Belfast Corporation Transport Dept., and Alexander Brown, a director of Davidson & Co. Ltd., Engineers and Ironfounders, Belfast. Both wrote of Edwards in the highest terms. Appointed P/O RAF VR, 19.7.1940. File ref: 339/43325.

Eldred 2/Lt. John Sturgess. Born 19.9.1894, at 71 Marine Parade, Sheerness-on-Sea, the second son of Paymaster Capt. Edward Henry Eldred CBE, Royal Navy, and Mrs Ethel Florence Hastings Eldred *née* Sturgess, The Gables, Petersfield, Hants. *Bond of Sacrifice*: 'grandson of Edgar Eldred, Esq., of Petersfield, and of the late Commander Richard Sturgess.' Educated at St Helen's College (September 1907 to December 1908); Cleveland House School, Weymouth (January 1909 to September 1910); private tuition with Mr Chevalier (September 1910 to January 1911); Woodville House, Norwich (from January 1911). Admitted to Sandhurst in late 1912. Gazetted a 2/Lt. in 3rd Leinster Regt, August 1914, and served for a short time at Tipperary and Cork. Joined 2nd RIR 27.10.1914 on attachment. Wounded 8.11.1914 and died at No. 11 General Hospital, Boulogne, 6.45 a.m., 27.11.1914. His father contacted the WO from Haarlem, Holland, 22.12.1914, requesting that the effects be sent to the Revd F.D. Sturgess, Yiewsley Vicarage, Middlesex. These included a cigarette case, a pawn ticket, and FF17.85 (£0.71). By the end of 1918 his parents were residing at Myrtle Cottage, Portchester, Fareham, Hants. Boulogne Eastern Cemetery, Pas de Calais, I.C.1. File ref: 339/11146.

Elphick 2/Lt. Kevin. Born 21.12.1896, the son of Oscar and Grace Elphick, 15 Ashchurch Park Villas, Ravenscourt Park, London. Educated at Stonyhurst where he was a Cadet in the OTC, 1909–11. Commissioned to 4th RIR 26.6.1915 and joined 2nd RIR in July 1916. Wounded in the arm and abdomen 28.9.1916 and died two hours after his admission to OC Special Hospital, Warloy. *Stonyhurst Roll of Honour*: 'The Military Chaplain of his brigade wrote: "The death of Lt. Elphick came to us as a great shock; we knew he had been wounded in the arm, but had not heard of any other injury. On his way down the trench he complained that he was feeling cold and done up. No one suspected, as far as we could judge, that he had received a serious wound. He was then brought off to the field ambulance. He must have sustained other injuries which were not manifest in the trench." ... His Colonel gave these further details: "He was holding, with his company, a line near Thiepval ... and was sniped through the arm in the early morning. I saw him when he was being brought to the dressing station, and his wound in the forearm appeared to be a slight one."' His father wrote to the WO, 5.10.1916, asking if Kevin's body could be brought home and buried next to his mother. The WO replied that the French authorities would not permit it. A statement from the Catholic Presbytery of Ashchurch Grove, Shepherd's Bush, 26 October, advised that there was no will. His surviving relations were his father (aged 59), and siblings Grace Marie (24) and Patrick Joseph (16). Warloy Baillon Communal Cemetery Extension, V.D.22. File ref: 339/73048.

Erskine Lt. Pakenham. Born 28.4.1889 at Jordanstown, the son of Pakenham and Barbara Erskine *née* Rogers, Fernville, Whiteabbey, Belfast. His father was a traveller. Educated at the Royal Belfast Academical Institution, 1900–3. The Headmaster wrote, 30.5.1915: 'he left for business after attaining a fair standard of education. This training has developed further by a successful experience in business affairs. Mr Erskine, I may add, has in addition to the ordinary attainments which a boy gains at school, a thorough knowledge of Spanish'. He was employed in the linen business, resided at Fernville, and was a Private in Queen's University OTC. Gazetted a 2/Lt., 3rd RIR, 10.4.1915. Height 5 foot 11 inches, chest 33–38 inches, weight 159 pounds. Disembarked in France 1.12.1915 and joined 2nd RIR. Promoted Lt. 29.2.1916. Attached to 74th TMB, admitted to a CCS 5.5.1916, and struck off the strength 19.6.1916 (according to the war diary). His file notes that he was with 74th TMB at La Boisselle, 7.7.1916, 'He is suffering from shell shock. He was blown up by an explosion of shell. Unconscious for a short time. Headache. Backache. Insomnia. Bad dreams. Tremor. Reflexes.' Left the unit that day and embarked Calais–Dover 16 July.

MBs at Olderfleet Hotel, Larne: 9.9.1916, he had been in their care since he had been invalided from France. 'He was suffering from general contusions of the abdomen and testicles and shell shock. He is still suffering from pain after meals with occasional attacks of pain and vomiting, although he has improved considerably during the past week; considering I had him operated on 18 months ago, his condition is not satisfactory.' 14 September, 'he has made a fair improvement ... There is some gastric discomfort after eating, and he is not able to take much exercise.' 18 October, 'He still suffers from insomnia and frequent attacks of indigestion.' 25 November, 'although improving, his nervous system is not yet normal and he suffers from insomnia.' He had recovered by the time he was sent on a grenade course in Dublin during January 1917. Later served with 3rd RIR. A letter from the Army Council to the Under Secretary of State, Colonial Office, 11.6.1919, advised that he had recently been employed with the King's African Rifles and demobilized 30.5.1919. Employed as a salesman, residing at Fernville. Granted permission, 4.7.1919, to proceed to South America so long as he went as a civilian and kept the WO advised of his address. File ref: 339/45903.

Evans Lt.-Col. John OBE. A Regular officer of the R. Inniskilling Fusiliers. Joined 2nd RIR as Second-in-Command 11.7.1916. Struck off the strength 14.3.1917. Mentioned in Despatches, *London Gazette*, 4.1.1917, 30.12.1918, and 8.7.1919. OBE, *London Gazette*, 3.1.1919.

Sprig of Shillelagh, journal of the R. Inniskilling Fusiliers, May 1922: 'It is with regret that we have to announce the departure of our Commanding Officer, Major J. Evans OBE, who was placed on half-pay on 27th inst. ... Major Evans was educated at Clifton College and was first appointed to the Regiment on 7th March 1894, from the Royal Military College, Sandhurst, joining the 1st Battalion at Dover. He was promoted Lieutenant on 6th August 1897, and was Assistant Adjutant to that Battalion in Londonderry in 1898. He served with the 1st Battalion in the South African campaign, 1899–1902, and was severely wounded at Pieter's Hill on 24 February 1900. Promoted Captain 16 November 1900, he was posted to the 2nd Battalion in South Africa, April 1901 and served with that Battalion until September 1913. During the period he held the Adjutancy of the Battalion from 29 August 1905 to 28 August 1908. He was appointed Adjutant of the Discharge Depot, Gosport, on 3 September 1913, and held this appointment until the outbreak of war. Promoted Major, 12 October 1914, during the Great War he served as Staff Captain, L. of C., British Expeditionary Force, from 5 October 1914 to July 1916. He was appointed Temporary Lt.-Col. in the Labour Corps from 11th November 1917 to 23 September 1918. Temporary Colonel and Labour Commandant (graded A.A.G.), 22nd Army Corps, British Armies in France, from 24 February to 25 May 1918. Temporary Lt.-Col. Labour Corps, 26 June 1918 to 7 May 1919. From July 1916 to April 1917 he served with the 2nd Battalion, The Royal Irish Rifles, and from May to October 1917 was employed as Instructor in the 2nd Army School. Posted to the 2nd Battalion at Portland in January 1920, and to command of the Regimental Depot at Omagh 6th March 1920.'

Sprig of Shillelagh, Spring 1943: ' ... died at his home, 62 Clifton Park Road, Bristol, on 6th November 1942 ... He saw service in South Africa, receiving twenty-six wounds at Inniskilling Hill. It is told how he complained jokingly at the dressing station that he had missed the Regimental number by one. Though badly knocked about he rejoined for duty some ten months later and saw the rest of the campaign through ... His many wounds began to tell on him in later life and during the last year or two he was seldom out of pain, but nevertheless remained game to the last.' His medals are in the regimental museum at Enniskillen. These include the Queen's South Africa Medal with five clasps (Transvaal, Relief of Ladysmith, Orange Free State, Cape Colony, Tugela Heights) and the King's Medal with two clasps. Closed file.

Farran Capt. Edmond Chomley Lambert. Born 3.10.1879, the son of Edward Chomley and Anne Hume Farran *née* Ryan, Knocklyon House, Templeogue, Co. Dublin. Educated at Dr Benson's School, Dublin. Obtained his BA and LL B from Trinity College, Dublin, 1902. Barrister, King's Inns, Dublin, 1904. In 1905 he was a L/Cpl in the South of Ireland Yeomanry, Dublin University OTC. Gazetted a 2/Lt. in 3rd RIR, 20.9.1914. Height 5 foot 11 inches, chest 33–36 inches, weight 147 pounds. Promoted Capt. 1.1.1915. Wounded and missing 16.6.1915. *Irish Times*, 26.6.1915: 'only left Dublin within the last few weeks ... He is the author of several legal text books.' WO casualty list of 17.7.1915: 'Letter received from Florence Harley, 11 Stationary Hospital, Rouen, stating that wounded soldiers in this hospital stated that Capt. Farran was killed about 16 June.' A letter was sent by Ms Harley on 12 July: 'They happened to have been in his company and were taken by Capt. Farran to make an attack on German trenches ... Capt. Farran was shot during the attack when returning to the trenches. Two men went out to look for him and found him dead. He was buried at Hooge.'

Letter from his sister, Elisabeth Mary, 27.7.1915: 'Will you be good enough to forward to US Embassy for communication to German Government an enquiry as to whether Capt. E.C.L. Farran ... is a prisoner of war in Germany.' WO subsequently sent an enquiry and the German Red Cross advised that he was not recorded in the POW lists. 4574 L/Cpl P. Connor, 5th RIR, was interviewed at Holywood Barracks, 7.9.1915: 'The Battalion were engaged in a charge on 16 June in which Capt. Farran took the lead, the informant's platoon were in the rear and the informant was wounded in the ankle before reaching the German trench. He crept back and on his way saw Capt. Farran, Sgt Major Courtney, Sgt Longhead and Cpl Laird all lying together. Sgt Major already dead. Informant lay beside him for some ten minutes and while he was there Cpl Laird died and soon afterwards Capt. Farran died also.'

2/Lt. Bennett at No.3 General Hospital, Le Treport, 18.8.15, said 'Lt. Kertland and Capt. Farran were both ... lost in June and I am afraid both were killed. There was a small attack at Bellewaarde Farm. We were in support and were moved up to consolidate and hold the first line of captured trenches. At 3.30 orders came from Capt. Farran's company to make another small attack. The Germans had not been crushed by the bombardment and a vigorous machine gun fire broke up the attack. A few were got but not, I think, very many. It is just possible but not probable that the Germans may have picked up some ... In the regiment we have very little hope for Capt. Farran or Lt. Kertland.'

Elisabeth advised WO that the Plaque and Scroll should be sent to her brother George P. Farran at Knocklyon House, then on active service in Palestine. The estate totalled £2,040. Menin Gate Memorial. File ref: 339/58010.

Fayle Capt. Oscar. Born 16.3.1888 at Merlin, St Mary's, Clonmel, Co. Tipperary, the son of Benjamin Fayle, Merlin, and Rebekah Davis Fayle, Millnar. Educated at Bootham School, York, and obtained his BA from Trinity College, Dublin, 1909. He had been a member of the OTC. Applied for a commission in August 1914. Height 5 foot 9½ inches, chest 36–39½ inches, weight 168 pounds, civil engineer, single. Address St Helen's, Highfield Road, Dublin. Gazetted a 2/Lt. in 4th RIR in August 1914. Joined 2nd RIR 31.5.1915. Posted to 31st Coy, RE, 14.9.1915. Lt. and a/Capt. 1916. His address at demobilization, 8.10.1919, was c/o Anglo-South American Bank, Antofagasta, Chile. Died 9.9.1958. File ref: 339/13042.

Fenton Lt. Peter Merton. An officer of 2nd RMF. Served with his battalion in France, 10.7.1915 to 12.10.1915. Joined 2nd RIR 9.1.1917. Wounded 1.2.1917. Probably transferred to the Seaforth Highlanders on disbandment of the RMF in 1922. Closed file.

Ferguson Major John Alex. Born 19.10.1872 at Belfast. Educated at the Royal Belfast Academical Institution, Queen's University, Belfast (Classics and Modern Languages), and the University of Louvain, Belgium. Served with 2nd South Staffordshire Regt from May 1900 to May 1902 when he resigned his commission. Joined 5th RIR, March 1907, and appointed H/Capt. 17.3.1908. Married his wife Muriel 14.7.1915. Home address 3 Kensington, Chichester Park, Belfast.

Arrived France, 22.5.1916, and joined 1st RIR three days later. Evacuated to the Base, 8.6.1916, with varicose veins. Embarked Calais–Dover 17 June. His daughter Valerie was born 22.6.1916. Reported to 5th RIR 31.8.1916. Joined 2nd RIR, 19.11.1916, and left, 30.12.1916, 'over age for front line' to go to Rouen as a Draft Conducting Officer. Embarked Le Havre–Southampton, 9.3.1917, on the *Gloucester Castle*. Cause, debility, having had influenza a short time previously. Home address, The Knoll, Craigavad, Co. Down. Found permanently unfit for general service due to age; fit for service with a Garrison or Labour unit abroad.

The WO ordered that Ferguson (5th RIR attached 3rd RIR) report to the Embarkation Commandant at Folkestone, 9 June, for passage to France. He was to be an Officer Instructor, Army of the Rhine. Appointed 10th Royal Hussars Education Officer, 11 June, and Hussars Brigade Education Officer, 31 July. Appointed Officer Instructor to 4th KRRC in India, 10.10.1919. The MB at Belgaum (Poona Division), 30.8.1920, was ordered to examine Ferguson for fitness to serve in the Army Education Corps. Found fit, but WO said his case had been carefully considered and it had been decided that he would not be appointed: 'educational qualifications good. No training as a teacher. Does not appreciate situation as regards Educational Training.' Address was his father's home at 75 Eglantine Avenue, Belfast. Discharged 16.7.1921, 5th RUR attached 4th KRRC, rated A. Elected to demobilize in India. File ref: 339/138948.

Ferris Capt. Andrew. Born 28.11.1889 at Main Street, Larne, Co. Antrim, the son of James and Aggie Ferris *née* McIlwaine. His father was a carpenter and builder. Educated at Larne Grammar School and the Arts School, Belfast Technical School. Applied for a commission 12.8.1914. Height 5 foot 11 inches, chest 33½–36 inches, weight 126 pounds, single, Presbyterian, civil engineer and surveyor. Address Rathmore, Larne. Passed a course of instruction as a 2/Lt. on 18.3.1915. With 4th RIR until 12.5.1915. Joined 2nd RIR 2.6.1915 and went to hospital, sick, the next day. MB at Queen Alexandra Military Hospital, London, 28.6.1915: 'This officer went to France with his regiment on 24 May 1915. He had previously for a fortnight been losing flesh and feeling weak. At Ypres he was not considered fit to do duty in the trenches, but was placed on the sick list on 5 June and was sent home on 17 June. He complained of weakness, polyuria and great thirst. No glycosuria, but he is thin and nervous and under his usual weight.' Arrived at Larne, 30.6.1915, with a note that he had also contacted measles. MB at Belfast 20.7.1915: admitted for polyuria. Reported to 4th RIR 18.9.1915. Promoted Lt. 20.11.1915.

Applied to join the RFC 4.5.1916: 'My qualifications are knowledge of internal combustion engines, including various aeroplane engines – Anzani, Gnome and Renault. Knowledge of construction of various aeroplanes. Ability to read a map accurately and knowledge of machine guns. I am extremely anxious that I should be attached to RFC as a pilot or equipment engineer.' A MB, 6 May, reported that 'his vision is not quite normal' but the problem could be corrected; colour sense and hearing were okay. CO, Belfast Garrison, 13 May, stated that he could be attached to the RFC: 'I also certify that he is a good map reader and field sketcher and that he has a knowledge of mechanical engineering'. Arrived at Reading, 20 June, for a preliminary course of instruction in aviation. Appointed Flying Officer 7.9.1916.

MBs: 2.11.1916, 'He has twice been at the Front, firstly with the infantry for one month. He was invalided home with polyuria and periodical neuralgia. He was home for one year, sent out beginning September in RFC, and now suffering vertigo, neuralgia and liability to be easily fatigued. KJ plus slight tremor of hands, nervous temperament.' 28.12.1916, he still complained of insomnia, suffered some asthmatic attacks at night, was still somewhat nervous and easily fatigued. 17.2.1917, his neurasthenia had improved. Promoted Capt. 1.1.1917. Instructions were issued, 8.3.1917, that his £75 fee should be refunded as he had obtained the Royal Aero Club certificate, number 2738. A note from Brooklands, 28.4.1917, stated that he had been there since mid-March. He had asthma with acute attacks at night. His daily limit of flying was two hours. Found permanently unfit as a pilot, 30.4.1917, and his flying pay was to cease. Major A.A.B. Thompson, OC 33rd (HD) Squadron, RFC, wrote to the President of the MB at Lincoln, 28.6.1917: 'This officer has been A/Adj to 33 (HD) Sqn while on light duty, having been passed permanently unfit for flying. Since he has been with this Squadron, however, he has made several ascents both as pilot and passenger without any ill effect. He has on several occasions been up over 7,000 ft and stayed there a considerable time. He is particularly keen on flying and his abilities as a pilot are above the average. I consider that if he could be given an opportunity of gradually accustoming himself to flying by being passed for "Graduated Flying" he would make a reliable pilot.' MB at 4th North General Hospital, Lincoln, 29.6.1917: suffering neurasthenia and asthma from 30 April; he had generally recovered and was passed fit for general service, but the 'question of fitness for flying reserved'. His brother James served as a Lt. in the RAF. File ref: 339/18333.

Festing Major Arthur Hoskyns CMG, DSO, FRGS. Born 9.2.1870 at the residence of his grandfather, Richard James Todd, 4 Gloucester Road, Regent's Park, London. He was the fourth son of Henry Blaythwayt Festing of Bois Hall, Addlestone, and Mary Eliza, eldest child of Richard James Todd of Great Eppleton Hall, Durham (Count of the Holy Roman Empire, created 1704; title not assumed in England). His other grandfather was Capt. Benjamin Norton Festing, RN, Knight of Hanover, who fought at Trafalgar. One of his uncles was Major-General Sir Francis Worgan Festing KCMG, GCB, ADC to Queen Victoria. Educated privately on the continent and at Sandhurst. Gazetted to the RIR, 11.2.1888, and served in the Nile Campaign of 1889. Seconded for service with the Royal Niger Company, 29.7.1895, and served as Adjutant to the Force in the Niger–Sudan Campaign of 1896–7, taking part in the expeditions to Egbon, Bida, and Ilorin. For his services, he was Mentioned in Despatches, *London Gazette*, 11.6.1897, and received the West African Medal with clasp

(Niger 1897). Promoted Lt. 3.7.1889, Capt. 15.1.1898, and Brevet Major 16.1.1898. Also received the Jubilee Medal. Served with the combined Imperial Troops (West African Frontier Force), and with the Royal Niger Company's troops 1898–9, being present at the operations on the Niger. Served in Borgu, and took part in the expeditions to Lapia, Argeyah, Ibouza, and Anam, being in command of the latter two. Again Mentioned in Despatches, *London Gazette*, 7.3.1899; received a clasp to his medal, and was created a Companion of the DSO, *London Gazette*, 7.7.1899: 'In recognition of services whilst employed in the protected territories adjacent to the Gold Coast and Lagos and on the Niger.' This was the first DSO to an RIR officer.

He was next on service in the South African War, 1899–1900. Took part in operations in the Orange Free State, February to May 1900; operations in the Cape Colony, south of the Orange River, 1900; in operations in Rhodesia May, 1900; operations in the Transvaal, west of Pretoria, July to November 1900. For a time he was in command of the 11th Mounted Infantry Bn, and on the Staff of the Rhodesian Field Force. Received the Queen's Medal with five clasps. Served in West Africa (Southern Nigeria), 1901–2, and in the Aro Expedition, commanding various columns with the local rank of Lt.-Col. from January 1901. Mentioned in Despatches, *London Gazette*, 12.9.1902; received the medal with clasp, and was created a CMG in 1902 for his services in the Aro Expedition. In 1903 he served as Base Commandant and Officer Commanding the Line of Communications in West Africa (Northern Nigeria), with the Kano–Sokoto Expeditionary Force. He was again Mentioned in Despatches, *London Gazette*, 31.7.1903, and received a clasp. Retired to the Reserve, 6.9.1905, with the substantive rank of Capt., having received a civil appointment under the Colonial Office in appreciation of his service.

Awarded the Royal Humane Society's bronze medal 1911: 'At 6 p.m. on 5.10.1910, a canoe, in crossing a swollen river at Nabugo, Gold Coast, was capsized and a native carrier was carried away, the depth being from 10 to 20 feet and infested with alligators. Awurdu Moshi went in and caught him but was unable to bring him in. Major A.H. Festing DSO, Royal Irish Rifles, then went in and brought both to land. (Case 38061).' Retired from the Civil Service 1912, and was afterwards employed by the Royal Niger Company in the Cameroons. He married Victoria Eugénie Valentine, Comtesse de Valette, in 1912 but she died the following year.

At the beginning of the Great War he served with 3rd RIR in Dublin and went overseas in December 1914, joining 2nd RIR as Second-in-Command, 5.12.1914.

Went on leave to the UK, 27.2.1915, and this was extended to 15.3.1915 due to illness. Joined 1st RIR, 21.3.1915, taking over the duties of Senior Major and Second-in-Command. Killed in action, 9.5.1915, and there are various reports of his death (*Bond of Sacrifice*): he was first wounded in the thigh, and was afterwards shot in the head and killed instantaneously while leading a charge ten yards from the German trenches. 7875 Bugler Gough: 'He was the bravest officer I have ever seen. He went over the parapet with a revolver in one hand and a stick in the other, just as if nothing had happened, walking quite coolly. We took the trench, and that night we searched and searched for Major Festing's body and could not find it. I saw him fall, and he was shot dead instantly. The Germans bombarded the trench horribly, and that may account for his body not being found.' *Burgoyne*: 'He was lying wounded in a German trench and refusing to be taken prisoner he blew his brains out. A brave officer and a fine soldier.' Ploegsteert Memorial. File missing.

Finlay Capt. Frederick Laird. Commissioned into 3rd RIR, 22.1.1913. Promoted Lt. 20.12.1913. Went overseas with 2nd RIR and was wounded 26.8.1914. *Lucy*: 'A young officer of B Coy had led an assault and had killed a German officer with his sword. The German officer had run him through the thigh in a duel.' B Coy commander, 26.10.1914, when he was taken prisoner. Promoted Capt. 1.1.1915. His medals are held in the regimental museum. Closed file.

Fisher Lt.-Col. Henry Francis Thornhill. *Records of Service*, Worcestershire Regt, compiled 1912: born 21.10.1871, the son of Revd W.F. Fisher, Shalfleet, Isle of Wight. Appointed a 2/Lt. in the Worcs Regt 13.8.1892; seconded for service with the ASC and transferred 1.10.1894; appointed Lt. 29.9.1895; seconded for special service in the Uganda Protectorate 21.1.1898 to 22.2.1900 (Medal with clasp); Capt. 20.9.1899. Served in the South African War, operations in Rhodesia, DAAG, Rhodesian Field Force 23.2.1900 to 6.4.1901; operations in Cape Colony, November, December 1900; in the Transvaal, and Orange River Colony December 1900 to August 1901; DAAG, South Africa, 7.4.1901 to 12.8.1901 (Queen's Medal with 5 clasps). Major 7.11.1906. Qualified in a course of instruction at the London School of Economics. Qualified as 2nd Class Interpreter in a modern foreign language. Retired from the ASC, 11.9.1912, and joined the Reserve of Officers.

Recalled at the beginning of the war and served with 5th Worcesters in the UK. Joined the BEF 5.12.1915. Left 2nd RIR, 8.5.1917 (noted as 3rd Worcestershire Regt), but there is no mention of when he had joined. Army List, December 1918, ASC Reserve of Officers, T/Lt.-Col. whilst commanding an Infantry Bn 20.11.1917. Awarded the French Bronze Medal of the Public Service. Lt.-Col., retired pay, by 1920. File missing.

Fitzgerald Major Gerald Vincent. Born 9.10.1892 at 21 Castle Road, Dundalk, Co. Louth, the son of Michael Vincent and Mary Elizabeth Fitzgerald. His father was a bank clerk and sub-manager. Educated at Bishop Foy's School, Waterford, and Cork Grammar School, which he left at Easter 1911. Religion, Church of England. He wrote a letter to the WO, 27.4.1912, from Belgrave Place, Cork, advising that he had served in the Cork Grammar School OTC for the previous two years, and asked for details of how to apply to join the SR. Commissioned to 3rd Leinster Regt 3.7.1912. Mobilized 5.8.1914.

Joined 2nd RIR 10.10.1914. Severely wounded 13.10.1914, GSW left eye. Embarked Calais–Dover aboard the *Copenhagen* the next day. Address shown as Bank of Ireland, Waterford. Admitted Cottage Hospital, Wimbledon, where the eye was removed. Promoted Lt. 2.1.1915. Mentioned in Despatches, 14.1.1915, 'for gallant and distinguished service in the field'. Numerous MBs certified him fit for home service only. Notes on his file in February 1915 show that he had not rejoined 3rd Leinsters, as he was meant to do, and the WO didn't know where he was. On 26.2.1915 he was ordered to rejoin at once. Promoted Capt. 8.5.1915. He was in the Fever Hospital at Cork as of 6 June. Eligible for an annual wound pension of £100. Seconded for service with the MGC 22.11.1915. MB at Military Hospital, Grantham, 13.12.1915: eye not yet healed. Returned to 3rd Leinsters 15.1.1916. He was a patient in No. 4 London General Hospital as of 28 March. A note, 12.5.1916, recorded that OC 3rd Leinsters said that Fitzgerald had been seconded for duty with the MGC and was not with his battalion. Certified fit for general service 5.12.1916.

Appointed T/Major 12.2.1918. Left unit 29.4.1918. Granted six months leave to England on a medical certificate, 22.8.1918, from the Machine Gun Centre at Bombay. Embarked HMAS *Brighton* 2.9.1918. Hospitalized at Taranto, 30.11.1918, 'seriously ill'. Disembarked Dover, 25.1.1919. Address in UK given as Holt & Co. MB 8.4.1919: fit A, to report to MGC Centre. Transferred from being an outpatient at Grantham Military Hospital to Wharncliffe War Hospital, Sheffield, 3 June. Applied for a permanent commission in the Regular Army

4.6.1919. Next of kin at this time was his mother. Discharged 16.12.1919, rated A1, single. Address 19 Idrone Terrace, Blackrock, Co. Dublin.

Served during the coal strike, 15.4.1920 to 6.6.1920, attached to No. 4 Reserve Bn MGC. Home address at this time, 29 Holland Street, Kensington. He wrote to the WO 20.7.1921: he was currently unemployed and living off his pension. He had seen that there were vacancies for recruiting officers, and asked if he was eligible. WO replied that openings were restricted to retired Regular Officers who had been commissioned from the ranks. WO letter 22.7.1922 notified of the impending disbandment of the Leinster Regt and enquired whether he wanted to relinquish his commission or transfer to another militia. Resigned 17.8.1922 retaining the rank of Major.

A letter in 1923 from Kitchener House for Officers and Ex-Officers, 59 Sloane Street, London, made a general enquiry about Fitzgerald, who was 'proceeding to Canada to try and make a fresh start in life'. WO gave a basic outline adding 'I am to add that Major Fitzgerald also served with the Auxiliary Division, Royal Irish Constabulary'. A file cover entry: 'We have nothing recorded against this officer beyond a note that he was struck off the strength of the RIC as an Absentee'. Applied for enrolment in the Officer's Emergency Reserve 24.9.1938 and was accepted; to be removed due to age 9.10.1947. Ministry of Labour to WO, 16.1.1940, asked for an outline of service regarding an application for temporary employment with the Post Office. File ref: 339/8817.

Forbes 2/Lt. John Robinson. Gazetted a 2/Lt. in 3rd RIR 26.6.1918. Joined 2nd RIR during October 1918. File missing.

Forster 2/Lt. Thomas Burton. Born at Wexford, 23.7.1886, the son of Major-General John Burton Forster CB and Olive Edith Mary *née* Sergent. Married Florence Elizabeth Johnston at Winnipeg, 24.3.1908, and they had a daughter, Florence Olive May Burton-Forster, born 13.4.1909. Served with 10th (1st Gwents) South Wales Borderers, Colwyn Bay. His will dated 18.1.1915 left everything to his wife at 178 Twelfth Avenue West, Vancouver. Applied for a commission 9.2.1915: rancher, height 5 foot 10¾ inches, chest 40–43 inches, weight 150 pounds. Permanent address Melrose, Ash Valley, Surrey. Commissioned to 3rd R. Irish 9.2.1915. His wife's address was PO Box 123, White Earth, Minnesota, or Cathedral, 121 Cathedral Avenue, Winnipeg, Manitoba. At this time his father was CO Division of Regiments in Lancashire. Joined 2nd RIR 4.10.1915. Went sick and admitted to FA 8.10.1915. Did not return to 2nd RIR and was posted to 2nd R. Irish 8.11.1915. WO telegram to General Forster, 57th or 59th Division, Canterbury, advised that his son was wounded 9th June and remained at duty, but was subsequently killed in action 10.6.1916.

History of the Royal Irish Regiment: 'Next night Lt. Forster was out again with his patrol and located two German working parties, both of which were dispersed by our Lewis gun fire ... When the battalion was in the trenches Lt. T.B. Forster and his scouts were out in front each night. On 10th they came under very heavy rifle and machine gun fire and Lt. Forster and three men were wounded. L/Sgt Michael Dreeling carried back L/Cpl Wright, then returned and carried in Lt. Forster and finally again went out under heavy fire to search for L/Cpl Walsh, who was missing and unfortunately could not be found. 2/Lt. Forster, a very promising young officer, died of his wounds shortly after he was carried in.' His widow received a pension of £100 per annum. She later re-married: Mrs Gilmour, 646 Walker Avenue, Winnipeg, Canada. Citadel New Military Cemetery, Fricourt, Somme, V.A.19. File ref: 339/27406.

Foster Major Henry William MC. Born 23.5.1861. Awarded the King Edward VII Coronation Medal 1902. Rose through the ranks of the RIR to QM 17.9.1902. H/Lt. 21.10.1903 having served 11 years 313 days in the ranks, and 12 years 203 days as a Warrant Officer. Awarded the King George V Coronation Medal 1911. H/Capt. 17.9.1912. Joined 2nd RIR (Capt. & QM) 3.6.1916. Promoted H/Major 1.7.1917. MC 1.1.1918. Left 11.3.1918, sick, and embarked Le Havre–Southampton 16 March. He was not considered fit for home service until the end of May when he wrote to the WO requesting permission to return to his unit. Instructed to report in writing to HQ London District, Horse Guards Annex, for temporary duty pending the result of his next MB. His current address was 89 Claverton Street, London SW1. Only fit for sedentary work until 6.5.1919 when he was found fit for home service. He wrote to the WO from The Oaks, Ilfield, Crawley, Sussex, 23.6.1919: 23rd Army Corps had closed down, he was no longer employed by the RE of that Corps, and requested orders. Advised that as he had attained age he was being placed on the retired list effective from 1.8.1919. Retired pay was at the rate of £250 per annum. Eligible for the Silver War Badge.

He wrote to the WO from Melrose, Brindley Heath, Surrey, 16.8.1924, applying for admission to a military hospital for an operation which he could not afford privately and that the condition, Hydrocele, was due to military service. The request was rejected as not being so attributable. His wife died 12.8.1944. Messrs Lamb & Co., Solicitors, National Bank Buildings, Nairn, Scotland, 26.8.1944, to Army Paymasters Office advised that Foster was admitted as a private patient to the Royal Asylum, Inverness, 'in:capax', and had previously been residing at Willowbank, Waverley Road, Nairn. Mr Peter Ford Lauder, Bank Agent, Bank of Scotland, was appointed Curator Bonis on Foster's estate. Admitted to The House of Daviot, Pitcaple, Aberdeenshire, 11.9.1944, and died there 21.11.1945. File ref: 339/5884.

Fowler 2/Lt. Francis Reginald. Born 3.8.1897, the son of John Busteed Fowler, a stockbroker, and Annie Louise *née* Hill, 9 Sunmount, Cork. Educated at Cork Grammar School, 1908–14, where he was a member of the OTC. General efficiency fair, musketry very good, and had some knowledge of semaphore. Employed as a temporary official at Cork Savings Bank. Applied for a commission 18.10.1915. Height 5 foot 8½ inches, chest 33–35½ inches, weight 128 pounds. Appointed 2/Lt. in 3rd Leinster Regt, 5.11.1915, and joined the School of Instruction at Cork. Joined 2nd RIR 24.7.1916. Wounded while with a fatigue party, 20.8.1916, but remained at duty. Killed in action 18.10.1916. Next of kin was his father at 8 Sidney Ville, Bellevue Park, Cork. Siblings, as of 31.1.1917, were Kathleen Lilian (aged 28), Sgt Richard Tarrant Fowler, ADMS Canadians (25), John Gerald, Canadian Record Office (21), Elizabeth Dorothy (15), Winifred Eveleen (13), Leonora Mary (10), and Arthur Irwin (9). Thiepval Memorial. File ref: 339/46707.

Fry Lt. George Frederick. Gazetted a 2/Lt. in 3rd RIR, 16.11.1915. Joined D Coy, 2nd RIR, 21.7.1916. Transferred to the RFC 27.6.1917. Promoted Lt. 1.7.1917. Closed file.

Gallwey Lt. Thomas Hinton Edward. Born 28.7.1896, the son of William and Frances K.I. Gallwey *née* Davis, Westcliff, Tramore, Co. Waterford. Educated at Mount St Benedict, Gorey, Co. Wexford, 1907–14. Applied for a commission in April 1915. Address Rockfield, Tramore, single, weight 177 pounds, chest 35½–38½ inches. Gazetted a 2/Lt. in 3rd RIR, 13.4.1915. Promoted Lt. 22.3.1916. Joined 2nd RIR 4.7.1916. Wounded, GSW right hip, 16.7.1916. Embarked Rouen–Southampton aboard the *St George*, 20 July, and admitted to the Countess of Pembroke's Private Hospital, Wilton House, Salisbury, until 6 August. MB, Fermoy, 5 September: the Medical Superintendent of Waterford stated that Gallwey had been attending at intervals since 11 August: 'On my first visit he had a wound on the right hip which was healing but still discharging purulent matter fairly freely. This wound healed rapidly under a simple surgical dressing and was quite closed and healthy before the end of the month. There seems to have been some injury to the nerves supplying the muscles on the outer and posterior aspects of the thigh and leg; for his walking and other movements were still considerably hampered on my last examination about a week ago.'

Gallwey wrote from Rockfield to the WO, 28.10.1916, to advise that his leave would end on 7 November and that he would be at Clonmeen, Banteer, Co. Cork. Posted to 3rd Garrison Bn, Northumberland Fusiliers, 24.2.1917, and to 2nd Garrison Bn, R. Irish, 1.3.1917. Reported to the Base at Boulogne, 24.8.1918, for duty as a cashier. Assumed duties as officer-in-charge under person-in-charge, as escort of silver from Northern France to Mediterranean ports. Admitted to No. 8 British Red Cross Hospital with influenza 28.10.1918. Proceeded to Rockfield on sick leave 13 November. Transferred to King George V Hospital, Dublin, for further treatment. He had suffered jaundice as a sequel to influenza and did not make a good recovery: attacks of vomiting and pain in the area of his liver. He was still not fully recovered and got pain in the gall bladder region. 'He is certainly improving steadily but is anxious to get clear of his troubles, if possible, at a quicker rate.' He had been on leave from France, 14.8.1919 to 28.9.1919, and stated that a doctor said he was fit for duty – he wanted a MB at the earliest opportunity. However, a note from Waterford MOH said that he 'is suffering from liver derangement attended with neurasthenia and loss of weight and is not, in my opinion, fit to resume duty for the present'. He was about to resign on account of ill health, 4.11.1919. File ref: 339/45904.

Garner Major Charles Wilson. Born 20.5.1888 at Christ's Church, Birkenhead, Chester. Enlisted as Pte 772 in 16th Public Schools Bn, Middlesex Regt, 17.9.1914. Height 6 foot, chest 37½–40½ inches, weight 135 pounds, single, stockbroker. Applied for a commission 4.12.1914. Major-General C.H. Powell CB, 36th (Ulster) Division, recommended Garner for a commission in 9th RIR. Commissioned 3.3.1915, promoted Lt. 27.2.1916, Capt. 2.7.1916, and Major 7.1.1917. *Belfast News Letter*, 4.1.1917: 'Captain C.W. Garner, son of Mrs E. Garner, 27 Drummond Road, Hoylake, was mentioned in Sir Douglas Haig's despatches (in *London Gazette*) "for distinguished and gallant service and devotion to duty".' A/Second-in-Command, 8/9th RIR, November 1917. Mentioned in Despatches, *London Gazette*, 4.1.1917, 25.5.1917, and 24.5.1918. Took over duties of C Coy, 2nd RIR, 11.6.1918. Discharged 12.4.1919, rated A1, married. Permanent address Hoylake, Cheshire. Belgian Croix de Guerre. File ref: 339/22390.

Gavin Lt. Robert Fitz-Austin. Born 26.11.1889 at Fatehgarh, Bengal, India, the son of George Fitzaustin and Ann Bennett Gavin. His father was a Capt. in 6th Bombay Cavalry. Having been educated by private tutor and at Wellington College, Berkshire (1902–7), he applied for admission to the Royal Military Academy, 6.5.1908. Gazetted a 2/Lt. 18.9.1909, and promoted Lt. 15.4.1913. Served in India with 1st RIR and returned with them to join the BEF. Wounded 10.3.1915: GSW to his left foot and to his face – the bullet entered his left cheek, passed through his nose, behind the nostrils, and exited on the right side. There were no fractures in either case. He was in hospital in London, where his mother returned from Rome to visit him. Reported to 3rd RIR for light duty, 29.4.1915. Joined 2nd RIR 28.6.1915. *Belfast News Letter*, 14.7.1915: 'He is a nephew of Lt.-Col. R.C.S. Macausland of Woodbank House, Garvagh, whose youngest son [2/Lt. O.B. Macausland, 1st RIR] was killed in action, 9th May 1915.'

Promoted Capt. 28.7.1915. Wounded and missing 25.9.1915. His mother, Mrs Hebard Hudson, advertised in the newspapers for information. Witness reports: 7071 Cpl P. Murphy reported that Gavin went over the top for a second time and was hit by a shell in no-man's-land and that several men saw this. He did not know whether the body was recovered as they never went back to the same trenches. CSM Field saw Gavin wounded before the attack but that he still led his men out. 20149 Rfn Darragh was told by Gavin's servant, Rfn Coleman, that he had been with Gavin when he was killed and took his watch so that he could give it to Gavin's mother the next time he went on leave. *Irish Times*, 1.10.1915 reported that he had relatives in Dublin. Menin Gate Memorial. File ref: 339/14940.

Getty 2/Lt. John Boyd OBE. Born 25.1.1894. Member of the UVF and of Freemason Lodge 280, Moyarget. Applied for a commission 19.6.1915 and 2.7.1915. Single, address Carrycroey, Stranocum, Co. Antrim. Gazetted a 2/Lt. in 17th RIR, 23.8.1915. Joined 2nd RIR 16.2.1916. 'Seriously wounded' by a high-explosive shell 18.3.1916. Admitted to No. 8 General Hospital, Rouen, 23 March. Embarked Le Havre–Southampton aboard the *Dover Castle*, 14.6.1916, and admitted to Lady Cooper's Hospital, Hursley Park, Winchester. MB 5 July: various wounds, patella 'destroyed' and removed. Discharged from hospital, 11 July, and granted leave. Admitted to Ebrington Military Hospital, Londonderry, 1.11.1916.

Granted a wound gratuity of £125. He advised, 8.3.1917, that he was in Tyrone County Hospital, Omagh. MB at Belfast, 27 March: he had lost all power of extension of his left knee; his left heel was raised from ground; the leg was wasted and his general health was poor. MB, 3 May: 'He will never be fit for anything but sedentary work.' The wound was classed as equivalent to the loss of a limb, very severe and permanent; granted a wound pension of £100 per annum. He wrote to the WO, 17 May: he had lost the use of his left leg; his right leg was 'practically useless', and he suffered recurring headaches from a skull fracture; requested an increased pension. MB 8.11.1917: he recently had another operation to remove pieces of bone from his left thigh; 'He is much run down from protracted operations and residence in hospitals, in bed most of day.' Relinquished his commission on grounds of ill health, *London Gazette*, 1.1.1918. A pair of surgical boots was issued at King George V Hospital, Dublin, 1.3.1918. He wrote to the WO, 19 March: his pension of £150 per annum had expired two days earlier and asked for a renewal. He advised, 28 April, that he had twelve operations to date and had been permanently hospitalized; no answer had been received about his pension and he requested another gratuity. MB at George V Hospital, 10.5.1918: the leg wounds were still discharging. WO replied that he had been paid £500 in gratuities which was the maximum possible and, in addition to his £100 pension, he was in receipt of £75 per annum from the Ministry of Pensions. Ordered to return to King George V Hospital for further treatment, 18.1.1919. A year later there had been no improvement. Obtained his LL B from Trinity College, Dublin, 1921. Married Jessie Cheyne 27.7.1925. His medals were issued to him 20.6.1951. Died 14.7.1976. His pension at that time was £1,232 and £36 per annum for his wife. Their address was Rosemead, 8 Demesne Road, Holywood, Co. Down. File ref: 339/41292.

Gibson Lt.-Col. Francis Marion Saunders MBE. Member of Freemason Lodge 1, Cork. Gazetted a 2/Lt. in 3rd CR 8.11.1913. Promoted Lt., 1.10.1914, and Capt. 2.2.1915. With the BEF, France, from July 1915. Joined 2nd RIR 1.10.1915 and was wounded the next day. Seconded for duty with the MGC 26.6.1916. Appointed T/Major 27.12.1917. Rejoined the BEF in October 1918. Transferred to 2nd Devon Regt 13.9.1922. Promoted Major, 7.2.1931, and given the brevet of Lt.-Col. 1.7.1932. Closed file.

Gibson 2/Lt. John Andrew. Born 31.5.1891. Applied for a commission in December 1914. Single, home address, Hillsboro, Co. Down. He had trained for thirteen months with South Belfast UVF. Gazetted a 2/Lt. in 17th RIR, 10.7.1915. Attended the School of Instruction until he joined 2nd RIR 16.2.1916. A confidential report by OC 2nd RIR, 9.4.1916, recommended Gibson be sent home. He was willing, but not an efficient platoon commander and unlikely to become one. He had an unformed character, a lack of ability to command and 'could never possess the confidence of his platoon in the field'. OC 25th Division: 'This officer is, under the circumstances, not only useless in the field, but a source of danger to the troops under him.' OC 2nd RIR: 'I recommend that the services of 2/Lt. Gibson be utilized at home for training purposes.' A letter from the office of the CiC France to the WO, 24.4.1916, advised that Gibson was to be sent home. Being unable to support the recommendation that Gibson be assigned to training, he should be allowed to resign his commission. Arrived in the UK 2.5.1916. The WO advised him that he had been sent home due to adverse reports. The recommendation that he should relinquish his commission had been approved and would be gazetted in due course. He wrote to the WO, 1.8.1921, saying that he was sent home for training duties due to unfitness caused by the strain of war. He complained of not having received any gratuity or other recompense for having served, and consequently suffered 'deprivation commercially'. The WO allowed a gratuity, as his resignation did not result from wilful actions on his part. File ref: 339/32234.

Gifford Major Herbert Llewellyn OBE. Served in the South African War in 1900 and received the Queen's Medal (Cape Colony clasp). Operations in Cape Colony, North of Orange River, including action at Faber Put. Capt., 3rd Dragoon Guards, 9.10.1901. Capt. from R. Garrison Regt, Egyptian Army, 11.3.1910. Appointed Capt. in 1st RIR and posted to 2nd RIR. Wounded 14.9.1914. Returned to the UK 6.10.1914. Promoted Major 1.9.1915. Rejoined 2nd RIR from 60th Bde 5.9.1915. Struck off the strength having gone sick 31.1.1916. Served on the Staff as GSO 2, 19.6.1916. DAAG, 67th Division, 20.6.1918. Awarded the OBE 12.12.1919. *Quis Separabit*, October 1929: 'Irish Riflemen past and present will learn with regret the death early in this year of Major H.L. Gifford OBE, who last served with the 1st Battalion in the Isle of Wight.' His widow, Lady Gooch, presented his medals to the Regimental Museum. Closed file.

Gill Major Fr Henry Vincent DSO, MC, MA, SJ. Born 8.7.1872. Educated at Clongowes Wood College, Co. Kildare, which he left in 1889. He trained under Professor P. Castelan SJ, at Louvain. Applied for an appointment as a chaplain 10.11.1914. Next of kin were his brothers: Major J. Gerald Gill, RAMC, 8 Castle Street, Carrick on Suir, Co. Tipperary, serving with the BEF as CO on HS *St Andrew*, and Richard A. Gill, 50 O'Connell Street Upper, Dublin. The latter was the address of the family firm of M.H. Gill & Son Ltd., publishers, printers, wholesale and retail booksellers, stationers, book binders, manufacturers of church goods and brass work, etc. Appointed Chaplain to the Forces, No. 4065, 4th Class (Capt.), 14.11.1914. Arrived at Boulogne Base 18 November.

  The Cross on the Sword: 'A Jesuit priest, Fr Henry Gill, was disappointed at being sent to a base hospital but made the best of things, as he reported to his Father Provincial: "Medical department wonderfully well organized. It is certainly not the kind of life to select as an amusement. I hope however that one may go nearer the fighting line." When Mgr Keatinge visited that hospital, Fr Gill had an interview with him on the subject of appointments ... and as a result was posted to 2nd Royal Irish Rifles and remained attached to the battalion until the end of the war. "The Commanding Officer gives every encouragement, but between being in the trenches and sudden moves it is not always possible to hold Mass. Confessions in fields, roadside, generally in several inches of mud ... Whole battalions have been to confession and Holy Communion in the last week to ten days ... The advantage of being attached to a regiment is that I am able to be up this far ... I thought it worth the risk to pay a visit to the most advanced line of trenches in order that my influence with the men might be greater. I know that this had excellent results. When the chaplain knows at first hand the conditions under which men live – and die, for several were killed soon after in the trenches I visited – he is better able to encourage the men to be patient."' Joined 2nd RIR 4.12.1914.

Irish Life, 24.9.1915: 'Father Gill SJ, who was Mentioned in Despatches, belongs to a well-known Dublin family. He gave up some very important scientific work in order to go to the front. He is an MA of Cambridge University, where he obtained a research degree through an important discovery in electricity.' Awarded the MC in the King's Birthday Honours, June 1916.

Orange, Green and Khaki: '[March 1918] At the same time, the adjutant of 15th Irish Rifles requested the Senior Chaplain 107th Brigade, Fr Henry Gill SJ, DSO, MC ... to conduct a burial service. Before Cambrai, such events would have been unthinkable.'

Witherow, March 1918: 'He was a fine-looking priest of middle age and very distinguished looking. He was a great help to us on the retreat because of the respect with which the French people treated him. He could get any billet he wanted in a village because the inhabitants were only too glad to have a priest in their house, both for his own sake and for the fact that his presence would be a guarantee that the property would be respected. I had some very interesting arguments with his reverence.' DSO *London Gazette*, 8.3.1918: 'For distinguished service in the field.'

He had been feeling the strain, especially due to his age, and went to No. 1 General Hospital as chaplain: 'About the beginning of August I got a letter telling me that Fr Irwin SJ (an Irishman of the English Province), a chaplain at the hospital at Etretat, was anxious to spend a few months at the front and that, if I wished to take his place, I could have the advantage of a rest and a change of work and surroundings in one of the most beautiful seaside places of Normandy.' Just before he returned to the Rifles, he spent two weeks with the Independent Air Force.

Letter to the Chaplains' Dept., WO, 8.10.1918, from Revd B.S. Rawlinson, Assistant Principal Chaplain, GHQ: 'Kindly note that the Revd H.V. Gill (RC), whose contract of service expires on 17th November 1918, has intimated his intention not to renew same. Report on his services is attached. Character: excellent. Physical fitness: v. good. General suitability for duty as an Army Chaplain: suitable to a very high degree. Other remarks: this Chaplain was S.C.F. [Senior Chaplain to the Forces] of a Division with 3rd Class rank from 6.1.17 to 8.11.17. His service in all respects has been satisfactory.' He had in fact renewed his contract but, as the war was ending, Fr Rawlinson held up the application and allowed it to be withdrawn. His letter (83) to the Fr Provincial, 30.11.1918: 'I am satisfied that I have done right though, strange to say, leaving the Battalion definitely is a wrench. The casualties have been simply enormous and I do not think anything tends more to create attachment than having the common danger.' Commission relinquished 7 December. Address St Francis Xaviers, Upper Gardiner Street, Dublin. WO, Chaplains' Department, wrote to him 17 December: 'I am directed to inform you that in recognition of the services rendered by you in the Army Chaplains' Department, approval has been given for your appointment as an Honorary Chaplain to the Forces, 3rd Class [Major].' *The Cross on the Sword*: '[Fr Rawlinson, the Vicar General:] "He seemed like a lost soul whenever you met him, but he was always there when wanted, and was afraid of no man. But his vitality had been much lessened by his experiences of the war years." Fr Gill spent the last thirteen years of his life as a Father Minister and spiritual father to the Leeson Street Jesuit community in Dublin.'

Died in Dublin 27.11.1945. *Quis Separabit*, May 1946: 'The Revd Gill was a distinguished scientist, as well as a very gallant officer. Throughout his life he retained a keen interest in scientific questions, and was a frequent contributor to various periodicals ... As a chaplain to a Bn in the line he was beloved by all. Quite fearless himself, his quiet generous personality did much to keep up morale during dangerous and uncomfortable times.'

Irish Times, 28.11.1945: ' ... was the eldest surviving son of the late H.J. Gill MA, a former member of the Irish Party, and head of the publishing firm of M.H. Gill and Son, Ltd. Born in Dublin in 1872, he was educated at Clongowes Wood College and University College, Dublin. He taught for some years at Clongowes and Belvedere, and studied for the priesthood at Louvain and Milltown Park, where he was ordained in 1906 ... Shortly after his ordination he spent two years at Downing College, Cambridge, where he worked at the Cavendish Laboratory, under Professor J.J. Thomson. Later he investigated the distribution of earthquakes in time and space, and communicated his theories to a meeting of the British Association in 1913. Throughout his life he retained a keen interest in scientific questions and was a frequent contributor to periodicals. A selection of his essays was published in 1943 under the title *Fact and Fiction in Modern Science*. He also wrote a short biography of the Jesuit physicist, Roger Boscovich, and two devotional works: *Jesuit Spirituality* and *Christianity in Daily Life*. On the day before his death he finished correcting the final proofs of a work on St Joseph.' File ref: 374/27281.

Gilliland Capt. Valentine Knox. Youngest surviving son of George Knox Gilliland DL, and Frances Jane Gilliland, Brook Hall, Londonderry. *Immortal Deeds*: 'He was formerly in the reserve of officers, and was posted to the Rifles in January ... nephew of Mr T.F. Cooke DL, Caw, a director of the Great Northern Railway.' *Irish Life*, 30.7.1915: 'At the outbreak of the war Captain Gilliland was posted to the 3rd (Reserve) Battalion Royal Irish Rifles, stationed at Dublin, and proceeded to the front on January 18th, having been promoted Captain two days previously from the rank of Second Lieutenant.'

Burgoyne: 'April 21st: About 3 p.m. Gilliland turned up at my dug-out with his face bound up. We'd both been using a periscope in his trench this morning and the trench isn't 80 yards from the enemy who are holding the edge of a wood at this point. They took no notice of our periscope then, but later when I'd left him they put a bullet in a sand-bag alongside it and when he removed it along the trench and looked through it again a bullet hit the top glass with such force that the fragments of the top glass smashed the lower glass and splashed into Gilliland's face cutting his nose and chin about, but nothing serious of course ... May 10th: Poor Gilliland was killed on the afternoon of the 7th. A sniper got him in the head from trench 46.'

Killed by a stray bullet 8.5.1915. Age 25. *Irish Times*, 12.5.1915: 'The deceased officer, whose father was the late George K. Gilliland DL, a former High Sheriff for County Londonderry ... His brother is Captain Frank Gilliland MA, of the 11th Service Battalion of the Royal Inniskilling Fusiliers. Just a week ago news reached Derry of the death of his cousin, Lieutenant W.M.M. Gilliland of the 2nd Battalion Royal Inniskilling Fusiliers, who was killed in action at the Dardanelles on April 30th, having been previously wounded at the battle of Le Cateau in August. On the day that Mrs G.K. Gilliland received the news of her son's death she also received a letter from him dated the 8th inst., in which he mentioned that the battalion was going into action.' His mother was notified that he was buried in Trench 47 near Hill 60. She administered the gross estate of £4,152. *Irish Times*, 4.6.1915 gave details of the memorial service held at All Saints' Church, Londonderry, the previous day. Menin Gate Memorial. File ref: 339/21403.

Godson Major Kenneth Lindsay. Promoted Lt., 2nd RIR, 15.11.1914, with seniority from 13.3.1915. B Coy. To hospital, sick, 11–24.3.1915, and 5.4.1915. Invalided home. Promoted Capt. 1.1.1917. Army List December 1918 shows him employed with an Officer Cadet Bn. Evacuated sick to Persia in July 1920 while serving with 2nd RIR in Mesopotamia during the Arab Rebellion. At the Depot 1923.

Quis Separabit, autumn 1964: 'Kenneth Godson died suddenly at his home at Fleet, Hampshire, on 24th June. He was born in 1895 and commissioned into the Royal Irish Rifles in Aug 1914. He served in the 2nd Battalion during the retreat from Mons ... Apart from a short tour at the Regimental Depot in the Isle of Wight most of his service was spent with the 2nd Battalion in Iraq, Egypt and India, until his retirement in 1931. In 1929 he married Miss Verity Hankin of Wellington, South India, who predeceased him. He was recalled on the Reserve of Officers in 1939 (with brevet of Major) and, in the course of service with the BEF was taken prisoner. "Cuthbert", as he was generally known, will be remembered as a gentle, kindly person, fond of music and of amateur theatricals. He was also a keen and proficient games player, particularly of cricket, at which he had been awarded a County cap for the Isle of Wight. The Regiment extends its sympathy to his son and daughter.' Closed file.

Goodman Lt.-Col. Henry Russell DSO. Born 18.8.1875, the eldest son of Mr J.F. Goodman, Dublin. Commissioned to 2nd RIR 7.3.1900. *Irish Life*, 14.5.1915: 'He served in the South African War, 1899–1902, being attached to the Army Service Corps from April 1900. He took part in the several operations in the Transvaal, Orange River Colony and Cape Colony from November 1900 to May 1902 and was slightly wounded. He received the Queen's Medal with four clasps and the King's Medal with two clasps.' Promoted Lt., 28.5.1903, and Capt. 28.6.1908. With 1st RIR in India from 1904 and was Adjutant 1907–9. Member of Freemason Lodge 25, Dublin. Joined 2nd RIR at Dover. Wounded 13.10.1914. *Lucy*: 'The dour old company commander ... came back, and raved and blasted up and down the road, looking for his horse. He even swore at the soldier who showed him the dead beast. Then he went off in a high temper to his company, where he himself was wounded.' Served as Assistant Provost Marshal in Belfast. Rejoined 2nd RIR 17.6.1915. Temporarily in command 23.6.1915. Promoted Major 1.9.1915. Stationed at the Curragh Camp, June 1916. Rejoined 2nd RIR, 24.11.1916, and took command the next day. By that time he was married. To FA 9.12.1917, and England 14.12.1917. See main text. Mentioned in Despatches 9.12.1914, 25.5.1917, and 12.12.1917.

DSO, *London Gazette*, 17.9.1917: 'For conspicuous gallantry and devotion to duty in commanding his battalion. The spirit and drive of his battalion during an attack and the splendid way in which they captured their own objective and then went on to the assistance of another battalion that was temporarily in difficulties, are to be entirely attributed to the personal influence and initiative of this officer. By excellent training he has improved the fighting efficiency of his battalion beyond all recognition, and prior to the attack his patrols penetrated the enemy's lines on several occasions, inflicting heavy casualties and gaining much valuable information.'

Quis Separabit, April 1929: 'By the time this number of *Quis Separabit* appears, we shall have said "Au Revoir" to Lt.-Col. H.R. Goodman DSO, who completed his tenure of command of the 2nd Battalion on March 22nd. Now in his thirtieth year of service, he leaves us after a distinguished and varied career … Obtaining his Regular Commission from the Militia, he joined the 2nd Battalion on March 7th, 1900, in South Africa, and very soon afterwards obtained his baptism of fire. It was a foregone conclusion that Major Sitwell would choose him to serve in the "Local" Mounted Infantry Company which was raised at Thaba 'Nchu early in 1901 and which worked in close co-operation with the 2nd Battalion. In this company he served with great distinction and was wounded in December, 1901, whilst assisting in the exceptionally brilliant little operation at Vlakplaats, where a handful of the "Local" Mounted Infantry turned 200 Boers out of a strong position. After the South African War, for which he got both medals, he served with the 2nd Battalion in Dublin, leaving for India to join the 1st Battalion. Arriving at Fyzabad in October 1904, he spent the next six years at that place, Meerut and Burma, and built up a high reputation as a horseman and horse master. For three years of this period he was Adjutant of the battalion.

'Coming home in 1911, after a short period of service with the Egyptian Army, he was ready to proceed with the 2nd Battalion to France in 1914, and thus for the second time was on active service with his original battalion. He commanded his company throughout the retreat from Mons – always thinking of his men before himself. At the Aisne, shortly after Col. Bird was wounded, Capt. Goodman, as he then was, was largely instrumental in stopping a German attack by bringing up men from the Worcestershire Regiment and turning the German's right. In the fight at La Basée in October he was severely wounded. For his work during this period he was Mentioned in Despatches. He rejoined the battalion in June 1915. Most of 1916 was spent in various Staff appointments, but the 2nd Battalion again welcomed him back early in December 1916, when he, now a Major and temporary Lt.-Colonel, took over command at "Plug Street". This famous area got particularly lively soon after his arrival. The "Raiding Season" had begun. For more than a year he continued to command the battalion. He led it at Messines, Ypres, and Cambrai. Old soldiers know how few commanding officers could boast of a complete year in command in France. During this period he was Mentioned in Despatches twice and awarded the DSO. The strain, however, told, and he had a breakdown in health which necessitated a rest from "Front Line" soldiering. The measure of his success can be measured best by the record of the 2nd Battalion during his period of command. This record was a very high one, as is well known.

'When peace time soldiering came back again, he commanded the Depot for three years, and on completion served with the 1st Battalion on the Rhine from September 1923 until the end of 1924, when he was promoted Lt.-Colonel and appointed to command the 2nd Battalion in India … As a horseman and horse master he is well known. He played polo for the County Dublin team in 1899, 1903, and 1904, and had the distinction of playing for Ireland against England in the latter year at Dublin. In India he captained the 1st Battalion team which played in the Infantry Tournament at Lucknow in 1906. Since his return to India he has endeavoured to promote the game within the 2nd Battalion both by precept and example … 'In saying "Au Revoir" to him we must not forget to include Mrs Goodman … To Patsy and Kathleen we would like to say that we hope we will see more of them in the future days.'

Retired in 1929 and resided at *Fairy House*, Totland Bay, Isle of Wight. Died of concussion following an accident which occurred while he was training a young horse, 21.5.1936. Closed file.

Gough 2/Lt. Ronald Albert. Enlisted as Pte 2239 in 5th Yorkshire Regt. Promoted 2/Lt. in 3rd RIR 28.11.1917. Joined 2nd RIR 16.2.1918. See main text. Wounded, gassed, 14.8.1918. Closed file.

Gransden 2/Lt. Victor Eric. Born 5.7.1896, the son of Samuel Henry and Lizzie Gransden, 2 St Columb's Court, Londonderry. His father was a contractor. Educated at Foyle College and First Derry Boys' School. Enlisted in 17th RIR 19.1.1916. Weight 126 pounds, height 5 foot 7 inches, chest 32–34½ inches, single. To No. 7 Officer Cadet Bn 5.10.1916. Discharged to a commission in 20th RIR 28.2.1917. At that time his height was recorded as 5 foot 5¼ inches and his weight as 110 pounds. Posted to 10th RIR. Killed while serving with 2nd RIR, 26.4.1918. *Irish Times*, 4.5.1918: 'Lieutenant Gransden was asleep in his dug-out in the headquarters in the outpost line, when a shell fell through the roof, and killed him instantly.' His father administered the estate, gross value £160. Minty Farm Cemetery, Langemark–Poelkapelle, West-Vlaanderen, III.A.3. File ref: 339/73109.

Gray Capt. Henry John. Born 11.7.1886. Served as No. 7561 with 2nd RIR. Promoted from Colour-Sgt to 2/Lt., 18.11.1914. *Burgoyne*, 14.1.1915: 'Gray at once moved his machine gunners up to me ... A German shell hit Gray's dug-out and blew it in just after he had left.' To FA from UK, 28.5.1915. Promoted Lt. 1.10.1915. Also served in France from 6.9.1915 to 7.4.1917, and from 11.12.1917 to 27.3.1918 when he was taken prisoner. T/Capt. 5.8.1918. Repatriated in December 1918. Ceased to belong to the Reserve of Officers 11.7.1936. Died 1966. Closed file.

Greacen Lt. Robert. Born 28.9.1894, the son of Robert and Madge Greacen, Aviemore House, Monaghan. His brother Walter, born 24.6.1892, ran the Western Arms Hotel in Monaghan. Another brother, Capt. Thomas Earldrid Greacen MC, born 27.9.1893, served with the Canadian Infantry, was managing director of Greacen & Co. Ltd., Wine & Spirit Merchants, Monaghan, and died in 1959. Educated at Campbell College, Belfast, 1908–13; Head Prefect 1913; Captain School's 1st XV 1911–13. Served Campbell College Junior OTC 1909–13, Colour-Sgt. Attested at Prince Albert as Pte A.40801 with 32nd Bn Canadian Expeditionary Force, 5.4.1915. At that time he was a member of 52nd Regt. Bank clerk, 5 foot ¼ inch, chest 34½–36½ inches, blue eyes, dark hair, bank clerk, Presbyterian. Applied at Shorncliffe, Kent, for a commission in 16th RIR about August 1915. Gazetted a 2/Lt. in 6th RIR, 8.10.1915, but posted to 4th RIR for further training, and ordered to report to the School of Instruction at Holywood. Promoted Lt. 1.7.1917.

Joined 7th RIR, 6.7.1917, and posted to B Coy. Wounded 16.8.1917 and embarked Boulogne–Dover two days later. MB at Prince of Wales Hospital, Marylebone, 15 September: GSW left arm during an attack, no bone or nerve damage. Wound healed. Reported to Carrickfergus 20 November. Joined 2nd RIR 15.8.1918. GSW right leg at Bailleul, 20.8.1918. Embarked Boulogne–Dover, 25 August, and admitted to No. 5 Northern General Hospital. MBs at Leicester: 9 September, granulated entry and exit wounds, no bone or nerve damage; 11 November, several boils on right leg. Discharged 14.1.1919, rated A, single. In 1938 he was residing at 108 Hadon Crescent, Hamilton, Ontario, Canada, and was engaged as a manufacturer's representative. A family bar was destroyed in the 1974 Monaghan bombing. By 1982 he was at Tullyleer, Monaghan. File ref: 339/44953.

Grey Lt. Thomas Henry. Born 19.12.1892. Applied for a commission, 6.1.1915. He was single and a member of the Sutton Volunteer Association. Commissioned to 5th RIR 6.5.1915. Home address, 3 Warrenpoint, Clontarf, Dublin, which was the residence of John J. Grey. Joined 2nd RIR, 3.4.1916, and was wounded 26.4.1916. Embarked Le Havre–Southampton aboard the *Asturias*, 28 May, suffering from a shell wound with septic poisoning in the left thigh. MB 12.6.1916: flesh wound, various incisions had been made for cellulitis and these had not yet healed. In King George V Hospital, Dublin, as of 30.7.1916, and was at home by 2 September. MB 15.12.1916: improving and could walk with the aid of two sticks. Employed in the Railway Transport Office in Dublin doing light office work. Promoted Lt. 1.7.1917. MB 19.7.1917: the muscles in his left leg were considerably wasted due to disuse. He was still working in the Railway Office as of 25.4.1918. MB at King George V Hospital, 6 May: he was improving, and classed C for six months. Ordered to return to his present duty at the Censor's Office, 85 Grafton Street, Dublin.

Married 14.8.1918. MB at Dublin 13.6.1919: he walked with a slight limp and could not fully extend his left knee; the leg muscles were wasted and he tired after walking a couple of miles. 'To resume his duties at Dublin.' Discharged 7.10.1919, occupation bank official. MB 23.4.1920: the wasting was less marked, he could flex his knee, but still walked with a limp and tired easily.

In 1938 he was Vice-Chairman of the Dublin Branch of the RUR Association. Died 27.8.1966 at his residence, 22 Victoria Road, Clontarf. His pension at the time was £89.60 per annum and £7.20 for his wife, Jenny. Balgriffin Cemetery. His medals were donated to the regimental museum. File ref: 339/48379.

Gribben Lt.-Col. Edward C. MC. Born 11.9.1891 at Holywood, Co. Down. *Belfast News Letter*, 1.9.1917, reported that he was a son of Mr E. Gribben, High Street, Belfast, and Mrs Gribben, Avondale, Cultra, Holywood. He was employed by the Chambers Motor Works, and was commissioned to 5th RIR 15.8.1914. Promoted Lt. 22.5.1915. Joined 2nd RIR 24.8.1915. Suffered severe shell shock during the autumn of that year. He may have served for a while with 1st York and Lancaster Regt.

Transferred to the RFC in 1917 and was posted to 70 Squadron flying Sopwith Camels. Scored five victories during July and August. RFC Communiqué No. 97, 17.7.1917: 'Five Camels of 70 Squadron encountered a very large formation of about 30 or 40 enemy aircraft. In the combat two Camels were lost but the other three continued the fight. Capt. N. Webb drove down two opponents completely out of control, and Lts E.C. Gribben and J.C. Smith each drove an enemy aircraft down out of control.' RFC Communiqué No. 100, 10.8.1917: 'Lt. E. Gribben, 70 Squadron, got on the tail of one enemy aircraft which spun down and crashed.' MC, *London Gazette*, 8.1.1918: 'For conspicuous gallantry and devotion to duty on offensive patrols. In every combat he has been most conspicuous, continually attacking superior numbers of the enemy, destroying some and driving others down out of control. He fights with great dash and skill, and whenever any machine of his formation is in difficulties, he is invariably at hand to render assistance.' Posted to Home Defence, flying night fighters with 44 Squadron. Reassigned to 41 Squadron as a flight commander, 2.10.1918. Wounded 4.10.1918 when he was forced down by a Fokker D.VII.

Promoted Lt.-Col. 1.11.1934. CO London Irish Rifles, residing at 9 Cromwell Road, London. *Quis Separabit*, November 1938: 'It is with profound regret that we find ourselves faced with the fact that Lt.-Col. E. Gribben MC, will be retiring in November ... Lt.-Col. Gribben came to us in 1930 with a very distinguished record ... He has been in command since 1934.' *Quis Separabit*, May 1939: 'We wish him the best of fortune in his new activities with the Royal Air Force.' Closed file.

Hackett Capt. Leäro Aylmer Henry MC. Son of Edward Augustus Hackett ME, M.Inst.CE, and Emilie Elliott Hackett, Clonmel, Co. Tipperary, and grandson of Thomas Hackett JP, Castletown, Ballycumber, King's County. Educated at the Erasmus Smith Abbey Grammar School, Tipperary. Appointed 2/Lt. in 4th RMF, 2.11.1901, and promoted Lt. 9.6.1902.

Resigned his commission 29.12.1906. Appointed Lt., 6th RMF, 10.2.1916, and transferred to 10th RIR 19.7.1916. MC, *London Gazette*, 14.9.1917: 'For conspicuous gallantry and devotion to duty in commanding his company during an attack. In conjunction with another company he knocked out an enemy strong point, capturing 30 officers and 70 of other ranks, also five machine guns. Throughout the day he set a splendid example of leadership.' Killed in action while serving with 2nd RIR, 24.4.1918. At that time his father was County Surveyor at the Court House, Clonmel. Effects included a £600 War Loan certificate. Gross value of the estate £780.

His brother, 2/Lt. Eric Adrian Nethercote Hackett, 6th R. Irish, was killed in action 9.9.1916. Both are named on the Abbey Grammar School War Memorial. Their sister, Venice Clementine Henrietta Hackett, was a VAD nurse and died 13.10.1918. The family address was Mountain View, Poulavanogue, Co. Waterford. Minty Farm Cemetery, Langemark, III.A.7. File ref: 339/70504.

Harmer 2/Lt. Hubert George. Born 16.2.1897 at Penge, Surrey, the son of George William Harmer. Attested in the Army Service Corps 7.10.1914. Height 5 foot 9 inches, chest 37–40 inches, weight 144 pounds, insurance clerk, single. Promoted Sgt 16.11.1914. To BEF France 13.7.1915. Applied for a commission 21.10.1916. Permanent address was his father's residence at 145 Ashley Road, Upper Parkstone, Dorset. Correspondence address, Sgt S/1/2307, No. 3 Coy ASC, 17th Divisional Train. Employed as Clerk, Supply Details. Returned to the UK 21.1.1917. Accepted for No. 1 MGC Cadet Bn, and ordered to report to Bisley, 1.3.1917. Found unsuitable for the MGC and transferred to No. 2 Officer Cadet Bn, Cambridge, 5.7.1917. Gazetted a 2/Lt. in 20th RIR 29.8.1917. Joined 2nd RIR 11.8.1918. To 12th RIR 25.2.1919. Promoted Lt. 1.3.1919.

Sentenced to be cashiered from the Army, 14.5.1919. Confirmed by CiC Army of the Rhine. First charge: 'When on active service scandalous conduct unbecoming the character of an officer and a gentleman, in that he, at Arnoldsweiler in an inn, on the night of the 1st–2nd April 1919, created an unseemly disturbance and without cause fired a revolver.' Second charge: 'When on active service, drunkenness, in that he, at Arnoldsweiler on the night of 1st–2nd April 1919, was drunk.' Pleaded not guilty but found guilty of all charges excepting that the discharge of the revolver was deemed to have been accidental. Pay ceased 30.5.1919. He wrote to the WO, 9.11.1925, asking for certified copies of his military discharge and service. This was required by the American Consular Service for the purpose of granting a visa for the USA. 'I was cashiered from the army but if this could be worded discharged I should be glad.' Address at this time was Carvesgate Cottage, Marlborough Road, Canford Cliffs, Bournemouth. A file cover note stated that the scandalous conduct 'did not seem to have been much more than a brawl' but the WO could not say that he had been discharged rather than cashiered. They replied saying they understood that the American emigration authorities no longer needed the certificate. File ref: 339/82052.

Hart Major John James MC. Born 22.3.1886. Promoted from 7937 Sgt to 2/Lt. in 2nd RIR 18.11.1914. Served with 2nd RIR, 13.8.1914 to 13.1.1915, and with 1st RIR, 18.5.1915 to 16.1.1916. A/Adjutant of 1st RIR August 1915. Placed on the sick list 2.1.1916. Attached to the Nigeria Regt. 19.12.1916. Served in British, German, and Portuguese East Africa, Nyasaland, and Northern Rhodesia. He was wounded and subsequently repatriated 14.2.1918, being awarded the MC, *London Gazette*, 13.8.1918: 'For conspicuous gallantry and devotion to duty. After his company commander had become a casualty, he took command of his company and handled it throughout the day with remarkable skill and courage. During the withdrawal he remained near the only gun which was in action, and himself worked a machine gun until finally he was compelled to withdraw, bringing his gun with him. His conduct under trying conditions has always been most commendable.' Left the Reserve of Officers 22.3.1936. In 1938 he was residing at Bramfield, Lower Green Road, Esher, Surrey.

Quis Separabit 1966: ' ... died in hospital near his home in Cobham, Surrey, on 22nd July 1966. He had been in failing health for some time and had just passed his eightieth birthday. He was one of a notable group who were commissioned in the regiment on the field of battle in France in November 1914 ... After a lengthy period of service in France and Belgium, he was transferred to German East Africa towards the end of 1916 and served with the Nigeria Regt WAFF and as Staff Captain of the West African Service Brigade. In these operations he was given the immediate award of the Military Cross.

'Not content with inaction after the Armistice, he managed to get to North Russia in 1919. On his return to England he was posted to the 1st Bn The Royal Ulster Rifles and in 1922 arrived in Cairo to serve with the 2nd Battalion. In 1927 he became adjutant of the Nilgiri Malabar Auxiliary Forces and on completion of that appointment he retired from the army in 1931. Johnnie Hart had always had a flair for administration and keeping accounts. Sure enough in 1936 he accepted an appointment in the Air Ministry as a Civilian Accountant officer. This led to his being commissioned in the RAFVR in September 1939 – he became a Squadron Leader and served until he was permitted to resign in May 1945 ... My wife and I recall the Hart's bungalow in the Nilgiri's S. India where hospitality was dispensed in true Irish style and naturally that also brings to mind the part which his wife, Corinne, played at that time in the happy regimental community at Wellington. Our deep sympathy goes out to her and to their daughter Joan at this sad time.' – General Steele. His widow donated his medals to the regimental museum. Closed file.

Haskett-Smith Lt.-Col. William Joseph Jerome Saccone. Gazetted into the RIR, 8.5.1901, and served in the South African War 1901–2, taking part in operations in Orange River Colony, August 1901 to 31.5.1902. Received the Queen's Medal with three clasps. Commanded G Coy. Promoted Lt., 14.6.1905, and Capt. 8.3.1910. Joined the BEF during October 1914, presumably with 2nd RIR, where he remained until February 1915. Returned to France, 5.7.1915, and joined 1st RIR 6.8.1915. To the UK, sick, 19.10.1915. Rejoined 2nd RIR 5.9.1916. Posted to 2nd South Lancashire Regt as acting Senior Major 5.10.1916. Served with 1st RIF, and was employed with the Tank Corps 1.1.1917 until August 1917. He resumed active service January 1918 until the end of the war, perhaps with 18th London Regt (London Irish). Hon. Secretary of the RUR Regimental Association in the mid 1930's. In 1938 he was residing at Ellerton Lodge, Ellerton Road, Copse Hill, Wimbledon. Died at Jersey 1961. Closed file.

Hayward Capt. Richard Benjamin. Born at Hampstead, Middlesex, 3.1.1873. Enlisted as Boy (Musician) 8952 in 2nd Rifle Bde 3.9.1887. Next of kin was his mother, Lilly Hayward, 9 Circus Road, Gospel Oak Fields, Kilburn, London. Height 4 foot 9⅝ inches, chest 27 inches, weight 77 pounds, Church of England. Appointed Bugler 3.12.1890. Reverted to Pte 28.1.1891. Appointed Bandsman 23.5.1895. Served in the UK until 22.9.1897 when he went to Malta. Appointed a/Cpl 16.4.1898. Posted to Egypt 12.7.1898 and Crete 21.9.1898. Promoted Cpl, 15.7.1899, and Sgt Bugler 24.8.1899. To South Africa 2.10.1899. Posted 1st Rifle Bde 21.5.1900 and returned to the UK. Posted to the Depot 9.10.1900. Married Nellie Matilda *née* Walden at Gosport 10.12.1904. Transferred to 1st RIR as 7872 Bandmaster 5.1.1905. His daughter, Lillian Walden, was born at Meerut the same day. Permitted to continue his service beyond 21 years, 25.4.1908. Permitted to extend his service from 27.2.1914 to 4.1.1920. Commissioned 2/Lt. in 1st RIR 4.11.1914. Medals at this time: Sudan (clasp Khartoum 1898); South Africa (clasp Defence of Ladysmith); Long Service and Good Conduct granted 2.6.1906.

Joined 2nd RIR 16.1.1915. To hospital, medically unfit, 2.4.1915. Embarked Boulogne–Dover aboard HS *St Andrew*, 18 April. Home address, 38 Holland Road, Maidstone. Served with 3rd RIR and promoted Lt. 27.5.1915. There followed a series of MBs until he was certified permanently unfit for general service but fit for home service. *Inglorious Soldier*: 'He was a quiet, grey-haired professional soldier with a grizzled moustache.' He took part in the attack against the South Dublin Union during the 1916 Rebellion and was recommended for gallantry by Major F.F. Vane. Appointed T/Capt. and Adjutant RIR Garrison Bn, 24.11.1916. Seconded for service as Adjutant 3rd Garrison Bn RIF, 13.1.1917. Mentioned in Despatches 25.1.1917. Placed on the half pay list due to ill health, 25.1.1919. He emigrated to Canada 1.4.1921; temporary address c/o Mr John Millar, 86 Colbeck Street, Runnymede Road, Toronto. He wrote to the WO, 1.6.1921, giving his new address as 364 Beresford Avenue, Toronto, Ontario, and sought permission to reside in the USA as he had a chance of work there. Later served as Regimental Bandmaster and Director of Music with the Queen's Own Rifles of Canada. File ref: 339/18917.

Hay-Will Capt. Noel George MC. Born 1887. Educated at Malvern and Sandhurst. Gazetted to the Cheshire Regt 1907. English, single, Roman Catholic, spoke German. Promoted Capt. 1914. Embarked for the BEF 2.12.1916. Joined C Coy, 13th Cheshires, 19.3.1917. Attached 2nd RIR 23.3.1917. Posted to 11th Cheshires. Awarded the MC 'For conspicuous gallantry and leadership during the operations on Westhoek Ridge from 31.7.17 to 6.8.17, and 11.8.17 to 14.8.17. During these periods, Captain Hay-Will commanded his company, which was holding an advanced position on the Westhoek Ridge, with great ability under extremely bad weather conditions and continual heavy shelling. Under these trying conditions Captain Hay-Will showed the greatest coolness and cheerfulness and set a fine example to his men. On the 12.8.17 and 13.8.17, Captain Hay-Will in the absence of his Commanding Officer took command of the Battalion which had just taken over a line of Battle Outposts. Under heavy shell fire, and constantly exposed to hostile machine gun and rifle fire, this officer personally reconnoitred the whole of his Battalion sector and obtained information of great value regarding our own and the enemy's disposition. The information obtained was absolutely essential for the successful co-operation of the artillery in repelling hostile counter-attacks which developed during that period.' File missing.

Healy 2/Lt. Dermot Joseph. Born at Finglas, Co. Dublin, 3.3.1888, the son of Hugh F. and Ellen Healy. His father was a civil servant. Educated at Blackrock College, Co. Dublin. Enlisted as Pte 9288 in the Inns of Court OTC 3.2.1916. Civil servant, height 5 foot 8 inches, chest 35–37 inches, weight 168 pounds, address 13 Sandymount Road, Sandymount, Co. Dublin. Applied for a commission 1.8.1916. To No. 7 Officer Cadet Bn, 11 August. 2/Lt., 5th RMF, 18.12.1916. Joined 2nd RIR 2.3.1917. Killed in action, 5.8.1917, attached to 74th TMB. Next of kin, father, aged 67, Sandymount Road. His mother administered the estate. Menin Gate Memorial. File ref: 339/68181.

Heron Capt. Charles. Served with Queen's University OTC. Member of First Killyleagh Presbyterian Church. Commissioned to 5th RIR 12.6.1912, and promoted Lt. 8.9.1914. Joined 2nd RIR 10.10.1914. Wounded 14.10.1914. *Down Recorder*, 31.10.1914: 'County Down Men.

Lt. C. Heron, who was drafted to the 2nd Royal Irish Rifles at the front early this month, has communicated to his father, Mr J. Heron JP, Tullyvery, that he lies in a London hospital with a bullet wound in one of his legs. When he was carrying a despatch his cycle was smashed by a shell, and he escaped with only slight concussion. Two days later he was hit, and lay for five hours, shells bursting all around, and causing several casualties. Before he was picked up by the medical corps he had the satisfaction of seeing his comrades clear the German trenches with the bayonet.' Promoted Capt. 17.4.1915 with 5th RIR. Adjutant Garrison Bn RIF 12.4.1916. Attached Royal Army Ordnance Corps. Still on Army List 1923 with 5th RIR. Closed file.

Hill Lt. William Carlisle MC. Born 24.6.1895, the son of R.C. and Catherine Hill, 101 Fitzroy Avenue, Belfast. His father was an official of the Belfast Harbour Board. *Belfast News Letter*, 14.6.1917, reported that he had been in the linen trade at Mulhouse Work. Appointed Pte 2/6th Black Watch, 28.12.1914. Address C Coy, 6th Black Watch, Western Barracks, Dundee; height 5 foot 8 inches, chest 35½–39½ inches, single. Gazetted a 2/Lt. in 19th RIR, 10.7.1915. Promoted Lt. 30.5.1916. Joined the BEF 19.7.1916. MC, 12.3.1917, for conspicuous gallantry and devotion to duty. *Irish Life*, 4.5.1917: 'He succeeded in moving his guns to defensive positions under very heavy fire. Later, in spite of heavy fire, he continued to fire a gun himself. He set a splendid example of courage and determination throughout.' Left 2nd RIR and attached to 74th TMB 18.3.1917. Killed in action 7.6.1917. Net estate of £79 administered by his mother. Menin Gate Memorial. File ref: 339/32235.

Hill-Dillon Col. Stephen Searle CBE, DSO. Born 27.11.1887 at Jesmond, Northumberland, the only son of John Dillon, Lyncombe Rise, Bath; Governor of HM Prison, Liverpool. Educated at Llandovery College, South Wales, and abroad. Entered Sandhurst and was commissioned in the RIR, 9.10.1907. Promoted Lt. 22.4.1909. Adjutant, 2nd RIR, 27.11.1913. Wounded 19.9.1914. *The Distinguished Service Order*: 'He was Mentioned in Despatches, and created a companion of the Distinguished Service Order (*London Gazette*, 18 February 1915): "Stephen Searle Dillon, Lt., Royal Irish Rifles". He was promoted Captain, 15 March 1915, and subsequently held the following appointments: Special appointment as Special Service Officer, 2 June 1915 to 18 March 1916; GSO 3, 5th Army Corps, April to August 1916; GSO 2, 5th Army Corps, August 1916 to November 1917; GSO 2, American Staff College, France, November 1917 to April 1918; GSO 2, 6th Division, April to June 1918, GSO 2, 2nd Army Corps, June to September 1918, GSO 2, 4th Army Corps, November 1918 to 5 February 1919; GSO 2, Irish Command, 6 February 1919. He was three times Mentioned in Despatches, and was given the Brevet of Major, 1 January 1918. Major Hill-Dillon (additional name of Hill assumed in 1916) married, in 1916, Gladys Muriel, daughter of the late Frances Heslop Hill, of Redenham, Hants, and Shroton, Dorset.'

Died in Co. Tipperary, 12.3.1981. *Blackthorn*, 1981: ' ... was awarded the DSO for "His services in connection with operations in the field". He was passed fit again for duty in 1915 and served as a Port Control Officer 1915–16 and as a General Staff Officer in France and Belgium 1916–19. He was appointed a General Staff Intelligence Officer GHQ Dublin 1919–22 and GSO2 War Office 1922–4 ... He rejoined The Regiment in 1924 having been appointed a Brevet Lt.-Col. in 1922 and served with 1st Bn The Royal Ulster Rifles stationed at Cologne, part of the British Army of The Rhine. After a short stay with the 1st Bn he left on posting to the 2nd Bn in India. While in India he shot big game and played polo. He was a good cricketer and rode as an amateur on the flat and over fences, also in Point-to-Points. He had racehorses which he rode with considerable success. Stephen believed in making racing pay. He had a rival, a brigadier, who rode and had similar views. They were not friends and on one occasion Stephen put the brigadier over the rails when trying to come through on the inside. The fact that there was no inquiry makes one think that each knew enough about the other to avoid publicity.

'He retired to the Reserve of Officers in 1925 and went to live at Redenham where he had horses with Percy Woodland. Not only did he ride many winners on his own horses but Percy got him outside rides. After 1930 Redenham was sold and he came to live at Hayes near Navan where he trained and rode with success. Many wondered at his wisdom of living in the South of Ireland only ten years after he had been an Intelligence Officer at GHQ in Dublin 1919–22. However, all was well. Many years later Mr Joe McGrath remarked to Lord Donoughmore "I was told to shoot that man. I am glad now that I didn't". Stephen and Joe worked together on racing matters and each respected the other. He was elected a member of the Irish Turf Club in 1934, elected a Steward 1939–40, 1946–9 and 1954–7. He was also elected a member of INHS Committee in 1953 and acted as a Steward 1935–8 and again 1950–3.

'He was recalled on 4th January 1940 for further War Service. His service during World War II was GSO2 1940–2 with HQ NID; the War Office and GHQ Home Forces. In 1942 he was appointed GSO1 and was at Allied Force HQ in North Africa and Italy from 1942 to 1945. He was promoted Acting Colonel 1943 and Temporary Colonel 16th March 1944. For his Services in World War II he was decorated with the OBE and later the CBE. He was Mentioned in Despatches, made an officer of the Legion of Merit (USA) and awarded the French Croix de Guerre with Silver Star and the Medaille de la Reconnaissance Française. After the war he found many good young horses for the Queen Mother from whom he got a Christmas card every year right up to the end. One of those horses was Devon Loch whom you might say won the Grand National. He married Miss Gladys Muriel Hill, in 1916, who survives him, together with his three daughters Muriel, Frances and Jean.' OBE 1939–46 Birthday Honours List. CBE awarded on the recommendation of the CiC (Royal Navy) Mediterranean. Closed file.

Hoare Capt. Edward James MC. Member of Freemason Lodge 40, Belfast. Promoted from Sgt 7957 to 2/Lt. in 3rd RIR, 1.10.1914, and to Lt. 15.3.1915. Rejoined 2nd RIR 24.4.1915 on return from a machine gun course. Wounded 16.6.1915. Promoted Capt. 1.1.1917. He was serving with 2nd RIR during the Arab Revolt in Mesopotamia. On 27.10.1920 several hundred Arabs carried out a night raid on the battalion's camp. *Graves*: 'Capt. E.J. Hoare, commanding C Company, could be seen walking the parapet directing the fire onto the Arab groups.' For this action he was awarded the MC 10.8.1921. Closed file.

Houlihan 2/Lt. Joseph John. Son of William Houlihan, Carnare, Fedomore, Co. Limerick. Attested Pte 12234 in the RAMC 20.4.1915. His will left all property to his father. To No. 9 Officer Cadet Bn at Gailes 2.8.1916. Gazetted a 2/Lt. in 3rd CR 16.12.1916. Joined 2nd RIR 21.1.1917. Left 19.4.1917, GSW right shoulder, and embarked Boulogne–Dover aboard HS *St Andrew* five days later. Reported to 3rd Reserve Bn Command Depot at Tipperary, 10 June. Certified fit for general service 22.10.1917. He was in hospital 22.4.1918. Returned to his unit 7.6.1918. GCM at Le Havre for drunkenness, 28.9.1918: found guilty and dismissed from the Army. File ref: 339/67410.

Howard Capt. William Edward Sharpe. Entered Trinity College, Dublin, 1910. Promoted Lt., 4th RIR, 13.6.1914. Left to join the BEF 14.10.1914. Joined 2nd RIR 2.6.1915. Wounded 16.6.1915. *Irish Times*, 22.6.1915: 'A telegram has been received from the War Office by Mr

Samuel Howard, Ardavon, Rathgar, formerly of Dungannon, stating that his eldest son ... has been wounded.' *Irish Times*, 25.6.1915: 'In a letter from his son in hospital in France, dictated to his nurse, he states that he had lost his left eye in the fight on the 16th inst. The bullet entered his head low down at the back, coming out through the eye. Lieutenant Howard writes cheerily and characteristically, and says "Sure one is tons".' Promoted Capt. 22.9.1915. *Falls*: 'The 4th Battalion likewise was concerned in the Easter Week Rebellion. It sent one company under Captain W.E.S. Howard, which formed part of a composite rifle battalion despatched from the north.' Still on Army List 1923. Closed file.

Howroyd 2/Lt. Frank William. Born Bradford, Yorkshire, 2.4.1882, the son of a contractor. Educated at Bradford Technical College. Married Haidee Elizabeth Gunn at Keighley, Yorkshire, 11.7.1908. Their daughter Diana Barbara Neary was born in London 31.12.1914. Enlisted as Rfn 3/9126 in 3rd RIR at Belfast, 27.5.1916. Height 6 foot 1 inch, chest 35½–38 inches, weight 172 pounds, actor, address 32 Cumberland Park, Acton, London. He had served for five years in 2nd West Yorks Volunteer Artillery. Appointed an unpaid L/Cpl, 22.7.1916, and a/Cpl 21.11.1916. Applied for a commission 1.12.1916. Correspondence address E Coy, 3rd RIR, Victoria Barracks, Belfast. Appointed a/Sgt 25.12.1916. Posted to No. 4 Officer Cadet Bn at Oxford 7.4.1917. Discharged to a commission, 31.7.1917, and served with 7th RIR from 7.10.1917. Joined 2nd RIR 14.11.1917. Left unit, 1.12.1917, pyrexia, fever of unknown origin. Admitted to No. 3 London Hospital, 8 December. Address 23 Goldsmith Road, Acton. Classified permanently unfit for any service on account of ill health and placed on the retired list 18.10.1918. Resided at 156 Marylebone Road, London NW1. File ref: 339/102656.

Hunter Lt. Walter Frederick MC. Commissioned in the R. Irish through Belfast University Contingent of the OTC, 8.10.1915. Brother of 2/Lt. Stanley Hunter, 8th RIR, wounded and taken prisoner in November 1915. Transferred to 8th RIR in 1916. *Belfast News Letter*, 13.6.1917: 'Wounded, is a son of Mr W.J. Hunter, 116 Eglantine Avenue, Belfast.' Promoted Lt. 1.7.1917. Posted to 2nd RIR. Wounded in action 6.9.1918. MC, *London Gazette*, 1.2.1919: 'For conspicuous gallantry and leadership on 6th September 1918 in the Messines Sector. During the operations this officer showed great dash and courage in leading his men forward. He was the means of his platoon rushing a machine-gun post, capturing the gun and killing the team. He is a very determined leader and showed great ability in handling his men.' Relinquished his commission on account of ill health caused by wounds, 2.9.1919. Regular Army emergency commission as an RUR Lt., 9.12.1940. H/Capt. 25.5.1945. File missing.

Hutcheson Lt.-Col. Robert Barrett. Obtained his BA from Trinity College, Dublin, 1907. Commissioned to 2nd RIR, February 1909, and promoted Lt. 1.1.1910. Joined 2nd RIR, 20.9.1914, and appointed a/Adjutant. C Coy. Promoted Capt. 18.3.1915. To hospital with concussion 7.5.1915. Mentioned in Despatches 30.5.1918. Promoted Lt.-Col., 1918, while commanding Com. Musketry School. French Croix de Guerre (Silver Star) 17.8.1918. Attached Labour Corps 1919. Italian Croce de Guerra 21.8.1919. Died 20.8.1966, aged 82. *Irish Times*, 24.8.1966: 'Peacefully at his residence, Prospect, Queen's Avenue, Old Colwyn, Denbighshire, North Wales ... Funeral service on Friday next at 11.30 o'clock in the Church of the Holy Trinity, Rathmines. Internment immediately afterwards in Mount Jerome Cemetery [Dublin]. No flowers. No mourning please.'

    Quis Separabit, winter 1966: 'R.B. or "Hutch" as he was affectionately called, joined the Royal Irish Rifles in 1908 and retired in 1925. I first met him when he was commanding a company in the 4th Battalion in 1916 and as a young and pretty green subaltern swallowed eagerly the rather lurid stories he told in the Mess about life in the Army before the Great War of 1914 ... He saw service in France and Belgium in the early months of the war but it was when attached to the Labour Corps in Italy and in charge of a Prisoners of War Camp that he did his most valuable work. In this appointment he had the rank of Lt.-Colonel and was awarded it on his retirement.' – General Steele. His medals are held at the regimental museum. *Thoms Directory* for 1912 lists a Mrs Hutcheson at 82 Palmerstown Road, Rathmines, Dublin. Closed file.

Inglis Capt. James Norman. Born 29.7.1887. Director of Inglis's Bakery. Served with Queen's University OTC. Permanent address, The Burn, Cregagh, Belfast. Enlisted in 6th RIR during December 1914. Height 5 foot 5 inches, chest 35–37 inches, weight 130 pounds, single, could ride 'motor cycles, not horses'. Promoted Lt. 28.1.1915. Served at Gallipoli from July 1915. Admitted to No.13 CCS with diarrhoea, 21 August, and transferred to Mudros. Invalided to the UK on HMHS *Canada*, 24.8.1915. Admitted to 1st London General Hospital, 29 October, convalescing from 'paratyphoid B complicated by suppurative double parotitis'. Still weak and granted leave of absence.

He wrote from Kilmona, Adelaide Park, Belfast, 6.4.1916, to a Major Warner stating that he had telephoned on 29.11.1915 for a transfer to the RFC, after an original application in June 1915. Stated that it seemed he would revert to 2/Lt. if he transferred. He had joined Belfast University in 1910 and held the rank of Cadet Sgt until he joined 6th RIR. Also held Machine Gun Certificate as well as knowing Wireless and Signalling. He wanted to know if it was necessary for him to lose rank, as he did not wish to transfer in that circumstance. Advised that if he entered the RFC as a Flying Officer he would not lose by the transfer. Reported for duty with 4th RIR 12.4.1916. Applied for a transfer as a Pilot or Temporary Observer in the RFC, 6.7.1916. Listed all his qualifications and experience, including Dollymount (Distinguished) Instructor's Certificate in the Vickers Light Gun, and added that he had been up in a plane since his return from Gallipoli. He was the inventor of a long-range Military Signalling Lamp (Patent 3586/12) used by the Government. It seems that he served for some time as an observer before being posted to 8th RIR. Promoted to Capt. Transferred to 2nd RIR about February 1918. Rejoined from Divisional Reception Camp 7.8.1918 and took command of C Coy. Left to join GHQ Supernumerary Wireless Department at the end of August 1918.

Letter to WO Medals Branch, 3.7.1923, from William E. Moss, Hillfield Park, Aldenham, Watford: 'I have been appealed to by a friend, Capt. Norman Inglis, to assist him in claiming his medals for overseas service. His original regimental record office was at Beggar's Bush Barracks, Dublin, but no longer exists; he was subsequently transferred to some RE unit in Palestine, and the precise procedure of his demobilization he has never fathomed.' File ref: 339/5300.

Innes-Cross 2/Lt. Sydney Maxwell. Son of Charles Innes-Cross DL, Dromantine, Newry, Co. Down. Gazetted a 2/Lt. 5.2.1913 from Sandhurst. *Lucy*, pre-war: 'The third officer was a small-sized young subaltern named Cross, a young English public school boy, as yet of no account, except that he was an officer of Irishmen who looked up to him in their ancient traditional clannish way, a way charmingly friendly, but rather pathetic, and perhaps out of date in a matter-of-fact country of very mixed peoples. In return this young officer got very fond of us, and our brogue amused him. He used to imitate us very well at the regimental concerts, in which he figured as no mean comedian.'

D Coy commander when the Germans attacked his line, 27.10.1914, and was reported missing. *Lucy*: 'It appears that there were a good many wounded in the section of the trench occupied by the corporal and the lieutenant. These could not be got away. There were also a few fit men who preferred to stay, and when the order came to retire the officer was loath to leave them. Ternaghan got him out of the back of the trench, but half-way to safety he stopped and turned about to go back to the front line. Ternaghan stopped too and grabbed him, urging him to escape, but he shook the corporal off, saying: "I must go back". But he did not get as far as the trench. Two Germans rose up just behind it, and, rushing him, killed him with their bayonets.'

Age 20. Brother of Lt. A.C.W. Innes-Cross of Airlour, Whauphill, Wigtownshire. *Down Recorder*, 27.5.1916: 'In the High Court, Dublin, on Monday, there came on for hearing an application by Lt. A.C. Wolseley Innes-Cross, Irish Guards, of Dromantine, near Newry, for letters of administration of the estate of his brother, 2/Lt. S. Maxwell Innes-Cross ... in presumption of his death ... Counsel said that a soldier who saw Lt. Innes-Cross in the trenches when they were rushed by the enemy was a prisoner in Germany. If the officer were alive he would be entitled to a legacy of £8,000. Mr Justice Madden said, having regard to the circumstances of the family, that this was not a matter of urgency, and he would let it stand generally.' Rue Petillon Military Cemetery, Fleurbaix, II.E.46. File missing.

Ireland Lt.-Col. Herbert Richard Hall MC. Born 1879, the son of Mr de Courcy Plunkett Ireland, Merton Hall, Borrisokane, Co. Tipperary. Native of Clonmel. Promoted Capt., 3rd Leinster Regt, 20.12.1914. Attached to 2nd RIR. MC awarded January 1916. *King's County Chronicle*, 23.3.1916: 'for conspicuous gallantry under heavy shell fire during an attack. He prepared the point of entry into the enemy's trenches, and organized the attacking parties with great coolness and resource.' Wounded 7.7.1916. Later attached to 2nd RMF. *Irish Times*, 1.4.1918: 'Col. Ireland, who was wounded on March 23rd, when he was commanding a battalion of the Royal Munster Fusiliers, was in his fortieth year and was the last surviving child of Mrs de Courcy Ireland, Borrisokane.' *Irish Life*, 26.4.1918: ' ... died on March 28th from wounds received in action on March 21st. He entered the Army in 1900, serving in the West Indian Regiment until 1912 when he retired. In December 1914 he was attached to the Leinster Regiment and was wounded in March 1915 and again in July 1917.' St Sever Cemetery, Rouen, B.6.15. File missing.

Ivey Major Thomas Henry DSO. Born 20.9.1881. Served in the ranks of the Coldstream Guards, 12.8.1914 to 2.11.1914, and was Mentioned in Despatches 9.12.1914. Promoted from 4091 CSM to 2/Lt. in the RIR, 1.10.1914, and promoted Lt. 15.3.1915. Returned to the front 29.6.1915 and was wounded 25.9.1915, while serving with 2nd RIR (being part of the machine gun section). *Irish Times*, 6.10.1915: 'Captain Thomas Ivey, Royal Irish Rifles, wounded in France, is 34 years of age and enlisted in his twentieth year in the Coldstream Guards, in which he was a Company Sergeant Major of thirteen years service when war broke out. He was with the Coldstreams in the advance to and the retreat from Mons, the fighting on the Aisne and the Marne, and between Ypres and Armentieres, and he received his commission in the Royal Irish Rifles just thirteen months ago, when he was mentioned in despatches. He was gazetted Captain on Monday last.' He returned to the front, 3.4.1917, and joined 1st RIR, 28.4.1917. Took over the duties of Second-in-Command, 19 June, and was appointed a/Major. He was in temporary command 1–9.8.1917, 9.10.1917 to 29.12.1917, and 4– 20.4.1918, being awarded the DSO and Mentioned in Despatches, 7.4.1918, *London Gazette*, 3.6.1918. From 20.8.1918 he was employed as Commandant of 36th Divisional Reception Camp until the end of the war. Closed file.

Jackson Lt. Patrick Arthur Dudley. Born 10.3.1897 at Fyzabad, India, the only son of Major Cecil Jackson JP, 8th Hussars, of Knapp House, Gillingham, Dorset, and Violet Emily Caroline, daughter of Col. Richard George Bolton, Royal Horse Guards (The Blues). Educated at Durnford, Langton Matravers, Eton, and crammed at Wrens. Applied for a commission 2.12.1914. Single, height 5 foot 8½ inches, chest 33½–36 inches, weight 152 pounds. Permanent address 70 Cadogan Place, London SW; correspondence address 9th RIR, Newcastle, Co. Down. Went overseas December 1915. Appointed to a Regular commission 23.6.1916. Wounded at Thiepval, 1.7.1916, while serving with 9th RIR; shrapnel left leg. Left 2nd Red Cross Hospital at Rouen and embarked Rouen–Southampton on *St David*. MB at 2nd Southern General Hospital, Bristol, 6 July: small entry and exit wound, slight not permanent. To 3rd RIR 11.9.1916. Joined 2nd RIR 9.12.1916. Killed in action 4.1.1917. Effect included an unopened letter to Miss F. Brockington, Calcutta. About this time his father went to India. The original wooden cross from his grave is kept in the Church of St Michael and All Angels, Thornton, Bucks. Hyde Park Corner (Royal Berks) Cemetery, Ploegsteert, A.2. File ref: 339/17025.

Jeffares Capt. Richard Thorpe. Born 1890, the fourth son of Michael H. Jeffares, Seskin, Leighlinbridge, Co. Carlow. Commissioned to 4th RIR 6.5.1911. Height 5 foot 11¼ inches, chest 34–36½ inches, weight 150 pounds. Promoted Lt., 20.2.1913, and Capt. 6.3.1915. Also served in German East Africa. His brother, 2/Lt. M.H. Jeffares, served with 1st RIR. Next of kin was his uncle, John Jeffares, Scarke House, New Ross, Co. Wexford

Free Press, 10.4.1915: 'Lt. Jeffares … had a narrow escape in the recent big engagement in France. A bullet struck the watch which was strapped to his wrist but fortunately did not do any injury beyond smashing the watch to atoms.' Invalided home from France on SS *Brighton* due to measles 14.5.1915. A MB, 29 June, noted that he had recovered but was suffering slightly from nervousness and insomnia. A letter to Uncle John, written at Carrickfergus, 10.10.1916, stated that he was awaiting a wire from the WO. He would come down on the way through Dublin and send all his kit and clothes by train when he gets his orders. He enclosed Army Form W3136 – only to be used if he was killed – for claiming a gratuity for officers killed in action. 'If I do go West spend some of it on Mick and Mary, Mary will want a helping hand and so will Mick.' He said he was nearly broke, but had few outstanding debts; he should be owed about £160 if the war lasted three years. He was thinking about possibly marrying Molly Ross, daughter of a solicitor in Belfast, after the war.

Rejoined 2nd RIR and later left for the Divisional Musketry School. Letter from Dick to Uncle John, 19.7.1917, about a new scheme of pensions and gratuities: officers were to receive an extra £100. He said that as his uncle was the next of kin, it would go to him. 'I would like you to hold on to it and spend it mostly on Mick if he gets safely through it all. Do as you like with it but give Mick first call and preference.' He said that he did not expect to get killed, 'but we are in a hot place at present. There is a hell of a fight coming off soon. Now you know my wishes and after all I look on you as my father and Boss. My other and real father I have no feeling for. We are still in the line strafing him and he is strafing us all days and nights. The din and noise is terrific and we suffer a lot but he suffers more … The whole place is chock and block of guns and all blazing away. I have got a few shell cases, solid brass, excellent vases or ash trays, in my valise.' He also sent his love to Aunt Cissie.

Rejoined 2nd RIR 25.7.1917. Wounded in action, 10.8.1917, while commanding B Coy. See main text. Admitted to No. 30 General Hospital, Calais, the next day. WO telegram 17 August: 'Capt. R.T. Jeffares Irish Rifles now diagnosed gunshot wound left forearm severe.' Discharged from hospital 5 September and rejoined 2nd RIR. WO telegram 6.10.1917: 'Regret to inform you Capt. R.T. Jeffares Irish Rifles reported Oct 6th admitted 33rd Casualty Clearing Station dangerously wounded head. Further reports will be sent on receipt.'

Free Press, 3.11.1917: 'Although only 27 years of age, he had a distinguished career. He received his early education in the John Ivory School, New Ross, after which he spent four years in the Kilkenny College, where he had a brilliant scholastic record. He received his commission in the Royal Irish Rifles in 1910 and, in 1912, was appointed to an important post in the Rhodesian Police. He was there until the outbreak of war in 1914 when he returned home to join his battalion and proceeded to Flanders shortly after his arrival. He went through several of the big engagements and was wounded in the early part of last August. He was on a visit home on a ten days leave in the latter part of September and shortly after returning to the firing line he received the fatal wound. For some time during 1916 he was Commandant of a bombing school in Ireland ... Another brother, Lt. M.H. Jeffares, Scarke House, is at home at present having been wounded early last August. A second brother of the deceased is a paymaster in the Navy and a sister a VAD Nurse in England.' Mentioned in Despatches *London Gazette*, 21.12.1917.

Gross value of his estate was £238. An invoice was submitted from T.G. Phillips, Military Tailors and Outfitters, 4 Dame Street, Dublin, for £16.70 and included: refitting of a jacket, metal stars, changing a jacket to rank of Major, and the German South West Africa medal ribbon. Colfer & Son, Solicitors, New Ross, requested the WO to pay money owed: 'We enclose copies of two letters written by the deceased to his uncle, our client, Mr John Jeffares of Scarke House, New Ross, Wexford. The deceased was brought up and educated by Mr Jeffares who is a wealthy man and has no need of the money. But he is most anxious to carry out the deceased's wishes with regard to the brother Mick.' £154.59 was sent in settlement. Effects returned included a cigarette case, wrist watch (broken); religious medallions, and tobacco pouch. Bethune Town Cemetery, Pas de Calais, III.J.16. File ref: 339/31057.

Jenkinson Capt. T.S. 4th RIF. Joined 2nd RIR 13.10.1915. Wounded accidentally by a Very Pistol 11.12.1915. Rejoined 30.1.1916. Wounded by shell fire 26.4.1916. Joined 1st RIF 11.12.1916. Admitted to 27th FA, 11.4.1917: severe GSW, fractured tibia, left knee. Admitted to No. 30 CCS, 12.4.1917, and to 24th General Hospital at Etaples the next day. Embarked for Dover aboard HS *St Denis*, 18 April. File missing.

Johnston 2/Lt. Roland Ivan. Born at Dalriada, 22.9.1885, the son of Samuel A. and Agnes Johnston, Dalriada, Jordanstown, Whiteabbey, Co. Antrim. Educated at Marlborough College, Wiltshire. Husband of Susan May Johnston, RR5, Fenwick, Ontario, Canada. Member of Freemason Lodge 282, Carrickfergus. Returned from Canada and enlisted as Sapper 2425 in the RE, 9.4.1915. Height 5 foot 10¼ inches, chest 39–42 inches, weight 168 pounds, automobile mechanic. Address Jennymount Mills, York Road, Belfast. *Irish Times*, 5.9.1918: 'He was a splendid all-round athlete and a member of the North of Ireland Football Club.'

Posted to the BEF and joined South Midland RE from 4/1st South Midland Field Coy 11.12.1915. Transferred to England, 6.1.1917, having applied for a commission. Gazetted to 3rd RIR 30.5.1917 and rejoined the BEF. Wounded while serving with 2nd RIR, 24.8.1918, and admitted to No.110 FA. Transferred to No. 62 CCS the next day: 'entry wound over spine of left scapula excised and enlarged. Scapula found severely comminuted. Several loose fragments of bone removed.' Admitted to No.8 Red Cross Hospital at Boulogne, 27.8.1918, and examined by Major W. Ashdowne, RAMC: 'Vomiting, jaundice and collapse on admission. Vomiting persists. Wounds on left back clean. Right back, chest unhealthy small wound. Chest – right chest – breath sounds absent. Heart displaced to right. Collapsed right lung.

Left air entry poor. Urgent dyspnoea. Collapse marked. Pulse rapid and weak.' Died at 5.10 a.m., 28.8.1918.

List of effects sent to his father included a tube of brilliantine and *Songs of a Sourdough*. His widow was residing at The Quoile, Downpatrick, Co. Down, 3.12.1918, when she applied for a pension. The executors were James Campbell, managing director, and Thomas James Sheppard, clerk, of Jennymount Mills. Estate valued at £1,675. Philip Johnston, Fairholm, 150 Worple Road, Wimbledon, wrote to the WO, 6.7.1922, seeking details of the death. Terlincthun British Cemetery, Wimille, Pas de Calais, II.F.11. File ref: 339/88980.

Jones Lt. George Dean Johnston. Born 10.6.1894. The Rector of Navan, Archdeacon of Meath, Ven. John Rennison, wrote a reference for him as a former pupil at The College, Navan, on 19.7.1911: 'I have always found him in every way satisfactory, he is a youth of more than average ability, and has passed most creditably in the Prep and Junior grades of the Intermediate Exam. His conduct has always been most exemplary and gentlemanly, he is thoroughly steady and can be relied upon for punctuality and attention to his work. I believe him to be most truthful and conscientious, and can speak of him in the strongest terms'. Applied for a commission 29.10.1915. Address Mount Charles, Slane, Co. Meath; height 5 foot 8 inches, chest 32–35 inches, weight 127 pounds, single, bank official in the Bank of Ireland, Navan. Commissioned to 3rd Leinster Regt in November 1915.

Joined 2nd RIR 24.7.1916. A/Adjutant June 1917. Promoted to Lt. in July 1917. Left unit 16.7.1917. Embarked Boulogne–Dover on HS *St Andrew*, 30 August. MB at No. 4 London General Hospital, 10.9.1917: 'He was blown up by a shell at Messines on 7.6.17. He was thrown and dazed. Headaches since, dizzy.' Applied from hospital in Kilkenny for a wound gratuity, 27.10.1917, and again from Mount Charles, 16.11.1917. MB at King George V Hospital, Dublin, 13.11.1917, 'His nervous symptoms are still well marked and he has not made much improvement during the last two months. Board are of the opinion that light sedentary duty, to occupy his mind, would benefit his general health.' Took up light duty as a Railway Transport Officer. MB 5.3.1918: 'Suffers from insomnia and frontal headaches. Neither condition is improving. Depression, pulse rapid, tremors especially in hands. Exaggeration of deep reflexes. No evidence of organic disease. Has lost weight, looks pale and ill.' Passed permanently unfit for any service. WO directed that he be placed on the retired list: 'A shell exploded near him on 7.6.17 and he was dazed afterwards and subsequently went through the fighting of the next twelve days; from that time he suffered headaches, insomnia, nervousness and loss of appetite, which has become worse over the last two months. Depressed, with tremor of hands, exaggerated reflexes, pulse 86 and losing weight.' Granted a wound gratuity of £250.

MB at Arbour Hill, Dublin, 5.9.1918: he had been at home since the last MB, unable to work. 'States that he is sleeping better and that headache is not so continuous. He is in better spirits, and looks much better, but still is weak and easily tired, and has pulse of 120, and still perspires easily. Knee reflexes exaggerated. His appetite is good, and he is putting on a little weight.' Army Pensions Office received a note of his death, 24.2.1967, from Ministry of Pensions and National Insurance. Pensionable disability neurasthenia; rate of pension at death £89.60. He left no wife or child. File ref: 339/48155.

Jones Lt. William. L/Sgt in the Irish Guards when he was promoted for services in the field to a commission in 7th RIR, 1.1.1917, joining the same day. *Belfast News Letter*, 13.3.1917, reported that he had been wounded. Rejoined 7th RIR, 31.10.1917, and posted to D Coy. Joined 2nd RIR 14.11.1917. Promoted Lt. 1.7.1918. Closed file.

Jonsson Major Aubrey Thomas. Born 1877. Gazetted a 2/Lt. in 3rd RIR 5.5.1902. Promoted Lt. 15.11.1902, and Capt. 1.10.1904. Joined 2nd RIR 26.10.1914 and was captured the next day. Promoted Major 18.9.1915. Interned in Holland from 6.2.1918. Repatriated to the UK 19.11.1918. Granted two months leave and then to report to 3rd RIR. Statement to the WO, 10.12.1918: He was captured 27.10.1914 at the road leading into Neuve Chapelle. The enemy broke through the left end of the trenches that morning. An order was passed down from Capt. Dickson, commanding the battalion, to retire at once in succession from the right. Capts Davis and Jonsson were last to leave the trench, and Davis was killed as he jumped onto the road. There was then heavy rifle fire from the enemy and many men were killed or wounded. He shouted to his men to push on in front, but they shouted back that it was impossible. He pushed on across the road and found a CSM and about eight men in a shell-hole. He asked how long ago they had lost connection and the CSM said about twenty minutes earlier. The CSM and about four of the men were wounded. CSM told him they could not get through the village as it was entirely occupied by the enemy. 'I then said if the men would follow me I would have a try. One of my men in front then volunteered to take a wounded man along, saying the enemy would not fire on the wounded and once he got into the village he would signal, this he did not do, but I have heard since that he escaped safely. As he reached the village two of my men jumped up to rush the village, but were killed. Finding myself surrounded and in this hopeless position I offered to lead the five or seven unwounded men on a hopeless charge for the name of the Regiment. This, they rightly replied, 'was no good' so we lay, hoping for relief, or later to get away under cover of darkness. At about four we were rushed and what remained of us captured ... I should like the honour of stating that the German General congratulated me on the bravery of the men of my Regiment. He indignantly informed me that for two weeks he had tried with great numbers, to take our position but had failed. He could not understand this, being aware that we had only a few men. I naturally misled him as to our strength.'

He wrote to the WO, 18.12.1918, from Hotel Mount Pleasant, Great Malvern, Worcestershire, acknowledging receipt of a rail warrant to join 3rd RIR and asked for his leave to be extended to 1.2.1919. He was recently divorced and, as he had not seen his daughter for four years, wished to have her with him until the end of her holidays. WO refused any extension. Reported to 3rd RIR 17.1.1919. Discharged 28.2.1919. No blame was attached to his capture. Resigned his commission 24.3.1920. File ref: 339/41247.

Joy Lt. Frederick Charles Patrick. Born 23.1.1892 at Seapatrick, Banbridge, Co. Down, the son of Robert and Elizabeth Joy. Educated at Highgate School (where he was in the OTC), and obtained his BA from Trinity College, Dublin, 1912. Resided with his brother, Robert Cecil Joy, a solicitor with the Bank of Ireland, at Grove House, Stillorgan, Co. Dublin. Applied for a commission 13.8.1914. Height 6 foot, chest 37–39 inches, weight 154 pounds, brown eyes and hair, chartered accountant, Church of England, single, permanent address Grove House. Joined at Naas, 15.9.1914, and discharged on appointment to a commission in 7th RDF, 29.9.1914. Gazetted a 2/Lt. in 3rd RIR with seniority to date from 15.8.1914. Promoted Lt. 8.5.1915. Joined 2nd RIR 1.4.1915. Killed in action 16.6.1915. His brother Cecil was next of kin and sole executor. Value of probate £1,101. *Banbridge Chronicle* 30.6.1915: 'Lt. Joy belonged to a family which has played a large part in the history of Belfast, the name still remaining in one of the streets and amongst them was a Chief Justice of Ireland. Lt. Joy's father, who died about 15 years ago, was a well-known citizen of Belfast ... A brother, Dr H.A. Joy, was a distinguished student at the Queen's College, Belfast, and took his medical degree in the Royal University with first class honours, afterwards becoming a surgeon in the Navy. Another brother, Mr W. Bruce Joy, who was well known in Belfast some years ago now resides in the Philippine Islands where he is engaged in business. He is married to a daughter of the late Mr A.B. Wilson, Maryville, Belfast. Mr Bruce Joy, the well-known sculptor, is also a connection of the same family.' Menin Gate Memorial. File ref: 339/26054.

Kearns Capt. Michael Christopher. Born c.1878, the son of a soldier. He had been a pupil at the Royal Hibernian Military School, Dublin, from 1.2.1890 to 5.10.1892. Joined the RIR as a boy soldier, No. 3691. Served in the South African War 1899 during operations in Natal, receiving the Queen's Medal with clasps. He later served with 2nd RIR as CSM and was wounded. Promoted 2/Lt., 1.10.1914, and attached to D Coy. *Immortal Deeds*: 'Lieutenant Kearns went out to France as a Colour-Sergeant; he is 6 foot 2 inches high, and a noted shot. He still retains his rifle. During an attack on the British trenches he picked off the leading ten Germans himself with the ten rounds in his magazine, reserving the fire of his platoon until the enemy came within short range. His skill and coolness saved the situation.' *Burgoyne*: 'At Ypres, in November, during the attack by the Prussian Guards, he bowled over fourteen of them himself. A very cool man, a most trustworthy soldier and a fine officer.' Mentioned in Despatches, 17.2.1915, 'for gallant and distinguished service in the field'. Promoted Lt. 15.3.1915. Joined 1st RIR 16.2.1918 and was struck off the strength 9.8.1918, no reason being stated. At the Depot 1923. Died in hospital at Bath 21.12.1947. Closed file.

Keating Major Patrick William. Commissioned to 4th CR 26.4.1913, promoted Lt. 1.5.1914, and Capt. 10.7.1915. Attached to the RMF. Appointed a Regular Capt. in the RIR, 29.8.1916, and attached to 7th RIR, 1.11.1916. Took over the duties of Adjutant 12.12.1916. Left unit 3.1.1917 for the Heavy Branch MGC, and attached to the Tank Corps as a/Major. Joined 2nd RIR 3.2.1918, and 1st RIR 21.10.1918. Returned to the UK 14.2.1919 prior to going overseas with 2nd RIR. Mentioned in Despatches 3.2.1920. Closed file.

Kelly Capt. David Herbert. Entered Trinity College, Dublin, 1913. Member of Freemason Lodge 9, Dungannon, Co. Tyrone. Commissioned to 3rd R. Inniskilling Fusiliers, 15.8.1914. Served with the Worcestershire Regt. Promoted Capt. 24.7.1915. Joined 2nd RIR 22.9.1915. Mentioned in Despatches, *London Gazette*, 15.6.1916. Wounded 16.7.1916 while serving with 2nd RIR. Educational instructor 1919. Closed file.

Kemp Capt. Albert Edgar MC, DCM. Born in Birmingham. Married Miss A. Gill of Dorking. Embarked for France with 2nd Worcestershire Regt in August 1914. At that time he was L/Sgt 10968. DCM, *London Gazette*, 16.1.1915: 'Acting-Sgt A.E. Kemp. For conspicuous gallantry and ability on 31st October at Gheluvelt, in the control of his men during the very critical engagement which resulted in the recapture of the village.' The depleted 2nd Worcs was the only reserve available for the counter-attack at Gheluvelt, which was successful, plugged the gap and prevented the Germans breaking through to the Channel ports. Commissioned in the field 19.7.1915 for distinguished service. Wounded by shell fire, 2.10.1915, while serving with 2nd RIR. Promoted Lt. 30.5.1916, and Capt. 16.9.1917. Employed with 7th RDF according to the Army List of May 1918. It is not known when he returned to 2nd RIR but he was with C Coy in August 1918. Wounded 1.10.1918. MC, *London Gazette*, 29.7.1919: 'For gallantry and devotion to duty south of Dadizeele on October 1st, 1918. He was commanding a company in the attack, during which he was wounded through both thighs. The situation being uncertain, and no officer being available to hand his command to, he refused to be evacuated until he was satisfied that all was in order. This necessitated his carrying on his duties for four hours after being wounded, when he was evacuated as a stretcher case.' Closed file.

Kennard Capt. John Adam Gaskell. Commissioned to 5th Rifle Bde, 15.8.1914, and joined 2nd RIR 5.12.1914. To hospital, 30.12.1914, then granted sick leave. He wrote to the WO, 8.2.1915, from his father's address at Belmore House, Upham, Hants: 'I was invalided with colitis and am now suffering from nerves. I am afraid my writing is not very good.' In another letter, 27 February, from 18 Adelaide Crescent, Hove, Brighton, he requested instructions for a MB and travel warrant as his leave was soon to expire. His father informed the WO, 6 March, that John was in Staffordshire, was far from well, unfit to travel, and was suffering from nerves. Reported to 5th Rifle Bde at Sheerness during April. Certified fit for general service 26.8.1915.

Posted to 2nd Rifle Bde and served as a Capt. Left unit, 1.11.1916, suffering from trench fever and debility. Embarked Le Havre–Southampton six days later. Ordered to report to the 5th Bn at Sheppey for light duty 19.6.1917. At this time he was at 15 Eccleston Square, London. His doctor sent a certificate saying Kennard was unfit to rejoin. He was working on recruiting duties 'in the M.A.R.O. and that is about all he can do – I feel sure that he would rapidly break down if he rejoins.' He wrote to the WO, 4.3.1918, from the Central London Recruiting Area, Great Scotland Yard, pointing out that he had been seconded to the Ministry of National Service, 15.11.1917, but had not received a war service gratuity. From the time he transferred to the Ministry his Army pay ceased and the WO refused any more funds. Restored to the establishment, 10.3.1919, and demobilized as a result of ill health. Address 17 Ashburnham Mansions, Chelsea. Age 37. The following month he was working as a director at Turner's Motor Manufacturing Co. Ltd., Wulfruna Works, Lever Street, Wolverhampton. Relinquished his commission, 1.4.1920. Served continuously during the coal strike, 13.4.1921 to 15.5.1921, at the Rifle Bde Depot. Using the headed paper of Fiat Motors Ltd., 43–44 Albemarle Street, London, he complained, 21.7.1921, that he had not received his £50 gratuity for serving during the strike. File ref: 339/17427.

Kennedy Capt. Herbert Alexander. Son of Margaret Kennedy. Commissioned 25.7.1891. Promoted Lt., 2.3.1896, and Capt. 10.4.1900. Retired 29.12.1906. Rejoined at the commencement of the war and was posted to B Coy, 2nd RIR. *Bond of Sacrifice*: '... who was a member of a naval and military family, was born at Bellary, India, and was the son of Major-General H.F. Kennedy, 60th Rifles (KRRC), of Bath, and grandson of Captain Kennedy, RN. He was educated at Bath, and after passing through the RMC, Sandhurst, received his commission in the 2nd Battalion Royal Irish Rifles in 1891. He served with his battalion in the South African War, his services there gaining him the Queen's and King's medals, each with two clasps. He was promoted Captain in 1900, and in 1906 joined the Reserve of Officers ... He was mortally wounded at Neuve Chapelle when leading his men in action on the 24th October, and died of his wounds at the Military Hospital, Bethune, on the 28th October, 1914. He married, in 1912, Dorothy, only child of the late Mrs Charles Collins, and cousin of Lieutenant-General Sir Aylmer Hunter Weston KCB, DSO.' In his will he left a considerable sum of money to the RIR Officers' Mess for sport, adventure and parties. This was well known to officers of the regiment as the Kennedy Trust – see Col. Becher. Bethune Town Cemetery, Pas de Calais, I.A.5. File missing.

Kertland 2/Lt. Edwin Blow. Born 29.1.1896, the son of Edwin Happer and Meta Blow Kertland, Dunnimarle, Knockdene Park, Belfast. Educated at Campbell College 1909–12. At that time he was living at 42 Eglantine Avenue, Belfast. Applied for a commission 5.8.1914. Apprentice manager, linen trade. Currently serving as a L/Cpl in Queen's University OTC. Permanent address was his mother's home at 8 Mount Pleasant, Belfast. Gazetted a 2/Lt. in 3rd RIF and employed at a training camp near Fannad Head. Joined 2nd RIR 10.2.1915. Slightly wounded 23.3.1915. Mentioned in Despatches. Wounded and missing 16.6.1915. Next of kin, widowed mother Martha, aged 47. He had three sisters: Anna Blow (17), Mary Patricia (14), and Jessie Graham (8). His uncle, Edwin Blow, c/o James Blow, 44 Textile Buildings, Linenhall Street, Belfast, wrote to the WO on behalf of Martha Kertland, 17.11.1915. Cox & Co. told him they could not release the balance of monies due until Edwin was declared dead. The family had a letter from Capt. Gavin, 2nd RIR, 3.8.1915, enclosing a report by 6688 Rfn Arthur McConville, C Coy 2nd RIR: 'Lt. Kertland was hit by machine gun fire and fell – he must have been mortally wounded as I lay beside him for seven minutes and he did not move.' Death accepted for official purposes 29.12.1915. His medals and citation were donated to the RIF Museum. RBAI Memorial. Menin Gate Memorial. File ref: 339/22334.

King Lt. Frederick John. He was a 2/Lt. in 4th R. Irish. Joined 2nd RIR 4.10.1915 for his first BEF posting. To hospital, sick, 21.2.1916. Closed file.

Kirkpatrick Capt. Drummond. Gazetted a 2/Lt. in 3rd RIR 15.8.1914. Promoted Lt. 8.5.1915. Joined 2nd RIR 28.6.1915 for his first overseas posting. Severely wounded by a shell 1.8.1915. See main text. Promoted Capt. 19.2.1916. Later served at the Depot. Resided at Kincraig, Belfast. He attended the 36th (Ulster) Division Officers' Old Comrades' Association annual dinner 1937. Closed file.

Knox Brigadier Fergus Y Carson DSO. Born in 1898, a son of the Revd David Browne Knox DD and Maude Carson Knox, The Manse, Whitehead, Co. Antrim. The Y in his name is not an abbreviation according to his son Jeremy: 'It was generally understood within our family that our grandfather had interjected Y at the appropriate moment during the baptism as a joke and had then insisted on its inclusion in the birth certificate.' Educated at the Royal Belfast Academical Institution and Coleraine Academical Institution. Commissioned to 4th RIR 10.7.1915. Height 5 foot 9 inches. Joined 2nd RIR 21.7.1916. Wounded while with a working party 16.7.1917. Promoted Lt. 15.12.1918, and Major 15.1.1936. In 1920 he married Jessie 'Ivy' Carroll, formerly Wilson, and they had two sons, David Brian (born 1932) and Richard Jeremy (1933). Served in Egypt, India, and the Sudan. At HQ 166th Infantry Bde, Lichfield, Staffordshire, in 1938.

Quis Separabit, no. 1, 1961: *Editorial* – 'During the 1914–18 War he served as a 2/Lt. with the Royal Irish Rifles, and from 1925 to 1928, he was Adjutant of the London Irish Rifles afterwards he held a similar post with the 2nd Battalion, The Royal Ulster Rifles, and commanded the Regimental Depot in 1938. He commanded the 2nd Battalion in the Belgian campaign in 1940, gaining the DSO and being Mentioned in Despatches. In May, 1941, he was promoted Brigadier and he commanded the Assault Brigade of the 50th Infantry Division in the Normandy landings. He was awarded a Bar to his DSO in 1944. He served with the Military Mission to Belgium and Holland, 1944–5, and was made a Knight Commander of the Order of Orange Nassau with Swords, and a Commander of the Order of Leopold II with Palm. In 1946 he was appointed to command Cyrenaica District, Middle East, and in 1947 Deputy District Commander Home Counties District. He retired in 1949 and was appointed to the RUC, retiring in 1957 because of ill health.' His first DSO was presented in the main square of Tourcoing by General B.L. Montgomery, 26.5.1940. He was head staff officer of the Ulster B Special Constabulary. Died at his home in Exmouth, Devon, 28.5.1961, after a long period of ill health.

Quis Separabit, no. 1, 1961: 'In Cairo "on the streets" in 1923 I saw him command his Platoon to the entire satisfaction of his men and the people he was keeping in order. Later on he did grand service with the London Irish Rifles and was one of General Bernard's band of Company Commanders in the 1st Battalion at Aldershot. But I regard it to be supremely fortunate that, in the design and working out of things, he came to command of the 2nd Battalion just as the flag fell in France in May, 1940. To my mind this was his "finest hour". He was ready for his responsibilities and he carried them out superbly in the advance into Belgium during the fighting there; especially at Louvain; and in the subsequent withdrawal. Indeed as a Commander he became a legend; that legend still persists and rightly so. General Horrocks tells in his book of the lesson Fergus taught him then. Around Louvain there were many rumours and two Riflemen came excitedly back to the Battalion "HQ" saying that disaster had befallen their Company. The CO calmed them down and told them to return; just as they were going he called them back and said "Here, have a cigarette". Together they smoked and back they went contentedly. That was a fine illustration of the art of command of men in battle ... With Jeremy amongst us [Lt.-Col. R.J. Knox], many will see the characteristics and outlook of Fergus as something continuing and very satisfying.' – General Steele. Closed file.

Kyte 2/Lt. Ernest Cockburn. Served in the ranks of 7th R. Inniskilling Fusiliers. Gazetted a 2/Lt. in 7th RIR, 15.9.1917, and joined the same day. To 2nd RIR 14.11.1917. Later employed as a Brigade Education Officer. Closed file.

Lane 2/Lt. Charles Henry. Enlisted as Pte 5928 in 5th Lancers 27.11.1905. Height 5 foot 7½ inches, chest 33–36 inches, weight 147 pounds, age 20, barman.

Next of kin was his mother, Alice Maude Patterson, East Indian Arms, Poplar. His brothers were Frederick John, Francis William, and Henry, and his sister was Mabel Putt. Posted to 12th Lancers in India, 5.9.1906. Admitted to hospital at Sialkot, 18.2.1908, with a slight contusion to the right thigh. There were three short admissions for malaria in 1908–9. Posted to South Africa 24.10.1910. Transferred to the Reserve, at his own request, before expiration of his period of service, 20.1.1912, and returned to the UK. Married Agnes Maud Anderson, 31.5.1913. Their daughter Ethel Mabel was born 15.4.1914.

Mobilized 5.8.1914 and posted to 12th Lancers as a L/Cpl. To the BEF France 15.8.1914. A/Cpl. 15.11.1914 and Cpl. 10.4.1915. Admitted to No. 5 Cavalry FA with influenza 7.10.1915. To Base Depot 20.1.1916. A/Sgt 18.7.1916 and promoted Sgt 6.1.1917. Commissioned in the field to 10th RIR, 19.6.1917, and took up duty three days later. Gassed by a shell, 14.8.1918, while serving with 2nd RIR. Admitted to No. 62 CCS, 21.8.1918, and died that day, aged 30. His home address was The Sir John Barleycorn, 39 Upper North Street, Poplar, London. Died intestate with a gross estate of £703. His widow wrote to the WO, 31.8.1918, requesting a death certificate as this was needed to transfer the business into her name. Arneke British Cemetery, Nord, III.E.7. File ref: 339/119133.

Laville Capt. Samuel Eustace Blythe. Popularly known as Tim. Lt. in 3rd Leinster Regt. Joined 2nd RIR 11.10.1914. Wounded 25.10.1914. Joined A Coy, 2nd Leinster Regt. Slightly wounded by shell fire at Hooge 14.8.1915. Commanding D Coy, 21.9.1915. Killed in action 18.8.1916 by shell fire at Guillemont. A telegram was sent to Laville, Magistrate, Supreme Court, Penang, Straits Settlements. His mother, Ellen (Mrs L.V. Laville), was residing at

99 Addison Road, Kensington, and was the sole beneficiary. Her income was a small pension. Commemorated at Bedford School Chapel. Peronne Road Cemetery, Maricourt, Somme, III.I.16. File ref: 339/9755.

Leach Capt. Ernest Walter Vindin. Born 5.2.1896 at 98 Rathgar Road, Rathfarnham, Co. Dublin, the elder son of Ernest William Leach LGB, a civil servant, and Isabel Madeline Leach. Attended Dublin High School 1908–11. Applied for a commission 19.11.1914. Height 5 foot 9½ inches, chest 34¼–36¼ inches, weight 134 pounds, medical student at St Andrew's College. Address, father's residence at Prospect House, Milltown, Co. Dublin. Correspondence address, Military Hospital, Newbridge, Co. Kildare, where he was employed. Additional applications for a commission were made 29.12.1914, 9.2.1915, and 19.2.1915. A WO memo, 4.3.1915, to OC Oxford University OTC advised that he was a Temporary 2/Lt., posted 10th South Staffordshire Regt, and had been transferred to 3rd RIR. Joined 2nd RIR and promoted Lt., 4.12.1915. Slightly wounded, 2.1.1916, but remained at duty. Appointed a/Capt. 16.12.1916. Killed in action 2.1.1917. Mentioned in Despatches 4.1.1917. Single and intestate. Effects sent to his father included a small testament and silver cigarette case. His father wrote to the WO asking if there was any compensation due as he had a large family to support. Hyde Park Corner (Royal Berks) Cemetery, Ploegsteert, B.10. File ref: 339/36439.

Leask Squadron Leader Patrick Alexander Ogilive. Gazetted a 2/Lt. in 3rd RIR 16.9.1914. T/Lt., 15.11.1914, and joined 2nd RIR 6.1.1915. To hospital, sick, 18.1.1915. Promoted Lt. 15.3.1915. Wounded 7.5.1915. *Burgoyne*: 'January 12th [1915]: Have left my last joined Subaltern, one Mr Leask from Canada, there … January 18th: … my Canadian hero, tells me he has to go to Hospital now for the "Itch". He thinks he got it coming over in the transport. Have told him not to come near me or any of my kit … May 6th: Jolly Leask, who was my Company grenade specialist, I selected to hold 47 and to make the attack with his grenade throwers. May 7th: Then I heard a shriek, and a "Mr Leask is kilt", and I saw Leask ploughing his way, arms and legs like a drunken man, fighting down the trench through the dead and wounded … I rushed forward and caught him by the shoulder and dragged him under cover. Poor chap, he was just a bit shaken but like the plucky fellow he is, recovered at once; he had a bad hit in the back of the head, and was wounded in the ribs too … Most of Leask's followers had been killed and wounded … I rejoined the 4th Battalion at Carrickfergus on July 2nd … Leask quite recovered, joined us a month later.' Transferred to the RFC 4.11.1915. Promoted Capt. 1.1.1917, and Major 25.11.1917. Later Squadron Leader, RAF. Applied to resign his commission in the RIR with effect from 1.8.1919 upon being appointed to a permanent commission in the RAF. File ref: 339/13992.

Lecky 2/Lt. John. Born 4.2.1892, the only child of the Revd Alexander Gourley Lecky and Mary McKinley Lecky, Feddyglass, Raphoe, Co. Donegal. His father was pastor of 1st and 2nd Ballylennon Presbyterian Church, Raphoe, where he was resident from 1878 (ordained 1872), being appointed Clerk of the Raphoe Presbytery in 1884, succeeding his father, Revd John Lecky (1803–85), who had held that post for the previous forty years.

Educated at Coleraine Academical Institution. Enlisted at Lurgan into 16th RIR, 6.2.1915. Engineer, height 5 foot 10 inches, chest 38½–41 inches, weight 154 pounds. Appointed L/Cpl 1.3.1915, a/Cpl 21.4.1915, and promoted Cpl 21.9.1915. Gazetted a 2/Lt. in 18th RIR, 6.12.1915, and transferred to England five days later. Joined 2nd RIR 10.6.1916. Killed in action 16.7.1916. His father administered the gross estate of £569. Effects included a cigarette case and St John's Gospel. Thiepval Memorial. File ref: 339/46662.

Leman Major John Frederick. Commissioned into the Worcestershire Regt in 1906 and promoted Lt. in January 1909. Attached to 2nd RIR 8.5.1917. Posted to 11th Lancashire Fusiliers 17.6.1917. This may have been a temporary move as no details appear in their war diary. Closed file.

Lennox 2/Lt. Alfred James. Born 1889, the only son of William James Lennox, 24 Abbey Street, Armagh. His father was a draper at 17 and 19 Market Street, Armagh. Educated at the Royal School, Armagh. Enlisted as Pte 2388 in D Coy, 6th Black Watch (Royal Highlanders) TF, Perth, 10.10.1914. Declared age 23 years 5 months, height 5 foot 8½ inches, chest 35½–38 inches. Embarked Folkestone 2.5.1915. Received a slight GSW to the shoulder, 1.6.1915, and was admitted to No. 1 FA 51st Highland Division at Locon, and to No. 7 CCS at Merville the next day. Transferred to No. 5 Train on the 4th, to No. 20 General Hospital on the 5th, and to a convalescent camp at Etaples 20.8.1915. Rejoined his unit 31.8.1915.

Discharged to a commission in 7th RIR, 28.11.1915, and posted to 2nd RIR, joining from the Cadet School 8.12.1915. Missing, believed killed, 19.1.1916. Reports on file state that he was killed on the 20th. His father wrote to the WO, 28.2.1916, that he had heard from the CO and from Capt. Kelly who 'do not quite close the door against the faint hope that our beloved son may have been only wounded when he fell, and may therefore be alive in the hands of the enemy'. An internal WO memo dated 30 June referred to 'List No. 131A' from the German Government to the American Embassy in Berlin: a list of British dead forwarded to the Foreign Office 20.3.1916. One man is 'Lenorx? 6 R.H.P. No. 2388'. This was taken as being Lennox and death was accepted for official purposes. Died intestate leaving an estate of £183. Witness statements: 7285 Rfn T. Compton, A Coy, at No. 23 General Hospital, Etaples, 14.7.1916, said he saw Lennox's body lying in a trench at Vimy Ridge. He had been killed by a HE shell and the head was separated from the body. Compton knew Lennox well and was in a traverse when the shell that killed him came over. Lennox was buried at 'Souci Valley' behind the trenches. 8205 Rfn Coates, aboard the *St David*, Boulogne, 12.7.1916, saw Lennox killed on January 19th. Lennox was in charge of a party of bombers of which Coates was one. They were in an enemy trench near Le Touquet on the left of Armentieres. A bomb came over and blew Lennox into the air. 'He was quite dead but his body was not taken back. The bomb fell in front of him and I remember I shouted to him, but he walked right on top of it and was killed outright.' Ploegsteert Memorial. File ref: 339/50623.

Leslie Lt. Kenneth Drysdale. Born in London, 15.12.1886, and educated at Uppingham. Enlisted as Pte 1743 in 18th Royal Fusiliers 2.9.1914. Height 6 foot 1½ inches, chest 34–36½ inches, weight 162 pounds, blue eyes, fair hair. Next of kin was his father, Andrew Leslie, c/o Randall Bros., Sherwood House, Piccadilly. Appointed L/Cpl 15.2.1915, promoted Cpl 8.5.1915, L/Sgt 9.7.1915, Sgt 27.10.1915, and posted to the BEF France 14.11.1915. Applied for a commission 9.3.1916. Single, electrical engineer. His father was a clerk. Returned to the UK, 23.3.1916, and went to No. 1 Officers Cadet Bn at Denham. Commissioned to 5th RIR, 7.7.1916, and posted to 7th RIR.

Left that unit, 20.10.1916, suffering from a hernia, and embarked Boulogne–Dover aboard the *St Denis* on the 26th. His address at that time was Stoke, Green House, near Slough, Berkshire. He wrote a letter to the WO from 1 Valley Road, Shortlands, Kent, 21 December, requesting a date for a MB; currently on leave to 29.12.1916. MB at the Royal Herbert Hospital, Woolwich,10.1.1917: ordered to report for light duty to 5th RIR. Certified fit for general service 28.3.1917. Hospitalized with venereal disease at the Military Hospital, Portobello Barracks, Dublin, 18.5.1917. He also required a surgical operation. Memo from OC 5th RIR to HQ, Northern District Irish Command, 29.10.1917: Leslie was still in hospital with VD. Noted as an efficient officer before hospitalization and was expected to remain so when discharged. Recommended retention in the services. MB 3.12.1917: hernia healed, syphilis treatment ongoing, gonorrhoea cured, fit for general service. Joined 2nd RIR 16.2.1918. GCM at Proven, 21.6.1918, on a charge of drunkenness and dismissed from the Army. Telegram from Provost's Office Boulogne to WO, 6 July, notified that 'Ex Lt. K.D. Leslie dismissed' would depart for Folkestone the next day. GHQ, France, advised WO that Leslie was dismissed, 5.7.1918, and officer's pay ceased that day. WO notice to Military Posting Officer 30.8.1918: Leslie was to be posted in accordance with current regulations for the posting of recruits, but not to the corps in which he previously served as an officer. Later served as Pte S/28410 in 2nd Argyll and Sutherland Highlanders. File ref: 339/60809.

Littledale Capt. Cyril Richard Evelyn. Born 15.1.1893, the son of Richard W.W. Littledale LL D, TCD, KC. Educated at Portora Royal School, Enniskillen, and Trinity College, Dublin, where he trained in medicine. Served three years in Dublin University OTC and discharged with the rank of Sgt, 8.8.1914. 'This is an extremely efficient and well trained Cadet NCO.' Height 5 foot 9 inches, chest 31–38 inches, weight 147 pounds, single. Applied for a commission 8.8.1914. Address, Murragh Hill, Killiney, Co. Dublin. Gazetted a 2/Lt. in the 3rd RDF 15.8.1914. Joined 2nd RIR 24.2.1915. Wounded 11.4.1915. Embarked Boulogne–Dover aboard the *St Patrick*, 17 April. Address 9 Fitzwilliam Place, Dublin, which was his parents' home. MB at Caxton Hall: superficial bullet wound to the scalp, otherwise 'in a fairly good state of health'. Injured at Dublin, 25 May, when he was thrown from his motorbike: large abrasion to his left knee and some fluid on the joint. Reported for duty with 3rd RDF 12 June.

Joined 1st RDF at Gallipoli 20.8.1915. Left unit 22.9.1915 with enteric fever and embarked Alexandria–Southampton aboard the *Dover Castle*. MB at King George V Hospital, Dublin, 18.1.1916: still suffering the effects of enteric fever and insomnia. Reported for duty with 3rd RDF at Cork, 19.2.1916. Posted to 9th RIR, 9.5.1916. Left unit, 23.8.1916, having been 'blown-up by trench fire' that day. 'He became shaky and unable to stand fire.' Embarked Calais–Dover aboard the *Dover Castle*, 26 August. Cause of return, neurasthenia. MB at 4th London General Hospital: 'He has slight tremor and much increased reflexes'. Unfit for eight weeks. A confidential report by OC 9th RIR, 6.9.1916: Littledale joined the battalion 19.7.1916 and it was immediately apparent that he had little experience handling men. Did not trust him to command a company so he did two tours of the trenches as second-in-command of a company. His Coy Commander reported that he 'did not know how to perform his duty properly and was of a much too nervous temperament for war, and not a good example to the men.' The OC had watched him during the second tour and was satisfied the report was correct. Noted that Littledale had also served in Dublin during the Easter Rising. Said he was appointed Capt. in September 1915. OC's opinion was that Littledale had not been properly trained, was not efficient, 'and in addition is not suitable for the command of men in the field ... I recommend that his services be dispensed with.' OC 36th Division wrote to IX Corps and recommended Littledale should be dispensed with or employed at home. CiC British Forces in France to WO, 20.9.1916, requested Littledale be removed from the establishment of 9th RIR and not be sent to serve in France again.

MB at Dublin: 31.10.1916, 'He suffers insomnia and deranged digestive system.' Reported for duty with 17th RIR, Ballykinler Camp, Co. Down, 15 December. Posted to ASC Motor Transport Depot at Grove Park 26.2.1917. Promoted Lt. two days later. To MT Depot at

Bulford 28.3.1917. MT attached 193 Section, 303 Siege Battery, RGA, 3 April. BEF 90th Heavy Artillery Group. 884 Coy Siege Park. Appointed a/Capt. 29.7.1917 and promoted Capt. 29.11.1917. Admitted to No. 3 Canadian Stationary Hospital, 9.1.1918, with a fractured metatarsal, right foot. This was caused by slipping in the cab of a lorry which had a floorboard removed due to a defective clutch. His foot was caught between the clutch and chassis of the lorry while trying to abandon the vehicle when it was out of control and about to crash. Invalided to the UK 26.1.1918. Posted to 348 MT Coy at Swindon, 24.5.1918. To Grove Park MT Depot Pool 1.9.1918. To BEF France, 3.10.1918, for MT duties with 79th Bde RGA. Court martialled at Bonn, 18.9.1919, with two other officers (same charge and outcome): Capt. J.B.S. Payne, RGA, and Lt. A.B. Tonnochy, London Regt TF. First charge: 'Committing an offence against the property of an inhabitant of the country in which he was serving in that he at Euskirchen, on the 21st August 1919, broke windows and glass the property of Herr Joisten an inhabitant of Euskirchen, situated on German Territory occupied by the British Army.' Second charge: 'Conduct to the prejudice of good order and military discipline, in that he ... took part in a riotous and unseemly disturbance in the hotel of Herr Joisten.' Found not guilty to charge one, guilty to charge two. Severely reprimanded. MB 9.8.1920: serving with 1154 MT Coy RASC in Belfast. 'General condition good. No signs of scars on scalp. No residual effects from Typhoid.' Demobilized 17.3.1921, rated A1, student, address, Atherstone, Temple Road, Dublin. Chairman of the British Legion, Dún Laoghaire, Co. Dublin, in 1947. Resided at 8 Richmond Grove, Blackrock, Co. Dublin. Died 3.9.1949 and buried at Dean's Grange Cemetery. File ref: 339/11989.

Lowry Capt. Gerald FRGS. Born 9.3.1890 at 58 Wellington Park, Belfast, the son of John and Agnes Lowry *née* Garrett. His father was a manager. Commissioned to 5th RIR 18.7.1911. With C Coy, 2nd RIR. He was shot in the head, through both temples, and blinded 25.10.1914. Repatriated to St Dunstan's Hospital where he remained until Christmas 1914, when he was temporarily the guest of Sir Beach Towse VC, at Goring-on-Thames. Towse had been blinded in the South African War. Promoted Capt. to date from 28.10.1914. He wrote to the WO, 22.1.1915, that in accordance with instructions received some weeks previously, he had that day reported to his nearest military station, Depot, Royal Berkshire Regt, at Reading. From 3.2.1915 his address was c/o Mr Arthur Pearson, 15 Devonshire Street, London. He had made arrangements with Lady Dudley to leave for the Riviera, 'for my health' on 25 February. There are a series of file notes, spring 1915, which say the MB had declared him permanently unfit for home service, but fit for light duty in maybe six months time. Nobody seemed to know what this light duty might be and notes went back and forth querying it. They wanted him taken off full pay as there was no point maintaining it. Placed on the half pay list at the rate of £0.35 per day. He was also awarded a gratuity of £280 for the loss of his sight. Half pay became effective 5.4.1915.

OC 5th RIR to HQ Irish Command 30.9.1915: Lowry had been engaged in a prosperous linen business. Mentioned half-pay rate and gratuity and asked that as he was totally incapacitated his pension should be set at the rate for a Regular Officer and not the reduced rate for SR Officers. Irish Command forwarded to the WO for 'consideration as a special case' and were advised that there was no difference in the rates. Lowry would receive not less than £300 per annum, wounds pension and retired pay, taken together. He would receive an addition to his wounds pension from 26.10.1915. Wound pension was set at £200 per annum. WO note: 'This officer might as well be taken off the half pay list and gazetted to retired pay. The rate is the same.' Placed on retired pay from 16.11.1915. He wrote to the WO, 9.12.1915, headed paper, The National Institute for the Blind, 224–8 Great Portland

Street, London, asking if he was entitled to an additional £150 per annum of which he had heard mention. WO advised that his combined retired pay and wound pension were more beneficial than the new rate. After two years training as a masseur he commenced work at Middlesex Hospital. Through fund-raising activities, he met many famous people including the Prince of Wales, General Pershing, and Charles Lindbergh. Practised as an osteopath in London, having qualified in 1925. Wrote several books including *From Mons to 1933*, *Helping Hands*, *A Place Among Men*, and *The Feet in Relation to Health*. Despite his disability, he continued to engage in physical activity including golf, horse riding, sailing, skiing, boxing, swimming, and gymnastics. File ref: 339/8472.

Loyd Capt. Edward Basil Kirkman. Served as Sgt 2650 in Lord Strathcona's Horse, Imperial Army. Gazetted to 2nd RIR which he joined 25.4.1916. Ordered to report to the India Office, London, 26.3.1917, and struck off the strength of 2nd RIR. To General List 4.5.1917, and Indian Army 20.6.1917. Mentioned in Despatches, *London Gazette*, 27.5.1917. Lt. and Capt. in 11th King Edward's Own Lancers. Awarded GSM with clasps for Iraq and Kurdistan. Closed file.

Lucy Lt.-Col. John Francis OBE. Born 1.1.1895 in Cork, the son of Denis Patrick and Kate Lucy *née* Coleman. His father was an unenthusiastic agent for the foundering family beef-breeding farm. He had two brothers and a sister. Enlisted as Rfn 9896 into the RIR with his brother Denis Patrick, 3.1.1912. Height 5 foot 7 inches, Roman Catholic. Joined 2nd RIR in September 1912. Appointed L/Cpl and promoted Cpl in 1914, A Coy. Denis was killed in action 15.9.1914. Made Orderly Room Sgt at the end of 1914. Sent home sick, late 1915, suffering from neurasthenia. Later served at the Depot and assisted at the defence of Trinity College during the Easter Rising. Promoted 2/Lt. 15.6.1917. Rejoined 2nd RIR 6.8.1917 and posted to B Coy. Wounded at a trench block by a German pineapple grenade during the battle of Cambrai, 7.12.1917: 'Shell wounds; very severe – knee, buttock, thigh, abdomen, back and forearm'. To No. 8 General Hospital, Rouen. Returned to the UK at the end of December. Promoted Lt. 15.12.1918. Later employed by the Ministry of Labour. Seconded to the King's African Rifles 1921–6 as a company commander and also served as Adjutant. Some of this time was spent in Nyasaland. Posted to Bombay as a staff officer 1928–32. Married Dorothea Mary Davis Jennings (died 15.9.1949, aged 49; middle daughter of Professor James George Jennings CIE, MA (Oxon) and Maud Walrond *née* Davis) there and they had three children, Denis Patrick (born 1929), John Francis (1931), and Mary Katherine (1933). Professor Jennings was the founding vice chancellor of Patna University in India.

Rejoined 2nd RUR at Gravesend in 1933. Retired 4.4.1935. Became a journalist in Dublin. His military memoirs were published in 1938. Introduction to *There's a Devil in the Drum*: 'After an unsuccessful venture into the world of business in Dún Laoghaire, he took up journalism and became a well known commentator and interviewer for Radio Éireann.' Rejoined as a Reserve Officer in August 1939 and served with the BEF in France as a staff officer in 1940. Evacuated via St Nazaire. Became a training officer and as a/Lt.-Col., took command of the 70th Young Soldiers' Bn, RUR, in January 1942. Awarded the OBE 1945. He was later a councillor for Cork City. Died 1.3.1962 at his residence, Ronayne's Court, Rochestown, Co. Cork.

Quis Separabit, Summer 1962: 'Active in everything he did, often unorthodox and of independent mind he was nevertheless a most approachable person and always ready to help the younger generation ... Retiring between the wars, he rejoined the Regiment in 1939 and subsequently took command of the 28th Leader Training Battalion at Holywood, Co. Down, an appointment which gave full scope to his abilities. Since his final retirement he had lived in Co. Cork where he played an important and active part in public affairs and particularly in the well being of ex-soldiers in the area. As an officer who continued to take an active interest in the affairs of the Regiment until his death he will be greatly missed and we extend our sympathy to his family and, particularly, to Major D.P. Lucy who follows him in the Regiment.' Denis Lucy was CO, Queen's University Belfast OTC, 1972–4. Seán Lucy was Professor of Modern English and Head of the Department of English, University College, Cork. In his latter years he lived in Chicago where he died in July 2001. Kate Davis *née* Lucy (MA, Trinity College) is a poet and musician residing in Dublin. Details provided by Denis Lucy. Closed file.

Lynch Lt. Gilbert Edwin. Born 1891, the son of Christopher and Eliza Anne Lynch, Somersby, Park Road, West Hartlepool. His father was a schoolmaster. Husband of Mary Clara Lynch of Hart, West Hartlepool, Co. Durham. Roman Catholic. Commissioned from Sgt, Northern Cyclists Bn, to 2/Lt., Northumbrian Division, Army Cyclist Corps, 19.10.1915. Promoted Lt., 30.8.1918, with seniority from 1.7.1917. Transferred to 7th Durham Light Infantry, 10.11.1917, and attached 7th RIR. Joined 2nd RIR 14.11.1917. D Coy commander. *Witherow*: 'An Englishman and a very nice man to work under.' Killed by shellfire 21.3.1918. Pozières Memorial. File missing.

McAlindon Capt. Thomas MC. Born at Lurgan, the son of Hugh and Sarah McAlindon, Derrytrasna, Lurgan, Co Armagh. His brothers were John, Patrick, Edward, Henry, and Denis. Enlisted as Rfn 9096 in the RIR (SR), 5.2.1908, and into the Regular Army 5.8.1908. Age 17 years 6 months, height 5 foot 5¾ inches, chest 32–34 inches, weight 116 pounds, labourer. Posted to 2nd RIR 11.9.1908. Appointed L/Cpl 20.5.1911 and promoted Cpl 10.10.1912. Reprimanded for not complying with an order at Tidworth, 31.12.1912. Unpaid L/Sgt 20.3.1914; a/Sgt Cook 22.4.1914; Sgt Cook 2.5.1914. Extended service to complete twelve years 9.6.1914. CQMS 18.6.1915. To No. 8 Ambulance Train and No. 14 General Hospital at Wimereux, 4.10.1915, GSW left knee. Discharged to Base Details, 6.1.1916, and to No. 3 Infantry Base 19.3.1916. Rejoined 2nd RIR 27.3.1916.

   Granted commission 25.3.1917 and commenced duty four days later. *War Diary* 10.8.1917: 'An enemy M.G. which had just come into action on the left at J.7.g.60.60 was successfully dealt with by B Coy. 2/Lt. T. McAlindon leading a determined rush put the team of the gun to flight.' *Belfast News Letter*, 1.12.1917, reported that he was appointed T/Capt. in August 1917. MC 26.9.1917: 'For conspicuous gallantry and devotion to duty. During an attack he was compelled, owing to casualties, to take over a strange company at a moment's notice. Shortly after the attack had commenced he encountered an enemy machine gun which was firing on and enfilading our waves. With great courage and initiative he dashed at it with his revolver and put the team to flight. This prompt and gallant action undoubtedly saved a number of casualties at a most critical point in the attack.'

   Wounded, 23.11.1917, and embarked Le Havre–Southampton 12.12.1917. MB at Caxton Hall, 21 December: he had sustained various bomb wounds to his buttocks and thighs. They were mainly healed with no bone or nerve damage. MB at Furness Hospital, Harrogate, 24.1.1918: wounds were healed. Recommended three weeks leave, then to report to 3rd RIR at Belfast. MB at Belfast, 25.3.1918: 'His wounds are healed but he has been 3 years and 3 months at the front and his nerves are not strong. He cannot concentrate his attention properly.' Certified fit for general service 24.7.1918. Admitted to Fargo Military Hospital, 2.9.1918, having been ill with enteritis for eight to ten days. 7.9.1918: 'Somewhat improved … very depressed and will not pull himself together.' 12.9.1918: 'His condition is worse'. 15.9.1918: 'During last 12 hours he has got rapidly worse. His toxic symptoms are quite intense, and he is dying.' Died at 9.15 a.m., 17.9.1918. Age 26. A list of effects included Exchequer Bonds totalling £243. Next of kin was his widowed mother who later resided at Derryloiste, Esky, Lurgan. His medical case sheets were sent to the Medical Research Committee, British Museum. Derrytrasna Roman Catholic Cemetery. File ref: 339/103552.

McArevey Capt. Joseph Bertrand MC. Born 25.2.1896 at Courteney Hill House, Newry, Co. Down, the youngest son of John Joseph and Teresa McArevey *née* Downey. His father was a cabinet maker. Educated at Clongowes Wood College, Co. Kildare, which he left in 1913. Studied medicine at University College Dublin and passed his first examinations, summer 1914. Applied for a commission 18.3.1915. Single, height 5 foot 10 inches, chest 32–35½ inches, weight 148 pounds, Roman Catholic. Member of the Royal College of Surgeons OTC. Gazetted a 2/Lt. in 3rd RIR, 20.3.1915. Qualified as a first class instructor of the Vickers gun. Embarked Southampton–Le Havre aboard SS *Huntscraft*, 10.3.1916, and attached to 74th Coy, MGC. Ordered to return to the UK and report to the WO in writing upon arrival. 'Considered unfit for service as MG Officer.' A later file cover entry: 'We also have a note that he was returned from the MG Corps and placed on our blacklist – presumably for inefficiency.' Proceeded to the UK 2.7.1916.

Joined 2nd RIR 29.10.1916. Appointed a/Capt., A Coy, 15.1.1917. MC 26.9.1917: 'While the battalion was holding the line, previous to the attack on Westhoek Ridge, this officer was indefatigable in work of consolidation in keeping the men fit, cheery and alert, especially during the time when the enemy was shelling the line. He organized his Company for the attack on Westhoek in an excellent manner, and though time was limited, every man knew his job. He showed great judgement in selecting the men for the difficult operation of storming the dug-outs at Westhoek, capture of which was essential for the success of the advance. He led his Company in the attack with great dash and skill, and on reaching the objective, quickly got them in hand and commenced consolidating. He worked under most tiring conditions on August 11th, all his officers and NCOs with the exception of one Lance-Corporal, having become casualties.'

Belfast News Letter, 31.8.1917, reported that his father was a JP, Chairman of Newry Technical Instruction Committee; member of Newry Harbour Trust, and Carlingford Lough Commissioner. His brother, Lt. John A. McArevey, a solicitor, was in the ASC. Applied for a Regular commission, November 1917. Recommended by Col. Goodman: 'Has commanded a company for over a year and has distinguished himself on all occasions. He was awarded the MC for his conspicuous gallantry at Westhoek Ridge. He is an extremely good Coy commander and his Coy has always been very efficient.'

Wounded, 23.11.1917, and embarked Calais–Dover 28.11.1917. *Belfast News Letter*, 28.11.1917, reported that he had suffered severe GSW to his head and left arm. Permanent commission antedated to 30.12.1915. Reported to 3rd RIR 16.2.1918. He applied to OC 3rd RIR, 24.3.1918, to be allowed to resume his medical studies at the Medical School, Cecilia Street, Dublin. Requested a wound gratuity, saying he was suffering headaches due to a head wound and had to wear glasses as his sight was permanently affected. Resigned his commission, 11.5.1918, with the honorary rank of Capt. Address 72 Lower Leeson Street, Dublin. He was not entitled to a gratuity. Mr J. Devlin MP, United Irish League, wrote to the WO, 12.8.1918, on behalf of McArevey, then residing at 100 Baggot Street, Dublin, appealing against the refusal of a gratuity. The WO pointed out that regular commissions carried pensions, and temporary commissions carried gratuities. By the end of October he was residing at 54 Adelaide

Road, and at 113 Upper Leeson Street during 1919. Requested a MB, 2.6.1919, as he thought he needed an operation for shrapnel still in his left arm. A gratuity was eventually granted under AO 85 of 1919, 23.9.1919, but not for his SR service. File ref: 339/45908.

McCallum Major John Dunwoodie Martin CBE, DSO. Born 2.9.1883, the eldest son of John McCallum, later Financial Secretary, National Education Board, Ireland, and a daughter of Revd J.D. Martin, Tullyallen, Co. Armagh. Educated at the Belfast Royal Academical Institution, where he was head boy in 1902, and Queen's University, Belfast. Graduated 1906 and practised as a solicitor at Belfast. Commissioned in the Territorial Force (Unattached List), for service with Belfast University OTC, 1.1.1909, and promoted Lt. 1.7.1909. Attached 1st Cheshire Regt 1–31.3.1910. Promoted Capt. 19.1.1912. Played badminton for Ireland 1913–14 and 1920–7. Applied for a temporary commission 20.10.1914. Height 5 foot 6¾ inches, chest 33½–37 inches, weight 138 pounds. Married Eveleen Lindsay, 1915, daughter of Lindsay Hill Lloyd, Belfast.

The Distinguished Service Order: 'Adjutant of 8th RIR, 1914. Proceeded to France 3.10.1915. He was present at the Battle of Thiepval, 1.7.1916, the Battle of Messines, 7.7.1917, and commanded his battalion at the Third Battle of Ypres 16.8.1917, the Battle of Cambrai 21.11.1917, and the Retreat at St Quentin, March 1918, and as Acting Lt.-Col., August 1917, commanding the 8th Bn The Royal Irish Rifles, and from 8.2.1918 to 12.5.1918, commanded the 21st Entrenching Battalion. During the final victorious advance in Sept., Oct., Nov., 1918, he commanded, temporarily, the 2nd Battalion, the Royal Irish Rifles, and the 15th (S) Battalion, the Royal Irish Rifles, until the latter battalion was withdrawn from the fighting with the 36th (Ulster) Division in the beginning of November. He was Mentioned in Despatches and awarded the French Croix de Guerre in December 1918.'

DSO, *London Gazette*, 22.9.1916: 'For conspicuous gallantry in action. As senior officer with the battalion he controlled the operations with great skill and courage. He organized the consolidating of the position, moving about utterly regardless of personal danger and encouraging his men.'

Promoted Major 6.8.1917. *Witherow*, March 1918: 'A more fearless officer I have never seen. When our men turned and lay down to fire on the enemy, the Major stood up directing the fire and this amid a whirl of bullets.' Took temporary command of 2nd RIR, 1.10.1918. Applied for a commission in the Regular Army, 27.3.1919. At this time he was serving with 15th RIR. Discharged, rated A, 14.12.1919, having last served with the Army of the Rhine. The WO wrote, 13.12.1921, offering him a Regular commission as a Capt. He replied that he could not accept the offer as he had been appointed a Resident Magistrate in Ireland and was currently commanding the Royal Irish (Special) Constabulary Camp at Newtownards, but asked to be placed on the Reserve of Officers list. CBE 1921. He lived at Warrenpoint and later moved to 41 Ormiston Crescent, Belfast. Died in hospital 14.1.1967.

Quis Separabit, Spring 1967: 'At the time of his retirement in 1954 he was the last serving Resident Magistrate appointed under the pre-1921 regime ... He was prominent in rugby football, hockey, lawn tennis and cricket while at university and joined the North of Ireland Club in 1903, playing cricket regularly until 1927. Major McCallum was admitted a solicitor in 1909 and was in private practice with his uncle until 1914. He took over the adjutancy of Queen's University Training Corps on the outbreak of war in August 1914. In the same year he became Adjutant of the 8th (Service) Bn The Royal Irish Rifles. In 1915 he went to France and remained with the 36th Division until the end of the war when he went as second in command to the 12th (Service) Bn The Royal Irish Fusiliers. At the opening of the Battle of the Somme on 1 July 1916 he displayed conspicuous gallantry and was awarded the DSO and

Mentioned in Despatches. Later in the war he held the rank of Acting Lt.-Colonel and in 1918 was decorated with the French Croix de Guerre. In 1920 he became a Resident Magistrate in Co. Clare – one of the most disturbed areas in Ireland – and returned to the North of Ireland in the same year as Commandant of the Royal Irish Constabulary Camp at Newtownards. For his services in this capacity he was awarded the OBE, which he received from King George V after the State Opening of the Northern Parliament in 1921, and was later awarded the CBE. He resumed duty as a Resident Magistrate in 1922. Major McCallum is survived by his wife.' They had no children. RM at Newry 1922–43 and Belfast 1943–53.

An appreciation by R.F.A.C.: 'If he thought that injustice had been done, he said so in plain words and he did not mind to whom he said them. Many stories are told of him in the way he fought with senior officers for the welfare of his men in the 1914–18 war. His physical courage was also of the highest order. He won a magnificent DSO on the Somme in 1916 and his OBE was gained when he was a Resident Magistrate for standing up in his car when he was ambushed and blazing away at his opponents.' *Who Was Who*: 'President International Badminton Federation 1961, President Badminton Union of Ireland.' File ref: 339/13911.

McCammond Lt. Cecil Robert Walter. Born 13.2.1899 at Ballygloughan, the son of Walter Edwin Carson McCammond and Emily Maud *née* Porter. At that time his father was a Capt. in 4th RIR. Educated at Rockport School, Co. Down, and St Bees School, Cumberland. Applied for a commission 30.4.15. Address was his parents' home at Innisfayle, Donegall Park, Belfast. He had served in St Bees School OTC until 31.3.1915. Presbyterian, height 5 foot 3 inches, chest 32–34½ inches, weight 124 pounds, age 16. Enlisted as Pte 17/1185 in 17th RIR 21.6.1915. Another application for a commission was made 22.10.1915. At this time he was a L/Cpl in 17th RIR, gave his age as 18 and address as Sissonfield House, Rathmines Road, Dublin. Commissioned to 19th RIR 3.1.1916 when he was still aged 16. He was in Dublin during the 1916 Rebellion. *Falls*: 'The alarm was brought by 2nd-Lieutenant C.R.W. McCammond, of the 19th Battalion, who was on leave from his own battalion on a visit to his father, Lt.-Col. W.E.C. McCammond [CO 3rd RIR] ... Lieutenant McCammond had been in Dublin, and about noon, when returning on horseback to barracks, was set upon by rebels at Portobello Bridge. These had established themselves in Davy's public house, which overlooked the bridge and commanded the Rathmines Road and Richmond Street. A number came out of the house to attack him, while others fired at him from the windows. Fortunately they were incredibly bad marksmen. Lieutenant McCammond got clear, only slightly wounded and rode on to barracks to give the alarm.'

Later joined the BEF. *Irish Times*, 16.9.1916: ' ... invalided home through shell shock.' Joined 3rd RIR 26.10.1916. Promoted Lt. 6.7.1917. Joined 2nd RIR 28.7.1917. *Irish Times*, 19.12.1917: ' ... has been admitted to hospital overseas. His condition is favourable and he is in no danger. He was blown up by a shell last week.' Rejoined 8.1.1918. Wounded 21.3.1918. *Belfast News Letter*, 25.3.1918, reported that he was admitted to hospital at Rouen, 23 March, suffering from a gunshot wound to the right ear and severe gas poisoning. Admitted to 2nd General Hospital, Bristol, 26.3.1918. The wound was a superficial abrasion but it was thought at the time that a shrapnel fragment might have penetrated his skull so he was sent to the UK. Found to be 'perfectly well' and granted leave until 22.4.1918. Rejoined 2nd RIR 17.6.1918. Wounded in action, 10.7.1918, with shrapnel wounds to his back and chest. *Irish Times*, 18.7.1918: ' ... is a son of Brigadier-General W.E.C. McCammond.' Embarked Boulogne–Dover 18.7.1918. MB at the Welsh Hospital, Netley, 26.7.1918: wounds severe, not permanent. Address, Innisfayle. Posted to No. 10 Camp, Durrington, 12.11.1918. Discharged 17.4.1919. Student, rated C1, single. WO letter to

McCammond at 16 Wandsworth Gardens, Belmont, Belfast, 6.10.1923: 'With reference to your letter of the 17th September last regarding your Army Medical records, I am directed to inform you there is nothing in the records of this Department to indicate that you suffered from a discreditable disease during your Army service.' There is no context to this and McCammond's letter is not on file. Applied to join the Officers Emergency Reserve 8.11.1939 and was accepted. File ref: 339/51001.

McConnell Lt. Harold Jeffrey. Born 25.7.1893, the son of William and Mary McConnell of Spokane, Washington, USA, and Lisnastrain, Lisburn. Nephew of Thomas McConnell, Ballinderry, and cousin of John T. McConnell, solicitor, Lisburn. Educated at Campbell College, and Pyper's Academy, Belfast. Enlisted in the R. Fusiliers, 3.9.1914, and applied for a commission, 28.4.1915, at which time he was Pte. 1804 in C Coy, 18th R. Fusiliers (Public Schools Bn) stationed at Epsom. Single, address Kensington House, Knock, Co. Down, employed by Cox & Co., Bankers, Charing Cross, London. Gazetted a 2/Lt. with 5th RIR, 15.6.1915, and arrived at the front, 6.6.1916, joining 1st RIR. Wounded 1.7.1916. *Belfast Telegraph*, July 1916, reported that he was the son of the late William McConnell of Lisburn, and the nephew of Mrs Robson of The Mount, Hill Hall, Lisburn. Served with 7th RIR until it was absorbed by 2nd RIR, 14.11.1917. Joined the RFC at Reading 31.12.1917. After a one month course he went to the School of Navigation and Gunnery and commenced with No. 98 Squadron (D.H.9 day bombers), 6.4.1918. Killed in action, 31.5.1918, and buried in Larch Wood (Railway Cutting) Cemetery, Ieper. Plot I.B.15. Next of kin was his sister, Miss J.S. McConnell, 12 Elmers Drive, Teddington, Middlesex.

McConnell Lt. William Clark. Born 26.2.1885 at Derryvolgie Avenue, Belfast, the youngest son of Robert John and Mary Elizabeth McConnell *née* Smylie. His father was an auctioneer. Educated at Stubbington House, Fareham, Hants; Nieuwied, Germany; City and Guilds of London, Finsbury Technical College. *Irish Times*, 17.7.1916: ' ... completed his term as an articled pupil at the Queen's Engineering Works, Bedford, afterwards taking a course of electrical engineering at the City and Guilds of London Institute. At the outbreak of war he was a partner in the firm of McConnell and Bailey, mechanical and electrical engineers, London E.' Applied for a commission 17.9.1914: single, height 5 foot 5¾ inches, chest 33–36¼ inches, weight 129 pounds. Appointed a 2/Lt. in 3rd RIR 14.10.1914. Promoted Lt. 31.7.1915. Joined 2nd RIR 7.10.1915. Killed in action 9.7.1916. *Irish Life*, 28.7.1916: 'son of Sir Robert McConnell, Bt., DL, Glen Dhu, Strandtown, Belfast. He was ... attached to a battalion of the regiment as machine-gun officer in September, 1915.' Letters of Administration granted the estate of £191 to Lisa McGown McConnell. The family solicitor was Alfred E. McConnell, 35 Royal Avenue, Belfast. Thiepval Memorial. File ref: 339/4142.

McCoy Lt. William. Served as Sgt 1603 in the Army Cyclist Corps at Gallipoli, 7.8.1915 to 30.9.1915; at Greek Macedonia, Serbia, Bulgaria, European Turkey and the islands of the Aegean Sea, 5.10.1915 to 30.6.1916. Commissioned from the ranks, 2.6.1916, and promoted Lt. 2.12.1917. Joined 2nd RIR 10.8.1918. Still on Army Lists 1921.

McDonnell, 2/Lt Martin Joseph. Born at Dunmore, Galway, 2.7.1892. Enlisted as Pte 7937 in the Irish Guards 28.4.1915. Tea planter, Roman Catholic, height 5 foot 10 inches, chest 35–37 inches, weight 139 pounds. Next of kin was his mother, Ina McDonnell, 29 Ailesbury Road, Dublin. He had served as a 2/Lt. in 4th CR, June 1911 to April 1912, 'resigned'. Posted to 2nd Irish Guards 28.4.1915. Promoted Cpl 14.9.1915. Embarked for the BEF

5.10.1915. Admitted to No. 97 FA and No. 23 CCS, 14.10.1915, with Impetigo. Admitted to No. 4 Stationary Hospital at St Omer, 22 October, suffering from debility. Rejoined 2nd Irish Guards 4.11.1915. L/Sgt 8.3.1916, and Sgt 17.5.1916.

Applied for a commission 22.7.1916. Address, Newpark House, Kilmeague, Co Kildare. Correspondence address, No. 16 Platoon, No. 4 Coy, 2nd Irish Guards, BEF. Granted a Regular commission and posted to 2nd RIR, 24.8.1916. Joined 3.9.1916. Wounded, 22.1.1917, and admitted to No. 2 CCS. A WO telegram advised his mother that he was dangerously ill: GSW both legs. Died 24.1.1917. Fr Gill wrote to the Fr Provincial at Dublin, 27 January, ref: CHP1/25(58): 'You will have heard of the death of Lt. McDonnell, who seems to have known you very well. It was very sad about him. A shell hit his dug out and smashed both his legs. I managed to get to him in time and to anoint him, he was perfectly conscious then, and the doctors hoped there was some hope. At the Clearing Station it was found that the only hope of saving his life was to take off both legs. He was however too weak to withstand the double operation, and sank gradually, and died on Wednesday last. He and his men were at Mass, and he received Holy Communion with them, the day before they went to the trenches. So thank God there is nothing to be troubled about. His mother will feel it very much. He was a splendid fellow and everybody liked him.'

At this time his mother was named as Mrs Ina M. Gaskel, Newpark, Kilmeague. His siblings were Francis James (23), Farrell Dermot (13), and Kathleen May (10), all living with their mother. Died intestate. *Irish Times*, 31.1.1917: 'He was a son of the late Mr Farrell McDonnell, Dunmore, Co. Galway, and Kilmeague, Co. Kildare, and a nephew of Mr James McDonnell, Chairman of Galway County Council, and Mr J.P. McDonnell, Clerk of the Tuam Union.' Bailleul Communal Cemetery Extension, Nord, III.A.194. File ref: 339/72252.

McFerran 2/Lt Maurice Anderdon MC. Born 10.10.1897 at 85 St George's Square, London, the elder son of John Cecil Grant and Helen Mary McFerran *née* Salt. His father was a linen manufacturer at The Drift, Antrim Road, Belfast. Grandson of John McFerran, The Barn, Carrickfergus, and Sir Thomas Salt, Bt., Weeping Cross, Staffordshire. BLGI. *Belfast News Letter*, 10.4.1918, added that he was a nephew of Lt.-Col. E.M.G. McFerran, OC Royal North Downs, and of James L. McFerran, Oakfield, Carrickfergus. Educated at Stancliffe Hall, Matlock, and Shrewsbury where he was a Pte in the OTC (left December 1915). To No. 7 Officer Cadet Bn, 29.5.1916, and gazetted a 2/Lt., 4th RIR, 26.9.1916. Address was his parents' house at Rickerscote House, Stafford. Correspondence address 1 Oriel Road, Fulwood, Sheffield.

Joined 2nd RIR 17.2.1917. Presented with his MC ribbon 27.1.1918. *London Gazette*, 5.7.1918: 'For conspicuous gallantry and devotion to duty. During three days' fighting he maintained touch between the leading companies and battalion headquarters. He went four times to the front line through a heavy barrage and brought back valuable information.' Killed in action at 10 a.m., 21.3.1918, near Grugies while 'trying to ascertain the situation'. Next of kin was his father, Major McFerran, C Coy, 6th Reserve Bn, RE, Irvine, Ayrshire, who administered a gross estate of £259. Remembered at St Thomas' Church, Walton. Pozières Memorial. File ref: 339/61848.

McGhie Lt. John Warnock. Born 16.9.1894. Applied for a commission 13.12.1915. Single, home address Ballyalton House, Downpatrick; correspondence address 24 Botanic Avenue, Belfast; employed in the linen business. Gazetted a 2/Lt. in 20th RIR, 6.1.1916. Served with 14th RIR. Promoted Lt. 6.7.1917. Appointed a/Capt., while OC C Coy, 31.8.1917. Joined 2nd RIR during October 1918. Released 1.2.1919. File ref: 339/50997.

McIntosh 2/Lt James Marshall. Born 1886 at Wrexham, Denbigh. Enlisted as Pte 8441 in the RWF 2.8.1904. Height 5 foot 5⅝ inches, chest 32½–35½ inches, weight 111 pounds, groom. Aged 18 years 1 month. The next of kin were his mother Annie, and younger siblings Martha and David, 3 Elephant Place, Market Street, Wrexham. Duplicate attestation papers in his file are in pieces in an envelope. A certificate noted that they were destroyed by white ants in the HQ of Rangoon Bde Office, February 1913. Posted to 1st RWF 19.11.1904. Charged with an offence at Aldershot, 26.11.1905: 'breaking into No. 2 Cookhouse' and 'Being found ... with a prostitute in Cookhouse at about 1.30 a.m.' Sentenced to eight days detention. Served in the UK until he was posted to 2nd RWF for service in India and Burma, 13.1.1906. Appointed an unpaid L/Cpl, 8.8.1906, and a paid L/Cpl 10.5.1907. Transferred as Rfn 9511 to 1st RIR, 1.10.1910, and appointed Pioneer Sgt. Awaiting trial by District Court Martial, 8.11.1910 to 4.12.1910, for conduct to the prejudice of good order and military discipline. No details are given. Sentenced to be reduced to the rank of Cpl 5.12.1910. At Maymyo, 24.7.1911, he applied for permission to discharge to his residence in India on the Reserve. He had obtained employment with the Burma Oil Company. Transferred to the Army Reserve in India upon payment of £10 for conversion of service, 23.9.1911. Married Margaret Gavagan at the Roman Catholic Church, Maymyo, 21.7.1912. His employment is shown on the marriage certificate as Superintendent, Fire Brigade. Witnesses were J.M. Jarre and Jane Gavagan.

Mobilized as a Cpl at the RIR Depot, Belfast, 25.1.1915, appointed an unpaid L/Sgt and posted to 3rd RIR. 'Not mobilized in India. Came to England on leave July 1914.' He had been in Burma prior to his return to the UK. There was no record of his ever having been granted leave to return to the UK. The WO queried this with Rangoon, as there had obviously been a delay in his mobilization. Rangoon replied that they could not answer the question and referred to his papers having been destroyed by ants, but whether there was paperwork granting or requesting leave to travel to UK was not known and it seemed unlikely that there ever was. It appears that he arrived in the UK during July 1914 but did not report his arrival until 25.1.1915. Posted to 2nd RIR, 20.4.1915, and promoted 2/Lt. 27.5.1915. Killed in action 16.6.1915. A letter from a/Adjutant Wakefield, 2nd RIR, to Frank Handley, executor of the will, 53 Smithdown Road, Liverpool, stated that McIntosh was killed at Hooge while leading his men in a charge. McIntosh had told Wakefield that he wished his kit to go to the Liverpool address. Dublin Records Office advised that the next of kin was his mother. There was some confusion between the WO and the India Office. Following a casualty list in the *Times* his wife had sought details via the office of the Lieutenant Governor in Burma, but the message came back to London as '2/Lt. J.M. McIntosh Royal Irish Regiment', to which the WO replied that they had no information. A WO letter to Miss Larder, 26 Broadbank, Louth, Lincolnshire, 30.7.1915, referred to her letter and advised that McIntosh was killed. Rangoon cabled the WO, 5 August, and queried J.M. McIntosh, RIR, and asked for information for his wife. The WO confirmed McIntosh was killed in action, and that the next of kin had already been notified. They reminded Rangoon that the query they had initially sent was for McIntosh of the R. Irish. His mother made an enquiry about the disposal of the will and effects. His widow wrote saying that she was in urgent need of funds and asked that the pension due to her be granted at the highest rate possible. The WO replied to his mother saying that all effects had gone to Handley and as far as they were aware there was no will. His widow was awarded a gratuity of £100 and an annual pension of £100. The estate was due £169.24 from Army funds. By March 1916 her address was c/o Major T. Fitzpatrick, Kirk House, Hedon, Yorkshire. In September 1916 she was staying at 26 Mornington Road, Ranelagh, Dublin. On 7.2.1920 she sought payment of £41 outstanding monies due. Address, c/o Miss Gavagan, White Cottage, Circular Road, Maymyo, Burma. She was living there with friends as her income was insufficient for her to live in England. She later resided at 1 Hurlingham Gardens, Fulham, London. Menin Gate Memorial. File ref: 339/3216.

McKay Capt. Herbert Donald. Commissioned to 4th CR 2.2.1914. Promoted Lt. 2.12.1914. Served in France, March to June 1915 and November 1915 to May 1916. Joined 2nd RIR 23.3.1916. Joined 5th CR and served in Greek Macedonia, Serbia, Bulgaria, European Turkey, and the islands of the Aegean Sea, October 1916 to September 1917. Promoted Capt. 19.1.1917. Left Salonika for Alexandria 10.9.1917. Served in Egypt, September 1917 to 31.10.1918. He was wounded during the war. Transferred to the KOSB 2.8.1922. Closed file.

McKee Lt. Patrick Joseph. Born Shankill, Antrim, 1.11.1888, the son of James and Ellen McKee *née* Morell. Baptized at St Mary's Catholic Church, Belfast. Educated at St Mary's Intermediate School, Belfast; Belfast Mercantile College, and King's College, London. Applied for a commission 17.3.1916. Address 49 Trevor Street, Holywood, Co. Down. Currently serving with Belfast University OTC. Enlisted as Rfn 9693 in 3rd RIR (10th Officers Cadet Bn at Gailes) 1.8.1916. Height 5 foot 7⅛ inches, chest 34½–37 inches, weight 137 pounds, Customs Warehouse Keeper, single. Gazetted a 2/Lt. in 3rd RIR 21.11.1916. Joined 2nd RIR 29.1.1917. Killed in action 10.8.1917. WO telegram advised his grandmother, Eleanor McKee, at Trevor Street. She was claimed to be the executrix, but it seems that no will existed. Solicitor's letter to WO outlined articles missing from the list of effects, with estimated values. These included a revolver £4, bayonet £3, and a silver cigarette case £3.25. Another solicitor's letter mentioned the missing equipment and said that a balance was due on the outfitter's bill for McKee's kit: the total was £45.48, deposit paid £15. As the Army balance due was only £2.43 there would be a debt outstanding against the estate. They asked for sympathetic consideration and the WO requested evidence of a verbal will. WO advised solicitors that McKee had received the full £50 uniform allowance so the WO would not cover any debts. Letters of administration showed a gross estate of £56 and the grantee was an uncle Frank McKee, 13 Howard Street, Govan, Lanark. Menin Gate Memorial. File ref: 339/67078.

McKeeman, Lt Francis Kennedy. Served as Pte 1230 in the South Irish Horse and later as 73107 in the Corps of Hussars. Gazetted a 2/Lt. in 3rd RIR 1.5.1918. Joined 2nd RIR 24.7.1918. Wounded in action during October 1918. Closed file.

McKeown Capt. William Wilson. Born 15.9.1885 at Mount Street, Ballymena, the son of Wilson and Susan McKeown *née* Cooney. His father was a solicitor. Educated at Ballymena Academy, Trinity College, Dublin, and King's Inns, Dublin. Applied for a commission 18.9.1914. Married, Barrister at Law. He had practised for 4½ years at Donegall Square Buildings, Belfast. Permanent address, c/o Alexander Govan Reid JP, Rathmore, Adelaide Road, Kingstown, Co. Dublin; correspondence address, 75 Highfield Road, Rock Ferry, Cheshire. Mr Reid was general manager of the Dublin and South Eastern Railway, Westland Row, Dublin. Gazetted to 4th RMF and served at home until he joined 2nd RIR 20.1.1917. Later attached to 2nd RMF. Left that unit, 4.10.1918, having been wounded during an attack on Le Catelet. His right hand was blown off by a shell, and the forearm was later amputated to leave a five-inch stump. Embarked Le Havre–Southampton 23.10.1918. Address Rathmore. Awarded a wound gratuity of £250. He moved to 26 Crosthwaite Park East, Kingstown, Co. Dublin, in April 1919. MB at the Prince of Wales Hospital, Cardiff, 3.10.1919: he had been fitted with a Carne's arm, 'Artificial limb causes no inconvenience'. Ordered to report to 1st RMF at Crownhill Barracks, Plymouth. Awarded a wound pension of £100 per annum from 4.10.1919. MB at Plymouth 13.12.1919: wound soundly healed, some debility due to wound and operation. Discharged, rated C, 24.12.1919. File ref: 339/27319.

MacLaughlin 2/Lt. James Leslie. Born 14.10.1896, the son of James MacLaughlin, Victoria Road, Londonderry. Enlisted as Rfn 17/431 in 17th RIR at Belfast, 29.4.1915. Height 5 foot 8 inches, chest 30½–34½ inches, weight 136 pounds, Presbyterian, clerk. Discharged to a commission in 17th RIR 4.10.1915. Joined 2nd RIR 16.2.1916. Wounded 7.7.1916: shrapnel wounds face, chest, right arm and hand. Embarked Le Havre–Southampton on HS *Salta*, 11 July, and admitted 2nd Western General Hospital, Manchester. MB 2.8.1916: the wounds were all superficial except for damage to the right middle finger and thumb. On sick leave at Londonderry until he reported to 17th RIR at Belfast, 2.10.1916. Ordered to report to OC Convalescent Hospital, Holywood, for duty and left 17th RIR, 18.10.1916. The hospital had nearly 500 men but only three Duty Officers. Posted to 8th RIR 15.1.1917.

Reported sick 10.4.1917 suffering from Dysentery. Embarked Boulogne–Dover aboard HS *Jan Breydel*, 23 April. Admitted 3rd London General Hospital, Wandsworth. MB at the Dysentery Convalescence Hospital, Barton-on-Sea, 15 June: no symptoms and improving; still had impairment of his wounded hand. Promoted to Lt., RIF, 1.7.1917. Embarked Southampton–Salonika 19.8.1917. Posted to 2nd RIF 14.9.1917. Embarked Salonika–Alexandria 17.9.1917. Admitted to hospital with tonsillitis 16.11.1917. Admitted Military Infectious Hospital, Shroubra, 26.11.1917 with Diphtheria. To Base Depot Kantara, from hospital, 6.1.1918. Rejoined 2nd RIF 14.1.1918. To demobilization camp 19.6.1919. Embarked Alexandria 29.6.1919. Discharged 14.7.1919, rated A, single. Address Ardken, Victoria Park, Londonderry. File ref: 339/45656.

McLaughlin Major William. Son of William Henry McLaughlin DL, and Emily Sophia *née* Dobbin, Macedon, Whitehouse, Co. Antrim. His father was principal of the firm of McLaughlin & Harvey of Belfast and Dublin. A brother, Trooper George McLaughlin, was killed in action at Lindley, 30.7.1900, during the Boer War. His eldest brother, Henry McLaughlin of Blackrock, acted on Lord Wimbourne's Irish Recruiting Committee. Another brother, Lt. A.M. McLaughlin, was killed in action while serving with 1st RIR, 9.5.1915. 2/Lt., 4th RIR, 21.11.1903; Lt. 19.5.1906, H/Capt. 3rd RIR, 21.1.1908. Joined 2nd RIR 21.11.1914. To Corps HQ at Bailleul 10.1.1915. To hospital, sick, 30.1.1915. Promoted to Major 2.10.1915. Remained with 3rd RIR and was still on the Army Lists in 1923. Closed file.

McMahon 2/Lt. Patrick. Born 8.11.1886, the son of Patrick McMahon, 3 Edward Street, Armagh. Educated at Skerry's College and Christian Brothers School, Armagh.; Employed as a cashier in the Belfast Bank at Buncrana. Enlisted in 6th Black Watch, 19.9.1914, and posted to A Coy. Height 5 foot 7¼ inches, chest 34¾–37¾ inches, weight 140 pounds, grey eyes, red hair. Applied for a commission 23.3.1915. Letter from Michael Cardinal Logue, Ara Coeli, Armagh, 14.3.1915: 'I have known Patrick McMahon from his early boyhood and have always found him a young man of high character and exemplary conduct. He is orderly, obliging, intelligent and earnest in doing any work committed to him. I believe he has strictly observed up to the present the total abstinence pledge which he took at his confirmation'. Discharged to a commission in 4th RIR, 11.6.1915.

Joined 2nd RIR 26.11.1915. Wounded, 9.7.1916 while Second-in-Command of A Coy. To Red Cross Hospital, Rouen, 28.7.1916. 'Wound on left hand, portion of shell skimmed across fingers making wounds on dorsum of three fingers. Suffered from shock as shown by nervousness and sleeplessness. These are considerably improved. Wounds of the fingers are healed with no resulting disability.' Transferred from Le Havre to Southampton 6.8.1916. Rejoined 13.3.1917. Wounded 10.6.1917, receiving gun-shot wounds in left side and arm, and died the following day at No. 2 CCS. *Irish Times*, 15.6.1917: 'He was a clerk in the Provincial Bank, Newry.' Unmarried. Effects sent to his father included a cigarette case, a religious medallion, and a rosary. Bailleul Communal Cemetery Extension, Nord, III.C.44. File ref: 339/48346.

Magenis 2/Lt. Richard Henry Cole. Born 20.4.1887 at Drumdoe, Crossna, Boyle, Co. Roscommon, the son of Edward Cole Magenis. Succeeded to the estates of his father in 1908. There was a family residence at Finvoy, Ballymoney, Co. Antrim, where he stayed during the hunting season. Educated at Radley College, Abington, Oxford, 1902–6. Gazetted a 2/Lt. in 3rd RIR, February 1908. *Bond of Sacrifice*: 'Mr Magenis was a cricket and football player, while hunting, shooting, tennis and fishing were amongst his recreations.' He was unmarried and had two sisters who resided at Boyle. The Magenises were landlords and owned the Craigs, Dirraw, the Knockans, and the Mullans. Left for France 26.8.1914, and joined 2nd RIR 7.9.1914. Killed in action 15.9.1914.

Roscommon Herald, 29.9.1914: 'Mr Magenis was prominently connected with social life in Boyle and was prominent in sporting circles, his horse *The Pagan* and others being successful at many race meetings in the West. He was for many years Master of the Rockingham Harriers. He lived at Drumdoe, Boyle, and was nephew of the late General Magenis [Finvoy Lodge], Ballymoney, and succeeded to the General's estates in Antrim, Down, and Roscommon.' Remembered in the Church of Ireland, Green Street, Boyle. La Ferte-sous-Jouarre Memorial, Seine-et-Marne. File missing.

Mallett Lt. Henry Charles. 9672 Sgt. Mallett, 2nd RIR, promoted 2/Lt. 23.2.1917. D Coy. Wounded in action 7.6.1917. Promoted Lt. 24.8.1918. Closed file.

Malone Capt. William Antony MC. Born 14.7.1884. Joined 4th RIR as a 2/Lt. 7.4.1906, and promoted Lt., 12.8.1909. Resigned 1910. Appointed Lt., 3rd RIR, 18.10.1914, and served with 7th RIR being promoted Capt. 8.11.1915. Embarked Boulogne–Folkestone 26.4.1916. Home address, 3 Pretoria Terrace, Harold's Cross, Rathmines, Co. Dublin. He was not found fit for general service until 1.2.1917. Rejoined 7th RIR 28.6.1917. To hospital 11.11.1917. Joined 2nd RIR 24.2.1918. MC, *London Gazette*, 26.7.1918: 'For conspicuous gallantry and devotion to duty during an enemy attack. He was in command of half a battalion, and showed great skill and coolness while resisting enemy attacks and while withdrawing his men. The clever handling of his men saved many casualties.' Left 2nd RIR with gastritis, 12.6.1918; embarked Boulogne–Dover and admitted to the London Hospital, E1, 20 June. Found fit for general service 21.1.1919.

Transferred to payment by the India Office 20.10.1919. Discharged 10.7.1921, having last served with the RUR, Sappers and Miners, in India. Rated A, married. Applied to join the Regular Reserve of Officers 6.11.1921. A note on his file states: 'We have nothing recorded against this officer beyond that at the end of 1914 he was concerned in a brawl at the lodgings of another officer, in respect of which the Army Council expressed their grave displeasure.' Admitted to the Regular Reserve Class 2 with seniority from 7.3.1916. His address as of 11.10.1923 was 60 Bedford Road, East Finchley, when he requested a year's leave of absence to travel to Kenya.

Applied to be discharged from the Reserve, 26.1.1928, due to total disability resulting from war wounds. Address, 8 Walton Road, Sidcup, Kent. A Ministry of Pensions report stated that he was suffering from 'severe neurasthenia of progressive type due solely to effects of war service ... Can't walk; can't stand; no power of right arm and only partial use of left. Unable to dress himself and requires assistance to attend to the calls of nature; very depressed at times and bursts into tears without cause; very irritable ... Mentality: depressed, emotional and hysterical.' He was retired, having been rated 100 per cent disabled. Died 12.10.1957. His widow, Sarah, resided at 220 Lower Kimmage Road, Dublin, and was not entitled to an Army pension. File ref: 339/60001.

Mansergh Capt. Robert Otway. Born 12.1.1885 at The Shrubbery, 9 St Andrew's, Hillingdon, Middlesex, the son of St George Dyson Mansergh and Alice Emma 'late Peel formerly Horner'. Religion Church of England. Educated at Eastmans Royal Naval Academy, Southsea. Appointed 2/Lt., 4th Militia Bn R. Irish Regt, in January 1904. Commissioned into 3rd RIR, 23.5.1906. Posted to 1st RIR and attached to 2nd RIR at Dublin, 1.7.1906. Embarked for India to join 1st RIR 5.9.1906. Promoted Lt., 7.2.1908. Arrived at Liverpool, 3.3.1911, on one year's leave. Posted to 3rd RIR at Belfast 23.10.1911. Joined 6th RIR at Dublin 21.8.1914. T/Capt., 15.11.1914, and Capt. 5.3.1915.

Served at Gallipoli from 7.7.1915 until 10.8.1915 when he was wounded in the left forearm by a grenade. Rejoined 6th RIR at Mudros, 30.9.1915, and took command, 2 October to 28 November, with the temporary rank of Major. Took the battalion to Macedonia, 5.10.1915, and was temporary Second-in-Command from 28.11.1915 until 1.2.1916, when he assumed command of C Coy. On 1.12.1915 he presided at the FGCM of 227 Pte Patrick Downey, 6th Leinster Regt, at Hasanli, Serbia. Downey was found guilty and later executed. To Malta, sick, 14.8.1916. To 3rd RIR at Belfast 20.11.1916.

Joined 2nd RIR 23.1.1917. To 25th Division HQ 12.4.1917. A MB at Le Havre, 9.5.1918, rated him category A: 'Officer is anxious to return to the line and the board considers him fit at his own request.' MB at Etaples, 9.10.1918, recommended sick leave to England. He wrote to the WO from Old Court, Waterford, 30 October, advising that his leave would expire 2 November and that 'I am fit to return to France'. Rejoined 2nd RIR and resumed command of D Coy 10.11.1918. To England, 14.2.1919, having volunteered for service abroad. Joined 3rd RIR at Rugeley, 16 April, and 2nd RIR at Thetford, 14 May. Embarked with 2nd RIR for Mesopotamia 18.9.1919. Wounded 7.10.1920. Applied to the Adjutant of 2nd RUR, 1.2.1921, for six months leave pending retirement. As of 23 May he would have fifteen years service and was entitled to a pension. His home address was stated as Rock Lodge, Ballyhooly, Co. Cork. The application was forwarded to HQ 55th Infantry Bde. Admitted to hospital at Baghdad, February 1921, where he remained for about two months suffering from jaundice and an enlarged liver. Offence committed 13 April: 'Drunkenness whilst a patient in hospital'; placed under arrest and later severely reprimanded. Left 2nd RUR and embarked Basra–Bombay–London, 12 May, arriving 11 July. Granted leave and went to Rock Lodge. Married during September 1921. About this time his mother's address was given as Old Court. He requested a MB with a view to receiving a disability pension due to an 'enlarged liver' incurred during the Arab revolt in Mesopotamia. A MB at Cork Military Hospital certified him permanently unfit for general service due to deafness and hepatitis. He retired with a pension of £150 per annum 13.12.1921. In 1931 he was still living at Rock Lodge. Died 1949. File ref: 339/6505.

Marriott-Watson 2/Lt Richard Brereton MC. Born 6.10.1895, the son of Henry Brereton Marriott-Watson (1863–1921). His father, born in Australia but spent his adult life in England, was a very famous writer of his day, specialising mostly in supernatural and historical fantasies such as *Hurricane Island, Marahuna* and *Chloris of the Island*. He also co-wrote a play, *Richard Savage*, with J.M. Barrie.

Enlisted as Pte 2346 in 5th The Queen's (Royal West Surrey Regt) 11.8.1914. Single, height 6 foot 1½ inches, chest 33½–35½ inches. Applied for a commission 19.10.1914, and appointed a 2/Lt. 9.12.1914. Posted to 13th RIR 23.9.1915. Took part in their night raid of 26.6.1916. An article he wrote about the raid was published in the *Irish Soldier* propaganda magazine in November 1918. War Diary 13th RIR at Thiepval, 1.7.1916: '10.20 a.m. Somewhere about this time I sent out 2/Lt. R.B. Marriott-Watson, the Intelligence Officer, to see if any information was forthcoming. He knew the ground well as he was Bn Scout Officer. He, however, was wounded and admitted to hospital.' To No. 8 General Hospital, Rouen, 3 July, GSW left shoulder. Embarked Le Havre–Southampton aboard RMS *Lanfrane* two days later. His home address at that time was given as Vackery House, Shere, Guildford, Surrey. MB at No. 2 Southern General Hospital, Bristol, noted that the bullet had passed through muscle, no bone damage. He wrote to the WO, 29 July, asking for a MB and gave his address as c/o Col. Cust, Danby Hall, Northallerton, Yorkshire. MB at Military Hospital, York, 9 August: wound healed but scar imperfect. 'Complains of being jumpy and easily tired.' Fit for general service 14.9.1916. Reported to 3rd RIR at Belfast. An informal letter from Major-General Sir E.O.H. Hamilton KCB, 22 Marloes Road, Kensington, 24.9.1916, to the WO stated that Marriott-Watson wanted a transfer to the Royal West Surrey Regt and asked it this could be fixed. This was not possible as there were already too many candidates.

Joined 2nd RIR 1.11.1916. MC *London Gazette*, 1.1.1917. To FA 10.1.1917 and admitted to No. 14 General Hospital at Wimmereux with severe trench fever, 20.1.1917. Rejoined 2nd RIR 20.12.1917. See main text. Missing in action 24.3.1918. The WO wrote to his father as next of kin, 18.7.1918: they received a Red Cross POW report that Capt. J.C. Bryans advised Marriott-Watson was killed in action. There is a small slip of paper on the file that states: 'Note for reviewers. This man became known as a poet. Preserve the file on review if the contents are worthwhile.' His best known poem is *Kismet*:

Opal fires in the Western Sky / (For that which is written must ever be)
And a bullet comes droning, whining by / To the heart of a sentry close to me.
For some go early and some go late / (a dying scream on the evening air)
And who is there that believes in Fate / As a soul goes out in the sunset flare?

Pozières Memorial. File ref: 339/2172.

Marshall Lt. Herbert. Born at Toronto 21.11.1887, the son of Mrs J. Marshall. His father was Irish, a builder by trade. Obtained a BA in Philosophy and Political Science, University of Toronto. Served in the University of Toronto Contingent, COTC, from 1.10.1914. Enlisted as Pte 82137 in 32nd Reserve Bn Canadian Expeditionary Force at Shorncliffe, Kent, 7.7.1916. Next of kin was his mother at Box 106, New Toronto, Ontario. Applied for a commission, 20.5.1916. Height 5 foot 10½ inches, chest 33–36 inches, weight 130 pounds, single, student, hazel eyes, light hair, Presbyterian. To No. 6 Officer Cadet Bn, Oxford, 5.9.1916. Discharged to a commission in 5th RIR, 18.12.1916. Joined C Coy, 2nd RIR, 13.3.1917. Wounded in action 7.6.1917: a bullet passed through his right loin. Embarked Calais–Dover two days later. Address, c/o Mrs M. Officer, Haslemere, Ash Grove Park, Cliftonville, Belfast. MB at Caxton Hall 28 June: both wounds healing, still unable to turn round. Reported to 5th RIR at Belfast 31.8.1917. Rejoined 2nd RIR, 16.2.1918, and posted to D Coy. *Witherow*: 'But my special chum was a Canadian called Marshall. He was very thoughtful and earnest and a graduate of Toronto University who had originally intended to study for the church.' Promoted Lt. 19.6.1918. Discharged 12.4.1919. Address, 102 Patterson Avenue, Toronto. Mentioned in Despatches 9.7.1919. File ref: 339/63991.

Martin Major Joseph. Born 8.5.1884 at Carmoney, Co. Antrim, the son of Joseph Martin. He had an elder brother William. Enlisted as Rfn 6842 in the RIR, 3.9.1902, and posted to the Depot. Next of kin was his father at 21 Aberdeen Street, Belfast. Height 5 foot 8 inches, chest 33–35 inches, weight 124 pounds. Posted to 2nd RIR 11.2.1903. Appointed L/Cpl, 26.6.1903, and promoted Cpl 12.11.1904. Gained a Master Cook's certificate at Aldershot, 8.4.1907. Sgt Master Cook 25.10.1907. Married Annie McGregor Campbell at Belfast, 9.1.1912. Colour-Sgt 5.12.1912. His daughter Maisie Lillian was born at Tidworth, 22.9.1913. He was a member of the battalion soccer team. Re-engaged 31.3.1914 and appointed CQMS. All service to date appears to have been at home.

To France with 2nd RIR. Commissioned in the field from RSM 1.10.1914. Posted to duty with 2nd South Lancs 17.11.1914. Mentioned in Despatches, 14.1.1915, 'for gallant and distinguished service in the field'. He received an extra regimental promotion to Capt. for further distinguished service. Left unit, 21.5.1915, invalided, ulcer in stomach. Embarked Le Havre–Southampton aboard the *Asturias*, 3 June. Gave his address as Fishmonger's Hall (a hospital), London, and his home address as The Mall, Downpatrick. Ordered to report to 3rd South Lancs at Moor Lane, Crosby, 26.8.1915. Returned to France sometime around January 1917 and was attached to 8th South Lancs. Left unit, 18.3.1917, and embarked Boulogne–Dover aboard the *Princess Elizabeth*, 23 March. Home address, Hopeville, Ashgrove Park, Belfast. Reported to 3rd South Lancs, Cowlarns Camp, Barrow-in-Furness, 31.5.1917. He wrote to the WO applying for a gratuity due to ill health. They replied stating that his abdominal problems had nothing to do with military service and the claim was inadmissible. He reapplied 7.7.1917 while he was serving at No. 1 School of Instruction for Infantry Officers, Brocton Camp, Stafford.

Certified fit for general service 10 September. Embarked for Italy and arrived at Padova, 20.4.1918. Served as an Instructor at GHQ School. Left his unit, 2nd South Lancs attached 89th Labour Group, Italian Expeditionary Force, 22.4.1919. Embarked Le Havre–Southampton, 1 May. Leave granted 14–25 May. Ordered to report forthwith to 3rd South Lancs at Wellington Barracks, Dublin, 27.8.1919. Admitted to King George V Hospital, Dublin, 8.9.1919. Found permanently unfit for service and was ordered to return home. He wrote to the WO, 9.2.1920, and asked to be retired from the Army. This was approved, 2 March, and he was granted the rank of Major. Served during the emergency, 10–14.4.1921, at the Depot of the Prince of Wales Volunteers, after which he was sent home. His address was 104 High Street, Sandgate, Kent. Remarried 2.10.1965. Died 10.10.1968. His widow was Mrs. Kathleen May Martin, 23 Teign View Road, Bishopsteignton, Devon. File ref: 339/13683.

Master Capt. Charles Lionel. Born in Ceylon, 24.3.1881, the son of William Edward Master, Kotmalie, Ceylon, and Jeanette, daughter of Samuel Newson Gissing. Nephew of Harcourt Master, Rotherhurst, Liss, Hants. Grandson of Lt.-Col. Harcourt Master, 1st Dragoon Guards and 4th Queen's Own Light Dragoons. Great-grandson of Lt.-Col. Harcourt Master, 52nd Foot. Educated at Bradfield College. Joined the RIR from the Louth Militia (where he served for six months), as 2/Lt., 5.1.1901. Promoted Lt. 28.3.1905, Adjutant 25.1.1908, and Capt. 28.6.1908. B Coy, 2nd RIR.

de Ruvigny: 'Served in the South African War, taking part in operations in the Orange Free State and Transvaal, August 1901–May 1902 (Queen's Medal with five clasps). On the outbreak of the European War, he went out with his regiment to France, took part in the retreat from Mons, and the subsequent engagements prior to meeting his death in action at La Couture, on 12 October 1914, from a shrapnel shell, when leading his company in the attack. He was buried at Vielle Chapelle; unmarried. He was mentioned for distinguished conduct in the field in Field-Marshal Sir John French's despatch of 8 October 1914 ... It was owing in a large measure to his tuition and untiring efforts that the Royal Irish Rifles turned out a [soccer] team which was a tower of strength for several years in regimental contests, and had the proud distinction of winning the Army Cup.' Mentioned in Despatches 9.12.1914. Brown's Road Military Cemetery, Festubert, IV.B.22. File missing.

Mathews-Donaldson Major Charles Lionel Grey MBE. Born 26.6.1890 at Clifton, Bristol, the son of Col. Charles George and Edith Blanche Mathews-Donaldson, 'Irish family'. Educated by Mr Bacon, Winton House, Aldershot (September 1901–March 1904), Wellington College (May 1904–June 1907), and by Mr Welch, Heath End, Farnham (February 1908–February 1909). Applied for admission to the Royal Military Academy 9.9.1909. At that time he was serving under his father in the Royal Anglesey RE. Their home address was 2 Cromwell Place, South Kensington. Gazetted a 2/Lt. in the RIR 25.3.1911.

Served with 2nd RIR and was wounded 27.8.1914. Embarked Rouen–Southampton aboard the *St Patrick* two days later. According to his file he was retiring from Nouvelles and was in Caudry village when a shell burst and killed four others with him; he remembered nothing more until he found himself in an Ambulance Wagon. MB at Woolwich 31 August: concussion from a shell-burst and was suffering headaches, buzzing in the ears, and could not stand bright light. 'He is very silent and not inclined to talk'. The paper is marked 'not wounded'. His father, 'Colonel Commanding Royal Anglesey RE (SR)', wrote to the WO, 3.10.1914, stating that his son was still confined to bed and enclosed a medical certificate. Promoted Lt., 13.10.1914. Charles wrote from Cromwell Place, 24 October, advising that he would not be able to attend a MB. His leave was extended to 30.3.1915. He again wrote, 15.3.1915, and asked if the MB could attend him at his home 'as I hope to be able to get away for a change on the 30th March'. The WO extended his leave of absence up to 26.8.1915 when a MB certified him unfit for general service for one year and home service for six months, but fit for duties as an ADC. Staff service, ADC (temporary), 13.11.1915, and promoted Capt. 28.11.1915.

His father wrote to the WO, 15.9.1916, from Beaumaris, Anglesey, stating that his son was seconded as ADC to the Governor of Tasmania. Charles wrote to the WO, 8.12.1916, from Government House, Hobart, Tasmania, asking for permission to resign his commission due to being permanently unfit. Appointed ADC to the Governor of Western Australia. His staff service ended and he was placed on the half-pay list, 23.3.1917, for twelve months and was then to be re-examined. He wrote from Government House, Perth, Western Australia, 22 May, asking to be allowed to retire from the Army on the grounds of permanent medical unfitness. Placed on retired pay 18.9.1917. MBE *London Gazette*, 3.6.1927 while ADC and Private Secretary to the Governor of the Windward Island 'for services in combating the recent fire at Castries, St Lucia.' Attended the Regimental Dinner in 1938. File ref: 339/7864.

Mayne Major Edward Colburn. Commissioned as a Lt. into 3rd RIF, 24.2.1886, and promoted Capt. 10.5.1893. Served in operations with the Sierra Leone Frontier Police, 1897–8, receiving a medal and clasp. Also served during the Boer War, 1899–1901, attached to 2nd

RIF, and received the Queen's Medal, with clasps for Orange Free State, Transvaal, and Natal. To the Reserve of Officers 12.8.1903. Joined 3rd RIF, 12.8.1914, and attached to 2nd RIR 6.12.1914. Joined 1st RIR 16.5.1915. Mentioned in Despatches 22.6.1915. CO of 1st RIR, 26.2.1916 to 14.4.1916. Resumed command of his Coy 19.5.1916. Took over the duties of Town Major at Millencourt and Vermelles, 23.6.1916. Later Railway Transport Officer at Dernancourt. To Etaples, 19.11.1916, as Instructor at No. 2 Training School. Arrived VIII Corps reinforcement camp, 5.1.1918. Area Commandant Hipshoek and St Jan-Ter-Biezen, 21.10.1918. Ordered to proceed to England and report to WO in writing upon arrival, 16.3.1919. Demobilized with the honorary rank of Major, 22.9.1919. Served during the coal strike 9–26.4.1921. Home address 11 Holland Road, London. File ref: 339/25047.

Mercer 2/Lt. Samuel. Born 16.2.1895 the son of Henry Cooke Mercer, 276 Shankill Road, Belfast. Enlisted 7.6.1915 as Pte 17/1066 in 17th RIR. Draper, employed in Messrs. John Arnott and Co., height 6 foot ½ inch, chest 33–35 inches, weight 140 pounds. Applied for a commission 27.9.1915. Gazetted a 2/Lt. in 17th RIR, 4.10.1915. Joined 1st RIR 16.8.1916. Embarked Le Havre–Southampton, 18 November, aboard SS *Dunluce Castle* with 'Trench Fever and General Debility.' The MB at 2nd Western General Hospital, Manchester, 18.12.1916, noted that pains began 2.11.1916, head and abdomen. 'He is now better. Has still occasional pains in legs. But is still weak.' T/Lt. 1.1.1917. Joined A Coy, 2nd RIR, 7.5.1917, and was wounded, 18.6.1917, while on daylight patrol near Warneton. GSW both legs; one bullet passed from side to side through both thighs, no bone damage. *Belfast News Letter*, 29.6.1917, reported that he had a brother, Walter, in the RAMC. Wrote from the UVF Officers Hospital, 60 Botanic Avenue, Belfast, 21.9.1917, stating that the wounds were healed but his left leg was useless and he had to use crutches. Another letter, 1.1.1918, advised that he was then walking with the aid of a 'stout stick'. A note dated 6 June states that Mercer was serving with an Armoured Car Section in Belfast. He was living at Claremorris, Co. Mayo, 28.6.1918. His address was the Free Library, Edward Street, Portadown, 12.8.1919. Discharged 11.7.1919. Last served attached Ministry of Labour. Address, 7 Albert Street, Bangor, Co. Down. Rated C1, single, civil servant. File ref: WO339/45658.

Mitchell 2/Lt. Arthur Gorman. Born 29.9.1896, the son of Arthur Brownlow Mitchell FRCSI (Lt.-Col. RAMC), 18 University Square, Belfast. His mother, Agnes Crawford Mitchell *née* Gorman, died when he was born. Educated at Campbell College 1908–14. Served Campbell and Queen's OTC. Matriculated at Queen's University, Belfast. He had two half-brothers: John Myles Mitchell (born 3.12.1902) and Charles Brownlow Mitchell (25.1.1906). He also had a half-sister. Applied for a commission, 21.4.1915. Single, first year medical student, height 6 foot ⅛ inch, chest 33–36 inches, weight 144 pounds, address 18 University Square. Gazetted a 2/Lt. in 5th RIR 8.5.1915. Joined 2nd RIR 14.4.1916. Killed by a sniper's bullet 13.5.1916. Ecoivres Military Cemetery, Mont St Eloy, Pas de Calais, I.K.18. File ref: 339/48382.

Mitchell Lt. Homer Dean MC. Born 16.2.1889 at Drummondville, Quebec. Educated at Nantucket High School, and Brown University, Providence, Rhode Island. Then went to McGill Unversity, Montreal. Attested as Pte 406 in the Canadian Overseas Expeditionary Force (Canadian Army Medical Corps, 3rd General Hospital) 13.3.1915. Next of kin was his aunt Mrs George Mitchell. Mechanical engineer, height 5 foot 6 inches, chest 33½–36 inches, weight 124½ pounds, grey eyes, brown hair, Presbyterian. Graduated from McGill with a B.Sc. in Agriculture, May 1915. Went to France in June. Applied for a commission 23.11.1916. Address No. 3 Canadian General Hospital (McGill), BEF. To No. 13 Officer Cadet Bn at Newmarket 9.3.1917.

Commissioned to 17th RIR 27.6.1917 and posted to 8th RIR. Wounded at Bourlon Wood with 8/9th RIR, 23.11.1917; struck by a rifle bullet which lodged under the skin at the back of his neck. Embarked Boulogne–Dover, 1.12.1917, and admitted to 2nd Western General Hospital, Manchester, where the bullet was removed. Reported to 17th RIR at Dundalk 23.1.1918. Rejoined the BEF in June. Attached 2nd RIR 24.8.1918. MC, *London Gazette*, 31.1.1919: 'In the Messines sector on 6th September, 1918, for conspicuous gallantry in action. He showed great skill and leadership, advancing with his platoon under heavy machine gun fire. During the advance his platoon captured three machine guns and destroyed the teams. He was wounded during the operation.' GSW right buttock, including a fracture and wound to the right thigh. Embarked Boulogne–Dover 19.10.1918. Promoted Lt. 27.12.1918. MB at the Military Hospital for Officers, Brighton, 17.10.1919: all wounds were healed but he was permanently unfit for military service. He could walk with the aid of a stick and wanted to be repatriated. Left for home 6.2.1920. File ref: 339/100625.

Moore Lt. Morgan Edward Jellett MC. Born 22.2.1894 at Letterkenny, Co. Donegal, the only son of Edward Erskine Stone Moore MD and Nina Margaret Jane *née* Jellett, The Haven, Teignmouth, Devon. His father was resident medical superintendent of Donegal District Lunatic Asylum. Educated at Aravon School, Bray, Co. Wicklow; Trinity College, Glenalmond (where he was captain of the school during his last year), and King's College, Cambridge, from October 1913. Applied for a commission 7.11.1914. Address, Asylum House, Letterkenny. Correspondence address, Heathville, Monkstown, Co. Dublin. Single, height 5 foot 10¾ inches, chest 33–36½ inches, weight 137 pounds. He had served 4 years and 1 month in Glenalmond OTC and 1 week in Cambridge University OTC. A certificate from Cambridge shows that he had passed parts 1, 2, and 3 of his first examination for Medicine and Surgery. Gazetted a 2/Lt. in 13th RIR, 12.11.1914. Granted a Regular commission 23.5.1916.

Took part in 13th RIR's night raid of 26.6.1916. Wounded 1.7.1916: shell wound right forearm and bullet wound (shrapnel) left buttock: severe not permanent. MB at Londonderry, 19.10.1916, noted that the forearm wound was still open causing restricted movement. Joined 20th RIR, 30.11.1916, and posted to 3rd RIR 26.4.1917. MB at Belfast, 16.2.1917, found him fit for general service but not in a tropical climate. At the time he was under orders for Salonika but, when he started taking quinine as a precautionary measure, he developed a severe reaction with tight and discoloured skin and could not wear his shoes.

Joined 2nd RIR 31.7.1917. *Irish Times*, 14.11.1918: 'He became acting adjutant the following October and was with them in the Cambrai offensive in November 1917.' Promoted Lt. 4.11.1917. Missing in action 24.3.1918. His father requested the names of captured RIR officers so that he could make enquiries. Capt. Bryans wrote from Berne, 8.7.1918, that Moore was wounded about 4 p.m.: 'I have grave fears about him.' 5919 Sgt (name unclear) was with 3rd RIR: 'When I saw the cruel deeds of the Huns I thought I would chance my luck in getting back through them, so I managed to escape through a break in the centre and with the help of God I got back safe.' Mr Moore was supplied by the WO with the names and camps of some prisoners for him to continue his enquiries: 14043 Cpl W. Ballard (Giessen), 11358 Rfn F. Burke (Cassel), 19925 Rfn H. Byrne (Friedricksfeld), 6902 L/Cpl T. Cairnduff (Stendal), 47632 Rfn G.H. Carpenter (Langensalza), 9174 L/Cpl D.L. Conoghan (Zerbst), and 9863 Rfn W. Hamilton (Münster III). They asked that he not make any reference to possible bad treatment by the Germans when writing because that 'would be certain to get these men into trouble'.

Appeared on an official list of war dead received from Germany via the Red Cross. Died 27.3.1918 in a German Field Hospital at Flavy-le-Martel: 'cause, shattering of both legs.

Buried cemetery there.' An additional list of repatriated men that had been captured 24.3.1918 was given to Mr Moore: 5486 T. Burton, 6454 J. Hooks, 4458 A. Gordon, 770 R. Keith, 5388 W. Heslop, and 15160 J. Lindsay. A statement was made by 9795 Rfn E. Thompson at the Depot, 4.3.1919: he was taken prisoner and detailed to carry German wounded to a barn near Cugny. When he arrived there he saw Lt. Moore, who was dead. He was ordered to remove Moore's boots and then bury him, which he did. Grand Séraucourt British Cemetery, Aisne, VI.E.9. File ref: 339/13908.

Moreland 2/Lt. James Alexander MC. Born 24.3.1896 at Cameron Street, Brookline, Massachusetts, the son of William J. and Mary Moreland *née* Smith. Educated at Ballymacareney National School, Banbridge. Employed on the staff of Messrs John Robb & Co., Castle Place, Belfast. Enlisted as Pte T3/031235 in the ASC, 7.12.1914, and posted to 4 Coy, 36th (Ulster) Divisional Train. Height 5 foot 5 inches, chest 32½–35 inches, weight 116 pounds, draper. Embarked for the BEF 4.10.1915. Promoted Cpl., 10.7.1915, and a/Sgt 10.10.1915. Reprimanded for not complying with an order given by a CSM 31.1.1916. Applied for a commission 8.11.1916. Admitted to No. 16 Officer Cadet Bn at Rhyl, 3.1.1917, and commissioned in 3rd RIR 25.4.1917. Went to the front, 20.7.1917, and joined 2nd RIR 6.8.1917. Applied for a permanent commission in the Indian Army, 29.7.1917. Appointed a/Capt., 26.11.1917 to 13.12.1917, while commanding a company. *Belfast News Letter*, 7.1.1918: ' ... distinguished himself in heavy fighting in which his Division was engaged in November last ... At present he is home on leave preparatory to joining the Indian Army.' MC 4.2.1918, *London Gazette*, 2.7.1918: 'For conspicuous gallantry and devotion to duty. He took command of three companies when the company commanders had become casualties, and reorganized them at a critical stage. He re-established communication in all directions and got his men into a position from which they were able to support other units.' Next of kin was his mother at Moss Side, Derriaghy, Dunmurry, Co. Antrim. His address at the end of 1917 was 15 Springfield Gardens, Springfield Road, Belfast. Embarked for India 13.2.1918. Relinquished his commission 25.3.1919 on appointment to the Indian Army. File ref: 339/83915.

Morgan, Lt. Ernest George. Born 9.7.1898, the son of Richard Morgan, a draper. Educated at St Nicholas, Belfast. Enlisted as Rfn 19/469 in 19th RIR 12.5.1916. Address was his father's house at 105 Ulsterville Avenue, Belfast. Height 5 foot 10½ inches, chest 32–34 inches, weight 125 pounds, Church of England, apprentice wholesale warehouseman. Posted to 18th RIR to serve as a Cadet, 11.7.1916. Applied for a commission 31.5.1917. Permanent address, Burmah Villa, Fitzwilliam Avenue, Belfast. Admitted to No. 7 Officer Cadet Bn 7.9.1917. Commissioned to 18th RIR 29.1.1918. From May to July 1918 he was unfit for service. Joined 2nd RIR 30.8.1918. Left 16.9.1918, embarked Calais–Dover on the 28th, and admitted to Eccleston Hospital with septic sinovitis. Rejoined at Salisbury Plain, January 1919. Attached to No. 4 Depot Company RASC, 16.6.1919. To RASC Training Establishment 25 August to 20 September. Promoted Lt. 30.7.1919. Discharged 17.3.1920, single, rated A. Address 15 Fitzwilliam Avenue, Belfast. File ref: 339/115225.

Morgan Capt. Samuel Valentine. Born 5.6.1880 at Church Street, Newtownards, Co. Down, the son of John and Elizabeth Morgan *née* Calwell. His father, a shoemaker, was later Sgt Instructor of Musketry in 3rd and 4th RIR. He was the eldest of eight children, the others being May (1883), John Joseph Leo (1884), Bridgetta (1888), Sydney (1890), Patrick Herbert (1892), Violet (1895) and Beatrice (1900–45). Enlisted 28.1.1896 as Boy No. 4717 at

Newtownards and was posted to 3rd RIR as a Bugler. Clerk, height 5 foot ½ inch, weight 92 pounds, chest 27½–30 inches, tattoo on the back of his left hand, fresh complexion, grey eyes, light brown hair. Re-posted to Details Bugler in 2nd RIR and appointed L/Cpl 1.6.1901. Promoted Cpl 1.10.1901; appointed L/Sgt 23.9.1902; posted to the Depot and promoted Sgt 4.1.1903. Served as Orderly Room Sgt with the Louth Rifles (6th RIR Militia) 1903–8. Lt.-Col. A.R. Cole-Hamilton's farewell message, 1908: 'Sgt S.V. Morgan, whose never-failing hard work, good temper, zeal, and tact have contributed so much to the excellent state of the battalion.' Posted to 3rd RIR, 28.6.1908, appointed Orderly Room Sgt, and promoted Colour-Sgt. QM Sgt 28.6.1911. Resided at Victoria Bar, Belfast. Married Rose Gertrude Marquess, North Street, Newtownards, a teacher, and daughter of John Marquess, farmer, at the Roman Catholic Church of St Malachy, 21.8.1911. Witnesses Daniel Joseph Marquess and Bridget Moran. Their son John Leo was born at Belfast, 6.8.1912. Recommended for a commission by his CO 28.9.1914. All service to this time was at home. Appointed to a Regular Army commission, 1.10.1914, and Adjutant 6.10.1914.

Irish Times, 11.2.1915: 'On parade yesterday of all officers, non-commissioned officers and men of the 3rd (Reserve) Battalion, Royal Irish Rifles, at Wellington Barracks, Dublin, under the command of Major F.M.G. McFerran, Brigadier-General F.E. Hill CB, DSO, Commanding 31st Infantry Brigade and Dublin Garrison, presented Lieutenant and Adjutant S.V. Morgan with the Long Service and Good Conduct Medal … In making the presentation General Hill said it was unique for a combatant officer to receive this distinction which was usually awarded to NCOs and men after 18 years service whose character was irreproachable. He further said that any soldier might earn the VC for an act of bravery committed on the spur of the moment, but it took a soldier 18 years to earn the Good Conduct Medal. Lieutenant and Adjutant Morgan was awarded the medal on 1st October 1914 on which date he was also gazetted to commissioned rank from the rank of Quartermaster Sergeant. General Hill quotes this officer to the rank and file as an example of how any soldier might rise from the ranks.'

Promoted Lt., 15.3.1915, and was appointed Adjutant. His brother, Lt. John Morgan, 2nd R. Inniskilling Fusiliers, was killed in action at Festubert, 16.5.1915. *Irish Life* 28.12.1917: 'Captain Morgan was … one of the officers in Portobello Barracks during the rebellion who gave evidence before the Commission of Inquiry.' He was ordered to the front but had been feeling ill. MB at Belfast, 23.12.1916: tonsillitis; he had been under treatment and was considerably debilitated. Applied for a posting to a school of instruction. His daughter Gertrude Elizabeth was born at 9 Court Street, Belfast, 23.1.1917. MB at King George V Hospital, Dublin, 28 March: deflected septum of nose. He had recovered and was recommended for fourteen days leave and then to rejoin his unit. Joined 2nd RIR, 7.5.1917, and made a/Capt., D Coy, 1.8.1917. Killed in action 10.8.1917. His family was well provided for as he left a good sum of money, had a considerable life assurance policy and his wife qualified for a widow's pension. The family moved to 53 Southwell Road, Bangor, Co. Down, and later to Southampton. Both children became teachers. Menin Gate Memorial. Additional details supplied by his grandson Hugh Pitfield. File ref: 339/21476.

Morris Brigadier-General Edmund Merritt CMG, CB. Born 15.6.1868, the son of Edmund Morris, Toronto. Married Lily, daughter of Major-General G.W. Shakespear. Gazetted a 2/Lt. in the Devonshire Regt 17.12.1890. Promoted Lt. 20.10.1892, Capt. 24.6.1899, and Brevet Major 29.11.1900. Served Tirah 1897–8, receiving the medal with two clasps. Served in the South African War 1899–1902 as Adjutant of Thorneycroft's Mounted Infantry. Received the Queen's Medal with six clasps and the King's Medal with two clasps. Mentioned in Despatches. Employed in South Africa until 1906. Promoted Major 22.11.1912. Brigade Major 5.7.1911 to 31.5.1915. Arrived and took command of 2nd RIR 1.6.1915. *War Diary* 23.6.1915: 'Major E.M. Morris, promoted Lt.-Col. of the 2nd Bn The King's Own (Royal Lancaster Regt) and left to join his new unit.' See main text. He commanded 1st Bn The King's Own in France for a few days having been posted in error. Then took the 2nd Bn out to Salonika where he was CO from September to December 1915. Brigade Commander (31st Infantry Bde) from 30.12.1915 to the end of the war. Mentioned in Despatches and awarded the Brevet of Lt.-Col. He commanded the Cairo Bde from 1.6.1919. Awarded the CMG 1916, CB 1919, and Order of the Nile. Retired 1923. Later was a JP for Suffolk and resided at Great Cornard, Sudbury, Suffolk. Died 1.1.1939. Closed file.

Morrogh Major John Dominick. 3rd R. Irish. He had previously been temporarily attached to 2nd RIR. Joined 2nd R. Irish at St Omer (HQ BEF) where the remnants of the battalion spent four months (November 1914 to March 1915) trying to get back to war strength following their disaster at Le Pilly on 20.10.1914. Took command of C Coy, 15.12.1914. Wounded at St Julien 9.5.1915. In Dublin with 3rd R. Irish during the 1916 Rebellion. Their regimental history contains the following: 'On the morning of the 27th April a party of picked shots under Major J.D. Morrogh succeeded in getting a good position on a roof top and thence inflicted casualties on the rebels in the Post Office. One shot wounded the rebel commander Connolly ... On the morning of the 28th a party under Major Morrogh and CSM Banks succeeded in capturing the republican flag from the roof of the Post Office.' Later served with 8th RIR. He was captured, 21.3.1918, while serving with 7th R. Irish. Medal roll shows 'France prior to 5/15. Star and medals returned name not added to roll.' Closed file.

Morrow Lt. Edwin. Born 22.5.1896, the son of Mr N.J. Morrow, Whitehall, Dhu Varren, Portrush. Enlisted as Rfn 18/590 in 18th RIR 19.10.1915. Height 5 foot 11 inches, chest 34–35½ inches, pupil at school, single. Applied for a commission, 28.2.1916. Posted to No. 7 Officer's Cadet Bn 5.4.1916. Discharged to a commission with 19th RIR 6.7.1916. Promoted Lt. 7.1.1918. Served with 14th and 15th RIR. Wounded while serving with 2nd RIR 30.7.1918: blown up and buried by a HE shell; wounded in the right thigh and face, with contusion of the right eye. Embarked Calais–Dover 4.8.1918. Rejoined 3rd RIR 30.11.1918. At this time his home address was Seaview, Farnham Road, Bangor, Co. Down. Applied for a wound gratuity, 21.11.1918, saying his right eye was useless. Granted £250. MB at Belfast 9.5.1919: wounds healed; no disability in his leg; no significant disfigurement due to facial wounds; eyesight 6/6 left eye, 2/60 right eye; no improvement likely. MBs at Belfast: 5.5.1920, 40 per cent disability; 2.8.1921, disability classed as severe and permanent, Morrow complained of depression in three week cycles. Pension of £100 granted annually until 29.7.1922. Wound pension taken over by Ministry of Pensions 5.10.1922. Died 29.1.1981, by which time his disability had been rated at 50 per cent; annual pension £1,203 plus age allowance £161.63. File ref: 339/57730.

Morton Capt. Thomas Matthew. A son of William and Annie Morton, Hollydene, Holywood, Co. Down, and younger brother of W.J.E. Morton below. His father was a manufacturer's agent. Commissioned to 5th RIR 2.7.1913. Junior Administration Officer, West Africa, 27.4.1914. Promoted Lt. 8.9.1914. Joined 2nd RIR from 4th RIR 4.11.1914. Reported sick 14.11.1914. Promoted Capt., 5th RIR, 20.2.1915. Joined 7th RIR 1.1.1917. To Indian Army 2.4.1917. Appointed a/Capt. 21.7.1917. Served with 3rd Gurkha Rifles. Promoted Capt. 5.5.1919. Closed file.

Morton Lt. William John Edward. Born 9.1.1888 and educated at Sullivan Upper School, Holywood. *Irish Life*, 28.1.1916: 'He had assisted his father, in his office in Belfast.' Applied for a commission 6.8.1914 and was gazetted to 5th RIR. Resided at 26 Fountain Street, Belfast. Embarked for the BEF, 3.5.1915, and was posted to 1st York and Lancs Regt. Promoted Lt. 22.5.1915. Joined 2nd RIR 24.8.1915 on return from three-weeks leave. Killed by shell fire 5.9.1915. *Irish Times*, 10.9.1915: 'He was a playing member of the North of Ireland Rugby Club. His brother, Captain T.M. Morton, is the Adjutant of the 5th Battalion Royal Irish Rifles at Hollywood.' Effects included a cigarette case and three pipes. His father was executor, gross estate £515. Menin Gate Memorial. File ref: 339/27470.

Moss Lt. William Philipson MC. Promoted from the ranks to 2/Lt. in 3rd RIR 14.10.1914, and to Lt. 31.7.1915. Joined 2nd RIR 7.10.1915. Slightly wounded and remained at duty on both 18.3.1916 and 28.4.1916. Wounded 7.7.1916. MC 1.1.1917. Spent the remainder of the war with 3rd RIR. File missing.

Mulcahy-Morgan Capt. Edward Spread. Son of John Edward Spread Mulcahy-Morgan BL, Lara House, Rathdrum, Co. Wicklow, by his wife, Susan, eldest daughter of the late William Bennett Campion KC, HM Sgt-at-Law. Educated at the Erasmus Smith Abbey Grammar School, Tipperary. Commissioned to 4th RIR, 5.4.1907, promoted Lt. 7.4.1910, and Capt., 3rd RIR, 10.10.1914. Wounded and missing, 27.10.1914, while serving with 2nd RIR. *Immortal Deeds*: 'When lying severely wounded in the back and arms by shell fire, he was only able to articulate: "Advance! Advance!" when approached by a non-commissioned officer who wished to help him.' His brother, Lt. Francis Campion Mulcahy-Morgan, 7th RIR, was born at Clondalkin, Co. Dublin, 5.3.1895 (fourth son), and killed in action 6.9.1916. Their father wrote to the WO, 15.12.1916: 'I am now proceeding to wind up the affairs of my other son Capt. E.S. Mulcahy-Morgan ... I have since heard from several returned soldiers whom I have interviewed that he was fatally injured, which I regret to know is true or we would long since have heard from him. I shall be glad to know if you will issue a death certificate in his case also. We never received either his pay or (£50) allowance while he was on duty in Dublin or Kingstown.' They had three brothers, Major William Edmund Victor, T.W., and N.R., and three sisters, Susan L., Martha K. and Albina I. Lara House was sold in the 1930s, converted to a hotel but burned down in the 1950s. Named on the Abbey Grammar School War Memorial. Le Touret Memorial. File missing.

Munn Lt. Norman Barry MC. Born 21.11.1896 at 45 Castlereagh Street, Belfast, the son of Dr R. Jackson Munn MB, B.Ch. His brother, Sydney Jackson Munn, was born 21.3.1898. Educated at Campbell College, 1910–15; 1st XI 1913–15 (Captain 1915); School Prefect; 1st XV 1913–15. School's Interprovincial at rugby and cricket. Joined Queens University OTC 21.10.1915. Applied for a commission, 2.12.1915, but was rejected by the selection board. Joined 19th RIR, 25.3.1916, as Rfn 19/412. Appointed L/Cpl 27.7.1916. Re-applied for a commission 12.9.1916. Height 5 foot 10½ inches, chest 33–36 inches, weight 148 pounds, medical student. Promoted Cpl 11.10.1916. Posted to No. 7 Officer Cadet Bn 3.1.1917. Commissioned 26.4.1917 and served with 10th RIR.

Joined D Coy, 2nd RIR, 2.4.1918. Wounded 2.6.1918, see main text. Embarked Boulogne–Dover 11.6.1918, GSW both legs and left arm. Address Ingleside, Woodstock Road, Belfast, which was his father's home. He wrote to the WO, 9 September, from the Officers Hospital, Palace Barracks, Holywood, Co. Down, requesting a wound gratuity. MC, *London Gazette*, 13.9.1918: 'For conspicuous gallantry and devotion to duty when in command of a night reconnaissance. The patrol was heavily bombed by the enemy, one officer being killed, whilst of the remainder, all were wounded except one. Although wounded himself in twelve places, he carried a wounded officer to a place of safety, and then went to the support line, returning with a stretcher party, all the while being under heavy machine gun and rifle fire. It was mainly due to his courage and resource that the whole patrol returned without leaving any identification in the hands of the enemy.' Promoted Lt. 26.10.1918. Appointed temporary commandant POW Camp New Bilton from 7.3.1919. As of 24.4.1919 he was serving in a POW camp at Dorchester. Rejoined 3rd RIR 23 July. Discharged 8.8.1919, rated C1. Queen's University, Belfast: MB, B.Ch., 1924. Resided at 22 Purley Oaks Road, Sanderstead, Surrey. Lt. in the RAMC 1942–3. Dr Munn's medals were donated to the regimental museum in 1968. File ref: 339/83501.

Murphy 2/Lt. Bernard Joseph. Born 4.8.1897 at Youghal, Co. Cork, the son of Dr Daniel Joseph Murphy LRCP, LRCS, LFPS, and Annie Murphy. Educated at Rockwell College, Cashel, Co. Tipperary, and was a bank clerk. Enlisted as Pte 5/7005 in 5th RMF, 31.5.1916, and posted to the Reserve. Single, height 5 foot 9½ inches, chest 31–34 inches, weight 115 pounds. Address was his father's house at Devonshire Villa, Youghal. Joined Dublin University OTC 1.6.1916. Applied for a commission 27.7.1916. Mobilized 28.8.1916 and posted to 7th Officer Cadet Bn 5.9.1916. Discharged to a commission in 5th RMF 18.12.1916. Joined 2nd RIR 22.3.1917. Wounded in action 10.8.1917 and died at No. 32 CCS 18.8.1917. Effects included a rosary, crucifix, spectacles, and a lock of hair. Brandhoek Military Cemetery No. 3, Vlamertinghe, Ieper, II.F.25. File ref: 339/69905.

Murphy Capt. Patrick MC. Born 29.12.1879 at Borrisokane, Co. Tipperary. Enlisted as Pte 1222 in 1st Irish Guards, 29.1.1902. Height 5 foot 9½ inches, chest 36–38 inches, weight 154 pounds, painter (another note said postman). Address at enlistment, South Terrace, Borrisokane. Next of kin was his mother, Kate Griffin. He had a younger sister, Mary Anne, at Thornvale, Moneygab, King's County. Appointed L/Cpl 3.10.1903. Posted to the Depot 29.1.1904 and granted Good Conduct pay the same day. Posted 1st Bn 10.10.1904. Promoted Cpl 26.9.1905. L/Sgt 23.6.1906. Contusion of knee 6.12.1906: he did not claim this as being due to military service; injury rated severe, not permanent. Reverted to Pte 10.1.1907 and transferred to the Military Foot Police as Pte 929 that day. Granted second Good Conduct Badge 29.1.1907. Retransferred to 1st Irish Guards 26.10.1907. L/Cpl 7.11.1907. Extended service to complete twelve years, 11.1.1909. Posted to the Depot 1.3.1909.

Married Jessie Randall at Farnborough 10.7.1909. Children born: Michael Edward at Caterham 11.4.1910, and Patrick James at London 24.3.1913. Promoted Cpl 7.5.1910. Posted to 1st Bn 10.8.1910. Unpaid L/Sgt 3.9.1910. Severely reprimanded for an offence at London 2.8.1911: neglect of duty as Sgt-in-Waiting; not warning a Cpl for Guards; not warning a man for Purbright. Paid L/Sgt 26.8.1912. Sgt 26.5.1913. Posted to the Depot 13.12.1913. Reengaged to complete 21 years, 22.1.1914. Posted to 2nd Bn 17.9.1914. Appointed CSM (Drill Sgt) 13.11.1914. Embarked Southampton–Le Havre 16.8.1915. All service until this time was at home.

Transferred to 2nd RIR as CSM 2/9771, 26.8.1916. Wounded in action 10.10.1916 but remained at duty as a/RSM. Recommended for a commission by Col. Goodman, 9.1.1917: 'I have seen this Warrant Officer in and out of the trenches. He is a very able man and thoroughly reliable under all conditions. I would like him as a 2nd Lt. in this Battalion.' Commissioned to 2nd RIR 1.2.1917. To Bde Grenade Coy 26.2.1917. Appointed a/Lt. without pay while commanding Bde Instructional Coy, 1.4.1917. Mentioned in Despatches, *London Gazette*, 25.5.1917 and 21.12.1917. A/Capt. 20.7.1917. To 74th Bde Instruction

Platoon 1.10.1917. Took over command of A Coy at the Bde School, 13.2.1918.

Wounded, GSW right calf, while serving with 2nd RIR, 27.3.1918. Clean perforating wound, 'bullet, rifle, passed through'. Admitted Liverpool Merchants Hospital, Etaples, the next day. Embarked for the UK aboard HS *Stad-Antwerpen*, 1.4.1918, and admitted 1st London General Hospital. MB 24.4.1918: wound healed, granted three weeks leave, then to rejoin 3rd RIR at Belfast. Promoted Lt. 1.8.1918. Ordered to rejoin the BEF, 16.8.1918, and to command a school in 66th Division. 'To remain seconded and to be A/Major whilst holding the post of Cmdt 66th Div Rec Camp from 1.10.1918 to 10.3.1919.' Appointed ADC to GOC 66th Division 21.3.1919. MC, *London Gazette*, 3.6.1919. Relinquished appointment 'on abolition of 66th Div 6.6.1919.' Retired with a gratuity of £1,500, *London Gazette*, 9.10.1919. Address, 8 Cambridge Buildings, Upper Gordon Street, Westminster, London.

Reported for duty to 1st RUR, Kensington Gardens, London, 9.4.1921, and was sent home to await instructions same date. Demobilization to date from 30.4.1921 (Coal Strike). Letter to Record Office, Irish Guards, Buckingham Gate, London, 2.2.1948, from John Griffin of Dovedale, 20 The Broadway, Lancing, Sussex: he was Murphy's step-brother and was trying to find him. Also referred to Murphy's sons who, he thought, were in the RAF during WW2. He had not heard from Murphy since 1922 and wanted to contact him purely for family reasons. RHQ Irish Guards advised of the transfer to the RIR and forwarded the request to the Infantry Records Office in Perth. They advised Griffin that if he sent a letter to Murphy in an envelope then they would forward it to the address known in 1921. File ref: 339/92332.

Murray Lt. Philip Ernest. Born 10.5.1889 at 31 South Circular Road, Kilmainham, Dublin, the son of Philip and Marie Aylward Murray *née* Styles. Educated at St Mary's College, Rathmines. Enlisted as Driver in the Dublin RFA Reserve, 17.2.1909, and purchased his discharge 12.3.1909. He was a member of the Irish National Volunteers. Applied for a commission 26.1.1915. Single, Private Secretary, Anchor Brewery, Dublin. Commissioned to 4th CR 24.2.1915. Served in France with 1st Pioneer Bn, attached 2nd Canadian Division. Joined 2nd RIR 8.4.1916. Wounded slightly 23.4.1916 but remained at duty. Wounded 9.7.1916 and admitted to No. 7 Stationary Hospital, Boulogne. A bullet passed through a larynxal ventricle causing paralysis of the right vocal chord. Home address, Tintern, Effra Road, Rathmines, Dublin, where his mother resided. Embarked Boulogne–Dover aboard HS *Cambria*, 13.7.1916, and admitted to the Royal Free Hospital, Grays Inn Road, London. Awarded a gratuity of £62.50. MB at King George V Hospital, Dublin, 31.10.1916, found him permanently unfit for general service in anything but a tropical climate. Reported for duty with 4th CR at Crosshaven 1.11.1916. Promoted Lt. 7.11.1916.

Left for India, 4.5.1917, having been seconded for service with the Indian Army. Stopped over at Durban where he was court martialled 16.3.1918. Charged with deserting on 1.1.1918; pleaded not guilty and found guilty: 'To suffer death by being shot.' Sentence confirmed and commuted by GOC South African Military Command at Cape Town 27.3.1918: to be cashiered and to serve three years penal servitude. The GOC recommended that when Murray returned to the UK 'the matter of clemency might be considered with a view to enabling this ex officer to regain his character from the ranks'. Embarked for England aboard the *Durham Castle*, 25.4.1918.

He made a petition from HM Prison, Wandsworth, 12.6.1918. On route to India they had stopped and encamped at Durban. Here he met a woman whom he became infatuated with and lived with her as her husband. His name was on the list to sail for India on SS *Caronia* on 3.1.1918 'but on the night of the 2nd January 1918, I unfortunately took too much absinthe, so that I was unable to withstand the blandishments of the lady referred to and instead of returning to camp and preparing for embarkation on the morrow I remained with her. When I came to my senses it was too late and I remained away until apprehended by the Military Police at Durban – being absent for two months in all.' He stated that other than this he had a clean record and had volunteered for war service. 'I was fighting for the Allied Cause in France, when others of my nationality and family were interned during the rebellion in Ireland.' He had to make an entirely fresh start in life and considered that being cashiered was punishment enough. He asked for the sentence to be reconsidered. The woman in question was Mrs J. Harcourt-Peace. He moved in with her in November 1917, in the house of Mrs Cordes, Palmer Street, Durban, and they used the name Mr and Mrs Harcourt.

His mother wrote to the WO, 19.6.1918, referring to a letter she had sent the previous week asking about her son's whereabouts. She had since heard that a lieutenant of his name was then a prisoner in Wandsworth on a charge of deserting, but she had a letter from her son in South Africa dated 23.11.1917 wherein he said that he would be in India by the time she received it. 'I think there must be a mistake somewhere.' She was ready to identify the man in prison, if required, and if it did transpire to be her son, then there must be some mistake. The WO confirmed the situation of Prisoner 379 and that the sentence would be reviewed at some future date. She wrote to the Home Secretary asking for the case to be reinvestigated, as she could not believe that he intentionally did wrong. She stated that his 'three brothers who were involved in the rebellion here in 1916 are all doing well now as loyal subjects here'. Despite Philip being wounded twice, he was being branded as a criminal. 'You know what an effect that will have on recruiting here if it becomes known, and I have been urging his brothers to join up as soon as ever we get Home Rule.'

She wrote again, 22.6.1918, to say that she had omitted to mention that Philip had been in hospital at Wynberg whilst in South Africa and also about this time he had received news of the death of his fiancée. She thought his mind was disturbed. She enquired about her son's pay, 29.7.1918, as there were debtors. In this letter she referred to him having suffered barbarous treatment on the journey back to the UK and said that this would make good propaganda for the Nationalists. 'Captain Redmond has launched an appeal for him.' The WO issued instructions, 27.8.1918, to the Governor of Wandsworth to release Murray and advised his mother accordingly. Released from Maidstone Convict Prison 2.9.1918.

Murray wrote to the WO, 5.9.1918, requesting return of the testimonials submitted with his original application for a commission, and asked if he would receive formal discharge papers. He wrote a letter and statement to be put before the Army Council, 25.9.1918, seeking reinstatement in the Army. He said that at his trial he wanted to avoid any scandal and had changed his plea to guilty at the last minute and dismissed his lawyer. The case continued with the not guilty plea already in place and he took no interest in the proceedings. He disputed some of the evidence and the interpretation of his actions.

Mrs Murray wrote to the WO 9.10.1918. Her son was entirely in sympathy with the Army, wanted to make good and 'to have another whack at the Hun'. He was anxious to be re-commissioned in the Army but feared that his appeal would be passed over. He currently depended on her for support and could not take up his old position because his previous co-employees were all Sinn Feiners. 'Without his original testimonials he cannot apply for another position, and I will not consent to his joining as a Private for I think that the fact of his release shows that his sentence was harsh and unjust.' She went on to say that he did his bit when all his former comrades and relations were in the Rebellion in 1916. 'They are nearly all now employed and doing well, while he, who turned his back on all their advice and cajolery to take his place in the fight for Right is shunned by them, without employment, and a burden to his own people.' She hoped that the Secretary of State for War would put in a good word with regard to Philip being re-commissioned. She wrote without Philip's knowledge. He was planning on moving to a climate that was better for his health. The Army Council advised him that they had considered the matter but could see no case for over-turning the findings of the court martial. File ref: 339/40580.

Noble 2/Lt. Richmond Samuel Howe. Born 2.5.1877 at Howe Mase, Castle Street, Great Torrington, Devon, the son of Samuel Richmond Noble, Congregational Minister, and Mary Isabella *née* Harrington. His father was Irish. Educated at Bradford, and Lincoln College, Oxford. Member of Freemason Lodge 10, Belfast. Applied for a commission 21.7.1916. Correspondence address Inns of Court OTC, Berkhampstead (since 28.1.1916). Manager and Secretary of an insurance society. To No. 7 Officer Cadet Bn 1.8.1916. Commissioned to 3rd RIR 22.11.1916. MB at Le Havre 26.4.1917: fit to return to duty having had pharyngitis and rheumatism. Joined 2nd RIR 1.5.1917. B Coy. Wounded by a HE shell 7.6.1917.
     Embarked Calais–Dover aboard SS *Newhaven*. MB at 1st South General Hospital, Birmingham, 13 July: 'There were extensive injuries on left side of face; eyeball was severely damaged and there is deafness. There were numerous small wounds of left forearm and hand. There were several flesh wounds of left buttock and both thighs. He was sent via CC Bailleul to 35 General Hopspital, Calais. After two days he was admitted here on 9 June 1917.' *Belfast News Letter*, 11.6.1917: 'Secretary of the Orange and Protestant Friendly Society [12 Victoria Street], he has been associated with it ever since its inception. He had made a special study of the National Insurance Act on taking up work with the OPFS, and is a recognized authority on the application and interpretation of the statute ... Mrs [Beatrice] Noble of Sheridan, Helen's Bay [Co. Down] received a telegram yesterday informing her that her husband was seriously wounded, and asking her to leave immediately to see him.'
     MBs at Belfast: 24.10.1917, the wounds had healed. 'Loss of teeth; temporary plate used; permanent plate required. Thigh wound healed, but has limp. 28.1.1918, 'Left eye has been enucleated. Right eye 6/36 without glasses, 6/9 with glasses. Unable to make his way about at night and he is unable to judge distance. Almost stone deaf in left ear ... Right eyeball very prominent and vision will probably deteriorate. Instructed to return to unit (Clandeboye). Has provided himself with artificial eye and dentures.' Placed on the Retired List due to ill health caused by wounds, *London Gazette*, 1.3.1918. 'Remaining eye weak without glasses; cannot resume civil employment immediately; his Directors have given him extended leave until the end of the year.' From May 1919 his address was *Lisnatore*, Suffolk, Dunmurry. MB 7.6.1919: 'Thinks there is some improvement since last Board. Now complains of loss of left eye and thinks right eye is somewhat affected. Also of recurrent severe headaches especially in cold weather. Is still somewhat nervous and apprehensive but has improved though he still avoids responsibility. No fits. Sleeps well at present. No battle dreams. Memory and concentration impaired. Temper irritable ... Scars on chin and cheek soundly healed, not adherent or tender and causing no facial deformity.' File ref: 339/67975.

Norman Capt. Geoffrey Schuyler MC. Son of George Schuyler Cardew and Ada Emily Norman. Gazetted to the RIR 5.10.1910, and promoted Lt. 11.2.1914. Wounded during the Battle of the Aisne 14–21.9.1914. Rejoined C Coy, 2nd RIR, 21.11.1914. To hospital, concussion, 10.5.1915, and returned to the UK four days later. Mentioned in Despatches 22.6.1915. Rejoined 5.8.1915, appointed Adjutant two days later, and promoted Capt., 1.10.1915. Slightly wounded but remained at duty 27.4.1916. Posted to 75th Bde HQ, 2.6.1916. Rejoined from Division 1.12.1916. Ceased as Adjutant 22.12.1916. MC 1.1.1917. Served in

British, German, and Portuguese East Africa, Nyasaland, and Northern Rhodesia, 25.10.1917 to 14.3.1918. Gained GSM, 'Nigeria 1918' clasp. *Lucy*, December 1915: 'The Adjutant, one of those gallant, reckless, and cheerful chaps who would go anywhere and do anything as a matter of course in war … He was of the cream of the fighting men, and I always admired him. He took a pride in never dodging shells. He marched upright about the trenches, and was admirably slow and supervising in the middle of the worst attacks. He was decorated for bravery, and his adventurous spirit, surviving the war, led him to join the French Foreign Legion, where he won further distinction and a commission for gallantry against the Tuaregs.' With the Foreign Legion during the 1920s. Later served as 48899 Capt. in 2nd London Irish Rifles/RUR. Died 30.7.1941, aged 50, and is commemorated on Golders Green Crematorium War Memorial. His medals are held in the regimental museum. Closed file.

O'Brien 2/Lt. Sidney Joseph Vincent. Born 9.7.1892 at Bridport, Dorset, the son of Andrew Stafford and Edith Blois O'Brien, 23 Bond's Hill, Londonderry. His father was Irish and a Customs and Excise officer. Educated at Summerhill College, Sligo, and NUI. Applied for a commission 3.7.1916. He was then in Dublin University OTC, height 6 foot 3½ inches, chest 37½–40 inches, weight 173 pounds, gentleman farmer (owner of a grazing farm). To No. 7 Officer Cadet Bn at the Curragh. Discharged to a commission in 5th RMF 18.12.1916. Joined 2nd RIR 27.2.1917. A Coy. Killed in action 7.6.1917. Estate, gross value £729, was administered by his father. Menin Gate Memorial. File ref: 339/67948.

Ogier Capt. Cyril Alfred MC. Born 1893. He was a clerk at Lloyds. 3rd Bn The Royal Militia of the Island of Jersey. Address, 31 Stopford Road, Jersey. Promoted Lt., 11.2.1914. Served in the BEF with 7th RIR from 20.12.1915 and was wounded 3.7.1916. GSW neck and left shoulder, and neurasthenia. He had an operation on his neck at Reading Military Hospital, 16 July, and then went on leave to Jersey. Reported to 4th RIR 12.10.1916. There was a second neck operation at Belfast, 27 October, after which he returned to Jersey. Found fit for general service, 19.7.1917, and returned to 7th RIR. Promoted Capt. 10.8.1917. Joined 2nd RIR 14.11.1917. Posted to 2nd Hampshire Regt, 29th Division, 6.1.1918. The Hampshire's regimental history, vol. 2: 'The 2nd Hampshire had to turn to and dig in SE of Croix de Poperinghe …· [17.4.1918] Seeing the troops in front wavering, Captain Ogier dashed forward with Z Company, arriving most opportunely just as the enemy were breaking into our line. His prompt and vigorous action was most successful, though he himself was badly wounded in the leg, the enemy were ejected and the line fully re-established.' For this action he was awarded the MC. GSW left thigh. Admitted to the Military Hospital at Devonport 30.4.1918. By June he was on light duty with 3rd Hampshires at Gosport when he was posted to 4th RIR. Reported for duty as Adjutant 52nd (Grad) Bn Hampshire Regt 31.7.1918. Discharged 4.11.1919. Single. Panamanian La Solidaridad, 3rd Class 17.2.1920. MB during May 1926 awarded a 100 per cent disability pension. GOC Jersey District to WO, 15.3.1927, advised that Ogier was to relinquish his commission on account of ill health caused by wounds. Died 15.4.1937 and buried at St Saviour's Churchyard, Jersey. File ref: 339/67672.

O'Lone Capt. Robert James. Born 1884 at Belfast, the son of John and Mary O'Lone, Castleview Road, Knock, Belfast. Siblings were John A., Harry Ralph, Walter Percy (below), Henrietta, Edith, Gertrude, and Clara. Enlisted in the RIR 29.3.1902; height 5 foot 2½ inches, weight 117 pounds, chest 32½–34½ inches, brown eyes and hair, plumber. Appointed L/Cpl 12.6.1902, Orderly Room Clerk 31.8.1902, Cpl in 2nd RIR 1.12.1903 and L/Sgt 12.8.1905. Orderly Room Sgt 30.9.1911. Married Gladys Louise Edwards at the Wesleyan Chapel,

Dover, 22.8.1912. QM Sgt 30.9.1914. Promoted 2/Lt. 20.6.1915. A/Adjutant 3.8.1915. T/Capt. with effect from 26.9.1915. Killed while visiting a listening post at 9.30 p.m., 11.11.1915. Mentioned in Despatches 1.1.1916. Next of kin was his widow at 4 Walpole Road, Twickenham. Their children were Robert John and Gladys Mary. *Irish Life*, 28.1.1916: 'He was the third son of Quartermaster-Sergeant John O'Lone [RIR], Victoria Barracks, Belfast, and Loughries, Newtownards.'

Buried in the military cemetery near the Police Control Motor Car Corner, Westhoek, north of Armentières. By this time his parents were residing at 63 Victoria Road, Bangor, Co. Down. Probate of the Will was granted to his father c/o Victoria Barracks, Belfast, and his brother Harry of 21 Edward Street, Portadown, a cashier. Gross value of the estate was £284. His widow later resided at 11 Grove Avenue, Twickenham, Middlesex. Tancrez Farm Cemetery, Ploegsteert, I.G.14.

Blackthorn, 1989, recorded the death of his son: 'Colonel Robert John O'Lone DSO, OBE, died peacefully at his home near Salisbury on 20 April 1989 aged 75. He was one of four generations of his family to have served in The Royal Irish Rifles / Royal Ulster Rifles ... Colonel O'Lone was commissioned in 1933 in the Third Queen Alexandra's Own Gurkha Rifles and saw his first active service on the North West Frontier of India. During the Second World War he took part in the Burma Campaign and was awarded the DSO for gallant and distinguished services. He was DAAG Northern Ireland District from 1948 to 1950 and commanded 6th Bn The Royal Ulster Rifles (TA) from 1952 to 1955, this was followed by a tour as GSO 1 at Headquarters Northern Ireland District. He was Commander of Cyrenaica Area 1960 to 1963 and finally before retiring in 1966 he became Inspector of Physical Training from 1963. He is survived by his widow Charmian and his married sons and daughter. His elder son Colonel [later Brigadier R.D.] Digby O'Lone was commissioned into the Royal Ulster Rifles in 1965 and subsequently commanded the 2nd Bn The Royal Irish Rangers from 1984 to 1987.' File ref: 339/32194.

O'Lone Capt. Walter Percy DCM. Born in 1890 at Belfast. Brother of R.J. O'Lone. Enlisted as Rfn 7511 in 2nd RIR 20.5.1905. Lisped slightly, freckled complexion, brown eyes and hair. Served at home until he joined the BEF. Appointed L/Cpl 20.8.1908, promoted Cpl 10.12.1910 and Sgt 6.2.1914. Wounded 15.9.1914, GSW to left hand. Appointed a/CSM 1.10.1914. Wounded 8.11.1914, GSW to left foot; toe amputated. Transferred to England 11 November. DCM 1.2.1915, *London Gazette*, 30.3.1915: 'For conspicuous gallantry on numerous occasions under most difficult circumstances, especially at Illies, and also for gallantry in voluntarily conveying most important messages under heavy rifle and shell fire on two occasions.' Posted to 3rd RIR 15.2.1915. Commissioned 9.4.1915. His parents were then at Loughins, Newtownards, Co. Down. Husband of Annie O'Lone, Belle Vista, Ballynahinch, Co. Down. Joined 2nd RIR 28.6.1915. Mentioned in Despatches. Appointed T/Capt. 28.7.1915. Wounded and missing 25.9.1915. Witness reports: 4980 Rfn William Clarke (17th Lancers attached 2nd RIR) was at the Princess Christian Hospital, Weymouth, 17.1.1916. He saw O'Lone struck by a bullet or bomb at Hooge and fall off the parapet into the German trenches at about 4 a.m. Clarke was about 3 or 4 yards from him while the battalion was charging. 2862 L/Cpl H. Fagan said that he saw him killed. 6222 Frank McKane said that Capt. O'Lone, D Coy, was killed and left in the German trench (this information was actually passed on by Bomber Nesbitt of 2nd RIR). Menin Gate Memorial. File ref: 339/26960.

O'Neill Capt. Robert Armstrong. Born 30.10.1879 at Ballymena, Co. Antrim. Served 18 months in the 13th Bn Imperial Yeomanry during the Boer War. Enlisted as Cadet 1112 in

16th RIR 8.6.1915. Height 5 foot 10 inches, chest 36–38½ inches, weight 162 pounds, electrical engineer, Presbyterian, single. Address *Norham*, Bladon Drive, Belfast. Next of kin was his brother, John Bowman O'Neill, 26 Cromwell Road, Belfast. Discharged to a commission in 14th RIR, 24.6.1915. Embarked for the BEF 4.10.1915. Wounded in the jaw and right hip, 1.7.1916, while attached to 109th TMB. Admitted to 108th FA, No. 3 CCS, and No. 3 General Hospital. Embarked HS *Salta* 8.7.1916. Reported to 3rd RIR 2.11.1916. His wounds were healed but he was having trouble with lumbago. MB at King George V Hospital, Dublin, 16.1.1917: deficiency of teeth in the lower jaw and required a plate. Joined No. 2 Infantry Section, 7.5.1917, but was admitted to No. 110 FA, sick, 10 May and subsequently to No. 58 FA, No. 53 CCS, No. 7 Stationary Hospital, and No. 39 General Hospital. Promoted Lt. 1.7.1917. Rejoined 109th TMB 17.7.1917. Returned to 14th RIR 24.12.1917. Joined 2nd RIR 29.12.1917. Posted to Base as unfit and admitted to No. 32 Stationary Hospital at Le Havre 6.5.1918. Medically classed B3 and posted for duty at the Base Depot 27.6.1918. The Electricity Dept., City and County Borough of Belfast requested, 24.6.1918, that O'Neill be released back to them as they had contracts with shipyards for Admiralty work and they needed him. His age was stated as 45 years 7 months. To HQ 3rd Army 12.8.1918. Assumed duty as Town Major of Arqueves 19 August. Belfast Council was advised that he would be released 28.9.1918. Classified as permanently disabled and resigned his commission. File ref: 339/42193.

O'Reilly 2/Lt. Herbert Wilson. Enlisted as Pte PS/1880 in the R. Fusiliers. Promoted 2/Lt. in 4th RIR, 15.6.1915. Joined 2nd RIR 26.11.1915. Wounded 19.1.1916 and died the following day in a FA. Bailleul Communal Cemetery Extension, Nord, II.B.72. File missing.

Orr 2/Lt. Walter Leslie. Born 6.4.1890 at 6 Knapton Terrace, Kingstown, Co. Dublin, the youngest son of Fingal Harman and Constance Emilie Orr (married 20.6.1883). His father was a merchant. Educated at Avoca School, Blackrock, and entered Trinity College, Dublin, 1908. He went to the Malay States about 1910 to join his brother in rubber planting, but was invalided home in February 1914. Served as a Private in the Malay States Volunteer Rifles from February 1912. Applied for a commission 3.11.1914. Single, address was his widowed mother's house at 16 Crossthwaite Park, Kingstown. Commissioned to 4th RIR, 17.11.1914. Joined C Coy, 2nd RIR, 14.7.1915. Killed in action 25.9.1915. Menin Gate Memorial. File ref: 339/35423.

Panter Lt.-Col. George William MBE, MP. The second son of George William Panter MA, The Bawn, Foxrock, Co. Dublin. Educated at Sedbergh School, Cumberland; Trinity College, Dublin (entered 1912 and served with the OTC), and Sandhurst. Commissioned 16.12.1914, and joined 1st RIR 20.3.1915. Later returned home and served with 4th RIR. Joined 2nd RIR 8.12.1915. Mentioned in Despatches 1.1.1916. Transferred to the RFC as an observer 8.3.1916. Lt. (Flying Officer) 30.5.1916. His left arm was shot off in an air action. Served with the RFC/RAF 1916–18. Appointed T/Capt. and Adjutant 26.3.1917. Employed Air Ministry 1918. MBE 3.6.1919. Served 1919–35 with the RUR in Italy and the Sudan, reaching the rank of Lt.-Col. In 1936 he was residing at Clooneavin, Warrenpoint, Co. Down. *Quis Separabit*, May 1938: 'We were delighted to see Major G.W. Panter MBE, MP, successfully contested the Mourne Division for the Northern Ireland Parliament.' Resided at Enniskeen, Newcastle, Co. Down. Retired as MP 1945 and died the same year. His children are Capt. Michael Panter (born 16.9.1936), Coldstream Guards, and Mrs Eveleigh Brownlow (15.9.1938). Closed file.

Patterson Lt. Richard Ferrar. Born 29.1.1888. Applied for a commission 8.12.1915. Received an Honours Degree from Cambridge. Schoolmaster, height 6 foot, chest 38–42 inches, weight 198 pounds. Address, Kilmore, Holywood, Co. Down. He had served in Oundale School Corps with the rank of Sgt, attached Northumberland Regt, 1903–7. Gazetted to 20th RIR, 5.1.1916, and was ordered to report to the School of Instruction, Queen's University, Belfast, 11.1.1916. Served with 8th and 9th RIR. Promoted Lt. 6.7.1917. Joined B Coy, 8/9th RIR, 16.9.1917. Joined 2nd RIR, 7.2.1918. Discharged 5.2.1919, rated A1, single. File ref: 339/51847.

Payne Capt. James Cecil Warren MC. Born 9.10.1882, the son of Somers and Edith Payne, Leecarrow, Passage West, Co. Cork. His father was a barrister. Educated at Mostyn House School, Parkgate, Chester (1887–1900). He was a banker. Applied for a commission 15.1.1915. A letter of recommendation from Lt.-Col. C.J. Lynch, OC 4th Scottish Rifles, included a note: 'He is of sober habits, has plenty of tact and understands Irishmen thoroughly. I think he will be quite an efficient soldier in a very short time.' He had served with the Rifle Cadet Corps attached 1st Volunteer Bn Cheshire Regt while at Mostyn House. Commissioned to 4th CR 13.2.1915.

Joined 2nd RIR 23.3.1916. He was partially buried by a shell that knocked him out, 2.9.1916. He was sent down to the Base for a rest and rejoined from hospital, 12 September, but 'on returning to duty he found he could not carry on and was sent home.' To FA, 19 September, and embarked Boulogne–Dover aboard HS *St Patrick*, 26 September. Home address was his father's residence at Carrigmahon, Monkstown, Co. Cork. The MB at Caxton Hall, 5.10.1916, noted that after two strenuous months he was beginning to feel the strain. 'Is now sleeping better and not so easily tired. Needs a short period of leave only.' MB at Cork Military Hospital, 4.11.1916: 'He is still suffering from symptoms of shell-shock.' Promoted Lt. 7.11.1916. Reported to 4th CR at Crosshaven 2.12.1916. Joined 6th CR at Locre, 31.12.1916. Left this unit, 25.3.1917, with German Measles. Embarked Boulogne––Folkestone, 7 April, and granted leave. Rejoined 4th CR in June. Joined 5th CR at Moascar, Egypt, 20.9.1917, and served in Palestine. Embarked at Port Said, Egypt, aboard the *Ormonde*, 23.5.1918, and arrived Marseilles, 1.6.1918. Appointed a/Capt. 23.6.1918. MC, *London Gazette*, 4.10.1919, while serving with 5th CR: 'For conspicuous gallantry and devotion to duty. In the attack on Le Cateau on the night of the 10th/11th October, 1918, his company was detailed to mop up the town. He organized his parties and personally led the most dangerous enterprises, continuing his task right through the night and till several hours after dawn, when he had thoroughly satisfied himself that the enemy could give no further trouble to the remainder of the battalion.' Discharged 30.5.1919, rated A1, single. Last served with 3rd CR. His older brother, Capt. Robert Leslie Payne DSO, a Regular Officer in the CR, was known as a drunk after the war and was blamed as being partly responsible for the 1920 Connaught Rangers mutiny in India. File ref: 339/40579.

Peebles Major Arthur Edmondson. Commissioned 8.7.1907. Promoted Lt. 1.4.1909. Wounded while serving with 2nd RIR, 15.9.1914. Employed at the Army Ordnance Depot. Promoted Capt., 15.3.1915, and Major 26.6.1923. Closed file.

Perry-Ayscough Capt. Henry George Charles. Born 11.11.1875, the son of the Revd G.P. and the Hon. Mrs E.S. Perry-Ayscough. Joined the South Cork Militia (3rd RMF) as a 2/Lt., 12.5.1900. Seconded for service with the 2nd Bn, West African Frontier Force, North Nigeria Regt, 1900, taking part in the expedition against the Chief of Tawari, and awarded the medal with clasp. *Irish Times*, 11.10.1915: 'In 1901 he was in Northern Nigeria taking part in the operations against the Munshis and Yerghums.' Served during the South African War in operations in the Transvaal, receiving the Queen's Medal with four clasps. Appointed Capt. in the Fermanagh Militia (3rd R. Inniskilling Fusiliers) June 1903. Resigned July 1907 with the honorary rank of Lt. He was employed in the Chinese Postal Service as Deputy Postal Commissioner from 1906. His pay was about £1,400 per annum. Applied for a Regular commission 8.11.1914. Single, permanent address c/o Messrs. Holt & Co., 3 Whitehall Place, London SW. Correspondence address 58 Southover, Lewes, Sussex, which was the residence of his sister, Alice Augusta Catherine Perry-Ayscough. Appointed Capt. in 4th CR 14.11.1914. Joined 1st CR at La Beuvriere, France, 9.1.1915. Admitted to Lillers Clearing Hospital with malarial fever 15.4.1915. Embarked Boulogne–Dover on the *St Patrick* 19 May. MB at No. 3 London General Hospital, 22.5.1915, noted that the malaria had originated in West Africa during 1900. Reported to 4th CR at Bere Island, Co. Cork, 28.6.1915. Joined 2nd RIR 23.9.1915. Wounded and missing 25.9.1915. *Irish Times*, 21.6.1916: ' ... son of the late Revd Perry-Ayscough MA, rector of Brabourne, Kent. Grandson of the third Lord Congleton ... When last seen, by a brother officer, he was leading his men against the enemy trenches. He passed over the parapet and was then seen to fall, and since then nothing has been heard of him.' Estate valued at £3,569. Menin Gate Memorial. File ref: 339/13024.

Phillips Lt. Harry. Born in Dublin 3.2.1893. He was in Rhodesia at the outbreak of war, having lived there for sixteen years on his father's farm, and been educated at St George's. Enlisted as Pte 1043 in 16th Public Schools Bn, Middlesex Regt, 26.9.1914. Height 5 foot 9 inches, weight 151 pounds, chest 34–36 inches, correspondent (journalist); he had been under Legal Articles, 'expired mutual consent'. Next of kin was his sister Miss S. Phillips, later Mrs B.L. King, c/o B.L. King, Government Veterinary Surgeon, Umtale, Rhodesia. Applied for a commission 1.2.1915. Gazetted a 2/Lt. in 5th RIR 2.5.1915. Joined 2nd RIR, 26.11.1915. Wounded by a bullet in the chest 19.1.1916. Embarked Le Havre–Southampton, 4 March, aboard the *Copenhagen*. MB at Caxton Hall, 13 March: a bullet had gone through the right side of his chest and most of the fifth rib had been removed. Peritonitis set in and, from 26 January to 10 February, his condition was critical. He had also sustained about ten small wounds from shell fragments. He wrote, 19.3.1916, from Mrs Hall Walker's Home, Regent's Park, London, advising that the MB had recommended that he travel to Rhodesia when well enough. He asked for a wound gratuity saying he had a rib removed and 'All hopes for my recovery were abandoned'. A certificate from the British Red Cross Society, 85 Pall Mall, 8 May, stated that he had a weak heart and was currently in Mrs Hall Walker's Hospital, Sussex Lodge. Lady Dudley would arrange his free passage to Rhodesia if the WO granted permission to travel. Phillips requested permission to proceed to Rhodesia via Cape Town 17.5.1916. His address would be c/o Mr S. Phillips, Meirles Hotel, Salisbury, Rhodesia.

Returned 15.9.1916 and joined 5th RIR. Applied for duty in South Africa, 3.1.1917, stating that a MB had recommended him for garrison duty in a warm climate. The WO advised GOC Troops in Sierra Leone, that he had been selected for duty with a West African unit and would soon depart from the UK. The WO sent a rail warrant, with orders to embark aboard SS *Apapa* at Princess Landing Stage, Liverpool, 21 February. Granted rank of T/Lt. while serving with the West African Regt. Promoted Lt. 1.7.1917. Left Sierra Leone on leave and embarked on SS *Akabo*, 5.12.1919. Applied for repatriation to Bulawayo 9.2.1920. MB at Caxton Hall the same day: slight limitation of movement to his right chest and some enlargement of the heart. He also had malaria in Africa. Injury classed severe and permanent. Embarked on SS *Saxon*, 5.3.1920. Discharged at the end of 'standardized voyage period'

24.3.1920. Single, law student. Died 9.4.1972, as the result of a fall, 'Overseas case'. His pension was then £123 per annum. His wife was not named but her address was 11 Mapu Street, Tel Aviv, Israel. Listed in *British Jewry Book of Honour*. File ref: 339/48384.

Phillips Lt. Percy. Born 19.6.1893, the son of Alice Phillips, 137 Bowyer Road, Saltley, Birmingham. His father was English. Enlisted as Pte 3302 in the Warwickshire Yeomanry, 16.10.1915. Height 5 foot 10 inches, chest 31–35 inches, accountant. Applied for a commission 20.11.1915. Correspondence address, HQ, Warwickshire Yeomanry, 3rd Line, Warwick. Permanent address, 123 Great Charles Street, Birmingham. Married 27.12.1915. Admitted to No. 5 Officer Cadet Bn, Cambridge, 14.4.1916. Commissioned to 5th RIR 5.9.1916. Joined 2nd RIR 26.10.1917. Wounded by a shell splinter 6.12.1917. Embarked Le Havre–Southampton, 16.1.1918, and admitted to 1st Southern General Hospital, Edgbaston. Promoted Lt. 5.3.1918. Assumed duty under the Ministry of Labour 22.10.1918. Applied to the WO, 11.12.1918, for a temporary pension as the wound to his left leg still did not allow him to walk properly. Address, 52 Selborne Road, Handsworth Heath, Birmingham. Paid a civil salary by the Ministry of Labour from 1.1.1919 and ceased Army payments. Discharged 25.6.1919. MB at Birmingham 26.6.1919: very limited flexion to left knee; treatment ceased, no further progress; 30 per cent disability; permanently unfit for military service. Address, 101 Ravenshurst Road, Harborne, Birmingham. Placed on the retired list due to ill health 10.8.1919. MB at Manchester 24.10.1919: disability then rated at 40 per cent. Address, 13 Shavington Avenue, Hoole, Chester. Died 20.2.1981. Disability at that time 90 per cent. Annual pension £2,165, Dependency allowance £37.08, CAA £461.44, Comforts allowance £200.74, Age allowance £357.16. Widow, Mrs Alice Gertrude Phillips, 10 Martello House, 2 Western Road, Canford Cliffs, Poole, Dorset. File ref: 339/57120.

Pigot-Moodie 2/Lt. Charles Alfred. Born 30.5.1890 at Westbrooke, Rondebosch, Cape Province, South Africa, the younger son of George and Rosa Pigot-Moodie. Applied for a commission 10.8.1914. Single, law student, had served as a Trooper in Oxford University OTC Cavalry (left June 1913). Address 10 Cadogan Gardens, Middlesex. Height 6 foot, chest 35½–38 inches, weight 154 pounds. *Bond of Sacrifice*: 'He was educated at Windlesham House, Brighton, at Harrow, and Magdalen College, Oxford, and was gazetted to the [6th] Rifle Brigade in August, 1914. He was a member of the Conservative Club.' Joined 2nd RIR 5.12.1914. Killed in action 13.1.1915. *Burgoyne*: 'He was in H3, our dangerous trench, and the bullet entered his neck and came down through his nose and he only lived about seven minutes after he was hit. Poor fellow, a real good sort – brother in the Scots Greys. He was over the day before yesterday to see his brother. He was probably supervising the repairs of his trench. So silly, poor fellow, to expose himself in open day.' Probate was granted to his sister Minna Sophia Pigot-Moodie, Cadogan Gardens. Estate valued at £25,914. Kemmel Chateau Military Cemetery, Heuvelland, West-Vlaanderen, A.3. File ref: 339/16568.

Pollock Lt. Norman Varien. Born 27.4.1894, the son of Hugh McDowell Pollock JP, and Annie M. *née* Marshall, 11 College Gardens, Belfast. Educated at Felsted School, Campbell College, and in Switzerland. His father was a member of the Belfast Board of Trade, Belfast Chamber of Commerce, a city magistrate, and later became the first Minister of Finance in the Government of Northern Ireland. Enlisted in the RIR 15.8.1914. Applied for a commission 9.9.1914. Single, height 5 foot 10¾ inches, chest 33½–36½ inches, weight 149 pounds. Left 3rd RIR, 30.7.1915, embarked Dublin–Southampton the next day and promoted Lt. Joined 1st RIR 7.8.1915. Struck off the strength, 23.10.1915, suffering from catarrh and jaundice. Reported for duty with 3rd RIR, 29 November. Joined 2nd RIR 13.8.1916. Left unit, 27.1.1917, on leave to the UK. A letter, 5 February, from James Graham MD, advised that Pollock was suffering from acute bronchial catarrh. ADMS, Belfast District, to Military Hospital, Belfast, 16.2.1917: a medical officer was to be sent to visit Pollock at home. The report on the same day stated that his cardiac action was very poor and that he was unfit to travel. Later served as a Lt. in the Gold Coast Regt, West African Frontier Force. MB at Coomassie, 14.1.1918: Very thin and anaemic; poor physique. Numerous attacks of fever had left him lacking both physical and mental energy. Unsuitable for service in Africa and unlikely to recover there; evacuated to the UK. Certified fit for general service 30.10.1918. From this date he came under Army funds for pay. Retired on account of ill health 4.3.1919. File ref: 339/61870.

Poole 2/Lt. Frank Tarbett. Born 3.12.1886 at Bishop's Castle, the son of a gentleman farmer. Educated at Newport Grammar School, Shropshire. Enlisted as Pte 19930 in 3rd King's Shropshire Light Infantry 29.1.1916. Single, farmer, Church of England, height 5 foot 8 inches, chest 33–35 inches. Next of kin were his mother Ellen at Roslyn House, Wellington, Shropshire, and Mrs R.E. Reynolds, Barry Island, Pembrokeshire. Applied for a commission and admitted to No. 1 Cavalry Cadet Squadron at Netheravon, 2.8.1916. Appointed to a commission in 1st Reserve Regiment of Cavalry 19.12.1916. Joined North Irish Horse 29.1.1917. To 17th Tank Bn 25.8.1917 to 15.12.1917. Joined 2nd RIR 11.8.1918. Wounded (gassed) 14.8.1918 and returned to the UK. Discharged 10.2.1919, rated C1. Last served with 4th RIR. File ref: 339/67259.

Price Lt. Ernest Dickinson. Born 20.3.1894 at Cappagh House, Co. Tipperary, the second son of Ivon Henry Price MA, LL D, and Margaret Emily *née* Kinahan. He had five brothers and two sisters. His father was District Inspector, Royal Irish Constabulary. Educated at Mourne Grange School, Co. Down, and St Columba's College, Dublin. Entered Trinity College, Dublin, 1912, and served with the OTC. Applied for a commission 10.8.1914 and appointed to 3rd R. Irish. Height 5 foot 9¼ inches, chest 35–38 inches, weight 147 pounds, address Tyrone House, Nenagh, Co. Tipperary. Joined 2nd RIR 4.10.1915. Applied for a permanent commission 31.1.1916. OC's recommendation added that Price had 'carried out a bombing offensive against the enemy in a most thorough manner some two months ago'. Appointed 4.3.1916. Wounded and died of wounds 19.3.1916.

Irish Life, 9.6.1916: 'Two of his brothers are also in the Army, a third in the Dublin University OTC and a fourth a Royal Navy Cadet at Osborne.' At the outbreak of war, his father was Assistant Inspector General, RIC, residing at 109 North Circular Road, Dublin, and became Intelligence Officer at Irish Military Headquarters, acting as intermediary between the military authorities, the Under Secretary, Dublin Castle, RIC and DMP. Held the rank of H/Major. Mentioned in Despatches and awarded the DSO in early 1917. Retired with the Brevet of Lt.-Col. Later lived at Greystones, Co. Wicklow. Cabaret-Rouge British Cemetery, Souchez, Pas de Calais, XV.K.13. File ref: 339/37448.

Proctor Lt. Leslie Horner. Born 27.7.1896 at 35 Salisbury Street, Westoe, South Shields, the son of Thomas John and Jane Proctor *née* Horner. His father was an oil merchant. Educated at Tynemouth Municipal High School and worked for a firm of electrical power suppliers 1911–14. Served as Cpl 710 in the Tyne Electrical Engineers (TF) until his release, 29.8.1916. Entered the RMC in September 1916. Height 5 foot 7½ inches, chest 34–36½ inches, weight 140 pounds. Address was his parents' home at 25 Cleveland Avenue, North

Shields. Commissioned to the RASC 1.5.1917. Joined 2nd RIR, 6.10.1917, and left to join the RAF 19.6.1918. To School of Air Gunnery, 7 September, and to the BEF 6 October. Joined No. 10 Squadron as an Observer 12.10.1917. Killed accidentally 17.11.1918. The squadron record book noted the aircraft type and number as A.W.B. 4185. Pilot Lt. W.K. Salton, with Proctor as observer, left on a test flight at 15.30 hours and, at 15.45 hours, 'Machine dived into house in Menin. Personnel killed. Machine totally wrecked.' Kortrijk (St Jean) Communal Cemetery, West-Vlaanderen, A.20. File ref: 339/70456 and AIR1/1373/204/22/32.

Rainey 2/Lt. William. Born 28.1.1887 at 15 Christopher Street, Belfast, the son of Robert and Mary Rainey. Enlisted as Rfn 8391 in 2nd RIR 6.11.1906. Height 5 foot 5¾ inches, chest 34–36 inches, weight 126 pounds, labourer. Next of kin was his mother at 60 Brownlow Street, Belfast. He had an older brother Robert. Appointed L/Cpl 22.7.1908, and promoted Cpl 7.12.1910. Posted to the Depot 1.8.1911. Married Sarah Dempsey 25.12.1911. Posted to 2nd RIR 1.10.1913. Appointed L/Sgt 28.10.1913 and promoted Sgt 30.1.1914. Wounded, GSW jaw, and admitted No. 10 General Hospital 24.9.1914. To the UK, 27 September, and admitted American Women's War Relief Hospital at Paignton. Posted to 3rd RIR 14.11.1914. Rejoined 2nd RIR, 26.10.1915. Granted leave to UK 23.9.1916 and admitted to hospital in Belfast, 4 October, with neurasthenia. Discharged 30.10.1916. Commissioned 18.2.1917. Second-in-Command of C Coy. Killed in action 23.11.1917. His widow lived at 63 Bristol Street. Children: William Henry (born 11.10.1912), Sarah Adeline (26.1.1914), and Warren Dempsey (3.8.1917). Cambrai Memorial, Louverval, Nord. File ref: 339/92886.

Raymond Lt. Arthur Augustus. Born 27.10.1896 at Chaddesley Corbett, Worcestershire, the son of Capt. Henry Warner Raymond (RIR retired 1892) and Isabella Georgina Maud *née* Wetherall. Educated at Wellington College, Berkshire, where he was in the OTC, West Watling Park, Cambridgeshire, and Sandhurst. Gazetted a 2/Lt., 3rd RIR, 1.10.1914. Address Brockencote, Binghley Road, Wimbledon. Next of kin was his sister, Patricia Margaret Evelyn, at the same address. Joined 2nd RIR 5.12.1914. Left 3.1.1915, suffering from blood poisoning, and returned to the UK. He had been cut by barbed wire in the legs and face on the night of 27.12.1914. Resided with his aunt, Miss E.A. Raymond, at 213 Cromwell Road, London. Rejoined 2nd RIR about April 1915. His batman was 5051 Rfn F. Hill. Slightly wounded, 16 June, but remained at duty. Killed in action by shell fire 1.8.1915. See main text. Buried behind a stable at Lankhof Chateau. Memorial in St Cassian's, Chaddesley Corbett, Worcs. Menin Gate Memorial. File ref: 339/15789.

Rea Lt. Vivian Trevor Tighe. Born 17.8.1891 at Mendoza, Argentina, the only son of Henry Tighe and Clare Tighe Rea, 1 Glandore Park, Belfast. His father was a steamship broker, Lagan Navigation Company, and Vice-Consul in Belfast for the Netherlands and Argentina, 80 High Street, Belfast. His sister, Muriel Vere, died 31.5.1911 aged 12. Educated at Campbell College, 1905–8, and Queen's University, Belfast, BA 1910 (Honours in Logic, Metaphysics and History of Philosophy). Joined 4th RIR in 1911, commissioned 10.2.1912, and was promoted Lt. 20.2.1913. Minister of religion. Entered Trinity College, Dublin, 1912. Joined 2nd RIR 10.10.1914. Killed in action 25.10.1914.

Burgoyne: 'Rae in the 4th Battalion lost his life because he would leave his trench during the day instead of waiting till nightfall.' *Lowry*: 'Vivian Rea, who was an old friend of OTC days ... and how greatly did I admire his pluck and character.' *Bond of Sacrifice*: 'Lieutenant Rea had been Scoutmaster of the Bangor (Co. Down) Troop of the Boy Scouts, for several years the first troop in Ireland, and was Honorary Secretary of the Ulster Scout Council and an earnest worker among young men ... His Scouts and fellow students at Trinity College are erecting a memorial window at Bangor (Co. Down) Parish Church to perpetuate his name.'

Irish Times, 9.11.1914: ' ... was a native of Bangor, Co. Down ... and a grandson of the late Mr Hugh Rea, of Clifton Lodge, Belfast, and the Northern Bank, Londonderry ... when war broke out he had almost completed his Divinity course. He won the Theological Society's Medal this year.'

Co. Down Spectator, 20.11.1914: 'Lieutenant Rea was taken to a chateau at the end of the village of Neuve Chapelle, about three hundred yards behind the trenches. The medical officer saw that the wound was fatal, and that the wounded officer was rapidly sinking. Lieutenant Rea spoke to the doctor, and on learning his condition charged him with a reassuring message to those at home. Shortly after he lapsed into unconsciousness, and died almost without suffering. After nightfall his body was interred, together with that of Captain Reynolds, in the grounds of the chateau ... At three o'clock on the following morning, the 26th ult., the chateau, which had been used as a base by the staff, and the cellars of which were utilized as a hospital for the wounded, was shelled and set on fire by the enemy. It was necessary to hurriedly remove the wounded, and shortly afterwards the building was reduced to ruins ... He rendered valuable assistance as an interpreter when not in the trenches owing to his fluent knowledge of the French language.'

Single, intestate, gross value of estate £288. His father asked for details of the place and circumstances of death, stated he had six relatives serving in the Army, Navy and RFC, and that the lack of details about casualties was preventing people from enlisting. His wife's health and possibly life depended on getting details of their son's death. He later received information from Capt. Dixon. Mr Rea wrote again, 25.9.1915, stating the advice that he had from Major Daunt was that Vivian's body had remained uncovered at Neuve Chapelle Chateau and that, after a German bombardment, it was covered by the rubble. Since then he had been endeavouring to get to Neuve Chapelle but as there had been no advance and the trenches were still, he understood, just a short way from the village, he had been unable to get there. He had since been told that there was a graves commission who undertook burials at the front and enquired that, if this was correct, then how would he get in touch with them. He would cover any expenses. The matter had preyed on his mind and affected his health. WO gave the address for the graves registration commission in France. The father died 22.4.1936 aged 78 and his mother 26.5.1922 aged 58. Guards Cemetery, Windy Corner, Cuinchy, Pas de Calais, IX.G.6. File ref: 339/8176.

Reilly Lt. John MM. 7036 Sgt Reilly, 2nd RIR, awarded the Military Medal for gallantry during the operations at Messines 7–22.6.1917. Promoted 2/Lt., 23.6.1917, and Lt. 23.12.1918. Closed file.

Reynolds Capt. Thomas James. Joined 2nd RIR 10.10.1914. Shot by a sniper 25.10.1914. *Bond of Sacrifice*: 'the second son of the late Thomas James Reynolds CE, Ceylon, and of his first wife, Margaret, eldest daughter of the late Dr Slevin, Longford, Ireland, and nephew of the late Deputy Surgeon-General Reynolds. He was born in Ceylon on the 19th January 1871, and educated at Terenure College, County Dublin; and Belvedere College, Dublin, joining the Militia in April 1900. He was employed with the Gold Coast Constabulary and the King's African Rifles from April 1900 to October 1902, during which time he took part in operations in Ashanti, for which he received the medal. He was promoted Lieutenant in

February 1902, and Captain in the Royal Irish Rifles in May 1909. From March 1910 to January 1911 he was an Adjutant of the Territorial Force, and in May 1914 was appointed Adjutant of the 3rd (Reserve) Battalion of his regiment. Captain Reynolds ... was a member of the Leinster Cricket Club, Dublin. He was unmarried.'

Irish Times, 30.10.1914: 'When appointed a Lieutenant in the R.D. Fusiliers he went to India where he eventually became attached to the Staff ... Captain Reynolds took out his degrees as an engineer in the College of Science, Dublin.' *Irish Times*, 4.11.1914: 'A solemn Memorial Service ... was held yesterday morning in St Mary's Roman Catholic Church, Rathmines. The Bishop of Canea presided, and the Solemn Requiem Mass was celebrated by Revd F.F. O'Loughlin CC (Chaplain to the Forces and cousin of the deceased officer). The 3rd Battalion Royal Irish Rifles, of which Captain Reynolds was the Adjutant, was represented by Lt.-Col. McCammond, 16 officers and 200 men. The 6th Battalion was represented by Lt.-Col. Bradford, 6 officers and 100 men. The Sacred Chant was impressively rendered by a special choir of priests.' Guards Cemetery, Windy Corner, Cuinchy, Pas de Calais, VIII.F.46. File missing.

Ricks 2/Lt. Leo Joseph. Born 21.12.1892 at Monasterevan, Co. Kildare, the son of Mr V.D. Ricks. Enlisted at Calgary as Pte 434001 in the Canadian Expeditionary Force, 30.12.1914. Single, salesman, height 6 foot, chest 34½–39 inches, blue eyes, light brown hair, Roman Catholic. He had served with the 103rd Regt at Calgary 1912–14. Promoted from Sgt in the CEF to 2/Lt. in 3rd RMF. Joined 2nd RIR 20.1.1917. D Coy. *Witherow*: 'He was a magnificently built Canadian standing over six feet in height, but the most depressing and gloomy companion one could wish for. The most shunned man in France was the man who was perpetually in a gloomy frame of mind. Things with him were always in a bad way or the Germans were going to attack, he was sure of it. This was a terrible sector, in fact nothing was right. He simply got on ones nerves until one longed to kick him out of the dugout. He was eventually got rid of by sending him to a school behind the lines to act as an instructor.' To UK, 15.2.1919, for repatriation to Canada. Closed file. Details from the National Archives of Canada, file ref: RG150, Assession 1992–93/166, Box 8263–42.

Robb Capt. George Cyril. Born 9.12.1894, the son of John Robb, *Tivoli*, Castle Avenue, Clontarf, Dublin. Attended Campbell College until 1912, then went to Trinity College, Dublin. He was a medical student at the time of his enlistment and a cadet in the OTC. Applied for a commission, 5.8.1914, and was gazetted a 2/Lt. in 3rd RIR, 15.8.1914. Promoted Lt., 8.5.1915, and joined 1st RIR, 18.5.1915. Returned to the UK suffering with pleurisy, 5 November. Joined 2nd RIR, 13.8.1916. Developed acute rheumatism, returned to the UK, 3 October, and was not declared fit again until 20.4.1917. Rejoined 1st RIR and took command of C Coy, 20.8.1917. Wounded, 19 September, GSW right forearm, and rejoined from hospital, 5 October, as an a/Capt. Wounded again, 30 November, by shell fire and transferred to England. Demobilized, 25.2.1918, and remobilized, 27.8.1918. Rejoined 1st RIR 7.12.1918, transferred to 12th RIR 22.2.1919. Discharged, 19.11.1919, and returned to Trinity College, receiving his B.Dent.Sc. and MA in 1922. Enrolled in the Officers Emergency Reserve 27.10.1938. At that time he was practising as a dental surgeon and residing at 22 Hoghton Street, Southport, Lancs. File ref: 339/47225.

Roddy Lt.-Col. Edwin L. Served with 2nd Cheshire Regt in India and was a Lt. by 1899. When the battalion embarked from Bombay, 16.11.1914, Capt. Roddy remained at Jubbulpore with 19 men to form a depot for the instruction of Territorials. Later rejoined 2nd Cheshires.

Their regimental history, *Ever Glorious* by Bernard Rigby, recorded: 'On 3rd October [1915], the Germans launched a full-scale attack along the length of 84th Bde line, but were repulsed. Major Edwin Roddy led a counter-attack, the men having fixed their bayonets. They were swept back. Bde HQ ordered fresh attacks, but the men had now gone beyond the point of endurance.' Took temporary command of 13th Cheshires at Beauval, 26.10.1916. Joined 2nd RIR as Second-in-Command 30.12.1916. To 172nd Bde 2.4.1917. Later served with 11th Cheshires. From 5.8.1918 he was in temporary command of 1st Cheshires for about a month. File missing.

Roe Lt. George Sweetman. Born 4.4.1880 at 108 Blatchingham Road, Hove, Sussex, the son of Fleet Surgeon Peter Mitchell Roe (listed as deceased on the birth certificate) and Georgina *née* Humfrey. *Belfast News Letter*, 19.1.1918, reported that he was the nephew of the late Revd Dr T.W. Roe, for many years vicar at Ballymacarrett. Attested at Valcartier as Pte 23354 in the Canadian Expeditionary Force, 19.9.1914. Single, clerk, height 5 foot 10¾ inches, chest 33–37 inches, blue eyes, brown hair, Salvation Army. He had served two years with the Coldstream Guards. Next of kin was his brother, Revd W.A. Roe, Bawnboy, Belturbet, Co. Cavan. Applied for a commission 5.10.1915, while he was serving as a Cpl in 1st Canadian Contingent. Gazetted a 2/Lt. in 6th RIR 9.12.1915. Joined 7th RIR 1.1.1917. To hospital with trench fever 11.2.1917. Later developed bronchitis but was certified fit to return to his unit 12.6.1917. Detailed by 7th RIR to meet 2nd RIR and conduct them to his battalion camp where both units were amalgamated, 14.11.1917. Wounded 3.12.1917 when he was blown up by a shell and fell on the duckboard, hitting his left knee against the edge. He was unable to walk properly and limped back to Bn HQ. Relinquished his commission on account of disability (sinovitis of the knee) 14.10.1918. Address 70 Wellington Road, Dublin. By April 1919 he was residing at 669 Elgin Avenue, Winnipeg. A wound gratuity was refused as it was slight, following on a severe injury which he received before being commissioned. File ref: 339/49584.

Rosborough Major James. Born Ferry Quay Street, Londonderry, 26.3.1870, the son of Andrew and Jane Rosborough *née* Babington. Educated at Foyle College, and Trinity College, Dublin, where he gained his BA in 1894. Also did 'one year's law course'. Commissioned in 3rd RIR Militia 8.6.1893. Height 5 foot 8½ inches. Promoted Lt. 10.6.1895. Posted to 6th RIR (Louth Rifles) Militia 3.6.1896. Mobilized during the South African War when he spent nine months home service at Sheffield and Aldershot 1899–1900. H/Capt. 18.10.1900. In West Africa and Gambia with the 2nd Bn Central Africa Regt, 1901: expedition against Fodi Kabba, medal and clasp. East Africa and Somaliland, clasp, 1902–4, with 1st King's African Rifles. Company Commander with 1st KAR at Nairobi and Nandi, East Africa, 1905–6. Mentioned in Despatches 18.9.1906. Seconded to the Louth Rifles 1906–8. Served Zanzibar and Nyasaland until 1910. Married Erdie Agnes McKinstry 21.1.1914. Mobilized at Holywood, 5.8.1914, and appointed second-in-command of 3rd RIR. Promoted Major 12.9.1914. His daughter, Dorothy Maureen Rosemary, was born 17.11.1914. Conducted 3rd RIR's 29th Reinforcement to Le Havre, 13.4.1915.

See Capt. Bowen-Colthurst. Sir John Maxwell, CiC Forces in Ireland, to WO, 2.7.1916: reported into the inquiry on the responsibility of Rosborough whilst in temporary command of 3rd RIR, 24–30.4.1916, during the absence of Lt.-Col. McCammond on sick leave. Rosborough did not effectively exercise his command during this period. Even allowing for the natural excitement due to the rebellion, the constant and anxious work, and want of rest, there was an utter absence of control, so much so, that it was possible for armed parties to leave barracks on missions without the knowledge of the CO. Adjutant S.V. Morgan had stated that at 10.40 p.m., 25.4.1916, Capt. Bowen-Colthurst had left the barracks with 25 NCOs and men, taking Sheehy-Skeffington with them. Morgan immediately reported this to Rosborough, who did nothing and stated that he could not recall this report. 'Major Rosborough is apparently rather deaf, and his commanding officer states that he is slow to appreciate events and take action, though in other respects he is a good officer. I consider that events show that Major Rosborough is inert, wanting in quick and sound judgement, and unfitted to command troops. I therefore recommend that Major James Rosborough ... be placed forthwith on the Retired List.'

An undated sheet signed by Col. H.V. Cowan CB, CVO, AAG Irish Command, stated that 3rd RIR was one of the best two, if not the best, of the 28 draft-finding battalions in Ireland. Credit was due to Col. McCammond who stated that he was assisted by Rosborough. Cowan supported Rosborough claiming that he thought he should be retained and that confidential reports on him are satisfactory. A file cover note, 6.7.1916: 'This is not a case for disciplinary action. Will you please deal with it?' Rosborough gave evidence at the court martial of Capt. Bowen-Colthurst and before the subsequent Simon Commission. He sent a letter of appeal to OC 3rd RIR. A letter to Lord Crewe from Revd Joseph McKinstry (Rosborough's father-in-law and a Presbyterian minister at Randalstown), 11 July, pleaded the case. WO to CiC Ireland: Rosborough must resign his commission but can retain his rank. Rosborough's resignation was dated 28 July. His wife petitioned HM The Queen on her husband's behalf. Rosborough wrote to the WO, 2 August, requesting a meeting with the Military Secretary. Address at the time was 20 College Gardens, Belfast. He was advised that the Military Secretary would see him on any afternoon. Revd McKinstry wrote to Andrew Bonar Law MP, 11 August, referring to a meeting they had the previous day and again pleaded the case. Bonar Law sent the letter to Lloyd George adding 'Carson is also interested in the case of Major Rosborough'. WO submitted a petition to the King: 'It is not recommended that Your Majesty may be pleased to issue any special instructions with regard to this petition'. McKinstry wrote directly to Lloyd George. Bonar Law proposed that no action be taken until the special commission in Ireland had reported. A memo dated 11 September advised that the commission of inquiry held by Sir John A. Simon KCVO, KC, MP, had completely cleared Rosborough's character regarding the affair and enquired whether any military employment had yet been found for him. WO to CiC Ireland: 28 September, stated that any action 'is suspended for the moment'; 6 November, the order to resign was cancelled.

Posted to 2nd RIR and joined 24.12.1916. Major A.V. Weir, 3rd RIR, in a letter to Capt. Bowen-Colthurst, 22.12.1916: 'Major Rosborough went out to the front last week. We went to see him off at the station. He was quite cheery but Mrs R says she does not think he will be able to remain long as he is not strong.' Struck off the strength of 2nd RIR, 25.3.1917: 'To be employed on the status of a PB Officer within the 1st Army area'. Assumed the duties of Town Major at Bully-Grenay the next day. Returned to the UK 23.10.1917. To 30th Liverpool Regt at Rugby 1.3.1919 and went with them to France 19.8.1919. Posted temporarily to Canterbury the same day, still shown as attached 30th Bn. Mentioned in WO Communiqué, September 1919. Proceeded to the UK for demobilization 27.1.1920. Education Officer / Instructor with 10th Hussars 23.10.1920. His father-in-law wrote to Sir Edward Carson KC, MP, thanking him for arranging this position. Applications by Rosborough for a permanent position as an Education Officer were rejected. Notes referring to his CO, Lt.-Col. Seymour, 10th Hussars, state that his opinion was that Rosborough was not up to the job: NCOs had been leaving his classes and going to an Army Schoolmaster. He wrote to the WO, 11.12.1920, applying for a position as Courts Martial Officer, but was advised that there were no positions of any sort available for him. A summary of service at this time gave his next of kin, other than his wife, as his sister Charlotte Babington Rosborough, Bellview, Buncrana, Co. Donegal. Interests were golf, agriculture and gardening. Discharged from the RUR, rated A1, 20.4.1921. Applied to become a senior cadet in the Royal Irish Constabulary in November 1921. There is a seven-page letter on his file to Stephen Walsh MP, Secretary of State for War, 22.7.1922, claiming compensation, which was rejected out of hand.

Resided 1931–49 at Dunrandal, 2 Norman Road, Kingsway, Hove, Sussex. Emigrated to Australia about 1950 and lived at 25 Billyard Avenue, Elizabeth Bay, Sydney, New South Wales. Died at the War Veterans Home, Narrabeen, NSW, 30.7.1957, and cremated two days later. Estate left to his son, Colin Babington Clarke Rosborough (commissioned King's Dragoon Guards, 12.10.1945), with a small annuity to his former wife, Lady Sarah Agnes Rosenthal. File ref: 339/27301.

Rose Major Richard De Ros MC, DL. *Thom's Directory* for 1912 lists him as a Deputy Lieutenant and previous High Sheriff for County Limerick, residing at Ardhue House, Limerick. Joined 6th RIR 20.10.1914. T/Lt. 28.10.1914, Capt. 13.1.1915, T/Major 9.9.1915 to 2.10.1915. Joined at Lemnos and took command of 6th RIR from 10.8.1915 to 30.9.1915. Commanded D Coy. Left unit 7.7.1916 and embarked Salonika–Malta 11 July. At this time he was unmarried. MB, 3 August: enteric fever. Embarked Malta–Southampton, 23 August, aboard the *Braemar Castle*. Joined 3rd RIR 24.12.1916.

Joined 2nd RIR, 17.6.1917, and appointed a/Major. MC awarded for gallantry during the Westhoek operations of June 1917, *London Gazette*, 8.1.1918: 'For conspicuous gallantry and devotion to duty. When temporarily in command of his battalion he assembled and led it to the assault with great dash and determination. The spirit and drive of this battalion in the assault and the splendid way in which they captured their objectives and threw out an outpost line close to our barrage deserved the utmost praise.' Granted sick leave 8.12.1917. Mentioned in Despatches 21.12.1917. Also resided at Dough, Lahinch, Co. Clare (1918 Absent Voters List). Rejoined 2nd RIR 14.1.1918. Temporarily in command 26.1.1918. Wounded by shell fragments 22 March: compound impacted fracture of skull (forehead, bone fragments removed from brain); fractured jaw; various penetrating wounds to chest. Embarked Boulogne–Dover, 16 April, and admitted to Lady Ridley's Hospital for Officers, 10 Carlton House Terrace, London. Awarded £150 wound gratuity. Bar to MC, *London Gazette*, 13.9.1918: 'For conspicuous gallantry and devotion to duty in command of the battalion. He made personal reconnaissances of the position after several officers were wounded – and was eventually severely wounded when attempting to regain touch with the unit on his left.'

WO advised by 2nd Scottish General Hospital, Edinburgh, 17.10.1918, that Rose had been instructed to continue treatment. Returned home, permanently unfit for military service, 13 December. Relinquished his commission 9.1.1919. Awarded a pension of £200 for the year to 21.3.1920. MB at Dublin, 13.2.1920, noted various scars but stated 'He is not suffering from Sciatica and there are no other ailments.' Pension of £100 awarded for the next year. Died at his home at Ardhue 16.1.1939. *Irish Times*, 17.1.1939: 'Funeral leaving … for London (for cremation). No flowers. Subscriptions instead to Peoples Dispensary for Sick Animals of the Poor.' File ref: 339/12582.

Ross 2/Lt. Kenneth. Born 1890, the son of George Harrison and Henrietta Matilda Ross, Cultra, Co. Down. Educated at Portora Royal School, Eastman's Naval School at Winchester, Queen's University Belfast (B.Sc.) and London University. He worked for six months at Woolwich Arsenal as an Analytical and Research Chemist. Single. Commissioned in 4th RIR

15.8.1914. Joined 2nd RIR with his brother, Melbourne, 28.6.1915. On the night of 15.8.1915 his patrol engaged a German patrol, killing one and capturing two of the 236th Regt. Wounded and missing 25.9.1915. Melbourne was killed in the same attack. Rfn Bevan: 'There were two officers, brothers, named Ross. One who belongs to A Coy was wounded, and the other who belonged to D Coy was killed. He was hit by a shell as we were retiring and I know for a fact that he was killed as I was quite near him at the time.' 6891 Sgt MacDermott: 'There were two brothers of this name in the battalion and one was killed and the other was wounded and missing. The one who was killed was killed in the first line of German trenches and we had to retire so we had to leave his body behind. There was no-one on our flanks and so it was impossible to hold the trench any longer and we left it at night ... The one who was wounded was left in the same line as Lt. Ross and he also had to be left there at night when we retired.' 9058 Sgt Graham: 'This officer was with me in the charge on 25 September at Hooge. I distinctly saw him killed. The shell burst amongst us and he was killed and buried by it. We had to retire so no more could be said about him but I am convinced that there is no hope of ever seeing him again in this world.' L/Cpl P. Oglesby, POW at Limburg, testified that he had seen Ross killed. 8157 Cpl Taggart: 'This officer was wounded in the charge of September 25th. He went on in the charge in spite of his wound and then was shot by machine-gun and riddled with bullets. He was buried at Ypres Graveyard I am most sure although I could not swear to it. He was leading his platoon and doing exceedingly well at the time. Everyone said that.' Estate administered by his father at William Street South, Belfast, and Cultra, Managing Director of W.A. Ross & Son, Aerated Water Manufacturers. Menin Gate Memorial. File ref: 339/18341.

Ross 2/Lt. Melbourne. Born 30.1.1885, brother of Kenneth, above. Educated at Portora Royal School. Member of Freemason Lodge 381, Holywood. Single, manufacturer (engaged in the family business). Gazetted to 4th RIR 15.8.1914. Joined 2nd RIR 28.6.1915. Killed in action 25.9.1915. 9410 T. Hills, D Coy, said that he had seen Lt. Ross blown to pieces. 'I was quite certain he was killed. It was early morning just before daylight just as the advance was beginning. I was only seven or eight yards from him. I have seen his people in Belfast and told them this.' The gross value of the estate was £1,508.

Industries of the North One Hundred Years Ago: 'W.A. Ross & Co., one of the foremost firms in Ireland. Founded 1879 by Mr W.A. Ross "who has been ably assisted from the first by his son". Products known in all parts of the world. Company works built over the artesian wells; spring well sunk to 226 feet. Many of the patents created by Mr W.A. Ross ... Produced a high class raspberry vinegar, prepared from berries from Ross's own garden at Craigavad, Cultra, Holywood.' Menin Gate Memorial. File ref: 339/18342.

Rossborough Lt. Reginald Allen. Commissioned into 3rd RIR 27.2.1915, and joined 2nd RIR 8.8.1915. To hospital, sick, 5.9.1915, and invalided home. Promoted Lt. 4.12.1915. Also served with the RMF. Closed file.

Rule Lt. Clifford. Born in the parish of Sherwood Forest, Nottingham, 22.11.1889, the son of Thomas and Elizabeth Mary Rule *née* Ross, 10 Crown Street, Sneinton, Nottingham. His father was an insurance agent. Educated at Wellington School, Somerset (January 1902–April 1903), and The County Secondary School, Brockley, Hilly Fields, London. Enlisted as Rfn 18709 in 13th RIR 14.9.1914. Height 5 foot 5⅝ inches, chest 32½–35 inches, weight 132 pounds, Baptist, clerk. Next of kin was his mother at The Moate, Holywood, Co. Down. Appointed L/Cpl 31.10.1914, and promoted Sgt 11.5.1915. To BEF France 3.10.1915. Applied for a commission, 1.3.1916. Occupation 'Director and Tea Merchant'. Posted to the Depot, 7 July, and to 20th RIR, 17 October. To No. 9 Officer Cadet Bn at Gailes, 5.5.1917, and to 18th RIR 12.7.1917. Commissioned to 3rd RIR 29.8.1917. Joined 2nd RIR 21.10.1917. Accidentally wounded, 1 November, but remained at duty. See main text. French Croix de Guerre a l'Ordre Brigade 11.12.1918. Posted to 12th RIR 25.2.1919. Promoted Lt. 28.2.1919. Discharged 17.9.1919, rated A, single, 'Tea Taster'. Relinquished his commission 1.4.1920. He wrote to the WO, 25.4.1938, asking for a record of his service for a job application. Address, 29 Cobham Road, Wood Green, London. Repeated his request, 6.5.1938, saying he was anxious for this information as he had been frequently unemployed. File ref: 339/102988.

Ryan Major George Julian DSO. Born 18.9.1878 at Tenby, Pembrokeshire, Wales, the second son of Col. George Ryan, RAMS, of Ashby Cottage, Ryde, Isle of Wight, and Louisa Clotilda, daughter of Major N. Colthurst-Brabazon, 83rd Regt. Educated at Elizabeth College, Guernsey, and was at the United Service College, Westward Ho!, North Devon from 1893. Entered Sandhurst in 1895. Commissioned to 2nd RMF, 8.9.1897. Promoted Lt. 11.3.1899. Served in the South African War, 1899–1902, and was employed with the Mounted Infantry in the advance on Kimberley, including the actions at Belmont and Modder River; operations in the Transvaal, June to 29.11.1900; operations in Cape Colony; Transvaal to March 1901; operations in Orange River Colony to June 1901. Mentioned in Despatches, *London Gazette*, 10.9.1901. Received the Queen's Medal with five clasps. Awarded the DSO, *London Gazette*, 27.9.1901: 'In recognition of services during the operations in South Africa.' Promoted Capt. 9.6.1906. Employed with the Egyptian Army, 6.2.1903 to 15.2.1910. Served in the Soudan, 1905, during operations against the Nyam Nyam tribes in the Bahr-el-Ghazal Province. *Bond of Sacrifice*: 'Here he did good work, and the Sirdar, Sir Reginald Windgate, brought his name to the notice of the Government.' Mentioned in Despatches, *London Gazette*, 18.5.1906, and received the Egyptian Medal with clasp.

In 1906 he took part in the operations at Talodi, in Southern Kordofan (clasp to Egyptian Medal). Participated and was wounded in operations in the Soudan, 1908, in the Blue Nile Province, with the force sent to punish the murderers of the Deputy Inspector and Police Commandant. He received the Brevet of Major, 7.11.1908, the Order of the Medjidieh and the Egyptian Medal with two clasps. Joined 2nd RMF in 1910. He served in France from 22.8.1914, and was made T/Lt.-Col., 21.1.1915. Took temporary command of 2nd RIR, 26–30.10.1914, then returned to 2nd RMF. Killed in action 23.1.1915. Mentioned in Despatches 22.6.1915. Unmarried. Guards Cemetery, Windy Corner, Pas de Calais, IV.B.45. File missing.

Scott Lt. Robert Clement MC. Commissioned to 18th RIR 23.8.1915. Served with 9th RIR. Promoted Lt. 1.7.1917. Joined 2nd RIR 6.2.1918. MC, *London Gazette*, 31.1.1919: 'For conspicuous gallantry in the Messines sector during the operations of 5th–6th September, 1918. The company commander having become a casualty, he immediately assumed command, and led his men with great determination through very heavy fire, and repelled a local counterattack. When the objective was taken, a party of the enemy which had been holding out in a portion of trench were driven out by him. His gallant leadership was a fine example to his men.' Posted to 12th RIR, 22.2.1919. Closed file.

Seth-Smith Major Hugh Eric Seth MC. Born 23.11.1887 at St Margaret's Mansions, Victoria Street, Westminster, the son of Charles Edward and Florence Maude Seth-Smith *née* Stevenson. His father was a Barrister. Educated at Malvern College and Brasenose, Oxford.

Member of the North of Ireland Cricket and Hockey Clubs. Applied for a commission 7.10.1914. BA from Oxford, schoolmaster at Rockport Preparatory School, Craigavad, Co. Down, and had served in the Inns of Court OTC. Permanent address, The Old Rectory, Bletchingley, Surrey. This was the home of Revd A.H. De Foutraine, Rector of Bletchingley. Gazetted 21.10.1914. Joined 2nd RIR and posted to B Coy 11.7.1915. Wounded, 9.8.1915, while in charge of a digging party. Embarked Calais–Dover aboard the *Dieppe*, 20 August. GSW right thigh, flesh wound. Reported to 4th RIR 27.10.1915. Promoted Lt. 15.3.1916. Joined 7th RIR 1.11.1916. Appointed Staff Capt., 25th Infantry Bde. MC, *London Gazette*, 1.1.1918. Disembarked at Boulogne with HQ 16th Division 31.7.1918. Admitted to No. 24 FA and No. 39 Stationary Hospital, 15.2.1919, with a corneal ulcer. Demobilized 10.4.1919, rated A1, single, address Bletchingley. After the war, he and H.W. Weaving toured Northern Ireland on a motor cycle and sidecar searching for a suitable house and estate to start a prep school. In 1921 they founded Elm Park School, Killylea, Co. Armagh, which lasted until 1954 when the remaining boys joined Rockport School. Died in 1946. File ref: 339/35424.

Sharkie Lt. Joseph Henry Faussett. The second son of Mr Joseph E. Sharkie, Park Avenue, Omagh, Co. Tyrone, and Mrs Sharkie, principal of Sion Mills National School. Church of England. Entered Trinity College, Dublin, 1914, as an engineering student. He and his brother Fred William Sharkie had been members of 2nd Bn, Tyrone Regt, UVF, and their father 'acted as camp secretary to the regiment at the historic camp held at Baronscourt about two years ago'. Commissioned to 4th RIR, 20.7.1915, from the OTC of Trinity College. Joined 2nd RIR 21.4.1916. Wounded in the right thigh, 13.5.1916, but remained at duty. Later joined 6th RIR at Salonika, 13.2.1917. Wounded in the head, hand, and thigh by shell fire at Kalendra Wood, 25.2.1917. Promoted Lt. 1.7.1917. Fred, born 12.9.1891, served with the 1st Canadian Contingent. Details in *Irish Times*, 19.5.1916, and *Belfast News Letter*, 7.3.1917. Received his MA in 1921. Also MAI, MICE, MIWE, M.Cons.E. Resided at 38 St Ives Park, Ringwood, Hants. Closed file.

Silver Capt. Bernard James. Born 15.6.1892 and was a motor engineer. Commissioned to 4th R. Inniskilling Fusiliers 3.7.1912. Promoted Lt. 20.12.1913. Attached to 2nd RIR in September 1914. Left 16.11.1914 suffering from influenza and chronic rheumatism, and embarked Boulogne–Southampton aboard the *Carisbrooke Castle*, 24 November. Reported to 4th Inniskillings at Buncrana, 27 December. Promoted Capt. 31.3.1916. Served in India and Burma from March 1916 to April 1920. He wrote to the Adjutant of 4th Inniskillings, August 1920, asking to be allowed to resign his commission as he then had a civil employment in Karachi and would be unable to attend annual training. Advised that he was discharged from No. 2 Armoured Motor Bde 31.3.1920. Rated A1, married. Address, 14 The Mall, Rawalpindi. Resignation approved 20.1.1921. On 22.5.1939 he asked if there were any positions available. Said he commanded No. 2 Armoured Motor Bde and had many years experience in motors and wireless. Any position considered, rank not important. Address 5 Luxmi Road, Dehra Dun. File ref: 339/9268.

Sinclair Lt. Herbert Darbishire. Born 30.5.1894, the son of Saul Sinclair, Inglewood, Adelaide Park, Belfast. Brother of 2/Lt. G.S. Sinclair, killed in action with 1st RIR. Nephew of Col. Thomas Sinclair CB, MD, FRCS, and John Sinclair of the Belfast Harbour Board. Educated at the Royal Belfast Academical Institution, and the Ecole de Commerce, Neuchâtel. Applied for a commission, 21.11.1914, having served 18 months in the UVF. Height 5 foot 9 inches, weight 144 pounds, clerk, fluent in French and German. Commissioned to 5th RIR

2.12.1914. Joined 2nd RIR 10.6.1916. Left 24.7.1916 and returned to the UK suffering from bronchitis. Joined C Coy, 1st RIR 18.12.1917. Severely wounded in the head and right forearm by a grenade when the Germans raided his trench, 1.3.1918. Admitted to No. 2 Red Cross Hospital at Rouen and later transferred to 3rd Southern General Hospital, Oxford. Moved to the Cottage Hospital, Southport, 2 May. Transferred to the Irish Command Depot at Tipperary, 2.8.1918. Underwent a further operation at the Central Military Hospital, Belfast, 4.9.1918. Demobilized 28.1.1919, rated C1. Later lived at 100 Broomielaw, Glasgow.

Sloane 2/Lt. William Ritchie. Commissioned to the RIR 26.6.1918. Joined 2nd RIR during October 1918. Posted to 12th RIR. FGCM, 30.5.1919: 'Drunkenness and scandalous conduct.' Found guilty and cashiered from the Army, *London Gazette*, 26.7.1919. Closed file.

Smiles Capt. William Alan. Born 29.4.1885, the son of William Holmes Smiles and Lucy Smiles *née* Dorling, Westbank, Strandtown, Belfast. His father, who died in 1904, founded (in addition to the Royal County Down Golf Club at Newcastle) with Gustav Wolff (Harland & Wolff) the Belfast Ropework Company, which was the largest in the world. His mother was half-sister to Mrs Beeton, the famous Victorian cookery expert. He had seven brothers and three sisters. *Irish Times*, 22.7.1916: 'Captain W. Alan Smiles ... a grandson of the late Dr Samuel Smiles, the celebrated author of *Self-help* and other books.' With Rossall Cadet Corps 1897–9. Qualified as a solicitor 1905 and practised at Belfast and Larne. Formerly Deputy Crown Solicitor, Co. Mayo, in 1908. Applied for a commission 15.8.1914. Height 6 foot 2 inches, chest 32–36 inches, weight 140 pounds. Commissioned to 9th RIR 23.9.1914, promoted Lt. 23.11.1914 and Capt. 1.1.1915. To 17th RIR 9.11.1915. Joined C Coy, 2nd RIR, 13.3.1916. Killed in action 9.7.1916. 10192 Rfn C. McDonagh, D Coy, reported that Smiles was killed instantly by a shell. 'I saw his body lying in the German 2nd line trench at about 9 a.m. I do not know whether the body was buried.' 2/Lt. J. Clarke saw him 'lying dead in a trench with shrapnel wounds in his back'.

Gross value of his estate was £1,382. Probate granted to his widowed mother, his sister Aileen, and his brother John Holmes Smiles, 37 Bedford Avenue, High Barnet. Thiepval Memorial.

Irish Times, 22.8.1917, reported the death of his brother: '2/Lt. Samuel Smiles, Royal Irish Rifles ... He came from South America to join the Army, and received his commission in December 1916, from Queen's University OTC, proceeding to the front in May last. Mr Smiles, who was 35 years of age, was a fine athlete, and won numerous golf prizes, including the Argentine Centenary Cup. He was a partner in the firm of M'Ewan and Smiles, Buenos Aires.' File ref: 339/14328.

Smylie Capt. Cecil Victor. Born 24.8.1891, the third son of Hugh and Elizabeth Ann Smylie *née* Hennessey, 17 Agincourt Avenue, Belfast. His father was a chartered accountant at 13 Donegall Square North, Belfast. Educated at Methodist College, Belfast. *Irish Times*, 18.7.1916: 'Before joining the Army he was engaged in his father's business as an articled clerk.' Enlisted 14.9.1914. Height 5 foot 6½ inches, chest 37–39½ inches, weight 158 pounds, fresh complexion, blue eyes, brown hair. Applied for a commission 12.4.1915 and appointed to 4th RIR 25.4.1915. Address Cromer, Cadogan Park, Belfast. Joined 2nd RIR 20.4.1916. Wounded 10.7.1916. MB at Belfast, 9.11.1916: suffering from headaches and rheumatic pains in his back, worsened by marching. Severe insomnia, bronchitis, and coughs. Promoted Lt. 1.7.1917. Posted to 2nd RIR from July 1917 until he returned home in February 1918 on being transferred to the MGC. Later served with 7th Bn MGC in the eastern war theatre.

Demobilized 16.11.1919. At that time his father's address was Castleavery, Adelaide Park, Belfast. His brother, Hugh, also served with the RIR.

Belfast Telegraph, 8.8.1960: 'The death took place yesterday of Captain Cecil Victor Smylie, Deramore Park, Belfast, after a very brief illness. Captain Smylie was a fellow of the Institute of Chartered Accountants in Ireland and senior partner in the firm of Messrs. Hugh Smylie and Sons. He was honorary treasurer of the Belfast Cathedral, and also of the Ulster branch of the Irish Rugby Football Union, of which he was a past president. Among many of his other activities he was a joint honorary secretary of the Lord Mayor of Belfast Coal Relief Fund, and a member of the executive committee of the "Not Forgotten" Association and secretary of the Northern Ireland War Memorial Building Fund. Captain Smylie was well known in rugby circles, being connected with Collegians, of which he was treasurer and a past president. He had also been captain of Collegians' I, II, III and IV 15's during his youth. He was a past president, one of the founders and an original secretary of Methodist College Old Boys' Association. During World War 1 he served with the YCV [14th RIR] and was presently honorary treasurer of the Belfast branch of the British Legion. Captain Smylie, who was a well-known Freemason, was WM of Eldon LOL No. 7 and secretary of the Arthur Square Masonic Hall trustees. He is survived by his wife, Mrs Edna Smylie, and his daughter, Patricia. Captain Smylie realized an ambition in seeing the commencement of the Northern Ireland War Memorial Building in Belfast. He had been secretary of the fund since the end of World War II.' File ref: 339/55782.

Smyth Capt. Charles Devaywis. Served in the South African War, 1902, during operations in Orange River Colony, April to 31 May, receiving the Queen's Medal with three clasps. Promoted 2/Lt. 28.1.1903, Lt. 9.7.1906, and Capt. 13.5.1910. Retired on appointment to 5th RIR, 23.11.1912. Joined 2nd RIR 10.10.1914 and was wounded three days later. Promoted Capt., 25.3.1916, and relinquished his commission that day on account of ill health. File missing.

Smyth Capt. George Bostall Jenkinson. Born 23.7.1890 at Milltown House, Lenaderg, Banbridge, the second son of James Davis Smyth and Charlotte Anna Smyth. The family was engaged in the linen industry. Church of Ireland. Member of Freemason Lodge 18, Newry. Commissioned to 5th RIR, 26.8.1914.

Smyths of the Bann: 'He was named after his grandfather George Bostall Jenkinson, an American from Newark, New Jersey. He was educated at Portora Royal School, Enniskillen (1903 to 1908) and Trinity College, Dublin, where he was a member of the Dublin Universities Officers' Training Corps, having the rank of Cadet. George studied for the Bar and was admitted as a student of King's Inns in the Michaelmas term of 1909, graduating from Trinity College Dublin in 1913 ... his enlistment papers stating that he was 5 foot 8 inches tall, weighed 10 stone, had chest measurements of 34 inches minimum and 36½ inches maximum ... Whilst serving as a 2nd Lieutenant with the 6th Battalion of the Royal Irish Rifles at Anzac on the Gallipoli Peninsula on 9 August 1915 he was severely wounded. His ankle was badly smashed by a bullet and his right leg was hit six times, 4 inches above his ankle having a considerable area stripped of skin. As a result he was laid up until the spring of 1916 and was considered unfit for service until 24 July 1916. He left Alexandria, Egypt, on 2 October 1915 on board the ship *Letitia*, bound for England.'

Promoted Lt. 1.7.1915. *Irish Times*, 23.8.1915: 'He is at present in the 19th Hospital, Alexandria, suffering from leg wounds. Lieutenant Smyth is a member of the Irish Bar, and went to the North-East Circuit.' Joined 7th RIR, 30.4.1917, and 2nd RIR 14.11.1917. Wounded 23.11.1917.

Smyths of the Bann: 'He was promoted to Acting Captain on 31st August 1917 and on 18th December he left Rouen for Southampton, arriving on the 19th and was conveyed to the 3rd Southern General Hospital in Oxford. On the same day he was transferred to the Sommerville Hospital suffering from bronchitis. He was discharged fit for home service on 12th January 1918 and given three weeks' sick leave, before returning to active service in France where he was killed in action near Courtrai on 22nd October 1918.' Rejoined 2nd RIR 30.8.1918 and took temporary command 1.10.1918. Mentioned in Despatches 28.12.1918.

Siblings were Charlotte (1882–1956), Douglas (1884–1960), and Ruth (1887–1960). Among many relations that served in the war were his first cousins: Lt.-Col. G.R.F. Smyth DSO, who was RIC Divisional Commander in Munster during the War of Independence and was assassinated by the IRA, 17.7.1920; Major G.O.S. Smyth DSO, MC, was a member of the 'Cairo Gang' intelligence unit during the War of Independence and was killed in Drumcondra while trying to capture Sean Tracey and Dan Breen, 12.10.1920. Harlebeke New British Cemetery, VII.B.17. File ref: 339/11541.

Somers Capt. William MC. Born 9.9.1889. Educated at Methodist College, Belfast. Member of Freemason Lodge 377, Newcastle. Applied for a commission 8.1.1915. Unmarried, cotton wholesaler, address 23 Suffolk Street, Dublin. Commissioned to 17th RIR 20.5.1915. Promoted Lt. 20.5.1915, and Capt. 2.7.1916. MC awarded while serving with 11th RIR. *London Gazette*, 14.9.1917: 'For conspicuous gallantry and devotion to duty when commanding his company. He engaged in personal combat with the enemy when mopping up the front line. His company captured over 100 prisoners and accounted for many others, as well as two machine guns and two trench mortars.' Also served with the Tank Corps. Joined 2nd RIR during October 1918. Struck off the strength on appointment as 107th Infantry Bde Intelligence Officer. Also served with 12th RIR. Resided at Sunnybank, Dundonald. File ref: 339/23612.

Soutry Lt.-Col. Trevor Lloyd Blunden DSO. Born 23.3.1878. Commissioned in the RIR 18.10.1899. Served in the South African War 1899–1902; was Mentioned in Despatches, received the Queen's Medal with three clasps and the King's Medal with two clasps. Captured by the Boers at Reddersburg but later freed by Lord Robert's advance. Promoted Lt. 1.3.1902, and Capt. 28.6.1908. *Belfast News Letter*, 7.10.1905, reported on the unveiling of the RIR Boer War Memorial at Belfast the previous day, when he formed part of the 2nd RIR guard of honour. He was called Capt. Thom in Lucy's book: 'He was a huge, tanned fellow, with a black moustache, quite handsome and distinguished looking. He seldom spoke, but he had a very critical eye, which did more to quell and hold us. In all matters he was extremely strict and very just. He was English.' Slightly wounded in the arm while serving with A Coy, 2nd RIR, 14.9.1914. Promoted Major 1.9.1915. DSO *London Gazette*, 1.1.1917: 'For distinguished service in the field.' Brevet Lt.-Col. 3.6.1918. Mentioned in Despatches 22.6.1915, 4.1.1917, 15.5.1917, 11.12.1917, and 30.5.1918. French Croix de Guerre (Silver Star) 17.8.1918. Italian Order of St Maurice and St Lazarus, Cavalier, 12.9.1918. File missing.

Spedding Major Charles Rodney Wolfe DSO. Born 25.4.1871, the only son of Capt. Benjamin Henry Spedding MRCS, LRCP, Edinburgh, and Mrs H.B. Spedding, of Bangor, Co. Down. Educated at St Columba's College, and Trinity College, Dublin. Commissioned into the RIR from the Militia, 23.12.1893. *Belfast News Letter*, 7.10.1905, described him as 'a well-known Belfast gentleman'. Promoted Lt. 6.10.1896, Capt. 1.3.1902, and Major 2.11.1911.

The Distinguished Service Order: 'He served in the South African War, 1899–1902, as Station Staff Officer [September to December 1900]; as Adjutant, 9th Bn Mounted Infantry,

28 December 1900 to 25 April 1901; as Staff Officer to General Bruce Hamilton's column of Mounted Infantry, 1901–2. He was present at operations in Orange Free State, March to May 1900; operations in Orange River Colony, May to November 1900; operations in Cape Colony, south of Orange River, 1899–1900; operations in the Transvaal, April 1901 to 31 May 1902; operations in Orange River Colony, 30 November 1900 to April 1901. He was Mentioned in Despatches (*London Gazette*, 10 September 1901, and 20 July 1902); received the Queen's medal with three clasps, the King's medal with two clasps, and was created a Companion of the Distinguished Service Order (*London Gazette*, 27 September 1901): "Charles Rodney Spedding, Lt., Royal Irish Rifles. In recognition of services during the operations in South Africa." He was invested by the King, 24 October 1902. He was promoted to Captain, 1 March 1902; was ADC to Major-General, Infantry Bde, Malta, 16 June 1906; commanded the 5th Bn Mounted Infantry, Harrismith, South Africa, 1912.'

Bond of Sacrifice: 'He was Chief Staff Officer after this [April 1901] to the late Major-General (then Colonel) Ingoville Williams, who commanded an Australian column until the end of the South African War ... Major Spedding married [1907] Constance Mildred Edith, younger daughter of Lt.-Col. T.G. Cuthell, late 13th Hussars, Goldhill Lodge, Surrey, and left a son and two daughters ... He was also a very clever trainer, always trained his own ponies, and won many races in India, Malta and South Africa.'

Missing in action 19.9.1914. Mentioned in Despatches 9.12.1914. His widow later resided at *Hawani*, Totland Bay, Isle of Wight. *Burgoyne*: 'During the battle of the Aisne he went back with a party to fetch rations up; that was the last the battalion saw of him. But he had to cross a bridge which was continually under hostile shell fire. Someone saw him urging his men across one by one, and shells bursting about, and all fear he was most probably knocked into the river and killed or drowned.' La Ferte-sous-Jouarre Memorial, Seine-et-Marne. File missing.

Spence Lt. Charles Henry. Member of Freemason Lodge 54, Belfast. Joined the BEF as Sgt 6952, 14.8.1914, and served until November 1914. Also served 25.5.1917 to 1.8.1917, and 25.5.1918 to 23.10.1918. Promoted to 2/Lt. in 2nd RIR, 18.1.1918. He was wounded during the war. Closed file.

Sprague Lt.-Col. Louis Charles. Commissioned 7.12.1895, promoted Lt. 27.11.1897, Capt. 10.12.1902, Major 11.12.1914, and T/Lt.-Col. 14.10.1915. Joined 2nd RIR 14.10.1915 and took command. In temporary command of 74th Infantry Bde 15.9.1916. Relinquished command of 2nd RIR on being transferred to England. Army List December 1918 shows him attached to 84th Training Reserve Bn. File missing.

Stanley 2/Lt. John Joseph. Born 23.9.1896 at Newcastle-on-Tyne, the son of John Joseph and Dorsey Stanley, 10 Seymour King Building, Kenley Street, Holland Park, London. Enlisted as Pte 23517 in 3rd Durham Light Infantry 25.1.1915. Single, optician, Church of England, height 5 foot 7¼ inches, chest 32–36 inches, weight 126 pounds. Posted to 2nd DLI, France, 26.1.1916. Commissioned in the field from the rank of a/CSM and joined 2nd RIR 18.9.1917. Killed in action 9.12.1917. Gross value of the estate was £165. His father was 11970 a/RSM on the Supernumerary strength of the Depot, DLI, with an address of Drill Hall, The Green, Sunderland. Fifteen Ravine British Cemetery, Villers-Plouich, Nord, II.C.1. File ref: 339/126053.

Stein 2/Lt. John Francis. Born 5.10.1885 at 7 Corrig Avenue, Kingstown, Co. Dublin, the only son of Robert Francis and Mary Josephine Stein *née* McDonald, Woodview, Blackrock,

Co. Dublin. Held an engineering diploma from the Royal College of Science, Ireland. Applied for a commission 11.5.1915. Single, height 5 foot 10½ inches, chest 36¼–38 inches, weight 148 pounds, vision 6/36 and 6/6, wore glasses. *Irish Times*, 5.10.1916: 'He was educated at Beaumont College, S.J., near Windsor, and, having completed his course as a civil engineer, he went out to practice his profession in Canada. Shortly after the commencement of the war he resigned his business in Canada, and returned to Ireland to join the Army. Having been three times rejected by a Medical Board on account of heart trouble, he finally succeeded in getting passed by another Board, and joined the Royal Irish Rifles about fifteen months ago, and having trained at Dollymount and gone through the Rebellion in Dublin in Easter week, he left for France in July last. While stationed at Rouen he was again medically examined, and two Boards declared that he was unfit, and he was offered a non–combatant military appoint-ment, but Lieutenant Stein insisted on being examined by another Medical Board, which passed him, and he was allowed to go to the front, where he met his death in action.' Commissioned to 3rd RIR 3.7.1915. Joined 2nd RIR 8.7.1916. Killed in action 28.9.1916. He had four sis-ters, two of whom were nuns at the Dominican Convent, Merrion Avenue, Blackrock. His widowed mother complained at the delay in receiving his effects but a file note states 'Irish kit refused admission to Ireland by GOC', presumably due to the state of the country after the Rising. Buried at Paisley Avenue Cemetery, Thiepval Wood, but in 1920 his remains were exhumed and interred at Lonsdale Cemetery, Authuile, Somme, IX.E.5. File ref: 339/55779.

Stewart Lt. James Alexander. Born 5.7.1892. Educated at Clongowes Wood College, Co. Kildare, 1904–9. Insurance Inspector for Scottish Provident Institution. Applied for a com-mission 5.9.1914. Addresses, 3 Upper Sherrard Street, Dublin. Height 5 foot 9¼ inches, chest 32–35 inches, weight 115 pounds, Roman Catholic, single. A recommendation from F. Conway Dwyer MD, FRCSI, President of the Royal College of Surgeons in Ireland, said that Stewart's grandfather had been a Cambridge Professor; the family was 'highly esteemed in Dublin and have always occupied a high social position.' Stewart was of the highest charac-ter and intelligence. His file also contains a recommendation from the Right Hon. Charles A. O'Connor KC, Master of the Rolls in Ireland. Commissioned to 3rd RIR. Promoted Lt., 31.7.1915.

Joined 2nd RIR 7.10.1915. Wounded 10.12.1915: he had been shot through the thigh. Gangrene of the foot necessitated its amputation 1.1.1916. A secondary haemorrhage caused amputation through the middle third of his thigh. Embarked Boulogne–Dover aboard HS *St David*, 22.1.1916. Home address, 59 Dartmouth Square, Dublin. Supplied with an arti-ficial leg at Queen Mary's Hospital, Roehampton. His address, as of 20.7.1916, was Ashville, Thormanby Road, Howth, Co. Dublin. Reported to 3rd RIR 5.8.1916. Eligible for a wound pension of £100 per annum. Reported for duty with No. 12 District Infantry Records Office, Cork, 16.1.1917. A memo from Lt.-Col. McNish, 5.4.1918, stated that Stewart was very will-ing and keen to do anything asked of him, but he was far too slow at handling paperwork to work in a records office: 'he is very slow indeed and work is delayed in consequence'. Stewart had said he would like a position of Messing Officer, which he had done before coming to Cork. A memo, 1.6.1918, from Col. E.V.D. Pearse, Records No. 12 District, was full of praise for Stewart and wanted him retained. He might have been a bit slow but he was conscientious, painstaking, and accurate. He had a slight speech impediment and did not always express himself clearly, so it was easy to misunderstand his ability until you knew him. 'He is by no means deficient in ability.' Col. C.C. East, Commanding No. 12 District, wrote to HQ Irish Command, 4.6.1918, withdrawing the previous recommendation. Discharged 25.3.1919, rated B3, married.

He wrote to the WO, 11.2.1938, from 62 Crag Path, Aldeburgh, Suffolk, requesting a summary of his military service as his son was applying for a scholarship. His address, 1.11.1957, was 1st Floor Flat, 34 Netherhall Gardens, Hampstead, London, when he requested another summary of his service as 'unfortunately, I have lost my medals'. File ref: 339/4141.

Stewart Lt. James Noel Greer MC. Born 25.12.1890 at Belfast, the son of Margaret Stewart. Educated at Belfast Mercantile College. Employed as a clerk with Belfast Corporation (at discharge he described himself as an Electrical Engineer). He had served as No. 2636 in the Royal Navy for six months (enlisted for 12 years, 25.5.1909, but purchased his release). Character marked 'VG', Stoker 2nd Class, HMS *Vivid*. Enlisted as Pte 1048 in the North Irish Horse 28.8.1914. Height 5 foot 7 inches, chest 32–35 inches, weight 124 pounds, Church of England. Promoted Cpl 1.12.1914. His will left £100 to Miss Agnes McIlwaine of Helen's Bay, Co. Down, and the remainder of his estate to his mother. To BEF, France, 1.5.1915, and attached to No. 9 Squadron RFC 14.1.1916. Reverted to Pte at his own request, 8.9.1916. Attached to 33rd Division for temporary duty 13.9.1916. Applied for a commission 13.2.1917. Correspondence address D Squadron, 1st North Irish Horse, 7th Corps Cavalry, BEF France. Home address was his widowed mother's residence at 19 Jubilee Avenue, Antrim Road, Belfast. Returned to the UK 26.2.1917. To No. 2 Officer Cadet Bn at Pembroke College, Cambridge, 5 May. Gazetted a 2/Lt. in 3rd RIR 29.8.1917. Joined 2nd RIR 21.10.1917.

Belfast News Letter, 3.12.1917, reported that he was wounded 23.11.1917. Left unit 9.2.1918. Embarked Rouen–Southampton, 21 February; cause of return, ingrown toenail and abscess on his left foot. Rejoined 2nd RIR 17.6.1918. MC for bravery on 29.7.1918 (see D.B. Walkington), *London Gazette*, 11.10.1918: 'For conspicuous gallantry and devotion to duty while leading a patrol. His patrol crawled out some 500 yards in daylight and surprised and rushed an enemy post of 12 men, killing 4, wounding 2, and making 4 prisoners. After bombing a small dug-out he then withdrew his patrol skilfully under heavy machine-gun fire. He showed great dash and disregard of danger.' Joined 2nd RIR cadre at Dunkirk 24.3.1919. Discharged 9.4.1919, rated A1, single. Enrolled in the Army Reserve of Officers, 15.7.1940, to be discharged due to age 25.12.1950. File ref: 339/105205.

Stoker Capt. Douglas Hyndford. Born 14.6.1893 at Carrigaline, Co. Cork, the son of Edward Beck and Elizabeth Morris Stoker *née* McOstrich, of Leecarrow, Passage West, Co. Cork. His father was a butter merchant. Educated at Dixon's Army College, Cork, and by private tuition. Applied for a commission 7.12.1913. Address, Clifton Grange, Douglas, Cork. Appointed 2/Lt., 4th R. Irish, 24.1.1914, and promoted Lt., 26.12.1914. Joined 2nd RIR 4.10.1915, went to hospital with dyspepsia the following day, and returned to the UK, 10.10.1915. Reported to 4th R. Irish at Queenstown, 20.3.1916. His elder brother, Lt. Edward Alexander Morris Stoker, 6th R. Irish, was killed in action 12.9.1916. Returned to France 23.10.1916 but was not considered fit. Placed on Base duties. Struck off the establishment of 6th R. Irish, 16.7.1917, and posted as a/Capt. with No. 118 POW Coy, France, attached to the Labour Corps 28.3.1918. Discharged 2.11.1919, rated A, single.

His address was c/o Kidd & Co., Grafton Street, Dublin, when he wrote to the WO, 21.6.1921. He had to leave his home in Cork a few months after he returned from France because of 'the recent trouble in Ireland ... my people in Cork were warned that I was not to return'. He was making arrangements to move to England and thought it advisable to resign his commission. He had not received his medals and thought that correspondence to his home was being interfered with. Resigned his commission on disbandment of the R. Irish,

14.7.1922. By 1926 Kidd & Co. had gone into liquidation and his new address was 78 Harcourt Street, Dublin. File ref: 339/10361.

Stone 2/Lt. Herbert William Degatau. Born 26.5.1879 at 8 Jew's Walk, Sydenham, Kent, the son of Waldemar and Alma Louise Schmidt *née* Degatau. His father was an underwriter. Educated at Westminster School and gained Oxford–Cambridge Higher Certificate 1896. He was a Pte in the Shanghai Volunteer Corps 1899–1904 and served during the Boxer Rebellion of 1900, receiving the China Medal. Enlisted as Pte PS/3673 in 19th R. Fusiliers, 14.12.1914, under the name Schmidt. Applied for a commission 30.4.1915. Single, permanent address, Uplands, Burk's Road, Beaconsfield, Bucks. Changed his surname to Stone by Deed Poll, 5.5.1915. Commissioned to 4th CR 25.5.1915. Admitted to No. 6 Red Cross Hospital, Etaples, with influenza, 5.1.1916. Joined 2nd RIR 8.2.1916. Killed by shell fire 26.4.1916. Probate was granted to his sister, Ethel Alma Schmidt. Gross value of the estate £718. Ecoivres Military Cemetery, Mont-St Eloy, Pas de Calais, I.G.15. File ref: 339/50572.

Strohm 2/Lt. Edward Charles. Born 23.1.1882 at Hanover Square. Educated at United Westminster and Kent County College, Herne Bay. Married Winifred Dora Eastman at Lewisham, 12.6.1907. There is a letter to Strohm in his file, dated June 1916, written on a page from a Field Service notebook from what appears to be OC 16th RIR (Lt.-Col. J. Leader): 'I was really glad to hear from you but find I can't advise anything. If you were at home in England you could of course get in at once. I would take you as a cadet in my Bn with pleasure. By the time you get this, however, we will have finished the war probably, but I don't know how many of us will witness the end.' 16th RIR were preparing for the Somme attack of 1.7.1916. Applied for a commission 27 July. 'Broker (Vancouver BC)', height 5 foot 8 inches, chest 36–39 inches, weight 155 pounds, father deceased. Permanent address, c/o Chappelle & Co. Ltd., 50 New Bond Street, London; correspondence address, 53 Thorn Beach Road, Catford, London.

Enlisted as Pte 8186 (later 762216) in 28th London Regt (Artists Rifles) 8.8.1916. His wife was at Chase, British Columbia. Reapplied for a commission 10.8.1916. Correspondence address, A Coy 2nd Artists Rifles (2/28th London Regt), Hare Hall Camp, Gidea Park, Essex. Posted to No. 15 Officer Cadet Bn, 30.9.1916. Transferred to the MGC Officer Cadet Bn, 6.12.1916. In March 1917 OC MGC OCB recommended he return to his former unit. Commissioned to 4th RIR 29.5.1917. Joined No. 9 Platoon, C Coy, 2nd RIR 7.8.1917. Wounded and taken prisoner at Cugny 24.3.1918. His post-war debriefing explained: The fog lifted about 10 a.m., weather fine, visibility fair. He was in support of C Coy about 50 yards behind the front line. Enemy 'planes passing over but no sign of our planes'. German machine guns were established on both flanks and the enemy advanced in short rushes. The British fire was very damaging all morning. In the afternoon enemy trench mortars came forward. About 2 p.m. the enemy were spotted about 2,000 yards to the right and well to the rear. About 3 p.m. they were also well to the rear on the left. Enemy trench mortar and machine gun fire was persistent by then. His men were running low on ammunition. At about 4 p.m. the enemy put down a very heavy bombardment which lasted half an hour. He saw an officer and about 20 men falling back which gave the enemy the opportunity to break through, which they did in a few minutes. The enemy seemed to pass straight through them and they were mopped-up by the second wave. 'I was taken about 5 p.m. I had no ammunition and what remained of my men had none.' Exonerated of blame for his capture. Repatriated 4.12.1918, rated A1. Discharged 13.3.1919. File ref: 339/69183.

Stuart Lt. Thomas Moore MBE. The eldest son of Mr R.C. Stuart, 87 Woodvale Road, Belfast. His father's business address was 13 Lombard Street, Belfast. Member of Freemason Lodge 421, Belfast. Enlisted as Pte 14/15984 in 14th RIR. Joined the BEF 6.10.1915. Promoted 2/Lt., 13th RIR, 20.11.1916. Wounded in action 23.11.1917 while serving with 2nd RIR. Admitted to No.20 General Hospital, GSW to the left forearm and gas poisoning. *Belfast News Letter*, 19.4.1918: 'Lt. Stuart was one of the original Young Citizen Volunteers and joined with his brother Jack (now in the Tank Corps) in Sept 1914 – both seeing service with the Ulster Division. Lt Stuart received his commission for services rendered in the Thiepval battle. He had previously been employed in the Rates Office in Belfast City Hall.' Promoted Lt. 20.5.1918. With 12th RIR in Germany 1919. Silver War Badge, 13.6.1919. Later MBE (Civil), Defence, and War Medal 1939–45, Queen Elizabeth II Coronation Medal 1953. Closed file.

Swaine 2/Lt. Henry Poyntz. Born 31.3.1890 at The Citadel, Cairo, Egypt, the elder son of Capt. Arthur Thomas Swaine, RIR (retired as a Col., 28.10.1904), and Cordelia Florence, only daughter of Hon. Justice Smith. His parents had married in September 1886 at Halifax, Nova Scotia. Privately educated at Ryde (1899–1904), Marlborough College (1904–7), Mr Kirschoffer in Camberley (from September 1907), and Mr Hodgson in Germany (from March 1908). Applied for the RMC 11.4.1908. Family address, The Cottage, Bowlhead Green, Milford, Surrey. Commissioned to the RIR 5.10.1910. Killed in action 15.9.1914. Single and intestate. At that time his parents were at Morris Lodge, Farnham, Surrey. RMC Memorial. La Ferte-sous-Jouarre Memorial, Seine-et-Marne. File ref: 339/7749.

Teele Capt. William Beaconsfield MC. Born 23.5.1886 at Enniskillen, Co. Fermanagh. Educated at Portora Royal School 1898–1904. Commissioned to 5th RIR 1904. Regular 2/Lt. 2nd RIR 9.4.1910, Lt. 12.9.1914, and Capt. 1.9.1915. Served with 6th RIR at Gallipoli. Attached to 3rd RIR until he was posted to 5th RIR, 1.2.1916. Joined 2nd RIR 17.8.1916. Posted to 10th Cheshire Regt for duty, 18.12.1916. Rejoined 2nd RIR 14.4.1917. To 25th Division 20.4.1917. Rejoined 2nd RIR 7.8.1918. MC, *London Gazette*, 31.1.1919: 'For gallantry leading his company in the Messines sector on 6th September, 1918. This officer commanded his company, which suffered heavy casualties early in the fight, but he continued to push his company on until the objective was reached. He gave early information of the enemy's presence on the left flank of the battalion. He quickly reorganized his company and destroyed any attempt made of local counter-attack by the enemy.'

He was married and resided at Enniskillen. Died after a brief illness 25.3.1975. *Blackthorn*, 1975: 'He was granted a regular commission in 1910 and joined the 2nd Bn with which he went to France in 1914 ... He was transferred to the 1st Bn The Royal Ulster Rifles in 1921 and served in Germany until he retired in 1925. He was appointed Area Commandant of the Ulster Special Constabulary, Co. Fermanagh, in 1934 and when the Home Guard was formed he became the Adjutant and Quartermaster of the 2nd Fermanagh Bn [1939–45].' Closed file.

Templeton Major & QM George. Served in the South African War, 1899–1902, during operations in Cape Colony 1899, Orange River Colony June–November 1900 and November 1900 to 3 May 1902. King's Medal with two clasps according to *Services of Military Officers 1920*. H/Lt., 3rd RIR, 17.9.1902. Army List 1912 shows QM 4th RIR. H/Capt. 17.9.1912. Joined 2nd RIR 6.1.1915. Struck off the strength 15.1.1916. Promoted Major 1.7.1917. QM 3rd RIR 1917–19. On retired pay by 1920. Closed file.

Thomas Capt. Edmond Meysey. Born in Carlow, 9.11.1886, the son of Jocelyn H.W. and Mary Wilhelmina Thomas, Belmont, Carlow. Baptized at the Anglican Church, Carlow, 28.2.1897. Educated at Stanmore Park, Middlesex, and Cheltenham College 1899–1904. He was a 2/Lt. in the Carlow Rifles, 8th (Militia Battalion) KRRC, when it was disbanded in 1908. Commissioned into the RIR 27.5.1908. Height 5 foot 8½ inches. Promoted Lt. 8.3.1910. Awarded King George V Coronation Medal 1911. In Lucy's book he was called Lt. Lomas: 'He was a gentle, loveable man, who, in contrast to the captain made a point of knowing us all, of asking us intimate questions, and who had the unusual and welcome attribute of praising us warmly when we did well; consequently we would have died for him, whereas we would have merely killed for the captain ... Lt. Lomas, our company second-in-command, had been taken away to look after the regimental transport. We missed him badly, our last Regular officer, and one of the best.'

Embarked for France with A Coy, 2nd RIR. Left unit, 20.12.1914, and went to hospital: rheumatism of the feet and his heart had been affected. Embarked Boulogne–Southampton aboard the *Carisbrooke Castle*, 24.12.1914. Address: Chequers Court, Butler's Cross, Berks. Appointed T/Capt. 18.3.1915. He wrote from Belmont, 29.5.1915, saying that he had no orders to report anywhere. Told to report at once to GOC, Western Division, at Belfast for light duty. Reported to 36th Division and was attached as Adjutant to 12th R. Inniskilling Fusiliers at Newtownards. Rejoined 2nd RIR 29.10.1916. To 75th Bde for attachment 28.12.1916 to 27.3.1917. Left 2nd RIR for the Staff of 2nd Army HQ 1.5.1917, where he remained as it joined the Army of the Rhine. Embarked Calais–Folkestone 27.3.1919 and given two months leave.

He wrote, 28.5.1919, from Rugeley Camp, to the Adjutant of 3rd RIR asking to be appointed Adjutant of 5th RIR when that battalion was reformed. A note, 31 May, gave his father as the next of kin; an alternative was his maternal aunt, Lady Boileau, Ketteringham Park, Wymondham, Norfolk. Mentioned in Despatches 9.7.1919. Applied to resign from the service, 22.10.1919, as he wished to assist his father in the management of his estate. Retirement approved 29.11.1919. Resided at 5 Solent Avenue, Lymington, Hants. Died at Lymington 3.1.1974. File ref: 339/7079.

Thompson Lt. Robert Albert Joseph. Born 8.7.1893, the son of William Sydney Thompson, Ballinacarriga, Kilworth, Co. Cork. Joined the Royal Irish Constabulary as Constable 66711 in 1912. Posted to Donegal 5.2.1913. Enlisted as Pte 6212 in 2nd Irish Guards 16.12.1914. Address, Letterdracawara, Co. Donegal. Church of England, height 5 foot 8¾ inches, chest 35–38 inches. To the BEF as a L/Sgt, 14.9.1915. Wounded, GSW left leg, 25.12.1915 and returned to the UK. Applied for a commission, 11.7.1916, while serving with 3rd Irish Guards, Warley Barracks, Essex. Single. Reported to No. 5 Officer Cadet Bn at Cambridge 9.8.1916. Commissioned to 3rd RIF 22.11.1916. Posted to 7th RIR 6.2.1917. Wounded 3.8.1917 when he was blown up and his ankle was badly contused. Joined 2nd RIR 14.11.1917. To England and struck off the strength, 29.11.1917, as his old wound was troubling him. Spent almost five months in hospital and rejoined 3rd RIF at Rugeley, 11.6.1918. Promoted Lt. 22.5.1918. In December 1918 he was described as 'a most useful officer with ability and professional knowledge, power to maintain discipline, tact and capacity for training'. Appointed a/Capt. from 4.11.1919 to 9.12.1919 while he commanded 69th Chinese Labour Coy, Labour Corps. Disembodied 3.3.1920, rated A, married, farmer. Address Shelfield House, Shelfield near Walsall. His son, Robert Henderson Thompson, 34 Stormont Park, Belfast, requested details of his file in 1991. File ref: 339/68014.

Thompson Capt. Thomas John Chichester Conyngham DSO. Son of John Thompson, Newry Street, Markethill, Co. Armagh. He was an assistant in Messrs J. Robb & Co., Castle Place, Belfast. Commissioned to 4th RIF, 25.3.1915, through Queen's University OTC, and attached 2nd RIF. Embarked for France 1.10.1915. Joined 2nd RIR 13.10.1915. Promoted Lt. 1916. Wounded 26.4.1916 but remained at duty. Promoted to Capt. An enquiry was held, 9.10.1916, into an injury he received in the field the previous night. He was with C Coy when he got a wound in his foot from a rusty bayonet. This was adjudged an accident. Rejoined 2nd RIR 27.10.1916.

War Diary 7.6.1917: 'It was then observed that the 9th L.N. Lancs were meeting with a stubborn resistance at Middle Farm. To assist in overcoming this opposition … Capt. T.J.C.C. Thompson, immediately pushed forward so as to work round the farm on the right flank and attack the enemy from his rear. Owing to the gallantry of OC B Coy this operation was entirely successful and the enemy resistance at the farm was completely broken.' See main text. For this action, in which he was wounded in the head, he was awarded the DSO, *London Gazette*, 16.8.1917: 'For conspicuous gallantry and devotion to duty. He led his company with great dash and success to their objective, afterwards by his initiative rendering valuable assistance to another unit by co-operating on their flank. The spirit and dash of his company were largely due to his personality and gallantry on this, as on all other occasions.'

Joined 36th Base Depot 25.8.1917, posted to 1st RIF 31.8.1917, then rejoined 2nd RIR 9.9.1917. Took command 22.3.1918. Killed in action 24.3.1918, aged 26. See main text. Twice Mentioned in Despatches. Capt. Bryans was a POW at Camp No. 41, 1.7.1918, when he wrote that Thompson was killed 300 yards south of Cugny. Correspondence relating to Letters of Administration was dealt with by the Revd J.W. Auchmuty, The Rectory, Markethill, as the father was 'illiterate'. Estate of £188. Thomas's sister, Mrs Annie Gardiner, Dinnahara, Markethill, advised that she had heard that her father got the money. She enquired whether this should have been divided as her father had married for a second time. Pozières Memorial. File ref: 339/40568.

Toppin Capt. Alfred Henry. Born 28.11.1883 at Colwyn Bay, the son of Percy and Margaret Mary Toppin *née* Frinston. Educated at Colwyn Bay College, North Wales. Applied for a commission 25.10.1915. Address Merrion Lodge, Merrion, Co. Dublin. Single, insurance official, height 6 foot, chest 33–37½ inches, weight 163 pounds. Commissioned to 3rd RIR 16.11.1915 and served during the Easter Rising. T/Capt. 6.9.1916 whilst District Bombing Officer. Brother of Capt. Aubrey John Toppin who served in India. Promoted Lt. 1.7.1917. Joined 2nd RIR 21.10.1917. Severely wounded in the leg at Marcoing, 13.12.1917, and embarked Rouen–Southampton five days later. He had been accidentally wounded by a bayonet whilst getting into a trench at night – the bayonet was fixed to a rifle propped against the side of a trench. He had also been exposed to mustard gas on the 11th and 13th December, which slightly affected his eyes and chest. Address was Rocklands, Dalkey, Co. Dublin. To 3rd RIF at Durrington 4.6.1918. Released from service 30.7.1919 having last served with 3rd RIR. File ref: 339/47753.

Tuckett Capt. John Reginald. The son of W.R. Tuckett, Loughborough. Commissioned 14.8.1914, promoted Lt. 15.11.1914, with seniority from 14.3.1913, and posted to France 10.12.1914. Joined 2nd RIR 24.12.1914. *Burgoyne* 16.1.1915: 'Tuckett hit, and badly, two snipers on their return to their trenches this morning at dawn, and they fairly pasted the twenty or thirty Germans who were shelled out of their trench about mid-day: and they said they saw several drop.' 23.1.1915: 'Tuckett is very young, and also, I think the trench has got on his nerves. Don't blame him a bit, most of our bad casualties have been there.'

30.1.1915: 'Tuckett and the servant thought themselves very clever last night. They had marked down a solitary fowl, and, at dead of night, they murdered it, plucked it, cut it up and had all the feathers and bones buried within an hour of the crime ... found a couple of feathers and raised Cain. She got into such a temper she broke a chair. Eventually they paid her 5 francs for the bird and she calmed down, and after all the bird was uneatable.' Returned to the UK, 22.2.1915, and rejoined 2nd RIR 28.6.1915. Wounded in the head, 25.9.1915, and admitted to hospital at Dorchester House, London. Rejoined 21.7.1916. A/Capt 16.8.1916. Wounded 13.10.1916. Staff Capt., Havre Base, 14.1.1917, and at DAQMG, Genoa, 22.11.1917 to 7.4.1918. Retired pay 1920 and recalled 1939. Died 30.10.1981, aged 87. Some of his photographs and effects are in the Ypres Museum. Closed file.

Turpin Lt. Dermod Owen MC. Born 28.10.1894 at Ludlow Street, Navan, Co. Meath, the son of Thomas Digby and Janie Turpin *née* Sumerville. Educated at the Royal School, Armagh. Enlisted as Rfn/Cadet 17/1412 at Belfast, 9.8.1915. Height 5 foot 8½ inches, expanded chest 33 inches. Gazetted a 2/Lt. in 17th RIR, 4.10.1915. Joined 2nd RIR 2.4.1916. Wounded 9.7.1916, GSW middle finger right hand and shell shock. *Irish Times*, 18.7.1916: 'His father, who is manager of the Portadown branch of the Belfast Bank, has since received a letter from him stating that he is in hospital in France, and that he is progressing satisfactorily.' Embarked Le Havre–Southampton aboard HS *Maheno* and admitted to East Lancs Red Cross Hospital, Worsley, Manchester, 6.8.1916. Granted leave ten days later. Applied for a Regular commission in the Indian Army (Gurkhas), 3.8.1917, but was rejected on medical grounds. Joined 3rd RIR 2.10.1916. Promoted Lt. and transferred to 15th RIR 22.1.1918. MC, *London Gazette*, 4.10.1919: 'Between Defrlyck and the Gaverbeek, on the 20th October, 1918, he was in command of the support company. He led his company forward under heavy fire and filled a gap which was threatening the flank, and consolidated his position. On the 22nd he again led his company through heavy fire and bombs from enemy aircraft. His courage and determination inspired all ranks and enabled them to gain their positions at a most critical time.' Later served with 12th RIR. Relinquished his commission 22.10.1919, rated A1. His address as of 29.3.1920 was Hibernian Bank, Rathfriland, Co. Down. Attended the Dublin Branch Annual Reunion in 1938. File ref: 339/45663.

Tydd 2/Lt. William John Sterne. Born at Crohan House 14.11.1896, the son of Francis Edward and Isobel Tydd *née* Davis, Crohan House, Clonmel, Co. Tipperary. His father was a solicitor at 179 Great Brunswick Street, Dublin. Educated at Clonmel Grammar School. Enlisted 20.8.1915 as Pte 435622 in A Coy, 50th Canadian Infantry. Height 5 foot 8½ inches, chest 31–34 inches, blue eyes, light hair, bank clerk with Bank of Canada. He had previously served one year in the RE Territorials. His parents were then residing at Richmond House, Clonmel. Reported to the CO of 4th CR at Bere on being commissioned 9.3.1916 (having been delayed for two weeks due to illness). To the school of instruction at Cork. Joined 2nd RIR 20.1.1917. GSW left thigh (compound fracture), 22.1.1917, and died at No. 2 CCS. His mother wrote to Col. H.E. Street CMG at the WO, 19.2.1917: 'He was only two days in France when he was sent up the line and was killed the next day'. Bailleul Communal Cemetery, III.A.193. File ref: 339/55477.

Tyndall Lt. Joseph Charles. Born 18.5.1892 at 84 Palmerston Road, Rathmines, Dublin, the second son of Joseph Patrick and Nellie Tyndall *née* Devane, 2 Eaton Square, Monkstown, Co. Dublin. His father was a solicitor. Educated Castleknock College, Co. Dublin. Joined 4th RDF, 17.10.1910, and was promoted Lt., 20.4.1912. Resided at his parent's house at Farmleigh, Stillorgan Road, Co. Dublin. *Irish Times*,6.3.1915: 'He returned from Australia with the Colonial contingent last December. He then went into training with the 4th Dublin Fusiliers in Sittingbourne.'

Burgoyne 19.2.1915: 'Last night I took some stores up to a blockhouse behind our lines and took Tyndall, a youngster in the Dublin Fusiliers SR who has just joined us, with me.' 3.3.1915: 'Tyndall ... was killed yesterday. He stood up and fired some say two, others four, flares from the same spot and one after another. Either he was spotted by a sharpshooter or it was a stray bullet, but he was hit in the face, the bullet shattering his spinal cord in the neck.'

de Ruvigny: 'Was killed in action at Kemmel, 2 March 1915, after a fortnight in the trenches; unmarried. His elder brother, Surgeon William Tyndall, RAMC, is now (1916) on active service in France.' At that time their father was stated to be of unsound mind. Gross estate £841. Kemmel Chateau Military Cemetery, Heuvelland, West-Vlaanderen, A.1. File ref: 339/9402.

Vance Col. Robert Lancelot. Born 27.8.1890, the son of the Revd Canon Vance, Rathronan, Ardagh, Limerick. Educated at Campbell College, Belfast, January 1904 to July 1908. Trinity College, Dublin: BA 1913, MB, B.Ch. 1915. Commissioned to 4th RIF, August 1914. Joined 2nd RIR 10.2.1915. Wounded 16.6.1915. Lt. in the Indian Medical Service, 1916. Promoted Capt. in July 1916. Mentioned in Despatches, *London Gazette*, 5.6.1919. His younger brother, 2/Lt. Charles Richard Griffin Vance, 3rd Cheshire Regt, was killed in action 11.3.1915. Promoted Lt.-Col. in 1934. Foreign & Political Dept. Address 1938: c/o Lloyds Bank, London, and British Legation, Kathmandu, Nepal. Later resided at Grange Leys, Quainton, Aylesbury, Bucks. Closed file.

Varwell Lt.-Col. Ralph Peter MC. A graduate of Cambridge University and commissioned to 2nd RIR 9.10.1907. Promoted Lt. 1.4.1909. Went to the front with A Coy, 2nd RIR. Wounded 15.9.1914. Promoted Capt. 15.3.1915. Mentioned in Despatches 22.6.1915, 20.5.1918, 20.12.1918; MC 4.6.1917; Brevet Major 1.1.1919; French Croix de Guerre 26.11.1919. *Services of Military Officers 1920* noted that he served in France 13.8.1914 to 23.9.1914 and 13.6.1916 to 11.11.1918; Gallipoli 26.11.1915 to 31.12.1915; Egypt 1.1.1916 to 18.3.1916; Egyptian Expeditionary Force 19.3.1916 to 6.6.1916. Retired in July 1930 and, on the advice of his doctor, went to live in South Africa in 1941.

Quis Separabit, Summer 1957: 'Ralph Varwell's accidental and tragic death in South Africa shocks all who had the pleasure of knowing him ... He was wounded in 1914 at the Battle of the Aisne and thereafter held various staff appointments in Gallipoli, Egypt and France until the Armistice ... "Ginger", as he was affectionately known ... was an officer of the "old school" and set himself a high standard in all he did ... A year or so after the First World War he returned to Regimental duty and assumed command of the Regimental Depot which suited him as well as he was suited to hold it, for he was able, among other activities, to indulge his favourite pastimes of shooting and fishing. But it was, I think, in India when he rejoined the 2nd Battalion that he was happiest, for besides shooting of infinite variety in that country he was able to ride every day and also to hunt with the Poona and Kirkee hounds.' – Brigadier G.H.P. Whitfeld. Closed file.

Vernon 2/Lt. William Wood. Born 18.9.1889 at Ballinasloe, Co. Galway, the son of St George and Jane Waring Vernon *née* Shilson. Educated at Rosse College, Dublin, Francis College, Mountbellew, and by private tuition. Employed at Bank of Ireland, Galway. Known as Billy. Enlisted 27.1.1915. Height 6 foot ⅞ inch, chest 36–38½ inches, weight 160 pounds. At that time he had eight siblings: Ernest George (aged 36), Bank of Ireland, Maryborough; James Daly (33), Bank of Ireland, Thurles; Gunner George Mostyn (20), RMA, HMS *Agincourt*; Herbert Scott (20); Violet Caroline (25); Amy Muriel (23); Ivy Marpin (20); Margaret Sarah (18). The family home was then at 17 Claremont Road, Sandymount, Dublin. Commissioned to 4th CR 24.2.1915. Joined 2nd RIR 8.4.1916. No. 11 Platoon. Killed in action 8.7.1916. 2/Lt. J.M. Clarke reported that he saw Vernon's body: there was a wound in the back of his head, which had been covered over, and he was later buried in the trench. 8134 Rfn J. Maher, No. 12 Platoon, stated that Vernon was killed in the third line of German trenches by an exploding whizz-bang: 'I saw it strike him and it killed him instantly.' Thiepval Memorial. File ref: 339/40581.

Wakefield Capt. Charles James. Son of John and Jane Wakefield, Stoke Poges, Slough, Bucks. He had a brother called Reginald. Educated by private tuition. Enlisted as Rfn 4798 in 1st RIR 13.7.1896, farm labourer, height 5 foot 4¾ inches, chest 33½–35½ inches, weight 121 pounds, Wesleyan. Appointed L/Cpl 15.3.1903. Promoted Cpl 16.1.1905. Posted to 2nd RIR 1.2.1906. Appointed L/Sgt 8.3.1907. Married Abigail Howse at Stoke Poges 1.4.1907. Children born: Abigail 5.8.1908, Charles 31.5.1910, John 13.8.1911, and Henry 19.8.1913. Promoted Sgt 3.5.1910 and CQMS 9.6.1913. Home service to 24.4.1897; South Africa to 15.4.1899; India to 31.1.1906; remainder at home. Regimental Employment Sheet, 8.8.1914: 'Always has been exemplary character. Excellent at accounts. A thoroughly good man in every way.' Commissioned 1.10.1914. Promoted Lt. 15.3.1915. A/Adjutant during the summer of 1915. Wounded 28.8.1915: shrapnel wound in the back and left knee, spine fractured. Home address, 8 Sefton Park Road, Stoke Poges. Reported to 3rd RIR 28.5.1916. Promoted Capt. 1.1.1917. Served East Africa and Rhodesia 29.9.1917 to 25.11.1918. A/Major, 20.3.1918 to 1.8.1918, and from 25.9.1918. Died of cerebral malaria 1.7.1920 while attached to 6th King's African Rifles. Buried Dar es Salaam (Upanga Street) Cemetery. Mentioned in Despatches *London Gazette*, 1.1.1916, 5.6.1919, and 29.11.1920. File ref: 339/13682.

Wale 2/Lt. Clifford Hardwicke. Born 1881 at 34 Little Pulteney Street, Westminster, the son of Henry Frederick and Annie Wale. Enlisted in 9th City of Londonderry Regt TF (Queen Victoria's Rifles), 8.8.1914. Height 5 foot 8½ inches, chest 34–37½ inches, age 22 years 9 months. Embarked for France 4.11.1914. To No. 15 FA 7.3.1915. 2/Lt., RIR, 23.4.1915. Joined 2nd RIR 29.4.1915. Wounded 16.6.1915: flesh wound through to inner part of left arm and slight graze on outer side of arm. Embarked that day via Boulogne–Dover. The wounds turned septic for a while and his finger movements were affected. Rejoined 8.12.1915. Killed in action 19.1.1916. At that time his parents were at 50 Dartmouth Park Road, London NW. The family consisted of his father (aged 55), mother (55), siblings: Mary Emma (26), Reginald Henry (23), Annie Ruth (22), and Vernon Howard (19). Their new address in May 1916 was Wulstanhurst, Hendon Lane, Church End, Finchley. Ploegsteert Memorial. File ref: 339/29439.

Walkington Lt. Dolway Bell MC. Born 10.8.1897. Educated at Methodist College, Belfast. Applied for a commission 30.9.1914. Permanent address, 33 Tates Avenue, Lisburn Road, Belfast; correspondence address, 10th RIR, Donard Lodge Camp, Newcastle, Co. Down. Gazetted a 2/Lt. in 10th RIR 22.9.1914. To 17th RIR 21.5.1915. Joined 9th RIR in the field 20.7.1916. Promoted Lt. 7.1.1917. Admitted to No. 56 CCS, 6 September, and to 1st American (Presbyterian) General Hospital, 24 September. Reposted to 10th RIR, 29

September. Discharged to duty, 10 October, and arrived at the Base 27.11.1917. MB at Harfleur 18.12.1917: debility and anaemia. Classified A on discharge from hospital. He had not received any medical treatment at the Base because he was sent away on conducting duty. 'Never feeling quite well.' MBs at Le Havre: 24.12.1917, anaemic and debilitated, to be retained at the Base for two months; 25.2.1918, shown as 8/9th RIR, fit for general service. T/Capt. 9–21 May. Admitted to hospital, 10 June, from Second Army Central School of Instruction. Joined 2nd RIR.

   War Diary, 29.7.1918: 'At 5.30 p.m. on this date a patrol was sent out under Lt. D.B. Walkington and 2/Lt. J.N.G. Stewart composed of 4 Other Ranks with the object of obtaining identification. The patrol left our Line at X.11.b.68.02. and made direct for X.12.c.01.23. At this point a German Post was found. The patrol rushed the post which appeared to be held by about ten men. 4 prisoners were taken. (1 NCO and three men) 2 of whom were killed in no-man's-land on the way back as they showed fight, when enemy machine gun opened fire. The remainder of the post were either killed or wounded. At this juncture the patrol was fired on by enemy machine gun but no casualties occurred. The patrol re-entered our Line at 7.45 p.m. at about X.12.c.28.16.' MC *London Gazette*, 15.10.1918. Later served with the Provost Staff and had jaundice in January 1919. Discharged 23.4.1919, rated A1, single, linen manufacturer. Address, 128 Eglantine Avenue, Belfast. File ref: 339/14295.

Wallis Lt. Timothy Charles MC. A son of Mr H. Boyd, Graylands, Horsham, Sussex, and 48 Holland Park, London. His brother, Lt. Duncan Boyd Wallis, 3rd CR attached 2nd RMF, died of wounds 24.7.1915. Commissioned to 4th CR 22.11.1916. Joined D Coy, 2nd RIR, 17.2.1917. MC awarded for gallantry during the Westhoek operations. *London Gazette*, 8.1.1918: 'For conspicuous gallantry and devotion to duty. When his company commander had become a casualty, he took command and led the company during an attack with great ability. After the objective was gained, he did excellent work in sending back reliable information, and in consolidating his line, and the coolness and resource with which he dealt with hostile counter-attacks inspired all ranks with the greatest confidence.' Promoted Lt. 22.5.1918. Entered Trinity College, Dublin, 1919, and received his BA in 1923. Later resided at 37 Arlington Lodge, Monument Hill, Weybridge, Surrey. Closed file.

Walsh Lt. Richard Stanislaus MC. Born at Bandon, 31.8.1890, the son of John Walsh, Eversleigh, Bandon, Co. Cork. His father was MP for South Cork. Educated at St Vincent's College, Castleknock, Dublin. Enlisted as Pte 26921 in 10th RDF 11.5.1916. Applied for a commission 25.7.1916. Merchant, single, height 5 foot 7½ inches, chest 32–35¾ inches, weight 135 pounds. Transferred to 11th RDF, 29 July, and to No. 7 Officer Cadet Bn 5.9.1916. Discharged to a commission in 5th RMF 18.12.1916.

   Joined 2nd RIR 27.2.1917. Wounded 10.8.1917 and awarded the MC for gallantry on that day. *London Gazette*, 8.1.1918: 'For conspicuous gallantry and devotion to duty. His company commander having been killed shortly before the attack, he took command, but, whilst making final preparations, was wounded in the head. He quickly got his wound dressed and returned to duty, his one object being to lead his company in the attack, which he did with great dash and ability until he was wounded for the second time. He set a fine example of grit and devotion to duty.' Embarked Calais–Dover, 31.8.1918. To Dublin Castle Red Cross Hospital: wounded by shellfire, right arm broken, effects likely to be permanent. He had several operations to his right arm and had lost a lot of bone. Grafting was not considered feasible. Placed on the retired list. Retrospectively promoted Lt. with effect from 19.6.1918. Wound pension of £50 per annum granted for one year then to be reassessed.

MB at Dublin 22.9.1919: the wounds were all healed but he still suffered from the loss of muscle and bone. Three fingers of the right hand could not be flexed. File ref: 339/69938.

Watson 2/Lt. James. Born 15.5.1889, the son of Alexander and Sarah Watson *née* Quin, Ashfield, Cornascriebe, Portadown. His father was a farmer. Educated at Portadown Academy and was a bank official with the Ulster Bank, Belfast.

Enlisted in 14th RIR 14.9.1914. Height 5 foot 8 inches, chest 37–40 inches, weight 139 pounds, ruddy complexion, grey eyes, black hair. To 15th RIR 7.8.1915, and applied for a commission 27.9.1915. To 17th RIR 3.10.1915. Gazetted a 2/Lt., 3rd RIR, 22.10.1915. Joined 2nd RIR 21.5.1916. Killed in action 7.7.1916. His mother administered the estate of £87. Bapaume Post Military Cemetery, Albert, Somme, I.D.15. File ref: 339/46060.

Watson 2/Lt. John Knox. Born 9.9.1898 at Glenavy, Co. Antrim, the third son of Hugh Henry Boyd Watson and Edith Sarah *née* Wilson. His father, a Quaker and native of Megaberry, was a mill owner and also had a bauxite mine at Ballyluggan near Portrush. Siblings were William Chambers, 40932 Rfn David Robert (RIR, wounded 5.3.1917), James Bain, Thomas Vince, Kathleen, and Dorothy. The family moved to England in 1903 and resided at 11 Clarendon Place, Leeds. Educated at Mirfield Grammar School. Enlisted at Belfast, 24.10.1916, and sent to Queen's University OTC. To 19th RIR Cadet Platoon 20.12.1916 and trained with No. 7 Officer Cadet Bn. Discharged to a commission in 3rd RIR 31.7.1918. Height 6 foot, chemical engineer, Church of England, 'scar of burn on front of chest and on front of abdomen' (as a result of falling into an open fire in childhood). Left No. 10 Camp at Durrington, 26.9.1918, and joined 2nd RIR. Wounded 22.10.1918. He was part of a force attacking an enemy farmhouse. When the objective had been achieved and the enemy dispersed, he was too ill with influenza to continue and fell unconscious. He was placed on a stretcher and, because the enemy counter-attacked, was hurriedly placed out of the way in the attic. The Germans held the position for a short while before being driven back. He was retrieved and admitted to 14th General Hospital, Wimereux, 29.10.1918. Last served with 3rd CR. Discharged at Ripon, 26.7.1919. Served during the coal strike with 1st York and Lancaster Regt 12–28.4.1921. Relinquished his commission 10.8.1921. Resided at Wivelsfield, 116 Kew Road, Richmond, Surrey.

After the war he worked and became director in the family business, Watson's Water Softeners Ltd., Natrol Works, Orphanage Road, Watford. Married Winifred Rose Polyblank 9.9.1931. They lived at Knox Cottage, Prowse Avenue, Bushey Heath, Hertfordshire, and had two sons, Hugh Charles (born 19.6.1932) and Ian Knox (24.5.1935). Died 9.11.1988. His worst memory of the war was when he was sprayed with the brains and blood of his batman who had been hit in the head by a sniper. Details provided by his son Hugh, who did part of his National Service with the RUR in Hong Kong during 1951. Closed file.

Watts Capt. Robert MC. Born 15.11.1888, the son of the Revd Robert Watts, Kilmacrenan, Co. Donegal. Educated at Campbell College, September 1899 to July 1906. Served one month with Queen's University OTC. Qualified as a solicitor 1912 and worked with his stepfather, Charles William Black, founder of the family firm of C. & J. Black, Solicitors. Applied for a commission 1.12.1914. Height 5 foot 7¾ inches, chest 34½–37 inches, weight 133 pounds, Presbyterian. Appointed 2/Lt., RASC, 1.12.1914, and attached for training to 36th (Ulster) Division. Joined the BEF 4.10.1915. Promoted Lt., 1.7.1915, and Capt. 2.5.1916. Employed with 36th Divisional Train. MC, *London Gazette*, 1.1.1917. Returned to the UK, 7.1.1918, posted to No. 2 Infantry School of Instruction, 12 January, and attached to the Infantry.

Joined C Coy, 2nd RIR, 12.7.1918. Appointed a/Adjutant, 10 August, and Adjutant 10 October. Bar to his MC, *London Gazette*, 1.2.1919: 'This officer made a very daring reconnaissance by night after the battle of 6th September, 1918, in the Messines sector. The left flank of the battalion was somewhat in the air, and there was a danger of the enemy surrounding it. He established the fact and the exact spot of the nearest post on the exposed flank. The information which he brought in enabled the left flank to be made perfectly safe against enemy attack, and so assured the front and support companies that no real danger of being surrounded existed. He performed most valuable service.'

Suffered influenza at Courtrai 23.10.1918. On sick leave from 10.11.1918. Left Belfast, 30 November, and rejoined 2nd RIR. Demobilized 11.4.1919, rated A1, address Ardnagrenna, Strandtown, Belfast. French Croix de Guerre a l'Ordre Division, *London Gazette*, 19.6.1919. Married Lydia Norah (1897–1980), a medical doctor, 15.11.1921. He was a partner in the family firm and residing at Tiverton, Quarry Road, Belmont, Belfast. He was also a Governor and Trustee of Campbell College. He had two sons, Robert Newell Crawford (born 1923) and Charles John (1927), both becoming partners in the legal firm. He was President of the Law Society of Northern Ireland in 1939. Died of a heart attack 19.5.1967. For over thirty years, until his death, he was solicitor to the Presbyterian Church in Ireland in succession to his stepfather. His son Robert held this post until his retirement in 1993 and his son, Roger, carried forward the family tradition as a partner in the firm. File ref: 339/21943.

Weaving 2/Lt. Harry Willoughby. Born 6.6.1885 at Cutteslowe, RSD, Oxford, the son of Harry Walker Weaving and Beatrice Anne *née* Armitage, Pewit House, Abingdon, Berks. His father was a brewer and maltster. Educated at Abingdon School. Obtained a classical MA at Pembroke College, Oxford. He was a protégé of Robert Bridges (1844–1930), who worked as a doctor in London until 1881 and was appointed Poet Laureate in 1913. Owing to illness, he did not start working until he was 30 and became a junior master at Rockport Preparatory School, Craigavad, Co. Down. Applied for a commission 7.10.1914. Single, address, Pewit House. Joined 2nd RIR 12.7.1915 and posted to D Coy. Admitted to hospital, 7 September, and evacuated Dieppe–Dover two days later; 'sickness (heart trouble)', which was his own description. Robert Bridges, Chilswell, near Oxford, wrote to the WO, 23 October: 'Lt. Weaving was invalided home. After one or two months in hospital he had six weeks leave, dating from September 23, which expires November 3. I make myself responsible for the following statements. (1) He should never have been passed as fit for active service. (This is confirmed by result.) (2) If he returns, he will break down again. I speak from personal knowledge (he is a neighbour), and I have a letter from an officer who was out with him in France asking me if I cannot make some statement of his case to the authorities to prevent a mistake. As Lt. Weaving's breakdown was heart failure – he fainted in the trenches, and his life was despaired of in hospital – it is possible that, since he seems to be recovering well, he may after some months of absolute rest make a fair show before the Board. Also, he need not be discharged as wholly unfit. He has high mental qualities, and is popular with the men. At least I judge this last to be so from his telling me that his contact with them was the pleasantest experience of all his life – so that it might be possible to transfer him to some home unit where he might instruct recruits – to which, especially after his actual experience of the trenches, he would seem to be particularly fitted. His own feeling is that he does not like the idea of being out of it, but is aware that he will break down and be only a burden if he should be sent out again. He is willing to do anything ... My being a Fellow of the R. College of Physicians may perhaps lend professional weight to my opinion.'

A MB, 3 November, deemed him permanently unfit for general service, and did not con-sider that his condition had been caused or exacerbated by military service. WO to GOC Irish Command: he was to be instructed to resign his commission on the grounds of ill health and to be thanked for placing his services at the country's disposal at a time of crisis. Resignation approved 18.11.1915 and he returned to teaching at Rockport School. In 1921, he and H.E. Seth-Smith founded Elm Park School, Killylea, Co. Armagh. His nickname was 'Willow'. He wrote about the Irish and English countryside, and his poetry became very popular. The following is an extract from *Flanders*:

> Man has his life of butterflies / In the sunshine of sacrifice,
> Brief and brilliant, but more / Guerdon than the honey flower
> And more glory than the grace / Of their gentle floating pace.

Died at Abingdon in 1976. File ref: 339/35428.

Webb Capt. Gilbert Watson. Born 1.3.1890, the son of Richard Thomas and Blanche Louisa Webb, Rath House, Shandon Park, Knock, Belfast. His brothers were W.T.H., Richard Randall, Hermann Watson and Karl Watson Webb. Educated at Campbell College 1901–6. Served in Belfast University OTC until 8.4.1910. Employed 7th Shropshire Light Infantry. Applied for a commission 7.8.1914. Single, height 6 foot, chest 34½–37½ inches, weight 149 pounds. Commissioned to 3rd RIR. Joined 2nd RIR 28.2.1915. Suffered a scalp wound by a rifle grenade, 8 May, admitted No. 1 British Red Cross Hospital at Le Touquet, and embarked Boulogne–Dover 15 May. He was also suffering from anaemia, his general health was 'low', and was not certified fit for general service until 16.7.1915. Reported to 3rd RIR.
    Promoted Capt. 27.11.1915. He was with the RFC at Reading as of 14.2.1916 and with No. 9 Reserve Squadron at Norwich by 2.3.1916. Joined the BEF with No. 22 Squadron. *Irish Times*, 22.8.1916: 'On recovering he transferred to the Royal Flying Corps and took his machine to France on the 4th May of this year, flying all the way.' Killed in action 1.7.1916. His file contains a transcript of a letter from Lt. W. Owen Tudor Hart, Northumberland Fusiliers attached RFC. He was Webb's observer. At 11 a.m. they had been up for about an hour and were six miles behind German lines. They saw an enemy plane above them and turned to attack it. Both aircraft fired together and Tudor Hart saw other machines approach-ing. He signalled Webb to turn but nothing happened. When he leant over Webb he saw that he had been hit in the groin or stomach. Webb had put the nose of the machine down and was heading for the British lines, but lost consciousness a few moments later. Their plane went partly out of control and Tudor Hart couldn't get to the rudder controls to straighten it. German aircraft were circling and firing but didn't hit them because of the erratic way their machine was flying. This went on for about fifteen minutes until they crashed. Tudor Hart broke his ankle. He said that Webb had died in the air about two min-utes after he had been hit. He spoke highly of Webb and said he himself was well treated by the Germans on the ground – he was first approached by infantry and then one of the German planes landed nearby and two officers came and spoke to him. They apologized for shooting him down, but they had to. He referred to them as sportsmen.
    The WO told his widowed mother that the aircraft was shot down near Bancourt, Bapaume. Achiet-le-Grand Communal Cemetery Extension, Pas de Calais, IV.Q.5. File ref: 339/24042.

Weir Major Arthur Vavasour. Born 1865. Gazetted to 1st RIR from the Militia 16.11.1887. On service up the Nile 1889. Promoted Lt., 3.7.1889, and Capt. 3.2.1897. Served in the South African War, 1899–1902, and was captured at Stormberg 1899. Freed during Lord

Robert's advance 1900. Operations in the Orange River Colony (June–November 1900); Cape Colony, South of the Orange River, 1899; Railway Staff Officer, Wolvenhoek, from 2.7.1900. Queen's Medal with three clasps and King's Medal with two clasps. Adjutant 6th RIR (Louth Rifles) 1903–5. Promoted Major 13.7.1906. Left 3rd RIR, 30.12.1914, for Bournemouth to take command of 7th Shropshire Light Infantry. Joined 2nd RIR and assumed command 28.4.1915. Took over the post of Commandant of 7th Bde Area, 30.5.1915. He was serving with 3rd RIR at Belfast by 22.12.1916. That day he responded to a letter from Capt. Bowen-Colthurst: 'This week we are shoving everyone out as soon as they are fit. I am very fit and they ought to let me go. I am a rabid teetotaller since May and feel all the better for it.' This letter is in the author's collection. Died 1937. *Quis Separabit*, May 1937: 'He retired from the service in 1918. To his son, who is serving in the Indian Army and who carried out his attachment with the 2nd Battalion at Poona, we offer our sincere sympathy.' File missing.

Weir Lt. Charles MC. Born 3.6.1892 or 1891 (both years appear on different forms). He was a farmer. *Irish Times*, 22.7.1916: 'He is a native of Ballindrait, Co. Donegal.' Applied for a commission in April 1915. Address, 59 William Street, Dublin. He had been in St Andrew's OTC, Dublin, since November 1914. Commissioned to 18th RIR 23.8.1915. MC, *London Gazette*, 24.1.1917, for services during the 1916 Rebellion. Sent to the BEF, 27.5.1916, and joined 2nd RIR 10.6.1916. Wounded, slight GSW, 7 July, and embarked Calais–Southampton, 12 July. Joined 18th RIR for duty 24 August. Transferred to the Reserve Regiment of Cavalry 20.12.1916. Joined 5th R. Irish Lancers in France, 23 February. Promoted Lt. 27.8.1917. Left his unit, 5th Lancers, 3rd Cavalry Brigade, attached British Cavalry Base (Training Squadron), 25.2.1918, due to a fractured scapula caused by a fall from a horse. Embarked Le Havre–Southampton, 29 February. Applied for a transfer to the SR, 5th Lancers, 22 April, and joined 1st Reserve Regt of Lancers two days later.

Rejoined the BEF, 15.5.1918, and was attached to the British Cavalry Training School. Left 26 August suffering from dysentery and embarked Le Havre–Southampton two days later. Rejoined 1st Reserve Regt of Lancers 2.11.1918. Admitted to Dublin Castle Red Cross Hospital, 14.12.1918, until he was taken on the strength of the Appointments Department, Ministry of Labour, 7.1.1919. Passed through Irish Command Discharge Centre 15.9.1919, rated V, single. Permanent address The Park, Ballindrait, Strabane, Co. Tyrone.

He wrote to the WO, 14.4.1921, offering his services in any military capacity. Though resident in Ireland he 'had to live in London for some considerable time owing to being threatened by the IRA'. A certificate was issued of service in the coal strike (18–23.4.1921) with the MGC Cavalry Reserve Regt. Home address, Cadogan Court Gardens, Sloane Square, London. Advised that there were no positions available. He replied that he was awarded the MC for services during the 1916 Rebellion and, news of it having 'leaked out', he was threatened with death and could not return home. He was prepared to serve in Germany or anywhere else. Being currently unemployed, he could not afford to live in London for long. Col. Jarvis, OC Cavalry MGC, was happy to reinstate him with WO approval. The Colonial Office wrote to the WO, 2.6.1921. Weir had applied for a position and they asked for a report. He asked for a record of his army service, 20.1.1923, as he was desirous of taking up an important position. His address was then 170 Clifton Park Avenue, Cliftonville Road, Belfast. File ref: 339/44468.

Weir General Sir George Alexander KCB, CMG, DSO. Born 1.12.1876, the son of Archibald Weir MD, of Malvern. Educated at Harrow and Trinity College, Cambridge. Promoted Capt. in 3rd Dragoon Guards, 11.1.1902, and Major 2.7.1912. Joined 2nd RIR as T/Lt.-Col. and assumed command 24.6.1915. Slightly wounded, 6 September, but remained at duty. Left 2nd RIR, 11 October, and was ordered to command 84th Infantry Bde, 1st Corps, with the temporary rank of Brigadier-General.

The Distinguished Service Order: 'He was Senior Tactical Instructor, Cavalry School, 29 June to 4 August 1914; Staff Captain, 4th Cavalry Brigade, BEF, 5 August to 9 October 1914; GSO2, 2nd Cavalry Division, BEF, 14 October 1914 to 23 June 1915; commanded the 84th Infantry Brigade, BEF, Salonika Army, British Salonika Force, 13 October 1915 to 21 March 1918; commanded the 19th Infantry Brigade, Egyptian Expeditionary Force, 3 April to 6 October 1918; commanded the 13th Cavalry Brigade, Egyptian Expeditionary Force, 7 October 1918. He served in the South African War, 1899–1901, with the Imperial Yeomanry; took part in the various operations in the Transvaal, Orange River Colony and Cape Colony, 30 November 1900 to August 1901. (Despatches, *London Gazette*, 10 September 1901 and 29 July 1902; Queen's Medal with four clasps). He served in the European War 1914–18; was wounded; Mentioned in Despatches; was given the Brevets of Lt.-Col. 1.1.1917, and Colonel 1.1.1918; was made Officer of St Maurice and St Lazarus, and was created a Companion of the Distinguished Service Order (*London Gazette*, 23 June 1915): "George Alexander Weir, Major, 3rd Dragoon Guards. For distinguished service in the field." Colonel Weir married, in 1917, Margaret Irene, daughter of Robert More, of Woodgate Place, Bexhill.'

Who Was Who: 'KCB 1934 (CB 1923), CMG 1919, DSO 1915. Late Col. 3rd Dragoon Guards; late Col. 3rd Carabiniers; Hon. Col. 8th Worcestershire Regt; DL Worcs. Major-General 1927; Lt.-General 1933; General 1937; Comdt Equitation School and Inspector of Cavalry 1922–6; GOC Bombay District 1927–31; Commander 55th (West Lancs) Division TA 1932–3; GOC the British troops in Egypt 1934–8 (GOCinC 1936); retired 1938 ... Croix de Guerre avec Palmes.' Residing at Link Lodge, Malvern Link, Worcs, when he died 15.11.1951. Closed file.

Whelan Capt. John Percy. Born in May 1879, the elder son of Joseph Whelan, Barna, Osbourne Park, Belfast. Educated at Loretto College, near Edinburgh (1891–8). Joined 3rd RIF Militia and, from them, was gazetted a 2/Lt. in 4th Royal Garrison Regt 12.8.1902. Promoted Lt. 21.3.1903. When the regiment was disbanded, July 1905, he was transferred to the RIR. Promoted Capt. 8.3.1910. *Bond of Sacrifice:* 'For over two years, from March, 1910, to November 1912, he was Adjutant of the 10th Bn London Regiment. Subsequently he was posted to the 1st Battalion of his regiment at Aden, whence he was invalided home shortly before the declaration of war with Germany ... Captain Whelan married Gladys Lily, youngest daughter of the late Captain John Wray Mitchell, of Aroughty Grange, County Roscommon, and left one daughter, Sheila Maureen, born July 1907.' Joined 2nd RIR 2.11.1914. Commanded 2nd South Lancs 17–24 November. Killed in action 11.12.1914. *Burgoyne:* 'Captain Whelan was hit in the chest yesterday and died in about two hours. He was out scouting round with a dog and a rifle. I hear he walked right in rear of the German trenches, and returned safely, and he was hit whilst walking about behind his trench, and in full view of the Germans.'

Irish Times, 18.12.1914: ' ... grandson of the late John Whelan of Rath, Co. Wicklow, and nephew of the late Mr Thomas Whelan, Assistant Inspector-General, Royal Irish Constabulary. The Whelans of Rath are an old Irish family, who held estates in the counties of Carlow and Wicklow, and is two miles from Tullow, in Carlow, with which county the Whelans were always closely associated ... Although on the sick list when hostilities were opened, he at once endeavoured to get to the front, but the doctors would not allow him to proceed on active service until about six weeks ago ... His father is well known in Belfast as the agent of the Bank of Ireland in the Donegall Place branch up till he retired last year. Deep sympathy will be extended to Captain Whelan's parents, his brother, Lieutenant C.B. Whelan of the [7th] King's Royal Rifle Corps, and his sister in their bereavement.' Menin Gate Memorial. File missing.

White Major Francis Konrad. Born 30.1.1882 at Priory, Worksop, the son of John and Hannah Jane White, Linden House. Enlisted 11.11.1903 in 2nd Northumberland Fusiliers. Height 5 foot 6½ inches, chest 33–35 inches, weight 137 pounds, tattooed female figure on left forearm, grey eyes, brown hair. He was travelling from Gravesend to Southampton for embarkation to Mauritius, 20.2.1904, when the troop train was wrecked at Gomshall in Surrey. He received compound fractures of the left femur, dislocated pelvis, and concussion. The fracture resulted in a half-inch shortening of the leg. Discharged at his own request 6.12.1904. Address 39 Sea View Terrace, Cleethorpes, Grimsby. Estate agent's clerk. Married Rose Emily Woodhead at Holy Trinity, Guildford, 7.6.1905. Children born: Marjorie Rose 15.12.1906, and Hugh Francis 5.4.1909. His wife was residing at her parents' home, Lindenthorpe, Semaphore Road, Guildford, when she wrote saying that she did not mind her husband going into the Army for a second time. 'I know he likes it, and being a very good scholar I am sure he will get on.' Rejoined 2nd NF, 29.5.1907, and to the Reserve 3.5.1912. Discharge notes state that he was a 'good clerk', 'wants to become a schoolmaster', and had been employed as 'an acting school-master Sergeant' from 4.5.1911 to 4.4.1912. At that time he was noted as being a watchmaker, residing at Lindenthorpe, 5 foot 7 inches tall, blue eyes.

Mobilized 5.8.1914, transferred to 3rd RIR (No. 8640), and joined 2nd RIR 15.8.1914. Slightly wounded 4.9.1914, GSW left groin. That day he was also 'knocked down by a German cavalryman and received an injury to the knee which set up synovitis'. Admitted No. 6 General Hospital with old hip fracture, 18.9.1914, and transferred to England via SS *Asturias*, 1.10.1914. Joined 1st RIR, 8.2.1915, and was wounded at Neuve Chapelle 10.3.1915, GSW both thighs. Promoted Sgt 1.5.1915.

Commissioned 3rd RIR 25.8.1915. Rejoined 2nd RIR 7.10.1915. To hospital, sick, 4–14 November. Back to hospital, 17 November. Marked 'Permanent Base' and struck off the strength, 24.2.1916. Promoted Lt. 10.12.1916, Capt. 8.2.1917, Staff (Quay Superintendent Staff) 1.11.1917, Major (Staff DAD of Docks) 29.3.1919 to 20.2.1923. Letter to WO, 28.8.1919, from RIR, Docks and Waterways, Rhine Army, Cologne, requested a war gratuity. Served until 28.12.1919. MB at Cologne, 9.2.1922, declared him permanently unfit for general service. Placed on half pay and restored to full pay whilst appointed as Assistant Director of Docks, BAOR. Appointed British Delegate of the Inter-Allied Navigation Commission 25.4.1922. Returned to Guildford 20.2.1923 and resided at 22 York Road. Retired 7.8.1923 and awarded a gratuity of £200 with a pension of £150 per annum. His older brother John Henry lived at Bonnetts Farm, Montreal, and his younger brother Frederick Charles at Butler Street, Sheffield. He wrote to the Paymaster General, 29.9.1931, complaining that his pension had been reduced to £111.50. 'It entails great hardship in my case as I have become lame in recent years as the result of my Army service, that I cannot get about only under great difficulty.' Died 9.9.1942 at Waterden Lodge, 27 Waterden Road, Guildford, of bronchial pneumonia and carcinoma of the lung. File ref: 339/35163.

White Lt. Henry Edwin. Born 14.11.1888. Educated at Mountjoy School, Dublin. Entered Trinity College, Dublin, 1913. Applied for a commission 12.7.1915. Single, works manager, height 5 foot 10¼ inches, chest 34–36½ inches, weight 144 pounds. Home address, Fort Lodge, Lisbellaw, Co. Fermanagh. Commissioned to 17th RIR 3.8.1915. Joined 2nd RIR 2.4.1916.

Wounded 25 April and 13 May. Embarked HMHS *Aberdonian*, Rouen–Southampton, 25 May. Cause of return, wounded, shell-shock at Vimy Ridge. MB at No. 4 London General Hospital, 28 May: shell shock and exhaustion, due to 'burial'. He moved from Fort Lodge to Langford House, Springfield Road, Brighton, 4 September. MB 18.9.1916: the headaches were less frequent and less severe; he was sleeping better, dreamed less frequently and his memory had improved. Still underweight. Returned to France in 1917 and joined 8th RIR, attached to 107th TMB. Left due to neurasthenia, 27 May, and embarked Boulogne–Dover aboard the *St David*, 13 June. Promoted Lt. 1.7.1917. Discharged 25.2.1919. Last served with 3rd RIR. Rated C1, married, residing at Brighton. File ref: 339/35879.

Whitfeld Lt. Arthur Noel. Born 20.12.1890 at The Rectory, Bradenham, Bucks, the eldest son of the Revd Arthur Lewis Whitfeld, Hughenden Vicarage, High Wycombe, and Mary Ellen *née* Curzon. Educated at Kent House, Eastbourne (1900–4), Malvern College (1904–8), and by private tutor. Applied for the RMC 25.4.1909. Commissioned 5.10.1910, and was promoted Lt. 17.3.1914. Went overseas with D Coy, 2nd RIR. Mentioned in Despatches 8.10.1914. Killed in action 14.10.1914. Died intestate. WO advised, 11.2.1915, that a mobile unit of the Red Cross Society had buried him at Vielle Chapelle. He was a brother of G.H.P. Whitfeld, 1st RIR. Vieille Chapelle New Military Cemetery, Lacoutre, Pas de Calais, V.C.7. File ref: 339/7751.

Whitmore Lt. Benjamin Elton. Born at Worcester 2.12.1878, the son of Joseph Elton Whitmore, 91 St John's Road, Dudley, Worcestershire. Enlisted at Dublin as Rfn 5083 in 1st RIR 29.4.1897. Attestation form shows Thomas Henry Rodgers marked as an alias for Benjamin Elton Whitmore. Single, height 5 foot 5⅛ inches, chest 33–35 inches, weight 119 pounds, clerk. Next of kin was his step-aunt Mrs Woodhouse, Knighton, Radnorshire, being later replaced with his father's name. Promoted Cpl 6.3.1898, L/Sgt 26.3.1901, and Sgt 15.11.1901. Signed a statutory declaration at Fyzabad, 6.10.1904, correcting enlistment to his real name. Posted to 5th RIR 16.11.1907. Colour-Sgt 11.11.1911. Served at Home to 24.11.1897; South Africa to 15.4.1899; India to 6.12.1907; Home to 5.3.1915. Appointed CSM 29.8.1914. Promoted 2/Lt. in the RIR 5.3.1915. Joined 2nd RIR 30.3.1915. To hospital, sick, 9 June, and embarked Dieppe–Dover aboard the *Dieppe*, 29 June. Address, The Mall, Downpatrick, Co. Down. Reported for duty to 4th RIR 12.8.1915. *Burgoyne*: 'Whitmore came down to us from the 2nd Battalion, sent home broken down.' Promoted Lt. 13.11.1915.

A/Capt. 3.8.1917 to 27.2.1919. Adjutant 5th RIR 30.1.1917 to 27.2.1919. Embarked Tilbury, 18.9.1919, and disembarked Basra 16.10.1919. Next of kin was his wife, 4 Riverston Terrace, Holywood, Co. Down. He applied to the Adjutant of 1st RIR at Karind, 2.6.1920, to resign his commission as his wife and three-year-old child were in Mesopotamia and he had three other children at school in Ireland. He was not paid sufficient to maintain his life as an officer, and had been offered a position in England. Requested leave to proceed to the UK pending his resignation being gazetted, and asked for passage to be arranged for himself, his wife and child. Embarked for the UK 7.10.1920. Address, c/o Mrs McDonald, Irish Street, Downpatrick. Retired with a gratuity of £1,500 to the Regular Army Reserve of Officers, 8.12.1920. File ref: 339/24122.

Wilkins Major Cyril Francis DSO, MC. Born 30.4.1890, the son of Mrs G. White, School Bungalow, Penton Road, Ahmednagar, India. Served in the South African War receiving the Queen's Medal with six clasps and the King's Medal with two clasps. He had been a L/Sgt with 2nd RIR. Promoted 2/Lt. 6.3.1915. Wounded and then served with 3rd RIR. Rejoined

2nd RIR 25.6.1915. Promoted Lt. 28.11.1915. MC *London Gazette*, 1.1.1917. Adjutant, 23.1.1917 to 5.3.1918. Left on attachment to HQ XI Corps 20.10.1917. DSO, *London Gazette*, 1.1.1918. Rejoined from 1st Army HQ, 6.2.1918. French Croix de Guerre 19.6.1919. Mentioned in Despatches 21.12.1917 and 20.12.1918. Served at the Depot at Armagh. After the war he spent most of his service with 1st RUR. Promoted Capt., 1.1.1923, and Major in 1933. He attended the 36th (Ulster) Division Officers' Old Comrades' Association annual dinner, 1931 and 1932, signing himself as 2nd RIR, HQ General Staff, 108th Infantry Bde. *Who's Who* named his wife as Norah, daughter of C.W. Outram, Silverleigh, Purley. Died at Alexandria while playing polo for 1st RUR, 15.5.1935.

Quis Separabit, May 1946: 'On Saturday, December 1st, 1945, at the Royal Military Chapel, Sandhurst, Lt.-Col. Henry Robert Dunlop Hill DSO, The Queen's Royal Regiment, son of Lt.-Col. H.W. Dunlop Hill DSO, Indian Army (retired), and Mrs Dunlop Hill, Pivers Hill, Camberley, to Brenda Elodie Outram Wilkins, WRNS, younger daughter of the late Major C.F. Wilkins DSO, MC, The Royal Ulster Rifles, and of Mrs Wilkins, Firlands Lodge, Camberley.' Closed file.

Williams Capt. Charles Beasley. Born 29.10.1894, the son of James Alfred and Emily K. Williams, The Willows, Northland Road, Londonderry. Brother of E.J. Williams below. Educated at Foyle College. Entered Trinity College, Dublin, as a Divinity student, 1913, and was in the OTC. Applied for a commission 7.8.1914. Height 5 foot 6½ inches, chest 34–36½ inches, weight 136 pounds, address Brookley, Castlerock, Londonderry. Gazetted a 2/Lt. in 3rd RIR, 15.8.1914, promoted Lt. 8.5.1915, and Capt. 17.5.1915. *Irish Life*, 24.9.1915: 'He left for the front with a draft of the 2nd Battalion on the 1st May last ... Captain Williams was a keen rugby footballer and a capital swimmer.' A Coy. Killed in action 28.8.1915 and buried near Ypres. Effects included two tobacco pipes. Estate of £210 administered by his father. Menin Gate Memorial. File ref: 339/26051.

Williams Lt. Ernest Joseph. Born 11.10.1892 in Londonderry. His father was a bank manager. Educated at Hoyle College, Londonderry, and Strand School, London. Matriculated at the University of London. Attested at Regina, Canada, 25.1.1915, as Pte 26440 in 46th Bn Canadian Infantry. Height 5 foot 11 inches, chest 33–35 inches, weight 154 pounds, Church of England. Transferred to 10th Bn Canadian Infantry, 28.8.1915, apparently on arrival in France. Applied for a commission 23 December. To No. 2 Officer Cadet Bn at Pembroke College, Cambridge, 25.2.1916. Commissioned to 5th RIR 7.7.1916. Joined 2nd RIR 13.9.1916. *War Diary*, 15.2.1917: '2/Lt. E.J. Williams slightly injured, remained at duty. Cause of accident: premature explosion of No. 5 Mills Bomb.'

Irish Times and *Belfast News Letter*, 23.2.1917: 'Mr J.A. Williams, actuary, Londonderry Savings Bank, has been notified that his second son, Lieutenant Ernest J. Williams, Royal Irish Rifles, has been accidentally wounded in France. Second Lieutenant Williams was in the service of the Bank of Montreal when the war broke out. He joined the Canadian Expeditionary Force, and after a winter's active service in France received his commission in the Royal Irish Rifles, going to the front again last August. His only surviving brother, Temporary Captain H.P. Williams [Harold Patton Williams MC], Royal Inniskilling Fusiliers, is at present on active service.' The other brother was 2/Lt. James Alfred Williams, RIR, born 1897, killed 6.9.1916.

C Coy, 2nd RIR. GSW right elbow 7.6.1917. Embarked Boulogne–Dover, 15 June, aboard HS *St David*. The MB at 1st Western General Hospital, Fazakerly, Liverpool, 3 July, stated there was no damage to bones or nerves. Certified fit for general service 24.10.1917 and ordered to rejoin his unit. Promoted Lt. 7.1.1918. Killed in action 15.10.1918 while serving with 1st RIR. Died a bachelor, intestate. Dadizeele New British Cemetery, Moorslede, II.B.1. File ref: 339/77314.

Williams Major Ronald Douglas MC. Born 20.9.1889, the son of John Williams, Dunmurry House, Belfast. Educated at Campbell College, 1898–1906. First Bursar, St Andrew's University 1906; BA Trinity College, Dublin, 1911. He was a son-in-law of Sharman D. Neill and brother-in-law of R.L. Neill, 1st RIR. Commissioned to 5th RIR 15.6.1915. Served with 8th RIR. His son, Robert Dermot MacMahon Williams, was born 26.12.1916. Promoted Lt. 1.7.1917. *Belfast News Letter*, 18.3.1918, reported that he was shot through the shoulder by a sniper, 12.3.1918. MC 31.5.1918. A/Capt. 5.11.1918. Joined 2nd RIR during October 1918. Governor of Campbell College 1920; CO Queen's University OTC 1921–8. Resided at Inverlough, Marino, Co. Down. Director of McBride & Williams (1933) Ltd., handkerchief producers. President Old Campbellians Society 1926–8. Resided at 46 Elmwood Avenue, Belfast. Died 7.6.1958. His brother John was Professor of History at St Andrew's University in 1929. Closed file.

Wilson 2/Lt. Charles Elliott. Born 1880 at Walton on Thames, Kingston, the son of J.W. Wilson. Enlisted as Pte PS/5932 in 20th R. Fusiliers, 2.9.1914. Age 35 years 11 months, travelling salesman. Height 6 foot, chest 33½–36½ inches, weight 156 pounds. Applied for a commission 17.5.1915. Permanent address Rockfields, Arlington Lodge, Eastbourne. Correspondence address, D Coy, 20th R. Fusiliers, Clipstone Camp, Notts. Commissioned to 18th RIR 21.5.1915. Joined 2nd RIR 10.6.1916. Wounded 7.7.1916: shrapnel wound left wrist, sprained ankle, injury to back. He fell into a German dugout due to the explosion of a trench mortar. Embarked HS *Salta*, Le Havre–Southampton, 10 July, and admitted to 2nd Western General Hospital, Manchester. Reported to 3rd RIR 28.9.1916. Embarked Southampton–Alexandria 4.12.1916. Joined 1st Garrison Bn R. Irish at Assiut 2.1.1917. T/Lt. 1.4.1917. Admitted General Hospital, Cairo, 15.11.1917, with phtysis. Rejoined his unit 5.12.1917; HQ Southern Canal Sector 17.12.1917; POW Camp Heliopolis, 17.2.1918; POW Camp Sidi Bishr, 16.5.1918; and Aliens Internment Camp Sidi Bishr 3.7.1919. Embarked HT *Valdivia* at Alexandria, 12.8.1919, for demobilization in the UK. Discharged 24.8.1919, rated B3, single, wine and spirit shipper. File ref: 339/781.

Windle Lt. Philip. Born Chesterfield 25.2.1893, the son of Henry Job and Annie Windle *née* Billinge. His father was a bank clerk. Educated at Gresham's School, Holt, Norfolk (1907–9). Applied for a commission, 17.6.1915. Address, Bank House, Heanor, RSO, Derbyshire. Single, clerk in Parrs Bank Ltd. Commissioned to 4th RIR 26.7.1915. Joined 2nd RIR 23.5.1916. Wounded, 9 July, and embarked Calais–Dover, 13 August, aboard the *Dieppe*. MB at Caxton Hall, 21 August: superficial shrapnel fragment wound to right chest, six inches long by one inch wide, 'Now healed'. Joined 4th RIR 14.11.1916. Promoted Lt. 1.7.1917. Joined 1st RIR, 8.11.1917. Suffered a shrapnel wound to his left hand, 27 November, and embarked Calais–Dover, 4 December. Address, Atlantic Hydro, Blackpool. He had lost the ring finger of his left hand and the second finger was 'useless'. MB at Blackpool, 9 October, graded him as medical rating F and sent him home. Classed medically unfit for further service and put forward to go on the retired list. MB, 24.1.1919: the disability was severe and permanent – no longer serving. Granted a £250 wound gratuity. File ref: 339/34543.

Witherow Capt. Thomas Hastings. Born 7.9.1890, son of the Revd William Witherow, *Koh-i-noor*, Bloomfield, Belfast. Educated at Campbell College, 1901–2. Obtained his BA from Queen's University. On 28.9.1912 he collected 22,160 signatures for the Ulster Covenant, nearly all at Westbourne Presbyterian Church. Commissioned to 17th RIR, 28.1.1915, and subsequently attached to 14th RIR at Randalstown. In May he was temporarily attached to the 36th (Ulster) Division Cyclist Coy. Joined 17th RIR in June and was appointed Bn Musketry Officer in January 1916. Took a draft to France in February and then returned to his unit. Promoted Lt. 28.10.1916. Sent to join the BEF 12.12.1916 and was attached to 8th RIR. B Coy Commander, 8/9th RIR, 17.10.1917 to 26.12.1917. Applied for a regular commission in the Indian Army 5.2.1918. Joined 2nd RIR, 7 February, and posted to command a platoon of D Coy. Temporarily attached to 9th Inniskillings during the retreat of March 1918. Took command of D Coy, 2nd RIR, 2.4.1918. To the General List, 4.7.1918, and attached to the Indian Army 13.8.1918. Promoted to Capt. 28.10.1919. Licensed by the Presbytery of Belfast, 16.5.1923, ordained a Presbyterian Minister at First and Second Markethill, 3.2.1926, and resided at The Manor, Markethill, Co. Armagh. Retired 30.4.1963. By 1982 his address was 7 Farnham Road, Bangor, Co. Down. His war memoirs are held by the Liddle Collection, reference GS 1774.

Blackthorn, 1990: 'A most remarkable combination of warrior and man of the cloth, The Revd Tom Witherow, The Rifles oldest known officer, died on 1 September 1989, aged 99 years. Son of the Revd William Witherow, Minister of Westbourne Presbyterian Church in East Belfast, he attended both Campbell College and RBAI, before going to Queen's University. He was a founder member of the OTC in 1908 and graduated with a BA in 1912 before passing to Magee University College, then completing his studies in The Presbyterian College, Belfast. He was commissioned in 1915 and posted to the 17th Battalion at Ballykinler where on account of his previous experience he was appointed Musketry Officer for the 107th Infantry Brigade. Because of holding this position he was retained at Ballykinler when the 36th (Ulster) Division moved to France. At the end of 1916 he was posted to the 8th (East Belfast Volunteers) Battalion and took part in the Battle of Messines in April 1917, the Third Battle of Ypres in July, and the Battle of Cambrai in November … The 2nd Battalion was in the trenches opposite St Quentin when the German offensive began in March 1918. Tom was attending a Company Commanders' Course at Corps Headquarters. He was promptly recalled, but had great difficulty finding his Battalion due to the confused state of fighting. On conclusion of the battle, the only survivors from the Battalion were the Commanding Officer, one other officer and himself. In May 1918 he was ordered to report to the India Office in London and was appointed to the 98th Infantry Regiment of the Indian Army. He saw active service during the Afghan War when the British were intent on minimising Russian influence in Afghanistan. In 1922 he resigned his Commission and entered the Ministry of the Presbyterian Church … Following the Evacuation from Dunkirk, The Revd Witherow was requested by the War Office to volunteer for active service again. He agreed to this and served in Great Britain as a Captain in the Pioneer Corps until he was medically discharged in 1942. However, he continued his connection with The Royal Ulster Rifles and he conducted a Service at the 36th (Ulster) Division Memorial on the fiftieth anniversary of the Battle of the Somme in 1966.' Closed file.

Wood 2/Lt. Walter. Born 1893 at Blythe, Northumberland. Enlisted as 1st Aircraftman 1276 in the RFC, 16.10.1913, aged 20 years and 1 month. Single, height 6 foot, chest 32–36 inches, weight 140 pounds, cable telegraphist. He had previously served in the OTC Royal Scots and was granted a free discharge to join the Northern Cyclist Bn 5.7.1910. Posted to No. 4

Depot RGA, 18.10.1913, and transferred to the RFC, 22.1.1914, as Air Mechanic 2nd Class with 6th Squadron. Went to France 12.8.1914. Served as 1st AM with 10th Squadron from 1.2.1915. Convicted for a civil offence, 12.3.1915, having issued a cheque in payment for a motor cycle without having an account with the bank on which the cheque was drawn. Bound over for twelve months on a £10 recognisance. Returned to France 23.7.1915. Joined 2nd RIR, 18.3.1916, having been given a commission from 1st Class Mechanic, 12.3.1916. To hospital, sick, 4.5.1916. Died of malaria at the Special Hospital for Officers, Kensington, 14.1.1920. His widow lived at 1 Walmer House, Walton Street, London. They had no children. Funeral expenses were paid by his mother, Margaret Wood, 27 Dale Street, Blythe. Buried at Blythe Cemetery, grave 2139. File ref: 339/57341.

Workman Lt. Edward MC. Born 4.12.1886 at Belfast, the only son of Frank and Sarah (daughter of John M'Causland) Workman. Educated at Charterhouse and Trinity College, Cambridge, where he graduated BA in Engineering with Honours, 1908. *de Ruvigny*: ' ... a member of the Ulster Club and of the Royal Ulster and the Royal North of Ireland Yacht Clubs, and steered his owns yacht successfully on many occasions. He was also a member of the County Down Staghounds and a keen motorist. Before the war he had been an enthusiastic member of the Ulster Volunteer Force, and during the grave political crisis of Easter, 1914, he rendered most practical valuable service to the Unionist cause.'

He had been an officer in 6th Bn, East Belfast Regt, UVF. Applied for a commission, 19.8.1914. Shipbuilder, height 5 foot 7¾ inches, chest 34–36½ inches, weight 139 pounds. Commissioned to 5th RIR. Joined 1st RIR 9.5.1915. Promoted Lt. 22.5.1915. Attached to A Coy, 2nd RIR, 24 August. Mentioned in Despatches 25.9.1915. On 19.1.1916 he took part in the raid at Le Touquet and was wounded by a blow to the head from a rifle butt. Admitted to No. 1 Red Cross Hospital (Duchess of Westminster's), Le Touquet, 21 January. A telegram from the hospital to WO warned that he was 'now dangerous' and 'may be visited'. The hospital advised WO, 24 January, that his parents had arrived and recommended that their daughter and her husband, Capt. D.C. Lindsay, 20th RIR, should be permitted to travel to France. Permission was granted.

Irish Times, 25.1.1916: 'He was reported to be dangerously wounded, but a letter received from him yesterday, written since he was wounded, does not put so serious a complexion on his condition.' Died of wounds, 26 January, 'Meningitis following wound on head by rifle butt' (compound fracture of skull).

Irish Times, 28.1.1916: ' ... was a director of the well-known shipbuilding firm of Workman, Clark and Co. Ltd., of which his father, Councillor Frank Workman, an ex-High Sheriff of Belfast, was one of the founders, and he resided with his parents at The Moat, Strandtown.'

Awarded the MC, 15.3.1916: 'For conspicuous gallantry under heavy shell fire during an attack. He organized and rallied attacking parties, and, although wounded himself, continued with great coolness to direct operations.' Etaples Military Cemetery, I.B.21. File ref: 339/49124.

Wright Lt. James McHardy MC. Commissioned to 18th RIR 30.1.1918. Joined 2nd RIR 24.7.1918. MC, *London Gazette*, 31.1.1919: 'For conspicuous gallantry and excellent leadership in action. During the operations on 6th September, 1918, in the Messines sector, this officer showed great dash and skill in leading his platoon. He captured an enemy machine gun and completely destroyed the crew. He set a fine example of courage and determination throughout the operation.' Posted to 12th RIR, 25.2.1919, joining the Army of the Rhine. Promoted Lt. 30.7.1919. Closed file.

Young Lt.-Col. Herbert Nugent DSO. Born 18.10.1882. Commissioned in the R. Inniskilling Fusiliers 8.1.1901. Promoted Lt. 13.1.1904, and Capt. 1.4.1910. Served in the South African War 1901–2, receiving the Queen's Medal with five clasps. Joined 2nd RIR, 22.9.1915, and was wounded three days later. *Irish Times*, 6.10.1915: 'His injuries include wounds in the arm and foot, and are understood not to be very serious. He is the eldest son of Major H.P. Young, [Riverston,] Leamington Spa (Indian Army retired list), a veteran of the Afghan War, 1879, and the South African War. Captain Young served in the South African War, and was severely wounded while serving with the mounted infantry. He also took part in the Northern Nigeria Expedition, 1906.'

Appointed T/Lt.-Col., 14.2.1916, and took command of 7th Inniskillings. Landed in France 18.2.1916. Gassed 27.4.1916. Wounded by a sniper at Leuze Wood, 6 September, and transferred to England. *Orange, Green and Khaki*: 'Young's wound was very serious and only the speed with which his devoted men got him out saved his life.' Mentioned in Despatches 13.11.1916. Awarded the DSO, *London Gazette*, 1.1.1917, 'for distinguished service in the field.' Rejoined 7th Inniskillings and resumed command 15.2.1917. Wounded by shrapnel 15 May. Assumed temporary command of 49th Infantry Bde, 18–22 August. Later served in Italy with 11th Notts and Derby Regt. Awarded a Bar to his DSO for service in Italy, *London Gazette*, 15.10.1918: 'For conspicuous gallantry and devotion to duty during an enemy attack. When the enemy, assisted by an intense bombardment, had penetrated part of the defences, he went round the front line, found out the situation, and established liaison with other troops, which greatly assisted in the organization of the counter-attack. Shortly after, when his Commanding Officer was wounded, he took command and handled the Battalion with great skill. His fine personal courage animated all ranks, and as all communication was broken, the battle was fought by the Battalion on its own, Major Young having all the responsibility on his shoulders. He performed splendidly.'

Took command of 11th Notts and Derby Regt when 25th Division was reformed with nine battalions and returned from Italy, 15.9.1918. Killed in action 25.10.1918. *The Sprig of Shillelagh*, journal of the Inniskillings, October 1918: 'He was well known in Belfast and Londonderry, and had rendered splendid service in Command of the 7th Battalion of his old Regiment in the Irish Division … He served also in China and Nigeria … Colonel Young married in 1915 Alison, daughter of James Richmond, of Haddon Rig, NSW, and Kippenross, Dunblane, and leaves a son and a daughter. He was killed instantaneously by a shell.' Awarded the French Croix de Guerre and the Italian Silver Medal of Military Valour 29.11.1918. Mentioned in Despatches 6.1.1919. His widow later resided at Craigantaggart, Dunkeld, Perthshire. Pommereuil British Cemetery, Nord, France, E.7. File missing.

Young Capt. Roy Allen MC. Born 31.10.1885 at Shankill, Co. Antrim, the eldest son of Robert Young JP. Brother of V.C. Young below. Enlisted into The Black Watch, TF, 1.5.1912. Architect. Embodied 5.8.1914. Appointed L/Cpl 1.10.1914. Commissioned to 4th RIR 17.1.1915. Joined 2nd RIR 30.12.1915. Promoted Lt. 29.7.1916. *Irish Times*, 21.7.1917: 'He married in 1915 Kathleen, only child of Mr and Mrs John Hale, Pond Park, Lisburn.' MC, *London Gazette*, 16.8.1917: For conspicuous gallantry and devotion to duty as signalling officer to his battalion. During an attack he handled the signal communications with great skill and complete disregard of danger, working insistently throughout the operations.' Appointed to a Regular commission as 2/Lt., 15.3.1918, with seniority from 17.11.1915; Lt. 1.1.1917, a/Capt. 20.7.1917, a/Adjutant 11.6.1918. Returned to the UK during October 1918. Served with 2nd RIR/RUR in Iraq and North West Persia 1919–20, and India until 26.2.1925. Retired 21.10.1925. *Blackthorn*, 1975: 'died on 17th March 1975, in Tasmania … His widow lives in Westbury, Tasmania.' Closed file.

Young Lt. Visto Clive. A son of Robert Young JP, Marmion, Holywood, Co. Down, and grandson of Samuel Young MP, Derryvolgie Avenue, Belfast, who was the Home Rule member for East Cavan. Brother of R.A. Young. Commissioned to 4th RIR 20.7.1915. Served at Carrickfergus before going to the front in 1916. Wounded during October 1916. Rejoined 7th RIR 16.12.1916. Wounded again during a counter attack, 8.3.1917, but remained at duty. *Belfast News Letter*, 17.3.1917, reported that he had four brothers serving in the war. One was 2/Lt. A.F. Young of the Cheshire Regt. Promoted Lt. 1.7.1917. Attached to 49th TMB, 28 September. Joined C Coy, 2nd RIR, 14 November. Mentioned in Despatches 21.12.1917. General Court Martial, 22.5.1918, on a charge of disobedience, leaving post, and Sec 40 – sentenced to be cashiered – commuted to a severe reprimand. Wounded in action 6.9.1918. Closed file.

SOME OTHER RANKS

Bailey 7483 Rfn Daniel Julien. Born St Michan's, Dublin, in 1887. Commonly known as Julien. He had two sisters, Mary Jane and Elizabeth. Educated at St Mary's School, Stanhope Street, and St Vincent de Paul School, Glasnevin, Dublin. Joined the Dublin City RGA Militia. He was an apprentice compositor at Mr John Falconer's, printers and publishers, 53 Sackville Street, Dublin. Enlisted in the RIR 7.4.1904. Height 5 foot 4¾ inches, weight 112 pounds, chest 32½–34½ inches, Roman Catholic, blue eyes, brown hair, fair complexion. Posted to 2nd RIR 19.8.1904. Deprived six days pay for absence, 5.3.1907. Sent to India to join 1st RIR 8.3.1907. Appointed unpaid L/Cpl 14.6.1909. In confinement, 15.10.1909, awaiting trial on charges of absenting himself without leave, an act to the prejudice of Good Order and Military Discipline, and losing, by neglect, his equipment and clothing. Convicted, 9.11.1909, given 84 days detention and fined £3. Served 8 years and 357 days, of which 5 years and 328 days were served abroad. Transferred to the Army Reserve at Gosport, 29.3.1913. He lived at 44 Craven Park, Harlesden, London, for a few months, then went to Canada, returning in October 1913. This was the residence of Mrs Katherine E. O'Dea to whom he was engaged. Temporarily employed at Paddington Railway Station, from 6.7.1914, loading and unloading vans.

Mobilized at Belfast 5.8.1914 and posted to 2nd RIR. Wounded and taken prisoner 15.9.1914. British Intelligence discovered that he had joined the Irish Brigade in Germany. Mrs O'Dea had been listed as his next of kin. The Metropolitan Police made discreet enquiries and reported, 16.9.1915, that she was then residing at 28 Berkhampstead Avenue, Wembley: 'Mrs O'Dea is a widow, has said that she was educated in Germany; she is described as a very fast woman and whilst she was living at 44 Craven Park was always entertaining soldiers. I have also been informed that Mrs O'Dea has two sons now serving in the British Army.' 6902 Pte James Scanlon, a repatriated POW of the Leinster Regt, made a statement, 15.8.1916: 'On one of these occasions when we went to the Brigade's quarters Bailey was there in his unteroffizier's uniform. He was actively urging men to join the Brigade and asked me to do so. I called him a traitor, whereupon he got up to strike me, I said "Yes, of course you would hit a wounded man." He then sat down again ... Some time about July 1915 Bailey came to our part of the camp in the same uniform with a belt and a side bayonet. The Irish prisoners crowded round him, and I saw them knock him down and kick him. The Germans came to his rescue and got him away. Several of our men were punished for assaulting Bailey.'

He came ashore at Banna Strand, Co. Kerry, from the German submarine U19, with Sir Roger Casement and Robert Monteith, 21.4.1916. He used the name Julien Beverley and was driven by car to the neighbourhood of Tralee. Arrested the next day and, on condition that he would be protected, provided selective information about the gun-running plot. Taken from Spike Island, Cork, under military escort, 6 May, to the Royal Irish Constabulary Depot, Phoenix Park, Dublin. Immediately moved to Scotland Yard and placed in Cannon Row Police Station. Transferred to Wandsworth Detention Barracks the following day. Gave evidence at the trial of Casement, *1916 Rebellion Handbook*: 'He was taken, with other Irishmen, to the camp at Limburg, where he was well treated for a time: "I saw Sir Roger Casement about April 1915 (the statement proceeded). He spoke to me about joining the Irish Brigade solely for the purpose of fighting for Irish freedom, and I joined so that I could get out of the country, and was made Sergeant straight away." Bailey went on to say that he was sent to Berlin at the end of March 1916 and, with a Mr Monteith, went to a school to get instruction in the use of explosives. After three hours he went to another place in Berlin to get further instruction. On the 11th he and Mr Monteith and Sir Roger Casement were driven to the War Office. There he was given a railway ticket, and the three of them went to Wilhelmshaven. There they were put on a submarine.'

When the charges were read out at Bow Street, 15.5.1916, Casement, pointing to Bailey, said: 'Well, that man is innocent. I think the indictment is wrongly drawn against him. Is it within my power to pay for the defence of this man? I wish him to be in every way as well defended as myself, and if he has no means to undertake his defence I am prepared to pay for his.' Their trial took place 26–8 June. After Casement had been sentenced to death, the Attorney General intimated that the charge of treason against Bailey was withdrawn. 'As he had throughout been but a subordinate, and had a good character in the Army, and having always denied any intention of helping the enemy, but, in the words of the Attorney General, took the course he did to get away from captivity in Germany, the Crown entered a *nolle prosequi*, and he was at once released.' Went to live with Mrs O'Dea but was subject to compulsory retention under the Military Service Act. Transferred to 3rd Wiltshire Regt, 1.7.1916, No. 31447. Transferred to 3rd Royal North Lancashire Regt, No. 26418, 17 July. Posted to their 2nd Bn, embarking at Davenport, 19 August. Disembarked at Kilwa, Tanzania, German East Africa, 29 September. Transferred to the RE as a Sapper 272845 and moved to the EEF at Alexandria, 9.3.1917. Employed as a platelayer, WR/143247, RE, in the Railway Operating Division. A/Cpl 24.5.1919. Mentioned in General Sir Edmund Allenby's despatches, *London Gazette*, 5.6.1919, for services during the period from 19.8.1918 to 31.1.1919. Embarked for home at Port Said 6.9.1919. Discharged from the RE Transportation Branch 8.12.1919. File ref: 339/26418; police file: MEPO 2/10668; Irish Brigade papers: WO141/9.

Bellis 3/4951 Sgt George H. DCM. *London Gazette*, 25.1.1918: 'For conspicuous gallantry and devotion to duty. During an attack he led his platoon with great dash and gallantry, and on reaching the objective went forward beyond the outpost line and cleared many enemy dug-outs. His assistance was invaluable to his company commander, and throughout the operation he showed the utmost gallantry and ability both in leading and reorganising his company.'

Bland 3/4956 Rfn James. The son of Joseph Gill Bland, a postman, and Margaret Bland, Cartmel, Lancs. He was baptized in the Priory 20.2.1887 and had a sister, Annie, born 1889. The family later moved to Front-row, Grange Fell. Enlisted at Morecambe in 16th Lancers, No. 7065. Later transferred to 2nd RIR and was killed in action 25.9.1915. *Barrow News*, 16.10.1915: 'He was about 28 years of age, and originally enlisted with two other chums in the 16th Lancers soon after the outbreak of war, and the trio were subsequently transferred to the Royal Irish Rifles. He was a native of Grange, and was a well-known footballer, having played for the Grange Tradesmen, and also for Lindale and Cartmel clubs.' His name appears on the Grange-over-Sands memorial. Menin Gate Memorial. Information supplied by Howard Martin.

Boylan 9107 Sgt Anthony. Born 1886 at Gillardstown, Collinstown, Co. Westmeath, the son of Patrick and Mary Boylan. Enlisted at Dublin. In Lucy's book he was called Sgt Benson: 'Benson was always cheerful, natty, and self-possessed. He was well educated and highly intelligent, and invariably showed a smile on his round red face. He was of small stature, but big-chested, and his breast pockets were neatly squared-off with notebooks, duty rosters, and rolls. He was highly conscientious and full of the joy of living at the same time. He was also one of the most efficient scroungers in the regiment, and extremely kind-hearted, dropping his winnings, ill-gotten or otherwise, into the hands of the private soldiers as he moved about them, always saying some little thing; a quip about a battered hat, a smiling injunction, or a reprimand. He joked his men into cheerful efficiency, and held us all in his capable hand. A daring fellow and the model of an infantry sergeant.'

Killed in action 26.10.1914. *Immortal Deeds*: 'He had a most genial disposition which endeared him to all, and in addition he had a good big heart. When in the trenches one day the men were worried by the groans of a wounded German lying in front of them. The presence of German snipers made it too dangerous for anyone to attempt to go out and bring him in. After a time Boylan said: "I can't stand it any longer, lads. The poor devil can't be left to die there; and surely they will never fire on me," and so poor Boylan left his trench, only to be riddled with German bullets.' Le Touret Memorial.

Byers 6858 CSM John Alfred MC. Born and enlisted in Dublin. CQMS. FGCM at Sancy, 4.9.1914, for neglect of duty and acquitted. Wounded June 1915 and killed in action 7.7.1916. MC, *London Gazette*, 19.9.1916: 'For gallantry and devotion to duty on several occasions. In particular when, under heavy bombardment, his company suffered heavy casualties, his cool devotion to duty set a striking example.' Thiepval Memorial.

Campbell 7436 Rfn William J.A. DCM. Born 1885 at Shankill, Belfast, and was an iron-moulder by trade. Presbyterian. Enlisted 1904. Awarded the DCM with 1st RIR, *London Gazette*, 5.8.1915: 'For conspicuous gallantry on the 9th and 10th May, 1915, near Rouges Bancs. Private Campbell led a patrol down a German trench to ascertain where the enemy's flank rested, and carried a message back under a heavy fire. He volunteered for every dangerous duty, and, although wounded in the shoulder, declined to go to the dressing station, giving a splendid example of devotion to duty.' Posted to 2nd RIR. Awarded a clasp to his DCM, *London Gazette*, 15.3.1916: 'For conspicuous gallantry when accompanying an Officer into the enemy's trenches. He showed an utter disregard of danger. He and the Officer captured one enemy Officer and one man, and Private Campbell killed two others himself.' This refers to the raid at Le Touquet in January 1916. The officer, Lt. E. Workman, was wounded and brought back by Campbell. Married Mary Davison in August 1918. He sold his medals to start up a coal delivery business that was never very successful. Moved from Brennan Street to Ainsworth Avenue in 1931. Children were Edward Workman, William, James, Greta, and Evelyn. The family fell on hard times and when he died, 3.5.1938, they were left destitute. The sons remained in Belfast. Details provided by Rory Stephens.

Carthy 7752 Sgt Michael DCM. *Belfast News Letter*, 15.3.1917, reported that he was presented with his DCM at Victoria Barracks, Belfast, the previous day: 'For conspicuous gallantry and resource during an assault. He led his men with great coolness, reorganized various parties, and clearing a communication trench of a strong party of the enemy, of whom he captured two.' *London Gazette*, 14.3.1916. This refers to the raid at Le Touquet in January 1916. He also served with 1st RIR and the Gold Coast Regt.

Conlon 9397 Cpl (a/Sgt) Peter DCM. Previously served with 1st RIR. *London Gazette*, 14.8.1917: 'For conspicuous gallantry and devotion to duty. During an attack, though wounded in both legs, he captured eight of the enemy single-handed, afterwards increasing the number to twenty, assisted by another man. He displayed great determination and complete disregard of all danger in this affair, which he reported to his company commander before having his wounds dressed.' Later promoted Sgt.

Cullen 4/2977 Sgt John. The 1901 Census shows that he was a Roman Catholic and a student boarder at the Royal Hibernian Military School. *de Ruvigny*: 'Third son of the late John Cullen, Royal Horse Artillery, by his wife Annie (29 Northbrook Terrace, North Strand, Dublin) daughter of Morgan Redmond. Born Dublin 18.7.1890. Educated at Royal Hibernian School, Dublin. Clerk. Enlisted at Dublin 12.1.1915. BEF France and Flanders from 28.6.1916; died in an ambulance station 18.6.1917 from wounds received at Messines. Buried at a farm east of Bailleul; unmarried.' Westhof Farm Cemetery, I.D.2., Heuvelland, West Vlaanderen.

Curtin 6/7759 Rfn John DCM. Awarded the DCM 7.6.1917. *London Gazette*, 14.8.1917: 'For conspicuous gallantry and devotion to duty. During an attack, having lost touch with his company, he collected four comrades and attacked a hostile machine gun in action. He killed the team and captured the gun, thereby saving many casualties in another unit which was then attacking. He showed splendid initiative and promptitude.'

Egan, 7635 Cpl William E. Resided at 14 Barrett Street, off York Street, Kingstown, Co. Dublin. Shot through the left wrist and captured by the Germans 28.10.1914. In hospital at Cologne, 8.11.1914 to 8.2.1915. During this time he was approached by Sir Roger Casement. Moved to Limburg Camp until his repatriation 3.2.1916. He was interviewed about his experiences, 10.2.1916: 'In my opinion Corporal Egan is a man of intelligence and reliability.' He made a statement to an MI5 officer 11.3.1916. Gave evidence at the Casement trial – see Daniel Bailey above. *1916 Rebellion Handbook*: 'William Egan ... another ex-prisoner, said he knew Bailey at St Vincent de Paul School, Glasnevin, Dublin, and later he was in Bailey's regiment. He was wounded and captured at Neuve Chapelle in October, and he again met Bailey at Limburg ... Witness identified Bailey and Quinless as two prisoners who joined the Irish Brigade ... There were 2,500 Irishmen in the camp, and only 52 joined the Brigade.' He named two other RIR men that had joined the Irish Brigade: 7708 Rfn J. Greer and 7576 Rfn R. Scanlon. Granted a Silver War Badge. Another repatriated POW, 9008 Rfn J. Mahony, 180 Oxmantown Road, Arbour Hill, Dublin, also identified these men to MI5. Irish Brigade papers: WO141/9.

Fitzsimmons 6322 Rfn Patrick. Born 4.10.1883 at 17 Terence Street, Ballymacarrett, Co. Down, the son of Bernard and Mary Anne Fitzsimmons *née* Harte. Siblings were James (born 1886), Bernard (1888), Catherine (1892), and Elizabeth (1896). Married Brigid (or Bridget) Keenan, 19.4.1905, at St Malachy's Church, Alfred Street, Belfast. Resided at 22 Market Street. Children were Alice (born 25.6.1906) and Bernard (7.10.1908). By 1908 he was residing at 27 Roy Street. Employee of Messrs W.W. Kennedy & Co., carriers, warehousemen and produce brokers, 24–26 Academy Street, Belfast. He was a Reservist in 4th RIR. Posted to 2nd RIR 7.11.1914. Killed in action 16.6.1915. His widow resided at 89 Stanfield Street and later at 9 Raphael Street, Belfast. Menin Gate Memorial. He is, apparently, buried in the grave at Poelcappelle attributed to 6322 Pte John Condon, 2nd R. Irish, who was claimed to be aged 14 and the youngest British soldier killed during the war. At the time of writing, some of the family details (provided by Aurel Sercu, Bloemendale11, B-8904 Boezinge–Ieper, Belgium) have yet to be confirmed.

Hughes 10234 Rfn John. Son of Patrick and Mary Hughes, Devlin Street, Fermoy, Co. Cork. *Irish Life*, 19.4.1918: 'Trustworthy information has recently become available concerning the murder of two soldiers – Private John Hughes, 2nd Royal Irish Rifles, of Fermoy, and Private T. Hands, 1st Royal Lancs Regiment – in the retreat of the British Army from Belgium in the early days of the war. Hughes, Hands and Private Moore, of the RAMC, were three of the many stragglers left behind at St Quentin fortunate in being given refuge in the houses of some kindly French inhabitants. At the instigation of a spy named Lemerhrer, who posed as a Lorrainer by birth, they were arrested on January 22nd, 1915, and tried. The charge was based on a proclamation, placarded a short time previously by the Germans, who ordered all hostile soldiers in hiding to give themselves up by a certain date. The court martial pronounced sentence of death, which was later confirmed by higher authority. Moore, as a non-combatant, was sent into Germany.

'The two prisoners, while awaiting their execution, were allowed to take exercise in the courtyard, where they are reported as strolling unconcernedly, "singing and whistling national airs." The death sentence was read to them in prison on the morning of the 8th of March. A French priest who spoke English administered the last rites of the Church. The execution took place at St Hilary Barracks, the firing squad being composed of six men, under Captain von Maretz. The municipality had been warned to have coffins in readiness, and a carpenter drove to the barracks and took the corpses away to the military cemetery in Panbourg St Martin. He was received by a typical German officer, Lieutenant Hams, who refused to allow the bodies to be buried, saying: "Take those swine away; we have no use for them." A fit burial place, however, was found for them in a cemetery close to the monument of those who fell in 1870, and the graves were covered with masses of flowers by the French population. The epitaph which they put up – "Shot by the Germans" – was torn down by the military authorities, who substituted "Victims of the war." But the graves were always kept in good order by the French, and flowers and wreaths continually placed on them.' St Quentin Northern Communal Cemetery, XIX.6.11.

Jardine 6305 L/Cpl James. The son of John and Margaret Jardine, Railway Street, Banbridge. Church of Ireland. *The Lads Who Marched Away*: 'He was a regular soldier before the war seeing service both in India and Africa. He attested into the Royal Irish Rifles at Lisburn on 3rd April 1901, aged just 19. He was transferred to the army reserve on 2nd April 1909, after having served for 8 years; 6 years and 220 days of this service being abroad. Prior to his enlistment in 1901 he was employed as a postman. He was a member of the Ulster Volunteer Force, acting as section leader in the Huntly Company, 1st Battalion West Down Regiment. During the early part of the war serving with the Royal Irish Rifles he received a bullet wound to the leg. He spent part of his recovery time at home in Banbridge before returning to the front.' Sent to St Bartholomew's Hospital, London. Died in hospital at Boulogne from gas poisoning, 31.5.1915. Boulogne Eastern Cemetery, VIII.A.60.

Lewis 5067 Rfn Taliesin. Resided at 15 Davies Street, Mount Pleasant, Porth, Rhondda, South Wales. He was a student at enlistment and gave the following account of his experiences, 22.7.1918, when he was aged 22. 'I was captured at Hooge on the 25th September 1915 with a few others, about 23 Irish Rifles, no officers, some time in the morning. Some of them were wounded. We were taken first along the Menin road to Menin, and stopped that night at Courtrai prison where we stayed until the 28th September, and then entrained for Germany, arriving at Münster on the 30th. Here we were first put in Isolation Block 2, vaccinated once and inoculated five times. I stayed here for about three weeks. This block only contained new prisoners. From there I went into Block 1, Münster II. Two or three days after arriving at Münster we were given an official printed card to send home. I wrote this and addressed it to my home address, but I do not know whether it arrived.

'My work in Block 1 was looking after horses at Petershafen, hours 7 a.m. to 6 or 6.30 p.m., with almost an hour and a half for dinner. On the 31st August 1916 I was sent out on kommando with 11 others to Dörentrup, attached to Sennelager, about 60 km from Bielefeld, which is a main junction for Münster and Sennelager. This kommando was a sand and clay works. At first we were the only prisoners, but later six other English came from Dülmen. I stayed here about seven months. The accommodation was for the first four months in a small room, very closely packed, not sufficient room to have our food in. It was a room above the outhouse of an inn. We had German iron beds, one above another, two blankets and a straw sack. After Christmas we were given two rooms in a cottage near by, after many complaints. We had no heating apparatus in the first room, but in the cottage we had a stove between the two rooms. Washing facilities were very bad, no means for a bath. Later we were given a tub and we had to carry our water from the inn; no soap was given us.

'The food consisted of acorn coffee, one small loaf per man per week and soup once a day; meat very seldom and in very small quantities; occasionally we had potatoes or sauerkraut if there were no potatoes; also turnips. We got parcels here, but they were frequently delayed at Sennelager. I do not think the parcels were pilfered except when they happened to have got broken. They were censored by the sentry at the kommando in our presence. The only clothes anyone got from the Germans were trousers. Our boots could be sent and repaired at Sennelager by having wooden soles put on them. We were supposed to receive clothes from England every six months, but two or three times mine must have gone astray and I did not receive any. The work was in a quarry. Each man had a pick and a shovel and had to clear away clay and stone. It was very hard work as we were not accustomed to it, six of us being students. The hours were 6 to 6, excluding mealtimes; half an hour for coffee in the morning, one hour for dinner, and half an hour for coffee in the afternoon. We worked six days a week.

'The Germans tried to make us work in the rain: we refused time after time, and the punishment was to make us stand to attention in the rain. There were one military and two civilian sentries. They treated us fairly well. The military sentry was in charge of the camp. I was once beaten by the military sentry with the bayonet for making a complaint. I threatened to report to the General in charge at Sennelager. I was forestalled, and I and five others were sent back to Sennelager for refusing to work. Five were punished with 14 days dark cells, and I was court-martialled and sentenced on a charge of threatening the sentry and refusing to work. I had done nothing of the kind and had only been making a complaint. I received 14 days cells. Awaiting trial I was 15 days in prison without knowing the charge. The prison was overcrowded and conditions very bad. A tub was put into the room at night for a latrine and this would overflow on to the floor. The condition of the prison was filthy. I remained at Sennelager for three months. 'I escaped my 14 days cells by going on kommando on the 30th June with about 10 others to Oelde. This kommando is near Gottalan, and the work was making a railway embankment. There were three kommandos here. One of these three kommandos was a Minden kommando, and this was the one I was in. We found 60 Russians there on our arrival. Conditions here were extremely bad. Accommodation was in a small theatre, about 80 men all told, Russians and British. The latrine was about 5 yards from the cookhouse. We had a bath once a week in the cookhouse at 3 a.m. on Sunday mornings in a hand bowl; no soap supplied. There were four or five sentries with a lance-corporal in charge who was a bully and treated us very badly without any provocation. I do not know his name. We slept on the floor on straw sacks; no blankets. There was no place for our food, so we had to put it on the floor. We had to keep the accommodation clean ourselves and for this we had a broom.

'The work was ordinary railway work; 12 hours work a day, six days a week. We received 60–70 pfg. a day here. The food was very bad, worse than at Dörentrup. Parcels came very irregularly. The sentries were continually asking us to sell them food, and if we would not they ill-treated us. If we went sick it was only with great difficulty we obtained leave to see the doctor. I had a bad attack of diarrhoea here and was allowed to get very bad before seeing the doctor. The Russians were not watched so much as we and they were continually escaping. The Russians had been here two years. Otherwise the Russians and British were treated alike. One of the Russians when escaping was shot, and the sentries made quite a good joke of it. There were several cases of dysentery owing to bad food. Three of us including myself were sent back to Minden on the 31st August for being bad workers and stayed there 10 days.

'On the 10th September I was sent with four other British to Hamm, known as Kommando 64, attached to Minden, a large kommando. I remained here until the 24th June 1918, when I escaped. Hamm is 30–40 kilom. south of Münster. There were about 80 French and 40 British divided into several working parties. Three parties of British and French combined worked on the canal. In my party were 18 English, and we worked in the town loading up cement from the wagons into barges. Occasionally I had to work at unloading barges of coal, using a crane. Accommodation was in a racing stable, wooden beds, straw sacks and two blankets. There were two cooking stoves, but no drying apparatus. On the cement party the task was to unload eight wagons a day. It would take from 7 to 4 p.m. with half an hour for breakfast and an hour and a half for dinner. When unloading coal the work was easier. This was my best kommando. When on the coal two men were allowed off each day and we worked on Sundays.

'The general treatment was fairly good. It was an exceptionally good kommando on the whole. We, however, existed on our own parcels and could not have lived without them. Letters were sometimes a month or more late and very irregular; we lost a good many of them. I remained here until the 24th June 1918, when I escaped into Holland with Lance-Corporal Doughty, 2/5th Lincolns, reaching there on the 2nd July.' Ref: WO161/100.

Lorimer 8066 Cpl Daniel. *Ballymena Observer*, 15.10.1915: 'Writing to his aunt, who resides in North Street, Ballymena, L/Cpl Dan Lorimer … said: "We had a big fight with the Germans and that is the reason I did not write sooner. I tell you it was rough. We cut them down like sheep as soon as we ran up to them. I reckon there were six or seven of them for every one of us. I reckon I was lucky as I never got a scrape. I was recommended for the DCM for bravery on the field and I am getting full corporal – that is two stripes." Corporal Lorimer has two brothers, Sergt John Lorimer and Pte David Lorimer, Inniskillings, and Rfn Willie Lorimer, 18th Royal Irish Rifles, with the army. His brother-in-law, Pte Bob Owens, is with the Highland Light Infantry.'

Ballymena Observer 24.12.1915: 'Corporal Dan Lorimer, 2nd RIR, has been wounded for the second time. Intimation to that effect has been received by his wife from L/Cpl P. O'Kane who states that the injury is not serious. Corporal Lorimer took part in the retreat from Mons and was in the Battle of the Aisne where he was wounded.' Mentioned in Despatches 1.1.1916. Later served as Pte 120299 in the RAF.

McAteer 7303 Rfn Patrick. Born at Antrim about 1886, the second of ten children of Robert and Mary Ann McAteer *née* Quinn. Enlisted at Belfast and served with the RIR before the war, then posted to the Reserve. Married Mary O'Connor at Ballyclare, 22.1.1909. The 1911 Ireland census shows: 'General labourer and pensioner from R. I. Rifles.' Emigrated to Scotland about 1912 where he was employed as a boiler furnaceman at the Carron Ironworks near Falkirk in Stirlingshire. Later moved to Denny, Stirlingshire, where he may have worked in a cloth mill, residing at 29 Milton Row. Children were Mary, John, and Patrick.

Recalled at the outbreak of war and went overseas with 2ND RIR. Killed in action 5.8.1917. See main text. Fr Gill wrote, 7.8.1917: 'Dear Mrs McAteer, You will already have heard of the terribly sad news. May you find comfort in the Sacred Heart of Jesus and with His Blessed Mother. I cannot say how much we all felt the death of your husband. He was killed almost instantaneously by a shell at rear when the attack was made. His last thought – he hardly knew he was hit – was for his duty. Ever since I came out here in 1914 I have known your husband. He was a good man and you may be sure he is safe. He was in charge of his horses when the shell came unexpectedly. He was buried by me near where the commanding officer, Col. Alston, was buried more than two years before. He frequently spoke of you and his children, and if God has not given him the happiness of going back to you it is because He has even greater happiness for you all in His own good time. Your husband's horses and turn out were the pride of the regiment and far surpassed anything else of the kind out here. I shall not forget him at my Masses, and especially that God may give you the grace and strength to accept patiently this heavy cross which He has sent you. May God bless you all. Yours very sincerely, H.V. Gill SJ, Catholic Chaplain 2nd R. I. Rifles.' Another son, Hugh Messines, was born 22.10.1917. His name appears on the Denny war memorial plaque. Dickebusch New Military Cemetery Extension, Ieper, West-Vlaanderen, Belgium, IV.A.5. Information provided by his grandson, Dan Malloy, Paisley, and granddaughter Patricia McAtee, Denny.

McAuley 2/Lt. Daniel Joseph. Born 8.4.1868 at 8 Upper Dorset Street, Dublin. Roman Catholic. Educated at the Central Model Training School, Marlborough Street, Dublin. Worked as a groom. Enlisted as Rfn 1225 in the RIR, 22.6.1885. Promoted Cpl 9.6.1891, Sgt 23.1.1892, reduced to Rfn 10.11.1892, Sgt 12.12.1894, Colour-Sgt 8.7.1895. Served with 1st RIR 1885–91; 2nd RIR to 1899, and 6th RIR (Louth Militia) until he joined the Reserve, 21.6.1906. A qualified Instructor of Gymnastics, he also served as QM Sgt aboard HT *Dunera* from 3.11.1905 to 29.1.1906. Married Agatha Elizabeth Callowhill at Malta, 8.7.1894. Their children were Daniel Joseph (1895–1923), Elizabeth (1898–9), twins Elizabeth Henrietta (1900–50) and Margaret Mary (1900–69), Mary Ellen (1902–70), and Mary Agnes (1909–73). He was a postman in civil life and resided at Ballymakellet, Co. Louth. Re-enlisted as 14562 a/Colour-Sgt at Dundalk with 7th RIR, 16.9.1914. Appointed QM Sgt, 1.4.1915, and posted to France 19.12.1915. Severely reprimanded, 13.8.1917, at Rouen: 'When on Active Service, neglect of duty, when NCO in charge of Billet. Failing to report to the QMS an accumulation of government rations in accordance with written rules.' Joined 2nd RIR 14.11.1917. Promoted from RQMS to 2/Lt., 14.8.1918, and served with the Labour Corps until he was demobilized 7.2.1920. Died in Edenappa, Jonesboro, Co. Armagh, in 1947 and interred at Castletown Graveyard, Dundalk, Co. Louth.

McAuley 9448 L/Sgt Daniel Joseph. Born Colaba, Bombay, India, 1895, the son of 2/Lt. D.J. McAuley, above. Enlisted at Dundalk as a boy soldier in 2nd RIR, 30.6.1910, aged 14 years 9 months. Appointed L/Cpl, 16.6.1914, and a/Cpl 29.11.1914. Posted to 3rd RIR 11.8.1914. Served with 2nd RIR, 12.11.1914 to 6.1.1915, when we went to the Depot. To 3rd RIR, 9 July, until he returned to 2nd RIR, 29 September. Reduced to Rfn by the CO, 17.4.1916, for not complying with an order and being deficient of ammunition. Wounded by shellfire at Vimy Ridge, May 1916. To 3rd RIR 1.8.1916. Returned to the front, 7 December, joined 1st RIR and posted to 2nd RIR, 12 December. Promoted Cpl 7.6.1917. Wounded again and served at Home from 2.12.1917. To 1st RIR 25.3.1918.

Transferred to 6th Wiltshire Regt (No. 27804), 29.3.1918. Taken prisoner during the German offensive, 10 April, being repatriated 28 November. Remained in the Army, 5562506 2nd Wilts, serving in Hong Kong (18.10.1919 to 25.1.1922) and India (12.2.1922 to 22.10.1922). L/Sgt 19.9.1919. Reduced to Cpl for '(1) when in arrest escaping and remaining absent from 11.10.p.m. till found in bed at 5.30 a.m. 8.7.1920 (6 hrs 20 mins) and (2) drunk in Barracks about 11.10 p.m.' L/Sgt 1.4.1921. MB at Bangalore, 23.5.1922: 'Date and place of origin of the disability: May 1916, France. Patient states he was wounded by shell fire on above date whilst in action on the Vimy Ridge. He was sent down the line and eventually reached England. He returned to the front after three months at home. He was again wounded and was eventually captured. His wounds did not trouble him again until December 1920, when he felt pain in the left thigh and found he could not get his leg straight. Shortly afterwards one of the scars gave way and a copious discharge escaped, this ceased and finally his leg appeared to become normal. He was admitted to this hospital 12.2.1922. He could not flex his leg and day by day appeared to be in increasing discomfort. He was X-rayed 20.2.1922 and 24.2.1922. Small foreign bodies were seen to lie in the region of the hip joint. An unsuccessful attempt was made to remove them on 24 February but nearly a pint of puss escaped which gave the patient relief. His present condition is directly due to wounds received in action ... Patient is thin and yellow looking. He has a more or less constant discharge from his hip since the date of his operation. The Skiagram shows two small foreign bodies. A series of plates reveals the fact that these bodies frequently change their position. An attempt at accurate localization was unsuccessful. I do not recommend further operative treatment in this country owing to climate conditions.' The Board recommended his removal to England. Posted to the Depot, 23.10.1922, and admitted to the Royal Victoria Hospital, Netley. Medical notes: 'Left thigh amputated through the hip joint, 17.1.1923, on account of massive sepsis around the joint and into the pelvis. He markedly improved for fourteen days, when he developed thrombosis in his veins of right leg and died of septicaemia, 17.2.1923, exactly a month after his amputation.' Details provided by Donal Hall.

McCrea Lt. Samuel DCM. Enlisted as Rfn 8985. Awarded the DCM while serving as a CSM with 2nd RIR. *London Gazette*, 24.8.1917: 'For conspicuous gallantry and devotion to duty in leaving our front line trench in broad daylight and proceeding to the assistance of a wounded officer. Assisted by two comrades he subsequently brought him in, and that the officer's life was saved is directly due to the prompt and heroic action of this warrant officer, under rifle and machine gun fire. He had previously done the same thing in broad daylight.' Promoted a Regular 2/Lt. 27.7.1918 and served with 15th RIR. Promoted Lt. Placed on Half-Pay List 1920.

McNeilly 7006426 Sgt Thomas. Enlisted in the RIR as Rfn 9363, December 1909, and retired from 2nd RUR November 1931. A painting hangs in the City Hall, Belfast, that shows McNeilly at the Cenotaph with arms reversed. When the people of Enniskillen were about to erect their war memorial, the sculptor looked through many photographs of soldiers but could not find one to his satisfaction. A friend recommended that he view the painting. This he did, sketched McNeilly from the painting, and then sculpted him for the Enniskillen War Memorial.

McTeague 8722 L/Cpl Thomas P. DCM. 'This NCO showed great courage, dash and initiative. Whenever any signs of resistance was offered in his line of advance, he immediately rushed to the danger. He set to flight and captured two pickets of the enemy. His example was truly magnificent and inspired all around him. After reaching the objective he carried an important message back to the Battalion headquarters. While crossing the enemy barrage, he was wounded; nevertheless he delivered safely the message. Instead of getting his wound dressed at the time, he immediately returned to his company and remained at duty doing excellent work for the remainder of the operation.' This was during the Westhoek attack.

Mahoney 9008 L/Cpl Joseph. Resided at 180 Oxmantown Road, Arbour Hill, Dublin. Wounded at Mons, GSW to the head, and suffered paralysis of his legs. Captured 29.8.1914. First taken by British stretcher bearers to a house and then to a convent at Mons where he received good treatment by the Belgians. After about six weeks he was sent by the Germans to the English hospital at Mons. Placed on a train on the night of 20 November and moved to Hofgeismar Reserve Lazarette near Cassel. 'We were very roughly handled when being put into the train, and the carriage was very dirty and verminous, but we were not interfered with during the journey. Very little food was given to us, and it was bad, stale, sour bread and black coffee. On arrival at Hofgeismar we were left in great cold on the platform unsheltered for about half an hour. In the wagon on conveyance to the hospital we were unprotected from the crowd. I was hit on the back by a stick and one man was struck on the head severely. I was in this hospital till 5th December. So far as I am personally concerned I have no complaint to make as to my treatment at Hofgeismar. My wound did not require dressing.' Transferred to Cassel Camp, 5 December, and to Limburg Camp four days later. This information was taken from a statement he made to the Red Cross regarding his treatment at Hofgeismar. Ref: WO161/98

Miller RSM David MBE, DCM, MSM. He was from Cork and had been Provost-Sgt of 2nd RIR in 1917 when he was promoted to RSM. Awarded the DCM, 3.6.1918, and Bar *London Gazette*, 16.1.1919: 'For conspicuous gallantry and devotion to duty during operations in the Messines sector on the 5th/6th September, 1918. The W.O. displayed great courage in supplying the front line with ammunition, food and water under heavy fire. Rations had been delivered at battalion headquarters on the night 5th/6th September, but it was inadvisable to withdraw carrying parties from the front line companies. He with a small party of men worked without ceasing until daylight the following morning, conveying under heavy shell and rifle fire food, water and S.A.A. to each company. Owing to his tireless energy every man was fed and ammunition delivered to all posts. His conduct was a great example and undoubtedly increased the morale of all ranks.'

Blackthorn 1977: 'Ex-RSM Davy Miller died at his home in Laughton, Essex, on 24 June 1977. He was appointed RSM of 2nd Bn in 1917 and held this important post for eighteen years until 1935, when he became Garrison Sergeant-Major of Chatham ... During the Arab Rebellion in Mesopotamia in 1921, one of the last Meritorious Medals for "devotion to duty" was bestowed on RSM Miller; after 1921 the MSM was only granted for long and meritorious service. In 1931, when the Battalion was in Madras, he was awarded the MBE. As well as being an outstanding RSM, he excelled as an athlete. In 1920 he was 100 yards champion of Mesopotamia and represented the Bn in most athletic events. His brother, Sergeant Jack Miller, who also served in The Regiment, was an international athlete who represented the country. RSM Miller had an immense reputation throughout the Army and when he retired in 1946 he was the Army's Senior WO1.

'Let us hope that, for its own sake, the modern British Army still contains Warrant Officers of the calibre of Davy Miller, for he was indisputably a legend. He was not typical in the sense that the towering, steady-paced Drill Sergeants of the Foot Guards are typical.

But in the blackness of his buttons and the alacrity of his movements he was tailor-made to his role – that of Regimental Sergeant-Major of a Rifle regiment. Of short, almost diminutive stature, he was himself the very epitome of a Rifleman.' – Lt.-Col. Pat Corbally.

Murray 7450 L/Cpl Henry. Mentioned in Despatches 9.12.1914. FGCM at Westoutre, 30.12.1914, on miscellaneous charges. Severely reprimanded, sentence quashed. *Irish Life*, 22.1.1915: ' ... had seen previous war service and is in possession of the Queen's Medal for the South African campaign. On his discharge he qualified as chauffeur and obtained employment with Mr J. McCaughey, Dunbarton, Belfast. On the outbreak of war he at once rejoined the Colours, and after distinguishing himself in the early portion of the campaign was unfortunately wounded at the battle of the Aisne and was invalided home.'

Quee 8556 Sgt Hugh Francis DCM. He was from Belfast. *London Gazette*, 14.1.1919: 'For conspicuous gallantry and leadership during operations in the Messines sector on the 6th September, 1918. He was Acting Company Sergeant-Major in command of company headquarters during the advance. While advancing he noticed an enemy machine gun. He at once rushed forward, killing one of the team, and the rest surrendered. This act of gallantry undoubtedly saved many casualties and inspired the men around him to continue the advance without a check.' Later served as a/CSM.

Quinn 8964 Rfn John. Born at Belfast, 8.6.1878, the son of Hugh Quinn, a teacher, and Susanna *née* McKinzie, Mill Street, Comber, Co. Down. He had served in the Militia with 4th Highland Light Infantry. Attested into the RIR at Glasgow, 5.3.1908, stating that he was born in 1883. Height 5 foot 7⅜ inches, 128 pounds, chest 32½–35 inches, Presbyterian, fresh complexion, brown eyes, black hair, labourer. Reported to the Depot at Belfast, 17 March, and posted to 2nd RIR, 2 June. Posted to 1st RIR in Burma 6.1.1909.
  His conduct sheet included the following: 11–17.4.1908: Absent without leave. 16.5.1908: Drunk. 1.6.1908: Absent off parade at Reveille and returning drunk at 6 p.m.; fined 63 pence and confined to barracks for 8 days. 25.7.1908: Drunk in barracks; fined 50 pence. 8.8.1908: Breaking out of barracks, drunk in the street, and improperly dressed; fined 50 pence and confined for 14 days. 10.8.1908: Absent from defaulters roll call at 9 p.m. and remaining absent until found drunk in the barracks at 9.30 p.m.; fined 50 pence and confined for 14 days. 16.2.1909: Maymyo. Drunk in barracks, fined 25 pence. 1.3.1909: Drunk in camp; fined 50 pence. 12.3.1909: Drunk and committing a nuisance in barracks; fined 50 pence and confined for 10 days. 1.5.1909: Drunk and creating a disturbance in his barrack room; confined for 8 days. 28.4.1910: Assaulting a man of the Army Hospital Corps; confined for 5 days. 29.10.1910: Being out of bounds in a Burmese brothel; confined for 5 days. 5.1.1911: Drunk and smuggling beer into barracks; fined 25 pence and confined for 5 days. 5.4.1911: Mandalay. Drunk and returning to barracks late; fined 38 pence and confined for 3 days. 1.4.1912: Nagpur. Drunkenness; Regimental Court Martial, 35 days detention. 14.12.1912: Kamptee. Drunk, creating a disturbance and being in possession of smuggled beer; fined 50 pence and confined for 5 days. 23.1.1913: Drunk and creating a disturbance in the local theatre; using filthy language to an NCO; fined 25 pence and confined for 12 days. 22.2.1913: Drunk and creating a disturbance in his bungalow; fined 50 pence and confined for 10 days. 8.4.1913: Drunk in barracks; fined 50 pence and confined for 4 days. 1.1.1914: Aden. Drunk and creating a disturbance in his barrack room; fined 50 pence and confined for 8 days. 28.1.1914: Drunk and creating a nuisance in his barrack room; fined 50 pence and confined for 10 days. 14.6.1914: Using obscene and filthy language to an NCO; confined for 10 days. 11.4.1915: Absent from

Divine Service; fined 10 days pay and confined for 10 days. 22–30.8.1915: Absent from Tattoo for 8 days; fined 8 days pay and 14 days Field Punishment No. 2.

Served with the BEF 6–26.11.1914. Returned to the UK and joined 3rd RIR. Joined 2nd RIR, 30.9.1915, and suffered a GSW to his left arm, 7.7.1916. Accidentally sprained his left ankle 29.3.1917. Married Jane Tattersall at St Peter's Church, Aintree, 30.11.1917. Her brother, 25109 Pte Alfred Tattersall, 1st King's Liverpool Regt, had been killed in action 15.11.1916. Transferred as Pte 564598 to the Labour Corps, 15.7.1918, and served with a POW Coy. His brother Hugh served with 6th RIR. Demobilized 20.2.1919 and was discharged with a 30 per cent disability ('bronchitis, asthma, malaria – aggravated') 4.3.1920. Good character. Granted a pension of 75 pence a week. At that time he was living at 75 Kingswood, Aintree, Liverpool. Children were John (born 1921, served with the Royal Artillery in North Africa during WW2), Hugh (1924–98), David (1928–2003), Eleanor (1922–92), Jean (born 1931) and Annie (1932–7). Died at Liverpool, 1.6.1940, and is buried at Kirkdale Cemetery, Aintree. Details provided by his grandson Bill Miles.

Taylor 2/8380 Sgt William H. DCM. *London Gazette*, 10.3.1916: 'For conspicuous gallantry and coolness in assisting an officer under heavy artillery and machine gun fire, to organize men of other units. When the Company Sergeant-Major was wounded, Sgt Taylor at once took his place, and by his courage and example assisted to keep the men steady under very trying conditions.' By 1938 he was residing at Athlone, Co. Westmeath.

Trueman 7174 Rfn Thomas DCM. Born Newtownards, Co. Down, where he was a member of the local district LOL No. 4. Awarded the DCM, 16.1.1916, for gallantry at Armentières: 'For conspicuous gallantry. He bombed the enemy in the most fearless manner, killing several of them. Later on his way back he picked up a wounded NCO of the Royal Engineers and carried him back to safety under heavy fire.' Newtownards District LOL No. 4: 'He was the first Newtownards man to be awarded a medal in the First World War, and the medal rests to this day with his grand-daughter in Newtownards … Thomas Trueman returned from the war to live out his days in the town until his death in 1987 aged 93.'

Wilson 6/10485 Rfn Robert DCM. *London Gazette*, 14.3.1916: 'For conspicuous gallantry and determination. He had taken four of the enemy prisoners, when one turned and threw a bomb at him while the rest ran away. Private Wilson thereupon bayonetted one, shot two, and made the fourth a prisoner again. All this was done single-handed.' This probably relates to the raid at Le Touquet in January 1916.

Wright 1/6436 L/Cpl Joseph A. DCM. *London Gazette*, 25.1.1918: 'For conspicuous gallantry and devotion to duty. After the objective of an attack had been gained, he saw a dugout with an enemy machine gun in action. With the utmost dash and gallantry he rushed the dug-out, shot the gunner and captured the gun and fifteen prisoners. He then mounted the gun and fired at the retreating enemy, by his pluck, initiative and gallantry saving a great number of casualties.' This refers to the Westhoek attack.

Bibliography

Belfast News Letter, daily newspaper published in Belfast.

Blackthorn (1969 –), Regimental Journal of the Royal Irish Rangers and the Royal Irish Regiment.

Bowman, Timothy (2003), *The Irish Regiments in the Great War: Discipline and Morale*, Manchester.

Bray, Brevet Major Edward William (1908), *Memoirs and Services of the Eighty-Third Regiment, County of Dublin, from 1793 to 1907*, London.

Burgoyne, Gerald Achilles (1985), *The Burgoyne Diaries*, London.

The Campbell College Register, 1894 to 1938 (1938), Belfast.

Caulfield, Max (1963), *The Easter Rebellion*, Dublin.

Clongowes Wood College, War List, Revised to January 1918 (1918), Kildare: *The Clongownian*.

The Clongownian (1917, 1918, and 1919).

Clutterbuck, Colonel L.A., editor, in association with Colonel W.T. Dooner and Commander the Hon. C.A. Denison (1916), *The Bond of Sacrifice*, 2 vols, London.

Corbally, Lt.-Col. M.J.P.M. (1961), *The Royal Ulster Rifles 1793–1960*, Glasgow.

Crawford, W.H. (Introduction, 1986), *Industries of the North One Hundred Years Ago*, reprinted Belfast, original published 1891.

Creagh, General Sir O'Moore VC, GCB, GCSI and E.M. Humphris (1924), *The Distinguished Service Order 1886–1923*, London.

Falls, Cyril (1925), *The History of the First Seven Battalions: The Royal Irish Rifles in the Great War*, Aldershot.

—— (1922), *The History of the 36th (Ulster) Division*, Belfast and London.

Fisher, James J. (1916), *The Immortal Deeds of our Irish Regiments: No. 2, The Royal Irish Rifles*, Dublin.

Foy, Michael & Brian Barton (1999), *The Easter Rising*, Gloucestershire.

Free Press, weekly newspaper published in Wexford.

Geoghegan, Brigadier-General S. (1927), *Campaigns and History of the Royal Irish Regiment*, 2 vols, Edinburgh.

Gibbon, Monk (1968), *Inglorious Soldier*, London.

'Gill, Fr H.V. SJ, DSO, MC, War Reminiscences of, 1914–1918', held by Irish Jesuit Archives, Dublin, unpublished.

Grand Lodge of Free and Accepted Masons of Ireland: Roll of Honour, the Great War 1914–1919. Anon. Reprinted London (2003).

Graves, Charles (1950), *The Royal Ulster Rifles*, Belfast.

The Great War, 1914–1918, Bank of Ireland Staff Service Record (1920), compiled by Thomas F. Hennessy, Dublin.

Hall, Brendan & Donal Hall (2000), *The Louth Rifles, 1877–1908*, Genealogical Society of Ireland, Dún Laoghaire, Co. Dublin.

Healy, T.M. (1928), *Letters and Leaders of My Day*, London.

Hitchcock, Capt. F.C. (1937), *'Stand To': A Diary of the Trenches, 1915–1918*, London.

Ireland's Memorial Records (1923), compiled by the Committee of the Irish National War Memorial, Dublin.

Irish Life, weekly magazine published in Dublin.

Irish Times, daily newspaper published in Dublin.

Johnstone, Tom (1992), *Orange, Green and Khaki: The Story of the Irish Regiments in the Great War, 1914–18*, Dublin.

Johnstone, Tom & James Hagerty (1996), *The Cross on the Sword: Catholic Chaplains in the Forces*, London.

Kincaid-Smith, Lt.-Col. M., *25th Division in France and Flanders*, reprinted London (2001).

Lake, Revd W.V.C. (c.1974), unpublished autobiography.

Laurie, Lt.-Col. G.B. (1914), *History of the Royal Irish Rifles*, London.

Lowry, Captain Gerald (1933), *From Mons to 1933*, London.

Lucy, John F. (1938), *There's a Devil in the Drum*, London.

McCandless, Paul (2002), *Smyths of the Bann*, Banbridge.

McClimonds, Tommy (2001), *The Lads Who Marched Away*, Banbridge.

Manual of Military Law (1914), War Office, London.

Methodist College, Belfast, *"M. C. B."* (1915–23).

Middlebrook, Martin (1978), *The Kaiser's Battle*, London.

Nesbitt, Ronald (1993), *At Arnotts of Dublin*.

Newry's War Dead (2002), ed. Colin Moffett, Newry.

O'Reilly, G.H. (2001), *History of the Royal Hibernian Military School Dublin*, Genealogical Society of Ireland, Dún Laoghaire, Co. Dublin.

Prisoner of War Statements, National Archives, WO161/98.

Quis Separabit (1928–68), Regimental Journal of the Royal Ulster Rifles, Belfast.

Register of the Alumni of Trinity College, Second Edition (1930), *Seventh Edition* (1962), Dublin.

Royal Air Force Communiqués 1918 (1990), edited by Christopher Cole, London.

Royal Flying Corps Communiqués 1917–1918 (1998), edited by Chaz Bowyer, London.

Ruvigny, Marquis de, *The Roll of Honour: A Biographical Record of Members of His Majesty's Naval & Military Forces who Fell in the Great War*, reprinted London (2000).

Samuels, A.P.I. (1918), *With the Ulster Division in France: A Story of the 11th Battalion Royal Irish Rifles*, Belfast.

Services of Military Officers 1920 (1920), Suffolk.

Soldiers Died in the Great War 1914–19, Part 67: The Royal Irish Rifles, HM Stationery Office (1921).

South African War Honours & Awards, 1899–1902, reprinted London (1971).

Taylor, James W. (2002), *The 1st Royal Irish Rifles in the Great War*, Dublin.

Thompson, Robert (1999), *Ballymoney Heroes, 1914–1918*, Bushmills.

—— (1998), *Bushmills Heroes, 1914–1918*.

—— (2001), *Portrush Heroes, 1914–1918*.

Thom's Official Directory, 1912 (1912), Dublin.

36th (Ulster) Division Officers' (Old Comrades') Association (1924–48), a scrapbook of the annual dinner, held by the Somme Association.

University of Dublin, Trinity College, War List, February 1922 (1922), Dublin.

Vane, Sir Francis Fletcher, Bt. (1928), *Agin the Governments*, London.

War Diary of the 1st Battalion The Royal Irish Rifles, National Archives WO95/1730 and WO95/2502.

War Diary of the 2nd Battalion The Royal Irish Rifles, National Archives WO95/1415, WO95/2247 and WO95/2502.

War Diary of the 6th Battalion The Royal Irish Rifles, National Archives WO95/4296, WO95/4835 and WO95/4580.

War Diary of the 7th Battalion The Royal Irish Rifles, National Archives WO95/1975.

War Diary of the 3rd Division, National Archives WO95/1375, 1377.

War Diary of the 12th Division, National Archives WO95/1823.

War Diary of the 25th Division, National Archives WO95/2224.

War Diary of the 7th Infantry Brigade, National Archives WO95/1413.

War Diary of the 74th Infantry Brigade, National Archives WO95/2245.

War Diary of the 107th Infantry Brigade, National Archives WO95/2502.

Weekly Irish Times (1998), *1916 Rebellion Handbook*, Dublin.

Whitfeld, Diary of Brigadier G.H.P., held by the Imperial War Museum, unpublished.

Who Was Who 1897–1990 (1991), London.

Witherow, Revd T.H. (1920), 'Personal Recollections of the Great War', unpublished memoirs in the Liddle Collection.

Note: Every effort has been made to obtain permission from the relevant copyright holders.

Index

Abbeville, 50, 122
Abeele, 75
Acheux, 89
Acq, 81, 83
Adams, F., 191
Adams, G.H., 191
Agnew, A.E.H., 191
Aire Canal, 51
Aisne, 37, 39–50 passim
Albert, 85–6, 90
Aldershot Camp, 94
Alexander, P.D., 102n., 191
Allenby, E.H.H., 74
Allouagne, 50
Alston, J.W., 57, 60, 70, 191
Anderson, Sgt A., 45
Anderson, A.M., 95, 192
Anderson, D.M., 68, 192
Andrews, W.E., 65–6, 70, 192
Annequin, 109–9
Anzacs, 89
Armagh Wood, 75
Armentières, 51, 75
Army,
    2nd, 127
    3rd, 109
    5th, 110, 117
Arnott, L.J., 193
Arras, 109
Artillery, 41st Battery, RFA, 32
    30th Bde, RFA, 34
Aubers Ridge, 51–2
Aubigny, 84
Auchel, 50
Auckland Infantry Regt, 2nd, 94
Audencourt, 31–2

Augy, 49
Aulnoye, 22
Aventure, 52
Averdoingt, 84
Avesnes, 24
Avricourt, 120

Bacquencourt, 111
Bailey, 7483 Rfn D.J., 18, 335–6
Bailleul, 75, 92, 94, 127
Bailleul-aux-Cornailles, 81, 84
Baillie, CSM W., 132
Bainbridge, Maj.-Gen., 92, 180
Baines, Sgt J., 45
Baker, A.L., 194
Ballard, 14043 Cpl W., 283
Bapaume, 109
Barastre, 109
Barclay, L.G.DeR., 195
Barcy, 36
Barrett, W., 196
Barton, C.E., 127, 196
Barton, T.E., 88, 197
Bassée, La, 51–8
Battershill, F.L., 198
Bavai, 28–9
Bavichove, 130
Beale, D.O.C., 198
Beauchamp, 110
Beaumetz-les-Loges, 110
Beaumont Hamel, 89
Beaurain, 30
Beaurevoir, 35
Beauval, 89–90
Becelaere, 129
Becher, C.M.L., 48, 60, 64, 129–30, 198

Beckett, 6876 Cpl W., 94
Bedford Regt, 61, 63
Belgian Army, 2nd Bn, 18th Regt, 123
Belicourt, 35
Bell, Rfn G., 86
Bell, S.A., 74, 90, 199
Bellewaarde, 59–75 passim
Bellis, 3/4951 Sgt G.H., 336
Bennett, G.G.M., 200, 231
Bennett, R.U., 88, 200
Berneuil, 89
Bertrancourt, 89
Bertry, 31
Bethell, F.H., 74, 200
Bethell, H.K., 91, 180
Bethisy, 49
Béthune, 50, 81, 107, 109
Beuvry, 108
Bevan, Rfn, 305
Bézu, 37
Bhurtpore Barracks, 19
Billancourt, 111
Billy-sur-Ourcq, 49
Bird, W.D., 18–20, 27–32, 35, 37, 39–48
    passim, 200
Birr Crossroads, 65, 99
Bizet, Le, 75–8
Bland, 3/4956 Rfn J., 336
Bland, J.G., 68, 201
Blérancourt, 36
Blighty Farm, 127
Bochcastel, 123
Boiscrête, La, 29
Bois d'Autrecourt, 35
Bois de Biez, 52
Bois Morin, 37
Boisselle, La, 85
Bond, T.R., 202
Bonneville, 84
Borcherds, D.B.DeA., 81, 202
Border Regt, 8th Bn, 94, 102
Bouillancy, 36
Boutigny, 36
Boves, 110
Bouzincourt, 85–6, 89
Bowen-Colthurst, J.C., 18–20, 35, 40–6,
    203–4, 225, 302
Boylan, 9107 Sgt A., 336–7

Boyle, J.K., 118, 204
Boyle, T.M., 205
Boyle's Farm, 128
Braddel, C., 205
Braisne, 37, 49
Bratby, W.D., 205–6
Bray St Christophe, 118
Bremerschen, 94
Brenelle, 37
Breton, 81
Bridcutt, J.H., 127, 129, 206
Brielen, 124
Brigades, 4th Infantry, 89
    7th, 24, 28, 30–2, 37, 39, 43, 55, 64, 82
    8th, 37, 51–4
    9th, 65
    13th, 61
    55th, 90
    74th, 75
    75th, 90, 99
    76th, 75
    85th, 64
    107th, 112, 115, 117, 120, 124, 127
    108th, 109, 111, 127
    109th, 123, 127
    139th, 81
Broomfield, A.A., 79, 206
Brown, E., 98, 101, 207
Browne, J.P., 207
Browne, L., 207
Bruce, Major, 31
Bryans, J.C., 119, 207, 283
Bryans, T.E., 207
Bulford Camp, 94
Burgoyne, G.A., 58, 63, 208
Burke, C.J., 208
Burke, 11358 Rfn F., 283
Burton, 5486 Rfn T., 284
Bus-en-Artois, 89, 109
Bussières, 37
Buttle, A.E., 129, 209
Byers, 6858 CSM J.A., 337
Byrne, 19925 Rfn H., 283

Cabaret Rouge, 82–3
Cachy, 110–11
Caestre, 90
Cairnduff, 6902 L/Cpl T., 283

Calverley, G.W., 74, 209–10
Calwell, W.H., 99, 127, 210
Camblain L'Abbée, 82
Cambrai, 109–10
Cambridge Road, 65
Cambrin, 107
Camdas, 90
Campbell, 7436 Rfn W.J.A., 337
Canada Huts, 60, 64, 106
Canaples, 84
Carabiniers, 4th, 126
Carpenter, 47632 Rfn G.H., 283
Carruthers, R., 102n., 210–11
Carson E.H., 110, 211
Carthy, 7752 Sgt M., 337
Caruth, J.G., 74, 211
Cassel, 126
Cateau, Le, 30–5
Caudescoure, 99
Caudry, 30–1
Cerseuil, 37
Charley, H.R., 34, 211–13
Chassémy, 37, 49
Chateau Stables, 72
Chateau Wood, 100
Châtres, 36
Chatterton, E.V.H.P., 213
Chatterton, G.A., 214
Chaulnes, 111
Chasseurs Alpins, 102nd, 121
Chaussoy-Epargny, 121
Chelers, 81
Cheshire Regt, 13th Bn, 75–92 passim, 101, 107–8
Chézy-en-Artois, 37
Chouy, 49
Ciply, 24
Clarbrough House, 129
Clark, W., 34, 214
Clarke, J.M., 86, 214, 308, 320
Clarke, 4980 Rfn W., 293
Clary, 31, 35
Cleary, Cr-Sgt P.J., 132
Clendining, H., 126, 214–15
Close, 4816 Rfn R., 59–60
Clytte, La, 60, 64
Coates, 8205 Rfn, 264
Cochrane, E.A., 124, 215

Cochrane, J.S., 79, 215
Coleman, Rfn, 239
Collings, A., 126, 215
Compton, 7285 Rfn T., 264
Condé, 24, 38, 49
Conlon, 9397 Cpl P., 337
Connon, A.R., 215
Connor, 4574 L/Cpl P., 231
Conoghan, 9174 L/Cpl D.L., 283
Considine, T.J., 68, 216
Contalmaison Wood, 86
Contescourt, 117
Coomber, G.S., 216
Cooney, C.R., 90, 216–17
Cordner, J., 124, 217
Cornwall Camp, 106
Corps,
    II, 31–2, 51, 75, 122, 124
    XVII, 81
    XVII, 110
Cory, Major, 31
Couillet, 110
Coullemelle, 121
Coulommiers, 36
Count Gleichen's Brigade, 37
Courte Croix, 94
Courtney, Sgt-Maj., 67, 231
Courtrai, 129
Coutek, 126
Couture, La, 51–2
Couvrelles, 49
Cowley, V.L.S., 38, 48, 217–18
Cox, P.G.A., 111, 120–1, 126, 218
Coyelles, 36, 49
Crawford, C.O., 121, 218
Crawford, J., 219
Crèche, La, 81, 94
Crécy, 36
Crépy-en-Valois, 49
Creslow Farm, 90, 92
Croix Barbée, 51–2
Crouttes, Les, 37
Crowley, T.P., 219
Crown Prince Farm, 78–9
Crozet Canal, 118
Cruickshank, 40960 Rfn R., 94
Cugny, 118–20
Cullen, 4/2977 Sgt J, 338

Cullen, P.J., 128
Cumming, H., 74, 219–20
Cupples, W., 74, 219–20
Curchy, 111
Curragh, 19
Curtin, 6/7759 Rfn J., 338
Cyprian Farm, 127

Daly, J.J., 220
Dammard, 37
Darling, C.H.W., 77, 220
Darragh, 20149 Rfn, 239
Daunt, R.A.C., 55, 220–1
Davies, P.J.L., 221
Davis, H.O., 221
Davison, A., 108, 221–2
Davy, H.S., 59, 222
Dawes, C.R.B., 40, 222–3
Deacon, C.H., 223–4
Delette, 99
Dickebusch, 60, 64
Digges La Touche, A., 74, 224
Division,
  2nd, 28
  3rd, 24, 34, 37, 47, 51, 75
  5th, 37, 51, 62
  7th, 56
  12th, 85
  25th, 75
  36th, 107–18 passim, 122n.
  Naval, 110
Dixon, C.S., 56, 224
Dobbie, W.J., 96, 224–5
Dobbin, W.L.P., 18, 117, 225
Doherty, CSM M.M., 132
Doherty, Sgt, 77
Dominion Camp, 99
Domqueur, 89
Donnet Post, 89
Doran, Maj.-Gen. B., 28, 75–6, 81
Dormey House, 63
Doulieu, Le, 56
Doullens, 110
Downing, W.M., 225–6
Dranoutre, 59
Drought, J.B.A., 226–7
Drummond, Lt.-Col., 28
Duffy, Sgt H., 132

Dunkirk, 131
Durant, H.N., 46, 227

Eales, C.H.H., 65–6, 227
Eames, T.B.G.F., 227–8
Eaton, W., 128, 228
Ebblinghem, 94
Ecluse, 37
Ecoivres, 84
Edwards, C.K., 228–9
Egan, 7635 Cpl W.E., 338
Eldred, J.S., 56, 229
Elincourt, 35
Elphick, K., 89, 229
Elverdinghe, 124
Elzenwalle, 60
Englebelmer, 89
Ennisfallen, 22
Erches, 121
Ermitage, 126–7
Erskine, P., 83, 229–30
Esquelbecq, 129
Essigny, 112, 117
Estouilly, 111
Estree-Blanche, 99
Etricourt, 110
Evans, J., 91, 230–1
Ewart, Sgt J., 60

Fagan, 2862 L/Cpl H., 293
Faremoutiers, 36
Farran, E.C.L., 65–6, 231
Fayle, O., 232
Feignies, 24
Fenton, P.M., 232
Ferguson, J.A., 177, 232
Fergusson, C., 75
Ferris, A., 232–3
Ferte Milon, La, 37, 49
Festing, A.H., 233–4
Field, CSM., 239
Finlay, F.L., 34, 55, 234–5
Fisher, H.F.T., 235
Fitzgerald, G.V., 52, 235–6
Fitzsimmons, 6322 Rfn P., 338
Flack, Sgt W., 45
Flamengrie, La, 30
Flavy-le-Martel, 118

Fletre, 75, 94
Floringhem, 50
Fluquieres, 111, 114, 122
Forbes, J.R., 236
Forceville, 89
Forster, T.B., 236
Foster, H.W., 237
Fournes, 52
Fowler, F.R., 90, 237
Fransu, 84
French Army, 128th Infantry Regt, 126
French, Sir J., 75
Frew, D.T.C., 75
Friend, L., 45–6
Fruges, 99
Fry, G.F., 95, 237
Fusilier Trench, 95

Gabion Farm, 128
Gallwey, T.H.E., 88, 237–8
Gamaches, 121
Garner, C.W., 124, 132, 238
Gavin, Lt. R.F.A., 74, 238–9
Gentelles, 110–11
German Armed Forces,
    3rd Bavarian Division, 95
    181st Bavarian Regt, 79
    75th Infantry Regt (1st Hanseatic), 24
    Prussian Guards, 56–7
    25th Regt, 104
    15th Regt (Prussian), 88
    64th Regt (Prussian), 45
    236th Regt, 72   , 305
    90th Reserve Infantry Regt, 102
    Uhlans, 32, 121
Getty, J.B., 81, 239
Gibson, F.M.S., 75, 239
Gibson, J.A., 240
Gifford, H.L., 38, 240
Gill, H.V., 58–9, 62–4, 70, 73–7, 79–82,
    85–9, 94–100, 104, 106–8, 111–22, 126–7,
    130–1, 240–2
Gilliland, V.K., 60, 63, 242–3
Gillman, 1/41145 Rfn W.C., 127
Givry, 24, 27, 29
Gloucester House, 90, 92
Gloucester Regt, 1st Bn, 123
Godewaer, 75

Godson, K.L., 243
Gomiecourt, 110
Gonnehem, 50
Goodman, H.R., 49, 52, 69, 912, 110, 179,
    243–4
Gordon, Lt.-Gen., 180
Gordon, 4558 Rfn A., 284
Goss, 9872 Rfn J., 22–4, 30, 32
Gough, General, 37
Gough, R.A., 127, 244
Graham, 9058 Sgt, 305
Graham, 5266 Rfn J., 197
Grand Rozoy, 37, 49
Grand Séracourt, 112, 115–17
Gransden, V.E., 124, 245
Gray, H.J., 245
Greacen, R., 245
Greer, 7708 Rfn J., 338
Grenadier Guards, 28
Grey, T.H., 82, 245–6
Gribben, E.C., 246
Griffith, C.R.G., 111n.
Grugies, 116
Gudgeon, 5/8207 Rfn W., 129
Guillaucourt, 111
Guerbigny, 121
Guiscard, 120
Gulleghem, 129

HAC, 72–3
Hackett, L.A.H., 124, 246–7
Haig, D., 90, 180
Haldane, A.L., 75
Halifax Camp, 102
Hall, 7446 Sgt W., 197
Halluin, 131
Halpegarbe, 52–4
Ham, 35, 111
Hamel, 115–17
Ham-en-Artois, 81
Hamilton, H.I.W., 20, 31
Hamilton, 9863 Rfn W., 283
Hampshire Regt, 2nd Bn, 111
Hangest-en-Santerre, 121
Hannebeeke, 101, 105
Happencourt, 112, 117–18
Harbonnieres, 111
Hargicourt, 35

Harmer, H.G., 247
Harmignies, 24
Harponville, 84, 90
Hart, J.J., 44, 247–8
Haskett-Smith, W.J.J.S., 248
Haut Pommereau, 52
Haute Poste Farm, 126
Hautvillers, 50
Havre, Le, 22
Hayward, R.B., 248–9
Hay-Will, N.G., 249
Healy, D.J., 249
Hedauville, 89
Hell Fire Corner, 129
Herlies, 51–2
Herly, 111
Hermies, 109
Heron, C., 52, 249–50
Herontage Chateau, 56
Hervilly, 38, 49
Hesdin, 50
Heslop, 5388 Rfn W., 284
Hessian Trench, 90
Heule, 129
Higgins, 7/1226 Sgt H., 128
Highman, Sgt A.J., 132
Hill 60, 61, 63
Hill, Rfn F., 299
Hill, W.C., 250
Hill-Dillon, S.S., 48, 250–1
Hills, 9410 T., 305
Hindenburg Line, 109
Hinges, 50–1
Hoare, E.J., 68, 251
Hobson, 17533 Rfn W., 25
Hooge, 56–7, 63–5, 69, 72–3
Hooks, 6454 Rfn J., 284
Hope House, 90
Houlihan, J.J., 251
Howard, W.E.S., 68, 251–2
Howroyd, F.W., 252
Hughes, 10234 Rfn J., 338–9
Hunter, W.F., 128, 252
Hunter's Avenue, 90, 92
Hussars, 15th, 24
Hutcheson, R.B., 252–3
Hutments Camp, 131

Inglis, J.N., 253
Innes-Cross, S.M., 55, 253–4
Ireland, H.R.H., 78–9, 86, 254
Irish Guards, 28
Irwin, F.J., 131, 241
Ivey, T.H., 74, 254

Jackson, P.A.D., 92, 255
Jacob, C., 130
Jardine, 6305 L/Cpl J., 339
Jasper Farm, 124
Jeancourt, 35
Jeffares, R.T., 102, 107, 255–6
Jenkinson, T.S., 77, 82, 256
Jerlaux, 47
Johnston, 8666 Rfn J., 58
Johnston, R.I., 127, 256–7
Jones, G.D.J., 257
Jones, W., 257
Jonsson, A.T., 258
Joy, F.C.P., 68, 258–9

Kearns, M.C., 259
Keating, P.W., 259
Keeper's Hut Barricade, 92
Keith, Rfn R., 284
Kelly, D.H., 88, 259
Kelly, 7550 Sgt J., 177, 179
Kemmel, 57, 59, 97
Kemp, A.E., 75, 129, 259–60
Kennard, J.A.G., 260
Kennedy, H.A., 55, 260
Kertland, E.B., 68, 260–1
King, F.J., 261
King Edward Trench, 129
Kirkpatrick, D., 70, 261
Klijtberg Hill, 130
Knox, F.Y.C., 99, 261–2
Kopje Farm, 126
K.O.S.B., 57, 69, 110
Koursk, 131
K.O.Y.L.I., 2nd Bn, 52, 63
Kruisstraat, 72, 75
Kyte, E.C., 262

La Fosse Margnet, 38
La Fosse Marguel, 44
Laird, Cpl., 231

Lancashire Fusiliers, 11th Bn, 75, 83–92 passim
Lancers, 9th, 24
Lane, C.H., 127, 262
Launoy, 52
Laville, S.E.B., 55, 262–3
Leach, E.W.V., 92, 263
Leask, P.A.O., 63, 263
Lebucquière, 109
Lecky, J., 88, 263
Leicestershire Regt, 4th Bn, 49, 81
Leinster Regt, 2nd Bn, 72
Leman, J.F., 264
Lendelede, 130
Lennox, A.J., 79, 264
Leslie, K.D., 264–5
Lévignen, 36
Lewis, 5067 Rfn T., 339–41
Lewisham Lodge, 90
Ligny, 31
Lihons, 111
Lille, 131
Lincoln Regt, 1/4th, 75
Lincolnshire Regt, 1st Bn, 52, 55
Lindenhoek, 59
Lindsay, Rfn J., 284
Littledale, C.R.E., 60, 265–6
Little Wood, 109
Locre, 56–9
Loisne, 51
London Regt,
  1/7th Bn, 83
  1/9th Bn, 91
  23rd Bn, 106
Long, Sgt T., 132
Longueil-Ste Marie, 50
Longhead, Sgt., 231
Lorimer, 8066 Cpl D., 341
Lowry, G., 20–4, 34–40 passim, 49, 55, 266–7
Loyal North Lancashire Regt,
8th Bn, 99
9th Bn, 75, 78, 83, 86, 90–1, 85, 101
Loyd, E.B.K., 267
Lozinghem, 50
Lucy, J.F., 20–2, 35–40 passim, 46, 54–7, 102–4, 109–10, 267–8
L'Usine Monbart, 22

Lynch, G.E., 117, 268
Maast-en-Violaine, 37
McAlindon, T., 101, 109, 268–9
McArevey, J.B., 109, 269
McAteer, 7303 Rfn P., 100n., 341–2
McAuley, D.J,
342
McAuley, 9448 L/Sgt D.J., 342–3
McBride, 5009 Rfn S., 91, 177–80
McCallum, J.D.M., 129, 270–1
McCammond, C.R.W., 108, 116, 126, 271–2
McClelland, Sgt T., 132
McConnell, H.J., 272
McConnell, W.C., 86, 272
McConville, 6688 Rfn A., 261
McCoy, W., 272
McCracken, F.W.N., 20, 27–8, 40
McCrea, Lt. S., 343
MacDermott, 6891 Sgt., 305
McDonagh, 10192 Rfn C., 308
McDonnell, M.J., 92, 272–3
McFerran, M.A., 116, 273
McGhie, J.W., 273
Machine Gun House, 78–9
McIntosh, J.M., 68, 274–5
McKane, 3056 L/Cpl F., 59, 293
McKay, H.D., 275
McKee, P.J., 102n., 275
McKeeman, F.K., 129, 275
MacKenzie, C., 52
MacKenzie, M., 77
McKeown, W.W., 95, 275
McKinley, 9471 L/Cpl G.T., 26
MacLaughlin, J.L., 86, 276
McLaughlin, W., 276
McMahon, P., 86, 98, 276–7
McMicking, Lt.-Col., 27
McNeilly, 7006426 Sgt T., 343
McTeague, 8722 L/Cpl T.P., 343–4
Maedelstede Farm, 57
Magenis, R.H.C., 37, 45–6, 277
Maher, 8134 Rfn J., 320
Mahoney, 9008 L/Cpl J., 338, 344
Mailly-Maillet, 89
Maisnieres, 121, 124
Maizicourt, 84
Maladrie, 29

Mallett, H.C., 96, 277
Malone, W.A., 277–8
Manche Copse, La, 127
Mansergh, R.O., 278
Marbaix, 22
Marcelcave, 111
Marche, La, 36
Marcilly, 36
Marcke, 130
Margny, 120
Marne, 36–7
Marriott-Watson, R.B., 92, 119, 180, 279
Marshall, H., 96, 126, 279–80
Martin, J., 280
Mary Redan, 89
Massey, A., 82
Master, C.L., 32–4, 51, 280–1
Mathews-Donaldson, C.L.G., 34, 281
Maubeuge, 24, 28
Maurice, F., 31
Maurois, 30
Mayne, E.C., 281–2
Mawhinney, Rfn, 68
Meaux, 36
Menin, 56, 64, 72, 100
Mercer, S., 99, 282
Merriman, A.D.N., 132
Merris, 56, 75
Mesopotamia, 132
Messines, 92–9
Meteren, 90
Metz-en-Coutre, 110
Micmac Camp, 106
Middle Farm, 95
Middlesex Regt, 31, 51
Miller, RSM D., 132, 179, 344–5
Miller, 7083 Rfn W., 219
Mirvaux, 84
Mitchell, A.G., 83, 282
Mitchell, H.D., 128, 282–3
Mœvres, 109
Molinghem, 99
Monchy, 81
Mondicourt, 110
Mons, 24–8
Mont Kokereele, 127
Mont Noir, 127
Mont St Aignan, 22

Mont St Eloy, 81
Montay, 30
Montêmafroy, 37
Montigny, 30–1, 34, 36
Moore, M.E.J., 119n., 283–4
Moorseele, 129
Moreland, J.A., 108, 284
Morgan, E.G., 284
Morris, G., 28, 285–6
Morgan, S.V., 18, 102n., 284–5
Morris, E.M., 64, 69
Morrogh, J.D., 286
Morrow, E., 126, 286
Morton, T.M., 286
Morton, W.J.E., 72, 287
Moss, W.P., 81–2, 86, 287
La Motte, Farm, 36
Mouquet Farm, 89–90
Mouscron, 130–1
Mulcahy-Morgan, E.S., 287
Munn, N.B., 124, 287–8
Murphy, B.J., 102n., 288
Murphy, P., 121, 288–9
Murphy, 7071 Cpl P., 239
Murphy, Sgt W.J., 45
Murray, 7450 L/Cpl H., 345
Murray, P.E., 81, 86, 289–91
Musgrave, H., 124

Nanteuil-sur-Marne, 37
Nesle, 111
Neufmoutiers-en-Brie, 36
Neuilly-St Front, 37
Neuve Chapelle, 52–4
Neuve Eglise, 58, 92, 129
Nieppe, 90–2, 94
Noble, R.S.H., 96, 291
Noote Boom, 94, 126
Norman, G.S., 49, 63, 82, 291–2
Noroy-sur-Ourcq, 49
North Staffordshires, 8th Bn, 86
Northern Bluff, 89
Nouvelles, 24, 28–9
Noyelles-sur-Mere, 50
Noyon, 35
Nugent, O.S.W., 111

Obélisque, 36
O'Brien, 1369 Rfn J., 197

O'Brien, S.J.V., 96, 292
O'Callaghan, Sgt F., 132
Occur Avenue, 95
Occur Support, 95
O'Connor, 9558 Rfn J., 26
Oglesby, L/Cpl P., 305
Ogier, C.A., 111, 292
Oise, 35, 50
O'Lone, R.J., 76, 292–3
O'Lone, W.P., 74, 293
O'Neill, R.A., 293–4
Onslow Trench, 95
Oosthove Farm, 94
O'Reilly, H.W., 79, 294
Oresmaux, 121
Orr, W.L., 74, 294
O'Sullivan, 7747 Rfn J., 197
Ostel Road, 39
Ouderdom, 106
Oulchy-la-Ville, 37
Oultersteen, 75
Ovillers, 30, 85–91

Panter, G.W., 294
Paris, 36
Passchendaele, 123
Passion Village, 99
Patterson, R.F., 295
Payne, J.C.W., 295
Peebles, A.E., 45–6, 295
Penchard, 36
Penin, 84
Pernes, 50
Perry-Ayscough, H.G.C., 74, 295–6
Peterborough Camp, 126
Petites Aulnois, 36
Phillips, H., 79, 296–7
Phillips, P., 110, 297
Piebrouck, 129
Pigot-Moodie, C.A., 59, 297
Pithon, 111, 118
Pioneer Camp, 99
Plat de Bois, 29
Platt, 4/7413 Cpl R., 67
Plessiel, 50
Ploegsteert, 90, 92, 98
Plugstreet Hall, 92
Plumer, H., 81

Pollock, N.V., 297–8
Ponchaux, 35
Pont Logy, 52
Pont Tugny, 118
Poole, F.T., 127, 298
Poperinghe, 64, 75
Portobello Barracks, 45
Portuguese Expeditionary Force, 107
Port Salut, 50
Pozières, 90
Price, E.D., 81, 298
Pringy, 36
Proctor, L.H., 298–9
Proven, 122, 126
Puchevillers, 89, 110

Quarries, 116–17
Quee, 8556 Sgt H.F., 345
Quesnoy, Le, 30
Quevy-le-Petit, 24
Quinn, 8964 Rfn J., 345–6

Radinghem, 99
Railway Cutting, 112
Raimbert, 107
Rainey, W., 45, 109
Ravelsberg, 94
Raymond, A.A., 68, 70, 299
Rea, V.T.T., 55, 299–300
Reading, 9641 G.A., 88, 94
Reading Station, 126
Rebais, 37
Reckem, 130
Reclinghem, 99
Red Tile House, 79
Redmond, J., 76
Regina Camp, 91–2
Regina Trench, 90
Regnauville, 50
Reilly, J., 132, 300
Reumont, 30
Reynolds, T.J., 55, 300–1
Richebourg St Vaast, 55
Ricks, L.J., 126, 301
Ridge Wood, 60–1
Risky Farm, 126
Road Camp, 126
Robb, G.C., 301

Rocquigny, 109–10
Roberts Farm, 127
Roddy, E.L., 301–2
Roe, G.S., 302
Romarin Camp, 92
Romeries, 30
Rosborough, J., 18, 302–4
Rose, R.DeR., 101, 112, 118, 304
Ross, Lt. A.B., 100, 102
Ross, K., 72, 74, 304–5
Ross, M., 74, 305
Rossborough, R.A., 305
Rossignol, 57, 129
Rotten Row, 90–1
Roubaix, 130–1
Rouen, 22
Rouge Croix, 52
Rouge Maison, 38–9, 44
Roulers, 65, 72
Roupy, 111
Royal Engineers, 78, 109, 124
Royal Fusiliers, 47
    5th Bn, 57
    22nd Bn, 107
Royal Inniskilling Fusiliers,
    2nd Bn, 131
    10th Bn, 112
    11th Bn, 112
Royal Irish Fusiliers,
    9th Bn, 127
    10th Bn, 110
Royal Irish Regt, 2nd Bn, 32–4
Royal Irish Rifles,
    1st Bn, 107, 116–131 *passim*
    7th Bn, 109
    8/9th Bn, 112
    10th Bn, 110, 114, 122
    11/13th Bn, 112
    12th Bn, 109, 131
    15th, 116–17, 124, 131
Royal Scots, 24, 27–8, 58
Royal Warwickshire Regt, 5th Bn, 88
Royal Welsh Fusiliers, 31
Royal West Surrey Regt., 19
Roye, 120
Rubrouck, 126
Rule, C., 129, 305–6
Runaway Farm, 126

Ryan, G.J., 55–6, 306

Sanctuary Wood, 57
Sailly, 50
St Andrew's Drive, 91–2
St Aubin, 24
St Eloi, 60, 69
St Hilaire, 22
St Ives Avenue, 92
St Jean, 72
St Léger, 84
St Nazaire, 36
St Quentin, 112, 116
St Quentin Cabaret, 94
St Rémy, 49
St Soupplets, 36
St Sylvestre, 129
St Waast, 26, 29
Salency, 35
Saleux, 121
Salvo Farm, 126
Sancy, 36
Sarnia, 22
Saulchoy-sur-Davenscourt, 121
Scanlon, 7576 Rfn R., 338
Schaexken-Fontaine Houck, 126
Scott, R.C., 306
Seaborn Camp, 124
Senlac Farm, 127
Senlis, 85–6
Serain, 34–5
Seth-Smith, H.E.S., 72, 306–7
Shaexhen, 90
Sharkie, J.H.F., 83, 307
Shrapnel Corner, 62
Siege Camp, 122, 124
Silver, B.J., 307
Simencourt, 110
Sinclair, H.D., 307–8
Sloane, W.R., 308
Smiles, W.A., 86, 308
Smith-Dorrien, H.L., 20, 55, 75
Smylie, C.V., 308–9
Smyth, C.D., 52, 309
Smyth, G.B.J., 109, 309–10
Soissons, 37
Somers, CQMS R.G., 121
Somers, W., 310

Somme, 85–91, 118
Somme Dugouts, 116
Sourdon, 121
South Lancashire Regt, 2nd Bn, 22, 37,
    48–52, 59, 62, 72
Southampton, 131
Soutry, T.L.B., 38, 310
Soyécourt, 35
Spanbroek Farm, 59
Spedding, C.R.W., 42–7, 310–11
Spence, C.H., 311
Spoil Heap, 109
Sprague, L.C., 75, 91, 177, 311
Stanley, J.J., 108, 311
Staple, 94
Stapleton, CQMS T., 132
Steenbecque, 107, 124
Steenje Camp, 124
Stein, J.F., 59, 311–12
Stewart, J.A., 77, 312–13
Stewart, J.N.G., 126, 132, 313
Stoker, D.H., 313–14
Stone, H.W.D., 82, 314
Strazeele, 75, 94
Strohm, E.C., 119n., 314
Stuart, T.M., 109, 315
Suffolk Regt, 2nd Bn, 69
Surrey Farm, 78
Swaine, H.P., 45–6, 315
Swan Chateau, 99–100

Taggart, 8157 Cpl., 305
Targette, La, 81
Tarlefesse, 35
Tatinghem, 94
Taylor, 2/8380 Sgt W.H., 346
Teele, W.B., 131–2, 315
Templeton, G., 315
Terdeghem, 127
Terhand, 129
Ternas, 81
Thiepval, 89
Thieushouk, 90
Thomas, E.M., 316
Thompson, 9795 Rfn E., 284
Thompson, R.A.J., 316
Thompson, L/Cpl S.V., 70–2
Thompson, T.J.C.C., 82, 95–7, 118–19, 317

Tibets Farm, 127
Tidworth, 19, 22
Titre, Le, 50
Toal, 4420 CSM W., 197
Todd, 8561 Cpl F., 177
Toppin, A.H., 317
Toronto Dugouts, 90
Touquet, Le, 76–8, 81
Touquet Berthe, 92
Tournehem, 94
Transloy, Le, 109
Tröesnes, 49
Troisville, 32
Tronquoy, 35
Trueman, 7174 Rfn T., 346
Tuckett, J.R., 74, 90, 317–18
Tunneller's Camp, 126, 129
Turner, ARQMS J., 132
Turpin, D.O., 86, 318
Tydd, W.J.S., 92, 318
Tyndall, J.C., 59, 318–19

Ulster Volunteer Force, 19
Usna Hill, 86

Vailly, 39, 43, 49
Vallennes, 121
Vance, R.L., 68, 319
Vanilla Farm, 127
Varesnes, 35
Varwell, R.P., 46, 319
Vauciennes, 36
Vaucourtois, 36
Vaumoise, 49
Velde, 75
Vendelles, 35
Verberie, 50
Vermand, 35
Vermelles, 52
Vernon, W.W., 86, 319–20
Vic-sur-Aisne, 36
Vielle Chapelle, 51
Vieux Berquin, 81
Villers Bretonneux, 111
Villers Cotterêts, 36
Villers-St Genest, 36
Vimy Ridge, 81
Voormezeele, 60

Wagner Camp, 124
Wakefield, C.J., 72, 320
Wale, C.H., 68, 79, 320
Walkington, D.B., 126, 320–1
Wallis, T.C., 108, 321
Walsh, R.S., 102n., 321–2
Warlincourt, 110
Warneton, 98–9
Watson, J., 86, 322
Watson, J.K., 322
Watten, 94
Watts, R., 132, 322–3
Weaving, H.W., 323–4
Webb, G.W., 63, 324
Weir, A.V., 60, 64, 72, 74–5, 324–5
Weir, C., 325
Weir, G.A., 69, 325–6
West Kent Regt, 57
Westhoek Ridge, 95, 100–6, 129
Westoutre, 57–9
West Riding Regt, 7th Bn, 89
West Yorkshire Regt, 8th Bn, 89
Wheatley Corner, 129
Whelan, J.P., 58, 326–7
White, F.K., 327
White, H.E., 82–3, 327–8
Whitfeld, A.N., 52, 328
Whitmore, B.E., 328
Wieltje, 72
Wiencourt, 111

Wigwam Copse, 127
Wilkins, C.F., 92, 328–9
Williams, C.B., 72, 329
Williams, E.J., 94, 96, 329–30
Williams, R.D., 330
Wilson, C.E., 86, 330
Wilson, 6/10485 Rfn R., 346
Wiltshire Regt, 1st Bn, 22, 38, 49, 59, 69,
    72–3
Windle, P., 86, 320
Witherow, T.H., 112, 114, 120–3, 331
Wolfhoek, 127
Wood, W., 331–2
Worcestershire Regt, 3rd Bn, 22, 32,
    48–50, 59–60, 64, 69, 72, 105
Workman, E., 78–9, 332
Wright, 1/6436 L/Cpl J.A., 346
Wright, J.McH., 332
Wytschaete, 57

York and Lancaster Regt, 2nd Bn, 72
Yorkshire Bank, 109
Young, H.N., 74, 333
Young, R.A., 177, 179, 333
Young, V.C., 128, 334
Ypres, 56, 65, 72–3, 76, 99, 106, 109, 129

Zillebeeke, 62, 72
Zollern Trench, 90
Zouave Valley, 83